ARCTIC OCEAN

LAPTEV SEA

BERING SEA

CHICAGO PUBLIC LIBRARY
BUSINESS / SCIENCE / TECHNOLOGY
400 S. STATE ST.   60605

W9-DDQ-746

CHICAGO PUBLIC LIBRARY

R01199 42105

Chicago Public Library

C
P L

Form 178 rev. 1-94

Kamchatka Peninsula

Petropavlovsk

SEA OF OKHOTSK

S.   R.

Sakhalin Island

Kuril Islands

Yenisey River

Krasnoyarsk

Komsomol'sk

Khabarovsk

MONGOLIA

Vladivostok

SEA OF JAPAN

NORTH KOREA

CHINA

JAPAN

Guide to the Soviet Navy

Guide to the Soviet Navy

FOURTH EDITION

By Norman Polmar

Naval Institute Press
Annapolis, Maryland

Copyright © 1986
by the United States Naval Institute
Annapolis, Maryland

All rights reserved. No part of this book
may be reproduced without written permission
from the publisher.

Library of Congress Cataloging-in-Publication Data

Polmar, Norman.
  Guide to the Soviet navy.

  Bibliography: p.
  Includes indexes.
   1. Soviet Union. Voenno-Morskoĭ Flot.
I. Title.
VA573.P598   1986   359′.00947   86-23584

ISBN 0-87021-240-0

Printed in the United States of America

CHICAGO PUBLIC LIBRARY
BUSINESS / SCIENCE / TECHNOLOGY
400 S. STATE ST.   60605

R01199 42105

To the memory of
Captains W. J. Holmes and K. G. Shacht—
naval officers, submariners, authors, and friends.

Whatever its original rationale, the Soviet Navy's postwar expansion has created an offensive-oriented blue-water force, a major element in the Soviet Union's global military reach that supports expanding Soviet influence from Nicaragua to Vietnam to Ethiopia. From the Baltic to the Caribbean to the South China Sea, our ships and men pass within yards of Soviet naval forces every day. But familiarity, in this case, is breeding a well-deserved respect; they are good and getting better.

What is particularly disturbing about the "fleet that Gorshkov built" is that improvements in its individual unit capabilities have taken place across broad areas. Submarines are faster, quieter, and have better sensors and self-protection. Surface ships carry new generations of missiles and radars. Aircraft have greater endurance and payloads. *And* the people who operate this Soviet concept of a balanced fleet are ever better trained and confident.

—John F. Lehman, Jr.
Secretary of the Navy
1986

Contents

Preface

This edition of *Guide to the Soviet Navy* describes the continued Soviet thrust to the sea as we approach the last decade of this century. As discussed in chapter 1 of this edition—The State of the Fleet—the Soviet Navy has already surpassed that of the United States in several important warfare areas and is challenging it in others. But the Soviet Navy is designed to support the political-military-economic goals of the Soviet state, and direct comparisons with Western navies can be misleading if not dangerous. Thus, comparisons of the Soviet and U.S. navies have been held to a minimum in this volume.

The significance of a broader view of a modern fleet has been articulated by Admiral of the Fleet of the Soviet Union S. G. Gorshkov, commander in chief of the Soviet Navy from 1956 to 1985:

> . . . we have had to cease comparing the number of warships of one type or another and their total displacement (or the number of guns in a salvo or the weight of this salvo), and turn to a more complex, but also more correct, appraisal of the striking and defensive power of ships, based on a mathematical analysis of their capabilities and qualitative characteristics.[1]

Thus, emphasis in this volume is given to naval weapons and electronics as well as to Soviet naval missions and tactics, operations and exercises, personnel, aviation, shipyards, and bases. These are important to an understanding of a modern fleet beyond simply counting and providing superficial descriptions of ships, as is done in most naval reference works.

Also provided are brief discussions of the Soviet merchant and fishing fleets, civilian research ships, the shipbuilding industry, as well as the navies of the other Warsaw Pact nations. All of these contribute to the effectiveness and in some respects the limitations of the Soviet Navy. While the success and effectiveness of some Soviet naval-maritime activities can be questioned, the "bottom line" is an increasing Soviet capability to use the seas to further national goals in peacetime, during periods of crisis, and at all levels of combat.

Because warships take many years to design and construct, and because Soviet institutions and policies are deeply rooted in history, in several chapters there are history sections to provide a perspective, albeit brief, on the development of the modern Soviet Navy. Much of the modern Soviet fleet's customs, traditions, and even attitudes can be traced directly to Peter the Great, tsar of Russia from 1682 until his death in 1725.

Peter, who expanded his nation's frontiers to the Baltic Sea and Pacific Ocean coasts, and temporarily at the time to the Black Sea, was succeeded by rulers who had only limited interest in navies. This was true even of Catherine the Great, who had married Peter's grandson and ruled Russia from 1762 to 1796, and awarded an admiral's commission to an American officer, John Paul Jones.[2] At the end of the eighteenth century a Russian squadron operated in the Mediterranean, with an amphibious landing on Corfu that wrenched that island from the French.

Subsequently, there were other Russian efforts to build a large fleet, but not until Josef Stalin became ruler of the Soviet Union in 1924 was there a Russian leader with the interest and commitment to build a major fleet. Stalin's legacy to the modern Soviet Navy was the high priority he gave to the rehabilitation of the shipbuilding industry and supporting activities after World War II, and the initiation of a major warship building program and the development of nuclear propulsion and missiles. Of his successors, Nikita Khrushchev provided the incentive and through Admiral Gorshkov the leadership for the development of a modern and innovative fleet.[3] Further, Khrushchev allocated re-

[1]Admiral Gorshkov, "Sea Power and the State," *Morskoy Sbornik* (no. 2, 1972), pp. 20–21.

[2]Jones had served in the American Navy from 1775 to 1788 when, having been denied flag rank, he accepted a commission as a rear admiral in the Russian Navy. He served in Catherine's fleet in 1788–1790, his brief tenure being surrounded by intrigue and scandal. (He died in Paris in 1792.)

[3]Upon Stalin's death in March 1953 the Soviet Union was ruled by a leadership collective, with Khrushchev rapidly assuming the key position of First Secretary of the Central Committee of the Communist Party; by 1956 he was in total control of the Presidium, as the Politburo was then known, and hence in control of the Soviet government.

sources to the construction of a major merchant fleet (an accomplishment that had evaded Peter the Great despite his attempts to do so).

Under Leonid Brezhnev, from 1964 until his death in November 1972, the Soviet Union embarked on a number of political, military, and economic activities in the Third World that made the Soviet Navy and merchant fleet important players on the world stage. Further, under Brezhnev the Soviet Union reached strategic weapons parity with and—by some measures—possibly superiority over the United States, with a significant portion of that capability found in strategic missile submarines.

As indicated in this edition of *Guide to the Soviet Navy*, these trends can be expected to continue to a significant degree even if the current leadership in the Kremlin does not fully understand the role of navies and merchant fleets to the extent that their immediate predecessors have.

I am in debt to many individuals and organizations for their assistance in preparing this edition. In particular, for the considerable advice and encouragement given by Rear Admiral Thomas Brooks, USN; Kensuke Ebata of *Jane's Defence Week*; Fred Rainbow, editor in chief of the Naval Institute *Proceedings*; Messrs. James Kehoe and Kenneth Brower of Spectrum Associates Inc.; and Dr. Milan Vego, a former Yugoslav naval officer.

Others who have provided assistance include A. D. Baker III, special assistant to the Secretary of the Navy; Joel B. Bloom, naval architect; Lieutenant Commander B. P. Boxall-Hunt, RN, Standing Naval Force Atlantic; Geoffrey Palmer of the public relations office of Commander-in-Chief Fleet at Northwood; Dr. Boris S. Butman; Robert A. Carlisle, formerly of the U.S. Navy Office of Information (CHINFO) and his assistants Journalist 2nd Class Joanne Thomas and Mrs. Patricia Toombs, as well as Commander Kenneth Pease, Lieutenant Paul Weishaupt, and Judith van Benthuysen of CHINFO; Dr. Norman Friedman, author and analyst *par excellence*; Ambrose Greenway, editor of *Soviet Merchant Ships*; Captain Wilhelm Grentzmann, Royal Danish Navy; Eric Grove, formerly of the Royal Naval College Dartmouth; Kohji Ishiwata, editor of *Ships of the World*; Commander Tyrone G. Martin, USN (Retired); Captain Jochen Mehner, Federal German Navy; Edward A. Michalski, Department of Defense (Public Affairs); Lieutenant Commander David Parsons, editor of the U.S. Navy's magazine *Approach*, and Commander Peter Mersky, of his staff; Commanders T. J. K. Sloane and F. N. Ponsonby, RN, of the Directorate of Public Relations (Royal Navy); Dr. Scott Truver of Information Spectrum Inc.; and Dorothy Washington of the U.S. Maritime Administration.

Michael Dodgson not only undertook a series of ship drawings specifically for this volume, but provided me with valuable commentary on those ships.

I have drawn extensively on the reference book *Flottes de Combat*, edited by Jean Labayle-Couhat, and English-language edition, *Combat Fleets*, translated and revised by A. D. Baker. I have also used the data bases developed for *The International Countermeasures Handbook*, published annually by EW Communications, Inc., and by staff of the Natural Resources Defense Council, especially Messrs. Thomas Cochran, William Arkin, and Jeffrey Sands.

I am also in debt to several photographers for their efforts, in particular Leo and Lisa Van Ginderen and Dr. Giorgio Arra. Many of their photographs that were not published here were invaluable for determining details of Soviet ships.

Also, I am grateful to the several Soviet naval officers who have provided assistance, among them the late "Nicholas Shadrin," who had critiqued some of the material in the earlier editions of this book and shared his own, unpublished writings with me.

As always, this book is the product of considerable effort by several members of the staff of the Naval Institute Press, in particular Carol Swartz and Moira Megargee, as well as Patty Maddocks, Linda Cullen, and Susan Artigiani. Finally, I remain in debt to Jan Snouck-Hurgronje who, when with the Naval Institute Press, asked me to undertake this project.

This book is updated and published at three-year intervals. The compilation of information and photographs for the next edition begins almost immediately. Material and comments for the next edition should be forwarded to the undersigned in care of the U.S. Naval Institute, Annapolis, Maryland 21402.

NORMAN POLMAR

Guide to the Soviet Navy

The submarine remains the most important warship in the Soviet Navy despite the development of aircraft carriers and advanced surface combatants. The Victor III-class SSN shown here is typical of the modern Soviet submarines, which in many respects outperform their Western counterparts. The Soviets are making major advances in the areas of acoustic detection and submarine silencing, two technologies in which the U.S. Navy has long been the world leader. (U.S. Navy)

1
State of the Fleet

The Soviet Navy of the late 1980s is at a crossroads in its development. A modernization program underway is clearly providing the Soviet Navy with leadership in several important areas of naval warfare, among them

- mine warfare
- anti-ship missiles
- nuclear/chemical warfare
- short-range amphibious assault

In addition, there are major Soviet efforts underway in the areas of submarine warfare and ocean surveillance, and leadership in these two vital areas of naval warfare could shift to the Soviets by the end of the century. Qualitative, and to some extent quantitative, assessments in these areas are more difficult.

With respect to submarine warfare, the massive Soviet submarine effort is clearly "closing the gap" between U.S. and Soviet undersea warfare capabilities. While two decades ago the quality of U.S. submarines was above comparison with Soviet undersea craft, the planned U.S. SEAWOLF/SSN-21 class is expected to be only five to ten years ahead of Soviet submarines in quieting and acoustic detection capabilities when completed in the mid-1990s. In most other criteria Soviet submarines are already superior to those of the U.S. Navy (see chapter 12). The ability of the U.S Navy to remain ahead in the important areas of submarine quieting and acoustic detection will depend upon astute leadership within the Navy and support by the Congress.[1]

In the area of ocean surveillance the U.S. Navy probably has a superior peacetime and crisis capability. This is due primarily to the seafloor Sound Surveillance Systems (SOSUS) and the new series of T-AGOS ships with Surveillance Towed Array Sonar Systems (SURTASS). However, both SOSUS and SURTASS are highly vulnerable during conflict. Other surveillance systems are more difficult to compare; the Soviets certainly lead in the important category of surveillance satellites and the use of passive intelligence collection ships (AGI). And, related to satellite surveillance, the Soviet Union has an operational Anti-Satellite (ASAT) system that can threaten the limited U.S. satellite surveillance capability while the U.S. Congress, at the time this edition went to press, had effectively halted U.S. development in this field.

(The U.S. Navy continues to have unquestioned leadership in several important areas of naval warfare, especially aircraft carrier operations, anti-air warfare, and probably anti-submarine warfare.)

The development of the Soviet Navy over the past two decades clearly provides the Soviet Union with an exceedingly useful force for supporting the nation's political, military, and economic ambitions, both along the Soviet maritime periphery and, increasingly, at great distances from the Soviet homeland. A recent U.S. assessment of the Soviet armed forces notes that, "The [Soviet] Navy's power, mobility, and capability for worldwide deployment give it the ability to support Soviet state interests abroad to a degree unmatched by other branches of the Soviet military."[2]

By comparison, the Vietnam War of the 1960s and the post-Vietnam administrations of Presidents Nixon, Ford, and Carter saw a general decline in U.S. Navy modernization programs. The Reagan Administration's touted buildup to a 600-ship fleet still provides the Soviet Union with an almost 3-to-1 advantage in total submarines, with a significant lead in nuclear-propelled submarines and strategic missile submarines.

During a period of relative stagnation and decline of U.S. naval programs in the 1960s and 1970s, the Soviet Navy underwent a metamorphosis. Under the astute direction of Admiral of the Fleet of the Soviet Union S.G. Gorshkov, commander in chief of the Soviet Navy from 1956 until 1985, the Soviet fleet changed from primarily a coastal defense force, based on World War II (and earlier) technologies, to a large, modern, far-ranging navy.

Indeed, with respect to relative size and continuation of investment in naval forces, the rate of development of the Soviet Navy during Admiral Gorshkov's three decades as CinC are unprecedented in the modern history of any nation. At the same time, there have been massive investments in the Soviet ocean research, merchant, and fishing fleets, all of which contribute to the Soviet Union's ability to use the seas more effectively.

The most dramatic manifestation of these continuing efforts was the launching in December 1985 of the first Soviet aircraft carrier—a nu-

---

[1] The quality of U.S. submarine personnel is considered to be superior to that of the Soviet Union.

[2] Secretary of Defense Caspar Weinberger, *Soviet Military Power 1985* (Washington, D.C.: Government Printing Office, April 1985), p. 91.

clear-propelled ship that is expected to displace some 70,000 or more tons; simultaneous with the launching, a second ship of probably the same type was begun. But the Soviet naval buildup is across the board: similarly impressive programs are underway in (1) submarines, (2) large surface combatants, (3) land- and ship-based naval aircraft, (4) small combatants, (5) weapon developments, especially in mines and anti-ship missiles, and (6) reconnaissance and surveillance. While less is known about developments in the area of naval space programs and anti-submarine warfare, there are indications of major progress here too, progress that some observers have even labeled as possible "breakthroughs." The large Soviet military space program includes significant naval-associated elements. Again, while details are lacking in the public discussion, the current program to build a new generation of large space event support ships—some nuclear propelled—indicates an increasing Navy involvement in this field. The Soviet Navy already operates a network of ocean surveillance and ship-targeting satellites that far exceed the West's efforts in this field. And there are increasing indications of a possible breakthrough in Soviet anti-submarine capabilities. *If* it is forthcoming in the "near" future, it may well be satellite related (see page 34).

In consideration of the future of Soviet naval developments, there are several other unknowns. Many of these are related to submarine warfare, especially developments in propulsion and hull materials; the experimentation with Wing-In-Ground (WIG)-effect vehicles; and the application of stealth (low-observable) technologies to naval missiles.

Analyses of recent Soviet Navy developments also include the continued increase in long-range (out-of-area) operations and the growing use of overseas naval and related air bases, especially in Syria, Vietnam, Ethiopia, and Cuba. While the at-sea time of Soviet ships remains far below that of the U.S. Navy, it should be noted that basic Soviet operating concepts are very different from those of Western navies. For example, while about one-third of the U.S. Navy is forward deployed, primarily in the Mediterranean, Western Pacific, and Indian Ocean, only about 15 percent of the Soviet Navy's ships are at sea at any given time. Rather, the Soviets stress a high degree of inport readiness, with large numbers of ships being able to put to sea during a crisis or pre-war period.

Also, Arctic waters, especially under the Arctic ice pack, have become a principal operating area for Soviet strategic missile submarines (SSBNs) and their protective attack submarines (SSNs). The Soviets have demonstrated considerable interest in under-ice operations, the newer Soviet SSBNs having features specifically for hiding under the ice where they are essentially immune to airborne/space detection as well as to surface ships. U.S. submarine ASW efforts in the Arctic would be severely limited by the effects of ice formation, marine life, and, in some areas, the shallow depths on acoustic performance.

There are certainly shortfalls and problems with the Soviet naval buildup. Ship systems are still seen to fail, and the Soviets have now suffered two nuclear submarine sinkings.[3] In addition, there have been several "problems" with Soviet nuclear plants at sea as well as ashore, with some Navy personnel suffering high levels of radioactive exposure.

Further, the construction of specialized naval replenishment ships has halted far short of probable requirements, while there has been at least a lull in the procurement of long-range amphibious ships. The development of relatively short-range, high-speed landing ships continues unabated, which, coupled with the modernization of Soviet Naval Infantry (marines), points to a significantly enhanced capability for amphibious assault against areas adjacent to Soviet territory.

Several factors can be expected to affect future growth of the Soviet Navy: the stagnated Soviet economy; the on-going modernization of the Soviet Ground Forces, Strategic Rocket Forces, and Air Forces; and the changes in political and naval leadership in the Soviet Union. With respect to the last, the men who ruled the Soviet Union from the end of World War II until 1972 (Stalin, Khrushchev, and Brezhnev) all had specific interests in the development of the Soviet fleet, while Brezhnev had strong personal ties to the Navy.[4] The men who have succeeded Brezhnev—Andropov, Chernenko, and now Gorbachev—do not appear to have had such ties. At the same time, Admiral Gorshkov, who had been personally chosen by Khrushchev to head the Navy, and during his almost 30-year tenure demonstrated his political savvy and effectiveness, has been replaced by a younger man, Admiral of the Fleet N.I. Chernavin. While Chernavin gives all indications of intelligence and capability, he lacks the emotional (i.e., World War II experience) and political ties that his predecessor enjoyed and was able to exploit on behalf of the Navy. (See Appendix B.)

The Navy will be hard-pressed to garner rubles and industrial and manpower resources at its previous rate in an environment of little national economic growth, increasing competition for new weapons from the other services (with the proposed U.S. Strategic Defense Initiative promising to play havoc with Soviet defense planning should the Kremlin leadership decide to develop a counter SDI system), and with a CinC of the Navy who lacks visible political "clout."

There is, obviously, considerable momentum in the on-going Soviet naval programs, and this factor, coupled with the full-employment, full-production nature of the Soviet military-industrial complex, will see a continuation of current building rates for at least the near term. Also, the Navy is perceived by many Soviet leaders to contribute directly to the defense of the homeland—the primary role of the Soviet armed forces. Soviet anti-carrier and anti-strategic missile submarine (SSBN) forces help to defend Russian soil against nuclear strikes from the West. At the same time, the Soviet Navy's SSBNs provide a strategic reserve that is important to the Soviet doctrines of fighting a nuclear war and—at any level of conflict—bringing about a conclusion to the conflict on terms favorable to the Soviet Union. The current Soviet programs to develop mobile ICBMs can be expected to reduce the importance of the SSBN strategic reserve, but not to alleviate its significance.[5]

---

[3] A November-class SSN was lost off Spain in 1970 and a Charlie I-class SSGN was lost off Kamchatka in 1983; most if not all of their crews are believed to have been rescued. (The U.S. Navy has lost two nuclear submarines, the Thresher [SSN 593] in 1963 and the Scorpion [SSN 589] in 1968; both U.S. submarines were lost with all on board. Both navies have also lost diesel submarines since World War II.)

[4] Brezhnev, as an army political officer, participated in a major Black Sea amphibious landing at Novorossiysk in 1943, and in the early 1950s, as a civilian, was head of the Navy's political administration.

[5] As of late 1985 Soviet submarine-launched strategic missiles carried almost 2,100 warheads or 23 percent of the total estimated strategic warheads available to the Soviet Union. At that time, the U.S. submarine force carried about 50 percent of the U.S. strategic warheads.

What could the impact be if (when?) the Navy loses the battle for the ruble in competition with other defense activities and with capital investment programs? (There is essentially no competition from the civil sector.) Which programs could be expected to survive? The submarine programs—general-purpose and strategic—will continue as the mainstay of the Soviet Navy. The Soviet fleet—despite Admiral Gorshkov's statements to the contrary—is not a balanced fleet, at least not in the Western sense. Soviet strategic missile and attack (torpedo and cruise missile) submarines are the principal striking force of the Navy in most combat scenarios. In peacetime submarines provide an invaluable intelligence collection capability and, unlike Western submarines, Soviet undersea craft are used to "show the flag" in a political sense. Further, the large industrial facilities allocated to submarine construction and support, the multiple types developed over the past few years, and the tradition of a large undersea fleet all argue in favor of the continued emphasis on this arm of the Soviet Navy.

Indeed, the role of submarines is increasing because of the effectiveness of their cruise and ballistic missiles, the ability to use off-board (remote) sensors to detect targets, and improved communication methods. The recent Soviet rate of development of new submarines and submarine-related systems is remarkable, with seven new combat types and two research submarines being built since 1980, in addition to several significant submarine conversions (see page 109).

Recent Soviet developments in nuclear-propelled attack submarines (the Mike, Sierra, Akula) are in some respects the major concern of Western naval leaders. However, the deployment of the Delta IV and Typhoon ballistic missile submarines, and indications of a major construction or conversion program for submarines to carry the SS-N-24 strategic cruise missile, plus deployment of the SS-N-21 land-attack cruise missile, demonstrate the breadth of Soviet submarine efforts.

Also, the Soviets have not abandoned the diesel submarine. The low cost of these craft (to build and to man), their ability to conduct *some* missions as well or better than a nuclear submarine, and their extremely low acoustic detectability have apparently led the Soviets to continue their construction. Indeed, the Soviets have recently expanded the Kilo-class diesel program from one shipyard to three. While some of this increase in construction will be for foreign transfer, it is obvious that the Soviet Navy intends to maintain a significant force of diesel submarines. (This, too, is in marked contrast to the U.S. Navy, where some self-serving flag officers have halted all objective consideration of diesel submarines for the U.S. Navy and even prevented their construction for key U.S. allies.)

This massive submarine effort provides the Soviets with opportunities to develop and evaluate a variety of technologies and operational concepts, allowing them to chose the best design(s) for series production. Also, the variety of types presents Western anti-submarine forces with the need to develop different tactics and possibly different weapons for dealing with various submarine performance envelopes and their other features.

The second most important component of the Soviet operating fleet is land-based aviation. The high priority accorded to Soviet naval aviation is evident, with a major portion of the bomber production in the Soviet Union being allocated directly to the Navy and several new naval aircraft have been produced in the past few years. During the last decade Soviet naval aviation has increased by some 50 aircraft per year, an impressive rate of growth.

A related factor is the continued development of naval weapons and electronics. The efforts in these areas continue at a high rate, as indicated in later chapters of this volume. Beyond developing improved systems of existing types, the new types of weapons demonstrate the scope of Soviet research and development programs. Of particular significance are the SS-N-24 strategic cruise missile, the submarine air-defense missile, and reports of the application of stealth technology to new missiles.

This makes the surface, amphibious, and support forces the principal candidates for reductions. In the mid-1980s there were four major surface combat programs underway—the KIROV-class nuclear-propelled battle cruisers, the SLAVA-class missile cruisers, and the UDALOY and SOVREMENNYY destroyer classes. This level of surface warship effort has not been seen in the Soviet Union since Stalin's fleet buildup died with him in 1953. The surface fleet—increasingly vulnerable to Western anti-ship missiles and increasingly expensive—is the most "fragile" component of the Soviet buildup. Also, from a political viewpoint, the vulnerability of surface ships, real and alleged, tends to make them primary targets for politicians.

There are some indications that the amphibious force has already taken some "hits," at least in terms of long-range assault ships. Only two of the large, multi-role IVAN ROGOV-class amphibious ships were built; on first look one could make a similar statement about support forces, especially the large replenishment ships, but this shortfall is partially compensated by the large and modern Soviet merchant marine. Also, in such areas as civilian icebreakers and research/survey ships, which are important for effective naval operations, one sees major building programs underway.

Soviet naval manpower appears to be increasing in quantity and in quality. Here too the future is not clear, as the European Russian population is not significantly increasing, while there is dramatic growth in the number of Asians in the Soviet Union. The Navy's officer corps and technicians come primarily from the European peoples, and there is demand for those with technical and management skills in virtually all aspects of Soviet industry. The Navy already conscripts most of its enlisted men for three years compared to two years for most of the armed forces. The solutions to this problem are not clear, although certainly, the required service for naval enlisted men could be extended for perhaps another year or so, or voluntary retention programs could be invoked.

Another aspect of the future of the Soviet fleet is its reactions to U.S. defense policies. In the past, Admiral Gorshkov was able to obtain support for his programs by providing forces to counter American threats—aircraft carriers and strategic missile submarines that could strike the Soviet homeland with nuclear weapons. After that, Soviet strategic missile submarines with long-range missiles were given the role of a strategic reserve striking force.

In late 1983 the Soviets used the Navy to respond to the U.S. decision to deploy Tomahawk and Pershing nuclear weapons in the Western Europe theater. Party Secretary Brezhnev and Minister of Defense Dimitri Ustinov on separate occasions had both declared that the Soviet Union would deploy missiles in ocean areas close enough to the U.S.

mainland so that their missiles would require only ten minutes to reach their targets—an "analogous" response to the U.S. nuclear weapons in Western Europe. Thus, additional Soviet SSBNs were deployed—albeit briefly—off the U.S. coasts.

Similarly the Reagan Administration's maritime strategy and fleet buildup were certainly used by Admiral Gorshkov to gain support from his political leaders. The announced U.S. Navy plan to attack Soviet SSBNs during the conventional phase of a war can only motivate the Soviets—who appear to consider most of their SSBNs as a strategic reserve—to build more strategic missile submarines and to develop the forces needed to defend them.[6] Some Western analysts have expressed the opinion that should U.S. cruise missile submarines (and possibly carrier forces) forward deploy into waters off the Soviet homeland in a crisis period, the Soviets could similarly send SSN/SSGNs into American waters carrying the SS-N-21 missile, the Soviet version of the Tomahawk land-attack missile. Or, should several Soviet strategic missile submarines be sunk in the conventional phase of a conflict, the Soviets could respond by attacking a U.S. aircraft carrier.

A final factor that should be considered in assessments of the Soviet Navy is the impact of recent Soviet espionage efforts. The James Walker spy ring—that operated within the U.S. Navy for 16 years—provided the Soviets with volumes of information on U.S. submarine and antisubmarine efforts as well as on all aspects of military communications, and Ronald Pelton of the National Security Agency gave the Soviets details of clandestine submarine operations, including communication intercept projects. When these efforts are tallied with those of other Soviet espionage activities against the United States and its allies, the impact on Soviet naval capabilities could be considerable.

The Soviet fleet today is large, modern, and highly capable and presents the nation's leadership with a number of options for direct and indirect military response to Western political-military actions. There are

[6] The Soviet Union has maintained its SALT I limit of 62 modern SSBNs since the agreement was signed in 1972; the U.S. Navy has never reached its limit of 44 modern SSBNs.

obvious qualitative problems—as there are with any complex weapons, and especially with Soviet systems that have historically lacked the level of quality control found in the West. Still, that fleet provides a powerful force for the Kremlin leaders, a force that has already been used in "peacetime" to support allies and intimidate enemies.

There are many questions about the future of the Soviet Navy. The current research, development, and production programs will further enhance the effectiveness of Soviet naval forces. This will be particularly true if, in the post-Reagan-Lehman period, there is the anticipated reduction in the rate of funding for the U.S. Navy. Increasingly, the Soviet Navy will provide the Kremlin leaders with improved means of accomplishing their international goals in peacetime as well as in war.

ORDER OF BATTLE

The accompanying table 1-1 lists the Soviet naval order of battle. The various symbols are indicated below the table. Direct comparisons of the Soviet and U.S. navies are difficult and have limited meaning because the ships differ in size, configuration, and purpose, and because the missions and tactics of the navies are different. Still, with these qualifications, comparisons can be instructive.

The column for the Black Sea Fleet has the Caspian Flotilla indicated by the + symbol.

The Soviet data for frigates and smaller ships include those units operated by the KGB Maritime Border Troops. U.S. Coast Guard cutters are not included because, in comparison to the KGB ships, they have very limited combat capabilities. Not included in the Soviet totals, however, are the KGB-operated armed icebreakers, oceangoing tugs, and minesweepers that are generally comparable to U.S. Coast Guard cutters.

U.S. Navy tabulations include Naval Reserve Force (NRF) ships and aircraft with the + symbol.

The U.S. Navy's 12 LHA/LPH-type amphibious ships are listed as helicopter carriers. The two Soviet ships in this category are the MOSKVA and LENINGRAD, which are combination helicopter–guided missile ships.

TABLE 1-1. NAVAL ORDER OF BATTLE, MID-1986

	Soviet Union					United States
	Northern Fleet	Baltic Fleet	Black Sea Fleet + Caspian Flotilla	Pacific Fleet	Total	
Submarines—Nuclear						
Modern strategic missile submarines					62	38
SSBN Typhoon class	4	—	—	—		
SSBN Delta classes	22	—	—	16		
SSBN Yankee classes	11	—	—	9		
Older strategic missile submarines					1	—
SSBN Hotel III class	1	—	—	—		
Attack submarines						
SSGN types	*	—	—	*	48	
SSN types	*	—	—	*	85†	94‡
Special-purpose submarines	*	—	—	*	4	4§
Submarines—Diesel-electric						
Strategic missile submarines						
SSB Golf classes	1	6	1	7	15	—
Attack submarines						
SSG Juliett class	*	*	*	*	15	—
SS types	*	*	*	*	~140	4
Special-purpose submarines	*	*	*	*	~ 15	1‖
Total submarines	185	45	35	120	~385	141
Aircraft Carriers	1	—	1	2	4	13
Helicopter Carriers	—	—	2	—	2	12
Battleships	—	—	—	—	—	3
Cruisers	11	4	9	14	38	31
Destroyers	16	16	20	15	65	68 + 1
ASW Frigates (Krivak classes)	7	7	8	13	35	101 + 12
Light Frigates/Frigates	40	22	37 + 5	41	145	—
Missile Corvettes	—	—	—	—	40	6
ASW Corvettes	—	—	—	—	91	—
Radar Picket Corvettes	—	—	—	—	3	—
Missile/Patrol/Torpedo Craft	—	—	—	—	270	—
Fleet/Ocean Minesweepers	—	—	—	—	130	3 + 18
Amphibious Ships	13	21	11 + 13	20	78	48 + 2
Naval Aircraft						
Carrier-based aircraft					155	1,250 + 150
Land-based strike aircraft					400	—
Land-based patrol/ASW/reconnaissance aircraft					335	400 + 100
All other naval aircraft					750	

*Exact disposition unknown.
†A few units are expected to launch the SS-N-21 land-attack cruise missile.
‡Most U.S. SSNs can launch the Harpoon and Tomahawk cruise missiles.
§Two former SSBNs converted to attack submarines/transport submarines; the research-configured SEAWOLF (SSN 575); and the small, deep-diving research submersible NR-1.
‖The deep-diving research submarine DOLPHIN (AGSS 555).

2
Glossary of Terms

These are mostly U.S. and NATO terms. In general, the use of U.S. ship designation symbols is avoided in this volume, except for submarines, because of the major differences in U.S. and Soviet naval ship designs and roles.

AA	Anti-Aircraft
AA-( )	NATO designation for Soviet Air-to-Air missile
AAW	Anti-Air Warfare
ACV	Air Cushion Vehicle
ACW	Anti-Carrier Warfare
AEW	Airborne Early Warning
AGSS	Auxiliary submarine (diesel)
AGSSN	Auxiliary submarine (nuclear)
ACV	Air-Cushion Vehicle
ACW	Anti-Carrier Warfare
AGI	Intelligence collection ship
AS-( )	NATO designation for Soviet Air-to-Surface missile
ASUW	Anti-Surface Warfare
ASW	Anti-Submarine Warfare
C³	Command, Control, and Communications
CBW	Chemical-Biological Warfare
CinC	Commander in Chief
DP	Dual-Purpose (for use against surface and air targets)
draft	maximum draft of hull at full load; generally *does not* include sonar dome projecting below keel
DWT	Deadweight Tons (cargo-carrying capacity)
ECM	Electronic Countermeasures
ehp	equivalent horsepower
ELINT	Electronic Intelligence
EW	Electronic Warfare
FCS	Fire Control System
full load	ship displacement complete and ready for sea in all respects, including all fuels, munitions, and provisions as well as aircraft
GFCS	Gunfire Control System
hp	horsepower
IGE	In Ground Effect (hover)
kgst	kilograms of static thrust
lbst	pounds static thrust
length	length overall
light	ship displacement without crew, fuel, munitions, or provisions, and without aircraft
LSM	medium landing ship
LST	tank landing ship
MAD	Magnetic Anomaly Detector
MIRV	Multiple Independently targeted Re-entry Vehicle
MOD	Ministry of Defense
MPA	Main Political Administration of the Army and Navy
NATO	North Atlantic Treaty Organization
n.mile	nautical mile (1.15 statute miles)
oa	overall (length)
OGE	Out of Ground Effect (hover)
OTH	Over The Horizon (targeting)
RORSAT	Radar Ocean Reconnaissance Satellite
SA-N-( )	NATO designation for Soviet Surface-to-Air Naval missile
shp	shaft horsepower
SIGINT	Signals Intelligence
SLBM	Submarine-Launched Ballistic Missile
SLCM	Submarine-Launched Cruise Missile
SNA	Soviet Naval Aviation
SOSS	Soviet Ocean Surveillance System
SP	Self-Propelled (artillery)
SP	Single-Purpose (gun suitable for engaging only surface targets)
SRF	Strategic Rocket Forces
SS	torpedo attack submarine (diesel)
SS-N-( )	NATO designation for Soviet Surface-to-Surface Naval missile
SSB	ballistic missile submarine (diesel)
SSBN	ballistic missile submarine (nuclear)
SSG	guided (cruise) missile submarine (diesel)
SSGN	guided (cruise) missile submarine (nuclear)
SSN	torpedo attack submarine (nuclear)
SSQ	communications submarine (diesel)
SSQN	communications submarine (nuclear)

SSR	radar picket submarine (diesel)	VDL	Video Data Link
SST	target-training submarine (diesel)	VDS	Variable Depth Sonar
standard	ship displacement complete and ready for sea with all munitions, provisions, and aircraft, but without fuels	VLS	Vertical Launch System
		VSTOL	Vertical/Short Take-Off and Landing aircraft
SUW-N-( )	NATO designation for Soviet Surface-to-Underwater Naval missile	VTOL	Vertical Take-Off and Landing aircraft
		wl	waterline (length)
3-D	three-dimensional (radar)		

The FRUNZE, second of the KIROV-class battle cruisers, shows her long, clean lines as she maneuvers at high speed. During the past two decades Soviet naval development has emphasized essentially all aspects of modern naval power. (Mitsuo Shibata)

3
Soviet Ship Designations[1]

The general arrangement of ships in this volume is by generic type, based on the U.S. Navy's ship classification scheme (e.g., cruisers, destroyers, frigates). Because of the major differences in U.S. and Soviet warship designs and roles, this volume does not use U.S. Navy ship-type designations—CG, CGN, DD, DDG, etc.). However, the similarity of submarine types does make it feasible to use U.S. submarine designations, such as SS, SSN, SSG, and SSGN.

During the post–World War II period the Western intelligence services developed two principal schemes for identifying Soviet naval ships:

(1) Submarines were assigned code letter designations; generally the phonetic words are used for the letters, as Alfa, Bravo, Charlie, and Delta. Major variations within the class are indicated by roman numerals, as Charlie I and Charlie II. The principal exception to this scheme is the Western use of the Soviet term Typhoon (*Tayfun*).

There has been no order in the assignment of the submarine code letters, the first having been Whiskey. Because of the massive Soviet submarine construction effort, by 1985 no letters remained available for assignment (even with one Soviet "name" being used for the Typhoon class). Accordingly, the code name Akula (Russian for "shark") was assigned to the next class observed. The current NATO designation scheme for submarines is discussed in chapter 12.

(2) Surface warships have been given K-series code names from the mid-1950s onward, as Kara, Kresta, Kynda. Again, roman numerals indicate principal class variants, as Kresta I and Kresta II. Since the late 1960s most new Soviet surface combatant classes have been generally identified by their Soviet names, as KIEV, KIROV, UDOLOY, and SOVREMENNYY. Lesser Soviet naval ships have been assigned names according to where they were built or first observed, such as the landing ships of the Polnocny class that were constructed at the Polnocny shipyard in Poland. Smaller ships are named for locations, insects, and children's nicknames. See specific classes for details.

The Soviet Navy's designations for its ships are listed below, in table 3-1. In addition to these designations, the Soviets use a "ship rank" (*rang korablya*) classification scheme based on the ship's purpose, firepower, displacement, and crew size. The seniority of the ships' commanding officers, the status of their crews, and their logistic support are based on this ranking. There are four ranks:

1st rank: nuclear-powered submarines, ASW cruisers (i.e., KIEV, MOSKVA), guided missile cruisers.

2nd rank: large and medium diesel submarines, large guided missile and ASW ships, destroyers.

3rd rank: small ASW ships, escort ships, medium amphibious warfare ships, ocean minesweepers, missile craft.

4th rank: ASW patrol boats, motor torpedo boats, gunboats, landing craft, coastal and harbor minesweepers.

Under Soviet naval regulations, first- and second-rank ships hoist the naval jack simultaneously with the naval ensign when not underway; the third- and fourth-rank ships do not fly a jack.

TABLE 3-1. SOVIET SHIP TYPE DESIGNATIONS

	Russian Terminology	English Translation
AK	Artilleriyskiy Kater	Artillery Cutter
BDK	Bol'shoy Desantnyy Korabl'	Large Landing Ship
BPK	Bol'shoy Protivolodochnyy Korobol'	Large Anti-Submarine Ship
BRK	Bol'shoy Raketnyy Korabl'	Large Missile Ship
BT	Bazovyy Tral' shchik	Base Minesweeper
DK	Desantnyy Korabl'	Landing Ship
DKVP	Desantnyy Korabl' Na Vozdushnoy Podushke	Air Cushion Landing Ship
EHOS	Ekspeditsionnoye Okeanograficheskoye Sudno	Expeditionary Oceanographic Vessel
EM	Eskadrennyy Minonosets	Destroyer
ENS	Elektrostanttsiye Nalivatel'noye Sudno	Electric Power Station Vessel
GKS	Gidroakusticheskoye Kontrol'noye Sudno	Hydroacoustic Monitoring Vessel
GS	Gidrograficheskoye Sudno	Hydrographic Vessel
KIL	Kilektor	Lift Ship
KR	Kreyser	Cruiser
KRZ	Korabl' Razvedyvatel'nyy	Intelligence Ship
KS	Kabel'noye Sudno	Cable Vessel
KSV	Korabl' Svyazey	Communications Ship

[1] A detailed discussion of Soviet ship types is provided in Arthur D. Baker III, "Soviet Ship Types," Naval Institute *Proceedings* (November 1980), pp. 111–17; (December 1980), pp. 115–20; and (October 1982), pp. 168–74. Also see Lieutenant Commander Charles E. Adams, USN, and A.D. Baker III, "Soviet Naval Ship Names," *Proceedings* (July 1979), pp. 113–19; and Commander Tyrone G. Martin, USN, "What's in a Name?" *Proceedings* (July 1974), pp. 117–18.

An Oscar SSGN (background) and a Victor III SSN maneuver on the surface in northern waters. The large Soviet submarine force exercises in multiple-submarine tactics as well as integrated air-surface-submarine tactics.

	Russian Terminology	English Translation
KTs	Kontrol'naya Tsel'	Controlled Target
KVN	Korabl' Vozdushnogo Nablyudeniya	Radar Surveillance Ship
LDK	Ledokol	Icebreaker
MB	Morskoy Buksir	Seagoing Tug
MPK	Malyy Protivolodochnyy	Small Anti-Submarine Ship
MRK	Malyy Raketnyy	Small Missile Ship
MT	Morskoy Tral'shchik	Seagoing Minesweeper
MVT	Morskoy Vodnyy Tanker	Seagoing Water Tanker
OS	Opitnoye Sudno	Experimental Vessel
PB	Plavuchaya Baza	Floating Base
PKA	Protivolodochnyy Kater	Anti-Submarine Cutter
PKR	Protivolodochnyy Kreyser	Anti-Submarine Cruiser
PL	Podvodnaya Lodka	Submarine
PLA	Podvodnaya Lodka Atomnaya	Submarine (nuclear)
PLARB	Podvodnaya Lodka Atomnaya Raketnaya Ballisticheskaya	Ballistic Missile Submarine (nuclear)
PLARK	Podvodnaya Lodka Atomnaya Raketnaya Krylataya	Cruise Missile Submarine (nuclear)
PLRB	Podvodnaya Lodka Raketnaya Ballisticheskaya	Ballistic Missile Submarine

	Russian Terminology	English Translation
PLRK	Podvodnaya Lodka Raketnaya Krylataya	Cruise Missile Submarine
PSKR	Pogranichniy Storozhevoy Korabl'	Border Patrol Ship
RKA	Raketnyy Kater	Missile Cutter
RKR	Raketnyy Kreyser	Missile Cruiser
SB	Spasatel'nyy Buksir	Rescue Tug
SBR	Sudno Bol'shogo Razmagnichivanya	Large Deperming Vessel
SDK	Srednyy Desantnyy Korabl'	Medium Landing Ship
SKR	Storozhevoy Korabl'	Patrol Ship
SR	Sudno Razmagnichivanya	Deperming Vessel
SS	Spasatel'noye Sudno	Salvage Vessel
SSV	Sudno Svyazyy	Communications Vessel
TAKR	Takticheskoye Avianosnyy Kreyser	Tactical Aircraft Carrying Cruiser
TKA	Torpednyy Kater	Torpedo Cutter
US	Uchebnoye Sudno	Training Vessel
VT	Voyennyy Tanker	Military Tanker
VTR	Voyennyy Transport	Military Transport
ZM	Zaggraditel' Minnyy	Minelayer

4
Command and Organization

During the past few years there have been several significant organizational changes in the Soviet armed forces as well as major reassignments of senior officers.[1] However, when this edition went to press the Navy had undergone only minor organizational changes; a number of senior naval officers had been reassigned, most notably the Commander in Chief (CinC) of the Navy, a post that had been held by one man for three decades.

The armed forces of the Soviet Union consist of five military services that are under the Ministry of Defense (MOD) plus the border guards of the Committee for State Security (*Komitet Gosudarstvennoy Bezopasnosti*—KGB) and the interior troops of the Ministry of Internal Affairs (*Ministerstvo Vnutrennikh Del*—MVD). The five military services, listed in their normal order of precedence, are:

Strategic Rocket Forces
Air Defense Forces
Ground Forces
Air Forces
Navy

The term *Army and Navy* is still widely used by the Soviet leadership to indicate all of the armed forces. For example, the military political directorate is called the Main Political Administration of the Army and Navy (MPA). However, on a practical and operational basis, the current MOD organization has five separate military services.

The Soviet state is founded on the concept of "top-down" control of the population, the Politburo of the Communist Party being the apex of the hierarchy. The Party is an entity officially separate from the national government, though in most respects it controls the government. Mikhail Gorbachev is General Secretary of the Communist Party and hence the ranking member of the Politburo.

THE HIGH COMMAND

Party control of the armed forces is exercised through the Defense Council (*Sovyet Oborony*). The Defense Council is the highest Soviet military-economic-political planning and decision-making body, respon-

sible for preparing the country for war.[2] Chaired by the General Secretary of the Communist Party (Gorbachev), the council consists of selected members of the Politburo, including the Chairman of the Committee for State Security (KGB),[3] and the heads of the Ministry of Defense, Council of Ministers, GOSPLAN (the state economic planning agency), and the Chief of the General Staff.

The Defense Council controls the defense budget and makes the decision to develop and deploy each major weapon system and major warship class. The appointments of senior officers and organizational changes must be approved by the Council. The Minister of Defense, currently Marshal of the Soviet Union S.L. Sokolov, and the Chief of the General Staff, currently Marshal of the Soviet Union S.F. Akhromeyev, are the only military officers who are members of the Defense Council.

In wartime the Defense Council would become the State Committee of Defense (*Gosudarstvenny Komitet Oborony*—GKO), essentially a war cabinet to oversee all aspects of the nation, including strategic leadership. At that time the General Secretary would assume the function of Supreme Commander in Chief of the Armed Forces. When it became the State Committee of Defense, others would probably join the Defense Council, including the Commander in Chief of Warsaw Pact Forces and the Party secretary for defense industry.[4]

The Soviet armed forces have both an administrative and an operational chain of command. The senior peacetime body of the armed forces is the Main Military Council (*Glavnyy Voyennikh Sovyet*) or Collegium of the Ministry of Defense (*Kollegiya Ministerstvo Oborony*), which is responsible to the Defense Council for military strategy and operations, including training and readiness. The Minister of Defense (Sokolov) heads this council. The members of the council include the 14 deputy ministers of defense—five military service chiefs and nine other senior defense officials (see figure 4–2). In wartime the council would become the Headquarters of the Supreme High Command or

---

[1] See, for example, William F. Scott and Harriet Fast Scott, "Command Structure," Naval Institute *Proceedings* (December 1985), pp. 42–44.

[2] Under the 1977 Soviet constitution the Defense Council is a state and not a Party institution.

[3] The KGB is also responsible for operating and protecting the communications systems of the Soviet state and political leadership, and for safeguarding nuclear warheads in transit to and at storage facilities.

[4] The Chief of the Military Industrial Commission or VPK (*Voyenno Promyshlenaya Kommisiya*).

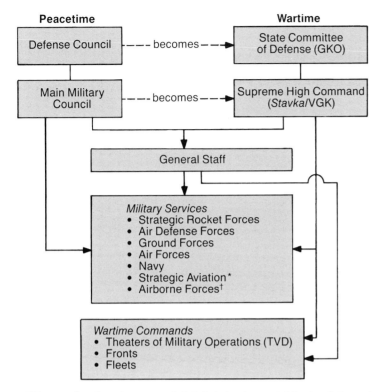

Peacetime		Wartime
Defense Council	- - - becomes - - →	State Committee of Defense (GKO)
Main Military Council	- - - becomes - - →	Supreme High Command (Stavka/VGK)

General Staff

Military Services
- Strategic Rocket Forces
- Air Defense Forces
- Ground Forces
- Air Forces
- Navy
- Strategic Aviation*
- Airborne Forces†

Wartime Commands
- Theaters of Military Operations (TVD)
- Fronts
- Fleets

* There are five air armies composed of strategic bombers and strike aircraft; these air armies are administratively part of the Air Forces, and operationally they are directly under the General Staff

† Airborne units are administratively part of the Ground Forces, and operationally they are directly under the General Staff.

Figure 4-1. Soviet High Command

Stavka, which would exercise direct operational control of the Soviet armed forces, either through the General Staff or directly through the various theater and front commanders.[5]

The General Staff is the executive agency for the Main Military Council in peacetime and for the wartime *Stavka*. It is charged with basic military planning for all of the services. Together the *Stavka* and General Staff form the Supreme High Command (*Verkhovnoye Glavnoye Kommandovaniye*—VGK). The Soviet General Staff was formally established in 1935 and was changed to its present form in 1942.

The Soviet General Staff differs significantly from the U.S. Joint Chiefs of Staff (JCS) in two respects: The JCS is composed of a chairman and the heads of the four U.S. military services, and it has a working staff of officers from the various services, generally individuals with no specialized staff training who are assigned for about two years at a time. In contrast, the Soviet agency is a professional planning staff, which consists mostly of "army" officers, with the key positions held only by officers who have graduated from the two-year course at the Voroshilov General Staff Academy, the highest professional military school in the nation. These are professional staff officers, who may spend their entire senior career on the General Staff or other major Soviet planning bodies. As representatives of the Soviet military viewpoint, they do not have to divide their loyalties between the staff and their parent service (to which they will return for future assignments) as their American counterparts do.

Although the Soviet General Staff is dominated by Ground Forces (army) officers, since 1972 a senior naval officer has served as a deputy

[5] *Stavka* was a tsarist term. Stalin established the first Soviet *Stavka* when the Germans invaded Russia in June 1941. During World War II the *Stavka* consisted of about 20 general officers. (In 1917, at the end of the tsarist regime, there were about 250 senior officers and officials in the *Stavka*.)

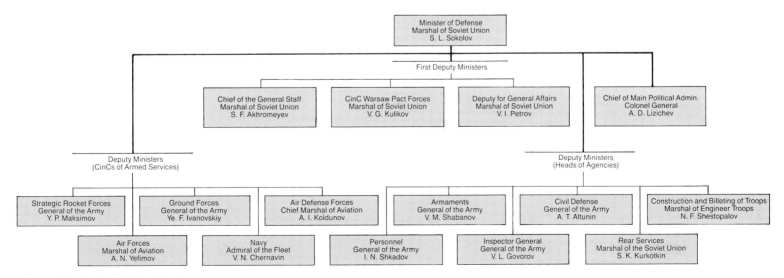

Figure 4-2. Soviet Ministry of Defense

The Soviet leadership today commands a fleet of large, highly capable warships that range over wide ocean areas in support of their political, military, and economic interests. This Kresta II—being looked at by a Royal Navy Lynx helicopter—typifies the modern Soviet warship: large, heavily armed, and laden with electronics. The Soviet command structure seeks to integrate these ships with the other components of the military establishment at essentially all levels of operations. (Royal Navy)

chief. Admiral N.N. Amel'ko, who had been CinC of the Pacific Fleet from 1962 to 1969, when he became a deputy CinC of the Soviet Navy, has served as a deputy chief of the General Staff for Naval Forces since 1978. Several other naval officers hold lesser positions on the General Staff.

MINISTRY OF DEFENSE

The direct control and administration of the armed forces on a daily basis in peacetime is the responsibility of MOD. The Minister of Defense exercises his duties through three 1st deputy ministers and 11 deputy ministers.

The 1st deputies are the Chief of the General Staff, the CinC of Warsaw Pact Forces, and a 1st deputy for general affairs. Five of the deputies are heads of the five armed services: the commanders in chief of the Strategic Rocket Forces, Air Defense Forces, Ground Forces, Air Forces, and Navy. The other deputies are responsible for Civil Defense, Personnel, Main Inspectorate, Rear Services, Armaments, and Construction and Billeting of Troops.

History. The current Soviet defense structure is based on the reorganization of 1953, when the MOD was established to direct the military services. During the next few years the other services and most other components of the current MOD were established in their current form. (The National Air Defense Forces—PVO-*Strany*—gained the status of a separate service in 1948 and was reorganized as the Air Defense Forces about 1980, incorporating the air defense troops of the Ground Forces; the Strategic Rocket Forces became a separate service in 1959.)

The first Minister of Defense under the 1953 reorganization was Marshal Nikolai Bulganin, a political officer with very limited military experience. He was succeeded in 1955 by Marshal Georgi Zhukov, the leading Soviet military hero of World War II. Zhukov was the successful architect of the defenses of Leningrad and Moscow and of the Battle of Stalingrad (now Volgograd). The latter battle is considered the turning point in the 1941–1945 war against Germany. Zhukov, the first professional soldier to head the Soviet defense establishment, was immensely popular in the Soviet Union. As Minister of Defense he was the first soldier to hold full membership in the ruling Presidium (as the Politburo was then called). Still, in 1957 the Soviet political leadership under Nikita Khrushchev ousted Zhukov from office because of fears that he was gaining too much power.

His place was taken by another professional soldier, Marshal Radion Malinovsky, who had been closely associated with Khrushchev during World War II. Malinovsky died in 1967 and the top defense post was given to still another professional soldier, Marshal Andrei Grechko. He too was given membership in the Politburo, but only with candidate (non-voting) status. After Grechko's death in 1976 the position of Minister of Defense went to Dmitri Ustinov, already a full member of the Politburo and the head of the defense industry.

Ustinov, a civilian ordnance specialist and industrial administrator, had been head of armament production in the Soviet Union since June 1941 and afterwards held a succession of senior positions in the defense industry and economic planning. Ustinov held the rank of engineer-colonel general before being appointed Minister of Defense in April 1976, when he was awarded the rank of General of the Army. Later that year the rank of Marshal of the Soviet Union was conferred upon him. He was a candidate member of the Politburo from 1966 to 1976, and a full member from 1976 until his death in 1984.

Marshal of the Soviet Union Sergei Sokolov, a professional army officer, was appointed to succeed Ustinov upon the latter's death in December 1984. In 1985 he was named a candidate member of the Politburo.

As noted above, a senior admiral has served as a deputy chief of the General Staff since 1972. Additionally, Admiral A.I. Sorokin has served as 1st Deputy Chief of the MPA since late 1981. He is believed to be the first naval officer to hold that position. Admiral Sorokin has served in the MPA since 1976 as one of several lesser deputy chiefs. (The chief of the MPA is an army colonel general.)

Also in 1981, Admiral of the Fleet G.M. Yegorov stepped down as Chief of the Main Naval Staff, a most important position that he had occupied since 1977. He then became chairman of the Central Committee of DOSAAF (voluntary society for cooperation with the army, aviation, and fleet), the national paramilitary training organization. Most Western analysts believe that his move was a demotion, resulting from the grounding of a Soviet submarine in Swedish waters in November 1981. The DOSAAF position has probably not been held before by a naval officer and thus may give the Navy added prestige and influence.

Several other admirals hold major non-Navy positions, among them Admiral A.I. Rassokho, Chief of the Main Directorate of Navigation and Oceanography within MOD, and Admiral N.I. Khovrin, a deputy CinC of the Warsaw Pact Naval Forces.

THEATERS OF OPERATIONS (*TEATRII VOYENNYKH DEYSTVIY*)

In peacetime the MOD administers military activities through four groups of forces (located in Czechoslovakia, East Germany, Hungary, and Poland), 16 military districts within the Soviet Union, and four naval fleets. In wartime the Soviets envision there being, in addition to strategic operations, three theaters of war—Western (European), Southwestern, Southern, and Far Eastern. Commanders and staffs are assigned to these four theater commands.

In these major theaters up to 13 theaters of military operations (TVD) would be established for unified direction of operations. The Soviets do not normally have commanders and staffs assigned to these TVDs, but would form their staffs from the groups of forces, major border military districts, and the MOD.

Currently there appears to be planning for five continental Eurasian TVDs, four naval or maritime TVDs, and four intercontinental TVDs. The maritime TVDs are the Atlantic, Pacific, Indian, and northern Arctic oceans. It seems likely that the maritime TVDs would be under a naval commander in wartime, while naval operations in waters such as the Baltic and Black seas would be part of the continental Eurasian TVDs. Reportedly, a Far Eastern TVD was activated in 1979, probably to formalize the command relationships, communications links, and logistics network for a future conflict in that area.

In wartime, headquarters would be established in some or all of the other TVDs as required to direct and coordinate combat and support

Admiral N.G. Kuznetsov. (U.S. Army)

Admiral S.G. Gorshkov. (Sovfoto)

Admiral V.N. Chernavin.

operations. The continental TVDs would direct the fronts (groupings of ground forces), the supporting air and naval units, and the military districts within the area. (The Soviet Union's 16 military districts include most military units, installations, and activities of the armed forces within their respective areas. All of the units of the Ground Forces and various support functions, including conscription and training, within Soviet borders are assigned to military districts.)

History. The concept of the TVD—i.e., as an intermediate level between the *Stavka* and the fronts (army groups)—was used briefly and ineffectively early in the war against Germany. More significantly, in March 1945 a theater command was established in the Far East in preparation for Soviet entry into the war against Japan.[6] This High Command of Soviet Forces in the Far East was "invested with broad authority for direction of combat operation" and had "a relatively autonomous character." The distance from Moscow to the new war zone and the limitations that distance put on communications led to the formation of this TVD, which directed three ground fronts, three air armies, the Pacific Fleet, and the Amur Flotilla in the war against the Japanese. Soviet experience with the theater command concept was limited. The success of the admittedly brief but complex and large-area campaign in the Far East has provided Soviet military leaders with a model for future theater command structures.

NAVY (*VOYENNO-MORSKOY FLOT*)

The Soviet Navy is an administrative organization (as are the other military services) as well as an operational command organization for forces afloat and related land-based aviation and marine units.

The CinC of the Soviet Navy is the equivalent of the U.S. Chief of Naval Operations and Secretary of the Navy. He is both a deputy minister of defense and CinC of the Navy. The CinC directs operations afloat and ashore primarily through four fleet commands plus the flotilla command on the inland Caspian Sea. There is evidence that the daily operational control of Soviet strategic missile submarines is vested in the Soviet General Staff (as is control of Soviet strategic aviation and airborne forces).

The current CinC of the Soviet Navy is Admiral of the Fleet V.N. Chernavin, who was appointed to the dual positions of deputy minister and naval CinC in December 1985. His predecessor was Admiral of the Fleet of the Soviet Union S.G. Gorshkov, who had served in that position for almost 30 years—from January 1956 until he was relieved by Chernavin. Gorshkov's tenure had spanned that of 13 U.S. secretaries of the Navy and nine chiefs of naval operations. Gorshkov had served in a single position longer than any other general or flag officer in the Soviet armed forces.[7]

---

[6] In February 1945 the Allies agreed that the USSR would enter the war against Japan three months after the end of the war in Europe, i.e., August 1945.

[7] The longest-serving U.S. Chief of Naval Operations since that position was established in 1915 was Admiral Arleigh Burke. He was in that office from August 1955 to August 1961.

Before assuming the CinC position, Admiral Chernavin was a 1st deputy CinC of the Navy and Chief of the Main Naval Staff. (Admiral of the Fleet N.I. Smirnov has been a 1st deputy CinC since 1974.) Chernavin's appointment to command the Soviet Navy was predicted when he became a 1st deputy in early 1982 (and was promoted from admiral to Admiral of the Fleet the following year). At the time of his appointment as Navy CinC Chernavin was 57 years of age (Gorshkov was 75 at the time and Smirnov was 68).

Admiral Chernavin served as Chief of the Main Naval Staff and 1st Deputy CinC only from 1982 until his appointment to Navy CinC a little less than four years later. Before that, Chernavin had command of the important Northern Fleet, holding the position from July 1977 until early 1982. In 1981 he was named a candidate member of the Central Committee. (One other naval officer is a candidate member, Admiral V.V. Sidorov, CinC of the Pacific Fleet. Admiral Gorshkov was a full member of the Central Committee, as are most deputy ministers of defense and a few other senior officers.)

History. Under the Communist regime a separate People's Commissariat (ministry) for the Navy existed briefly in 1918, then again from December 1937 through World War II.

In February 1946, when decisions were being made to initiate a major fleet building program, the Navy was integrated into the People's Commissariat for the Armed Forces, whose title was changed on 15 March of that year to Ministry for the Armed Forces. Four years later, in February 1950, this unified ministry was divided into a War Ministry and a Navy Ministry, again placing the Navy high command in a position of parity with the Army. Finally, the supra-level MOD was established in 1953, with the Navy becoming a subordinate service.

The basic organization of the Soviet Navy is shown in figure 4–3. The headquarters is a highly centralized organization with several deputy CinCs supporting the CinC. Current operations and long-range planning are the province of the Main Naval Staff, which in some respects is comparable to the U.S. Office of the Chief of Naval Operations.

The other deputy CinCs appear to have specific responsibilities and supporting organizations, but not all have been publicly identified. The Soviet Navy does not appear to have deputy CinCs for warfare areas or "platforms," like the U.S. Navy's deputy chiefs of naval operations for air, surface, and submarine matters. Rather, the principal deputy commanders in the Soviety Navy are for:

combat training
naval educational institutions
rear services (logistics)
shipbuilding and armaments

Although technically not a deputy CinC, the head of the Navy's political administration has the stature of one. This post has been held since 1981 by Admiral P.N. Medvedev. Other senior officers within Soviet naval headquarters include:

Commander of Naval Aviation
Commander of Naval Infantry and Coastal Defense
Chief of Naval Air Defense
Chief of Hydrographic Services
Chief of Auxiliary Fleet and Salvage-Sea Rescue Service
Chief of Firefighting Service
Chief of Inventions Bureau
Chief of Personnel Directorate

The officers now holding these posts are listed in appendix A.

Naval Headquarters directs fleet operations through four fleet com-

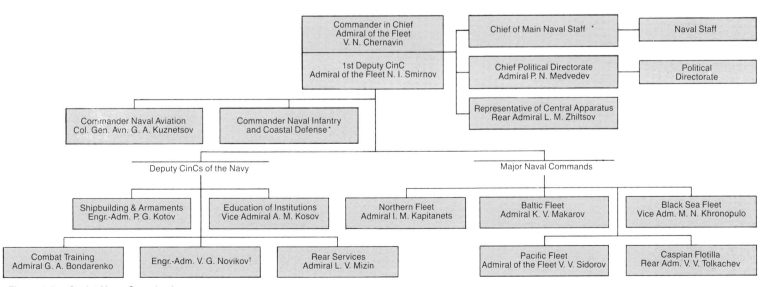

Figure 4-3.   Soviet Navy Organization

manders (see chapter 5) except that a forward-deployed squadron (*eskadra*) appears to be operationally under the direct control of Naval Headquarters. And, as noted above, strategic missile submarines are under the operational control of the Soviet General Staff.

The Military Council of the Navy consists of the CinC, the 1st Deputy CinC, the Chief of Main Naval Staff, the Chief of the Political Directorate, and possibly some of the other deputy CinCs. The council appears to be an advisory body to the CinC providing a senior forum for discussions of major policy issues, especially those that transcend political and specialized areas.

SPETSNAZ FORCES

The Soviet Union maintains a large force of special warfare forces, known by the Soviet acronym *Spetsnaz*. These forces are controlled by the Main Intelligence Directorate (*Glavnoye Razvedyvatelnoye Upravlenie*—GRU) of the Soviet General Staff.

The *Spetsnaz* forces conduct reconnaissance and special warfare missions in "peacetime" as well as in war. Peacetime operations, such as the assassination of Afghanistan's president in December 1979, are under the direction of the KGB.

There are *Spetsnaz* brigades of some 900 to 1,300 officers and men assigned to each of the four groups of forces in Europe as well as several of the major military districts. There are also four naval *Spetsnaz* brigades that are assigned to the four fleets (see chapter 9). According to a former Soviet intelligence officer, there are a total of 20 *Spetsnaz* brigades plus 41 separate companies.[8] Thus, total strength of *Spetsnaz* forces is at least some 30,000 troops within the Soviet armed forces (which total over five million men and women in the five military services).

KGB MARITIME BORDER TROOPS

The KGB Maritime Border Troops protect Soviet maritime borders against penetration by foreign agents or paramilitary forces and prevent Soviet citizens from leaving by water without proper authorization. The troops operate patrol ships and craft in most if not all of the nine border districts. Details on the Maritime Border Troops and descriptions of their ships and craft are provided in chapter 25.

[8] Viktor Suvorov [pseud.], *Inside Soviet Military Intelligence* (New York: Macmillan, 1984), p. 173.

The missile test ship PROVORNYY, converted from a Kashin-class destroyer to carry the SA-N-7 missile system, keeps tabs on a U.S. NIMITZ (CVN 68)-class aircraft carrier. Like most surface combatants, she is heavily armed and mounts an impressive array of electronic equipment. (U.S Navy)

5
Fleets and Flotillas

The current Soviet naval organization consists of four fleets and one flotilla. The Caspian Flotilla is the only survivor of the 12 lake, sea, and river flotillas that existed in the Soviet Navy during World War II. In peacetime the fleets are administrative as well as tactical organizations.

Each fleet and the Caspian Flotilla has a headquarters that is generally similar in organization to that of Naval Headquarters (see figure 5–1). Each fleet has its own naval aviation, naval infantry, coastal defense, and special warfare (*Spetsnaz*) components. The fleets' warships are organized into brigades and divisions. When ships are formed into a specific grouping or task force, they are designated an *eskadra*, literally, a squadron. This grouping can be semi-independent command, as the Fifth *Eskadra* in the Mediterranean, commanded by a vice admiral, the principal control of its operations vested in Naval Headquarters in Moscow and not in the fleet headquarters. The Soviet naval forces

in the Indian Ocean, assigned from the Pacific Fleet, form a similar *eskadra*.

NORTHERN FLEET

The Red Banner Northern Fleet is the largest of the three European fleets and in several respects is the most important.[1] Based mainly in the Kola Peninsula and White Sea areas, the Northern Fleet has more direct access to the Atlantic than do the Baltic and Black Sea fleets, and is thus responsible for wartime operations in the Atlantic and Arctic regions. In addition, the Northern Fleet normally provides submarines

[1] The Order of Red Banner has been awarded to various Soviet units and activities for exemplary service in wartime. The Baltic Fleet was cited for its role in the Revolution of 1917, and all four fleets and the Caspian Flotilla were cited for their service in the Great Patriotic War (1941–1945). The Baltic Fleet is formally referred to as the Twice-Honored Red Banner Baltic Fleet.

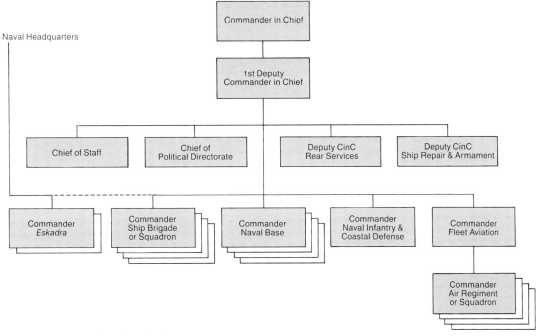

Figure 5-1.   Soviet Fleet Organization

The four Soviet operating fleets are, increasingly, composed of a balance of air, surface, submarine, and amphibious forces. However, the composition of each fleet is tailored for specific geographical constraints and mission requirements. The Northern and Pacific fleets, for example, operate the Navy's VSTOL aircraft carriers. Here a KIEV-class carrier, a Kresta II-class cruiser (left), and a Kashin-class destroyer refuel from the BEREZINA.

for operations in the Mediterranean Sea because the Montreux Convention of 1936 imposes restrictions on submarine transits between the Black Sea and the Mediterranean.

Russia's longest and most inhospitable coast is in the Arctic region. The waters are largely icebound in the winter, except for a 70-mile stretch of the Kola Peninsula, which includes the major ports of Pechenga and Murmansk. The region is subjected to long winter nights; in the Murmansk area the sun does not rise above the horizon from mid-November to mid-January.

History. At the beginning of the reign of Peter the Great, the father of modern Russia as well as the Russian Navy, the northern region was the country's only access to the sea.[2] Although Peter soon undertook

[2] Peter I was born in 1672. He became tsar under a regency at age ten, sharing the throne with a weak-minded older brother, Ivan V. The latter died in 1689, and Peter ruled alone until his death in 1725.

A contemporary French diplomat, de Campredon, cited Peter's military accomplishments in these words:

> . . .through inconceivable labour and patience, he has managed to form some excellent military and naval officers, a body of splendid soldiers, an army of more than 100,000 regular troops, and a fleet of sixty vessels, including twenty of the line. Russia, whose very name was scarcely known, has now become the object of attention of the greater number of powers of Europe, who solicit its friendship.

The above is quoted from British military historian Christopher Duffy's excellent *Russia's Military Way to the West: Origins and Nature of Russian Military Power, 1700–1825* (London:

campaigns to gain access to the Baltic and Black seas, the Arctic coast remained vital to Russian trade. During World War I the ports on the northern coast provided the route for Allied aid to the tsarist regime and then for the landings of U.S. and British troops during the Civil War (1917–1920).

The first major Soviet naval units to be assigned to the region were the patrol ships SMERCH and URAGAN and the submarines DEKABRIST (D-1) and NARODOVOLYETS (D-2), which transited the newly completed Baltic–White Sea Canal from Kronshtadt to Murmansk in the summer of 1933. This was the start of the Northern Naval Flotilla. Reinforcements of ships and submarines followed, and in September 1935 a flight of MBR-2 flying boats was transferred to the Kola Gulf to begin naval air operations in the northern area.

The flotilla was reorganized as the Northern Fleet on 11 May 1937. At the start of the Great Patriotic War in June 1941, the fleet had 15 submarines, 8 destroyers, 7 patrol ships, and numerous lesser craft, plus 116 naval aircraft. It was thus the smallest of the four fleets when the Soviet Union entered World War II. (Those naval forces in the White Sea area were organized as the White Sea Flotilla in August 1941.) The Northern Fleet participated in extensive combat operations against

Routledge & Kegan Paul, 1981), p. 40. Duffy also notes, "The Russian navy was possibly the proudest of Peter's creations. . . ." (p. 36).

German naval forces off of northern Norway and Finland. The Arctic operating area was important to the United States and Britain for convoys carrying war material to the Soviet Union.

In the initial postwar period the Northern Fleet was considered of secondary importance to the fleets in the Baltic and Black seas. This situation changed in the late 1950s when, under Admiral S.G. Gorshkov's direction, the naval forces that would operate in the Atlantic during war were shifted to the Northern Fleet, where they would have more direct access to the open sea.

Today the Northern Fleet has almost 50 percent of the Soviet Navy's submarines, some 26 percent of the surface warships (frigates and larger units), about 27 percent of the naval aircraft, and 26 percent of the naval personnel. The Pacific Fleet is slightly larger than the Northern Fleet in all categories except for submarines. The Northern and Pacific fleets share all of the Navy's nuclear submarines and ballistic missile submarines (except for the six Golf-class SSBs assigned to the Baltic Fleet and the Golf V missile trials submarine in the Black Sea Fleet).

Beyond operations in the Atlantic, the Northern Fleet probably has the responsibility for amphibious operations, should they be undertaken, against Norway, Iceland, and the North Sea approaches to the Danish Straits. Periodically, amphibious ships from the Northern Fleet have entered the Baltic for multi-fleet amphibious exercises.

Admiral I.M. Kapitanents has been CinC of the Northern Fleet since mid-1985. He previously served as a 1st deputy commander and then CinC of the Baltic Fleet. His predecessor in the Northern Fleet, Admiral A.P. Mikhaylovskiy, had held the position for less than four years. (See appendix A for a list of the senior flag officers within the fleets.)

Northern Fleet headquarters is located at Severomorsk, just north of the large port of Murmansk on the Kola Peninsula. In May of 1984 there was an accidental fire and explosion at the Severomorsk weapons depot where most of the Northern Fleet's reserve missiles are stored. A large portion of the depot was destroyed.

BALTIC FLEET

The Twice-Honored Red Banner Baltic Fleet was the principal Russian naval force for most of the period from the time of Peter the Great until early in the tenure of Admiral Gorshkov as CinC of the Soviet Navy.[3] Because the Baltic Fleet's access to the open sea is through waters controlled by NATO navies (the waters of Denmark, Norway, and West Germany), Admiral Gorshkov directed a redeployment of naval forces. As a result, those air, surface, and submarine forces with wartime assignments in the Atlantic were shifted to the Northern Fleet.

The Soviet naval forces in the Baltic are intended almost exclusively for operations in that area. The major exceptions are those ships undergoing trials and training in the huge Leningrad shipbuilding complex and training facilities. Thus, the principal missions of the Baltic Fleet in wartime appear to be supporting army operations and conducting landing and other naval operations to gain control of the Danish Straits. Amphibious operations and certain other Soviet naval activities would be supported by the East German and Polish navies. At the same time, the Soviet and other Pact forces would seek to deny use of the Baltic to the NATO navies.

[3] Admiral S.G. Gorshkov served as CinC of the Soviet Navy from January 1956 until December 1985.

The Soviet Navy's nuclear-propelled strategic missile submarines, like this Delta II-class SSBN, are assigned to the Northern and Pacific fleets, where they have more direct access to the open seas. A Shelon-class torpedo retriever is at the right.

The ASW cruiser-helicopter carrier LENINGRAD, assigned to the Black Sea Fleet, steams through the Baltic in conjunction with a fleet exercise that also brought the VSTOL carrier KIEV into that sea. The fleets in the Baltic and Black Sea are intended for operations in those waters and also in the Mediterranean. (West German Navy)

In 1980 and again in 1981 a task group of Soviet, East German, and Polish ships passed out of the Baltic through the Danish Straits and conducted exercises in the North Sea. These exercises have continued as non-Soviet Warsaw Pact naval missions have extended beyond the Baltic. This move may be partially political, a counter to the long-established NATO multi-national naval maneuvers in the Atlantic and the recent extension of West German naval operational areas to the North Sea.

The Baltic is of major importance to the Soviet Union as a commercial shipping route from the western Russian industrial region to European and world ports. In addition, Leningrad is the transshipment point for the express container route from Japan across the Soviet Union by train and then by ship to Atlantic nations. From a military viewpoint the Baltic forms the northern flank of the Central Front, while the Soviet shipyards on the Baltic are vital to the Soviet fleet in a prolonged conflict.

Much of the northern Baltic, including the Gulf of Finland where Leningrad is located, the Gulf of Riga, and the Gulf of Bothnia, are frozen during the winter. Low clouds in the autumn and winter months limit air operations in the region.

History. Russian influence in the Baltic area dates to 1703, when Peter the Great established a city in the marshes of the Neva River where it enters the Gulf of Finland. Naming this city St. Petersburg and making it the capital of Russia, he sought to bring Western influence to the country and envisioned St. Petersburg as a "window on the West." (The city's German-sounding name was changed to Petrograd in 1914, on the eve of World War I, and subsequently to Leningrad after Lenin's death in 1924.) In 1721 forces under Peter, relying heavily on assistance from British and other foreign naval specialists, defeated the Swedes in a series of battles in the Gulf of Finland. These victories established Russia as a Baltic power and a principal European state. Russian activity and interests in the region grew rapidly under Peter's successors. The Baltic was a major theater of combat for German and Russian naval forces in World War I. During the Bolshevik (Communist) Revolution that erupted in October 1917 against the Kerensky government, sailors from the Baltic Fleet were in the forefront of the revolutionaries. The crew of the cruiser AVRORA, moored in the Neva River, refused orders to get underway and fired blank rounds to signal the start of the Bolshevik assault on the Winter Palace (the Hermitage), site of the government that had replaced the tsarist regime in Russia.

Throughout Russia sailors were in the forefront of the Revolution. And sailors soon formed the core of the *Cheka*, or "extraordinary commission," established by Lenin to punish "spies, traitors, plotters, bandits, speculators, profiteers, counterfeiters, arsonists, hooligans, agitators, saboteurs, class enemies, and other parasites." The *Cheka*—responsible for the death of some 50,000 Bolshevik enemies from 1917 to 1922—was the forerunner of the KGB

Although sailors had helped spark the Revolution in 1917, by 1921 many were disillusioned with Lenin's form of dictatorship. In February they rioted in the city and seized control of the island naval base of Kronshtadt, on Kotlin Island in the Gulf of Finland. The gulf was frozen over and the island was taken by Bolshevik forces after a series of bloody assaults across the ice. The Baltic in 1918–1920 was also the scene of extensive British naval operations against the Communists, including highly successful torpedo boat attacks against anchored Russian battleships.

Between the two world wars Leningrad became the industrial and training center of the Soviet Navy. In June 1941, at the outbreak of conflict, the Baltic Fleet was the largest of the Soviet naval forces, consisting of 2 battleships, 4 cruisers, 21 destroyers, 65 submarines, and numerous lesser craft, supported by 656 naval aircraft. German naval forces almost immediately gained control of the Baltic as German armies pushed north and east from Poland, eventually encircling Leningrad (and being stopped almost within sight of Moscow). Pro-German Finland assisted in the war against the Soviet Union.

The Germans laid anti-submarine minefields and nets across the entrance to the Gulf of Finland to stop Soviet submarines from operating in the Baltic. These measures, plus German naval forces and the winter ice, limited the effectiveness of the Baltic Fleet. During the three-year seige of Leningrad the large-caliber guns of the battleships and cruisers trapped in the port were used to provide fire support for Soviet ground forces.

After the war Leningrad's shipyards and other naval facilities were rebuilt, having had high priority as part of Stalin's fleet rehabilitation.

Today the Baltic Fleet consists primarily of combat forces intended for wartime control of the area, amphibious assaults against West German or Danish positions, the support of Soviet ground operations, or the control of vital waterways. (The Danish island of Bornholm is considered a prime target of Warsaw Pact amphibious assault.) The Baltic Fleet is currently assigned 12 percent of the Soviet Navy's submarines, 16 percent of its surface warships (frigate and larger), 16 percent of its aircraft, and about 19 percent of its personnel.

The operational submarines normally assigned to the Baltic Fleet are all diesel-electric craft, although it does have nuclear submarines for training as well as trials, overhaul, and modernization. During September–October 1976 six Golf II ballistic missile submarines (SSBs) were shifted from the Northern Fleet to the Baltic to provide a sea-based theater nuclear strike capability. Each carries three SS-N-5 Serb missiles. Periodically one of these submarines travels out of the Baltic and back to the Northern Fleet area for missile test firings. In 1982 at least four diesel-propelled Juliett cruise missile submarines (SSGs), each armed with four SS-N-3 Shaddock missiles, shifted from the Northern Fleet to the Baltic. These boats replaced older Shaddock missile submarines of the Whiskey class.

While the Baltic Fleet is intended principally for Baltic operations, its

The Soviet Navy and the KGB Maritime Border Troops operate large numbers of small combatants in all fleet areas, such as this Osa II missile boat and, at far left, Nanuchka II missile corvette. These craft are important for offensive operations as well as coastal security. (Courtesy *Joint Services Recognition Journal*)

diesel-electric attack submarines do conduct periodic training patrols in the North Sea and in waters to the west of Great Britain.

The disproportionate share of personnel assigned to the Baltic Fleet can be attributed to the large numbers of officers and enlisted men attending various schools in the area and assigned to surface ships and submarines under construction in the several shipyards along the Baltic Sea and Gulf of Finland.

The Red Banner Leningrad Naval Base is the nation's largest naval complex, with a number of major schools and other training facilities (see chapter 9) as well as several large shipyards (see chapter 30). Leningrad also has the Central Naval Museum (housed in the imposing stock exchange building of the tsarist era) and the Central Naval Library, with its collection of about one million volumes. Headquarters for the naval base is located in the historic Admiralty building, whose distinctive gold-coated spire dominates the skyline of the lower Neva River.

The Baltic Fleet is under the command of Admiral K.V. Makarov. He assumed that position in early 1985 with his predecessor, Admiral I.M. Kapitanets, being detached to take command of the Northern Fleet. Makarov had been the Chief of Staff of the Baltic Fleet, apparently serving in that post with the rank of vice admiral from early 1983 until his appointment as CinC of the fleet. Admiral Kapitanets, in turn, had been assigned to command the Baltic Fleet in 1981 when the fleet's CinC, Admiral V.V. Sidorov, was suddenly ordered to take command of the Pacific Fleet (see below).

The fleet's headquarters is located at Baltiysk (formerly Pillau) near the Lithuanian port of Kaliningrad (formerly Königsberg).

BLACK SEA FLEET

The Red Banner Black Sea Fleet is responsible for operations in the Black Sea and, more significantly, it provides surface warships and aircraft for operations in the Mediterranean Sea as the Fifth *Eskadra*. The Black Sea Fleet, however, does not provide submarines for Mediterranean operations. As already noted, the submarines for the Mediterranean are provided by the Northern Fleet. Because of the significance of Black Sea–Mediterranean operations, the Black Sea Fleet has a greater proportion of large warships than the Baltic Fleet, although— unlike the Baltic Fleet's operational area—the Black Sea is essentially a "Soviet lake" with Turkey the only potentially hostile nation bordering the sea.

Black Sea ports are second only to those of the Baltic in handling Soviet maritime imports and exports. As in the Baltic, there are major shipyards located along the Black Sea coast. Despite its relatively southern location, some Black Sea ports, including the leading port of Odessa, are frozen for about six weeks of the year, as is the smaller Sea of Azov, immediately north of the Black Sea. Still, the Black Sea climate is the best in the Soviet Union, with many resorts located along the coast, several for naval personnel. Good flying weather is a major reason the Navy's air training center is located in the area.

History. Russian naval activities on the Black Sea can be traced to 1783, when ships from the Sea of Azov visited the village of Akhtiar

(renamed Sevastopol' the following year). Subsequent Russian interest in the area led to a series of wars with Turkey during the late eighteenth and nineteenth centuries, with British and French naval forces at times being allied with those of Turkey. The Russians were highly innovative in tactics and weapons during their battles with the Turks, introducing rifled shells among other developments. During this period shipbuilding became a major activity along the Black Sea coast, especially at Nikolayev on the Yuzhnnyy Bug River, a short distance from the sea.

At the start of this century many sailors of the Black Sea Fleet, like their comrades in the Baltic, were consumed by revolutionary fervor. In the abortive revolt of 1905 there was a much-publicized mutiny on board the battleship POTEMKIN, an event made immortal in Sergei Eisenstein's classic film of 1925.[4] During the Russian revolution of 1917 and the subsequent Civil War, the British and French landed troops on the Black Sea coast to support the anti-Red forces in the area. After the success of the Communists and the withdrawal of foreign fleets, the remnants of the Black Sea Fleet fled to North Africa, where they were interned.

In May of 1920 the newly established Bolshevik regime organized the Naval Forces of the Black Sea and Sea of Azov. These forces were redesignated the Black Sea Fleet on 11 January 1935. During the 1930s the Black Sea region regained its importance in the shipbuilding and maritime industries. At the outbreak of the Great Patriotic War in June 1941, the Black Sea Fleet was the nation's second largest, with 1 battleship, 6 cruisers, 3 destroyer leaders, 14 destroyers, 47 submarines, and 625 land-based aircraft. During the early stages of the German invasion of the Soviet Union in 1941, German troops assaulted the Ukraine. German land-based aircraft were the primary threat to the Soviet ships supporting the Red Army. The Germans pushed through the Ukraine and along the Black Sea coast, finally being stopped at Novorossiysk in late 1942. During the German offensive the ports and shipyards along the Black Sea were devastated.

The surviving Soviet ships and naval aircraft then supported the Soviet counteroffensive. Several naval flotillas were established in the Black Sea area by the Soviet high command during the war, among them the Azov and Danube flotillas. Both flotillas saw extensive combat under the command of then-Rear Admiral Gorshkov. Also, L.I. Brezhnev, General Secretary of the Communist Party from 1964 until his death in 1982, saw action with the Black Sea Fleet as a political officer during an amphibious landing by the 18th Army.

After the war the shipyards in the Black Sea region were rapidly rehabilitated to help rebuild the Soviet fleet. The formation of NATO in 1949, and the fact that Turkey and Greece successfully resisted Communist takeover efforts, seemed to deny the Black Sea Fleet easy access to the Mediterranean through the Turkish straits. Still, in 1958 the Soviets deployed naval forces into the Mediterranean. These were submarines that in 1960 were based, with a tender, at Vlore (Valona), Albania. The following year, as a result of the Sino-Soviet dispute, the Soviets were forced to abandon Vlore, leaving behind two Whiskey-

---

[4] More properly, the KNIAZ POTEMKIN TAVRICHESKI. She was renamed the PANTELIMON after the mutiny and the BORETZ ZA SVOBODU in May 1917.

class submarines that had been seized by the Albanians. The loss of this base pointed up the limitation of Soviet naval logistics, and Soviet combatant forces were not again deployed to the Mediterranean on a sustained basis until 1964.

From that time on Soviet naval forces have operated continuously in the Mediterranean, with surface ships and aircraft coming from the Black Sea Fleet and submarines from the Northern Fleet (see chapter 10). By the early 1970s the Soviets had an average daily strength of 50 or more naval units in the Mediterranean. This force, designated the Fifth *Eskadra,* reached a peak strength of some 73 surface ships and 23 submarines during the October 1973 confrontation with the United States in the Yom Kippur War in the Middle East.[5] Efforts to obtain support bases for the Soviet Mediterranean squadron centered on Egypt (until the Soviets were ejected in 1973) and continue in Syria. Air bases are available to the Soviets in Libya as well as Syria.

The typical composition of the Fifth *Eskadra's* 50 or so naval units is as follows:

7	torpedo attack submarines
2	cruise missile attack submarines
12	cruisers, destroyers, and frigates
1 to 3	minesweepers
1 to 3	amphibious ships
approx. 25	auxiliary ships, including survey, research, and intelligence collection ships

Soviet combat operations in the Black and Mediterranean seas would be supported by land-based aircraft from bases in the Crimea. In addition, cruiser-helicopter carriers of the MOSKVA class are based in the Black Sea and operate regularly in the Mediterranean, as do the KIEV-class aircraft carriers when they are in the Black Sea area. The Black Sea Fleet also has the largest cruiser-destroyer force of any of the Soviet fleets. In total, the Black Sea Fleet has 26 percent of the Navy's major combatants (frigates and larger) but only 9 percent of the Navy's submarines, with no nuclear or ballistic missile units except for one Golf SSB missile trials submarine. The Black Sea Fleet has 27 percent of the Navy's aircraft—including most of the Navy's training planes—and 20 percent of the personnel.

The Black Sea Fleet is commanded by Vice Admiral M.N. Khronopulo, who took command in mid-1985. Prior to that, from December 1981, he was the fleet's 1st deputy commander. Khronopulo replaced Admiral A.M. Kalinin who had only been appointed to command of the Black Sea Fleet in June 1983. The removal of a fleet CinC after only two years was unprecedented. Kalinin is reported to have been retired. (He was appointed Chief of Staff of the Baltic Fleet in 1979 and that fleet's 1st deputy CinC two years later, and was named to command the Black Sea Fleet two years after that; in May 1975 he commanded the two Soviet destroyers that visited the port of Boston.)

Before Kalinin the Black Sea command had been held by Admiral N.I. Khovrin, appointed in early 1974; he left in 1983 to become the

---

[5] At that time the U.S. Sixth Fleet in the Mediterranean had some 60 ships, but the fleet's 3 aircraft carriers provide a superior surface striking force.

Warsaw Pact's deputy CinC for naval forces.

The fleet headquarters is located at Sevastopol'.

CASPIAN SEA FLOTILLA

The Red Banner Caspian Sea Flotilla is primarily a small patrol force operating on the world's largest inland sea, which is shared with Iran. Under Peter the Great, Russian forces fortified portions of the Caspian coast and built a fleet that gained the ports of Baku and Derbend by treaty. Subsequently Baku was lost, only to be recaptured from Persia in 1816. Later treaties gave Russian warships the exclusive right to the sea, although Persia continued to hold the southern coast and Iran continues to operate patrol boats in the area.

Russian and Soviet naval operations on the Caspian continued with the construction of a canal from the Black Sea permitting the rapid transfer of ships up to destroyer size between the two bodies of water. Although naval activity on the Caspian is limited, there is considerable shipping with most of the cargo being oil and grain. Offshore oil wells in the Caspian contribute significantly to the Soviet Union's petroleum production.

The Caspian Flotilla currently operates 4 Riga-class frigates, 1 light frigate, 5 patrol ships, 20 lesser patrol craft, 25 minesweepers of various sizes, 13 Polnocny-class LSMs, 15 smaller landing craft, and several auxiliary ships. No aircraft are assigned to the flotilla. Total personnel strength is about 4,000 officers and enlisteds.

The Caspian Sea Flotilla is commanded by Rear Admiral V.V. Tolkachev, who has his headquarters at Baku. He has been commander of the flotilla since mid-1984. Before that he was the flotilla's chief of staff. The Caspian Flotilla was commanded by Vice Admiral G.G. Kasumbekov from 1977 to 1984.

PACIFIC FLEET

The largest of the four Soviet fleets and the one with the largest operating area is the Red Banner Pacific Fleet. Whereas in war the three European fleets would oppose the United States and NATO forces, the Pacific Fleet would oppose the People's Republic of China as well as the United States and its allies (South Korea, Japan, and possibly other nations, depending on the wartime scenario). The peacetime responsibilities of the Pacific Fleet include operations throughout the Pacific, and the fleet provides most of the ships that deploy in the Indian Ocean.

There has been a significant buildup of the Pacific Fleet during the past few years because of the unsettled political situation in Southeast Asia, the Soviet invasion of Afghanistan in 1979, the turmoil in the Persian Gulf region, and the continued unrest along the eastern coast of Africa. The principal mission of the Pacific Fleet, of course, is defending the Soviet Siberian coast, second only to the Arctic coast in length. In general, the Soviet Pacific coast provides more direct access than European coasts to the open oceans. The major port complex of Vladivostok opens into the Sea of Japan with four major straits giving egress into the Pacific. The Soviets control one exit (Kuril Strait), and another separates Japan and the Russian-held island of Sakhalin (La Pérouse), while the two other exits are controlled by Japan and Japan

Three Polnocny-class landing ships of the Pacific Fleet practice unloading PT-76 amphibious tanks during a 1982 exercise. The Pacific Fleet's naval infantry was recently enlarged and reorganized to division size. Along with the transfer of two VSTOL carriers, a battle cruiser, and other modern surface combatants to the Pacific, this buildup of amphibious forces provides a significant "power projection" capability for the Pacific–Indian Ocean areas. (Sovfoto, Sergei Kozlov)

and South Korea (Tsugaru and the Korean straits, respectively). Their blockade by the West is unlikely, except in the most extreme circumstances, because of the dependence of Japan and Korea on maritime trade. The second major naval port in the Far East is Petropavlovsk, on the coast of desolate Kamchatka. Most of the Pacific Fleet's submarines are based there, where they have direct access to the Pacific Ocean.

The Soviet Siberian coast has several ports vital to Soviet trade. These ports move cargo to and from European Russia (reducing the load on the severely limited trans-Siberian railway). They facilitate the economic and politically lucrative trade with the Third World nations of western South America, Southeast Asia, India, the Middle East, and eastern Africa.

History. Russians reached the Pacific coast of Siberia in significant numbers in the mid-seventeenth century. The towns of Anadyr' and Okhotsk were founded in 1649. The area grew in importance at a rapid pace, largely because of trade with China and then Japan. Commodore Matthew Calbraith Perry, Commander of the U.S. East India Squadron, forced the opening of Japan in 1853–1854 to preempt a Russian squadron in the area and prevent the tsar's officers from reaping the benefits of a treaty with Japan. The Okhotsk Flotilla was formed in 1731, then reorganized and renamed the Siberian Naval Flotilla in 1856. In addition to the flotilla, the 1st Pacific Squadron was established. At the start of the 1904–1905 war with Japan, the Russian Navy had 7 of its 15 modern battleships based at Port Arthur (the Japanese Navy had 6 modern battleships then in commission).

The Russo-Japanese War of 1904–1905 was a disaster for the Pacific Squadron as well as for a large reinforcing fleet sent by the Russians from the Baltic and Black seas. The Japanese triumph at the Battle of Tsushima on 27 May 1905 destroyed Russian naval power in the Pacific and established Japan as a world power. After the war the Russian Navy in the Far East consisted of the weakened Siberian and Amur flotillas. After the Revolution of 1917, Japanese and American troops landed at Vladivostok to support anti-Communist forces and help remove a Czech army in central Russia that the Allies wished to transport to the European theater. The Japanese left Siberia in 1922, after which the Soviets formed the Vladivostok ship detachment and the Amur Naval Flotilla in the Far East. These organizations were disbanded in 1926, with the ships and craft being assigned to the border guards and the new Far Eastern Naval Flotilla. The naval units were organized as the Naval Forces of the Far East in April 1932, and on 11 January 1935, as Soviet forces in the area increased, the title Pacific Fleet was assigned.

Pacific Fleet aircraft were involved in the fighting with Japan in Manchuria in the late 1930s. Ships moved troops and material and evacuated wounded. When the Great Patriotic War began in Europe in June 1941 the Pacific Fleet consisted of 14 destroyers, 91 submarines, numerous lesser craft, and some 500 aircraft. These units were essentially idle during the war, with 147,000 men from the fleet being sent as ground troops to the European theater.

When the Soviet Union attacked Japan in August 1945, the Pacific Fleet had 2 cruisers, 13 destroyers, and 78 submarines, plus other ships and craft and 1,549 aircraft. During operations against Manchuria and Korea, in the final days of the war, the fleet attacked Japanese shipping and supported ground operations with air attacks and logistic support.

Several amphibious landings, largely unopposed, were made at ports along the coasts of Korea, Sakhalin, and the Kuril islands. Some were undertaken in conjunction with parachute landings.

In January 1947 the Pacific Fleet was divided into the Fifth Fleet (headquartered at Vladivostok) and the Seventh Fleet (headquartered at Sovetskaya Gavan'). They were reunited into a single Pacific Fleet in 1953. Significant long-range operations of the Pacific Fleet began in 1959 when a SVERDLOV-class cruiser and two destroyers visited Djakarta, Indonesia. This was the harbinger of Soviet naval assistance to the Sukarno government in Indonesia. It included the transfer of a SVERDLOV cruiser, 12 Whiskey-class submarines, 8 destroyers, 8 escort ships, 12 Komar-type missile craft, and other naval material. (Sukarno's fall from power in 1965 ended Russian influence in the island nation.) Soviet naval operations expanded in the Pacific during the 1960s and spread into the Indian Ocean, with major ship and missile transfers to the Indian Navy contributing to that force's startling success against Pakistan in the 1971 war between the two nations.

The Soviet Pacific Fleet observed U.S. operations in the Vietnam War with great interest. Soviet intelligence collection ships (AGIs) periodically operated in the Gulf of Tonkin, with one AGI usually on station off Guam to observe the U.S. Polaris submarine base and detect B-52 bomber missions taking off from the island. Warnings of raids against Communist forces in Vietnam were broadcast moments after the planes took off. Soviet naval ship visits to Communist Vietnam began in March 1979, calling at the northern port of Haiphong and the southern ports of Da Nang and Cam Ranh Bay. Bear-D naval reconnaissance aircraft began flights from Da Nang in April 1972, flying missions over the South China Sea, including flights over U.S. naval ships. Reportedly, in this period the Soviets also began improvements to facilities at Kompong Som in Cambodia.

During the 1970s the Pacific Fleet began receiving first-line units at about the same time as the Soviet European fleets. This was highlighted by the transfer of the MINSK, the second of the KIEV-class aircraft carriers, to the Pacific in June 1979. The carrier was accompanied by the IVAN ROGOV, the largest amphibious ship in the Soviet Navy. Four guided missile cruisers (one Kresta I, one Kresta II, and two Karas) plus several lesser surface warships and submarines also joined the Pacific Fleet from 1978 to 1980.

Another KIEV-class carrier, the NOVOROSSIYSK, transferred to the Pacific Fleet in 1984, followed in 1985 by the nuclear-propelled battle cruiser FRUNZE, the second ship of the KIROV class. The buildup and modernization of the Pacific Fleet is continuing.

By 1985 the Pacific Fleet could boast almost one-third of the Soviet submarine force (including 25 of the 62 modern strategic missile submarines), 29 percent of the major surface warships (frigate and larger), and the largest of the fleet air arms, with 30 percent of the total SNA aircraft. Some 33 percent of the Navy's manpower is assigned to the fleet.

Admiral of the Fleet V.V. Sidorov commands the Pacific Fleet with his headquarters at Vladivostok. He took the CinC position after Admiral Ye.N. Spiridonov and several other senior Pacific Fleet officers were killed in an air crash in European Russia on 7 February 1981. (Spiridonov held the fleet command for less than a year and a half before his death.) Sidorov was serving as CinC of the Baltic Fleet when ordered to take command of the Pacific Fleet on short notice; he had commanded the Baltic Fleet since July 1978. A surface warfare specialist, he had earlier served as Chief of Staff of the Pacific Fleet. As a fleet admiral he is the highest ranking of the four fleet commanders and, with Admiral Chernavin, one of the two naval officers who are candidate members of the Central Committee of the Communist Party.

6
Missions and Tactics

Soviet naval missions have evolved continuously since World War II.[1] At this time they remain oriented primarily toward strategic strike and the defense of the homeland. However, there is increasing emphasis on supporting Soviet activities in the Third World.

At the same time, there are major improvements being made to capabilities in all combat areas—anti-surface, anti-submarine, and anti-air warfare, plus theater/tactical nuclear and chemical operations. Some analysts have called specific attention to recent Soviet developments in anti-ship missile defense and postulated developments in Soviet anti-submarine warfare.

MISSIONS

During the past decade, with the availability of the Delta and Typhoon classes of strategic missile submarines, the mission of "attack against the shore" by submarine-launched ballistic missiles has become the principal mission of the Soviet Navy. Included in this mission, depending upon the scenario of the crisis or conflict, are strategic missile submarines that serve in the roles of deterrence, pre-emptive strike, warfighting, and strategic reserve.

The large number of SSBNs in the Soviet fleet, their relatively high survivability, their large weapons payload, and their ability to strike targets in the United States from Soviet home waters or from under the Arctic ice pack, make them highly attractive to Soviet planners.

Second to this strategic attack mission, the principal mission of the Soviet Navy—as well as of the other Soviet armed services—is the defense of the homeland. This latter mission has led to a tactical style that tends to pervade all naval missions. Although the Navy has gone through a series of radical changes in organization and leadership as well as some changes in mission, the consistency of tactical style in the Soviet Navy is remarkable.

It would appear in 1986—as it did more than 50 years earlier—that the basic tactical concept of the Soviet Navy is to attack any hostile ship attempting to approach within striking range of the Soviet land mass or sensitive sea-air space. The concepts of concentration of force and of all-arms strike developed during the post-Revolution decade also remain in force today. These concepts, of course, have been transmuted considerably, so that the attack may now be mounted far from the Soviet coast and the target may now be a U.S. strategic missile submarine rather than a hostile battleship approaching the coast. However, conceptual similarities and their theoretical consequences remain.

Profound differences between Soviet and Western naval "styles" have important analytical consequences. Soviet warships with characteristics somewhat similar to Western types often have very different roles and should not be counted as analogous to those Western ships. Perhaps the most significant point here is that the fundamental Soviet mission has been, and remains, the defense of the homeland, and the perimeter of that defense is continuously expanding.

In the early 1960s, strategic strike by submarines was added to the list of primary Soviet naval missions. In turn, the defense of those missile submarines and—with deployment of the SS-N-8 missile in Delta SSBNs—the "sanctuaries" within which the missile submarines might operate became an additional mission. The defensive mission—"prosubmarine" operations—is alien to American naval thought. U.S. attack submarines as well as strategic missile submarines operate independently, employing stealth and communications silence for their survivability and hence their effectiveness.

The Soviets have a different approach to the subject. This is due in significant part to geography. Soviet attack submarines must reach the open seas through straits or "choke points" where they could be vulnerable to interdiction. But there is also an historical precedent. Admiral S.G. Gorshkov, commander in chief of the Soviet Navy from 1956 to 1985, wrote of the U-boat campaign in the Atlantic during World War II that "despite the exceptional threat to submarines by ASW forces, the German naval command did not conduct a single operation or other specially organized combat actions directed at destroying these forces, which doubtlessly reduced the intensity of the [German U-boat] communications battle."[2] And, one of the main reasons why the U-boats

---

[1] This chapter is based in part on research by Dr. Norman Friedman for the Hudson Institute discussion paper "Soviet Naval Tactics" (20 May 1982) and an expansion of the author's lectures "Thoughts on Soviet Naval Developments" and "Soviet Use of the Sea."

[2] Admiral Gorshkov, *Red Star Rising at Sea* (Annapolis, Md.: Naval Institute Press, 1974), p. 100. This is a compilation of translations of the 11 articles by Admiral Gorshkov that originally appeared in *Morskoy Sbornik* [Naval Digest] in 1972–1973 and were reprinted in the Naval Institute *Proceedings* during 1974. It was unprecedented for the serving head of the Soviet Navy to publish a series like this. The articles were revised and reprinted in book form, again under Gorshkov's byline, as *Morskaya moshch gosudarstva* [The Sea Power of the State] (Moscow: Voenizdat, 1976), and in English by the Naval Institute Press in 1979.

An Il-38 May anti-submarine/patrol aircraft overflies the U.S. aircraft carrier MIDWAY (CV 41) in the Western Pacific. The principal missions of the Soviet Navy now appear to be nuclear strike and defense of the homeland. Naval aviation—including the May aircraft—can contribute to both of these missions; for the former, the May helps to protect Soviet SSBNs from Western attack submarines. (U.S. Navy)

did not achieve victory "was that the submarines did not receive support from other forces, and above all from the Air Force, which would have been able both to carry out the reconnaissance for the submarines and destroy ASW forces. . . ."[3]

While some Western analysts contend that statements like this are hyperbole, a ruse to gain more support for surface warships, this cannot be entirely true, as such language is found often in internal Soviet naval documents. And the use of such forces to destroy or distract an enemy's ASW forces certainly is logical. Finally, the indications that the Soviets do intend to form a protected "haven" or "bastion" for strategic missile submarine operations in the Arctic region further supports Admiral Gorshkov's contentions.

There appears to be no strain of Soviet naval thought, on either the mission or the tactical level, parallel to Western concepts of sea control. On the mission level, the Soviet Navy under Gorshkov rejected Mahan's theories, which form the basis of U.S. naval thought (although Mahan is often quoted by U.S. naval officers who have not actually read him). Admiral Gorshkov wrote, "The Mahan theory of 'control of the sea,' considered indisputable, according to which only a general engagement of major line forces could lead to victory. . . . did not at all take into account not only the near-future prospects, but even the notable trends in the development of naval technology."[4]

Rather, Gorshkov preferred a Russian naval strategist and historian, Rear Admiral V.A. Belli, who wrote:

[3] Ibid., p. 103.

[4] Ibid., p. 40.

To achieve superiority of forces over the enemy in the main sector and to pin him down in the secondary sectors at the time of the operation means to achieve *control of the sea* in a theater or a sector of a theater, i.e., to create such a situation that the enemy will be paralyzed or constrained in his operations, or weakened and thereby hampered from interfering with our execution of a given operation. . . .[5]

In reality, Mahan's concepts had little practical application for the Soviets during the 1920s and 1930s because they lacked capital ships and their maritime activities were limited. By the 1950s the availability of radar, effective communications, long-range aircraft, advanced submarines, guided missiles, and even nuclear weapons for the war at sea made Mahan's concepts even more questionable. Coupled with geographic considerations and other factors, modern technology has given Mahan little if any relevance in the Soviet Navy of the Gorshkov era.

On the tactical level of sea control, the Soviets certainly wish to protect their own coastal shipping and their oceangoing units from West-

[5] Ibid., p. 71. Rear Admiral Belli, at the time a Captain 2nd Rank, made the statement in his thesis "Theoretical Principles of Conducting Operations" at the Naval Academy [i.e., Soviet naval war college], 1938.

ern naval attack. But in general they appear to view the sea in wartime as a jungle, with all or most warships subject to rapid destruction. Recent decisions to build relatively large and expensive surface combatants, such as aircraft carriers and the nuclear-propelled battle cruisers of the KIROV class, may lead to reconsideration of this tactical issue, but the current makeup of the Soviet fleet generally reflects earlier tactical concepts.

Indeed, the development of these ships fits more with a new Soviet naval mission, first espoused during the 1960s when Soviet naval forces began regular, and in some cases sustained, deployments in noncontiguous seas—the Mediterranean and Caribbean seas, the Indian Ocean, and most recently, the western Pacific. These are mainly missions to show political presence and project force in the Third World. To quote Admiral Gorshkov again, speaking of forward operations in peacetime:

Friendly visits by Soviet seamen offer the opportunity to the peoples of the countries visited to see for themselves the creativity of socialist principles in our country, the genuine parity of the peoples of the Soviet Union and their high cultural level. In our ships they see the achievements of Soviet science, technology and industry. Soviet mariners, from rating to

The KIEV-class aircraft carriers, the largest warships yet completed in the Soviet Union, were justified primarily for anti-submarine operations; their RBU-6000 and SUW-N-1 ASW weapon launchers and Ka-25 Hormone-A helicopters are visible here. But so too are the ship's gun and missile systems that—with her Forger VSTOL aircraft—provide a multiple combat capability.

Soviet sailors exercise in CBR protective gear. The Soviet Navy appears to be better trained and prepared to fight in chemical and nuclear environments than are most Western navies.

admiral, bring to the peoples of other countries the truth about our socialist country, our Soviet ideology and culture and our Soviet way of life.[6]

Only polemics? Unlikely. The Soviet Union, with approximate strategic and conventional weapons parity with the United States, is seeking to gain advances in the Third World, and as Oliver Cromwell remarked, "A man-of-war is the best ambassador." Now the Soviets have gone a step beyond sending sailors as ambassadors. In a less-publicized exposition on naval cruises, Admiral Gorshkov was more pointed:

> Further growth in the power of our navy will be characterized by an intensification of its international mission. While appearing within our armed forces as an imposing factor in regard to restraining imperialist aggression and ventures, at the same time the Soviet Navy is a consolidator of international relations. . . .[7]

For several years the Soviet Union has used proxy troops in Africa, the Middle East, and Southeast Asia, armed with Soviet weapons and sometimes directed by Soviet advisors. Soviet merchant ships and, to a more limited degree, naval ships have supported these activities. The Soviet Navy has used amphibious ships to move Third World troops in the Middle East, while warships steaming offshore have provided political support as well as collected intelligence for allies.

The naval and merchant fleets now being built will permit—in Western terms—"force projection" in the Third World. According to Gorshkov, "The Soviet Navy, in the policy of our Party and state, acts as a

factor for stabilizing the situation in different areas of the world, promoting the strengthening of peace and friendship between the peoples and restraining the aggressive strivings of the imperialist states."[8] In accordance with this thinking, new missions have been assigned to the Soviet Navy. In probable order of development, they are:

early 1950s Coastal Defense/Anti-Amphibious*
1950s Anti-Carrier*
1960s Anti-Western Sea Lanes*
Anti-Polaris*
Strategic Strike

1960s–1970s Forward Deployments for Political Considerations
1980s "Force Projection"—Support to Third World Countries

(Asterisks indicate "defense of the homeland" missions.)

TACTICS

Defense of the homeland being a primary Soviet mission, the primary naval operation is to destroy enemy warships attempting to enter the defensive area. This, in turn, requires a combination of (1) reconnaissance and surveillance to detect the intruder, (2) command and control to bring superior forces to attack at the proper time and location, and (3) effective strikes against the target ship or group of ships. These three areas have been well developed by the Soviet Navy.

History. The evolution of contemporary Soviet doctrine and tactics started with the problems faced immediately after the Revolution and Civil War. The new socialist state had neither the capital ships nor the industrial base to build an effective fleet. At the same time, threats from the sea were a major concern, as Britain, France, Japan, and the United States had used their navies to support anti-Bolshevik forces during the Russian Civil War.

Soviet naval forces were only gradually built up, and then in the context of a military program that emphasized ground and air forces. Once Soviet industrialization had begun in earnest, it was far easier to build light craft and then small warships. Although former tsarist officers continued to call for a battle fleet as a prerequisite for effective naval defense, a "young school" (*molodaia shkola*) of Soviet naval theorists attempted to turn this weakness into a tactical strength by a combination of limiting the naval mission and at the same time enforcing combined-arms operations.

The debate was considerable. V.I. Zov, naval commissar from 1924 to 1926, personally criticized members of the "old school." In an address at the Soviet Naval Academy (i.e., war college) in 1925 he declared:

> You speak of aircraft carriers and of the construction of new types of ships . . . at the same time completely ignoring the economic situation of our country and corresponding conditions of our technical means, completely ignoring the fact that perhaps tomorrow or the day after we will be called

[6] Admiral Gorshkov, *The Sea Power of the State* (Annapolis, Md.: Naval Institute Press, 1979), p. 252.
[7] Admiral Gorshkov, "Naval Cruises Play Role in Training, International Relations," *Bloknot Agitatora* (no. 8, April 1973), pp. 3–6.
[8] Gorshkov, *Sea Power of the State,* p. 277.

The Soviet Union has an insatiable appetite for intelligence, with the Navy conducting overt and covert collection activities. This Victor III-class SSN was observing a U.S. escort ship when she ran afoul of a towed sonar array. Here the Soviet intelligence ship NAKHODKA and the U.S. destroyer PETERSON (DD 969) stand by off the coast of South Carolina in 1983. (U.S. Navy, Lt. Comdr. J. van Carpenter)

on to fight. And with what shall we fight? We will fight with those ships and personnel that we have already.[9]

Thus, the concept of sea control in the Western sense was largely abandoned. In its place came pure coastal defense, with the advantages to be gained by tight coordination of the forces that could be afforded: coastal guns, land-based aircraft, light craft, and mines. Submarines and offshore pickets—designated *Storozhevoy Korabl'* (SKR), or "guard ship," by the Soviets—were, it appears, seen primarily as a means of detecting enemy ships entering the guarded area.

Stalin began to build a conventional, blue-water surface fleet in the

[9] Quoted in Commander Robert W. Herrick, USN (Ret.), *Soviet Naval Strategy* (Annapolis, Md.: U.S. Naval Institute, 1967), p. 10; the Zov speech was printed in the May 1925 issue of *Morskoy Sbornik*.

late 1930s. By that time a heavy industry base existed in Russia, and Soviet support of the Republicans in the Spanish Civil War of 1936–1938 and the limited campaign against Japan in 1937 demonstrated the need for major naval forces to support Soviet foreign policy. World War II halted Stalin's building program, but he sought to promote it again after the war.

It is remarkable in retrospect that there appears to have been no development of tactics for blue-water operations, even with the few large ships available. For example, the Soviets spent little if any effort on developing anti-submarine tactics for the screening of large ships, even when the SVERDLOV-class cruisers appeared in the early 1950s. The destroyers built in that period were primarily armed for and exercised in the anti-ship role, not ASW (or, for that matter, even air defense).

Similarly, not until the *Okean* exercises of 1975 did the Soviets demonstrate major interest in escorting oceangoing convoys and amphibious groups. Previous naval escort activities appear to have been oriented to either coastal operations or simulating Western tactics.

Before the war the Soviets employed submarines, guard ships, and land-based aircraft to detect intruders in Soviet territorial areas. They reported to a central commander ashore who could maintain a plot of the combat area and coordinate the attack. This type of command and control led directly to the present Soviet command structure and what is called in the West the Soviet Ocean Surveillance System (SOSS), which seeks to make available to a fleet commander a full picture of the potential battle area. (The SOSS is discussed below.)

An important concept in centralized targeting by Soviet forces is the "circle of uncertainty." Target data are generally fleeting: an enemy ship or force is reported at a specific point for a brief period. Its movement after that may be random and may well be unknown. In this situation there is an expanding circle of uncertainty around the original datum in which the target may be found. The longer the delay in reaching the target area, the larger the circle and the more difficult the subsequent search and reacquisition.

The Soviets have often emphasized high speed in their attack platforms and missiles precisely because of this problem. There is a great difference in the circle of uncertainty for a Mach 2 missile compared to a Mach 0.8 cruise missile at, for example, 200 miles (320 km), and the need for the high speed (with all its design penalties) testifies to continued Soviet reliance on centralized targeting and an attempt to avoid the need for mid-course guidance, which may be difficult or impossible in a combat environment.

Rigid, centralized tactical control has several advantages. First, in the early Soviet period it enhanced political control of military units, which for many years appeared to come before military effectiveness in priority. Second, a central commander could, at least in theory, make the most effective use of available weapons. Initially small attack craft, submarines, and land-based aircraft were the main striking force of the Soviet Navy; individually they would not be effective against an enemy's capital ships, but under centralized control their potential effectiveness was enhanced considerably. Centralized control also permitted a reduction in the search and targeting requirements for individual units (radar, sonar), so that more units could be procured for a given cost.

Soviet naval tactics, in contrast with traditional Western tactics, have thus become statistical in character—or to use the Soviet term, "scientific." The combination of centrally collected intelligence and centrally controlled attack forces continues as the basis of Soviet naval practice, although a trend toward decentralization has become apparent in the past few years. In virtually every tactical context, the attack is delivered all at once, often along several different axes, in an effort to overwhelm the defenses of the target ship or group of ships. Also, the strike is delivered at almost maximum weapon range. Increases in stand-off weapon range and speed permit earlier attacks sooner than would be possible if the attacking ships or aircraft had to close with the target; moreover, these increases facilitate strikes by more ships or aircraft within a given area.

The longer weapon range contributes to another key Soviet tactical concept, that of surprise or, in Admiral Gorshkov's words, "the battle for the first salvo." This is a favorite topic of Soviet tactical discussions. One Soviet military writer recently used this definition:

> Surprise is one of the most important principles of military art. This principle consists in choosing the time, means and methods of combat actions allowing to deliver a surprise blow at the enemy and thus to a certain extent to paralyse his will to resist. Surprise gives the possibility to achieve maximum result with the minimum spending of manpower, equipment and time.[10]

Addressing this concept, Admiral Gorshkov wrote:

> "the battle for the first salvo"—is taking on a special meaning in naval battle under present-day conditions (conditions including the possible employment of combat means of colossal power [nuclear weapons]). Delay in the employment of weapons in a naval battle or operation inevitably will be fraught with the most serious and even fatal consequences, regardless of where the fleet is located, at sea or in port.[11]

Citing Western analysis to explain or justify Soviet beliefs—a common ploy in Soviet writing—a recent text notes that the combat potential of a force can be increased two and a half times if it attains surprise.[12] At the same time, a Soviet naval officer has cited Western naval specialists as believing that "under present-day conditions the probability of attaining surprise in the first operations by time, axis, and location has *increased considerably in comparison with the past*."[13] [Emphasis added]

The combat concepts of (1) centralized control, (2) comprehensive intelligence and reconnaissance, (3) increasing weapon ranges, and (4) surprise are applicable to almost all phases of Soviet naval tactics. These include anti-surface, anti-submarine, and anti-air warfare as well as missile strikes against hostile territory.

ANTI-SURFACE WARFARE

The Soviets have exercised forces in the Anti-Surface Warfare (ASUW) role with land-based strike aircraft flying coordinated, multi-plane, anti-ship missile strikes.

Prior to the strikes there are extensive reconnaissance and intelligence collection efforts. As sufficient data on the target ships is received at the appropriate headquarters, the strike aircraft are launched toward the predetermined datum, under centralized control. The aircraft generally fly high enough for the lead plane to acquire the target with its own missile control radar, although missiles that can lock on after launch reduce this requirement. All aircraft in the wave then lock their missiles on the target. The aircraft—possibly coming from several directions, either simultaneously or in series, and even from different bases—will generally launch their missiles together or in waves in an effort to overwhelm defenses.

---

[10] Colonel B. Frolov, Ph.D. Candidate of Sciences (History), "Surprise," *Soviet Military Review* (no. 9, 1980), pp. 27–29.

[11] Admiral Gorshkov, *Red Star Rising*, pp. 131–132.

[12] Captain 1st Rank A. Aristov, "Surprise-Factor Effect on the Success of Combat Actions, at Sea," *Morskoy Sbornik* (no. 1, 1985), pp. 16–23.

[13] Aristov, "Surprise-Factor Effects," pp. 16–23.

While naval aircraft are primarily employed in the anti-ship role, during exercises strategic strike aircraft have also performed this role. (See chapter 8.)

Surface and submarine missile attacks are coordinated with the strike aircraft when possible. Tactics of the surface force are analogous to those of the strike aircraft. Attacks are controlled either from a headquarters ashore or from a command ship. This is especially true of small combatants—missile and torpedo boats—that are merely attack platforms acting with external targeting data under the directions of a central commander.[14]

There are obvious problems in coordinating air, surface, and submarine attacks. However, improved communications and longer-range and higher-speed missiles do facilitate such coordination. Again, in exercises the Soviets have attempted to synthesize such tactics. In the anti-carrier phases of the *Okean* 1970 exercises, the Soviets sent aircraft against simulated U.S. carriers in the waters between Iceland and Britain, while simultaneously in the Far East naval strike aircraft flew against simulated U.S. carriers in the Western Pacific.

In the context of the first salvo concept, these exercises, in pitting their warships against U.S and allied task forces, provide the Soviets the opportunity for updated targeting. Shortly before the planned strike, the accompanying Soviet ship or "tattletale" moves away from the target ships. This maneuver prevents the distraction of incoming Soviet missiles from their real targets. Also, the departing tattletale can participate in the missile strike (this probably accounts for the rear-firing missiles in the modified Kashin and Kildin destroyer classes).

Multi-platform ASUW tactics are receiving new attention in the Soviet Navy as new surface warship classes emphasizing the anti-ship role are joining the fleet. The Kynda (1962) and Kresta I (1967) classes, their principal armament being anti-ship missiles, were followed by several cruiser and destroyer classes whose weapons were heavily oriented toward ASW. But three major surface ship classes have now emerged with heavy anti-ship armament: the Sovremennyy (1981), the Slava (1983), and the nuclear-propelled battle cruiser Kirov (1980). However, it should be taken into account that several destroyer and ASW cruisers built in the 1960s and 1970s have the SA-N-1 and SA-N-3 surface-to-air launchers, both of which can be used against surface targets, according to Soviet statements.

With respect to submarines in the anti-shipping role, at least through the 1950s Soviet submarines acting in the coastal defense role were closely controlled by headquarters ashore. This was a continuation of prewar Soviet practices. In a related matter, the Soviets appear to have developed the "flying torpedo"—an underwater-launched anti-ship missile—to give these submarines greater stand-off range against intruders. Note that these submarines are best employed with off-board sensors and centralized control to coordinate missile strikes. Recent developments, especially the SS-N-19 missiles fired from the Oscar-class SSGN, significantly increase Soviet capabilities because of the submarine's high submerged speed, the long range of its missiles, and

the large number of missiles that are carried in this class (compared to eight in the Echo II and Charlie classes).

(The older, surface-launched SS-N-3/12 submarine missiles were developed with the land-attack SS-N-3c, intended for strategic attack against the United States. When the SS-N-3/12 is used in the anti-ship role, the submarine must remain on the surface for many minutes after launching to send target update data to the missile while in flight.)

A final consideration in ASUW is the possible use of land-based ballistic missiles against enemy ships. Soviet coastal defense forces have surface-to-surface cruise missiles for use against ships in the coastal defensive zones, possibly out to a couple of hundred miles. (See chapter 9.) Obviously, ballistic missiles have long offered the advantages of longer range and shorter flight time; but initially a ballistic missile could not be guided in flight against a moving target, and the time delay from target acquisition to missile arrival at the datum could be considerable—enough to permit the target ship to escape, especially if the mode of surveillance could not provide an exact location. The limited accuracy of the early ballistic missiles would further reduce possible effectiveness.

There is ample evidence that at least from the early 1960s, when the classic work of Marshal V.D. Sokolovskiy, *Soviet Military Strategy*, was published, the Soviets have been considering the use of land-based ballistic missiles against surface ships.[15] By the late 1960s the Soviet Navy was developing a submarine-launched ballistic missile, the SS-NX-13, apparently for use against surface ships. (This weapon was fully developed but not deployed; see chapter 27.)

Relatively recent developments in ballistic missile technology, especially the Multiple Independently targeted Re-entry Vehicles (MIRV) and the Maneuvering Re-entry Vehicle (MaRV), coupled with improvements in ocean reconnaissance and high-speed communications, have opened up new possibilities for the use of ballistic missiles against naval forces at sea. While Soviet professional writings of late have not discussed this subject, there are other indications of continued Soviet interest in this regard. For example, on 2 April 1982 the Soviets fired six SS-20 intermediate-range ballistic missiles into the Barents Sea. These firings are believed to have been related to a naval exercise in the same general area.

Available technology offers the potential for land- and ship-launched ballistic missiles to be used against surface forces. In particular, multiple, maneuvering, and homing warheads for ballistic missiles, plus the ability to re-target the "bus" or warhead dispenser while in flight, will increase the threat to Western naval forces.

ANTI-SUBMARINE WARFARE

Contemporary Soviet ASW has developed along similar tactical lines.[16] At least into the 1970s most ASW forces were organized into brigades

---

[14] A detailed description of missile and torpedo boat tactics is found in Dr. Milan Vego, "Tactical Employment of FPBs," Naval Institute *Proceedings* (June 1980), pp. 95–98, and (July 1980), pp. 106–11.

[15] Marshal of the Soviet Union V.D. Sokolovskiy, *Voyennaya Strategiya* [Military Strategy] (Moscow: Voyenizdat, 1962). The book was revised and republished in 1963 and 1967. Sokolovskiy was Chief of the Soviet general Staff from 1953 to 1960. A comparative analysis of the three editions is contained in Harriet Fast Scott, *Soviet Military Strategy* (London: Macdonald and Jane's, 1968).

[16] A detailed discussion of contemporary ASW methods is found in Donald C. Daniel, "Antisubmarine Warfare in the Nuclear Age," Orbis, (fall 1984), pp. 527–52.

controlled by commanders ashore. In search-and-attack operations, all of the ships defending an area would transmit their sonar data to a shore-based computer that would assign them attack courses and speeds, thus determining the appropriate point for attack. Then, the computers would go to sea in a cruiser or destroyer, designated a *Bol'shoy Protivolodochnyy Korabl'* (BPK), or large anti-submarine ship. BPKs thus became command ships for ASW groups.

The development of the MOSKVA-class helicopter carriers in the 1960s was in line with these ASW tactics. The carrier would bring many units (helicopters) into an area to attack a U.S. Polaris submarine initially detected by long-range, surface ship sonar or possibly by other means. This concept was abandoned, and the MOSKVA class was halted at two ships because of the increasing range of Polaris missiles and the large number of U.S. missile submarines, and because the MOSKVA probably was not performing as well as expected.

Nevertheless, the MOSKVAS and their Hormone-A anti-submarine helicopters did give the Soviet fleet its first experience with ship-based aircraft while taking to sea a significant ASW capability. The experience with the MOSKVAS was essential to the development of the subsequent KIEV-class aircraft carriers.

Also in 1967, the first Kresta I missile cruiser went to sea, carrying a single Hormone-B helicopter for missile targeting. This was the first Soviet surface combatant (other than the helicopter ship MOSKVA) to have a full helicopter support capability. The ship design was altered to that of an ASW ship with the Kresta II, which appeared in 1970. This ship carries a Hormone-A ASW helicopter and SS-N-14 ASW missiles in place of anti-ship missiles, demonstrating a significant advance in Soviet ASW doctrine for surface forces.

The Soviets have shown considerable interest in helicopter ASW. They have operated helicopters in this role from ashore and afloat as their principal means of attacking submarines at "medium" ranges, i.e., 30–40 n.miles (55–74 km). The Soviet enthusiasm for helicopters can be seen in the Mi-14 Haze, developed specifically for land-based ASW operations, and in the multiple helicopter capacities of the newer surface combatants KIROV and UDALOY. Writing on ASW tactics, a Soviet specialist explained the enthusiasm:

> The participation of helicopters in the search for submarines. . .not only widens the field of "visibility" of the warship carrying it but also substantially increases the ship's capability for conducting protracted tracking of a detected enemy. [Also] it increases the reliability of the employment of ASW weapons. And if it presents no great problem to a submarine to avoid a surface ship, the situation changes radically when a shipborne helicopter comes into the picture. Having a significantly greater speed than a submarine, [the helicopter] puts the submarine in a far more difficult situation. . . .[17]

Systematic airborne ASW tactics were developed in the late 1960s as new ASW aircraft became operational, beginning with the Il-38 May. The tactics were analogous with air anti-ship tactics: the land-based ASW aircraft would fly out to a datum, release sonobuoys to reacquire and

localize the target, and then attack. Limitations in the technique included the short range of Soviet sonobuoys, meaning that aircraft could rarely reacquire the target. Nor could the Il-38 carry enough weapons to achieve the "saturation" effect of surface ships firing anti-submarine rockets or releasing depth-charge patterns.

The later and larger land-based Tu-142 Bear-F ASW aircraft may have been developed to overcome this limitation. The turboprop bomber carries large numbers of sonobuoys to reacquire and hold contact with a submarine and also carries a large weapons payload.

Whereas the U.S. Navy considers its nuclear-powered attack submarine (SSN) primarily as an anti-submarine platform, the first Soviet SSN class (November) was not developed for the anti-submarine role. The high-performance Alfa SSN, developed shortly afterwards, may have been originally intended as an anti-submarine craft; it had the high speed to close rapidly to within torpedo range of intruders. The Victor and later classes of attack submarines (completed from 1967 onward) are generally considered ASW craft in the Western sense, i.e., they are intended for trailing enemy submarines and possibly serving in anti-submarine barriers. The Soviets also use diesel-electric attack submarines in this role.

Soviet attack submarines have been observed working with surface forces, apparently in the ASW role. While the U.S. Navy has put forward the concept of employing the high-speed LOS ANGELES (SSN 688)-class submarines in direct support of surface task forces, the Soviets have envisioned their SSNs in this role for a longer period. The SSN, in coordination with surface ASW ships or aircraft, is a deep, relatively quiet sonar platform. Once a target submarine is detected, the SSN could itself attack or—after communicating with other "killer" forces—withdraw from danger during the ensuing surface or air attack.

A related factor in Soviet submarine ASW is the large size of the Soviet attack submarine force. Multiple units could operate against U.S. undersea craft. For example, as a Soviet submarine attempts to transit a U.S. submarine barrier, a U.S. submarine might be unaware that a second, quieter Soviet submarine is in turn trailing the first, masking its own noise signature, waiting for the American craft to attack the transitor, thus revealing its presence and location.

The concept of "breakout" or breaking through U.S. anti-submarine barriers, is important in Soviet strategy. All three Soviet ASW platforms—aircraft, surface ships, and attack submarines—can be employed to help submarines break through NATO ASW barriers as well as to "defend the homeland" against Western strategic missile submarines. With the advent of the Delta-class SSBN in 1972, which could strike targets in the United States from Soviet home waters, a new operational capability evolved. Soviet missile submarines from the Northern Fleet would no longer have to transit narrow, and hence potentially dangerous, passages into the Atlantic. Instead, "sanctuaries" could be established in home waters where the missile submarines, defended by a combination of surface ships, submarines, and land-based aircraft, would be safe from American SSNs.

From a political viewpoint, this role of protecting SSBN sanctuaries may have justified the KIEV-class aircraft carriers. The ships, along with the BPK series of cruisers and destroyers, supported by land-based

---

[17] Captain 1st Rank N. Vo'yunenko, "Concerning Some Trends in the Development of Naval Tactics," *Morskoy Sbornik* (no. 10, 1975), pp. 21–26.

aircraft, provide an increasing open-ocean ASW capability. However, without the sea floor Sound Surveillance System (SOSUS) available to the United States (at least in the early phases of a war), and without the sensor and computer capabilities available in the West, Soviet ASW is generally thought to be many years behind Western ASW.

Two principal categories of sensors are considered in submarine detection: acoustic and non-acoustic.

Acoustic. Western ASW is based overwhelmingly on acoustic detection, i.e., sonars. Advances in acoustic detection are becoming increasingly more difficult as submarines grow quieter and the oceans grow noisier with the background sounds of offshore oil drilling, coastal fishing, shipping, and other activities. Moreover, environmental prediction techniques are telling submariners (as well as ASW forces) more about ocean conditions, making it easier for them to hide.

Future advances in acoustic detection will be based primarily on computer technology, and here the West is far ahead of the Soviet Union. As a result of computer research, and of buying and stealing computer technology from the West, Soviet advances in this field are expected. But at some point even computer advances will become subject to the diminishing returns of acoustic detection.

Non-acoustic. While the Soviets have a large investment in acoustic submarine detection, they more heavily research other detection methods: thermohydrodynamics, magnetics, chemical contaminants, and direct observables. Some authorities believe that *if* a breakthrough in non-acoustic detection is forthcoming, the breadth of the Soviet research effort would give them the advantage.

There are some who would suggest that the Soviets are close to a breakthrough in ASW. Professor James McConnell, of the U.S. Navy-sponsored Center for Naval Analyses, has written a noteworthy paper on this subject, after researching Soviet writings.[18] In particular, McConnell cites writings that claim the Soviets will achieve an effective anti-submarine capability by the late 1980s: "Experience indicates that the Soviets do not normally discuss the capabilities for an option until the arrival of the doctrinal/planning period in which the capabilities are to be put into operation. (Perhaps that is because only then do personnel have a 'need to know.')"[19] Professor McConnell does not, in his unclassified writings, indicate the specific means by which the Soviets could achieve a high non-acoustic detection rate, but it is known that Soviet efforts in this field are significant. This, the Soviet tactical concept of "netting" several sensors and weapons to compensate for individual shortcomings, and the depth of Soviet understanding of physics and oceanology, suggest that the potential in this field is significant.

Americans are not unaware of such developments. In 1985, for example, the U.S. Chief of Naval Operations said that scientific obser-

vations from an American space shuttle (orbital) flight the year before had perhaps revealed submarine locations. A Navy oceanographer on the flight "found some fantastically important new phenomology [sic] that will be vital to us in trying to understand the ocean depths," the admiral explained.[20] While not releasing details of the observations, which were called "incredibly important to us," a Navy spokesman implied that "internal waves"—left by a submarine's underwater transit—were involved. There are also indications that developments in synthetic aperture radar fitted in aircraft and satellites could contribute to submarine detection.[21] The Soviets are known to be working on projects in both internal wave detection and synthetic aperture radar.

McConnell also addresses the subject of striking at submarines once they are detected at long range. In particular, he calls attention to the shelved submarine-launched SS-NX-13 ballistic missile as potentially having ASW application, although other weapons could be candidates. Other Western analysts have also raised the SS-NX-13 potential.

Regardless of the specific means by which the Soviets would hunt Western SSBNs, to do so is important for them. Increasing concern on SSBN vulnerability in 1984 led the U.S. Congress to secretly vote $10 million for the Central Intelligence Agency to determine how susceptible U.S. strategic missile submarines are to Soviet ASW forces.

Anti-submarine warfare is of continuing—and increasing—importance to the Soviet Union. Western strategic missile submarines pose a potent threat to the Soviet homeland. In addition, the Soviets seek to protect their own SSBNs, which are believed to form the primary component of the Soviet strategic missile reserve. Finally, as the Soviets use the seas for long-range political and commercial activities, they must defend their own surface forces from Western and Third World submarines.

ANTI-AIR WARFARE

The development of Anti-Air Warfare (AAW) in the Soviet Navy has differed significantly from that of the U.S. Navy. American concepts of fleet air defense evolved in the Pacific during World War II, from the use of carrier-based fighters and massive shipboard anti-aircraft gun batteries. By the end of the war the U.S. Navy was developing radar pickets and surface-to-air missiles to combat the Japanese *kamikaze* threat.

In marked contrast, the Soviet fleet's coastal operations from 1941 to 1945 were almost always under the protection of land-based fighter aircraft. With a large land-based naval fighter force, limited long-range operations, and a lack of modern technology, there was essentially no advanced AAW development in the Soviet Navy during the first postwar decade.

This situation changed in the 1950s with the revolution in Soviet military affairs. The missile and related developments of the national air

[18] James M. McConnell, "A Possible Change in Soviet Views on the Prospects for Anti-Submarine Warfare" (Alexandria, Va.: Center for Naval Analyses, January 1985); reprinted as "New Soviet Methods for Antisubmarine Warfare?" Naval College *Review* (July-August 1985), pp. 16–27. Also see Captain 1st Rank A. Partala, Ph.D. (Technical Sciences), "Possibilities of Space-Based Radar Detection of Submarines," *Morsky Sbornik*, (no. 8, 1985), pp. 88–90.
[19] McConnell, p. 8.

[20] "Shuttle Flight Yields Data on Hiding Subs," *The Washington Post* (22 March 1985); " 'Transparent' oceans are more opaque," *The Washington Times* (22 March 1985).
[21] Edgar Ulsamer, "Penetrating the Sea Sanctuary," *Air Force Magazine* (September 1984), p. 29. Such reports were officially denied by the U.S. Department of Defense, e.g., Walter Andrews, "Soviet ability to target subs is denied," *The Washington Times* (17 August 1984).

defense force, along with the loss of the Navy's fighter arm, led to the accelerated development of ship-based air defenses.

Beginning with the new missile ships that went to sea in the early 1960s, the Soviets armed several classes with the SA-N-1 Goa surface-to-air missile. This missile was adopted from the ground-based SA-3, a low- to medium-altitude weapon. The trend at the time was to adopt army missiles and other weapons for naval use; the SA-N-1 was followed by the SA-N-2, converted from the ground-launched SA-2; the SA-N-3, from the SA-6; and the SA-N-4, from the SA-8.

Similarly, ground-based radars and fire-control systems were modified for shipboard use. (In some cases they were unsuccessful; while the SA-2 was one of the most important Soviet missiles, used extensively in Vietnam and the Middle East conflicts, the naval SA-N-2 was fitted to only one ship, the DZERZHINSKIY, and it was a failure.)

These missiles supplemented the anti-aircraft and dual-purpose guns in Soviet warships. Without ship-based aircraft, the Soviets were unable to achieve the defense-in-depth of U.S. naval forces. Still, shipboard AAW received significant emphasis, as indicated by Soviet leadership in developing close-in, rapid-fire guns and, with the SA-N-9, missiles for defense against attacking cruise missiles. Another significant event was the introduction of vertical launchers for AAW (the SA-N-6), with the attendant advantages of firing rate, flexibility, and protection, which conventional single- and twin-arm launchers do not have. The Soviets are also developing submarine-launched air defense missiles.

The availability of the KIEV-class Vertical/Short Take-Off and Landing (VSTOL) carriers from 1975 on has not resulted in a real ship-based fighter capability. The ships' Yak-38 Forgers, however, do provide an intercept capability against maritime patrol aircraft like the U.S. P-3 Orion, British Nimrod, and French Atlantic. This could be a highly significant capability in some scenarios. Also, the British experience with the Harrier VSTOL in the Falklands conflict indicates that the KIEV-class ships, with the Forger or the expected advanced VSTOL aircraft, could have significant capabilities against Third World air forces.

Most authorities believe Soviet naval air defense unquestionably lags behind that of the United States because of U.S. carrier-based fighters and radar aircraft (i.e., the Navy E-2 Hawkeye as well as the Air Force E-3 AWACS, which have operated with naval task forces). Soviet shipboard radars, missiles, and guns, as well as such tactical concepts as target data exchange among ships, are improving. And, an airborne early-warning aircraft is reported under development for use from the now-building nuclear aircraft carriers.

There is one area of AAW in which the Soviets are unquestionably ahead of the West—nuclear-armed missiles. Western intelligence believes that the SA-N-3, and probably the SA-N-1 and SA-N-6 in some ships, can carry nuclear warheads. This would enhance air defense against large-scale air strikes. (While analyses have indicated that a nuclear AAW capability would enhance U.S. force survivability, relatively few U.S. ships are fitted to fire the outdated Terrier-BTN nuclear missile, the only such weapon available to Western navies.[22])

The Soviets are increasingly aware of the need for effective AAW and, especially, for defense against attacking cruise missiles, as specific weapon and sensor developments related to AAW suggest. In 1982 the position of Chief of Naval Air Defense (initially filled by a rear admiral) was established at Naval Headquarters. This move coincided with the reorganization of the national air defense forces, reflecting an overall Soviet recognition of the need for more effective air defenses.

NUCLEAR AND CHEMICAL WARFARE[23]

Discussions of Soviet tactics must include theater/tactical nuclear weapons and chemical weapons, both of which appear to be fully integrated into all levels of Soviet naval forces and planning. The Soviet Navy is armed with a variety of nuclear weapons and regularly conducts offensive and defensive exercises. While there is less public information concerning the potential use of chemical weapons by the Soviet Navy, the massive chemical warfare capability of the Ground Forces, the apparent use of Soviet-made chemical and toxin weapons in Afghanistan, Kampuchea (Cambodia), Laos, Yemen, and possibly the Iraq-Iran War, and the Soviet Navy's extensive nuclear and chemical defense training all point to a significant capability in this field as well. (There is also considerable Soviet activity in research for biological warfare.)

The Soviet armed forces began developing their nuclear doctrine in the mid-1950s, after the death of Stalin. Previously, Stalin had believed that the geographic expanse and manpower reserves of the Soviet Union would more than compensate for Western superiority in nuclear weapons. Although he gave high priority to the development of such weapons, Stalin prevented military leaders from realistically considering how to use them or even how to defend against them. This new examination of nuclear issues is labeled a "revolution" by the Soviets.

The initial Soviet nuclear doctrine postulated that any war with the West would inevitably escalate to a strategic nuclear exchange. This concept was quite in line with Khrushchev's defense policies, which sought to reduce large (expensive) conventional forces in favor of a minimal strategic force, primarily ICBMs, and "unconventional" efforts against the West—for example, wars of national liberation and foreign trade.

In the post-Khrushchev era this attitude has been modified considerably. Writing in *Krasnaya Zvezda*, the daily newspaper of the Ministry of Defense, a Soviet general officer in 1976 warned that a conventional conflict in Europe "carries with it the constant danger of being escalated into a nuclear war."[24] This appears to be the central theme of contem-

---

[22] Previously the U.S. Navy also had a nuclear version of the ship-launched Talos surface-to-air weapon, which was in service from 1958 to 1978. The nuclear version of the Terrier missile (BTN—Beam-riding, Terrier, Nuclear) entered service in 1962. It is generally considered an obsolescent weapon. A nuclear version of the Navy's Standard SM-2 missile is in development.

[23] There has been minimal discussion in the United States on the subjects of nuclear and chemical war at sea on either an official or unofficial basis. One of the few published articles on this subject by a U.S. naval officer is Captain Linton F. Brooks, USN "Tactical Nuclear Weapons: The Forgotten Facet of Naval Weapons," Naval Institute *Proceedings* (January 1980), pp. 28–33. This article draws heavily on research of the BDM Corporation, published in part as "The Soviet Navy Declaratory Doctrine for Theater Nuclear Warfare" (Washington, D.C.: Defense Nuclear Agency, 30 September 1977). Also see Lieutenant Commander T. Wood Parker, USN "Theater Nuclear Warfare and the U.S. Navy," Naval War College *Review*, (January–February 1982), pp. 3–16.

[24] BDM, p. 10.

porary Soviet views on theater/tactical nuclear weapons: the officer's article claims that (1) war in Europe is the principal factor in Soviet non-strategic planning, and that (2) there is a distinct danger of conventional conflict escalating to nuclear conflict. But the same article also implies that should a NATO conflict reach a nuclear phase, it need *not* necessarily reach an all-out, intercontinental nuclear exchange between the Soviet Union and the United States.

An American analysis of Soviet military writings in this field concludes:

> One of the striking aspects of Soviet military literature is the heavy emphasis given to nuclear war fighting and the minute detail with which certain of its combat aspects are addressed. This is particularly true in those writings dealing with the ground-air campaign in the continental land theater, but it also carries over into the Soviet naval professional literature. The net impression is that the Soviet military has faced up to the reality of nuclear warfare, focused on it in their military schools and academies, and at least worked out the theory of how it should be fought and won. There is abundant evidence that the Soviets have designed and structured their forces in accordance with their theoretical writings, giving the impression that these writings have rationalized concepts that were later incorporated into doctrine.[25]

This attitude is reflected in the Soviet Navy by the relatively large number and variety of tactical nuclear weapons in the fleet.[26] These include "offensive" anti-ship weapons and "defensive" anti-aircraft and anti-submarine weapons, apparently deployed in ships ranging in size from the Nanuchka and Tarantul classes of missile corvettes to the large KIEV-class aircraft carriers. Tactical nuclear weapons of various types are also carried in Soviet attack/cruise missile submarines and aircraft.

Nuclear weapons appear to offer two major offensive advantages over conventional weapons in war at sea. First, whereas multiple hits with conventional weapons would probably be required to sink a cruiser or an aircraft carrier, the same task could be performed by a single nuclear weapon, of even small size. Second, a defense against nuclear weapons would require a 100 percent effectiveness, since a single penetrating missile or "leaker" could destroy the target.

A lesser factor is the number of anti-ship weapons that a ship could carry. Basic Soviet military policies dictate that *some* nuclear weapons will be carried. Any mix of nuclear and conventional would limit the launching ship to firing only conventional weapons in a conventional exchange; but all weapons—conventional as well as nuclear—could be used in a nuclear exchange.

From the Soviet perspective, the use of nuclear weapons in the AAW role would deter concentrated U.S. air attacks against ships, while in ASW operations a nuclear weapon could compensate for the target submarine's area of uncertainty or the limited effectiveness of conventional weapons. Another consideration is the potential use of high-altitude bursts of nuclear weapons to create Electro-Magnetic Pulse (EMP) effects that could seriously degrade the electronic and optical systems of ships and aircraft over large ocean areas. Underwater nuclear bursts could similarly reduce sonar effectiveness, creating a condition known

as "blue out." Soviet writings demonstrate a familiarity with all of these aspects of nuclear engagement.

Soviet naval readiness for nuclear warfare also includes significant defensive measures. The design of Soviet warships incorporates Chemical-Biological-Radiological (CBR) defensive measures. Warships, even the small Osa missile craft, have protective "citadels," areas that can be sealed to provide a safe, controlled atmosphere, with overpressure to keep out contaminants. Naval ships also have periscopes and other equipment for conning from sealed bridges, CBR washdown devices, and additional features to facilitate survival in a nuclear or chemical environment.[27] Observations of Soviet ships also indicate some hardening features, such as protection of radar wave guides (cables) from blast damage and the EMP effects of nuclear explosions. However, such protective features are not universal in Soviet warships.

A third area of Soviet nuclear preparedness is training and fleet exercises. Soviet naval personnel carry out CBR defense training on a regular basis, and nuclear defensive and offensive maneuvers are a regular part of fleet exercises.

Thus, Soviet naval weapons, warship configurations, and training and exercises point to a major capability for fighting a theater/tactical nuclear conflict at sea. It must be noted, however, that *all* known Soviet writings on this subject accept that nuclear weapons would *first* be used on land before they were released for use at sea.

Almost all of the nuclear defensive features point to a chemical warfare capability as well. Again, the munitions and protective measures of the Soviet Ground Forces have a considerable chemical capability. An official U.S. government evaluation states:

> The USSR is better prepared to conduct operations in a chemical environment than any other force in the world. Soldiers receive extensive chemical defense training. Most combat vehicles are equipped with a chemical protective system and a chemical detection alarm system. Chemical defense troops with specialized detection and decontamination equipment are found throughout the ground forces. . . .
>
> The Soviet Union continues to test, produce, and stockpile chemical weapons. The Soviets have developed the doctrine, plans, personnel, and equipment to support their use of chemical weapons.[28]

An earlier statement noted: "In Soviet military doctrine, toxic chemicals are associated primarily with theater warfare. The basic principle is to achieve surprise by using massive quantities of chemical agents against unprotected troops or against equipment or on terrain to deny its use."[29]

Chemical munitions can inflict considerably more casualties per weapon than can conventional, high-explosive munitions. This means that chemical weapons offer the opportunity of very high effectiveness per hit without escalation to the nuclear weapons threshold. It is safe to say that the Soviet Navy is prepared for the use of theater/tactical nuclear

---

[25] BDM, p. 21–22.

[26] See chapter 27 for a list of Soviet naval weapons believed to have nuclear warheads.

[27] The only U.S. surface warship configured to operate in a nuclear-chemical environment was the destroyer HERBERT J. THOMAS (DD 833), modified in 1963–1964 and discarded in 1974 (transferred to Taiwan).

[28] Secretary of Defense Caspar W. Weinberger, "Soviet Military Power, 1985" (Washington, D.C.: Department of Defense, 1985), pp. 71–72.

[29] Secretary of Defense Caspar W. Weinberger, "Soviet Military Power" (Washington, D.C.: Department of Defense, 1981), p. 38.

weapons and chemical weapons, while the U.S. Navy's surface forces are highly vulnerable to their use.

ELECTRONIC WARFARE

The Soviet Navy's own reliance on "real-time" transmission of reconnaissance and targeting data, the Soviet need for effective Command, Control, and Communications (C³), and the comprehensive Soviet understanding of the potential vulnerabilities of U.S. military C³ activities have led to a heavy emphasis on Electronic Warfare (EW). The Soviet term for offensive and defensive EW, *radioelectronnaya bor'ba* (Radio Electronic Combat or REC), covers the detection of hostile electronic transmissions, as noted above, but also the neutralization or destruction of the electronic threat and the protection of Soviet systems.

Offensive EW includes jamming and spoofing as well as destroying hostile communication centers and radars, using a variety of systems from Soviet shore-, air-, surface-, land-, and possibly submarine-based systems. One U.S. Navy communications security specialist has speculated that the Soviet Golf and Hotel submarines converted to special communications craft (SSQ/SSQN),

> may have a REC mission in addition to, if not in place of, their postulated C³ function. What could be more perfect than a jamming/deception platform that you would probably not detect until it started transmitting? Even then, given the confusion that even a partially successful IFF [Identification Friend or Foe] spoofing, pulse jamming, deceptive repeating or intrusion incident generates, the submarine would probably remain undetected, especially if the source could not be seen on radar.[30]

Several Soviet publications have stressed the need to strike Western C³ installations at the onset of a conflict. While public Soviet discussion in this area of naval warfare is limited, an official U.S. Army evaluation of Soviet REC estimates that the goal of this activity is to destroy or disrupt at least 50 percent of an enemy's command, control, and weapon-direction systems by either jamming or disruptive fires.[31] In addition to missile and gunfire (and the potential use of nuclear weapons in the EMP mode), Soviet techniques employed in offensive EW are radar jamming by barrage and spot "noise," chaff, and decoys; electronic jamming of command guidance systems by pulse and simulation techniques; and radio-communications noise jamming of AM and FM signals.

A variety of defensive EW techniques have also been discussed, stressing Communications Security (COMSEC) and Electronic Counter Countermeasures (ECCM). For example, although the Soviets must insure effective radio communications, to the extent possible radio operators will change power, modulation, and antenna direction along with frequency. In addition to command ships and communications submarines (SSQ/SSQN), Soviet naval communications achieve a high degree of survivability through redundant and hardened communication centers ashore. In the Soviet tradition, Naval Headquarters, the fleet command centers, and probably naval communication stations all have fully equipped backup facilities.

Radar operators will similarly change frequency, power, polarization, and modulation to reduce vulnerability. And, of course, the Soviets stress Emission Control (EMCON) with all electronic and communication equipment. Finally, the Soviets employ anti-radar "camouflage" when possible by doing such things as creating false targets or blending into the terrain and background.

The West has seen several examples of Soviet REC effectiveness, especially when the Soviets invaded Czechoslovakia in 1969 and when Egyptian crossed the Suez Canal in the 1973 Yom Kippur War.

INTELLIGENCE AND SURVEILLANCE[32]

Intelligence and surveillance are vital to successful military operations. In particular, Soviet naval operations being centrally controlled, the commander of a fleet or force or theater must have all possible information on the disposition—especially the location and status—of enemy forces as well as his own forces.

There are three separate and distinct agencies that collect intelligence for various naval requirements. These are the KGB, the GRU, *Glavnoye Razbedyatel'noye Upravleniye* (the Chief Directorate of the Intelligence of the Soviet General Staff), and the Naval Intelligence organization. The last consists of an intelligence directorate of the Main Naval Staff in Moscow and intelligence directorates of each of the four fleet headquarters. The fleet directorates support operating forces within their areas, operate intelligence collection ships (AGIs), aircraft, and other naval and civilian assets, and make the results of their intelligence gathering available to the Main Naval Staff as well as to the GRU.

Obviously there is duplication and overlapping between the KGB, GRU, and naval intelligence activities. But this is not necessarily a shortcoming. Efficiency and cost-effectiveness have never been part of the Soviet attitude toward intelligence. More is always better, and duplicative intelligence operations serve to check one another.

The general relationships and information flow between naval intelligence activities are shown in figure 6-1. In wartime there would be an additional reporting/direction route for the headquarters of the theater of operations. Each fleet intelligence directorate (*razvedyvatell'noye upravleniya*) has five divisions to carry out its functions (figure 6-2). Note that the third division is charged with the *Spetsnaz,* or special operations activities within the fleet area. These forces conduct covert actions and intelligence collection activities, similar to those of the U.S. Navy's SEALs (see chapter 9).

From an operational viewpoint, the Soviet Ocean Surveillance System (SOSS)—a Western term—is the principal means of keeping track of Soviet and foreign naval and air forces. It is fed by a variety of surveillance and reconnaissance activities, among them the Navy's op-

---

[30] Lieutenant Commander Guy Thomas, USN, "Soviet Radio Electronic Combat and the U.S. Navy," Naval War College *Review* (July–August 1982), pp. 16–24. This is an excellent discussion of Soviet REC. Also see Dr. Norman Friedman, "C³ War at Sea," Naval Institute *Proceedings* (May 1977), pp. 124–41.

[31] Department of the Army, *Soviet Army Operations* (Arlington, Va.: U.S. Army Intelligence and Threat Analysis Center, 1978), p. 5–81

[32] There has been little meaningful writing in the public literature on this subject. Exceptions include Commodore Thomas A. Brooks, USN, "[Soviet] Intelligence Collection," Naval Institute *Proceedings* (December 1985), pp. 47–49, and Dr. Norman Friedman, "Real-time Ocean Surveillance," *Military Technology,* (no. 9/84 1984), pp. 76–81. Also see Viktor Suvorov [pseud.], *Inside Soviet Military Intelligence* (New York: Macmillan, 1984); the author was a GRU officer who defected to the West.

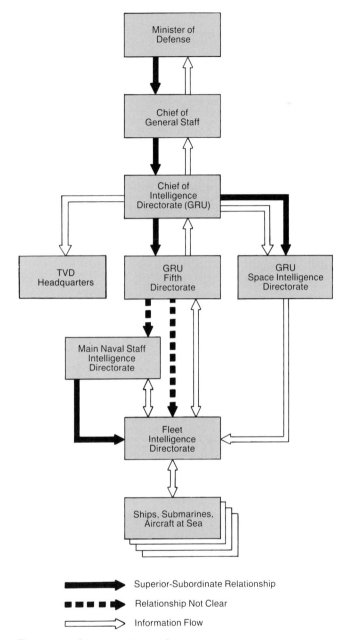

Superior-Subordinate Relationship

■ ■ ■ ■ ▶ Relationship Not Clear

⟹ Information Flow

Figure 6-1. Soviet Intelligence Command Relationships

erating forces (aircraft, surface ships, and submarines) and specialized information collection activities. The principal contributors to SOSS are aircraft, radio intercept, satellites, surface ships, submarines, and "spies."

Aircraft. The Soviet Navy employs specially configured An-12 Cub, Il-18 Coot, Tu-16 Badger, and Tu-20 Bear aircraft for ocean reconnaissance and surveillance. The most notable aircraft are the long-range,

four-turboprop Bear-D aircraft, which conduct radar and Electronic Intercept (ELINT) reconnaissance missions and have the ability to transmit radarscope data to missile-launching platforms through a video data link. Although the approximately 45 Bear-D aircraft in service would be highly vulnerable in wartime, their range (enhanced by in-flight refueling and overseas basing) makes them an invaluable component of SOSS during peacetime and crisis periods. Deploying to and from Cuba, these planes regularly fly along the U.S. Atlantic coast to conduct electronic surveillance.

The Tu-16 Badger flies in Soviet naval markings in several reconnaissance configurations, again using radar and ELINT collection systems. While lacking the Bear's range, the Badger can be refueled in flight and has a higher speed. (This reconnaissance aircraft is not the same as the Badger electronic countermeasure aircraft, which supports strikes against surface forces.)

Reconnaissance-ELINT variants of the An-12 Cub and Il-18 Coot transports are also employed to seek out surface naval forces, mainly for the purpose of collecting data on electromagnetic emissions from Western ships.

Radio Intercept. The Soviets operated a network of land-based radio intercept stations prior to World War II. After the conflict, employing captured German technology, they built an elaborate High-Frequency Direction-Finding (HF/DF) network given the code name Krug (German for "ring" or "circle").

This system, installed along the land and sea borders of the Soviet Union, seeks to intercept transmissions from surface ships and submarines and to triangulate their positions. Some overseas HF/DF stations have also been established, notably in Egypt during the period of close cooperation between the armed forces of the two nations (1956 to 1973), in Vietnam, and in Cuba.

Satellites. The Soviets began testing satellites for ocean surveillance since about 1968, with an operational system at least since 1974. The Soviets currently employ three types of satellites for ocean surveillance: (1) "ferreting" or ELINT vehicles that can detect and "lock on" electronic signals from ships, providing location and, possibly from radar signals, information on the type of ship; (2) Radar Ocean Reconnaissance Satellite (RORSAT) vehicles that use active radar to detect ships; and (3) photographic satellites that can eject exposed film packets when over the Soviet Union.

There are several operating modes for satellite reconnaissance. The satellites are often operated in pairs, of one or both types, to enhance coverage or to permit the passive ELINT satellite to "key" the RORSAT to specific targets of interest. These satellites use battery, solar, or nuclear energy as power sources.[33]

These and other satellites are in extensive use by the Soviet armed forces for tactical and strategic (for example, early warning) reconnais-

[33] The nuclear-powered RORSAT with the Soviet designation Cosmos 954 malfunctioned in January 1978, going into an uncontrolled re-entry and spreading debris over northern Canada. The Soviets resumed the oribiting of nuclear-powered satellites in April 1980 at the initial rate of two or more per year. Radioactive portions of another nuclear surveillance satellite, the Cosmos 1402, began breaking up in December 1982 and crashed into the Indian Ocean in January 1983.

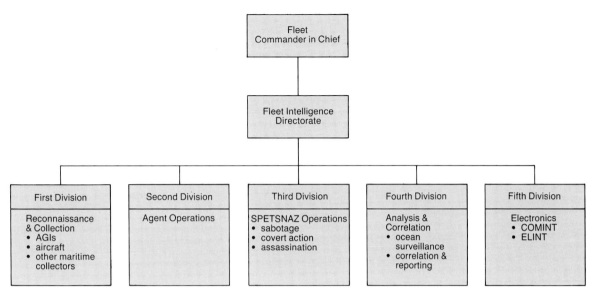

Figure 6-2. Fleet Intelligence Directorate

sance and surveillance. The Soviets made extensive use of reconnaissance satellites to keep track of the 1973 war in the Middle East. When four reconnaissance satellites orbited during a 12-day period in early October, it apparently had something to do with the Arab-Israeli conflict that erupted on 6 October 1973. Similarly, the Soviets increased their satellite collection during the Iranian and Afghan crises, which began in 1979, and during the Falklands war and the massive Israeli invasion of Lebanon, which occurred in 1982. Beginning on 2 April 1982, the day the Argentines seized the Falklands, the Soviet Union orbited a then-record number of reconnaissance and strategic early-warning satellites. At least eight strategic warning satellites were put up between that time and early June (the Israelis invaded Lebanon on 6 June). One reconnaissance satellite was kept in orbit for 50 days, again a Soviet record at the time.

The Soviets have also sent photographic satellites into orbit, but details of their ability to track warships have not been addressed in the public forum.

In early statements about its anti-satellite program, the U.S. Department of Defense said Soviet ocean surveillance satellites were the primary target. According to a U.S. defense official, "The principal motivation for our ASAT [Anti-Satellite] program is to put us in a position to negate Soviet satellites that control Soviet weapon systems that could attack our fleet."[34]

The Soviet Navy also makes use of satellites for communication and navigation. And one American observer has raised the issue of Soviet employment of manned satellites for ocean reconnaissance/weapons control. This, he notes, could be the *ultimate* force multiplier. In this context, the large Soviet investment in missile-range instrumentation ships and Space Event Support Ships (SESS)—some now under construction are nuclear propelled—is intended to serve as the "link" between future manned satellites and naval forces afloat and ashore.[35]

Surface ships. More than 50 specialized "intelligence collectors," designated AGI by Western intelligence, are in Soviet naval service.[36] While sometimes depicted in the press as disguised fishing trawlers, the AGIs are naval units, readily identified by their naval ensign and electronic antennas, and are manned by naval personnel. The large Bal'zam AGI class is armed with defensive guns and missiles, while several other AGIs have been backfitted with SA-N-5/SA-7 Grail heat-seeking missiles.

AGIs normally keep watch off the U.S. strategic submarine base at Holy Loch, Scotland, and off the southeastern coast of the United States— a position that permits surveillance of submarine bases at Charleston, South Carolina, and at Kings Bay, Georgia, and of the missile activity off Cape Canaveral, Florida. AGIs also operate in important international waterways, such as the Strait of Gibraltar, the Sicilian Straits, and the Strait of Hormuz. And AGIs regularly keep watch on U.S. and other NATO naval exercises.

Of course, Soviet warships also conduct surveillance of Western forces. Those Soviet ships and AGIs engaged in close trailing operations are generally referred to as tattletales.

In addition to naval ships, SOSS can be expected to make use of information obtained from state-owned and centrally controlled merchant and fishing fleets, and especially from the large Soviet research

[34] Testimony of Dr. Seymour Zeiberg, Deputy Undersecretary of Defense (Research and Engineering) for strategic and space systems, before the Committee on Armed Services, House of Representatives, 27 March 1979.

[35] Commodore Thomas A. Brooks, USN, "The Ultimate Force Multiplier," Naval Institute *Proceedings* (July 1985): pp. 137–39.

[36] The U.S. Navy discarded its passive intelligence-collection ships after the capture of the Pueblo (AGER 2) by North Korea in 1968 and the accidental Israeli attack on the Liberty (AGTR 5) during the 1967 Middle East War.

fleets. The last consists of ships and aircraft engaged in academic oceanographic and polar research, which supports the nation's civilian and military space and atmospheric research programs.

Submarines. Submarines, being capable of visual, radar, acoustic, and ELINT collection, especially in areas where aircraft and surface ships cannot operate, make highly useful intelligence platforms. They are particularly effective in garnering acoustic data from other undersea craft as well as from surface ships.

In addition to observing Western naval exercises, Soviet submarines regularly conduct reconnaissance off Western ports. In November 1983 a Victor III-class submarine was apparently observing a U.S. escort ship employing a towed-array sonar some 470 n.miles east of Charleston, South Carolina, when the submarine fouled the array and was disabled. (The submarine was towed to Cuba for repairs.)

Spies. The KGB and the GRU also gather information on Western naval movements and activities. They appear to do everything from placing agents in Western defense organizations to reading articles that discuss naval deployments, exercises, and port visits.

The information collected by the various components of SOSS are correlated at command centers in the four fleet headquarters and at Naval Headquarters in Moscow. These centers have hardened, highly survivable communications facilities with alternate facilities ready to serve as a backup, ensuring the rapid intake of intelligence data and the rapid outflow of directions to fleet and tactical commanders. Although Soviet tactics are highly dependent upon communications, once hostilities start it is possible that Soviet forces may be *less dependent* on command direction than are Western naval forces because of the Soviets' relatively rigid doctrine and tactics.[37]

In addition to these fixed facilities, the cruiser-command ships ADMIRAL SENYAVIN and ZHDANOV, the KIROV-class battle cruisers, and several submarine tenders are fitted with sufficient C³ systems to process and employ the products of SOSS.

Intelligence and surveillance are essential for Soviet naval forces to successfully carry out their missions.

---

[37] For a more detailed description of Soviet C³ systems and concepts, see the special issues of *Signal* [Journal of the Armed Forces Communications and Electronics Association], December 1984 and December 1985.

Soviet ASW forces include attack submarines, as this Victor II, and ship-based aircraft, as this Hormone-A hovering nearby. Less obvious are other components of the Soviet anti-submarine effort, including possibly satellites and land-based ballistic missiles.

7
Operations and Exercises

The expansion of exercises and operations have followed closely on the acquisition of more capable ships and aircraft by the Soviet Navy and an expansion of Soviet political-economic interests into the Third World. According to the U.S. Department of Defense,

> The Soviet Navy is the most visible element of the Soviet Union's forward military presence. The Navy has vastly increased its capabilities since the mid-1960s for the projection of power. Except for combat forces in Afghanistan, no other Soviet military asset has played as significant a role in Soviet policy toward the Third World. Soviet Naval forces can play roles of major significance in power projection in peacetime—with missions ranging from showing the flag to threatening strategic areas and waterways—in regional conflict, as well as in the initial period of global hostilities.[1]

Into the early 1950s most of the Soviet Navy's surface warships and submarines were based in the Baltic. Exercises were conducted only in Soviet coastal waters, while port visits by warships beyond Eastern Bloc nations were not carried out until after Stalin's death in March 1953. The following year—in July 1954—the new cruiser ORDZHONI-KIDZE and two destroyers visited Helsinki, and a month later the cruiser ADMIRAL USHAKOV and four destroyers paid a visit to Stockholm. The cruisers were of the large, graceful-looking SVERDLOV class. While Nikita Khrushchev would describe them as being suitable only to carry admirals on port visits, they were in fact very useful in that role. These ships were the mainstay of Soviet operations out of coastal areas for more than a decade.

These visits to neutral countries were expanded in October 1955 when the commander of the Baltic Fleet, Admiral A.G. Golovko, led the new cruisers SVERDLOV and ALEKSANDR SUVOROV and a quartet of destroyers to Portsmouth, England. This was the first visit of Soviet warships to a Western nation in the decade since the end of World War II. More significant politically, six months later, the cruiser ORDZHONIKIDZE, accompanied by two destroyers, carried Soviet leaders Khrushchev and N.A. Bulganin to Portsmouth for a state visit.[2] (This was the last visit of a Russian warship to England until 1976 when a Kashin-class destroyer called at Portsmouth in commemoration of the 20th anniversary of the end of World War II.)

When Khrushchev came to power in the mid-1950s, the Northern Fleet, with headquarters at Severomorsk on the Kola Peninsula, had only a few surface ships and about 30 submarines—less than 10 percent of Soviet underwater strength at that time. Under the Khrushchev-Gorshkov regime, the Northern Fleet's submarine arm was rapidly reinforced. For operations against the U.S. Navy or NATO forces, Soviet submarines could more easily transit the Greenland-Iceland-United Kingdom (GIUK) gaps to reach the Atlantic Ocean than they could through the Danish Straits.

Today, more than 180 submarines are assigned to the Northern Fleet, or almost one-half of the Soviet submarine inventory. Similarly, the Pacific Fleet, with more direct access to open seas, has been built up, and now shares virtually all of the Soviet Navy's nuclear-propelled and ballistic missile submarines with the Northern Fleet. Further, the Pacific Fleet provides the surface ships, submarines, and aircraft for operations across the Pacific, in Southeast Asian waters, and in the Indian Ocean.

The Black Sea Fleet has also been augmented to provide the surface ships and naval aircraft for deployments into the Mediterranean. (The submarines assigned to the Mediterranean *Eskadra* are from the Northern Fleet.)

After Admiral S.G. Gorshkov took command of the Soviet Navy in early 1956, he admonished his admirals to emphasize at-sea training. By the 1960s Soviet ships and squadrons were ranging farther from their home ports than at any time since the Russo-Japanese war of 1904–1905.[3]

---

[1] Secretary of Defense Caspar Weinberger, *Soviet Military Power 1985* (Washington, D.C.: Government Printing Office, April 1985), p. 115. The best public analysis of recent Soviet naval operations is Commander Bruce W. Watson, USN, *Red Navy At Sea: Soviet Naval Operations on the High Seas, 1956–1980* (Boulder, Colo.: Westview Press, 1982).

[2] During this visit Lionel Crabb, a retired British naval diving expert, at the behest of the Secret Intelligence Service (MI6), dived into Portsmouth Harbor near the Soviet cruiser, apparently to examine her underwater hull form. His headless body was later found floating in the river.

[3] In October 1904–May 1905 a Russian squadron from the Baltic and Black Sea fleets steamed 18,000 miles (28,800 km) to the Tsushima Strait between Japan and Korea, where the Russian force was decisively defeated on 27 May 1905 by a Japanese fleet.

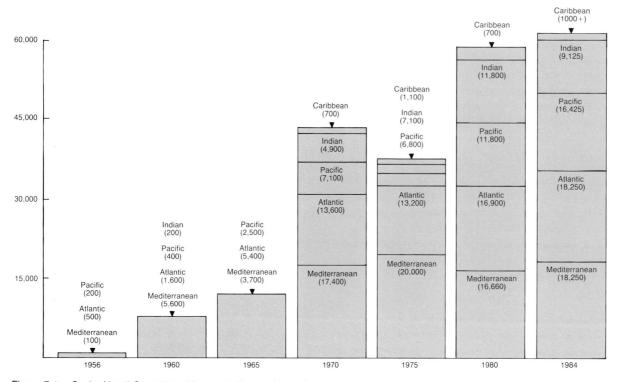

Figure 7-1.   Soviet Naval Operations (days out of coastal areas)

The periodic fleet training exercises not only sailed farther from Soviet territory but also, in time, became more complex. A joint command and staff exercise code-named *Sever*—Russian for "north"—was held in the North Atlantic, and the Baltic, Norwegian, and Barents seas in July 1968. East German and Polish ships joined the Soviet units in the first major naval exercise of Warsaw Pact nations and the largest Soviet naval exercise to that time. *Sever* included "eastern" and "western" fleets simulating Soviet and NATO naval groups meeting in combat, plus convoy escort, anti-submarine, and amphibious operations, with land-based naval aircraft participating. On 16 July a simulated Western amphibious force, under a Polish naval officer, carried out landings in the Baltic. Polish troops came ashore first, followed first by Soviet Naval Infantry and then by East German troops. The following day another amphibious group, under Soviet command, conducted a larger landing on the Rybachiy Peninsula. Apparently only Soviet troops were brought ashore in this second, larger landing.

This was the harbinger of still larger and more complex exercises that would come in the 1970s and 1980s. Almost every year of the past decade has seen more Soviet ships at sea, steaming farther from the Soviet homeland and remaining at sea for longer periods of time. This extension of blue-water operations has brought about an increased use of overseas ports and facilities and open-sea anchorages where Soviet ships cannot easily use foreign bases; it has also caused the development of the techniques and equipment needed for deploying ships

at sea (such as afloat support of ships and underway replenishment). This "peacetime" application of Soviet naval forces on the world's oceans has been summed up by James Cable, a distinguished British political scientist, in an essay "Political Applications of Limited Naval Force":

> In time of peace, a superior warship on the spot can achieve results not obtainable in other ways and without regard to the purpose for which the ship was built. What counts is the existence of the Soviet Navy, not the original motives of its builders. To be precise, what counts is the existence of ocean-going surface warships . . . when the object is to threaten force rather than use it, and if you have to employ violence to do it at a level which will not provoke [nuclear] war.[4]

BALTIC SEA

The Soviet Navy has a large number of ships in the Baltic Sea that are primarily dedicated to (1) performing naval missions in the Baltic during a non-nuclear conflict, such as seizing the island of Bornholm and the Danish Straits and supporting ground forces moving westward through Germany; (2) supporting naval training activities in the Leningrad area; and (3) conducting training and sea trials for the products of the Baltic

[4] This essay appeared in *The Soviet Union in Europe and the Near East: Her Capabilities and Intentions,* a report of a seminar sponsored jointly by Southampton University and the Royal United Services Institute, Milford-on-Sea, in March 1970. Mr. Cable, who spent 20 years in the British diplomatic service, expanded these views in his *Gunboat Diplomacy* (New York: Praeger Publishers, 1971).

The KIEV-class VSTOL carriers, like the NOVOROSSIYSK shown here underway in the Pacific, have permitted an extension of Soviet naval operations with limited tactical aircraft support. The two nuclear-propelled, full-deck carriers now under construction at Nikolayev will further extend that capability. The KIEVs, like their predecessors of the MOSKVA class, have a heavy weapons armament. (Mitsuo Shibata)

A modified Kashin makes a high-speed turn in heavy seas. Although the Soviet fleet in the Baltic Sea includes a large number of small combatants, there are at least 18 cruisers and destroyers in that sea. (U.S. Navy)

shipyards. In a theater nuclear exchange the Fleet's Golf-class SSBs can provide a limited nuclear strike capability.

Cruisers and destroyers are normally the largest warships in the Baltic. As of early 1986, there were one each of the Kresta I, Kresta II, Kynda, and SVERDLOV classes there—the smallest cruiser force in any of the four Soviet fleets. Major warships built or overhauled at the Admiralty and Zhdanov shipyards carry out their sea trials in the Gulf of Riga and in the Baltic.

And, periodically, there are major exercises in the Baltic that bring in ships from other fleets. For example, during the Zapad (West) '81 exercise in September 1981, the VSTOL carrier KIEV and the helicopter carrier LENINGRAD operated in the Baltic, the first time such ships had entered that sea. The large amphibious ship IVAN ROGOV, which had recently returned from the Pacific, was also among the 60 Soviet naval units that participated in the exercise, the largest peacetime maneuvers ever held in the Baltic. During Zapad '81 Soviet amphibious ships and merchant ships landed some 6,000 marines (Naval Infantry) and ground troops along the coast, a short distance from the Polish border. The landings were conducted by the Baltic Fleet's Naval Infantry regiment and by components of the "Proletarian-Moscow-Minsk" Guards Motorized Rifle Division, stationed in Leningrad.

In addition to the IVAN ROGOV, the troops were carried in Alligator and Ropucha LSTs from the Northern and Black Sea fleets as well as from the Baltic Fleet. The landings also demonstrated a variety of new equipment, including air-cushion landing vehicles, Mi-24 Hind helicopters, and T-72 tanks.

This landing, near Baltiysk on the Lithuanian coast, was the site of several previous exercises, but being only 15 miles (24 km) from the Polish border and in view of the unrest in Poland at the time, it took on special significance. Official Soviet statements cited more than 100,000 troops participating in the Baltic coast exercise. Zapad '81 was observed by the Soviet Defense Minister and ministers from the other Warsaw Pact nations, Cuba, Mongolia, and Vietnam. However, no ships from other Warsaw Pact navies participated in the exercise.

BLACK SEA-MEDITERRANEAN SEA

Probably the first sortie of Soviet warships into the Mediterranean after World War II occurred in May-June 1956 when the Black Sea Fleet commander, Admiral V.A. Kasatonov, led the new cruiser MIKHAIL KUTUZOV and two destroyers on a visit to Albanian and Yugoslav ports.

Soviet cruisers continued to make periodic visits into the Mediterranean. In particular, in October 1957 the cruiser ZHDANOV visited the Syrian port of Latakia which, coupled with Soviet arms transfers to Egypt that began the year before, marked the beginning of Soviet political-military activities in the Middle East.

More port visits to Albania and Yugoslavia followed, in part related to Soviet efforts to obtain naval bases in those communist states, thereby reducing the need to send ships through the Turkish Straits, which Soviet leaders feared could be easily closed in wartime. This became a major concern when Turkey joined the Western Alliance (NATO), formally tying Turkish defenses to the United States and Britain. A port was made available in Albania for Soviet ships from about 1958, and in 1961 several Whiskey-class submarines and a tender were briefly based there (see page 495). However, deteriorating relations with Albania and Yugoslavia ended all hopes of the Soviets maintaining a permanent naval presence in the Mediterranean.

In mid-1964 Soviet warships initiated a continual presence in the Mediterranean when a cruiser and two destroyers passed southward through the Turkish Straits. The move came shortly after President Johnson had advised the Turkish prime minister that if Turkish forces landed on trouble-plagued Cyprus, and the Soviet Union responded with military moves, Turkey could not count on the United States to come to its defense. This was a watershed in Turkish-American relations. Following this event, the Turkish Foreign Minister visited the Soviet Union for a week of discussions. Unquestionably, the passage of Soviet ships through the Turkish-controlled Dardanelles was discussed and restrictions were eased. Increased Soviet-Turkish economic relationships also followed.

During 1964, the Soviets probably maintained an average of five naval ships in the Mediterranean. Thereafter, deployment into the Mediterranean continued at a gradually increasing rate, with an "intelligence collector—" a trawler-type ship especially modified for electronic spying—or a warship normally dogging the U.S. and British aircraft carriers in the area. Periodically, submarines and sometimes their support ships would also be sighted in what previously had been considered an "American lake." In 1966, for example, a Soviet submarine tender in company with surface warships and submarines visited Egyptian and Algerian ports.

SVERDLOV-class cruisers made the first major port calls by Soviet warships in the postwar era. The surviving SVERDLOVS still serve effectively in the "political presence" role, in this instance the command ship ZHDANOV during a port visit to Toulon. With awnings spread, the cruiser, and the Kashin-class destroyer KRASNYY KRIM lying alongside, host visitors. (L. & L. Van Ginderen)

MIDDLE EAST

Direct Soviet interests in the Middle East began in 1956 when the Soviet government undertook a massive sale of arms to Egypt, with Czechoslovakia serving as the "middle man" for the sale (see appendix D). Two SKORYY-class destroyers as well as torpedo boats were transferred to Egypt that year, and there was some exchange of Soviet and Egyptian naval personnel in conjunction with the sale. Coupled with the occasional Soviet warship visits to Syrian and Egyptian ports, this led to significant interest in the Middle East by the Soviet Navy.

During the June 1967 Arab-Israeli conflict, a steady stream of Soviet ships passed through the Dardanelles, until there were about 70 Soviet ships in the Mediterranean. From 1967 until 1972, Soviet Badger reconnaissance aircraft, Mail ASW flying-boats, May patrol aircraft, and Cub ELINT aircraft were based in Egypt to support Soviet naval activities in the eastern Mediterranean. (Many of these planes had Egyptian markings.) Some Badgers were also sighted on runways in Libya, reportedly using the concrete strips at Wheelus, the former U.S. Air Force base that sprawls across the Libyan desert, and Blinder bombers were operating out of Iraqi airfields.

The Soviets again rapidly reinforced their naval forces in the Mediterranean during the Yom Kippur War in October-November 1973. Within a few days of the outbreak of hostilities, the Soviet *eskadra* began to receive additional ships, reaching a peak in early November of 5 cruisers, 14 frigates and destroyers, 6 escort ships, 2 Nanuchka-class missile corvettes, 8 amphibious ships, 38 intelligence and support ships, and 23 submarines, several of which were nuclear propelled. There were 88 anti-ship missiles in the Soviet force, exclusive of air-launched missiles that could be carried on Badger bombers flying from bases in the Crimea. This Soviet force of 96 ships confronted a U.S. Sixth Fleet that totaled some 60 ships.

The relative combat capabilities of the two fleets were difficult to compare. The Soviets had superiority in ship-to-ship missiles and submarines, while the U.S. Navy possessed considerable striking power in the fighters and attack planes on board the Sixth Fleet's three aircraft carriers. But a precedent had been established: the fall of 1973 was probably the first time that a Soviet naval force in a crisis area was larger—and significantly larger—than the U.S. naval force in the region. The U.S. Sixth Fleet commander at the time, Vice Admiral Daniel Murphy, reported:

Part of the Soviet *eskadra* at Kythira anchorage in the Mediterranean during the 1973 Yom Kippur War. A Kashin-class destroyer steams by a Kotlin and a second Kashin, a pair of Nanuchka missile corvettes, and the electronics-laden BASKUNCHAK, a space event support ship. (U.S. Navy)

The U.S. Sixth Fleet and the Soviet Mediterranean Fleet were, in effect, sitting in a pond in close proximity and the stage for the hitherto unlikely "war at sea" scenario was set. This situation prevailed for several days. Both fleets were obviously in a high readiness posture for whatever might come next, although it appeared that neither fleet knew exactly what to expect.[5]

The Soviets maintain a large *eskadra* in the Mediterranean, supported by naval aircraft flying from bases in the Crimea, Syria, and Libya and, at times, from ships. While the Soviets were forced to abandon bases in Egypt in 1973, the current Soviet military presence in Syria includes use of the port of Tartus with naval air deployments to Tiyas airfield. A Soviet submarine tender and a small oiler and water carrier are based at Tartus, while May ASW aircraft and, at times, other naval aircraft periodically deploy from Tiyas.

[5] Quoted in Admiral Elmo R. Zumwalt, Jr., USN(Ret), *On Watch* (New York: Quadrangle—The New York Times Book Co., 1976), p. 447.

Libya, which has received numerous Soviet aircraft and naval units, including submarines, regularly allows Soviet naval aircraft to operate there. Of late, May ASW aircraft have been flying from a Libyan airfield.

During periods of regional conflict or tension, Soviet ships often enter friendly Mediterranean ports to deter hostile attacks. This has been true of Egyptian and Syrian ports during Arab-Israeli wars, and a Soviet submarine tender entered the Libyan port of Tripoli in February 1986 when it appeared that U.S. naval forces in the Mediterranean might strike Libya in response to President Muammar Qaddafi's support of terrorist activities.

THE *OKEAN* EXERCISES

Two years after the *Sever* exercise, the Soviet Navy alone undertook operation *Okean* (Ocean), the largest naval exercise to be held by any navy since World War II. *Okean* '70 was conducted during April and May 1970, with some 200 surface ships and submarines, plus several hundred land-based aircraft, participating.

The exercises were conducted simultaneously in the Atlantic and Pacific regions, including the Barents, Norwegian, Baltic, Mediterranean, and Philippine seas, and the Sea of Japan. In the main operating areas the exercises followed the same sequence: (1) deployment of forces, (2) anti-submarine warfare, (3) anti-carrier warfare, and (4) amphibious landing. In the anti-carrier phase, simulated air strikes were flown against Soviet task groups in the Atlantic and Pacific. The Badgers of Soviet naval aviation struck at the simulated U.S. carrier groups in the North Atlantic and North Pacific within a few minutes of each other. Although this was a preplanned schedule, the strike was a remarkable achievement in planning and execution. Surface missile ships and submarines also simulated attacks against the carrier groups.

Interestingly, there were several Soviet surface ships and submarines in the Indian Ocean during *Okean* '70, including a Kynda-class missile cruiser. However, the Soviets did not consider that area part of the exercise, nor the subsequent task group sent to Cuba. (During the height of *Okean,* two pairs of naval Bear-D reconnaissance aircraft flew from a Northern Fleet base nonstop to Cuba. The first two Bear-Ds conducted reconnaissance of Soviet surface forces in the North Atlantic late on 21 April, the day before the simulated attacks against the Western carrier group.)

Okean '70 had several purposes. Marshal Andrei Grechko, then Minister of Defense, who observed the landings on Rybachiy Peninsula with other Soviet and Warsaw Pact officials, declared: "The *Okean* maneuvers were evidence of the increased naval might of our socialist state, an index of the fact that our Navy has become so great and so strong that it is capable of executing missions in defense of our state interests over the broad expanses of the World Ocean." For the Soviet Navy the *Okean* exercises were conducted "to test and make further improvements in the combat training level of our naval forces and in staff operational readiness." And, coming at the 100th anniversary of Lenin's birth, *Okean* also had a psychological purpose, demonstrating that the Soviet Navy was a full component of the communist system.

But most significant, *Okean,* along with a large exercise of Soviet Ground Forces, came at the end of the five-year defense-economic program. Thus, *Okean* was a "report" to the Soviet government and people of the capabilities of the Soviet Navy; it was intended to impress the political leadership that the huge investments in ships and aircraft had in fact benefited the Soviet Union.

Five years later, in April 1975, there was a similar multi-ocean exercise, dubbed *Vesna* by the Soviets and *Okean* '75 in the West. Again, there was a series of evolutions in the Atlantic and Pacific regions, involving some 200 naval ships and submarines, plus numerous aircraft. Major convoy defense exercises were conducted in the Barents Sea and Sea of Japan. These were possibly to evaluate Soviet convoy-defense as well as anti-convoy tactics. Several overseas bases were used by naval aircraft in April 1975, with Bear-D reconnaissance aircraft using an airfield in Guinea, May ASW aircraft and Cub recce/ELINT aircraft flying from Somalia, and Cubs using the airfield at Aden. (Bear-D aircraft also operated over the Indian Ocean, flying from bases in the Soviet Union.)

Significantly, the cruiser-helicopter ships Moskva and Leningrad, which had major roles five years earlier, were not at sea during the *Okean* '75 exercises.

After *Okean* '70 and '75, the Soviet Navy continued large-scale annual exercises as part of the regular training cycle for naval forces. The carrier Kiev joined in major exercises for the first time in 1976 as did other new ships. A major *Okean*-style exercise was expected to occur in the spring of 1980, as had happened at the conclusion of the previous Soviet five-year plans. During the year there were several small exercises, and there was a major Soviet naval presence in the Indian Ocean as well as in the Mediterranean. But there was no *Okean* '80.

The reasons may have been the potential danger of a super-power confrontation because of the high state of U.S. military readiness and related operations in the Indian Ocean due to the Iranian hostage situation, and the fear of further antagonism of the West following the Soviet invasion of Afghanistan in 1979. However, one senior U.S. intelligence officer has noted that the Soviet Navy by that time had demonstrated its ability to conduct multi-ocean exercises, and that an *Okean* would not be worth the time and expense. Most likely, *Okean* '80 did not occur for a combination of these reasons.

But the Soviet fleet was not idle. In July 1981 there was a large amphibious operation in the eastern Mediterranean, a joint Soviet-Syrian exercise in which 1,000 Soviet marines were landed. Also that summer, a combined Soviet-Polish-East German naval maneuver was held in the Baltic, and the massive, all-Soviet *Zapad* '81 landing was carried out that fall in the eastern Baltic. These maneuvers and exercises were particularly important because of their location and timing. They demonstrated that the combat training of the Soviet Navy had reached the point where it could respond directly to crises.

In 1983 there was another large-scale, multi-ocean series of exercises. Although smaller than those of *Okean* 1970 and 1975, this 1983 operation included more than 40 surface warships and a large number of submarines. There was the now-traditional emphasis on simulated anti-carrier strikes in defense of the Soviet homeland. But highly significant, there were also simulated attacks against convoys. These exercises included the highest-ever observed level of participation by Soviet merchant ships—about 40 of them—the Soviets apparently practicing tactics for defending their own convoys against attacks by Western naval and air forces.

There were also extensive air support operations in the 1983 exercise, with naval aircraft flying from Cuba, Ethiopia, Libya, Syria, and Vietnam as well as from Soviet bases.

The following year there was an even larger series of exercises. The spring 1984 operation was conducted primarily by the Soviet Navy's three Western fleets. This time there were more than 140 surface ships, including the new nuclear-propelled battlecruiser Kirov, and over 40 submarines participating, along with a large number of naval and air forces bombers that fanned far out over the Atlantic. There were simultaneous but less intensive exercises in the Pacific region.

The reasons for the large-scale 1983 and 1984 exercises are not fully clear. Again, the principal reason may well have been political. With the accession of Yuri Andropov to the head of the Politburo in November 1982 and of Konstantin Chernenko succeeding him in February 1984, along with other changes in the Soviet political leadership, the Soviet Navy may have felt the need to impress the nation's leaders with the capabilities and importance of the Soviet fleet.

ATLANTIC AND CARIBBEAN SEA

The Soviet exercises in the Norwegian Sea slowly extended southward. Beginning in 1959, when Fidel Castro took control of Cuba and began negotiations with the Soviet Union for economic and military assistance, there was interest in the Caribbean. Except for submarines, however, apparently no Soviet warships operated in the Caribbean during the 1960s. During the 1962 Cuban missile crisis, six Soviet diesel-electric submarines operated in the Caribbean area, all of which were located and identified by U.S. anti-submarine forces.

Then, in mid-June 1969, two diesel submarines, a nuclear-propelled attack submarine of the November class, and a submarine tender departed the White Sea base area, steamed around North Cape, and down into the Atlantic. Almost simultaneously, a surface force consisting of a Kynda-class missile cruiser, a missile frigate, and a missile destroyer passed through the Turkish Straits, transited the Mediterranean, and exited into the Atlantic. The submarine and surface groups rendezvoused off the Azores on 3 July, and after fueling from two Soviet tankers, steamed westward. The nine ships then entered the Caribbean, and remained for almost a month of exercises and port visits. This is believed to have been the first visit of a Russian squadron to the Western hemisphere since the American Civil War.

Almost a year later, in April 1970, during the height of the multi-ocean *Okean* exercises, a pair of Bear-D naval reconnaissance aircraft from the Northern Fleet flew to Cuba. Two additional pairs of Bear-D aircraft flew to Cuba during 1970, initiating the periodic deployments of Bear-D and later Bear-F ASW aircraft into Cuba.

Also in April 1970, a Kresta-class missile cruiser and a destroyer broke away from the *Okean* exercises in the North Atlantic and steamed southwest, being joined en route by a nuclear-propelled cruise missile submarine, two diesel attack submarines, and a submarine tender. This force entered the Caribbean and conducted exercises and port calls during May.

In September 1970, a third Soviet squadron was en route to the Caribbean. It consisted of a missile cruiser, a missile destroyer, a submarine tender, an oiler, and an LST. The landing ship carried two barges that subsequently were identified as submarine support barges. The LST entered Cienfuegos Harbor to unload the barges and other equipment believed to be for servicing submarines. This visit brought a public warning from the Nixon Administration that the Soviet Union "can be under no doubt that we would view the establishment of a strategic base in the Caribbean with the utmost seriousness." Two weeks later the submarine tender left Cienfuegos. The ship remained in Cuban waters, and on 15 October the tender entered the port of Mariel, 25 miles (40 km) west of Havana. The barges remained at Cienfuegos, and construction continued on various shore facilities for servicing naval forces.

Additional Soviet naval forces have visited the Caribbean, including a diesel-propelled ballistic missile submarine of the Golf class. However, no nuclear-propelled ballistic missile submarine is reported to have entered the area. In March-April 1984—as part of the 23rd Soviet naval deployment to the Caribbean—the helicopter carrier LENINGRAD and one of the new UDALOY-class ASW destroyers participated in the Caribbean operations, raising the deployments to a new level of capability.

These operations in the Caribbean demonstrate Soviet political in-

On the doorstep of the United States, a Soviet task force conducts an underway replenishment in the Caribbean. Deployments of Soviet warships began in 1969; these ships, making a 1985 deployment are, from left, a Krivak ASW frigate, a SOVREMENNYY anti-ship destroyer, the replenishment oiler DESTR, and another Krivak. (U.S. Navy)

Soviet visitors to the sunny Caribbean: a Kildin missile destroyer, a Kynda missile cruiser, and a Kashin missile destroyer; a Ugra-class submarine tender is in the background as a Soviet task group visits Havana. Such visits have political and military value to the Soviet Union. (Soviet Navy)

terest in the region as well as support for the Castro regime. From a military perspective, they familiarize Soviet forces with the region and provide training for the Cuban Navy. In wartime, Soviet ships, submarines, and aircraft in the area could attack U.S. cargo ships carrying Army units from ports on the Gulf of Mexico to Europe.

WEST AFRICAN OPERATIONS

On the eastern side of the Atlantic, the Soviets have also been maintaining essentially a continuous patrol of warships off the central African coast since late 1970. The presence of Soviet warships in the Gulf of Guinea, and probably directly off the Ghanian coast, coincided with the release by the Accra government of two Soviet fishing craft impounded some months earlier. There appears to have been a direct relationship between the Soviet warships and the release of the fishing craft.

In the aftermath of a Portuguese-backed attack on Conakry, Guinea, in November 1970, the Soviet Navy appears to have begun a regular patrol of the area in support of Guinea, and Soviet naval aircraft have been operating from Guinea. Conakry was subsequently used as a refueling base by Soviet Bear reconnaissance aircraft (see chapter 8). Although access for Bear aircraft has been terminated, the Soviets continue to use the Conakry harbor on a routine basis.

Farther south, in Angola, a former Portuguese colony, an uprising in 1974 sparked a long-term revolution. The Soviets supported the MPLA organization in the conflict, with Cuban combat troops being flown in by Soviet planes, their arms being delivered by Soviet merchant ships. Despite covert American aide to another faction, the MPLA was successful in establishing a communist government for Angola. Angola became the next base for Soviet naval aircraft, an important factor after use of the Conakry airfield was denied in 1977.

The Soviets have continued to maintain a small naval squadron of some five to eight naval units off the west African coast. In addition to being in a position to support events in Angola, the force sits astride the oil route from the Arabian Sea to Western Europe.

A Cuban Koni-class light frigate crosses astern of the ASW helicopter carrier LENINGRAD during the August 1984 Soviet deployment to the Caribbean. The LENINGRAD is the largest Soviet warship to have operated in the area. These surface ship deployments are generally accompanied by submarines. (U.S. Navy)

PACIFIC OCEAN

Soviet naval forces travelled far beyond the Far East area of Soviet Siberia and Communist China as early as 1959, when a SVERDLOV-class cruiser and two destroyers visited Jakarta. Subsequent political and naval discussions between the Soviet Union and Indonesia led to the transfer of a large number of warships and auxiliaries to the latter, among them a SVERDLOV-class light cruiser, a dozen Whiskey-class submarines, eight destroyers, eight escort ships, a dozen Komar missile boats, numerous torpedo and patrol craft, and support ships. Sukarno's later alignment with Communist China and his dramatic fall from power in 1965 ended the close Soviet association with Indonesia. After that, Moscow began talks with the city-state of Singapore, apparently aimed at obtaining permission for Soviet warships to join Soviet merchantmen in using the British-built dry docks of that port.

In general, exercises and operations by the Soviet Pacific Fleet were limited in scope compared to those of the three European fleets. They were constrained mostly to the Sea of Japan and the Sea of Okhotsk. The first operation that was truly reactive to U.S. activities occurred in January 1968, shortly after the North Koreans seized the U.S. intelligence ship PUEBLO (AGER 2). The Soviets sortied 16 ships—including intelligence ships and auxiliaries—into the Sea of Japan, maneuvering them between the Korean coast and the U.S. carrier group that had been dispatched to threaten the Koreans. The U.S. force was larger, including the nuclear-propelled aircraft carrier ENTERPRISE (CVAN 65). Mr. Cable observed,

> . . . the Soviet ships could neither have prevented a nuclear strike against North Korea nor even have defended themselves. But it was a discrete, yet unmistakable indication of Soviet interest and concern in American reactions. . . . Indeed, in so far as it was intended to symbolize Soviet commitment to the defence of North Korea, it may even have been a more effective threat than that posed by the greatly superior American fleet. It was also a striking instance of the occasional willingness of the Soviet Government to divert their ships to tasks which are both intrinsically risky and are likely to increase tension with the United States even at a moment of crisis.[6]

Less publicized Soviet naval operations in the Pacific, including the deployment of Yankee-class missile submarines to the eastern Pacific from about 1970, were followed by an open demonstration of Soviet naval capabilities in the Pacific phase of the *Okean* exercises of April-May 1970. A surface and submarine task force—led by a SVERDLOV-class cruiser—steamed south to the Philippine Sea, while there were extensive maneuvers, including long-range air strikes, closer to Soviet shores.

In the fall of 1971 a Soviet task force sortied across the Pacific and passed through the Hawaiian Islands, coming within sight of Oahu. This force consisted of a Kresta-class missile cruiser, two missile-armed destroyers, a nuclear-powered cruise missile submarine, two diesel-electric attack submarines, and a tanker.

Soviet naval operations in Southwest Asia expanded in the late 1970s when Soviet naval and air units began using the sprawling American-built air and harbor facilities at Cam Ranh Bay, Vietnam. Cam Ranh Bay is now the center of the largest concentration of Soviet naval forces outside of the Soviet Union. Naval strike, reconnaissance, and ASW planes operate from the base, which also has a squadron of protective fighter aircraft. The base brings Badger and Backfire aircraft within unrefueled striking range of the important Indonesian straits as well as all of Indochina, Indonesia, the Philippines, and the southern coast of China.

INDIAN OCEAN

The Indian Ocean became increasingly interesting to the Soviet Navy in the 1960s. This was due in part to the dependence of the West and

[6] Cable, p. 142.

Japan on Middle East oil, much of which exits through the Strait of Hormuz into the Indian Ocean, and Soviet logistic support for the North Vietnamese that relied heavily upon merchant ships that sailed primarily from Baltic and Black Sea ports through the Suez Canal (and after June 1967 around Africa) and across the Indian Ocean to Haiphong.

The Soviet Union first gained major access into the Indian subcontinent when Soviet leaders helped mediate the Indian-Pakistani conflict in 1965. Because of Pakistan's links with both the United States and Communist China, India was a most desirable ally.

Soviet ships had occasionally visited Indian Ocean ports, especially Massawa (Ethiopia) on the Red Sea. Early in 1968, a SVERDLOV-class cruiser, two missile-armed destroyers, and an oiler visited ten ports in eight countries of the area. The significance of these cruises was indicated by the presence of Admiral Gorshkov when a missile destroyer visited Massawa, Ethiopia, in January 1967, and at Pacific Fleet visits to Bombay and Madras early in 1968. (Soviet forces had used bases in Somalia, but they were abandoned for political reasons.)

Admiral Gorshkov's visit to India in February 1968 marked the beginning of massive Soviet naval assistance to that country. Since then, the Soviet Union has transferred to the Indian Navy several Foxtrot-class submarines, Kashin-class missile destroyers, Osa missile boats, various other craft, and a submarine tender. Soviet technical assistance has enlarged the capabilities of the Indian east coast naval base at Viskhapatnam.

Soviet-Indian political relations reached a high point in August of 1971 with the signing of a Treaty of Friendship, Peace and Cooperation. Among its various articles, the treaty provides that each nation "undertakes to abstain from giving any assistance to any third party that engages in an armed conflict with the other party. In the event of either party being subjected to attack or threat thereof . . . [the countries] shall immediately enter into mutual consultation with a view of eliminating this threat and taking appropriate effective measures to ensure the peace and security of their countries." Four months later, India invaded and overran East Pakistan; Soviet-provided missile boats sank several Pakistani naval and merchant ships and bombarded shore facilities.

In the aftermath of that conflict the nation of Bangladesh was established in what had been East Pakistan, and the Soviets were quick to offer political and economic assistance. During the India-Pakistan war a number of merchant ships had been sunk in the harbors of Chittagong and Chalna, while the Pakistanis had laid mines off the former port.

The Soviet Navy was called upon to sweep the mines and salvage the sunken ships. Beginning in early April 1972, a total of 22 minesweepers, salvage ships, and support ships arrived in Bangladesh waters. The salvage operations took almost two years. While there were reports that the Soviets were stalling while seeking permanent use of port facilities, the delay was more likely due to the limitations of Soviet salvage gear. The mine-clearance operation was easier and accomplished on a more realistic schedule. Both tasks provided valuable experience for the Soviet Navy.

Following the Bangladesh mine clearance, Soviet minesweepers and a support ship steamed for the Gulf of Suez where, in mid-July 1973,

they rendezvoused with the helicopter carrier LENINGRAD, which had transited around Africa, coming from the Black Sea. On board the LENINGRAD were Mi-8 Hip helicopters configured for aerial minesweeping. This force then began a four-month minesweeping operation in the Straits of Gubal as part of the multi-nation operation to open the Suez Canal. In this operation the Soviet force suffered from high winds, and one minesweeper was damaged in a mine explosion. (Simultaneously, a U.S. Navy helicopter minesweeping force was clearing the northern end of the Canal in Operation Nimbus.)

More recently, in the mid-1984 mining of the Red Sea by a Libyan merchant ship—using Soviet-provided bottom mines—South Yemen apparently requested Soviet assistance in sweeping the Bab al Mandeb for suspected mines.[7] Yemen at the time had a former Soviet T-58 minesweeper. Two Soviet minesweepers from the Black Sea fleet transited the Suez Canal en route for South Yemen, followed shortly by a task force consisting of the helicopter ship LENINGRAD, a cruiser, and a destroyer. The minesweepers reportedly conducted sweep operations, but no observations of minesweeping helicopter flights from the LENINGRAD were publicly noted.

Soviet installations have been established on the island of Socotra, just east of the Gulf of Aden and astride the southern entrance to the Red Sea and the Suez Canal. The island, belonging to the former British protectorate of Aden, once contained a British air base; subsequently, Aden, part of communist South Yemen, has been opened to Soviet ships and aircraft, military and civilian.

Today Soviet naval aircraft regularly fly missions over the Indian Ocean from Aden international airport and from the Al-Anad military airfield in South Yemen (as well as from bases in the Soviet Union), while Asmara in Ethiopia is also available to Soviet aircraft.[8] A naval repair and replenishment facility has been established at Ethiopia's Dahlak Island in the Red Sea, with Aden harbor and Socotra Island also being used by Soviet naval ships. At Dahlak there is a maintenance and fuel depot as well as an 8,500-ton floating dry dock operated by the Soviets. A submarine tender and other auxiliaries are based there.

These bases at the southern end of the Suez Canal-Red Sea route place the Soviet Navy in an excellent position to interdict shipping through that vital waterway, and not far from the tanker routes between the Arabian Sea and western Europe and Japan.

In 1970, the government of Mauritius, a former British colony east of Madagascar, signed a treaty with the Soviet Union providing port facilities for Soviet fishing craft. Soviet warships soon were anchoring in Mauritius ports as well. During the Okean naval maneuvers in April 1970, a missile-armed cruiser and other Pacific Fleet warships made prolonged port visits there.

These bases and anchorages facilitate the Soviet deployment of naval forces in the Indian Ocean region. Soviet ships now operate regularly in the Indian Ocean, coming primarily from the Pacific Fleet.

---

[7] See Dr. Scott C. Truver, "Mines of August: an International Whodunit," Naval Institute *Proceedings* (Naval Review, (May 1985), pp. 94–117.

[8] Eritrean rebels destroyed two Soviet May ASW aircraft at the Asmara airfield in May 1984.

The Indian Ocean *eskadra* now consists of 20 to 25 units—surface warships, submarines, amphibious, and auxiliary ships—periodically reinforced for exercises and during crises.

For the foreseeable future the scope of Soviet fleet exercises and operations can be expected to continue to increase. These activities support national political-economic interests, and also provide at-sea training for naval forces. Although the overall size of the Soviet fleet will not increase, and may decline slightly, the Navy will be better able to sustain overseas operations because of the availability of foreign bases and improvements in equipment reliability coupled with larger, longer-range warships.

Of particular significance will be the submarine forces, which have already been employed in support of political as well as military requirements. The rapid deployment of British nuclear-propelled attack submarines at the outset of the Falklands War in 1982 was carefully observed by the Soviet Navy. A future crisis or conflict in the Third World may well see a similar Soviet move. At the same time, the dispatch of several Soviet SSBNs into the Atlantic in response to the U.S. move to place Pershing and Tomahawk missiles in Western Europe demon-

The Soviet Navy deploys submarines in peacetime to many areas of the world for both military and political purposes. The latter role was the reason the two Foxtrot SS-type submarines and the Oskol-class repair ship visited Algiers in 1968 (top facing page). Two Foxtrots and an Echo II-class SSGN accompanied surface warships and a tanker, shown here (bottom facing page) refueling a SAM Kotlin destroyer that cruised the mid-Pacific in mid-1971, coming within sight of the Hawaiian Islands (a shadowing U.S. frigate is at far right). These submarine operations have not been without casualty; above, a Victor II SSN that collided with a merchant ship while trying to make a submerged transit of the tricky Strait of Gibraltar. (Dieter Jung; 2 views U.S. Navy)

strates a Soviet readiness to deploy strategic missile submarines for political reasons.[9]

The Soviet development of under-ice operating techniques in the 1970s now permits the Typhoon and Delta IV SSBN classes to use essentially all of the Arctic Ocean as an operating base. When under ice those submarines are immune to many Western ASW detection systems, while Western attack submarines operating under the ice ex-

perience degrading acoustic conditions and other limitations in tactics and communications.

A final comment on Arctic operations is the continued Soviet development of nuclear-propelled icebreakers that extend the Arctic transit season from Murmansk to Far East ports for the transit of warships as well as merchant ships. Again, geography has dealt the Soviets many disadvantages for their naval operations. Still, at-sea deployments in peacetime, the development of long-range ships, the acquisition of overseas naval and air bases, and the political realities of Soviet relations with certain neighboring nations, have all permitted the Soviet Navy to become an effective oceangoing force.

[9] Soviet Yankee-class SSBNs had initiated missile submarine patrols off the Atlantic coast of the United States in 1968 and off the Pacific coast in 1971. Earlier the less-capable Golf and Hotel missile submarines had operated in the North Atlantic and North Pacific.

Naval aviation is an important component of all aspects of Soviet naval operations. The recent qualitative and quantitative growth of SNA has been significant, both in terms of land-based capabilities, as this Il-38 May patrol/ASW unit, and ship-based capabilities. (Soviet Navy)

8
Naval Aviation

The modernization programs of both Soviet military aviation and the Soviet Navy in the 1980s are benefiting Soviet Naval Aviation (*Aviatsiya Voyenno-Morskogo Flota*). Significant qualitative and quantitative improvements are being made to Soviet Naval Aviation—referred to as SNA in the West—and at considerable cost. At the same time, there has been an increase in long-range, overseas naval air operations.

Soviet naval aviation (SNA) is the world's second largest naval air arm and flies some 1,650 aircraft, more combat aircraft than the air forces of Britain, France, or West Germany. The current strength of SNA is shown in table 8-1. The number of aircraft has been increasing at the rate of some 50 per year, with additions in most categories. Of particular significance has been the allocation of one-half of the Tu-22M Backfire strike aircraft directly to SNA.[1] At the same time, new fixed-wing fighter/attack, anti-submarine, and electronic aircraft as well as helicopters are joining SNA

In the offing is a new series of aircraft for the nuclear-propelled aircraft carrier now being constructed. Western intelligence analysts predict that the new carrier will embark fighter or fighter/attack, anti-submarine, reconnaissance, and Airborne Early-Warning (AEW) aircraft. Most of these functions could be performed by variants of the Ka-27 Helix helicopter, except that the fighter role is expected to be performed by modified Su-27 Flanker or MiG-29 Fulcrum aircraft, and the AEW role by a new fixed-wing aircraft.[2] A variant of the Su-25 Frogfoot aircraft may also be flown from the carrier. In addition, a new Vertical/Short Take-Off and Landing (VSTOL) aircraft is believed to be in the development stage; it would succeed the Yak-38 Forger, which now flies from the Kiev-class aircraft carriers.

At the same time, the construction of a nuclear carrier, following the four Kiev-class VSTOL carriers, marks a huge allocation of funds, manpower, and shipbuilding facilities. This program is in many respects the most remarkable aspect of the Soviet naval buildup initiated in the late 1950s (see chapter 13).

---

[1] All aircraft designations in this volume are Soviet military or design bureau designations and NATO code names. See chapter 26 for an explanation of the designation scheme and for aircraft characteristics.

[2] Rear Admiral John L. Butts, USN, Director of Naval Intelligence, testimony before Armed Services Committee, U.S. Senate (26 February 1985), pp. 2–3; Commodore William Studeman, USN, Director of Naval Intelligence, comments at Center for Naval Analyses conference, Washington, D.C. (13 November 1985).

TABLE 8-1. SOVIET NAVAL AVIATION, EARLY 1986*

Type	Aircraft
Strike/Bomber Aircraft	(400)
Backfire-B/C	125
Badger-C/G	240
Blinder-A	35
Fighter/Fighter-Bomber Aircraft	(135)
Fitter-C	75
Forger-A/B	60
Electronic and Reconnaissance Aircraft	(135)
Badger-D/E/F/H/J	80
Bear-D	45
Blinder-C	few
Aerial Tankers	75
Badger-A	
Anti-Submarine Aircraft	(205)
Bear-F	60
Mail	95
May	50
Helicopters	(335)
Haze-A/B	105
Helix-A	50
Hormone-A	120
Hormone-B	60
Hip	few
Transport/Training	400
Total Aircraft	1,650

*Totals are rounded.

Related to these force developments, during the past few years there has been a continued expansion of Soviet naval air operations. Of particular concern to Western planners has been the extensive use of the large air base at Cam Ranh Bay, Vietnam, by Soviet strike, reconnaissance, and fighter aircraft. This has complemented the ongoing Soviet naval air operations over the Atlantic (using bases in Cuba and Angola), the Mediterranean (flying from Libya and Syria), and the Indian Ocean (operating from Ethiopia and South Yemen).

History. Russian naval officers have shown strong interest in aviation since the end of the nineteenth century. A naval air arm was established

Low and slow, a May patrol/anti-submarine aircraft flies over the Arabian Sea. SNA complements the Soviet Navy's surface ships and submarines in long-range operations over the world's seas and oceans. (U.S. Navy)

in 1912 and during World War I the Russian Navy flew a large number of aircraft with some floatplanes being based on board merchant ships. Soviet military and naval aviation were highly innovative prior to the Revolution of 1917 and the ensuing Civil War—Russians experimented with helicopters, built the world's first four-engine aircraft, flew aircraft armed with recoilless cannon as well as more conventional weapons, and pioneered the field of aerial photography for military purposes.

After production halted during the Civil War, the number of opera-tional aircraft fell until by the early 1920s only a handful could be con-sidered as effective in combat. Subsequently, the rebuilding of Red air forces received high priority; the naval air arm was rebuilt as part of the fleet programs of the 1930s. Late in that decade there was an effort to obtain plans and components for aircraft carriers in the United States, but this did not come to fruition (see chapter 10).

When the Soviet Union entered World War II in June 1941—referred to by them as the Great Patriotic War—naval aviation was reported to have 1,445 aircraft, although they were mostly outdated types.[3] During the war naval aircraft flew missions in support of maritime operations, but also carried out other missions on a regular basis, directed by ground and area commanders. A few "strategic" missions were flown by the Navy, as on the night of 7–8 August 1941, when five Il-4 bombers left a base in Estonia to make a token and ineffective raid on Berlin. (The British had flown the first air raids against the Berlin area in August 1940.)

Soviet naval aircraft flew exclusively from land bases during the war.

According to Soviet sources, at the end of the war there were 1,495 aircraft assigned to the Pacific Fleet alone. This demonstrates the importance accorded to air support of naval operations. Most of the naval aircraft were of indigenous design and manufacture; however, 185 were the ubiquitous PBY/PBN Catalina flying boats, transferred to Russia in 1942–1943. This was followed by licensed Soviet production of the type, designated GST. The aircraft industry profited from the spoils of war as German technology, machinery, and aircraft engineers were brought to the Soviet Union. The unfinished German aircraft carrier GRAF ZEPPELIN was loaded with booty and taken in tow across the Baltic, destined for Leningrad, but she sank in rough seas because of a heavy load. The fleet rebuilding program Stalin initiated in the late 1940s was to include aircraft carriers, but none were laid down before the buildup was halted in 1953.

Even after the halt of Stalin's shipbuilding program in 1953, Nikita Khrushchev, his successor, wrote in his memoirs: "Aircraft carriers, of course, are the second most effective weapon in a modern navy (after submarines). I'll admit I felt a nagging desire to have some in our own navy, but we couldn't afford to build them. They were simply beyond our means."[4]

Rather, after World War II the Soviet naval air arm concentrated on land-based aircraft. Postwar Soviet Naval Aviation reached a peak strength of several thousand aircraft in the late 1950s, with large numbers of land-based strike aircraft supported by fighter aircraft, which could also be employed to protect naval installations from American carrier strikes. In the late 1950s SNA was stripped of its fighters, and they were assigned to the national air defense force. This reduced the Navy to a nadir of about 750 aircraft.

By the late 1950s land-based bomber aircraft were being armed with air-to-surface missiles for use against enemy ships. The first such weapon was designated AS-1 Kennel by Western intelligence. It was credited with being able to deliver a high-explosive warhead against surface ships or ground targets some 63 miles (100 km) from the launching bomber. These weapons were initially carried by Tu-4 Bull piston-engine bombers, the Soviet copy of the American B-29 Superfortress. Subsequently, the Kennel and other anti-ship missiles were carried by the Tu-16 Badger turbojet bomber.

In 1959–1960 the Soviet strategic air arm transferred most if not all of its missile-armed Badger medium bombers to the Navy for the anti-ship role. (The only missile-armed bombers retained by strategic aviation at the time were the long-range Bears.) By the mid-1960s SNA had some 400 Tu-16 Badger medium bombers and 100 older Il-28 Beagle light/torpedo bombers. The remaining 250 naval aircraft were patrol, ASW, transport, and utility aircraft, including some helicopters.

SNA has increased steadily in quality and quantity. In the early 1960s the large, four-turboprop Tu-20 Bear entered Soviet naval service in the Bear-D variant. Some 300 Bears were produced during 1961–1962 for the Soviet Air Forces, all bombers with B/C carrying land-attack missiles. The naval Bear-D carried no weapons (except defensive guns), but was a long-range reconnaissance and missile targeting aircraft. Significantly, during the 1960s and 1970s the Bear production line was kept open only for the Navy; the Bear-F, configured for ASW, entered service in the early 1970s.

In the late 1960s two other important naval aircraft entered service, the Ka-25 Hormone—an ASW helicopter in the A model and a missile-targeting helicopter in the B model—and the Il-38 May, a maritime patrol/ASW aircraft resembling the U.S. P-3 Orion. From 1974 on the Badgers were supplemented in the missile strike role by the new Tu-22M Backfire, a variable-wing aircraft, capable of Mach 1.9 at high altitude and Mach 0.9 at sea level. SNA lacked fighter aircraft for several years, but in 1975 the Yak-38 Forger VSTOL fighter-attack plane entered naval air service. About 1976, SNA began acquiring Su-17 Fitter-C ground-attack fighters; the first unit was established in the Baltic Fleet, followed a few years later by a Fitter-C unit in the Pacific Fleet. These planes are suited for the support of amphibious landings and attacks against small, high-speed combat craft.

AIR OPERATIONS

The first significant flights by naval aircraft from bases outside the Soviet Bloc began in the 1960s when SNA aircraft began flying from airfields in Egypt. At that time Soviet aircraft were also being transferred to Egypt, and a variety flew reconnaissance missions against the U.S. Sixth Fleet in the Mediterranean with Egyptian markings but Russian flight crews. By 1970 there were also reports of Badgers and possibly other naval aircraft on Libyan airfields. The use of Egyptian airfields ceased in 1973, but SNA aircraft continue to make extensive use of bases in Libya and Syria.

The first truly long-range efforts by SNA began in 1963 when the Soviets began an intensive series of mid-ocean flights over U.S. aircraft carriers. Between 27 January and 27 February Soviet planes flew over five carriers, in both the Pacific and Atlantic oceans—the USS CONSTELLATION (CV 64) was looked over by Soviet reconnaissance planes some 600 miles south of Midway Island, the FORRESTAL (CV 59) just south of the Azores. The aircraft were generally detected some 200 miles from the U.S. ships, and they were "escorted" in by U.S. fighters. U.S. Navy officials stated that the flights were probably intended to "convince the Russian people that carriers were obsolescent," although it is difficult to believe that there is public interest in such activities. More likely these were surveillance and training flights, which have continued.

The first major overseas landings by SNA aircraft took place during the *Okean* multi-ocean exercises of April 1970, when a pair of Bear-D

---

[3] On 1 July 1941 the U.S. Navy had 3,955 aircraft in service.

[4] Nikita Khrushchev, *Khrushchev Remembers—The Last Testament* (Boston: Little, Brown & Company, 1974), p. 31.

The Tupolev Bear is a large, graceful aircraft—the largest flown by the Soviet Navy and in production longer than any other combat aircraft in history. This view of a Bear-D, being watched by a U.S. Navy F-14A Tomcat, shows the aircraft's large turboprop engines with contra-rotating propellers, Big Bulge radome under the fuselage, and the ventral and tail 23-mm gun turrets. (U.S. Navy, Lt. Dave Parsons)

reconnaissance aircraft took off from the Kola peninsula, flew around North Cape and down the Norwegian Sea, over Soviet ships operating in the Iceland-Faeroes gap, and then continued south to land in Cuba. This nonstop flight of more than 5,000 miles (8,000 km) marked the first time that Bear aircraft had landed outside of Soviet Bloc countries. After a few days the Bears returned to their home base. In late April another pair of Bear-D aircraft flew into Cuba, and a third pair made the flight in May 1970, establishing a regular pattern for such operations. There was an average of five such flights per year until 1981, normally with two Bears in each flight (with four making the trip in September 1972 and three in July 1973).

In 1973 pairs of Bear aircraft began flying into Conakry, Guinea. On several occasions Bears in Cuba and Bears in Conakry appear to have carried out coordinated reconnaissance over the south and central Atlantic. Soviet aircraft ceased flying out of Conakry in 1977, and the pattern changed as Bear-D flights began to use the airfield at Luanda, Angola. These flights crossed the Atlantic between Cuba and Angola.

Since 1981 the presence of Bears in Cuba has been virtually continuous, with the aircraft using the San Antonio de los Baños military airfield since November of that year. Bear-F ASW aircraft joined the Bear-D flights to Cuba in 1983. These Bear flights provide long-range

navigation training and are a familiarization for the aircraft crews. The Bears also conduct surveillance and ELINT collection along the coast of North America, generally flying 200 to 250 miles offshore.

Naval air operations over the Indian Ocean usually originate from bases in the Crimea and include flights over Iran. During the 1970s a major base complex was available to the Soviets at Berbera in Somalia, but they were soon evicted from that country and began using a base in Ethiopia instead. Naval aircraft also fly from South Aden (the People's Democratic Republic of South Yemen). There is now an almost continuous presence of May patrol/ASW aircraft at bases in those countries. The movement of Soviet troops into Afghanistan in late 1979 opened the possibility of SNA forward bases being established in that country at some future date, increasing operational capabilities over the Indian Ocean.

In the Pacific, long-range flights from Far Eastern bases have been supplemented since 1974 by Bear operations from the former U.S. air bases at Da Nang and Cam Ranh Bay in Vietnam. From 1979 Bear-D/F aircraft flights have been continuous, soon followed by flights of Badger strike and electronic aircraft, ASW aircraft, and, finally, fighters. During 1985 there was an average of two dozen naval aircraft at Cam Ranh Bay at any given time—10 Badger strike aircraft, 6 reconnaissance/electronic Badgers, and 8 Bear-D/F aircraft. Also, since late 1984 the Soviet Air Forces has deployed a squadron of MiG-23 Flogger-C fighters to Cam Ranh Bay to defend the Soviet base complex.

COMMAND, ORGANIZATION, AND STRENGTH

The overall commander of Soviet Naval Aviation, on the staff of the CinC of the Navy in Moscow, is currently Colonel-General of Aviation G.A. Kuznetsov, who took that post in mid-1982. A career naval aviator, he had commanded naval aviation in the Northern Fleet from 1966 to 1975, then served as Chief of Staff of Naval Aviation from 1975. His rank, colonel-general, is approximately equivalent to that of full admiral.

Within each of the four fleets there is a naval air force commander with a general of aviation rank. The senior staff of SNA and each fleet air force includes a first deputy, chief of staff, chief of the political department, and senior engineer.

The current SNA strength of about 1,650 aircraft represents a net increase of over 200 aircraft since 1980. An estimated 70,000 officers and enlisted men are assigned to SNA, representing 16 percent of the Navy's total personnel.

The composition of the four fleet air arms varies with geography and mission. For example, anti-ship strike aircraft and patrol/ASW aircraft are assigned to each fleet. Long-range Bear reconnaissance and ASW aircraft are found only in the Northern and Pacific fleets, where their great range provides large-area search capabilities; Backfire strike aircraft are assigned to the Baltic, Black Sea, and Pacific fleets (not to the Northern Fleet); and Fitter-C fighter-attack are found in the air arms of the Baltic and Pacific fleets.

Within the fleet air arms are regiments and squadrons, with bomber regiments of some 28 to 30 aircraft believed to include three strike squadrons and a few ECM aircraft.

The KIEV-class aircraft carriers are assigned to the Northern, Black Sea, and Pacific fleets, bringing to their operating areas complements of Forger Vertical Short Take-Off and Landing (VSTOL) aircraft and Hormone and Helix helicopters. Both of the MOSKVA-class helicopter ships, with Hormones embarked, are in the Black Sea Fleet. Several classes of cruisers carry Hormone-A ASW helicopters or Hormone-B missile-targeting helicopters, with some Hormone-C utility variants also being seen on board ship. The Hormone's successor, the Helix, was first seen at sea in 1981 on board the ASW destroyer UDALOY and then the VSTOL carrier NOVOROSSIYSK.

The major SNA bases are believed to be located at:

Northern Fleet—Arkhangel'sk, Belusha-Guba, Murmansk, Pechenga, and Severomorsk.

Baltic Fleet—Baltysk, Bykov, Kaliningrad, and Riga.

Black Sea Fleet—Donuslav Lake, Gvardeyskoye, Nikolayev, and Oktyabryskoye.

Pacific Fleet—Alekseyevka, Vladivostok, Aleksandrovsk-Sakhalinsky, Petropavlovsk, and Korsakov.

In some instances these are base complexes; for example, four separate naval airfields are at Petropavlovsk on barren Kamchatka Peninsula, according to some reports. Also, there is a naval air research facility at Saki in the Crimea, where since at least 1979 there has been an outline of a carrier flight deck used for developing carrier launch and recovery procedures and equipment. The Soviet Air Forces provide basic and technical training for naval aviation. The Levanskiy SNA school at the Nikolayev complex provides specialized naval air training.

NAVAL AIRCRAFT

Bomber/Strike Aircraft. SNA's anti-ship strike role developed in the 1950s to counter American aircraft carriers, which were, at the time, justified primarily for the nuclear strike mission against the Soviet Union.[5] Called Anti-Carrier Warfare (ACW) by the U.S. Navy, anti-ship strike continues to be a high-priority Soviet mission.

The principal aircraft employed in the anti-ship role are the Tu-16 Badger and, increasingly, the Tu-22M Backfire. There are some 240 Badger-C/G aircraft in SNA, each capable of carrying two AS-2 Kipper or AS-5 Kelt missiles with ranges up to about 135 miles (220 km). These planes may also be capable of launching the newer AS-6 Kingfish air-to-surface missile.

The Tu-22M Backfire-B has been in SNA service since late 1974, with the latest aircraft of this type to enter service being the Backfire-C variant. This aircraft has been the subject of considerable controversy in the United States because of its possible use in the strategic attack role against North American targets. However, the fact that from the start of Backfire deliveries one-half of the planes have gone directly into SNA regiments and not the strategic air arm suggests that these are theater and not strategic strike aircraft. If they were intended for the strategic role, the strategic air arm would undoubtedly have been given more of the early Backfire production run to replace the outdated Bear and Mya-4 Bison long-range bombers.

The Backfire represents a particularly potent aircraft because of its high speed, long range, and ability to carry two of the AS-4 Kitchen missiles and possibly the AS-6. In the anti-carrier role, Backfires flying from bases in the Kola Peninsula could attack ships in the North Atlantic through an arc intersecting Gibraltar to the coast of Labrador. Backfires from bases in the Crimea could reach throughout the Mediterranean. In the Pacific, Backfires from Petropavlovsk bases could reach the Philippine Sea and the western-most Hawaiian islands. Flying from Cam Ranh Bay, Backfires (as well as Badgers) can cover the entire Indonesian archipelago.

The Badgers and Backfires were designed for in-flight refueling, as are the naval Bear. Refueling probes have been removed from the

TABLE 8-2. SOVIET NAVAL AVIATION FLEET ASSIGNMENT

Fleet	Aircraft Assigned
Northern Fleet	440
Baltic Fleet	270
Black Sea Fleet	435*
Pacific Fleet	500

*Includes aircraft assigned to the naval training establishment.

[5] U.S. aircraft carriers first carried nuclear weapons (in the Mediterranean) in 1950; they were withdrawn from this primary role about 1962 when U.S. land-based and sea-based ballistic missiles became available in large numbers.

The performance of the Yak-38 Forger is not impressive; still the aircraft provides a useful capability for operations beyond the range of land-based tactical aircraft. The Forger initially flew from carriers only in the VTOL mode; however, since the early 1980s they have been seen making short takeoffs, as in this montage of operations on the MINSK. (Courtesy *Joint Services Recognition Journal*)

Backfires under a Soviet-U.S. agreement; they could, however, be fitted into the aircraft within a few hours.

Backfire production continues at the rate of about 30 aircraft per year, these being divided about evenly between the SNA and Soviet Air Forces. The number of bomber-type aircraft in SNA has increased by some 50 aircraft over the past five years, indicating that the older Badgers are not being replaced by Backfires at a one-for-one rate, but rather the strike force is being increased as well as qualitatively improved.

A new high-performance bomber, given the NATO code name Blackjack, is under development and could enter operational service by 1988. A significant number of these aircraft will probably go to naval aviation. Indeed, the design of the aircraft may well have been based to a major extent on SNA requirements.

In addition to the Blackjack, there is at least one other long-range bomber under development in the Soviet Union. This aircraft, assigned the bureau designation Tu-160, is reported to be a bomber version of the Tu-144, the fixed-wing Supersonic Transport (SST) that entered Soviet commercial service late in 1975. This aircraft, assigned the NATO code name Charger, has reportedly reached a speed of Mach 2.4. A total of 13 commercial SSTs were built, including prototypes. A bomber version would have been extensively redesigned, reversing the usual practice of adopting commercial variants from military aircraft. Regardless of whether the Tu-160 is a true bomber adaptation of the Tu-144, and no matter what its exact status is, the Tupolev design bureau is unquestionably continuing to develop advanced bomber aircraft, which will have features for naval use. The Blackjack will be the next bomber aircraft to enter service with at least one more bomber design in the offing.

Beyond the missile-armed strike aircraft, SNA still operates a small number of Badger-A and Tu-22 Blinder-A bombers that carry free-fall bombs. These aircraft would probably be used against ground targets in support of amphibious operations or to support ground forces in combat. They could also be employed in reconnaissance and tanker roles.

The other bomber-type aircraft in SNA that are employed to support strike aircraft include 75 Navy-flown Badger-A tankers that can refuel other Badgers.

Fighter-Attack Aircraft. Two types of fighter aircraft are in SNA service, the land-based Su-17 Fitter-C and the carrier-based Yak-38 Forger-A/B. The Fitter is a ground-attack aircraft with a regiment of about 40 planes based in the Baltic; another Fitter regiment is being set up in the Pacific Fleet, with a total of some 75 planes in naval service by 1986. As noted above, these are probably intended to support amphibious landings and attack small, high-speed naval craft.

The KIEV-class aircraft carriers operate the Forger VSTOL aircraft in the fighter and attack roles. Two variants have been observed at sea, the single-seat A and the two-seat B. With only four KIEVs being constructed, the total Forger inventory will be about 60 aircraft, plus training and other pipeline aircraft.

The Forger, which has lift-plus-cruise engines, is considered less efficient than the ship-based Harrier VSTOL attack aircraft, flown by Britain's Royal Air Force and Fleet Air Arm, the U.S. Marine Corps, and the Spanish Navy. A follow-on VSTOL fighter-attack aircraft is under development in the Soviet Union and will succeed the Forger in the KIEV-class carriers. (The small elevators of the MOSKVA-class helicopter ships prevent them from operating the Forger, although the MOSKVA served as trials ship for the plane.)

It is anticipated that fighter-type aircraft now in service will be adopted for operations from the new, nuclear-propelled aircraft carrier.

Electronic, Reconnaissance, and Targeting Aircraft. Several specialized electronic and reconnaissance aircraft are flown by SNA. There are approximately 90 bomber-type aircraft now in service (Bear-D, Badger, and Blinder aircraft) plus a few modified cargo-type aircraft (Cub and Coot). Also in service are some 60 Hormone-B helicopters for shipboard use in the over-the-horizon missile targeting role.

In many respects the most remarkable Soviet aircraft is the giant Bear.[6] This graceful-looking aircraft has large, swept-back wings and four turboprop engines turning contra-rotating propellers. The Bear-D has an unrefueled range of up to 9,000 miles (14,400 km) and is fitted for in-flight refueling! This aircraft, with a prominent under-fuselage radome (NATO designation Big Bulge) makes radar and electronic sweeps of ocean areas and can relay target information via Video Data Link (VDL) to missile-armed surface ships and submarines. The approximately 45 Bear-D aircraft are assigned to the Northern and Pacific fleets.

The Badger-D/E aircraft are employed in the photographic and electronic reconnaissance role. The Badgers in the "recce" roles can be identified by camera ports or electronic pods under their wings and "blisters" or electronic domes on their fuselages.

The SNA also flies the Badger-H/J aircraft in the ECM role. This role calls for some aircraft to accompany the strike planes in close formation and others to stand off from the ships being attacked to jam or confuse defensive radars. These planes have powerful on-board radar jammers and also can drop chaff. (The built-in ECM capabilities of the Backfire apparently permit it to operate without the need for specialized jammer escort planes.)

A small number of Tu-22 Blinder-C aircraft are used in the photo-electronic reconnaissance role.

The Cub-C variant of the An-12 transport aircraft has been configured for the ELINT role, as has the Coot-A variant of the Il-18 transport. The Cub-C, sometimes in civil *Aeroflot* markings, has periodically overflown U.S. naval forces. The Coot-A is a modification of the transport model of this aircraft, not a variant of the Il-38 May that was originally based on the Il-18.

Another naval reconnaissance and targeting aircraft is the Hormone-B helicopter. This ship-based aircraft, operational since 1967, is carried in several guided missile cruisers plus the KIEV-class carriers to provide over-the-horizon targeting for the SS-N-3 and SS-N-12 anti-ship missiles. Only about two dozen of these helicopters are in service. (A modification of the Big Bulge radar is fitted in this helicopter.)

When this edition went to press, it was not known publicly if the larger Helix ship-based helicopter will be adopted for the reconnaissance and targeting role.

Another aircraft in this category is the carrier-based Airborne Early Warning (AEW) aircraft believed to be under development for the new nuclear carrier. It is expected to be a twin-engine, piston or turboprop plane developed specifically for the carrier/AEW role.

Anti-Submarine Aircraft. At this time SNA flies an estimated 95 Be-12 Mail flying boats, 50 May aircraft, and 60 of the Bear-F variants in the maritime patrol/ASW role.

The Mail—dubbed *Chaika* ("seagull") by the Soviets—and the Japanese *Shin Meiwa* are the world's only flying boats that remain in first-line naval service.[7] They are assigned to all four fleets while the giant Bear-F aircraft are in the Northern and Pacific fleets.

The May, developed from the Il-18 commercial transport, first appeared in its naval configuration about 1970. Relatively few Mays were

---

[6] For a brief history and appraisal of the Bear see Norman Polmar, "The Ubiquitous 'Bear,' " Naval Institute *Proceedings* (December 1985), pp. 54–59.

[7] The Chinese Navy still flies several Soviet-built Be-6 Madge flying boats, but these are being phased out of service. The U.S. Navy's last first-line flying boat, the P5M/P-5 Marlin, was phased out of service in 1967.

Yak-38 Forger fighter-attack aircraft parked on the deck of the VSTOL carrier NOVOROSSIYSK. The large hatch hinged back covers the lift-engine intake; the aircraft at right (No. 26) is a two-seat Forger-B model. These aircraft have not been completely satisfactory, and a new VSTOL fighter-attack aircraft is believed under development. (Mitsuo Shibata)

built compared with their U.S. Navy counterparts, the P-3 Orions, which continue in production (more than 500 Orions have been delivered to the U.S. and allied navies and air forces). From the available information, it is not clear whether May production was limited because SNA was not satisfied with the plane or because a more capable ASW platform was being developed (or planned). Some Western analysts have speculated that the May simply could not carry sufficient sonobuoys and torpedoes for the long-endurance ASW mission. The Bear-F remains in production, more than three decades after the first flight of the first Bear prototype in the summer of 1954. (The Navy Bear-F and the Air Forces Bear-H, a strategic missile carrier, continue in production, while the Bear-G is being converted from earlier Bear-B/C bombers. The Bear-G carries the AS-4 missile.)

The An-12 Cub is being used as a test platform for ASW systems. Little has appeared in the Western press about this role of the plane.

Helicopters are employed extensively for ASW, the Hormone-A being carried for that purpose in the MOSKVA and KIEV aviation ships, the UDALOY destroyers, and the KIROV, Kara, and Kresta II cruisers. About 150 Hormone-A helicopters, which first became operational about 1967, are in service.

Hormone-A production stopped a few years ago, and the improved Kamov-designed Helix ASW helicopter is now in series production.

Also relatively new to SNA is the larger, land-based Mi-14 Haze, an amphibious derivative of the Mi-8 Hip transport helicopter. The Haze is too large for shipboard use, being unable to fit on the elevators of the MOSKVA and KIEV classes. Rather, it was developed to replace the outdated Mi-4 Hound for shore-based ASW operations. Over 100 Hazes appear to have been delivered.

Minesweeping, Utility, and Training Aircraft. The Soviet Navy adopted several Hip helicopters for the minesweeping role, probably starting in the early 1970s. The helicopter carrier LENINGRAD carried a pair of these helicopters into the Red Sea in 1973–1974 for minesweeping operations at the southern end of the Suez Canal.

Subsequently, the Haze has been observed in the minesweeping role, being designated Haze-B by NATO.

The Soviet Navy also flies several Mi-8 helicopters in the transport and utility role. The transport helicopters have been observed with Naval Infantry markings during amphibious exercises; the Mi-8 as well as the Hormone-C and Helix-C helicopters have been seen on the cruiser-

Modern Soviet cruisers and destroyers carry Ka-27 Helix or Ka-25 Hormone helicopters for ASW and over-the-horizon targeting of anti-ship missiles. This is a Hormone-A on board the destroyer UDALOY, which can carry two of these helicopters. Note the flight control "greenhouse" at right, between the ship's twin hangars.

flagship ADMIRAL SENYAVIN, the IVAN ROGOV amphibious ships, and several auxiliary ships.

In addition to the operational aircraft described above, SNA has some 400 transport, training, and utility aircraft. These service the fleets and Navy Headquarters in Moscow and provide specialized naval aviation training, the last mostly in the Black Sea Fleet area.

STRATEGIC AVIATION

The Soviet Air Forces have a mission to support maritime operations with the most significant contribution being the strategic air arm (formerly designated *Aviatsiya Dalnovo Deistviya* or Long-Range Aviation). In the early 1980s Soviet strategic aviation was reorganized into five air armies, directly subordinate to the Supreme High command. (The armies are under the administration of the Air Forces.)

The bomber aircraft assigned to these air armies are 130 Backfire, 125 Bear, and 45 Bison long-range aircraft; 360 medium-range Badger and Blinder aircraft; and 450 relatively short-range Su-24 Fencer attack aircraft. All are capable of carrying nuclear weapons as well as conventional bombs.

Also assigned to these air armies to support the bomber aircraft are some 530 tanker, reconnaissance, and electronic warfare planes. According to a statement by U.S. officials, the Bear and Bison bombers in particular can be used against maritime targets, although other aircraft of the Air Forces have been observed in maritime exercises, and Blinder and Bear-E reconnaissance aircraft have flown missions against Western naval task forces.

The aircraft of these five air armies provide a significant capability for over-ocean reconnaissance, minelaying, and anti-ship operations.

A Badger-D electronic reconnaissance aircraft, showing its unusual nose configuration housing the Short Horn radar with electronic "blisters" under the fuselage. The Badger is flown in larger numbers by SNA than any other bomber-type aircraft. (U.S. Navy, Dana Barclay)

9
Naval Infantry, Coastal Missile-Artillery, and Spetsnaz Forces

The Soviet Navy has three ground-combat arms, the Naval Infantry, which corresponds in many respects to the U.S. Marine Corps and Royal Marines; the Coastal Missile-Artillery Force, which helps to defend key points from seaborne assault; and *Spetsnaz* forces, which are somewhat akin to the U.S. Navy's SEALs and the Royal Marines' Special Boat Squadron. Each of the four Soviet fleets has units of all three combat arms assigned to support operations in their respective areas.

During the past few years all three of these specialized combat arms have increased in size. The Naval Infantry has grown from an estimated 12,000 men in 1980 to about 18,000, while the Coastal Missile-Artillery has increased from some 8,000 to an estimated 14,000 in the same period. There have also been additions to the *Spetsnaz* forces, although details are lacking, and it is possible that some of the reported increases in Naval Infantry have actually been in the other forces. A continued modest growth in the size of the Naval Infantry is predicted by U.S. defense officials.

Possibly as significant as the additional personnel, the Naval Infantry structure has been significantly changed in the past few years, with the forces assigned to the four fleets raised to higher organizational levels. The three European fleets (Northern, Baltic, Black Sea) now have marine brigades vice regiments, and the Pacific Fleet has a division vice brigade. At the same time, the Naval Infantry units are receiving new weapons and vehicles, while the steady production of high-speed assault craft provides an improved assault capability. Within the range of these craft, they compensate for the relatively slow growth in the capabilities of the larger, long-range amphibious ships (see chapters 20 and 21).

When viewed in the context of other on-going Soviet modernization programs, e.g., naval aviation, surface ships, and submarines, the current investment in amphibious and coastal defense forces is substantial.

NAVAL INFANTRY

The primary mission of Naval Infantry (*Morskaya Pekhota*) is to gain control of territory adjacent to important straits and other waterways; this would be done through independent amphibious landings, or as the spearhead for combined marine-army operations, or in concert with airborne troops. The secondary mission is to defend naval bases and captured coastal territory.

The Soviet Naval Infantry currently has a strength of some 16,000 officers and enlisted men.[1] This represents a continued growth over the past few years. The relatively small size of the Soviet marine force when compared to the U.S. Marine Corps, its distribution among the four Soviet fleets, and the limited capacity of Soviet amphibious ships would tend to prevent its being employed in large-scale landings, in the manner planned by the U.S. Marine Corps. The Soviet Navy's leadership has carefully stated that the Naval Infantry is not intended to be employed in the American style. For example, Vice Admiral K.A. Stalbo, Soviet naval historian and theorist, has written:

> The experience of our Navy in landing naval forces during the Great Patriotic War [1941–1945] attests to the fact that in those years the Soviet school of the art of the amphibious landing of troops was built up and was crystallized in the course of battle, having developed along its own paths, which differ considerably from the paths taken by the naval art of the foreign navies, primarily the U.S. Navy.[2]

History. In 1705 Peter the Great established the first naval infantry regiment for his newly created fleet on the Baltic. The regiment had a total of 45 officers and 1,320 soldiers, organized in two battalions of five companies each. The creation of the regiment is considered the birth date of the Russian marine force (officially celebrated on 16 November). One of the first victories of the Russian marines came a year later when they captured the Swedish boat ESPERN in a boarding fight. And, beginning in 1707, the marines as well as large numbers of soldiers were used repeatedly in landings along the coasts of Finland and Sweden, and on offshore islands in the Baltic during the latter stages of Peter's lengthy conflict with Sweden (1700–1721).

Russian marines subsequently fought at sea and ashore, with a significant number being in the Russian fleets that periodically operated in the Mediterranean. They helped capture the city of Navarino in 1770 and the fortress of Beirut in 1773, and several islands in the Ionian Sea and the fortress of Corfu in 1798–1800. The number of marines in the

---

[1] The U.S. Marine Corps strength in 1986 is 198,000; the Soviet Naval Infantry is the third largest marine force, the South Korean marine force having 22,000 men.
[2] Rear Admiral K.A. Stalbo, "The Naval Art in the Landings of the Great Patriotic War," *Morskoy Sbornik* (no. 3, 1970), pp. 23–30. Subsequently promoted to vice admiral, Stalbo is a doctor of naval sciences, an honored scientist, and a state prize laureate.

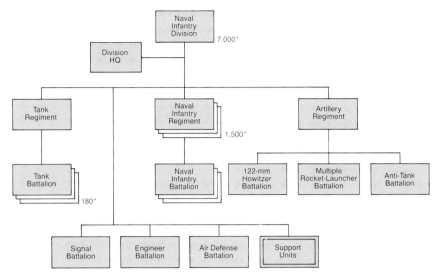

*Approximate number of personnel.

Figure 9-3.   Naval Infantry Division

battalions and separate batteries. Command and support functions for the brigade are provided by several small companies.

The Pacific Fleet's division has a strength of about 7,000 men, with each of its three regiments containing some 2,000 men. The division also has a tank and an artillery regiment, plus several support battalions (see figure 9-3).

The principal components of the brigades and regiments are:

Infantry Battalions. Each of the infantry battalions has some 400 men, organized primarily into three infantry companies of about 100 men each (see figure 9-4). Each company has three platoons.

Transportation for the battalion is provided by 34 armored, amphibious assault vehicles of the BTR-60PB type.

Each battalion also has a mortar platoon, with three 82-mm or 120-mm mortars, and an anti-tank platoon with AT-3 Sagger or AT-5 Spigot guided missiles.[6]

(The BTR-60PB is an amphibious/armored personnel carrier. It is a wheeled vehicle with a loaded weight of 21,000 pounds, and carries a crew of two plus 12 troops. A turret with one 14.5-mm and one 7.62-mm machine gun is mounted, with some vehicles fitted to carry SA-7 Grail anti-aircraft missiles or AT-3/5 anti-tank missiles.)

Tank Battalion. The tank battalion (figure 9-5) has one medium tank company, with ten T-54/55 or the newer T-72 tanks, and three light tank companies, each with ten of the amphibious PT-76 light tanks.

(The T-54 medium tank entered service in 1959, with the improved T-55 version operational from about 1961. The T-55 tank weighs 36

tons and has a 100-mm main gun with a crew of four. Diesel-powered, it can ford water 18 feet/5.5 m deep with a snorkel that can be rapidly installed by the crew.)

(The T-72 is a main battle tank that entered service with the Soviet Ground Forces in 1976 and was probably introduced into the Naval Infantry shortly afterward. Weighing some 41 tons, the T-72 has a smoothbore 125-mm cannon. The tank has automatic loading for the main gun, reducing the crew to three men.)

(PT-76 is a fully amphibious light tank that weighs 14 tons with a 76-mm gun fitted and a crew of three.)

Howitzer Battalion. The brigades' artillery components consist of self-propelled howitzer, rocket launcher, and anti-tank battalions plus an air-defense battery.

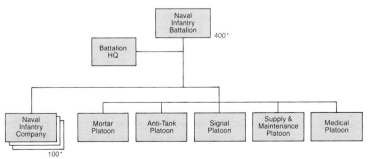

*Approximate number of personnel.

Figure 9-4.   Naval Infantry Battalion

[6] SA for Surface-to-Air missiles and AT for Anti-Tank missiles are Western designations; all others used here are Soviet nomenclature.

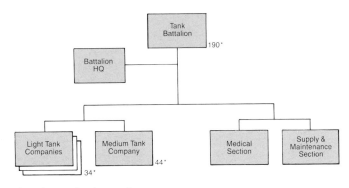

* Approximate number of personnel.

Figure 9-5. Naval Infantry Tank Battalion

T-54B medium tank.

The recent addition of the 122-mm M-1974 self-propelled howitzer battalion represents a significant improvement in marine firepower. The battalion probably has three firing batteries, each with six guns, for a brigade total of 18 weapons.

(The M-1974 gun is a 122-mm howitzer mounted on a light armored vehicle for high mobility weighing 20 tons. The firing range is estimated at nine miles. The gun crew is 4–5 men.)

Rocket-Launcher Battalion. The rocket-launcher battalion has 18 BM-21 multiple rocket launchers, descendants of the infamous "Stalin's organ" of World War II.

(The BM-21 is a truck-mounted, 40-tube, 122-mm rocket launcher. Range is about 22,500 yards and manual reload time is ten minutes.)

Air-Defense Battery. Anti-aircraft defense of the brigade is provided by this battery, consisting of one platoon armed with four ZSU-23-4 Shilka, self-propelled, quad 23-mm guns, and one platoon equipped with SA-9 Gaskin guided missiles on four BRDM-2 armored vehicles.

(The ZSU-23-4 is a potent short-range anti-aircraft weapon with integral fire control radar mounted on tank chassis. The rate of fire is about 200 rounds per minute per barrel. The SA-9 is carried and fired from a canister, four of which are mounted atop the BRDM-2. It is an infrared-homing missile with a maximum range of some 8,800 yards. In addition to these vehicle weapons, there are several SA-7 Grail man-carried rocket launchers in Naval Infantry units.)

T-72 main battle tank.

Anti-Tank Battalion. This unit has 18 multiple-rail AT-3 Sagger or AT-5 guided missile systems mounted on BRDM-2 vehicles. (There are also several SPG-9 73-mm recoilless rifles and AT-3 man-carried guided missiles in the brigade.)

Reconnaissance Company. The brigade's reconnaissance company has three PT-76 light tanks and nine BRDM-2 reconnaissance vehicles.

(The BRDM-2 is a wheeled amphibious personnel carrier weighing 15,400 pounds loaded, which carries four men and provides protection

PT-76 light tank. (Sovfoto)

BTR-60PB armored personnel carrier.

M1974 122-mm self-propelled howitzer.

ZSU-23-4 self-propelled air-defense gun.

against small-arms fire. A 14.5-mm and a 7.62-mm machine gun are mounted in a rotating turret.)

Engineer Company. These troops are used primarily to clear underwater and land obstacles in the assault area. K-61 amphibious cargo vehicles are used by these engineers, but they also land by BTR-60P vehicles, helicopters, and high-speed boats in advance of the assault waves.

At the division level there is a tank regiment (thought to contain three standard tank battalions), three infantry regiments (each with three rifle battalions), and an artillery regiment (comprised of several battalions). Details of these organizations are not publicly available; for example, when there were separate regiments in the fleet they consisted of some 2,000 officers and men, but that number included a tank battalion (190 men) and two artillery batteries (totalling more than 100 men). The divisional regiments are smaller and some of the support units that were assigned to the regiments are now at the division level.

Similarly, the principal components of the division's artillery regiment have not been published. The division does have an air-defense battalion with SA-8 Grechko surface-to-air missiles. This is a low- to medium-range missile with the missile and associated radars mounted on a six-wheeled amphibious vehicle. The launcher itself consists of six missile rails (enclosed, in the SA-8B version), with six reload missiles carried in each vehicle. The effective ceiling of the missile is between 150 and 20,000 feet.

PERSONNEL

The Naval Infantry has distinctive fatigue uniforms, consisting of black coveralls with blue-and-white-striped tee shirt visible at the open neck and a circular anchor insignia on the left sleeve. The marines also wear a black beret with an anchor insignia on the left side and a red star in front. The enlisted dress uniform is almost the same as for the rest of the Navy, with some differences in cut and color.

Military rather than naval ranks are used by the Naval Infantry (and Coastal Missile-Artillery Force). As noted above, the senior officer is a major general (one star) with probably colonels commanding the brigades, a major general commanding the Pacific Fleet's division, and lieutenant colonels or majors commanding the battalions. Naval Infantry officers are graduates of higher military rather than higher naval schools, with a number of officers known to be graduates of the Baku Higher Combined Arms Command School.

Enlisted men are conscripted into the Naval Infantry for two years, the same as for the Soviet Ground Forces. Training for Naval Infantry personnel concentrates on amphibious landings, although most types of ground combat tactics are also taught.

Selected personnel receive parachute training. Other marines perform in the swimmer/underwater demolition roles, which also require specialized training. The relationship, however, of these specialized marines and *Spetsnaz* forces is not clear.

An Aist at high speed in the Baltic Sea. The U.S. Navy's first landing craft air-cushion vehicle entered service in 1985, about 15 years after the first (smaller) Soviet amphibious ACVs entered service. (West German Navy)

COASTAL MISSILE-ARTILLERY FORCE

The Soviet Navy's Coastal Missile-Artillery Force has received far less publicity than the Naval Infantry. There are some 14,000 men currently assigned to coastal defense, a significant increase from a low of about 8,000 men in the early 1980s.

A few years ago the Coastal Missile-Artillery Force was reported to consist of three missile battalions with the Northern Fleet, six battalions in the Baltic Fleet, and five battalions each in the Black Sea and Pacific Fleet. It is not publicly known how many battalions are organized at this time.

The missile battalions are believed to be armed with the SSC-1b Sepal anti-ship missile, with range of at least 250 n.miles (460 km). This is a land-launched version of the SS-N-3 Shaddock missile. The 15 to 18 missiles in each Sepal battalion are carried on eight-wheeled, transporter-launcher vehicles. This provides a high degree of mobility, even over rough terrain, with road speeds up to 50 mph (80 km/h). (The smaller Samlet anti-ship missile, previously used for coastal defense, has been phased out of Soviet service.)

Coastal defense guns are also used by the Coastal Missile-Artillery Force. The older weapons have been discarded; the more modern guns reported in service include the advanced M-46 130-mm gun with a range of approximately 22 miles (35 km), using fixed ammunition. There may also be a few anti-aircraft gun and missile units in the Coastal Missile-Artillery Force.

In addition, coastal defense exercises are periodically conducted by the Ground Forces. Again, motorized rifle battalions are most often cited in accounts of these coastal defense maneuvers, although there has been some mention in the Soviet press of mountain infantry battalions being employed in this role.

SPETSNAZ FORCES

The Spetsnaz forces are somewhat similar to U.S. special operations forces, e.g., the Navy's SEALs and the Army's Green Berets. The Soviet troops are trained and equipped to carry out a number of sensitive missions, among them clandestine reconnaissance, sabotage or destruction of targets behind enemy lines, and assassination. As noted in chapter 4, these forces are controlled by the Main Intelligence Directorate (GRU) of the Soviet General Staff. Within each of the four fleets there is a naval Spetsnaz unit; official U.S. sources state that these are brigade-size units. This would place the strength of the naval Spetsnaz forces in each fleet at about 1,000 men, although some of these may be included in the fleet's Naval Infantry numbers.

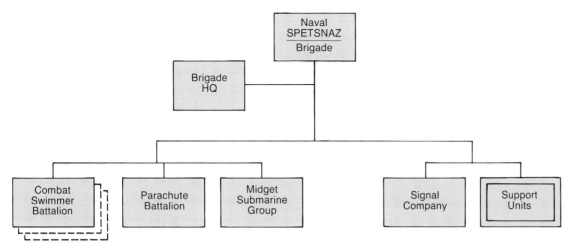

Figure 9-6.   Naval *Spetsnaz* Brigade

Each fleet brigade is estimated to consist of one or more battalions of combat swimmers and parachutists, a midget submarine group, plus a signals company and support units (see figure 9-6).

During wartime, according to official U.S. statements,

... small 5–12 man teams would be transported to a target area by aircraft, submarine, or surface ship and would be inserted immediately prior to hostilities. Their training includes parachuting, scuba diving, demolition, sabotage, surveillance, and target selection, as well as languages.

Once deployed, naval associated *Spetsnaz* would conduct reconnaissance and tactical operations against a wide variety of naval targets, such as ship and submarine bases, airfields, command and intelligence centers, communication facilities, ports, and harbors, radar sites, and—of primary importance—nuclear weapons facilities.[7]

[7] Secretary of Defense Caspar Weinberger, *Soviet Military Power 1985* (Washington, D.C.: Government Printing Office, 1985), p. 104.

The Polnocny is the largest class of amphibious ships in the Soviet Navy. This Polnocny-B variant is fitted with side troughs for explosive line and stern chutes for unmanned towing craft for use in clearing obstacles and mines from landing areas. There is a twin 30-mm mount forward of the bridge, and four SA-N-5 launchers are installed.

10
Personnel and Training

The manpower of the Soviet Navy continues to show a gradual increase, while there is evidence of an improvement in quality among the career personnel—the warrant ranks and officers.

The Soviet Navy has approximately 443,000 officers and enlisted men and women on active duty in 1986. This is some 341,000 less than the number in the U.S. naval services, which consist of about 586,000 men and women in the Navy and 198,000 in the Marine Corps. Discounting the Soviet marines and coastal defense troops, the Soviet Navy has approximately 175,000 fewer people than the U.S. Navy.

The Soviet Navy's personnel are allocated approximately as follows (percentages are rounded):[1]

Afloat	169,000	(38%)
Naval Aviation	70,000	(16%)
Naval Infantry	18,000	(4%)
Coastal Defense	14,000	(3%)
Training	46,000	(10%)
Shore Support	126,000	(28%)

There have been significant increases in Soviet naval manpower during the past few years. There had been a sharp reduction during the early 1970s, with Western intelligence reporting a Navy strength of 470,000 at the start of the decade but only 427,000 about five years later. The major reductions in that period were 10,000 cut from coastal defense forces and 45,000 from shore support activities. In the same period there was a significant increase in the naval air arm, with Soviet Naval Aviation going from about 40,000 to 50,000 men. From its strength in the mid-1970s the Navy's manpower has increased by some 35,000 men, most of them going to afloat assignments and to naval aviation, and lesser numbers to the naval infantry and coastal defense troops. In the past few years, however, the trend has been a reduction in the forces afloat and an increase in the shore establishment.

In the last few years the Soviet Navy's manpower has remained about stable. A reduction in personnel assigned to ships and the shore establishment has permitted an increase of some 7,000 men in naval aviation, 6,000 in coastal defense, 6,000 in shore support, and 3,000 in naval infantry.

[1] All personnel figures are as estimated by Western intelligence; changing methods of estimating may account for differences of as much as 10 to 15 percent over a period of time.

MILITARY SERVICE

The Soviet Union's Law on Universal Military Service is the basis for naval service. This law, last revised in 1981, states that all male citizens of the Soviet Union must perform at least two years of military service beginning at age 18. Navy shipboard personnel and men conscripted for the Strategic Rocket Forces, however, must serve for three years on active duty. (Prior to 1967 conscription was for three years, and shipboard duty required a four-year term.)

The conscription pool is based on an 18-year-old population that has generally completed the Soviet Union's required 10-year secondary school system. (The Soviet Union provides free education at all levels, including institutions of higher learning, instruction in minority languages as well as Russian, coeducation at all levels, and a uniform course of study. According to Soviet statements, over 90 percent of the men entering Soviet naval service have completed secondary education, although there are some indications that this percentage is lower.)

Draft deferments are provided for family, medical, or educational reasons. Exemptions are more difficult to obtain, generally being given to men with a physical disability or a serious criminal record, to married men with two or more children, and to men who are the sole support of elderly parents or siblings. The extent to which deferments and exemptions are granted because a man's skills are needed in the civilian sector is not clear.

Under Soviet conscription there is a call-up twice a year, in May-June and in November-December, with about 450,000 men drafted for all of the armed services in each call-up. Conscription, reserve programs, and support activities for all of the armed services are directed by the 16 military districts that encompass all areas of the Soviet Union (see chapter 4).

Service in the Soviet Ground Forces (i.e., army) is extremely arduous and spartan. Despite the longer term of naval service and the possibility of long cruises, the other services—especially the Navy—are often preferred. Those men with physical or psychological problems not sufficient to exempt them from military service are assigned to duties usually performed in Western navies by civilians, such as cargo handling and facility maintenance. This accounts in part for the large size of the Soviet Navy's shore establishment.

Enlisted men can be held beyond their official two- or three-year

Soviet officers and sailors on the bridge of a Petya I-class light frigate look at American Navymen looking at them. The Soviet Navy has demonstrated increasing professionalism over the past decade, with longer range and more complex operations, and increased readiness. (U.S. Navy, PH2 D. Beech)

period for up to six months of additional service. Men who wish to reenlist are usually placed in the warrant (*michman*) program (see below).[2] Very few sailors are allowed to remain on active duty as enlisted men beyond their initial service, in part because of the requirement to take in large

numbers of conscripts on a continuous basis. The number of men remaining as petty officers has been estimated by some Western sources to be as low as 1 or 2 percent. These are generally men who do not have the qualifications to enter the *michman* program.

Men who have completed their obligatory service and certain individuals who have received exemptions are required to serve in the

[2] Adopted from the English term "midshipman."

Ceremonies like this morning flag-raising ceremony on board Pacific Fleet cruisers are an important part of Soviet military life. From left are the VARYAG, TALLINN, and TASHKENT, with probably the PETROPAVLOVSK at far right. (Sovfoto, Sergei Kuzlov)

reserves up to age 50. All reservists are subject to periodic recalls to active duty for a total of up to two years of active service, the exact amount of time and the assignment being decided largely by the military district and varying with the category of reservist. There is evidence that the reserve program is hindered by resentment, both by the reservists who dislike the recalls and other requirements, and by active personnel who make only limited use of reservists who are recalled.

The military service law also provides for the conscription of women from age 19 to 40 who are trained in medical and other specialties. Women are not normally drafted, and very few serve in the Navy in a professional role. The use of women in the Soviet armed forces is limited also by the high percentage employed in the civilian sector as well as by the cultural and religious problems related to Asian and minority women working outside of their homes or villages.

Most women in naval service appear to serve primarily in administrative, communication, supply, and medical roles. Only a few have been seen on board naval ships. In 1978 several women sailors were observed in the helicopter carrier MOSKVA; an Italian journalist described them as "solid Russian girls in white uniform-dresses, certain are pretty, all at ease and treated with great gentility by the male crew, who evidently spoil them a little."

(Women served extensively in the Soviet army and air forces during World War II, and many saw extensive combat. In the postwar period the Soviets have had several woman test pilots and the world's first woman cosmonaut/astronaut, Engineer-Colonel Valentina Tereshkova, who flew 48 earth orbits in June 1963. No female naval aviators have been identified in the postwar period.)

Another problem related to military service is the decline in the birth rate of the Russian and Ukrainian portions of the Soviet population and hence the increase in the number of conscripts from Asian and minority groups. The latter lack upbringing in a technical environment, and many speak Russian very poorly (and in some cases not at all). This problem is becoming more acute. A U.S. defense analyst has observed, "From the standpoint of socialization and education, however, those same young men who are least desirable from a narrowly military perspective are also those most in need of the socialization and vocational training offered by the military experience."[3] Significantly, the Soviets do not allow the need to use such people in the military to threaten combat effectiveness or the political stability of units. Specific minorities who lack language or technical competence, and certain other groups who may be politically questionable, are not allowed to serve in sensitive positions (e.g., assignments with communications, intelligence, nuclear weapons) or certain front-line units.

In the long view the Soviets can solve this minority problem by selective personnel assignments (an option not fully available to U.S.

[3] Dr. Ellen Jones, "Soviet Military Manpower: Prospects in the 1980s," *Strategic Review* (fall 1981), pp. 65–75; and "Minorities in the Soviet Armed Forces," *Comparative Strategy*, vol. III, no. 4 (1982), pp. 285–318.

There are relatively few women in Soviet naval service. These young women are radio specialists and have been cited as being outstanding in political and military training.

personnel managers), reduction of the number of legal deferments, extending naval service for all conscripts by six months as allowed under the existing law, or a change in the law affecting the length of service. However, extreme care must be taken that any action to help the military manpower situation does not adversely affect the civilian sector, which has shortages in some technical disciplines.

PRE-SERVICE TRAINING

The reduction of required service in the 1967 law, coupled with the basic Soviet concept of political indoctrination for all citizens, has led to a comprehensive pre-military training program. Closely related are military sports and political activities.

There is military-patriotic training at all levels and in numerous aspects of Soviet life, often depicting the struggle between the Soviet Union and the Western world. Official Soviet literature is inundated with such statements as, "School children . . . must know the real danger which imperialism poses to mankind. The work done in a school by way of military-patriotic indoctrination must prepare students in practical ways to overcome difficulties during times of possible severe trials."[4]

To support this concept, the Soviet Union has developed an intensive program of pre-conscription military training. It begins at the pre-school level with cartoon comics depicting military heroes and continues throughout the required ten years of school and the year between completion of public school and call-up into the armed forces. History books emphasize the importance of the military in Russian history, the children visit war memorials and military museums, and retired military persons visit schools for presentations and talks. There are part-time, voluntary, paramilitary training programs for children as young as age nine or ten.

Civil-defense training begins in the second grade and continues throughout the educational career of most Soviet youth. (The Soviet civil-defense program is under the direction of a senior military officer and is a part of the Ministry of Defense.) During the last two years of school, all male students in the 9th and 10th grades (normally ages 16 and 17) participate in a compulsory pre-military training program of 140 formal hours. Courses are given in military history, the wearing and care of uniforms, small arms (with live munitions, including hand grenades), and radio and radar operation. Field exercises of several days' duration are also conducted as part of the program.

In the year between leaving high school and being called into active service, the young men participate in a part-time military program with courses in driving, vehicle maintenance, and communications. Although training does not always prepare men for the branch of service they will enter, those who will go into the airborne forces are often given preliminary parachute training; prospective submariners may receive a submarine familiarization course; and those who are to go into Navy diving work participate in the following program ". . . during their period of training at the Naval Club, the future divers learn a great deal and acquire many practical skills. They must be able to read drawings and schematics; draw sketches and measure underwater structures; and carry out rigging, assembly, repair and construction work while submerged. They must possess a good knowledge of the principles for conducting photographic, movie-making and television work, while submerged."[5] These training programs are for young men in school, working in factories, or on the farms prior to induction. Soviet press statements indicate that one conscript in three has a technical specialty before entering active service.

The various pre-service paramilitary activities are conducted by the Little Octobrists (ages 6–9), Young Pioneers (ages 10–15), the Komsomol (Communist Youth League, ages 14 and up), and DOSAAF (Voluntary Society for Cooperation with the Army, Aviation, and Fleet). The programs are conducted through the military districts, with all groups participating in war games as a part of the yearly round of activities, obviously tailored to the members' age and level of training. The Young Pioneers participate in zarnitsa or "summer lightning" games. Introduced in 1967, these include familiarization with army weapons, including firing with dummy ammunition, CBR defense, first aid, drill, and reconnaissance tasks.

The pre-military training programs vary in their degree of success, in part because of different attitudes and approaches within the separate military districts. With respect to civil defense, the general public attitude is not serious and there are major material deficiencies, in part because

[4] N. P. Aksenova, "On the Effectiveness of Military-Patriotic Indoctrination of School Children," Sovetskaya Pedagogika (February 1972), pp. 46–51.

[5] Engineer-Captain 1st Rank Ye. Shikanov, "Conquerors of the Depths," Voennyie Znaniia (February 1973), pp. 36–37.

Preservice military training in the Soviet Union begins on a voluntary basis with the start of primary school, and there are required programs for male students in high school and between graduation and being conscripted. These young seamen are preparing for a cruise on the Dnepr´ River. Although shortcomings exist in these programs, they contribute significantly to the "military environment" of the Soviet society. (Sovfoto, V. Granovsky)

of general shortages and poor organization and management—traditional Russian problems. In the physical-training programs the administrators tend to be overindulgent and inconsistent, often passing young men who should fail or who are marginal in order to fulfill the program's pre-established norms. With respect to actual pre-induction military training, there is a range of quality. There are reports of inadequately prepared instruction, overworked instructors, significant absenteeism, lack of equipment, and improper facilities. However, there is evidence of major efforts to upgrade the areas in which there are failings, and the overall programs must be considered successful in that they provide the draftee with some knowledge of the military before he enters active service. As periodically noted in the Soviet press, these pre-military programs do result in the average Soviet man being far different from his Western counterpart when he is called into active service at the age of 18.

From the viewpoint of military training, the most significant program is DOSAAF, which has several thousand units that provide pre-conscription training to some one-third of the young men entering the Soviet armed forces. Some aspects of DOSAAF activities are considered as only one step removed from active military service.

ENLISTED MEN

The Soviet Navy is a conscript navy, the sea-going sailors being called up for three years, and those who serve ashore conscripted for two years. Once on active duty, most conscripts will undergo an initial Navy training program that can vary from four or five weeks to as long as six months; some with previous DOSAAF or technical training may go directly to fleet assignments, and a few go directly into the *michman* program.

Each of the four fleets conducts its own basic training and assigns enlisted men. "Boot camp" of four or five weeks is devoted mostly to close-order drill, small arms, regulations and traditions of the service, individual CBR defense, and, of course, the ubiquitous physical training and political indoctrination. Upon completion of this brief recruit training, the conscript takes the formal military oath and becomes a full-fledged member of the Soviet Navy. At this point those sailors destined for menial or support jobs ashore—because of physical or political reliability problems or lack of aptitude—or who have previously acquired technical skills (from DOSAAF or other programs) go to their permanent duty stations.

Those men slated for duty afloat or who require more technical schooling attend specialist training, which is normally of five months duration. Men going to nuclear submarines receive nuclear training in addition to their specialty course. The fleet is confronted with a paradox: The reduction in first-term service to three years reduces the time available for training, while the complexities of modern equipment and operations require that personnel be more highly qualified than previously. One result is more intensive on-the-job training (OJT in the Western vernacular) and making more use of pre-service military training. During his active service the typical sailor will only work on one piece of equipment at one duty station, permitting the Navy to make maximum use of the time he is available.

The Soviet sailor is narrowly trained by U.S. standards, although he is increasingly encouraged to expand his knowledge beyond his narrow specialty. Stability in the assignment of officers to ships and stations and the emphasis on specialist qualifications make up for this lack of versatility in the conscripts.

Conscripts begin service with the rank of seaman or *matros* (see table 10-1). The majority of seamen can expect to be promoted one

TABLE 10-1. ENLISTED RANKS

Naval Rank	Military Rank
Chief Petty Officer (*Glavnyy Starshina*)	Senior Sergeant
Petty Officer 1st Class (*Starshina Pervoy Stati*)	Sergeant
Petty Officer 2nd Class (*Starshina Vtoroy Stati*)	Corporal
Senior Seaman (*Starshiy Matros*)	Private 1st Class
Seaman (*Matros*)	Private

grade, to senior seamen, by the time they have completed their three years of service. A first-term seaman may be promoted to petty officer second class and possibly even first class if his billet calls for that rank and he can pass the qualification tests, or if he is able to attend additional specialized training. The billet availability seems to be the key factor. Although there is a procedure for enlisted men to extend service for two years and hence become eligible for first class or chief petty officer status, few take this option, preferring instead to remain in the Navy in the warrant rank if they can qualify, or leaving the Navy and taking their technical knowledge to industry.

First-term servicemen live a spartan life compared to Western sailors; pay is low, food is simple, alcoholic beverges are forbidden, and there is little, or in some cases no, off-base liberty. However, an annual leave is given to visit home, and on base or board ship there is a variety of

Soviet sailors stand about before falling in at a naval training base near Kiev. They carry the well-known 7.62-mm AK-47 assault rifle. The large turnover of enlisted men—who can be retained for only two or three years—is a major problem of the Soviet Navy. (Peter Hrycenko)

social and cultural activities. In general, naval life is less harsh and less demanding than in the Ground Forces. The families of first-term servicemen have special privileges, such as work being found for their wives and being exempt from the tax on married citizens with few or no children. Family housing assistance and guarantees of post-service employment also help the servicemen. Of course, he may learn a technical skill while in the Navy that could be in great demand by the civilian economy when he leaves the Navy.

During his shipboard service the first-term sailor undergoes a year of training and specialist qualification. This training year is a carefully planned program in which the sailor becomes integrated first with his ship or unit, then with small formations, and, finally, with fleet exercises.

While Commander in Chief of the Navy, Admiral Gorshkov, stated ". . . our fleets conduct strenuous training the year round. In classrooms, on gunnery ranges and in simulators, on ships and in units (*chasti*), our seamen gain sound knowledge and the ability to handle machinery and systems and intricate weapons.

"Ocean cruises and distant voyages serve as the highest stage of this training."[6]

Combat training in the Soviet Navy is highly centralized and conducted in accordance with a detailed annual, monthly, weekly, and daily plan. The importance of combat training and continuity of training is evidenced by there being a Deputy CinC for Combat Training with the rank of full admiral. Admiral G.A. Bondarenko has held this position since 1973. (The Deputy CinC for Educational Institutions and the Chief of the Navy's Personnel Directorate are vice admirals, reflecting the importance accorded to training; see appendix A.)

Shipboard training encompasses a wide range of activities. Because of the large number of draftees the Navy must accept twice a year, a very detailed plan is worked out for the training cycles of each type of ship. In the first phase the crew engages in both theoretical and practical training in classrooms and simulators ashore, and aboard ships in port.

After review by the ship's squadron or division staffs, the ship moves to the second, at-sea training phase of the training cycle. This includes steaming exercises and live firings of all (conventional) weapons. Again, there is an examination at the end of the phase.

The third phase consists of small numbers of ships operating together, carrying out formation steaming and multi-ship exercises. After approval by higher command, the ships move into the fourth phase, in which larger groupings of ships conduct exercises. The duration of the phases and the specific evolutions vary with the type of ship. Also, the phase can be determined by the percentage of new crewmen on board.

Specialist qualification, which is independent of rank, is awarded on the basis of examinations in a man's skills. A man who qualifies as a specialist receives extra pay, and his qualification may be withdrawn for disciplinary reasons. Enlisted specialist badges, which indicate 1st, 2nd, and 3rd class and master specialist, are worn on dress uniforms. (The experience required for the master specialist is too extensive for a first-term conscript to acquire.) The number of men in a crew who

have specialist qualifications contribute to the standing of the ship or unit in the Navy-wide socialist competition.

Socialist competition within the Navy calls for the entire crew of a ship, unit, or base to strive for specialist qualification. This system of officially recognized rivalry originated in the civilian economy and is now an integral part of military training. It relies on moral incentives, honorary awards, and exhortations to stimulate servicemen and units to improve their skills, operational performance, discipline, and even political education. It involves meeting or exceeding "norms" in almost every facet of naval activity, from the quality of food served in the messes to the accuracy of missile firings. (To some extent it is reminiscent of the intensive competition in the U.S. Navy for battle efficiency "E" awards in the 1920s and 1930s, when everything legally permissible was encouraged to gain a ship or aircraft squadron a coveted "E.")

During a competition the crew of the nuclear submarine 60 LET VELIKYO OKTYABR "analyzed the results of the previous training year and in endeavoring to reinforce the achieved successes, approved new socialist obligations."[7] The submarine crew's new socialist obligations included:

- Reducing by 15 percent the time required for bringing the equipment, weapons, and the ship as a whole into a state of combat readiness . . .
- Seeing to it that 75 percent of the departments and services are outstanding
- Having each crew member become a class specialist, 20 percent of the sailors should gain the qualifications of master, and 70 percent 1st and 2nd class. The number of 1st-class missile troops and sonar operators should be increased by 50 percent.

The submariners' pledges for the following year included cultural and political promises as well as proposals for military achievement, including "to have a permanent amateur artistic collective and on the long voyages to systematically organize amateur artistic concerts," and "to constantly study the military, revolutionary and labor traditions of the Communist Party, the Soviet people and their Armed Forces, and the experience of political indoctrination. . . ."[8]

A report of the achievement of the Krivak-class frigate BODRYY, commended as the first ship in the fleet in the mid-1970s, cited that the crew "overfilled their Socialist commitments: 92 percent of their men have become class specialists, and one-third of them have mastered a related specialty. Aboard the ship eight out of ten men have been declared by their CO to be outstanding in combat and political training."[9]

There is a standard scoring scheme for socialist competition, the ships and units having high scores being rewarded and publicized, while "laggards" are exposed to public censure and pressure is brought to force them to improve. Failure to achieve "norms" can bring even stronger penalties. One ship—identified only as "X" in the Soviet military press—

---

[6] Admiral Gorshkov, "Ocean Cruises—School of Combat Training," in Rear Admiral N.I. Shablikov, et al., *Okean—Manevry Voyenno-Morskogo Flota SSR* [Okean—Maneuvers of the USSR Navy] (Moscow: Military Publishing House, 1970), p. 11.

[7] "New Scope for the Socialist Competition/High Dependability for the Ocean Watch," *Krasnaya Zvezda* (23 November 1978), p. 1.

[8] These "pledges" are highly publicized throughout the Navy and in national political publications.

[9] "Large ASW Ship Bodryy Lauded," *Krasnaya Zvezda* (1 December 1974), p. 1.

While taking on stores, the crew of an Echo II-class submarine takes advantage of the sunshine during a warm day in the Pacific. Recreation opportunities for Soviet sailors are limited ashore as well as afloat. (U.S. Navy)

Low pay and severe restrictions on free-time activities for Soviet enlisted men lead to the encouragement of musical and other do-it-yourself recreation. These sailors have organized a jazz band to play American-type jazz—highly popular in the USSR—as well as Russian music. (Soviet Navy)

failed to fulfill certain commitments. The "defects" in the ship were examined, and as a result during late 1980 the ship's commanding officer, V. Churikov (no rank was given), was relieved of his post and reassigned with a demotion, while officers (again no rank given) V. Volk, V. Dmitriyevskiy, L. Seregin, and others were made "answerable to the party."

Enlisted men who achieve outstanding individual ratings are rewarded with decorations, are publicized, and are given additional home leave. Petty officers and warrant officers whose sub-units have achieved excellent results may be promoted or given preference in admission to higher naval schools that would graduate them as commissioned officers. Another form of award for outstanding performance is to notify an enlisted man's former place of employment of his exemplary performance, a significant action because many sailors will return to their previous job when they leave the Navy. Departments, ships, and units that are cited by the fleet command as the year's best get to fly a special pennant or banner, and their officers can expect such an achievement to help advance their careers.

Since the rewards for success and penalties for failure are greatest for career warrant officers and commissioned officers, there is some falsification or exaggeration of achievements. The most serious competition is sometimes between officers, and this can lead to friction and

The crew of a Golf II-class SSB practices fire fighting and damage control during exercises off the coast of Japan. Smoke pots billow up while the Sorum-class tug MB-25 comes to the submarine's assistance. Training in the Soviet Navy is becoming increasingly complex. (Japanese Maritime Self-Defense Force)

tension. Thus, the greatest positive results of socialist competition are probably at the individual and sub-unit level, where skills can be increased in return for direct and important personal benefits.

Again, only a few sailors remain on active duty in an enlisted status beyond the required conscription period (with extensions adding up to six months to the required two or three years). Most sailors are discharged into the reserves, in which they serve up to age 50. A sailor who is selected for retention is generally appointed to warrant rank.

WARRANT RANKS

The warrant rank or *michman* was first introduced in the Russian Navy in 1716 and was used almost continuously until 1917 as the initial officer grade, corresponding to 2nd lieutenant in the army. The Soviet government reintroduced the rank of *michman* in the Navy on 30 November 1940 as the highest rank for petty officers (*starshinii*).

The status of warrant rank in the Soviet armed forces (*praporshchik* in the other military services) was changed to a separate category on 1 January 1972. The program is open to qualified enlisted men under age 35. Most have completed a term of service as a conscript, but some with sufficient prior training are recruited directly from boot camp, and some are former servicemen who have returned to active duty from the reserves. The reason for establishing warrant ranks at this level appears to have been the need for more career enlisted men, especially those with technical experience. Previously there was no formal program for training enlisted men after their first term of service. The importance and success of the *michmanii* program was indicated when, in early 1981, the senior warrant rank (*starshi michman*) was established in the Navy, to be conferred on men who have served as warrant officers for five years or more, with at least one year in positions normally staffed by officers or senior warrant officers.

After their appointment, the *michmanii* attend specialized, generally technical schools for one or two years, after which they usually go to an operational unit for their commitment of five years of post-training service. Subsequent multi-year enlistments are then possible until retirement age is reached.

On board ship the *michmanii* are assigned to each division, normally as the deputies to junior officers with direct command authority over petty officers and seamen. For example, an unmodified Kashin-class missile destroyer has a peacetime complement of approximately 20 officers, 20 *michmanii,* and just over 200 enlisted men. When possible, on board ship and at naval bases the *michmanii* have a separate mess. Along with having a distinctive uniform, special privileges, and higher pay than enlisted men, the *michmanii* represent the most technically competent group within the Soviet Navy.

OFFICERS

Soviet naval officers belong to an elite group that enjoys numerous privileges and opportunities while having a key role in Soviet defense and political strategies. The principal sources for the approximately 2,000 officers who are commissioned in the Soviet Navy every year are:

Higher Naval Schools	85%
Civilian Higher Schools	5%
Technical Institutes	10%

However, many naval officers begin their "career" at the age of 15 when they enter the Nakhimov secondary school in Leningrad.[10] Originally four schools were established in 1944 for the sons of deceased naval officers. Three of the schools have been closed down, and from

[10] Vice Admiral Povel Stepanovich Nakhimov won a major victory over a Turkish fleet at Sinope in 1853; his name is also given to a higher naval school and to a guided-missile cruiser.

the mid-1960s the remaining Nakhimov school in Leningrad has served as an officer "prep" school for specially chosen young men, generally the sons, nephews, or other relatives of naval officers and Communist Party officials. These students are accepted at Nakhimov for the last two years of secondary school, as preparation for higher naval schools.

At the Nakhimov school the cadets receive academic, military, and political training. Upon graduation from the Nakhimov schools the young men join graduates of other secondary schools and a select number of enlisted men in attending one of 11 higher naval schools, the equivalent of the U.S. Naval Academy.[11] These schools, their location, and areas of specialization are shown in table 10-2.

Of the five schools that educate surface line officers, the Frunze school is the most prestigious, tracing its heritage to naval cadet training that began in St. Petersburg in 1752. Two higher naval schools are dedicated to line engineering, and one each to shore engineering, radio-electronics, submarine warfare, and political affairs. All of the schools have a five-year course of instruction except for the political school, which offers a four-year curriculum. These higher naval schools provide

[11] In the Soviet Union there are approximately 140 higher military schools for all services that provide officer education for the armed forces; there are four such schools in the United States—the Naval, Military, Air Force, and Coast Guard academies.

TABLE 10-2. HIGHER NAVAL SCHOOLS

School	Location	Specialization
F. E. Dzerzhinsky Higher Naval Engineering School	Leningrad	line engineering
M.V. Frunze Higher Naval School	Leningrad	surface line
Kaliningrad Higher Naval School	Kaliningrad	surface line
Kiev Higher Naval Political School	Kiev	political
S.M. Kirov Caspian Higher Naval School	Baku	surface line
V.I. Lenin Higher Naval Engineering School	Pushkin (near Leningrad)	shore engineering
Leninsky Komsomol Higher Naval School of Submarine Warfare	Leningrad	submarine warfare
S.O. Makarov Pacific Higher Naval School	Vladivostok	surface line
P.S. Nakhimov Black Sea Higher Naval School	Sevastopol'	surface line
Sevastopol' Higher Naval Engineering School	Sevastopol'	line engineering
A.S. Popov Higher Naval School of Radio-Electronics	Petrodvorets (near Leningrad)	radio-electronics

a highly specialized education, the first two years being devoted primarily to basic, naval-related subjects and undergraduate studies; the remaining three years emphasize areas of specialization, with the result that Soviet naval officers are more technically educated and more specialized than their Western counterparts. Most naval officers will spend their career in the specialized field in which they were instructed at the higher naval school.

Practical training includes long-range cruises in warships and special training ships, the cadets receiving a "distant cruise" badge afterwards. Physical fitness is stressed at sea and ashore. An article describing the Popov Higher Naval Radio-Electronics School states that, "At the school they have a fine sports palace with a swimming pool, open sports area, and a firing range. Almost all of the students have sports ratings. In the past five years alone they have prepared here more than 20 masters of sports and hundreds of first-class sportsmen. Many students have often become champions and prize-winners of the armed forces, Leningrad, RSFSR [Russian Soviet Federated Socialist Republic] and USSR."[12]

Motivation is also stressed during an officer's education. The following comment by a ship's political officer illustrates this attitude: "Motivation comes first, the technology can come later . . . without motivation, technology is worthless." This motivation carries over to an officer's use of technology: "There is, first of all, the ship commanding officer's personal responsibility to the Motherland and the people for his use of the latest weapons and equipment. However, the responsibility is not limited to his service duties of controlling the ship and weapons. This responsibility is also determined by his role in training and educating his subordinates, in inculcating in them a high sense of duty to their Motherland."[13]

[12] Captain 1st Rank (Reserve) V. Nikolayev, "Named for A.S. Popov," *Voyennyye Znaniya* (no. 5, 1978), pp. 18–19.
[13] Rear Admiral G. Kostev (Assistant Professor), "The Ship's CO," *Soviet Military Review* (no. 8, 1979), pp. 16–17.

Two captains 3rd rank on board a SAM Kotlin-class destroyer. Their superiors are among the elite of Soviet society, and the incentive for these men to perform well and gain promotion is considerable. (U.S. Navy)

Graduates of higher naval schools are awarded an academic degree similar to the American baccalaureate and are commissioned as officers, in most instances as junior lieutenants. After graduation the new officers generally go on to their duty stations. The opportunity to proceed immediately to advanced education is available only to exceptional graduates. More than half the Soviet naval officers, however, will receive post graduate education at a later stage of their careers, with a significant number achieving a level roughly equivalent to a doctorate in the West.

The other major academic sources for Soviet naval officers are civilian higher schools (i.e., colleges) and technical institutes. These are generally four- and two-year establishments, respectively. There are reserve training programs at some of these schools, the instructional staff consisting of active service, reserve and retired officers, and civilians. Upon commissioning, these officers are generally sent to sea and spend their initial four to six years in a specific shipboard department (see below). During this period the young officer seeks to attain qualification in his speciality area, and he will seek to move to assistant commander (department head). Most officers will move up within their specialist area. Failure to serve in an executive or command position does not limit promotion and upward career movement. For example, a navigation specialist can serve as a ship, division, brigade, and fleet navigator, being promoted even while serving in the same position if his performance merits it. This policy sometimes results in rank inversion, and at times officers of senior rank will work for more-qualified juniors.

Soviet ships have up to seven "command" and four "staff" departments. The command departments, designated BCh for *Boevayie Chasti* and headed by assistant commanders of the ship, are BCh-1 navigation, BCh-2 missile and/or gunnery, BCh-3 mine and torpedo, BCh-4 operations, BCh-5 engineering. BCh-6 air, and BCh-7 command and control. The four staff departments are S.1-R electronics, S.1-Kh chemical, S.1-m medical, and S.1-S supply. An officer who goes on board ship will probably serve in the same department during his entire time in that ship, and when he goes to another ship, he will usually be in the same department as well.

Most graduates of higher naval schools are assigned to cruisers, destroyers, and frigates; graduates of the Leninsky Komsomol submarine school go to submarines. Graduates of the Dzerzhinsky and Pushkin engineering schools are assigned to BCh-5 departments in surface ships and submarines. Some outstanding graduates are immediately assigned as department heads, executive officers, and after brief service and additional training, even commanding officers of small combatants. These latter officers generally have an edge in subsequent promotion and major command assignments.

In the larger ships the outstanding heads of departments compete for the position of executive officer, with the BCh-1 generally having the edge. The commanding officer often selects, or at least approves, the selection of the executive officer (called assistant commander or *starpom* in the Soviet lexicon). By tradition, the executive officer of a ship usually becomes her commanding officer. The Soviet method of preparation of these officers for command consideration was described as:

> The commanding officer trains commanding officers. This rule . . . corresponds to the well-known principle in the Navy that the leader personally trains his subordinates. There is something else to be remembered also: It is a Navy tradition to pass command know-how along to one's successors. It is a truly happy commanding officer who turns his ship over to his senior assistant (Executive Officer). Needless to say, this is only possible when capable, promising officers are appointed (by the COs) as senior assistants and the commanding officers work hard and thoughtfully to prepare their replacements.[14]

There are also formal classes for prospective executive and commanding officers, but little has been published about these. Before he is formally selected, an officer must undergo a series of practical examinations in various naval areas that are administered by the staff officers of the command to which the ship is attached. He must also pass an interview with the division or other senior commander. The examinations are rigorous, with some candidates failing. At least one officer with previous command experience is known to have failed the examination.

After taking command of a ship, an officer undergoes a lengthy process to qualify for "independent command." During this process the division commander or a "flag specialist" with previous command experience will frequently ride the ship and observe the newly appointed CO. The rider may countermand or modify orders, as he deems appropriate. Thus, the new CO is taken through the annual evolution of exercises and training, and sometimes makes operational deployments with a flag specialist on his bridge before he is fully certified for command at sea. This practice is quite alien to Western navies.

The Soviet Navy wishes its COs to be independent, but it is a limited independence: to execute the assigned mission in conformity with the operational plan. Further, the Soviet concept of initiative is, in the opinion of some Western observers, confined to being creative in carrying out the assigned mission in the face of changed circumstances and/or the absence of orders from superiors.

The commanders of major warships (frigates and larger) range from captain-lieutenants to captains 1st rank, with at least two strategic-missile submarines being identified as having rear admirals as commanding officer. From the mid-1970s onward there have been several "deep" selections for commanding officer, with captain-lieutenants serving as commanders of several Krivak ASW ships and Kashin guided-missile destroyers. These officers have nine years or less of commissioned service, and some are under 30 years of age. This is approximately two ranks lower than frigate and destroyer commanders in the U.S. Navy. (There has been a similar reduction of unit commander ages

[14] Captain 1st Rank I. Gordeyev, "Who is Training Our Replacements?" *Morskoy Sbornik* (no. 12, 1981), pp. 44–48. Also see Officer Ye. Chernov, "We Raise Commanding Officers," *Morskoy Sbornik* (no. 3, 1981), pp. 33–38. Captain William Manthorpe, Jr., USN, has analysed Soviet CO selection and training in "Attaining Command at Sea," *Naval Institute Proceedings* (November 1975), pp. 97–98, and "Command Competence," *Proceedings* (December 1985), pp. 44–46. Several other meaningful articles on Soviet officer training have appeared in the *Proceedings* during the past few years, authored by Manthorpe, Captain James W. Kehoe, USN, and Dr. Robert C. Suggs.

in the Soviet Ground Forces, where there are regimental commanders as young as 32 and division commanders only 38 years old.)

Although young officers given such major assignments may not gain the staff experience of their Western counterparts, the use of general and naval staffs by the Soviet Union alleviates the need for all officers to be rotated through as many positions ashore as their Western counterparts. This, in turn, allows the Soviet line officers more fleet experience.

The fleet commanders in chief and ship and unit commanders have a major voice in officer promotion and assignment, much more so than their counterparts in the U.S. Navy. Advancement through captain 3rd rank is reported to be essentially automatic in the Soviet Navy. Selection for captain 2nd rank and above is apparently done by the Main Naval Staff. Those officers failing this selection generally remain on active duty until age 45.

Postgraduate education/training is generally a requirement for promotion to senior naval rank, and most officers are required to take competitive examinations for entry to advanced educational programs. Exceptions include outstanding graduates from higher naval schools, who are exempt from some portions of the examinations. The entrance examinations for a military academy may be taken up to three times.

Candidates for flag rank generally attend the Naval Academy in Leningrad, named in 1976 for the late Marshal Grechko (formerly the Order of Lenin Naval Academy).[15] This Leningrad institution, founded in 1828, is similar in concept to the U.S. Naval War College, but attendance confers more prestige and is more significant to an officer's career than is the American institution.[16] Line officers up to age 38 and engineering officers up to age 35 are accepted for resident graduate study, while officers are accepted for non-resident correspondence courses up to age 40. Candidates are required to pass entrance examinations in specialized areas and in a foreign language.

In addition to its advanced academic curriculum, the Naval Academy conducts studies and analyses for naval headquarters, and helps to develop strategy and tactics for the Navy. Potential flag officers may also attend the prestigious Voroshilov General Staff Academy in Moscow, where broad strategic, economic, and policy issues are addressed. The Voroshilov school has a two-year course (compared to the one-year course at the similar U.S. National War College and the Industrial College of the Armed Forces).

The higher naval schools offer graduate courses, both in residence and by correspondence, the length of courses varying from 12 to 18 months. Correspondence students are exempt from certain duties in order to study. There are some naval postgraduate institutions, in particular the Krylov engineering institution—a technical school that has no counterpart in the United States except perhaps the civilian Mas-

Then-Rear Admiral A.M. Kalinin, later commander of the Black Sea Fleet, shares a joke during the visit of two Soviet destroyers to the port of Boston in 1975. The long tours of sea duty for Soviet line officers are compensated for, in part, by a lower operating tempo than in the U.S. Navy and by certain material benefits. (U.S. Navy)

sachusetts Institute of Technology (MIT)—and the Naval Officers Technical School on Kronshtadt Island, Leningrad. In addition, naval officers receive specialized advanced education and training at the numerous schools operated by other services.

The Soviet military academies and higher military schools are commanded by general or flag officers, with several other senior officers on their teaching staffs.

Those naval officers who fail promotion to the next higher rank may be retired. However, there is considerable flexibility in the system, because officers can be promoted while in the same position. There are published retirement ages: active service for all junior officers currently lasts at least until they reach age 40; for captain 2nd and 3rd rank the retirement age is 45; for captain 1st rank age 50; for rear admiral and vice admiral age 55; and for admiral and admiral of the fleet age 60. There have been numerous exceptions, the most notable being Admiral Gorshkov, who retired as Commander in Chief of the Navy in December 1985, shortly before his 76th birthday.

[15] The full name of this institution is Naval Order of Lenin, Ushakov and October Revolution Academy *imeni* Marshal of the Soviet Union A. Grechko.

[16] There are believed to be 18 military academies in the Soviet Union; there are nine approximately equivalent schools in the United States: the Naval, Air, Army, and National war colleges, the Industrial College of the Armed Forces, the Armed Forces Staff College, the Army and Air Force command and staff colleges, and the Naval Postgraduate School.

Upon retirement most officers are transferred to the reserve where they serve up to ten years. These officers are subject to annual call-up, but this happens infrequently.

OFFICER RANKS

Line officers of the Soviet Navy have traditional naval ranks, with seven grades of commissioned rank below flag ranks compared to six in the U.S. Navy. This rank structure reflects the early German naval influence on the Russian Navy. Exact comparisons with U.S. ranks are difficult. For example, a Soviet captain 1st rank has the broad sleeve stripe of a commodore or rear admiral (lower half) in Western navies yet still wears the shoulder insignia of a colonel, his nominal army equivalent. The issue is further complicated because the Soviet military services do not have a brigadier rank; their one-star military rank is major general.

History. The military rank of admiral was introduced into the Russian Navy by Peter the Great in 1699, and the grades of rear (*kontr*), vice (*vitse*), and full admiral were used over the years with minor variations. (Although tsar Peter held military and naval ranks, he was only a captain in the Russian Navy until his 1709 victory over the Swedish army at Poltava. Only after that triumph—the first by Russian forces against a major European army—did he take the rank of rear admiral in the Navy and promote himself from colonel to lieutenant general in the army. The tsar did not assume the rank of full admiral until after his victory over Sweden in 1721.

The admiral grades fell into disuse at the start of the Soviet regime. Position titles were used for senior naval officers until late 1935 when the ranks of *flagman* (flag-officer) 1st and 2nd grade were introduced. "Admiral" was still not acceptable to the Communist regime; at that time, the term "general" was also avoided in the Red Army, but five army officers were named Marshal of the Soviet Union in 1935. The various grades of general and admiral were belatedly introduced in the Soviet armed forces on 7 May 1940, when seven Soviet naval officers were given admiral rank: N.G. Kuznetsov, the chief of naval forces, and I.S. Isakov and L.M. Galler, both at naval headquarters, were made admirals; the commanders of the Baltic and Pacific Fleets became vice admirals; and the commanders of the Northern and Black Sea fleets became rear admirals. S.F. Zhavoronkov, head of naval aviation, became a lieutenant general (two stars) at the same time. Many more flag officers were appointed during the war. The senior political officers assigned to the armed forces were given general or admiral ranks in December 1942.

The rank of admiral of the fleet (*admiral flota*) was also introduced in the Soviet Union on 7 May 1940. It was abolished on 3 March 1955 with the introduction of the rank of Fleet Admiral of the Soviet Union, but was reestablished on 28 April 1962 and corresponds to the military ranks of general of the army and marshal of an arm or service.

Admiral of the Fleet of the Soviet Union (*Admiral Flota Sovetskogo Soyuza*) is the highest rank of the Soviet Navy and corresponds to the rank of Marshal of the Soviet Union. It was introduced on 3 March 1955 and on that date was awarded to Isakov, the leading Soviet theorist of the 1930s, and Kuznetsov, who directed Stalin's fleet buildups of the late 1930s and early 1950s. On 28 October 1967 it was awarded to S.G. Gorshkov, 12 years after his being named CinC of the Soviet Navy.

The grades of captain 1st, 2nd, and 3rd rank (*ranga*) existed in the Russian Navy from 1713 to 1732, and again from 1751 to 1917, and in the Soviet Navy since 22 September 1935. Historically, these officers held the rank corresponding to the rank of the ship they commanded (*rang korablya*). Thus, a captain 2nd rank normally commanded a second-rank ship (see chapter 3 for current Soviet naval ship ranks).

In the Soviet Navy the rear, vice, and full admirals have insignia similar to their Western contemporaries and in most instances hold comparable positions. The flag rank issue becomes confused because the Soviet Navy has two admirals of the fleet on active duty in 1986, a rank not now held by serving officers in Western navies. The admirals currently in this grade are Admiral Chernavin, the CinC of the Navy, and Admiral Smirnov, the 1st deputy CinC (see appendix A; in the recent past the CinCs of the Northern and Pacific fleets have been admirals of the fleet).

An *approximate* comparison of Soviet military and naval ranks with U.S. ranks is provided in table 10-3. The Northern and Pacific fleets have generally been commanded by admirals and the Baltic and Black Sea fleets by vice admirals. In the U.S. Navy the area fleet commanders are admirals (Atlantic and Pacific Fleets) and the numbered fleet commanders are vice admirals (Second, Third, Sixth, Seventh). Thus, it seems reasonable to equate a Soviet admiral with the U.S. flag officer wearing the same insignia.

Direct comparisons of lower officer ranks are also difficult. For example, the commanding officers of some Soviet warships hold a similar rank to their American counterparts. However, cruisers of the MOSKVA, SVERDLOV, Kara, and Kresta II classes are mostly commanded by captains 2nd rank, while ships of their size in the U.S. Navy would have captains in command.

Senior instructors of the Soviet Navy have their rank prefixed with the term *professor* (professor) and engineering officers have the prefix *inzhener* (engineer).

The specialized branches of the Soviet Navy—Naval Aviation, Naval Infantry (marines), Coastal Missile-Artillery Force, *Spetsnaz,* Medical Service, and Rear Services—have distinctive uniforms and military ranks, separate schools, and other institutional trappings. These services are fully integrated into naval organizations in the same manner, for example, as U.S. Navy medical personnel are assigned to the Marine Corps units, and the Fleet Marine Forces are components of the U.S. Atlantic and Pacific fleet commands.

POLITICAL ACTIVITIES

The military establishment is in many respects the most powerful segment of the Soviet society, with probably more influence on the society than the educational, agricultural, or even industrial sectors. Because of this, the military has always been carefully watched and controlled by the Communist Party. During the past few years, however, there is increasing evidence that the Party now believes that the military establishment has become fully integrated with respect to ideals and goals.

TABLE 10-3. OFFICER AND WARRANT RANKS

Soviet Navy	Soviet Military and Specialized Naval Branches	Approximate U.S. Navy Rank
Officer Ranks		
Admiral of the Fleet of the Soviet Union (*Admiral Flota Sovyetskoga Soyuza*)	Marshal of the Soviet Union	Fleet Admiral
(none)	Chief Marshal Chief Marshal of Aviation	(none)
Admiral of the Fleet (*Admiral Flota*)	Marshal Marshal of Aviation General of the Army	Fleet Admiral
Admiral (*Admiral*)	Colonel General Colonel General of Aviation	Admiral
Vice Admiral (*Vitse Admiral*)	General Lieutenant General Lieutenant of Aviation	Vice Admiral
Rear Admiral (*Kontr Admiral*)	General Major General Major of Aviation	Rear Admiral
Captain 1st Rank (*Kapitan Pervogo Ranga*)	Colonel	Captain
Captain 2nd Rank (*Kapitan Vtorogo Ranga*)	Lieutenant Colonel	Commander
Capital 3rd Rank (*Kapitan Pervogo Ranga*)	Major	Lieutenant Commander
Captain Lieutenant (*Kapitan Leytenant*)	Captain	Lieutenant
Lieutenant (*Leytenant*)	Lieutenant	Ensign
Junior Lieutenant (*Mladshiy Leytenant*)	Junior Lieutenant	Ensign
Warrant Ranks		
Senior Warrant (*Starshi Michman*)	Senior Ensign	Warrant Officer or Chief Petty Officer
Warrant (*Michman*)	Ensign	Warrant Officer or Chief Petty Officer

More than 90 percent of all naval officers are believed to be members of the Communist Party or *Komsomol*—probably a higher percentage than in the other armed services. For a naval officer, membership in the Party is essential to obtain command or hold other important or sensitive positions.

History. As explained above, the Communist Party has traditionally exercised close control over the military establishment. Although sailors were in the forefront of the ill-fated 1906 revolution as well as the Great October Revolution of 1917, by 1921 the Baltic Fleet sailors at Kronshtadt were demanding free elections by secret ballot, freedom of the press and speech, the abolition of Bolshevik control over land use, and a "true people's revolution." The discontent of the Baltic sailors led to riots among Leningrad workers. The Bolshevik leaders and Red Army officer candidates attacked the Kronshtadt naval base, connected to the

mainland by ice. After 18 days the base fell, and with savage brutality the Bolsheviks executed or sent to Siberia several thousand sailors and the workers who had allied with them. There followed a long period of distrust of the political reliability of the fleet.

The loyalty of former tsarist officers was also a problem for the new Communist regime. Because of the lack of command experience and technical knowledge among the Communists, the ex-tsarist officers had to be used in military units. The result was the assignment of military commissars (*voyenkomi*) to each ship and unit to ensure that all orders by commanding officers were politically as well as militarily correct. At each subunit there were political instructors or *politruks* to indoctrinate soldiers and sailors in Party tenets. (Some former tsarist officers, especially I.S. Isakov and L.M. Galler, did serve in the most senior positions of the Soviet Navy.)

In June 1924, the new head of the armed forces, M.V. Frunze, abolished the dual-command system in favor of "unity of command" (*yedinonachalye*), in which the commanding officer no longer needed to have all orders countersigned by the political officer. This scheme took several years to institute fully. In each unit, however, there was a political assistant to the commander who was independent in virtually all respects.

The situation changed again in the late 1930s with Stalin's massive purges of the Soviet political and government leadership, which spread to the military establishment in 1937. Political commissars were reintroduced in June of that year, and "military councils" were established at all command levels, generally consisting of the commander, chief of staff, and political commissar. Decisions were made in the name of the council, with all three (or sometimes more) officers signing such orders—and sharing responsibility for them. In June 1940 as war approached, the concept of unity of command was again introduced, only to be abolished a year later when Germany invaded the Soviet Union and the dual-command system was reinstituted.

By the fall of 1942, when the German armies had been fought to a halt and Stalin was satisfied with the political reliability of most Soviet officers, he again ordered unity of command. But the October 1942 policy established an assistant commander for political affairs, in essence the system that continues today. These political officers were given military ranks in December 1942.

In general, there was distrust, if not actual hatred, for the political officers on the part of many naval officers. During World War II Navy Chief Kuznetsov discussed military matters with the chief political officer of the Navy, I.V. Rogov, "cautiously." Rogov was known as "Ivan the Terrible" in the fleet, his nickname a reference to the savage tsar of the sixteenth century who, partially mad, murdered his son. Another view of the Soviet Navy's political officers comes from a discussion of operations in the Baltic during the war:

> It very frequently happened that when a Russian vessel was sunk the survivors, fearing their commissar, refused to be taken on board, and would not give up their resistance until the commissar had been shot. . . . This is how it was, for example, on 14 September 1943 when six survivors were sighted after a [Soviet] PT boat went down in the Baltic Sea. As the German boat approached, the commissar shot two of his people floating

in the water, and the other three could not be taken aboard until after the commissar was shot dead.

When [the] large transport *Josef Stalin,* which had around 4,000 men on board, was stranded in the Gulf of Finland, the Russian survivors hanged their commissar.[17]

After the war the concept of one-man control continued, with political officers serving as assistant or deputy commanders at every level of command. The current Soviet policy has been stated in the following words by the then head of the Main Political Administration of the Army and Navy:

> One essential condition for the establishment and maintenance of stable order in all units is strict observance of the Leninist principle of one-man command. In the Army and Navy it is more necessary than anywhere else to ensure the strictest unity of action of large masses of people, their subordination to the will of one man. As evidenced by the one-half century of the Soviet Armed Forces, one-man command is the most effective method of troop control, particularly in a combat situation. It ensures really efficient, centralised [ok-np] and reliable direction of operations, achieve-

ment of victory in war and the necessary level of fighting efficiency and combat readiness in peacetime.

> One-man command plays an especially big role today, when the Army and Navy are armed with nuclear weapons and other up-to-date combat means. . . .[18]

Political activities within the Soviet armed forces are directed by the Main Political Administration (MPA), established in its present structure in 1946. The MPA is also a department of the Central Committee of the Communist Party, making it responsible to the Party leadership outside of the military chain of command. Political staffs subordinate to the MPA were then established within each service. As indicated in figure 10-1, under the MPA each military service has a political directorate. The Chief of the Navy's Political Directorate is a senior flag officer, who is at the level of Deputy CinC of the Navy. (The late Soviet leader L.I. Brezhnev, as a civilian, was head of the Navy's Political Directorate in the early 1950s.) The Navy's Political Directorate, in 1986 under Admiral P.N. Medvedev, supervises the political officers assigned to the fleets and specialized branches of the Navy, and to all units, and ships.

[17] Captain Erwin M. Rau, Federal German Navy, "Russia and the Baltic Sea: 1920–1970," Naval War College Review (September 1970), pp. 23–30.

[18] General of the Army A.A. Yepishev, *Some Aspects of Party-Political Work in the Soviet Armed Forces* (Moscow: Progress Publishers, 1975), pp. 197–98.

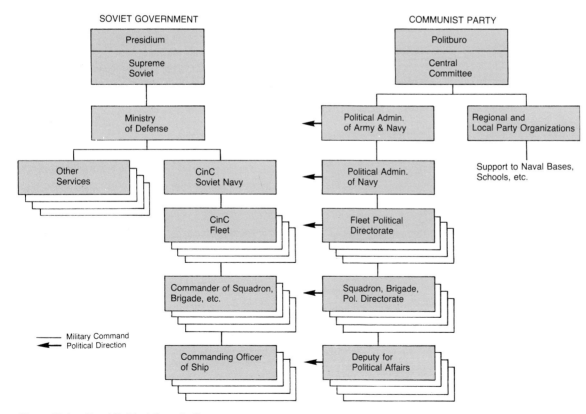

Figure 10-1. Naval Political Organization

The commanding officer of a ship or unit is personally responsible for his men's political attitudes and activities. Within each naval command (ashore and afloat) there is a political officer (*zampolit*) who serves as an assistant commander but additionally has his own chain of command up to the Navy's Political Directorate. The *zampolit's* duties aboard ship are diverse: he directs the ideological indoctrination of the crew; monitors the political reliability of the officers and enlisted men; ensures that Party directives are carried out; enforces discipline; and acts as both "chaplain" and social worker for the crew. Under the direction of the commanding officer, he is responsible for the morale of the crew. A shipboard political officer holds formal sessions regularly for the enlisted men and for officers on a periodic basis. Beyond these meetings there are continual "agitation and propaganda" activities, described as:

> Agitation and propaganda work is designed to instil in the personnel profound conviction in communist ideals, Soviet patriotism, proletarian internationals, uncompromising hatred for the enemies of communism, to strengthen their ideological staunchness and resistance to bourgeois influence in whatever form. An uncompromising struggle is being daily waged against hostile ideology and the aggressive essence and schemes of imperialism are unmasked.
>
> The basic methods of agitation and propaganda work conducted in the Soviet Navy include:
> —printed agitation and propaganda through books, pamphlets, leaflets, magazines and newspapers;
> —oral agitation and propaganda through lectures, periodic reports, talks and consultations;
> —poster agitation.[19]

Thus, the *zampolit* has a direct and integrated role in the operations and life of a ship. If a ship or unit performs well, the political officer will share credit with the commanding officer and his other assistants; if they do poorly, the political officer as well as the commanding officer will suffer. Also, according to a U.S. Navy evaluation, "In recent years . . . there has been a trend toward giving the political officer practical naval experience as a line officer prior to his entry into the political field."

The overlap of the naval and political areas reflects the current high degree of confidence of the Communist Party leaders in the reliability and loyalty of the armed forces. This is to be expected after more than 70 years of Communist rule and achievements. The last significant challenge to Party control over the military came in the early 1950s when Marshal Zhukov attempted to limit the influence of political officers over military decision making. However, since the unsettled period that followed Stalin's death in 1953 and the resulting "revolution" in military affairs, the political-military situation has settled down, and the political officers are generally considered a part of the service "team." This has resulted in significant "cross-fertilization" between the line and political officers, with some political officers eventually being given ship commands. Despite this integration of the *zampolit* into the "regular navy," the political officer retains his separate and direct line of communication to his political superiors up to the MPA and the Party leadership.

The Navy's political officers are trained at the Kiev Higher Naval Political School, one of several similar schools set up in 1967 for the different services. The four-year curriculum at the Kiev school stresses the political aspects of the armed forces, with emphasis on agitation and education in the fleet. Some naval line training is provided, but the newly commissioned political officers clearly do not have the same level of training as do graduates of the ten other higher naval schools. After service in the fleet and ashore, senior political officers of all services receive graduate-level instruction at the Lenin Military Political Academy in Moscow.

The relationship between the professional naval officer and the Party's other means of control over the military—the Committee for State Security (KGB)—is less than cordial. The KGB, as noted in chapter 4, includes the Maritime Border Troops whose units are responsible for the security of the Soviet Union's long coastlines. There are other special KGB troops that deal with the Navy, such as those responsible for the security of nuclear weapons.

The KGB is charged with counterespionage against both internal and foreign enemies. Reportedly, officers of the Third Directorate of the KGB, which is responsible for counterintelligence within the armed forces, are assigned to all branches of the military; they generally wear standard military uniforms, but are readily known as KGB officers and report only through the KGB chain-of-command. In the Navy, uniformed KGB officers are assigned to large surface ships. Covert KGB officers are assigned throughout the Navy, however, and operate a network of "informers."

Within the units and ships the KGB officers recruit men to report directly to them. According to one KGB defector, a former captain assigned to a motorized rifle regiment in East Germany, he was instructed that "when recruiting informers, you must not only convince them but also compel them to work for us. The KGB has enough power for that." And, he added

> The KGB had the rights and the power needed. If it was an officer [wanted as an informer], then his career could be threatened (without KGB approval no officer can be sent to a military academy or get promotion). With regular [enlisted] servicemen it was even simpler; they could just be dismissed from the army. Any Soviet citizen's life, too, could be threatened; he could be barred from an institute or from work in any undertaking, or be forbidden to travel abroad.[20]

While the political officers are considered part of the Navy contributing to the performance of ships and units, the KGB officers are only regarded with distrust and resentment.

Despite the unity of the Communist Party and the armed forces in their goals, there is still some political unrest. Indeed, there is some evidence of this throughout the Soviet Union, mostly related to the privileges of Party leaders at all levels and to the nation's continued economic problems. On rare occasions this political unrest surfaces. Probably the most dramatic example of the post-Stalin period occurred at the Baltic port of Riga on the night of 7–8 November 1975, as

[19] Admiral V.M. Grishanov, ed., *Man and Sea Warfare* (Moscow: Progress Publishers, 1978), p. 30.

[20] Aleksei Myagkov, *Inside the KGB* (New York: Ballantine Books, 1981), p. 82.

crewmen of the Krivak-class frigate STOROZHEVOY mutinied.[21] With many of the crew ashore following festivities celebrating the Great October Revolution, the ship's political officer, Captain 3rd Rank V.M. Sablin, another officer, and several petty officers and conscripts, seized control of the warship. They got the ship underway, and steered her down the Daugava River toward the Gulf of Riga.

One non-mutineer managed to jump over the side and swim ashore. The sailor was initially believed drunk and was ignored by authorities. Meanwhile, early on the morning of the 8th the ship glided into the Gulf of Riga and set a course for the Swedish island of Gotland some 200 miles (320 km) away.

The alarm was finally raised when one of the officers held prisoner in the STOROZHEVOY got free and was able to radio a frantic message to Riga. Moscow was called immediately and, reportedly, the CinC himself (Admiral Gorshkov) directed that the ship be stopped or, if that was not possible, sunk before she reached Swedish waters.

Aircraft were dispatched to find the ship, and nine Soviet warships joined in the hunt. The STOROZHEVOY was found, and after she ignored signals from reconnaissance aircraft, bombers were dispatched. French reports cited the planes actually attacking the ship, inflicting damage and killing and wounding about 50 crewmen before the mutineers surrendered. Other reports said the ship received only superficial damage with no casualties, while some sources indicated that the aircraft attacked a second Krivak that was chasing the STOROZHEVOY and that a total of 50 men were killed—15 in the STOROZHEVOY and 35 in the second Krivak. In any case, the STOROZHEVOY was captured from the mutineers.

Zampolit Sablin was executed by firing squad in Moscow following his trial before the Military Division of the Supreme Court of the Soviet Union, as were several enlisted men. Another officer was sentenced to 15 years in a labor camp. After a conspicuous cruise in the Baltic just outside of Swedish territorial waters, as if to demonstrate the loyalty of the ship, the STOROZHEVOY was transferred to the Pacific Fleet.

No other overt instances of unrest in the Soviet Navy in the recent past are known. Indeed, the opposite appears to be true among the Navy's officers, who are increasingly part of the elite of the Soviet Union. A postscript to the STOROZHEVOY mutiny comes from a Swedish military officer:

> Those who think this shows weakness are a little stupid. There is not a point of weakness. This demonstrates a will and a skill in making decisions. It shows the Russians are strong enough to do what is necessary.[22]

PAY AND BENEFITS

There are two basic types of compensation paid to Soviet naval personnel: minimal pay to conscripts and a relatively high pay to career servicemen, most of whom are warrant officers and commissioned officers.

The lowest ranking conscript, the seaman or *matros,* receives 3 rubles 80 kopecks per month while a senior seaman, depending upon his assignment, receives between 5 rubles 20 kopecks and 6 rubles 80 kopecks per month basic allowance.[23] An additional supplement is paid for specialist qualification, 1 ruble for third class, 2 rubles 50 kopecks for second class, and 5 rubles if the sailor qualifies as a specialist first class. Petty officers and some senior seamen earn 10 to 20 rubles per month plus specialist pay if they are in certain specified billets. In addition, three rubles per month are paid for sea duty during a sailor's first two years of service, and six rubles per month in the third year—as apparent compensation for serving longer than men in the other services. Thus, a conscript who becomes head of a subunit could earn as much as 30 rubles per month during his last year of service, still much less than the average Soviet worker in industry. Further, the additional money does not appear to compensate for the added responsibility and work of being head of a subunit.

Sailors are provided with food, minimal clothing, and limited medical care. Free recreation and cultural activities are provided, often interrelated and stressing political themes. Specific recreation activities stressed in the Navy include choir singing, do-it-yourself hobbies such as painting and handicrafts, and amateur acting. Discussions and reading are encouraged, with ship and station libraries stocked especially with books "dealing with political subjects, books on military history, the memoirs by outstanding military leaders, literature on the navies and armies of capitalist countries as well as books of fiction are all popular with Soviet navymen. While at sea during a prolonged cruise the men particularly appreciate magazines, satirical and comic publications."[24]

The sailor who is promoted to warrant rank can earn some 200 to 240 rubles per month, well above the income of the average Soviet worker.

Pay for commissioned officers is comparatively high and a major incentive for a naval career. Officer pay is based on commissioned status, rank, and length of service, with substantial supplements for sea duty, submarine duty, assignment to remote areas (Northern and Pacific Fleet regions), and education. The most significant component of this pay package is position pay. The approximate officer pay scale is shown in table 10-4. The basic pay for an officer is related to his having professional status with a degree in engineering; the rank pay is referred to as "star pay," a reference to his shoulder board insignia.

Within the variations of basic pay, the more important the position held the higher the basic pay. The combined basic and rank pay are increased for longevity at the rate of 5 percent for each five years up to 25 percent; submariners receive a bonus of 15 percent, with duty in nuclear-propelled submarines earning 20 percent; and sea duty in surface ships adds 30 percent. The special rates for service in the Arctic or Pacific regions vary with the location—about 15 percent more for duty in Vladivostok and up to 50 percent more for assignment in Murmansk or Petropavlovsk.

[21] There has been little authoritative writing in the West about the STOROZHEVOY mutiny. Probably the best work is the thesis by Lieutenant Gregory D. Young, USN *"Mutiny on STOROZHEVOY: A Case Study of Dissent in the Soviet Navy"* (Monterey, Calif.: Naval Postgraduate School, March 1982); the thesis was the basis of the popular article by Thomas B. Allen and Norman Polmar, "The Hunt for the *Storozhevoy,*" *Sea Power* (Navy League), January 1985, pp. 13–19.

[22] Quoted in Bernard D. Nossiter, "Soviet Mutiny Ended Swiftly," *The Washington Post* (7 June, 1976), p. 18.

[23] The official exchange rate is approximately 1 ruble = $1.40.

[24] Admiral Grishanov, *Man and Sea Warfare,* p. 174.

10-4. APPROXIMATE OFFICER PAY SCALE (Monthly Rate)

Rank	Basic Pay	Rank Pay
Lieutenant	120–150 rubles	120 rubles
Senior Lieutenant		130 rubles
Captain Lieutenant		140 rubles
Captain 3rd Rank		150 rubles
Captain 2nd Rank		160 rubles
Captain 1st Rank	190–300 rubles	180 rubles

TABLE 10-5. OFFICER CAREER ASSIGNMENTS

Years of Service	Rank	Typical Assignments
19 to 25	Captain 1st Rank	Military Academy of the General Staff (student) Brigade Command (small combatants) Division Command (cruisers/destroyers) Fleet Navigator CO strategic missile submarine CO KIEV (aircraft carrier) CO Sverdlov (cruiser)
14 to 21	Captain 2nd Rank	Naval Academy (student) Higher Naval School (instructor) Division Command (small combatants) CO Kiev (aircraft carrier) CO Moskva (helicopter carrier) CO Sverdlov (cruiser) CO Kara/Kresta/Kynda (cruiser) CO destroyer CO large landing ship
9 to 16	Captain 3rd Rank	Postgraduate Studies CO Kara/Kresta (cruiser) CO submarine tender CO destroyer CO Krivak (frigate) CO large landing ship CO large minesweeper XO surface combatant Department Head of surface combatant
5 to 12	Captain Lieutenant	CO Krivak (frigate) CO minesweeper CO small missile combat XO destroyer XO frigate Department Head of submarine
2 to 8	Senior Lieutenant	CO small combatant XO small combat
0 to 5	Lieutenant	XO small combatant
0 to 2	Junior Lieutenant	sea duty

Despite having to pay significant taxes and dues to the Communist Party (if a member), an officer's pay is significant by Soviet standards. Captains and flag officers earn from 500 to 2,00 rubles per month and have considerable non-monetary benefits, as befits the elite of a society.

Housing and medical service are provided free to all servicemen. Every year an officer receives one free round trip to any location in the Soviet Union, and if he is to use one of the Navy's resorts, primarily along the Black Sea coast, his wife and children travel free.

While regulations prescribe housing standards for servicemen, in some cases they are known to be substandard, especially for conscripts.

TABLE 10-6. SOVIET VERSUS U.S. NAVAL OFFICERS

	Soviet Union	United States
Pre-military training	Extensive	None
Political indoctrination	Extensive	None
Scope of education	Specialized	General
Sources	Higher Naval Schools 85% Other Institutions 15%	Naval Academy 10% NROTC 11% College & OCS 79%
Shipboard assignment	Very Specialized	Semi-Specialized
Technical Work	Hands-on	Managerial
Rotation	4 to 6 years	2 to 3 years
Shore duty	Minimal	Extensive

(However, the same situation exists in the U.S. armed forces.) The daily food ration in the Soviet Navy is stipulated at providing 3,000 to 4,000 calories, the highest allocation going to nuclear submarine crews. There are reportedly 40 special diets for Soviet servicemen, especially developed for men in arctic and tropical climates (on board ship or ashore), aviators, submariners, etc. The quality is reported to vary widely, with limited variety and few fresh vegetables and meat reported in some articles in the Soviet press. In part as a supplement, military cafes, post exchanges, and mobile stores at many bases provide "luxury" food items such as fresh fruit and vegetables in addition to staples.

These benefits are supplemented by certain social services in the Soviet Union. A childless wife of a sailor or warrant officer is exempt from paying the income tax levied on other childless workers. If there are children, they are provided with day care or kindergarten places, a benefit worth about 400 rubles per year. Special efforts are made to find housing and work for wives, and to help integrate them into new surroundings when the Navy moves families to base areas or home ports if the sailor is assigned to a ship. And when the conscript leaves the Navy, efforts are made to ensure that he is employed.

Still, embezzlement, poor quality, poor service, and poor management reduce the value of many benefits and services intended for conscripts. But because the Soviet armed forces have a high priority in Soviet society, major efforts are under way to remedy these problems. Nevertheless, the problems reflect the overall conditions of the Soviet state. state.

The situation with respect to non-monetary benefits is much better for officers. The housing, goods, and services are of relatively high quality. Senior officers, like officials of the Communist Party and important foreigners, have the use of special shops to purchase otherwise unavailable foods and goods, including imported products. Soviet naval officers are normally given 30 days of paid leave per year; senior officers and those who are assigned to remote areas or perform arduous duty receive 45 days per year. Special arrangements facilitate their travel, and recreation and vacation centers are available for them, including villas for senior officers on the Black Sea coast, the Soviet riviera. As one young Russian woman is said to have told an American officer, "A Soviet officer is a hell of catch."[25]

[25] Colonel Donald L. Clark, USAF (Ret.), "Who Are Those Guys?" *Air University Review* (May–June 1979), pp. 47–65.

The giant Typhoon SSBN, the world's largest submarine, demonstrates the Soviets' long-standing interest in undersea craft as well as their highly innovative submarine designs. The Soviets are making significant progress in several technology areas in which the West had been preeminent. The two flap-like projections between the Typhoon's sail and upper rudder are part of the towed communications buoy arrangement.

11
Fleet Development

The Soviet Navy is well into what may be considered the fourth stage of fleet development of the post–World War II era. The current Soviet ship design and shipbuilding effort has surprised many Western analysts and naval planners by the allocation of resources and the original approach taken by the Soviets. The result has been, in the words of the Director of U.S. Naval Intelligence:

> The transition of the Soviet Navy from a short-war, limited endurance force to one capable of fighting over the long haul at greater distances in either a conventional or nuclear environment should be largely complete by 1995.
>
> The Soviet Navy of the near future will also provide the Kremlin with a more effective instrument for expanding its influence and conducting coercive diplomacy in peacetime.[1]

The massive fleet building program initiated by Stalin after World War II was intended to provide a navy to secure the seas adjacent to the Soviet Union, to prevent an amphibious assault against Soviet territory, and to support possible moves by the Red Army into bordering states.

As soon as the major shipyards could resume work, the unfinished hulls of the prewar and wartime programs were rushed to completion. These programs were principally the light cruisers of the CHAPAYEV class and various destroyers, submarines, and lesser craft; however, the unfinished hulls of the battleships and battle cruisers laid down in 1938–1940 were scrapped.

Simultaneous with the rejuvenation of the shipyards, the various ship design bureaus were rehabilitated, and plans were prepared for a new generation of Soviet warships. These would become the first phase of the postwar development of the Soviet fleet.

PHASE I—STALIN PERIOD

These postwar ships would be based largely on existing designs, with some updating from captured German drawings, equipment, and ships, plus the assistance of former German technicians being used by the Soviets. By the late 1940s the keels for the first of these new designs were being laid down. Professor Michael MccGwire, a former British intelligence officer, has calculated that under Stalin's direction a 20-year shipbuilding plan was developed. Although the credible data are limited, MccGwire has postulated the number of ships that were to have been completed by the late 1960s. His estimates and data from other sources are shown in table 11-1.

Stalin's program would have produced a massive, albeit highly conventional, fleet. The Soviets began building the first postwar capital ships to be laid down by any nation—the STALINGRAD-class battle cruisers. These ships were to displace some 38,000 to 40,000 tons full load, carrying a primary armament of 12-inch guns. Subsequently, the design was revised to provide surface-to-surface missile launchers (retaining some 12-inch guns). The lead ship probably was started at the Nikolayev south shipyard on the Black Sea in early 1949.

Several of the CHAPAYEV-class light cruisers begun before the war were completed, as were many lesser ships of the wartime building programs. At the same time, the new cruiser, destroyer, and submarine classes were initiated. Two years later, in July 1951, when Admiral N.G. Kuznetsov was reappointed to head the Navy, he told the fleet's senior officers that the future of the Navy was bright and that in the near future the Soviet Union would construct aircraft carriers.

TABLE 11-1. POSTULATED SHIPBUILDING PLAN, 1946-1965

Type	Class	Lead Ship Completion	Total Planned	(Actually built)
Aircraft Carriers	(new design)	1956(?)	4+	—
Battle Cruisers	STALINGRAD	1955(?)	4+	—
Light Cruisers	CHAPAYEV	1949	5	5
Light Cruisers	SVERDLOV	1952	24	14
Cruisers	(new design)	1958	16	—
Destroyers	SKORYY	1950	80	72
Destroyers	Tallinn	1955	12	1
Destroyers	Kotlin	1955	36	39*
Destroyers	(new design)	1958	80+	—
Submarines	Whiskey	1952	336	231
Submarines	Zulu	1952	36	26
Submarines	Quebec	1955	96+	30
Submarines	(new designs)	1958	720+	—

*Includes 12 ships completed with SS-N-1 missile (Kildin and Krupnyy classes). See Chapter 27 for details of Soviet missile designations.

Statement of Rear Admiral John L. Butts, USN, before the Seapower and Force Projection Subcommittee, Senate Armed Services Committee, 26 February 1985, p. 24.

An unfinished SVERDLOV-class cruiser in the late 1950s, probably at the Marti (now Admiralty) shipyard in Leningrad prior to being scrapped as part of the post-Stalin cutbacks in large warship construction. Alongside is the Belgium-built merchant ship STANISLAVSKY.

Of more immediate concern to Western military planners in the immediate postwar period was the specter of some 1,200 Soviet submarines that could be operational by the 1960s if the Soviets could attain the German building rates of World War II. The medium-range Whiskey had been designed before the war ended, but plans were modified to take advantage of German wartime technical developments. The ocean-going Zulu demonstrated more German influence, with several features being adopted from the highly advanced Type XXI U-boat. The Zulu's successor, the Foxtrot (operational from 1957), was even further developed, and became widely used by the Soviet Navy as well as by several Third World navies.

The follow-on, medium-range Soviet submarine, the Romeo (operational from 1957), also incorporated German technology, while the smaller Quebec, a coastal submarine, would have a closed-cycle power plant to permit use of diesel engines underwater to charge batteries without the need to raise a snorkel breathing tube. This concept also had German origins.[2]

[2] After World War II the U.S. and British navies investigated closed-cycle diesel plants based on the German Walther concept. The British built two experimental submarines with this propulsion system, HM/Submarines EXPLORER and EXCALIBUR. The only U.S. craft built with such a closed-cycle (non-nuclear) system was the midget submarine X-1.

A SVERDLOV at sea in 1983, more than three decades after the lead ship was completed. These attractive ships are reminders of the large but outdated fleet that the Soviet Union began producing almost immediately after World War II. More important than these ships to the modern Soviet fleet was the rapid rehabilitation of the shipbuilding industry. (U.S. Navy, PH2 D. Beech)

In the event, Stalin's death in March 1953 brought this ambitious shipbuilding program to an almost complete halt. Within days, stop-work orders were sent out to some yards, and several major revisions were made in the program during the 1953–1955 period. The battle cruiser STALINGRAD was about 60 percent complete in 1953; the ship is believed to have been launched and expended in missile tests. While five of the CHAPAYEV-class cruisers, which had been started before the war, were completed, only 14 of the planned 24 light cruisers of the SVERDLOV class were finished. Significantly, large numbers of the destroyers and submarines were completed, although not all that were planned. The proposed aircraft carriers were never started.

Of great significance for the future Soviet fleet, Stalin's ambitious program did provide the industrial and design base for building a large navy.

PHASE II—KHRUSHCHEV PERIOD

Khrushchev and his colleagues who inherited the mantle of Stalin moved rapidly to cut back the naval rebuilding effort.[3] There was little opposition to the reductions. Early in his tenure as Party Secretary and hence head of the ruling Politburo, Khrushchev reassigned several of the recently rebuilt and new shipbuilding facilities to construct merchant ships instead of warships.

He then directed the Navy to seek more innovative weapons in place of large surface warships—with low-cost, high-firepower ships that could

---

[3] See "The Navy" in Nikita Khrushchev, *Khrushchev Remembers—The Last Testament* (Boston: Little, Brown & Co., 1974), pp. 19–34. While the accuracy of this volume has been questioned, being considered by some authorities a KGB effort, the work does seem to reflect the Soviet viewpoint.

counter Western naval forces. Khrushchev would later write quite candidly how he wanted to build large ships: "I'll admit I felt a nagging desire to have some [aircraft carriers] in our own navy, but we couldn't afford to build them. They were simply beyond our means. Besides, with a strong submarine force, we felt able to sink the American carriers if it came to war. In other words, submarines represented an effective defensive capability as well as reliable means of launching a missile counterattack."[4]

Admiral Kuznetsov continued to advocate the construction of a large, conventional surface fleet and argued against Khrushchev's position. Finally, Kuznetsov was fired; Admiral S.G. Gorshkov became Deputy Commander in Chief of the Navy in mid-1955 and officially succeeded Kuznetsov as CinC in January 1956. Khrushchev directed Gorshkov to scrap the fleet's battleships and cruisers, and to build instead a fleet of smaller, missile-armed ships and submarines that could defend the Soviet Union against Western naval-amphibious attacks. Of particular concern to the Soviet leadership were the American aircraft carriers, which could launch nuclear-armed strike aircraft against the Soviet Union.

The Soviets described this period as a "revolution" in military affairs, as nuclear weapons and other advanced technologies belatedly became a subject for discussion by the Soviet military leadership. Within the next few years Admiral Gorshkov disposed of the outdated battleships and older cruisers and initiated or accelerated the advanced weapon programs. Soviet shipyards produced swarms of the Komar and then Osa missile boats, armed with the short-range SS-N-2 Styx missile, and several destroyers were completed with the 100-n.mile (185-km) SS-N-1 Scrubber/Strela anti-ship missile. The Kennel surface-to-surface

---

[4] Ibid., p. 31.

The Soviet Navy in the postwar period led the world in the development of anti-ship missiles, such as this SS-N-2 Styx being fired by an Osa I missile boat. This well-publicized photo clearly shows the massive firepower packed into the 215-ton ships—four missiles and two rapid-fire gun mounts—unprecedented when the first Osa went to sea in 1959.

missile was developed for use in larger ships, but was unsuccessful and evolved into the AS-1 air-to-surface weapon.

Subsequently, the more-capable SS-N-3 Shaddock missile was developed, originally for submarine use in the strategic land-attack role (and possibly for surface launch in the land-attack configuration). The Shaddock went to sea in the anti-ship version in 1962 in the Kynda-class missile cruisers. Labeled a rocket cruiser (*raketnyy kreyser*) by the Soviets, the Kynda demonstrated the progress made by Admiral Gorshkov in "selling" new surface ships to the Soviet leadership. Preparations were also put forward for building a still-larger Shaddock missile cruiser design.

During this phase of fleet development the Soviet Navy put to sea a strategic strike force. Initially diesel-electric submarines were armed with nuclear torpedoes to strike American coastal cities. More significant, and more practical, the Soviets used captured German technology to develop both guided (cruise) and ballistic missiles for launching from submarines against land targets. The SS-N-3 Shaddock cruise missile was surface-launched, with a land-attack range of more than 400 n.miles (735 km) carrying a nuclear warhead.

Initially Whiskey-class submarines were converted to fire the Shaddock—first the single-cylinder type, then the twin-cylinder type, and finally the "long-bin" configuration, which had four tubes fitted in an enlarged conning tower. Some Western sources report that 72 of the Whiskey long-bin conversions were planned (only seven were actually completed, as were seven of the earlier conversions). Subsequently, new-construction Shaddock submarines were begun—the diesel Juliett (SSG) and nuclear Echo I/II (SSGN) classes.

Almost simultaneously the Soviets developed submarine-launched ballistic missiles. Tests were undertaken with Army-developed ballistic missiles of the Komet series. The first submarine-launched ballistic missile to become operational was the SS-N-4 Sark, a surface-launched weapon with a range of some 300 n.miles (645 km). Several Zulu-class diesel submarines were converted to carry two of these missiles, followed by the new-construction, diesel-propelled Golf (SSB) and nuclear Hotel (SSBN) classes.

Thus, the Soviets simultaneously built both diesel and nuclear submarines for the cruise- and ballistic-missile roles. Further, the SSGN and SSBN designs were developed at the same time as the first Soviet nuclear-propelled submarine design, the torpedo-armed November class. This large and multiple-design nuclear submarine program demonstrated (1) early Soviet belief in the effectiveness of nuclear submarines, (2) the decision to put large numbers of missile-armed submarines to sea as rapidly as possible, (3) the desire to use all available submarine shipyard capacity, and (4) possibly the limited availability of nuclear reactor plants. The size of the Soviet nuclear submarine program can also be seen when by 1970 the Soviet Union surpassed the United States in numbers of these submarines.

Although the capabilities of the Sark ballistic missile in the Soviet SSB/SSBNs were severely limited, especially when compared to the U.S. Polaris that would follow shortly, the Soviet Navy had in fact deployed a submarine-launched ballistic missile before the United States.

The Soviet Navy also led the world in the deployment of ballistic missiles at sea, although the early missile submarines—like this Zulu-class SSB—had severely limited capabilities. Here the SS-N-4 Sark missile is elevated prior to firing; note the open hatch and holding cradle.

The November-class SSN was the Soviet Navy's first nuclear-propelled submarine, going to sea less than four years after the USS Nautilus (SSN 571). The Soviets initiated SSBN and SSGN programs almost simultaneous with the November. This is the lead ship of the class, the Leninskiy Komsomolets, at the North Pole in 1962.

This strategic submarine effort of the Soviet Navy was stopped short of its apparent goals. The establishment of the Strategic Rocket Forces (SRF) as a separate service in late 1959 caused a cut back or quite probably a termination of the SSB/SSBN programs. Only eight Hotel SSBNs were completed along with 23 of the Golf SSBs, and plans for more advanced ballistic missile submarines were shelved.[5]

Under both tsars and commissars, Russia had demonstrated a major interest in submarines. While the Soviets failed in this period to build the 1,200 submarines that U.S. intelligence estimated could be built by the late 1960s, a large number of undersea crafts were produced. The medium-range Whiskey-class diesel boats were mass-produced at four yards, and when the last was completed in 1957 an estimated 231 had been built; 90 had been launched in a single year, an ominous indication of Soviet industrial potential just a decade after World War II had ended.

While the Whiskey program was under way the larger Zulu diesel attack boat and the Quebec coastal submarine were being built, albeit in smaller numbers. The Quebec's closed-cycle diesel plant was not successful, with several accidents occurring; the submarines were mod-

ified to operate as conventional diesel-electric craft, and served into the 1970s. Counting some older boats of wartime design, this massive submarine effort provided a peak strength of some 475 submarines by 1958, after which there was a decline as the older craft were retired at a faster rate than new construction.

One other significant submarine development was initiated in this period—the Alfa SSN. This advanced-technology undersea craft was begun by the late 1950s, even before the first Soviet nuclear submarine had gone to sea. The Alfa's revolutionary design includes an advanced reactor plant with a liquid-metal heat-exchange medium (in lieu of pressurized water) and a titanium pressure hull (instead of steel); these have resulted in the Alfa being the deepest-diving and fastest combat submarine yet built by any navy.

There are three possible explanations for the development of the Alfa. First, the Alfa may have been intended as a high-speed "interceptor," to dart out from base upon warning of an enemy warship approaching the coast. Another explanation may be found in the American press of the time, which estimated—incorrectly—that the U.S. submarine Skipjack (SSN 585), launched in 1958, had a top speed of 45 knots. Finally, the Alfa may be the result of a Soviet multi-track approach to the development of nuclear propulsion. If this theory is correct, one

---

[5] Components for an additional Golf SSB were transferred to Communist China and assembled there.

development track produced the pressurized-water reactor used in the Hotel, Echo, and November classes, while a separate program track led to the liquid-metal reactor of the Alfa.[6]

PHASE III—REACTING TO U.S. THREATS

The late 1950s saw a concentration of Soviet naval efforts on the anti-carrier mission. With the loss of the strategic land-attack mission, the cruise-missile submarines of the Whiskey, Juliett, and Echo II classes were shifted to the anti-ship role, being rearmed with the SS-N-3a version of the Shaddock. Both the Juliett and Echo II classes continued in construction for several years after the cancellation of the Golf (SSB) and Hotel (SSBN) programs. The Julietts and Echo IIs were provided with the Front Door/Front Piece radars for missile guidance and video data links to receive targeting data from long-range Bear-D reconnaissance/targeting aircraft.

Air-to-surface missiles were also being developed for the anti-carrier role; bombers were transferred from the Air Forces to the Navy to be armed with these weapons for the anti-carrier role (see chapter 8). There may also have been some initial interest in this period in developing sea-launched ballistic missiles for the anti-ship role, and there was some discussion in Soviet literature of employing land-based ICBMs in this role.

But Khrushchev's plan to reduce the size of the Soviet Union's conventional military forces in favor of a nuclear striking force (operated by the SRF) and to "fight" the West in the Third World fell apart when John F. Kennedy became president of the United States in January 1961. Kennedy, elected in a campaign that publicized a "missile gap" because of the Soviet Sputnik and missile test successes, began a buildup of U.S. strategic and conventional military forces. He accelerated the development of the Polaris submarine-launched ballistic missile and the Minuteman ICBM, giving them the highest priorities, increased the number of naval ships in commission, and built up forces, most notably the Army's Special Forces, to fight Soviet-sponsored insurgents in the Third World.

This U.S. strategic buildup was most dramatic. The situation created consternation in the Kremlin and led to major reconsiderations of Soviet defense planning. The recently decided Soviet defense policies emphasizing ICBMs were found wanting, as was Soviet missile development, which was encountering technical problems. Several revisions in defense planning were initiated, and in a move to overcome shortfalls in the ICBM program, Khrushchev ordered medium-range missiles and nuclear-capable bombers to be based secretly in Cuba. The ensuing Cuban missile crisis of October 1962 demonstrated that (1) the United States was willing to use conventional military force against the Soviets in the Western Hemisphere, (2) the U.S. strategic offensive weapons could overwhelm those of the Soviet Union, and (3) the Soviet Navy was unable to support an overseas adventure.

---

[6] A similar two-track effort had been initiated in the United States, with the liquid-metal project being cancelled after technical problems, although the project offered the promise of higher reactor power. This plant, using liquid-sodium as the heat-exchange medium, was operational from 1957–1958 in the USS Seawolf (SSN 575); a land-based prototype was also built at West Milton, New York.

Even while the Soviet missiles and bombers were still being withdrawn from Cuba, Deputy Foreign Minister V.V. Kuznetsov told an American official, "we will live up to this agreement, but we will never be caught like that again." Soviet military programs were accelerated, long-range plans were revised, and in March 1963 there was a top-level realignment of the country's economic management—just three months after a long-planned reorganization had occurred. A new Supreme Economic Council was set up, headed by Dmitri Ustinov, long-time head of armament production. This appointment gave military planning clear priority in the national economy after Khrushchev's earlier attempts at a more-balanced approach. Within the defense establishment, in the aftermath of the Cuban missile crisis a new chief of the Soviet General Staff was named in early 1963 and there were indications that Khrushchev, age 71, might soon step down. (He was forced to do so in October 1964.)

The events of 1961–1963 had considerable impact on the Soviet Navy. The significance of the Navy within the armed forces was enhanced, for naval forces could help to counter the U.S. Navy's Polaris submarines, could help to redress the "missile gap" that had in fact existed in favor of the United States, and might make future incursions into the Third World more successful.

With respect to shipbuilding programs, the construction of Kynda-class missile cruisers was halted after only four units were built; plans for a larger Shaddock-armed ship for the anti-carrier role were abandoned. The anti-carrier effort would be left mainly to aircraft and submarines armed with cruise missiles. The Kyndas were replaced on the building ways at the Zhdanov shipyard in Leningrad by the interim Kresta I class, which has one-fourth of the Kynda's missile load; however, the Kresta I has improved anti-aircraft and helicopter capabilities. After only four of these ships were built the matured Kresta II design appeared. The Kresta II is an anti-submarine ship, with long-range ASW missiles (SS-N-14) replacing the Shaddock anti-ship missiles.

At the same time as the Kresta program, the Nikolayev south shipyard in the Black Sea area was producing the MOSKVA-class hermaphrodite missile cruiser-ASW helicopter carriers. These ships, the first true aviation ships to be built in the Soviet Union, were intended to counter the U.S. Polaris submarines in regional seas adjacent to the Soviet Union. The MOSKVA was completed in 1967 and her sister ship, the LENINGRAD, was finished the following year. They were incapable of coping with the Polaris submarines, for by that time the U.S. Navy had 41 strategic-missile submarines, at least half of which were always at sea. Also, the Polaris A-3 missile, which became operational in 1964, had a range of 2,500 n.miles (4,600 km), reducing the potential effectiveness of the MOSKVA with her short-range ASW helicopters. At the time the MOSKVA program halted, the Navy was planning a larger, more capable aircraft carrier.

The Kresta II and contemporary Kara ASW ships could effectively serve as command ships for ASW forces seeking to protect Soviet submarines from Western anti-submarine forces, especially U.S. nuclear attack submarines. The pro-submarine mission seems to have been the rationale for several major Soviet programs of this period. It should be noted that while specialized anti-ship weapons, like the SS-

Another example of Soviet innovation in ship design is the MOSKVA-class combination missile cruiser and helicopter carrier. At right is a Kashin-class missile destroyer, the first oceangoing warship with all-gas-turbine propulsion. (U.S. Navy)

N-2 Styx and SS-N-3 Shaddock, were not fitted in these ships, the SA-N-1 and later SA-N-3 surface-to-air systems do have an anti-ship capability.

And the Soviets continued to produce large numbers of submarines. The production of earlier types—nuclear and diesel—continued. Three major classes of nuclear submarines were begun in the early 1960s, the second generation of such craft. The Echo I/II cruise-missile submarines, which were required to launch their Shaddock missiles from the surface, were followed into service by the more-advanced Charlie-class SSGN. The initial Charlie I is armed with eight, short-range (30-n.mile/55-km) SS-N-7 cruise missiles, but these can be fired while the submarine remains completely submerged; the subsequent Charlie II has the longer-range (60 n.miles/110-km) SS-N-9 missiles. This class, however, has not been completely successful.

The contemporary Victor torpedo-attack submarine (SSN) was a superior craft, believed to have been developed specifically for the anti-submarine role, as have essentially all U.S. Navy SSNs. With a maximum speed of some 33 knots, the Victor was the world's fastest operational submarine when it entered service in 1968. The improved Victor II/III classes followed.

The third new submarine type of the period was the Yankee strategic-missile submarine. As noted above, Soviet SSBN development slowed or was possibly halted completely with the 1959 defense decisions, with the last of the Golf/Hotel submarines being completed in 1962. Following the initiation of the U.S. strategic buildup, the Cuban missile fiasco, and

problems in Soviet ICBM development, the Soviet SSBN program was given new life. The immediate result was a new submarine design closely resembling the U.S. Polaris submarines, to which NATO assigned the confusing code name *Yankee*. Armed with 16 missiles in two rows of internal tubes abaft the sail structure, the design of the Yankee shows evidence of having been hastily completed and ordered into construction with the highest priorities. Production was undertaken at two yards, Severodvinsk in the Arctic followed by Komsomol'sk in the Far East.

The first Yankee SSBN was completed in 1967, the year that the 41st and last U.S. Polaris/Poseidon submarine was completed. Yankee production reached a peak of ten units in 1970, after which it slowed as the yards prepared for the follow-up on Delta-class SSBN. This latter undersea craft, which began to enter service in 1972, was the world's largest submarine built up to that time.

More significant than the size, the Delta SSBN carried a very long range missile, initially the SS-N-8 with a range of more than 4,000 n.miles (7,360 km). This meant that Delta submarines could remain in Soviet coastal waters of the Barents Sea and Sea of Okhotsk while targeting virtually the entire United States. This capability would invalidate Western ASW concepts that called for intercepting Soviet SSBNs (as well as attack submarines) as they transited from their base or patrol areas to missile-launching positions.

Additional torpedo-attack and cruise-missile submarine classes were begun during the early 1960s, continuing the Soviet policy of not only

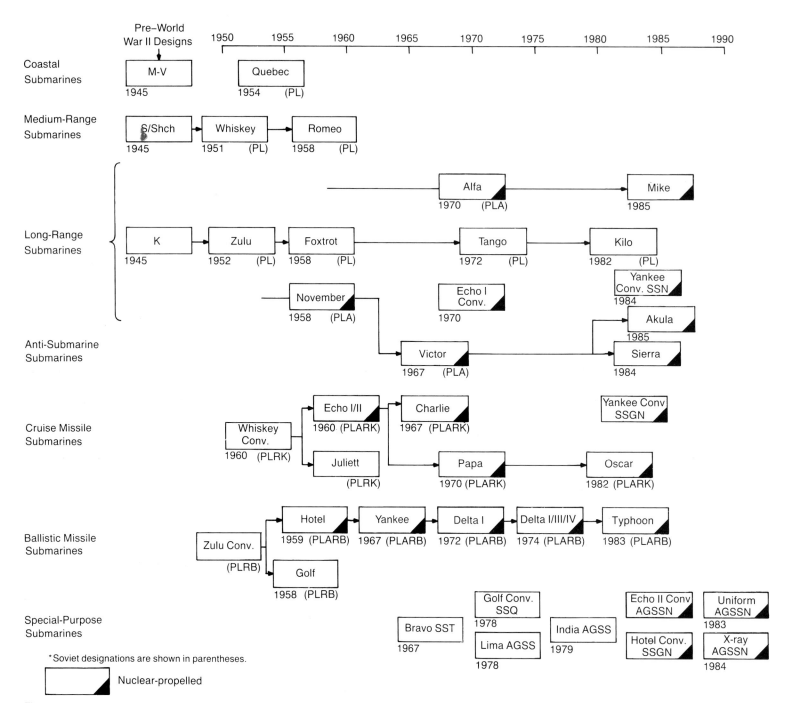

Figure 11-1.   Submarine Development

building large numbers of submarines, but also developing multiple classes. The Papa of this period is a one-of-a-kind cruise-missile submarine, larger and faster than the Charlie SSGN.

Diesel submarine construction also continued in Soviet yards. The U.S. Navy had abandoned the construction of diesel combat submarines in the late 1950s. The Soviets apparently believed that diesel submarines could undertake some missions as effectively, or more so, as nuclear submarines. It has also been suggested that Soviet industry simply could not produce the number of reactor plants needed for an all-nuclear undersea force.

The long-range Foxtrot diesel submarines have been followed by the further improved Tango-class SS (operational in 1972); construction of this class has now been followed by the Kilo class, the first of which entered service in 1982. Also built in this period were the four Bravo-class submarines, which are specialized target-training craft (SST). These serve both as targets for ASW forces and to train submariners, while having some combat capability. (The Soviets continued to build specialized support and research submarines in significant numbers, with two of the most unusual being the pair of India-class rescue and salvage submarines, completed in 1979–1980, which carry rescue/salvage submersibles and can support saturation diving operations.)

Thus, the Soviet Navy continued to emphasize submarine construction. Their production rate slowed in the late 1950s as the nuclear programs were instituted, and again in the late 1960s as the shipyards geared up to produce the second-generation nuclear submarines. Only seven submarines were completed in 1971: five Yankee SSBNs, one Charlie SSGN, and one Victor SSN. This was the smallest number of submarines built in any year since 1945. (The previous year—in 1970— an estimated 19 submarines were completed, all but one of which were nuclear powered.)

During this third phase of postwar Soviet naval development, the Naval Infantry ("marines") was reactivated in the Soviet Navy (see chapter 9). Construction was begun of specialized ships to carry and land these troops—the Polnocny LSMs at the shipyard by that name in Gdansk, Poland, and the Alligator LST at Kaliningrad in the Soviet Union.

Finally, sustained deployments were beginning in the Mediterranean Sea and the Indian Ocean, and the periodic visits of warships to the Gulf of Mexico-Caribbean area and to African ports created new requirements for at-sea replenishment ships. Previously, almost all fuel and supplies transferred to Soviet warships on the high seas came from merchant ships; however, starting with the fuel-munitions ship BORIS CHILIKIN (completed in 1971), the Soviets have increasingly employed specialized underway replenishment (UNREP) ships, an often overlooked but vital component of fleet development. The six CHILIKIN-class ships were followed by the single large BEREZINA, comparable in some respects to the U.S. Navy's AOE/AOR ships.

PHASE IV—THE MODERN SOVIET FLEET

In 1970, after observing a major Soviet military exercise, Party Chairman L. I. Brezhnev declared, "No question of any importance in the world can be solved without our participation, without taking into account our economic and military might." Whereas Stalin had avoided involvement in the Third World, and Khrushchev's "adventurism" had too often failed, Brezhnev seemed determined that the Soviet Union would have an active role in the Third World. The Soviet Union supported emerging and established socialist states, and carried out other Soviet goals in the Third World, including efforts to counter Western influence and activity.

Algeria, Angola, Cuba, Egypt, El Salvador, Ethiopia, Iraq, North Korea, Libya, Nicaragua, Somalia, Syria, Vietnam, and both North and South Yemen have all became recipients of Soviet attention in the 1970s and 1980s. In some cases Soviet combat troops have been present (as in Cuba and, until 1972, in Egypt); more often, surrogate troops (especially Cubans, but often with East German, Vietnamese, or Soviet advisors), have been used, and Soviet merchant ships carrying weapons and supplies are always in evidence.

Increasingly, Soviet naval ships have also been present. Admiral Gorshkov, when he was CinC of the Navy, had strongly supported this role (see chapter 5). By 1970, when Brezhnev made the statement cited above, decisions had already been made to construct still another generation of Soviet warships—including the first aircraft carriers to be built by the Soviet regime and the first nuclear-propelled surface warships.

By late 1971 the U.S. reconnaissance satellites overflying the Soviet Union brought back evidence of an aircraft carrier under construction at the Nikolayev south yard, where the MOSKVA and her sister ship LENINGRAD were constructed. The following December the ship was launched, revealing the largest warship yet built in the Soviet Union. Named KIEV, the 43,000-ton ship is a true aircraft carrier, with an angled flight deck and a large starboard island structure. But there the similarity to Western aircraft carriers ends.

The KIEV is fitted with heavy batteries of anti-aircraft, anti-submarine, and anti-surface weapons, plus Gatling-type, rapid-fire guns for close-in defense against cruise missiles. The anti-ship weapons are the SS-N-12, an improved version of the Shaddock with a range of some 300 n.miles (555 km).[7] Also the KIEV lacks the catapults and arresting wires of Western carriers that permit the operation of conventional aircraft. Instead, the KIEV carries a composite air group of some 35 Yak-38 Forger VSTOL aircraft and Ka-25 Hormone/Ka-27 Helix helicopters. The Forger, a transonic fighter-attack aircraft, was the second VSTOL combat aircraft to go to sea, the first having been the Anglo-American Harrier.

The decision to build the KIEV and her sister carriers seems to have been taken at the Politburo level about 1965. The decision would have been made at the highest level of government because of the major capital allocations of facilities, materials, and people required for these ships. A major factor in these decisions was the mission for the carriers. The fact that the KIEV is limited to a relatively small number of aircraft, of inferior types when compared to U.S. carrier aircraft, strongly indicates that the KIEV and her sister ships were not intended to counter Western carriers. Rather, two other roles appear more probable. First,

---

[7] The KIEV was the first aircraft carrier of any nation to be provided with significant anti-ship weapons since the U.S. carriers LEXINGTON (CV 2) and SARATOGA (CV 3) beached their 8-inch (203-mm) guns in 1940–1941.

the Soviet "pro-submarine" mission of supporting and protecting Soviet submarines, especially SSBNs, has been cited by Western analysts as an obvious rationale for the ship. Looked at in isolation, this thesis has some validity. However, the subsequent construction of larger aircraft carriers, the anti-ship weapons mounted in the KIEV, and the lack of a fixed-wing ASW aircraft for the KIEV reduce the credibility of the pro-submarine role.

A more likely rationale for the KIEV-class carriers is the increasing Soviet activity in the Third World. By the late 1960s the U.S. Department of Defense had announced the decision to reduce the American carrier force to 12 ships, and the Royal Navy as well as other NATO fleets were giving up their conventional aircraft carriers. At the same time, the number of airfields available to the United States in the Third World was declining. As a result, one or more KIEV-type ships in the right place at the right time could have considerable influence in crisis or combat situations.

Shortly after the lines of the KIEV became visible in satellite photography, there were indications that another large warship was being built at the Baltic shipyard in Leningrad. Although the Baltic yard had not constructed warships since the SVERDLOV cruiser program, the yard was building the nuclear-powered icebreakers of the ARKTIKA class. The new Baltic ship was the KIROV, a nuclear-powered missile cruiser. Displacing 28,000 tons, the KIROV is the largest warship except for aircraft carriers built by any nation since World War II. Here again, the KIROV demonstrates a highly innovative design. The ship has vertical-launch anti-aircraft (SA-N-6) and anti-ship (SS-N-19) missiles, the latter giving the KIROV, like KIEV-class carriers, a stand-off strike weapon. In addition, the KIROV carries anti-submarine and close-in defensive weapons, as well as several helicopters.

The role of the KIROV has also perplexed Western naval analysts. Most suggest that the KIROV class is intended to serve in a surface action group—that is, with cruisers and destroyers—or as a principal carrier escort ship. In the opinion of the author of this volume, the KIROV would be superfluous to a task group with a KIEV-type carrier. Rather, the KIROV's weapons, sensors, and command facilities make the ship more likely to have been developed as a screening ship for a nuclear carrier, with the latter delayed because of the need to use the same building dock that was constructing the four KIEV-class carriers. Further, at the risk of "mirror imaging" the American task force concept, a KIROV built to screen a carrier would have more anti-aircraft weapons and less anti-ship capability than the KIROV.

More probably, the KIROV and the other ships of the class will be employed as the core of surface action groups, operating in Third World areas where the ability of the United States to project tactical air power from carriers or land bases is limited.

The VSTOL carrier KIEV has been followed by three sister ships built at the Nikolayev south shipyard. Even as the fourth unit was being built, the graving dock where construction took place was being lengthened, and components were being assembled in the yard for a larger, nuclear-powered carrier. The new ship was laid down shortly after the fourth KIEV was launched in 1982.

This nuclear-propelled carrier, again the largest naval ship built in the Soviet Union, was launched in December 1985, almost simulta-

In addition to innovative ships, the Soviets have produced advanced weapon systems, as these 30-mm Gatling guns, being maintained by sailors on board a Kresta II-class missile cruiser.

neously with Admiral Gorshkov retiring after his unprecedented three decades as CinC of a major fleet. In announcing the nuclear carrier's launching, the U.S. officials revealed that a second ship of the class had been started. While details of the types of aircraft that this ship would operate were lacking when this edition went to press, the carrier will operate fixed-wing, high-performance aircraft, definitely employing arresting wires. Whether the nuclear carrier will have catapults or, initially at least, ski ramps for takeoff of the high-performance aircraft is not clear (see chapter 13).

Simultaneous with these capital ships, the Soviets initiated three

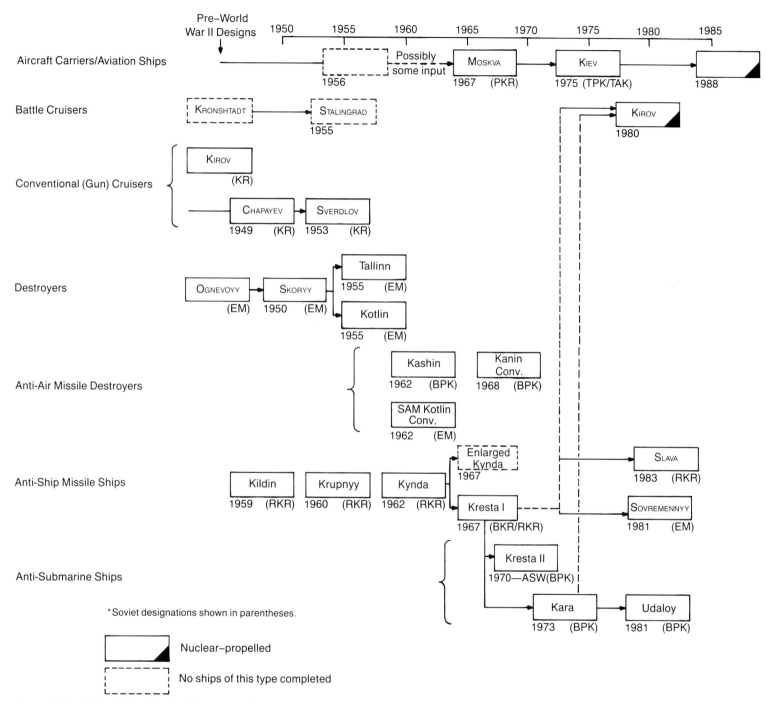

Figure 11-2.   Major Surface Warship Development

other cruiser-destroyer classes: the Slava, an anti-ship missile cruiser; the Sovremennyy, and anti-ship missile destroyer; and the Udaloy, an anti-submarine destroyer. With four yards engaged in building these four cruiser-destroyer classes, this is the largest surface combatant effort undertaken in the Soviet Union since the Stalin era.

In this fourth phase of postwar fleet development, the Soviets have continued an intensive submarine construction program. In the period 1981–1985 seven combat submarine designs were completed:

SSBN	Typhoon
SSBN	Delta IV
SSGN	Oscar
SSN	Mike
SSN	Akula
SSN	Sierra
SS	Kilo

Also, two special research submarines were completed, and Yankee-class SSBNs, removed from the strategic-missile role, were converted to attack submarine and to cruise-missile submarine prototypes.

The Typhoon was the largest undersea craft yet built by any nation (some 25,000 tons submerged displacement) and also showed a highly innovative design. Party Chairman Brezhnev revealed to President Ford at their November 1974 meeting in Vladivostok that the Soviet Union was building a giant strategic-missile submarine, the *Tayfun*. Brezhnev claimed that the new SSBN was a response to the U.S. Trident program. The Soviets continued to build the Delta SSBNs, with the Delta IV class being still larger than its predecessor and carrying a new missile.

Similarly, the Oscar SSGN, displacing about 14,500 tons submerged, is about half again the size of the American Los Angeles (SSN 688)-class attack submarines. The Oscar presents a new level of threat to Western naval planners, being armed with 24 SS-N-19 anti-ship missiles or three times the number of missiles carried by the earlier Echo II and Charlie SSGN classes. Further, the SS-N-19 combines the best features of the Echo II missiles (long range) and the Charlie missiles (underwater launch).

The simultaneous development of the Mike, Sierra, and Akula SSN designs once more indicates the depth of Soviet submarine development capabilities. Possibly they are competitive prototypes with only one or two intended for series production. This theory is supported by the fact that only one SSN was launched in 1985, apparently the smallest number put in the water in a single year since the start of the Soviet nuclear submarine program.

With respect to diesel attack submarines, as this edition went to press the Kilo SS program had been expanded to three shipyards. This indicates that a large number of these craft will probably be built for both Soviet and foreign use.

A final submarine type of particular interest is the conversion of three Golf diesel ballistic-missile submarines and at least one Hotel nuclear submarine to special communications configurations (SSQ/SSQN). These submarines appear to be configured to serve as emergency command ships or communications relay ships for fleet or area commanders.

In this fourth phase of Soviet fleet development the construction of amphibious and auxiliary ships has slowed considerably. Construction of over-the-beach LST and LSM classes continued into the 1970s, and in 1978 the first of two Ivan Rogov-class ships was completed. The Rogov is a highly capable amphibious ship, the first Soviet unit with a docking well for carrying air-cushion vehicles and the first with a helicopter landing area and hangar. Coupled with continued Soviet merchant ship construction, these "amphibs" provide a steady increase in the ability of the Soviet Union to move troops and equipment by sea and to mount amphibious assaults. A new LST class is being built in Poland, but only two of the Rogov-class ships were built.

The construction of specialized naval replenishment ships ceased after the one Berezina. A few additional tankers have been taken into the Navy from the merchant shipbuilding program, but the Soviet Navy still lacks effective Underway Replenishment (UNREP) ships on the scale of the U.S. Navy or even the Royal Navy. The compensating factor is the very large, flexible, and always available, state-controlled Soviet merchant and fishing fleet.

One other naval program is significant in this period, the extensive Soviet work in advanced technology hull forms. The Soviet Union has the world's largest fleet of civilian and military hydrofoils and Air-Cushion Vehicles (ACV). The latter include a major program of ACV landing craft, with several designs having been produced and in large numbers. The 250-ton Aist class provides a high-speed amphibious strike capability with a range of several hundred miles that is without equal among other amphibious forces.

A related development has been Soviet work with Wing-In-Ground (WIG) effect ship, called an *ekranoplan* in Russian. These resemble flying boats that travel over the water in the ground effect created by their own wings and hulls. A large WIG observed in the Caspian Sea in the 1970s was estimated to be a Navy program. That craft, with turbojet engines mounted in the wing roots, was estimated to weigh several hundred tons and was dubbed the "Caspian Sea Monster." Its reported speed is 300 knots at a cruise altitude of 20–25 feet (6–8 m).

A smaller WIG has also been identified, this having a single, tail-mounted tractor turboprop engine, plus two small gas turbine engines for takeoff. This craft is said to cruise between 150–250 knots, with a maximum speed of some 300 knots. This smaller craft has been reported to have been fitted with two or more launchers for the SS-N-22 anti-ship missile. This craft has been given the NATO code name Orlan (see page 108).

The naval role or roles for these craft have not been publicly identified. Obviously, the provision of SS-N-22 missiles indicates an anti-shipping role; others that have been suggested that merit consideration include amphibious assault and anti-submarine warfare.

INSTITUTIONAL FACTORS[8]

Friedrich Engels, who with Karl Marx wrote the *Communist Manifesto* (1847), the blueprint for the later Bolshevik movement in Russia, ad-

---

[8] This section is in part adopted from the author's report "Factors That Have Influenced the Soviet Navy—Potential Lessons for Aegis Shipbuilding", (30 April 1981), prepared for the U.S. Navy's Aegis shipbuilding project manager. Also see Arthur J. Alexander, *Decision-Making in Soviet Weapons Procurement* (London: International Institute for Strategic Studies, 1978; Adelphi Papers no. 147 and 148); Alexander Boyd, *The Soviet Air Force* (London: Macdonald and Jane's, 1977); and Colonel Oleg Penkovskiy, *The Penkovskiy Papers* (New York: Doubleday, 1965).

dressed the relationship of warships to the countries that produce them: "A modern warship is not merely a product of major industry, but at the same time is a sample of it. . . ."[9] The modern warships and other systems of the Soviet Navy are the product of numerous institutional factors of the Soviet Union. These factors include:

National Leadership. The leadership of the Soviet Union is very stable by Western standards. In the postwar period major military and industrial decisions have been vested mainly in the First Secretary (later General Secretary) of the Communist Party and in the Politburo.

During the long period of Stalin's leadership (1924–1953) there were innumerable occasions when he personally made design and procurement decisions. Admiral Kuznetsov wrote that ". . . without Stalin no one ventured to decide the large questions concerning the navy."[10] British historian Albert Seaton analysed Stalin's decision-making:

> Soviet writers are agreed that Stalin took a personal and directing role in the development of army equipment. Indeed, according to [Marshal G.K.] Zhukov, no single pattern of armament could be adopted or discarded without Stalin's approval. . . .

And,

> [Colonel-General K.A.] Vershinin said in 1948 that Stalin alone made the final decisions in aircraft development, and this is supported by the air[craft] designer Yakovlev's account. . . .[11]

For the subsequent Khrushchev period (1953–1964) we have the late Party chairman's own words to describe his decision making. After learning that the United States was placing ICBMs in underground silos, he took action:

> I summoned the people responsible and said, "Now look what's happened! The Americans have begun to dig the ballistic missile shafts which I proposed a long time ago. Let's get started on this program right away."[12]

Khrushchev continued, describing how he personally inquired about digging techniques and equipment, and how he was "proud of my role in originating the idea and later seeing [that] the conversion [to underground ICBM silos] was begun."

Decision making by senior Soviets with respect to specific weapons continued in the Brezhnev era. It acquired a different aspect after 1965 when Dmitri Ustinov was made a candidate member of the Politburo. His background in armament development and then his becoming a full Politburo member and Minister of Defense in 1976 implied that defense policy and hardware could be discussed more freely in the Politburo, without the need to call in outside experts.

Decision making at the Politburo level coupled with the stability of the leadership of the Soviet Union tend to ensure that policy and hardware decisions by national leaders will be carried out. In the post-Khrushchev period there appears to have been less "interference" with naval programs from a technical viewpoint. This is probably due in large part to the relationship of Brezhnev, the late Prime Minister Kosygin, and Politburo member Romanov with the Navy's leadership. Still, the increasing forward operations of the Navy and the related political implications probably make naval activities a periodic subject of Politburo discussions.

The stability of Soviet leadership—military as well as political—has been impressive by Western standards. Brezhnev served as head of the Party from 1964 until his death in 1982, Ustinov as Minister of Defense from 1976 to 1984, and Marshal of the Soviet Union N.V. Ogarkov as the Chief of the General Staff from 1977 to 1984. Admiral Gorshkov was CinC of the Navy from 1956 to 1985. The Navy's chief engineer—in charge of shipbuilding and armaments, Engineer Admiral P.G. Kotov—has held his post since 1966 (before which he was the deputy). This longevity suggests that projects that win top-level approval will be pursued. But also those projects rejected by the leadership must wait long periods before a change in administration will provide another opportunity.

Long-Range Planning. The Soviet Union has longer range planning in the defense and industrial sectors than Western nations. The entire Soviet economy is based on long-term, integrated planning. Whereas the United States has a five-year defense plan that is "extended" annually to add the "next" year, the Soviet five-year plan is for a finite period. Thus, while American leaders can repeatedly postpone difficult decisions or projects until the later years of the five-year program, the Soviet scheme provides for a specific period and end-of-plan accounting process.

In addition, the Soviet planning cycle is tied in with all aspects of society, including all military services and other defense agencies. Hence, a long-range naval construction effort would be linked to steel production, transportation, coal matters, commercial shipbuilding, etc.

Employment Policies. Full employment is a basic goal of the Soviet state. The Soviet constitution guarantees the right to a job. Thus, in the eyes of the Soviet leadership, the admission of unemployment would indicate the failure of this guarantee. Accordingly, once a factory or product line is established, it is difficult to close it down without major political implications. This may, in part, explain the continued production of outdated and even obsolete hardware. The Tupolev-designed Bear aircraft is an example of the very long Soviet production runs, the plane having been in continuous production since the mid-1950s—longer than any other combat aircraft in history.

There is also significant worker stability because Soviet citizens are generally not permitted to change jobs in critical industries without authorization, and factories and bases in remote areas are able to pay higher wages than those in more-desirable regions.

Copying Technology. The Soviets have traditionally copied Western technology—by whatever means available. This began during the reign of Tsar Peter I (see chapter 30) and continues today. There are several classic examples of the Soviets doing this, from allies and enemies alike. At the end of World War II the Soviets carted off much of Eastern

[9] F. Engels, *Izbrannyye Voyennyye Proizvedeniye* [Selected Military Works] (Moscow: Voyenizdat, 1957), p. 17.

[10] Admiral Kuznetsov, "On the Eve," *Oktyabr'* (no. 9, 1965), pp. 158–189; also see no. 8, 1965, pp. 161–202 and no. 11, 1965, pp. 134–137.

[11] Albert Seaton, *Stalin as Military Commander* (New York: Praeger, 1976), pp. 87–89.

[12] Khrushchev, op. cit., p. 49.

Europe's surviving industrial facilities as well as German technology, scientists, and technicians. In the same manner, American equipment was copied, including radars on U.S. ships transferred to the Soviet Navy and the U.S. B-29 heavy bombers that, after bombing raids against Japan, landed in Siberia and were interned.

The Soviets continue to seek Western technology by overt and covert means. The covert activities by the KGB and GRU seek information on virtually all Western military and industrial activities. Both agencies have established regular "legal" collection networks through various attachés in Western countries, and through extensive spy networks that attempt to penetrate Western military services, industry, and even government bureaus. The results of these efforts regularly appear in Soviet military systems. The Soviets are thus able to take advantage of Western developments while saving Soviet industrial and research resources that would have otherwise been invested in those areas.

Overt collection methods include the outright purchase of material and the vast amounts of information on technology published in the Western press and professional journals. In the naval-maritime area, the Soviets have purchased numerous merchant and fishing ships from the West as well as marine engines, computers, and electronics.

Production Rates. The Soviets have always stressed quantities of military equipment. Despite the ravages of war from 1941 to 1945, by the end of the conflict some 40,000 aircraft per year were being produced in the Soviet Union. About 80 percent of these were single-engine fighter and ground-attack aircraft, mostly of wooden construction. It was still a major achievement when one considers the manpower problems, shortages of materials, the severe weather conditions, and the fact that most of the plants producing aircraft and engines had been removed from European Russia and reestablished in the Urals early in the war.

After the war there were significant shifts in the types and numbers of aircraft produced, but the level of effort remained high. For example, in 1950 the Soviet aircraft industry produced about 4,000 MiG-15 turbojet fighters, 1,000 turbojet bombers, and several hundred Tu-4 Bull four-engine piston bombers, plus a number of other aircraft. While these totalled significantly less than the number of aircraft produced five years earlier, the effort was probably similar in terms of man-hours and resources required. This relatively high production rate of aircraft continues. For example, during the past few years Soviet military aircraft production has been greater than all NATO nations combined.

The same is true of Soviet production of tanks, artillery, and many other categories of military equipment. From a naval viewpoint, the Soviets outproduce the West in submarines and small combatants (missile, patrol, torpedo, and mine ships and craft). The West, however, produces more major surface combatants (frigate and larger) and more auxiliary ships than the Soviet Union.

The submarine building rate is particularly significant. In 1955 Soviet shipyards launched an estimated 81 submarines at the peak of the Stalin production effort; in 1984 Soviet yards launched nine submarines, eight of them nuclear-propelled units. Of the 1955 launchings, 62 were of the Whiskey class with a 1,050-ton standard displacement. These were diesel-electric craft, armed only with torpedoes. The 1984 submarines included a Typhoon SSBN with a standard displacement of

TABLE 11-2. SOVIET AIRCRAFT PRODUCTION, 1981-1985

Aircraft Type	1981	1982	1983	1984	1985	NATO* 1985
Bomber	30	35	35	50	50	2
Fighter and Attack	1,350	1,100	950	800	650	550
Anti-submarine	10	10	5	5	5	5
Helicopter	800	800	550	600	600	525
Transport	350	300	250	250	250	300
Utility/Trainer	50	50	10	10	0	300
Totals	2,590	2,295	1,800	1,715	2,055	1,682

*Includes the United States, but not France or Spain.

TABLE 11-3. SOVIET MISSILE PRODUCTION, 1981-1985

Missile Type*	1981	1982	1983	1984	1985	NATO† 1985
ICBM	200	175	150	75	100	0
LRINF	100	100	125	125	125	175
SRBM	300	300	500	500	450	50
SLCM	750	800	650	700	700	800
SLBM	175	175	100	50	100	75

*ICBM = Intercontinental Ballistic Missile; LRINF = Long-Range Intermediate-range Nuclear Force (formerly medium- and intermediate-range ballistic missiles); SRBM = Short-Range Ballistic Missile; SLCM = Sea-Launched Cruise Missile; SLBM = Submarine-Launched Ballistic Missile
†Includes the United States, but not France or Spain.

perhaps 20,000 tons, the rough equivalent of 19 Whiskey-class submarines, and an Oscar SSGN of about 10,000 tons standard displacement, equal in tonnage to more than nine Whiskeys. This displacement ratio provides a very rough approximation of the resources involved. Also, beyond being larger, the newer submarines have mostly nuclear propulsion as well as more complex electronics and more advanced weapons, than the earlier submarines, demonstrating the continuation of a high level of effort in this category of industrial endeavor.

Another consideration in Soviet shipbuilding is the extensive use of Polish and, to a lesser extent, other Eastern European shipyards to build amphibious, auxiliary, and merchant ships. This provides the Soviet shipbuilding industry with a high degree of flexibility while allowing them to concentrate to the degree desired on warship programs.

Quantity versus Quality. The Soviet Union is a land of quantity versus quality. Numbers are important and, indeed, are the means by which much of the Soviet military-industrial complex is graded. A given factory or industry is generally rated on the basis of numbers of units produced; quality is a secondary consideration. The grades thus given become the basis for promotions, pay increases, bonuses, and special privileges.

This numbers mentality results in the Soviet Union having more equipment of certain types than can be used by the active military establishment. This provides equipment for the reserves as well as ready equipment to replace combat losses and for foreign transfer. As an example, after the 1973 war in the Middle East the Soviet Union was able to provide rapidly several thousand tanks to Egypt and Syria to replace their losses, and was doing the same for Iraq in the early 1980s to replace losses in the Iraq-Iran conflict.

This approach to producing large numbers of units has also led to the practice of replacing rather than repairing damaged equipment and platforms at the unit or organizational level. This, in turn, reduces the maintenance requirements in Soviet units, always a problem with the short-term draftees that comprise the vast majority of the Soviet armed forces. At the same time, this emphasis on the production of "things" that can be easily counted, such as tanks and aircraft, sometimes leads to component shortfalls, that is, "things" that cannot be as easily counted and are thus shorted in favor of producing more of what can be counted against "norms" and quotas.

Component Similarity. Soviet design agencies and industry seek to provide similar components for successive generations of systems and platforms. Components appear to change only for specific reasons, such as product improvement or availability because of production-line changes. Accordingly, some components and systems have a long service life over successive classes of platforms.

There are obvious advantages to this scheme in terms of production costs, maintenance, spares, training, and personnel assignment. However, when there are limited production facilities or other problems with widely used components, there are bottlenecks. This appears to be the current situation with respect to integrated circuits; too many Soviet military (as well as civilian) systems are in need of advanced circuitry and too few production facilities are available.

Component Availability. Related to the issue of component similarity there are limited selections of components available, at least by Western standards. A design bureau cannot simply look through catalogues or phone up component producers to obtain minor but critical components for new systems. The Soviet industrial system limits the numbers and variety of equipment produced; relatively few components or systems are developed on speculation—that is, developed because they *may* be used or even needed.

As a result, new systems tend to make use of existing components, or for prototype systems the laboratory or factory may produce the components on an individual basis. While this is highly inefficient by Western standards, it may be the only way in which a Soviet producer can obtain a key component within required time constraints.

Innovation. The Soviet military-industrial environment simultaneously encourages and retards innovation. It encourages innovation because the various design bureaus, with one or more specializing in the development of different weapons and platforms, are continually producing new designs. These may or may not be put into production, but that is irrelevant to the purpose of these bureaus.

For all of the reasons cited above, however, innovation in the weapons and platforms being produced is difficult, and hence it is avoided when possible. This is acceptable to the armed forces because of manpower limitations on using and supporting new and more complex equipment. This is not to imply that innovation is opposed in principle—rather, that change must contribute to force or unit effectiveness and at not too great a cost. To quote the plaque that was alleged to be displayed in Admiral Gorshkov's office, "Better is the Enemy of Good Enough."

Soviet versus U.S. Defense Research and Acquisition. These factors have led to a current Soviet research and acquisition process that is in many respects quite different than that of the West. While the defense organizations of the Soviet Union and United States are quite different, there are some similarities in their military research and acquisition process. These similarities have been identified as a research base of developing technologies; senior management review and decision of major systems during specific phases of development; rigorous testing during all phases of development; and comparative periods for full-scale weapon development in both countries.

The differences, however, appear to be more significant:

(1) The Soviet Union has a single, top-level weapons development oversight agency, the Military Industrial Commission (VPK), that combines certain functions of various agencies of the U.S. Department of Defense, the Congress, and private industry.

(2) Approval for major weapons systems in the Soviet Union is made by the Politburo (if appropriate) and by a joint decree of the Central Committee and the Council of Ministers. These are the only top-level approvals required in the Soviet Union, whereas there are several major approvals in the United States, including the various milestones of the Defense Systems Acquisition Review Council (DSARC) of the Department of Defense, and less formal reviews by the Office of Management and Budget (OMB) and several congressional committees with major systems being considered by the entire House and Senate.

(3) Once a program is approved by the joint decree, appropriate resources are allocated within the Soviet military and industrial communities. Within the United States each program is "revisited" annually because of Congressional approval requirements.

(4) A major segment of Soviet industry is dedicated to defense programs, which programs unquestionably enjoy top priority. In the United States defense contractors compete for business under market conditions that are highly restrictive and, in some respects, retard innovation.

(5) The senior people involved in the Soviet research and acquisition process remain in the same position for long periods. The American system provides for frequent changes in defense and industry management.

MAINTENANCE AND SUPPORT

The maintenance and support of equipment in the fleet have been traditional problems for the Soviet Navy, in part because of the Soviet economic practice of producing "units" rather than spare parts, problems with workmanship and quality control, and personnel limitations.

The West's estimates of the success of the Soviet Navy in maintaining and supporting military equipment vary considerably. Undoubtedly some of the more critical comments are based on the appearance of some Soviet ships. Flaking paint and rust stains are sometimes used as the criteria for negative judgments; another criterion sometimes used is the time at sea of individual Soviet ships compared with American units, as well as the Soviet practice of towing ships to or from deployment areas. Observing appearances and operating modes may not be an entirely accurate means of measuring actual maintenance levels and the resulting readiness.

For example, the Soviet Navy seems to place less emphasis on the

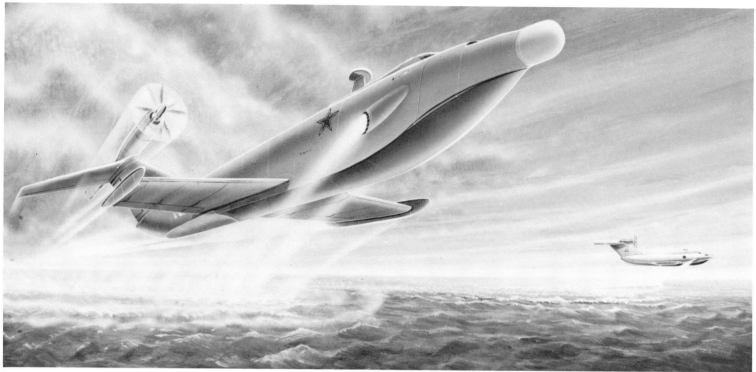

An artist's concept of what is believed the first operational Soviet Wing-In-Ground (WIG) effects machine, given the NATO code name Orlan. Resembling a large flying boat, this craft is believed intended for ASW; however, WIG craft are also suitable for amphibious assault, and this version has been observed undergoing trials with SS-N-22 anti-ship missiles.

appearance of their ships—except during port visits—than does the U.S. Navy. Rather, the Soviet emphasis seems to be on keeping the equipment working. This has been a traditional attitude. For example, Rear Admiral Kemp Tolley, when assistant naval attaché in Moscow during World War II, recorded the following in his diary about the Soviet crews that brought former U.S. and British naval ships around North Cape to Arctic ports:

> Our people found the Russian sailorman can be a complex fellow. By nature slovenly, they kept their ordnance, engineering, and most mechanical equipment clean, plentifully greased and operative. Not energetic, they were physically capable of great hardship. They were "heavy handed" in operating, maintenance and repairing of equipment; wasteful of spare parts, tools and supplies. Mechanical sense was crude, jumping to conclusions child-like that they knew-it-all, to the hazard of the inanimate gear they were working on.[13]

This attitude, coupled with the conservative design of their equipment—built with the level of technical competence of the sailor in mind—indicates that the equipment the Soviets have in their ships is kept in working order. (Officers and warrants perform most of the technical maintenance tasks on board ship, a necessity because of the short term that enlisted men serve in the Navy; see chapter 10.) At the same time,

the operating mode of the Soviet fleet tends to conserve equipment and other resources whenever possible. In February 1982, the U.S. Chief of Naval Operations told a congressional committee,

> . . . the Soviet concept of material readiness stresses conservation of resources by limiting the use of military equipment in peacetime. They apparently believe that limited use is the best way to ensure that equipment will be ready on short notice during a crisis. That is one reason the Soviets normally keep a smaller percentage of their forces deployed than we do, and why Soviet deployed forces generally maintain lower operational tempos.[14]

Still, the Soviet Navy does suffer from the general maintenance and support problems that plague all aspects of Soviet society. Throughout the society there are too often examples of poor workmanship, insufficient quality control, shortages of parts, and lack of personnel competence or incentives to do the job properly. The only mitigation is that within the Soviet society the armed forces have the highest priorities for men and material (after certain Party-related activities), and during the past two decades the Navy has received the "cream" of those resources.

Thus, for at least the near-term the Soviet Navy appears capable of maintaining and supporting the fleet that has been developed since World War II.

[13] Rear Admiral Kemp Tolley, USN (Ret.), *Caviar and Commissars* (Annapolis, Md.: Naval Institute Press, 1983), p. 170.

[14] Admiral Thomas B. Hayward, USN, before the Senate Armed Services Committee, 25 Febuary 1982, Hearings, Part 2, p. 1147.

12
Submarines

The Soviet Union has the world's largest submarine force. Some 385 submarines are in service, almost three times the number of undersea craft in service with the U.S. Navy. Table 12-2 lists the submarines currently believed to be in service, in the order of their appearance in this volume.

Also significant, the Soviets are believed to have up to seven different submarine classes in series production at four shipyards; this is an unprecedented submarine construction program:[1]

TABLE 12-1. SOVIET SUBMARINE CONSTRUCTION

Shipyard[2]	Class		Lead Ship Completed
Severodvinsk	SSBN	Typhoon	1983
	SSBN	Delta IV	1985
	SSGN	Oscar	1981
	SSN	Mike	1985
Komsomolsk	SSN	Akula	1985
	SS	Kilo	1982
Gor'kiy	SSN	Sierra	1984
	SS	Kilo	
Admiralty (Leningrad)	SSN	Sierra	
Sudomekh (Admiralty)	SS	Kilo	

The introduction of one diesel and six nuclear submarine classes since 1980 signifies an intensive Soviet submarine design and development effort. For example, the three SSN classes introduced in a three-year period represent three different designs, at least two types of reactor plants, and two different hull materials. In addition, since 1984 at least one Yankee SSN and one SSGN conversion have become operational and two research/special-purpose submarines have been completed, the Uniform AGSSN and the X-ray, apparently a smaller, nuclear-propelled craft. The Uniform and X-ray were completed at the Admiralty Sudomekh yard (Leningrad) in 1983 and 1984, respectively.

The reasons for this intensity and diversity of effort are not completely clear, but certainly such actions by the Soviets indicate that the submarine is the principal ship type in their naval doctrine and strategy.

The large number of classes in production and service impose a heavy support and training burden on the Soviet submarine force. However, they do afford significant design and development experience—not available in the West—and force Western anti-submarine forces to

counter them with greatly differing characteristics and capabilities.

The rate of submarine construction in the Soviet Union has slowed during the past few years. This may be due, in part, to a changeover to new designs or simply to the larger size and complexity of newer submarines, which each consume a greater amount of a given allocation of resources. The recent rate of construction has been ten submarines of all types per year. The current Soviet construction capability is estimated by Western intelligence to be 20 nuclear submarines per year on a normal work schedule, if component manufacturers can support that effort.

(By way of comparison, the U.S. Navy has two submarine classes under construction at two shipyards: the Los Angeles [SSN 688] at the Newport News yard in Virginia and the Electric Boat/General Dynamics yard at Groton, Connecticut; and the Ohio [SSBN 726] at the latter yard. These classes first entered service in 1974 and 1981, respectively. The next U.S. submarine class, the Seawolf SSN, will probably enter service about 1996.)

Several additional classes will probably be introduced into Soviet service in the future. The new classes could be expected to include a cruise missile submarine (SSGN), which would carry the SS-N-24 missile, and a new diesel attack submarine (SS/SSG). These classes are addressed later in this chapter. With less certainty, one can also predict the construction of another SSBN class and a new SSGN class.

The new SSBN design is seen as an effort by the Soviets to avoid a reduction in strategic submarine numbers while adhering to the SALT agreements on Submarine-Launched Ballistic Missiles (SLBM) and separate Re-entry Vehicles (RV). For example, in numbers of missiles, one Typhoon with 20 SLBMs equates with 1.25 Yankee/Delta III SSBNs or 1.75 Delta I submarines. Thus, the follow-on SSBN could carry 12 to 16 missiles. (The U.S. Ohio class carries 24 Trident SLBMs.)

The prediction of still another SSGN class is based on the large size and high cost of the Oscar SSGN. This class is now being built at the rate of one submarine every two years. Even a doubling of this effort will not provide sufficient units to replace the earlier Juliett SSG and Charlie and Echo II SSGN classes when they are retired.

While the quantitative data of the Soviet submarine program are known, the qualitative characteristics are less so. In general, Soviet submarines tend to be faster and deeper diving, and they carry greater weapon payloads than their U.S. counterparts. Soviet acoustic detection equipment (sonar) has historically been evaluated as inferior to U.S. systems; Soviet submarine noise levels have been considerably higher.

The Soviets are making improvements to hull-mounted sonars, and the introduction of towed-array hydrophones in the Victor III class in

---

[1] The only other example of this many classes being in production at one time is the Japanese submarine construction program of World War II.

[2] The Admiralty and Sudomekh shipyards were administratively merged in 1972 to form the United Admiralty Shipyard. They are listed separately below. See chapter 30.

TABLE 12-2. SOVIET SUBMARINE FORCE, 1986

Type	Class	Active	In service	Notes
Ballistic Missile Submarines				
SSBN	Typhoon	4	1983	in production
SSBN	Delta IV	2	1985	in production
SSBN	Delta III	14	1975	
SSBN	Delta II	4	1974	
SSBN	Delta I	18	1973	
SSBN	Yankee II	1	1978	
SSBN	Yankee I	19	1967	being deactivated
SSBN	Hotel III	1	1965	SS-NX-8 test ship
SSB	Golf V	1		SS-NX-20 test ship
SSB	Golf III	1		SS-NX-8 test ship
SSB	Golf II	13	1958	other units in reserve
Guided Missile Submarines				
SSGN	(new design)	—		in development/SS-N-24 missile
SSGN	Yankee	1	1985	converted from SSBN; test ship for SS-NX-24
SSGN	Oscar	3	1982	in production
SSGN	Papa	1	1970	prototype
SSGN	Charlie II	6	1973	
SSGN	Charlie I	11	1968	
SSGN	Echo II	26*	1962	
SSG	Juliett	15*	1961	
Attack Submarines				
SSN/SSXN	Yankee	13	1984	converted from SSBN; status of some units uncertain
SSN	Akula	1	1985	in production (?)
SSN	Mike	1	1985	in production (?)
SSN	Sierra	1	1984	in production (?)
SSN	Alfa	6	1979	prototype was dismantled
SSN	Victor III	21	1978	
SSN	Victor II	7	1972	
SSN	Victor I	16	1968	
SSN	Echo I	3*	1970	converted from SSGN
SSN	November	12*	1958	other units in reserve
SSXN	Hotel II	4	1962	former SSBN; status uncertain
SS	(new design)	—		in development
SS	Kilo	9	1982	in production
SS	Tango	20	1972	long-range submarine
SS	Foxtrot	~50	1957	long-range submarine
SS	Romeo	8	1957	medium-range submarine
SS	Zulu IV	1*	1952	long-range submarine
SS	Whiskey	~50*	1949	medium-range submarine
Auxiliary/Experimental/Special Mission Submarines				
SSQN	Hotel	1		converted from SSBN
SSQ	Golf	3		converted from SSB
AGSSN	X-ray	1	1984	small research submarine
AGSSN	Uniform	1	1983	
AGSSN	Echo II	1		converted from SSGN
AGSS	India	2	1979	rescue/salvage submarines
AGSS	Lima	1	1978	experimental submarine
AGSS	Foxtrot	few		oceanographic survey
AGSS	Zulu IV	few		oceanographic research
AGSS	Whiskey	few		research submarines
SST	Bravo	4	1967	target/training submarines
Total diesel-electric units		~185		
Total nuclear-propelled units		~200		
Total submarines in service		~385		

*Indicates additional units are in reserve.

1978 indicated a significant increase in the potential detection effectiveness of Soviet submarines. Also, after seeming to ignore submarine self-silencing measures for many years—except for anechoic coatings—the Soviets have recently demonstrated considerable interest in this area. The latest submarine classes have turbine machinery mounted on "floating rafts" acoustically isolated from the hull. This arrangement, which was introduced in the U.S. Navy in 1961 with the THRESHER (SSN 593) class, is considered a major step in reducing the machinery noises in nuclear submarines.

Another method of submarine quieting practiced by the Soviets is the extensive use of anechoic coatings. This technique is the underwater equivalent of "stealth" technology, using echo-absorbing, rubber-like materials to cover the hull to reduce the effectiveness of acoustic homing torpedoes. Both the Germans and Japanese had experimented with such coatings for submarines in World War II, but the Soviets were the first to employ anechoic coatings on a significant basis to reduce torpedo effectiveness, beginning at least in the late 1960s. (Soviet submarines have also been reported to use acoustic decoys and possibly jammers, again with the purpose of defeating attacking acoustic torpedoes.)

Soviet submarines could also benefit from extensive under-ice operations as conditions in the Arctic reduce sonar effectiveness. Both submarine and torpedo active/passive sonars are adversely affected by the ice, especially by downward ice projections and Arctic marine life, as well as by the shallow depths occurring in some of the northern regions.

Soviet progress in attack submarines was summed up in 1985 by the Director of U.S. Naval Intelligence:

> Over the past five years, the Soviets have launched an unprecedented number and variety of nuclear attack submarines. The emphasis in construction has clearly shifted from ballistic missile units. We believe this construction program is being driven primarily by Moscow's intention to close the technological gap between Soviet and Western submarines. Since the introduction of the Victor III class SSN, the Soviets have steadily reduced the technological inferiority of their newest submarines.[3]

The Soviet advances in submarines have made it increasingly difficult for Western ASW forces. Little of this has been publicly discussed; however, in a 1981 colloquy between a U.S. senator and the U.S. Navy's Deputy Chief of Naval Operations (Surface Warfare), Vice Admiral William H. Rowden, the senator noted that the new submarines of the Alfa class can travel at "40-plus knots and could probably outdive most of our anti-submarine torpedoes." He then asked what measures were being taken to redress this particular balance.

The admiral replied, "We have modified the Mark 48 torpedo. . . to accommodate to the increased speed and to the diving depth of those particular submarines." The admiral was less confident of the U.S. Mark 46 lightweight torpedo used by aircraft, helicopters, and surface ships: "We have recently modified that torpedo to handle what you might call the pre-Alfa. . . ."

In addition to the relatively high speeds, deep operating depths, and progress in the acoustics area (sonars and quieting), Soviet submarines

[3] Rear Admiral John Butts, USN, Director of Naval Intelligence, statement before Senate Armed Services Committee, 26 February 1985, p. 9.

An artist's concept of the Typhoon SSBN, typical of several highly innovative Soviet submarine designs of recent years. The Typhoon is the only SSBN class with the missile tubes forward of the sail structure. Most views of a Typhoon belie the ship's large size—as long as the Washington Monument is tall. (Painting by Richard Allison)

are also difficult ASW targets because of their multiple compartments, large reserve buoyancy, and, especially, their double-hull design (i.e., an outer protective hull and the inner, stronger pressure hull, with buoyancy tanks and equipment between them; in diesel submarines this space is used for fuel, and in the Oscar-class SSGN it also houses the SS-N-19 missile tubes). These features can significantly reduce the effectiveness of the Western lightweight torpedoes, like the U.S. Navy's Mark 46 and planned Mark 50, and the British Stingray, all of which have relatively small warheads.

A final consideration in submarine technology is the fact that the Soviets have *not* depended on the theft or commercial acquisition of Western technology for their submarine development. According to Melvyn R. Paisley, the U.S. Assistant Secretary of the Navy for research,

The Soviet submarine technological advances for quieting, strengthened double hulls, higher speed, higher reserve buoyance, and deeper operations are advances which are by and large not stolen or bought from the United States. Some technologies, [classified deletion], are Soviet design decisions which are different from our decisions. Other technologies, [de-

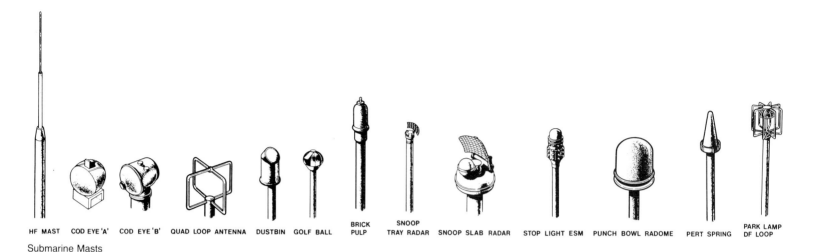

HF MAST   COD EYE 'A'   COD EYE 'B'   QUAD LOOP ANTENNA   DUSTBIN   GOLF BALL   BRICK PULP   SNOOP TRAY RADAR   SNOOP SLAB RADAR   STOP LIGHT ESM   PUNCH BOWL RADOME   PERT SPRING   PARK LAMP DF LOOP

Submarine Masts

leted], are the result of Soviet engineered high power density material and high strength hull material. The Soviets are ahead of the U.S. in these technologies.[4]

Rather, it is in the area of acoustics as well as production methods that the Soviets have sought the West's submarine-related technology. And, it is in acoustics that the long-active Walker spy ring may have made a major contribution to Soviet knowledge.

The Soviet submarine force has continued to experience operational problems and losses. In addition to the November-class SSN that sank off the coast of Spain in April 1970, a second nuclear submarine, a Charlie I SSGN, sank off of the Kamchatka Peninsula in the Bering Sea in 1983. (The latter submarine was salvaged.) There have also been several diesel submarine losses, most notably the Golf SSB that went down in 16,500 feet of water in the mid-Pacific in 1968 and was partially salvaged by the U.S. Central Intelligence Agency.[5]

Armament: Soviet combat submarines built since World War II have 21-inch (533-mm) torpedo tubes. Additionally, the Echo I/II, Juliett, and November classes have stern tubes for 16-inch (406-mm) torpedoes.

Torpedo tubes of approximately 26-inch (650-mm) diameter are reported to be fitted in the Oscar, Akulka, Sierra, Mike, and Victor II/III classes for launching the SS-N-16 ASW missile in addition to large-diameter torpedoes. See chapter 27 for additional notes on these weapons. The estimated torpedo "loadout" is indicated in brackets in the accompanying tables. This number indicates weapons in the submarine's tubes and reloads in the adjacent torpedo room(s), both torpedoes and tube-launched missiles.

Essentially all Soviet submarines—probably including strategic missile craft—have the capability of laying mines through their torpedo

tubes. Two naval mines can generally be carried in the space required for one 21-inch "long" torpedo, although there are some larger mines in service that may replace torpedoes on a one-for-one basis.

Three attack submarine classes have been identified by the U.S. Navy as probable candidates for carrying the SS-N-21 "Tomahawksi" land-attack missiles. They are the Akula, Mike, and Sierra SSNs. A single Victor III with a cylindrical structure forward of the sail has been reported as an SS-N-21 trials ship.

Also, the Soviets are developing at least two surface-to-air missiles for use from submarines. (See chapter 27.)

Classification: Soviet submarine type designations are explained in chapter 3. Because U.S. and Soviet submarine roles and missions are similar, U.S. submarine type designations are used in this volume (e.g., SS, SSB, SSBN).

Design: Modern Soviet combat submarine designs are characterized by relatively high submerged speeds, deep operating depths, and double-hull construction. (All submarines described in this chapter have a double-hull configuration except where noted.) The double-hull construction, which features an outer, partially flooding structure around the inner pressure hull, provides a "stand-off" distance to help defeat torpedo attack. This configuration also provides a large reserve buoyancy on the order of 30 to 40 percent.

Engineering: All Soviet nuclear-propelled combat submarines are believed to have two nuclear reactors except for the Charlie I/II and the Alfa classes. This accounts, in part, for the high speeds of Soviet nuclear submarines.

Names: Soviet submarine classes have been assigned letter designations by the U.S.-NATO intelligence community. Phonetic words are generally used for these letters, such as Alfa for *A* and Bravo for *B*. The exceptions are the Typhoon, which is the Soviet term for the craft (Russian *Tayfun*), and Akula, a Western code name used when all 26 letters of the alphabet had been exhausted (*Akula* is the Russian word for shark).

[4] Melvyn R. Paisley, Assistant Secretary of the Navy (Research, Engineering & Systems), testimony before Committee on Appropriations, House of Representatives, 2 April 1985, Part 7, p. 424.

[5] Four U.S. submarines have sunk since World War II: the nuclear submarines THRESHER and SCORPION (SSN 589), lost with all on board, and two diesel submarines, with only one civilian technician lost.

BALLISTIC MISSILE SUBMARINES

TYPHOON

DELTA IV

DELTA III

DELTA II

DELTA I

YANKEE II

YANKEE I

GOLF II

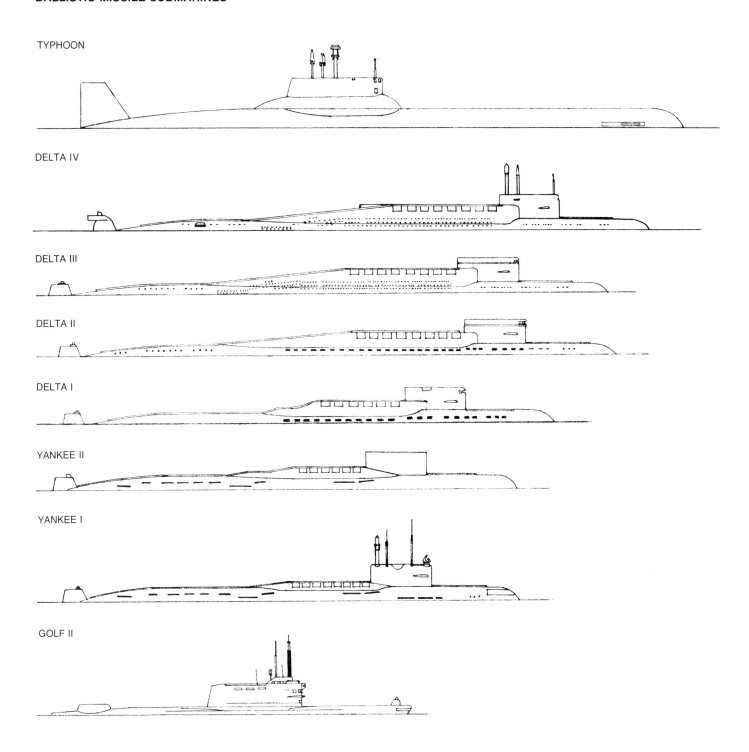

4+ NUCLEAR-PROPELLED BALLISTIC MISSILE SUBMARINES (SSBN): TYPHOON

Name	Launched	Completed
(unit 1)	Sep 1980	1983
(unit 2)	Sep 1982	1984
(unit 3)	Dec 1983	1985
(unit 4)	1984	1986
(units 5–8)	building and planned	

Builders:	Severodvinsk
Displacement:	
	25,000 tons submerged
Length:	557 ft 7 in (170.0 m) oa
Beam:	82 ft (25.0 m)
Draft:	42 ft 8 in (13.0 m)
Propulsion:	steam turbines; approx. 100,000 shp; 2 shafts/7-bladed propellers
Reactors:	2 pressurized water
Speed:	
	25 knots submerged
Complement:	approx. 150
Missiles:	20 SS-N-20 SLBM
ASW weapons:	torpedoes
Torpedoes:	... 21-inch (533-mm) or 26-inch (650-mm) torpedo tubes (fwd)
Radars:	Snoop series
Sonars:	low-frequency

The letter *U* (Uniform) has been used twice, initially for the Victor II-class SSN, then for a one-of-a-kind auxiliary submarine.

The assignment of the code name *Yankee* to the first modern Soviet SSBN class has caused confusion with the public and, at times, the Defense establishment. The term *Russian Yankee* is sometimes used in an effort to reduce confusion.

The Typhoon is the largest undersea craft constructed by any nation, being almost half-again as large as the U.S. Trident strategic-missile submarines of the OHIO class, which displace 18,700 tons submerged. The submarines are approximately the same length, but the Typhoon is almost twice as broad (with the OHIO having a single-hull design and

a beam of 42 feet). The lead ship of the Typhoon class was reportedly laid down in 1975, indicating a relatively long construction period for a Soviet submarine, possibly due to the complexity of the ship. That submarine began sea trials in June 1981 and became operational in 1983.

The U.S. Department of Defense estimates that eight units will be in service by the early 1990s. These submarines are in the Northern Fleet.

Classification: Soviet PLARB type.

Design: The Typhoon arrangement differs considerably from previous SSBN designs. There are *two* large pressure hulls arranged side by side, encased in the outer hull. This arrangement provides a high buoyancy reserve (possibly as much as 40 percent of total submerged displacement) and increased survivability because of the "stand-off" distance between the inner and outer hulls. Placing the missile tubes forward also alleviates the complexity of structure, piping, and wiring in a large missile compartment between the ship control compartment and the engineering spaces. The inner pressure hulls may be modifications of the Delta-class hull.

The torpedo tubes appear to be mounted in the bow, indicating a separate pressure hull for the torpedo-tube room forward. The 20 large vertical tubes for SLBMs are fitted between the hulls, *forward* of the sail structure. The location of the large sail indicates still another (fourth) pressure hull amidships for the submarine's control spaces.

The Typhoon appears to be designed for operations under ice. It would surface through the Arctic ice pack to launch missiles. The under-ice features appear to include the flat, protected top of the sail structure, retractable bow diving planes, and protected propeller shafts. (While the previous Delta and Yankee classes have had sail-mounted diving planes, the Typhoon has bow-mounted planes in part because the position of the sail structure aft of the mid-point of the submarine is unsuitable for control planes.)

Engineering: Like all Soviet SSBNs, these submarines have twin propeller shafts (all Western SSBNs are single-shaft submarines.)

Missiles: The lead ship of this class is reported to have launched two missiles within 15 seconds during firing trials in October 1982.

A Typhoon SSBN: the outer hull encases two inner pressure hulls, arranged in parallel; the missile tubes are forward, between the main pressure hulls. (1984, Ministry of Defence)

2+ NUCLEAR-PROPELLED BALLISTIC MISSILE SUBMARINES (SSBN): DELTA IV

Name	Launched	Completed
(unit 1)	Jan 1984	1985
(unit 2)	1984	1986
(unit 3)	building	
(unit 4)	building	

Builders:	Severodvinsk
Displacement:	10,750 tons surface
	13,550 tons submerged
Length:	508 ft 5 in (155.0 m) oa
Beam:	39 ft 4 in (12.0 m)
Draft:	28 ft 6 in (8.7 m)
Propulsion:	steam turbines; 50,000 shp; 2 shafts/7-bladed propellers
Reactors:	2 pressurized water
Speed:	24 knots submerged
Complement:	approx. 120
Missiles:	16 SS-N-23 SLBM
ASW weapons:	torpedoes [18]
Torpedoes:	6 21-inch (533-mm) torpedo tubes (fwd)
Radars:	Snoop Tray
Sonars:	low frequency
	towed array

This is the latest modification of the basic Delta design, further enlarged to accommodate the advanced SS-N-23 missile, although the design is only 16 feet longer than the Delta III. The submarine has features for under-ice operation, and the "turtle back" aft of the sail structure has been further enlarged.

These submarines are in the Northern Fleet.

A Delta IV underway, showing the lead on her upper rudder for a towed sonar; farther forward, just before the missile tubes, is the housing for her communications buoy. She carries the SS-N-23, a missile considerably larger than the U.S. Poseidon or Trident I missiles. The Delta IV and the larger Typhoon classes apparently are configured for under-ice operations. (1975)

This artist's concept shows a Delta IV surfaced in the Arctic icepack launching an SS-N-23 missile. The construction and continued improvement of the Delta SSBN series simultaneous with Typhoon SSBNs and their associated missiles demonstrate the major Soviet commitment to sea-based strategic systems. Note the height of the "turtleback" missile structure aft of the sail and the submarine's high freeboard.

14 NUCLEAR-PROPELLED BALLISTIC MISSILE SUBMARINES (SSBN): DELTA III

Name	Completed
(2 units)	1975
(4 units)	1976
(2 units)	1977
(2 units)	1978
(1 unit)	1979
(1 unit)	1981
(1 unit)	1982

Builder:	Severodvinsk
Displacement:	10,500 tons surface 13,250 tons submerged
Length:	508 ft 5 in (155.0 m) oa
Beam:	39 ft 4 in (12.0 m)
Draft:	28 ft 6 in (8.7 m)
Propulsion:	steam turbines; 50,000 shp; 2 shafts/5-bladed propellers
Reactors:	2 pressurized water
Speed:	18 knots surfaced 24 knots submerged
Complement:	approx. 120
Missiles:	16 SS-N-18 SLBM
ASW weapons:	torpedoes [18]
Torpedoes:	6 21-inch (533-mm) torpedo tubes (fwd)
Radars:	Snoop Tray
Sonars:	low frequency

These are similar to the previous Delta-class submarines but are larger to accommodate 16 of the improved SS-N-18 missiles. One unit is named 60 LET VELIKYO OKTYABR.

Seven units are in the Northern Fleet and seven are in the Pacific Fleet.

Classification: Soviet PLARB type.

Design: The "hump" or "turtle back" deck aft of the sail is higher than in previous classes to allow space for the longer SS-N-18 SLBMs.

4 NUCLEAR-PROPELLED BALLISTIC MISSILE SUBMARINES (SSBN): DELTA II

Name	Completed
(4 units)	1974–1975

Builder:	Severodvinsk
Displacement:	10,000 tons surface 12,750 tons submerged
Length:	508 ft 5 in (155.0 m) oa
Beam:	39 ft 4 in (12.0 m)
Draft:	28 ft 3 in (8.6 m)
Propulsion:	steam turbines; 50,000 shp; 2 shafts/5-bladed propellers
Reactors:	2 pressurized water
Speed:	18 knots surfaced 24 knots submerged
Complement:	approx. 120
Missiles:	16 SS-N-8 SLBM
ASW weapons:	torpedoes [18]
Torpedoes:	6 21-inch (533-mm) torpedo tubes (fwd)
Radars:	Snoop Tray
Sonars:	low frequency

This was an interim modification of the Delta I design, lengthened to accommodate 16 tubes but not capable of accommodating the later SLBMs intended for the Delta class. All four units are in the Northern Fleet.

Classification: Soviet PLARB type.

Delta III SSBN. The twin safety tracks for crewmen to clip onto when working on deck are readily visible; the twin hatches are machinery related.

The Delta III is easily identified by the height of the "turtle back" over the missile hatches compared to earlier Soviet SSBNs. The basic design of the Delta classes is derived from the Yankee class, the first advanced Soviet SSBN.

Delta II-class SSBN.

Delta II SSBN. Note the flow of water through the limber holes in the outer hull. Most Soviet submarines are double-hulled, with an outer, partially free-flooding hull, and an inner, protective pressure hull.

18 NUCLEAR-PROPELLED BALLISTIC MISSILE SUBMARINES (SSBN): DELTA I

Name	Completed
(1 unit)	1972
(4 units)	1973
(6 units)	1974
(2 units)	1975
(2 units)	1976
(3 units)	1977

Builders:	Komsomol´sk
	Severodvinsk
Displacement:	9,000 tons surface
	11,750 tons submerged
Length:	459 ft 3 in (140.0 m) oa
Beam:	39 ft 4 in (12.0 m)
Draft:	28 ft 6 in (8.7 m)
Propulsion:	steam turbines; 50,000 shp; 2 shafts/5-bladed propellers
Reactors:	2 pressurized water
Speed:	18 knots surfaced
	25 knots submerged
Complement:	approx. 120
Missiles:	12 SS-N-8 SLBM
ASW weapons:	torpedoes [18]
Torpedoes:	6 21-inch (533-mm) torpedo tubes (fwd)
Radars:	Snoop Tray
Sonars:	low frequency

The Delta is an enlargement of the previous Yankee SSBN design, intended to launch the larger SS-N-8 ballistic missile. The Delta I was the world's largest undersea craft when the first unit was completed in 1972. The subsequent Delta designs were further enlarged to accommodate 16 missiles, four more than the Delta I carried.

These were the last SSBNs built by the Leninskaya Komsomola shipyard at Komsomol'sk in the Far East. All subsequent ballistic missile submarines have been constructed at Severodvinsk on the Arctic (White Sea) coast.

Nine of these submarines are in the Northern Fleet and nine in the Pacific Fleet.

Classification: Soviet PLARB type.

Design: This class has steps at the after end of the "hump" or "turtle back" deck above the missile compartment. The later Deltas have flat, angled decks.

Stern aspect of Delta I SSBN with the sail-mounted diving planes readily visible. The Yankee and Delta SSBN classes and the India-class auxiliary submarines are the only Soviet undersea craft with sail-mounted diving planes. The spear-like mast is a satellite navigation antenna with the NATO code name Pert Spring.

Delta I-class SSBN. (1973)

20 NUCLEAR-PROPELLED BALLISTIC MISSILE SUBMARINES (SSBN): YANKEE I/II

Name	Completed
. . . . . .	1967–1974

Builders:	Komsomol´sk
	Severodvinsk
Displacement:	8,000 tons surface
	9,600 tons submerged
Length:	429 ft 5 in (130.0 m) oa
Beam:	39 ft 4 in (12.0 m)
Draft:	28 ft 10 in (8.8 m)
Propulsion:	steam turbines; 50,000 shp; 2 shafts
Reactors:	2 pressurized water
Speed:	18 knots surfaced
	27 knots submerged
Complement:	approx. 120
Missiles:	16 SS-N-6 SLBM in Yankee I
	12 SS-N-17 SLBM in Yankee II
ASW weapons:	torpedoes [18]
Torpedoes:	6 21-inch (533-mm) torpedo tubes (fwd)
Radars:	Snoop Tray
Sonars:	low frequency

The Yankee was the first "modern" Soviet SSBN class, being similar to the earlier U.S. and British Polaris designs, whose initial units were completed in 1960 and 1967, respectively. Thirty-four Yankee SSBNs were completed from 1967 to 1974. Subsequently, under the terms of the missile submarine limitations of SALT I, 14 Yankees have been retired from the strategic role until 1985 to compensate for newer SSBNs

(there is a 62-submarine limit under SALT I). The former SSBNs are listed separately in this chapter as guided missile (SSGN) and torpedo attack (SSN) submarines. Additional Yankees should be deleted from the SSBN role at the rate of one or two per year as the Delta IV and Typhoon classes are completed.

Of the current Yankee I force, 10 are in the Northern Fleet and 9 in the Pacific Fleet; the single Yankee II is in the Northern Fleet.

Class: The above completion dates are for the entire 34-ship class. The construction rate of this class reached a peak of 10 submarines completed in 1970, compared with a U.S. maximum annual rate of 13 Polaris SSBNs completed in 1964.

Most of the Yankee I SSBNs and the single Yankee II are in the Northern Fleet. The remainder of the class is in the Pacific Fleet.

Classification: Soviet PLARB type.

Conversion: One Yankee SSBN has been modified to carry the enlarged, solid-propellant SS-N-17 missile. Note that the number of missile tubes was reduced from 16 to 12 when the submarine was modified to the Yankee II configuration.

Design: These were the first Soviet submarines to have sail-mounted diving planes vice bow planes. The Yankees have a smaller rise to the top of the hull aft of the sail, over the missile tubes, than in the later Delta classes. Some Yankees have an angled edge at the forward base of their sail for a sonar installation.

Engineering: The Yankee uses a propulsion plant similar to that of the Victor SSN. This plant is estimated to generate 50,000 shp (compared with 15,000 shp for the S5W reactor plant in the U.S. Polaris-Poseidon submarines). Accordingly, the Soviet SSBNs are significantly faster than their Western counterparts.

The Yankee II has been converted to carry the SS-N-17 ballistic missile, the only submarine armed with that weapon. A Brick Pulp antenna is raised at the after end of the sail structure.

Yankee I-class SSBN; the bow "sonar window" is unpainted.

Sail structure of a Yankee I SSBN. This craft has a slanted addition at the forward edge of the sail structure. The hatches for several antennas are open, with the large, forward hatch opening revealing the retractable Cod Eye-B celestial sight.

Yankee I SSBN with sail-mounted diving planes at a "down angle." These submarines are based on the original U.S. Polaris SSBN design of the late 1950s.

1 NUCLEAR-PROPELLED BALLISTIC MISSILE SUBMARINE (SSBN): HOTEL III

Name

. . . . . .

Builders:	Severodvinsk
Displacement:	5,500 tons surface
	6,400 tons submerged
Length:	426 ft 5 in (130.0 m) oa
Beam:	29 ft 6 in (9.0 m)
Draft:	23 ft (7.0 m)
Propulsion:	steam turbines; 30,000 shp; 2 shafts/6-bladed propellers
Reactors:	2 pressurized water
Speed:	20 knots surface
	25 knots submerged
Complement:	approx. 80
Missiles:	6 SS-N-8 SLBM
ASW weapons:	torpedoes
Torpedoes:	6 21-in (533-mm) torpedo tubes (fwd)
	4 16-in (406-mm) torpedo tubes (aft)
Radars:	Snoop Tray
Sonars:	medium frequency

One Hotel II submarine was converted in 1969–1970 to a test ship for the SS-N-8 missile (for the Yankee SSBN). The submarine was lengthened almost 50 feet to accommodate the larger missiles and associated equipment. The Hotel III is in the Northern Fleet.

Four other Hotel-class submarines apparently remain in Soviet service, one as a communications submarine (SSQN) and four whose status is unknown (listed in this volume as SSXN). See pages 158 and 148, respectively.

A Hotel II SSBN at sea. There were no unclassified photos of the one-of-a-kind Hotell III available when this edition went to press. All other Hotels have been retired from the ballistic missile role in accordance with the SALT II accords. (Royal Navy)

1 BALLISTIC MISSILE SUBMARINE (SSB): GOLF V

Builders: (see Golf II listing)
Displacement: 2,300 tons surface
                       2,700 tons submerged
Length: 328 ft (100.0 m) oa
Beam: 27 ft 11 in (8.5 m)
Draft: 21 ft 8 in (6.6 m)
Propulsion: diesel-electric; 6,000-bhp diesels/5,300-shp electric motors; 3
                       shafts
Speed: 17 knots surface
                       12–14 knots submerged
Range: 9,000 n.miles at 5 knots
Complement: approx. 80
Missiles: 1 SS-N-20 SLBM
ASW weapons: torpedoes
Torpedoes: 10 21-in (533-mm) torpedo tubes (6 fwd 4 aft)
Radars: Snoop Tray
Sonars: medium frequency

This is a former Golf II-class submarine converted in 1974–1975 to serve as test ship for the SS-N-20 missile for the Typhoon-class SSBN. The Golf V is the only ballistic missile submarine in the Black Sea Fleet.

1 BALLISTIC MISSILE SUBMARINE (SSB): GOLF III

Builders: (see Golf II listing)
Displacement: 2,900 tons surface
                       3,300 tons submerged
Length: 360 ft 10 in (110.0 m) oa
Beam: 27 ft 11 in (8.5 m)
Draft: 21 ft 8 in (6.6 m)
Propulsion: diesel-electric; 6,000-bhp diesels/5,300-shp electric motors; 3
                       shafts
Speed: 17 knots surface
                       12 knots submerged
Range: 9,000 n.miles at 5 knots
Complement: approx. 90
Missiles: 6 SS-N-8 SLBM
ASW weapons: torpedoes
Torpedoes: 10 21-in (533-mm) torpedo tubes (6 fwd 4 aft)
Radars: Snoop Tray
Sonars: medium frequency

This is a former Golf I-class submarine converted in 1973 to serve as test ship for the SS-N-8 missile of the Delta I/II SSBNs. The submarine was lengthened some 33 feet in the conversion. It is in the Northern Fleet.

The single Golf III SSB with elongated sail structure.

13 BALLISTIC MISSILE SUBMARINES (SSB): GOLF II CLASS

Name	Completed
. . . . . .	1958–1962

Builders:	Komsomol sk (7 units)
	Severodvinsk (16 units)
Displacement:	2,300 tons surface
	2,700 tons submerged
Length:	328 ft (100.0 m) oa
Beam:	27 ft 11 in (8.5 m)
Draft:	21 ft 8 in (6.6 m)
Propulsion:	diesel electric; 6,000-bhp diesels/5,300-shp electric motors; 3 shafts
Speed:	17 knots surface
	12–14 knots submerged
Range:	9,000 n.miles at 5 knots
Complement:	approx. 80
Missiles:	3 SS-N-5 Serb SLBM
ASW weapons:	torpedoes
Torpedoes:	10 21-in (533-mm) torpedo tubes (6 fwd 4 aft)
Radars:	Snoop Tray
Sonars:	medium frequency

These Golf I-class submarines that were modified to the Golf II configuration with installation of the underwater-launch SS-N-5 missile. During September–October 1976 six Golf II submarines were shifted into the Baltic, the first time ballistic missile submarines had been assigned to that fleet. The other seven Golf II units are in the Pacific Fleet.

Class: A total of 23 Golf-class submarines were built, being armed with the SS-N-4 Sark SLBM. The above dates and shipyards apply to the entire class. Of these, 13 were modified to Golf IIs, those being completed from 1961 to 1971. In addition, three units were converted to trials ships for new SLBMs: the Golf III to test the SS-N-8, the Golf IV to test the SS-N-6, and the Golf V to test the SS-N-20. The Golf IV has been scrapped.

Three additional submarines were converted to a special communications configuration (SSQ) and are listed separately in this chapter.

One Golf I submarine was lost at sea in the mid-Pacific in 1968 with her entire crew. Portions of the submarine were raised in 1974 by the U.S. Central Intelligence Agency, which used the built-for-the-purpose lift ship HUGHES GLOMAR EXPLORER (later given the U.S. Navy designation AG 192).

Three submarines retaining the basic Golf I SSB configuration have been scrapped.

The plans and some components for an additional Golf SSB were given to China and assembled there. The submarine was launched in 1964. (It was the test platform for China's SLBM program.)

Classification: Soviet PLRB type.

Golf II SSB with communications masts raised. The low structure abaft the conning tower houses a communications buoy; the lower set of "windows" on the conning tower are sonar antennas. There is an extensive sonar installation in the bow. (1976).

Golf II SSB. These submarines provide a theater nuclear strike capability in the Baltic and Far East areas. (1984, Japanese Maritime Self-Defense Force)

Golf II SSB. The submarine's escape and rescue hatches, forward and aft, are ringed with luminescent paint; tethered emergency buoys are fitted aft of the two hatches. (1977).

BALLISTIC MISSILE SUBMARINES: (SSB) ZULU V CLASS

The former Zulu-class attack submarines converted to carry the SS-N-4 Sark missile have been stricken; six SSB conversions were completed between 1956 and 1959. An earlier, one-tube interim SSB conversion carried the Army's Scud short-range ballistic missile. See the Zulu IV listing with attack submarines.

GUIDED/CRUISE MISSILE SUBMARINES

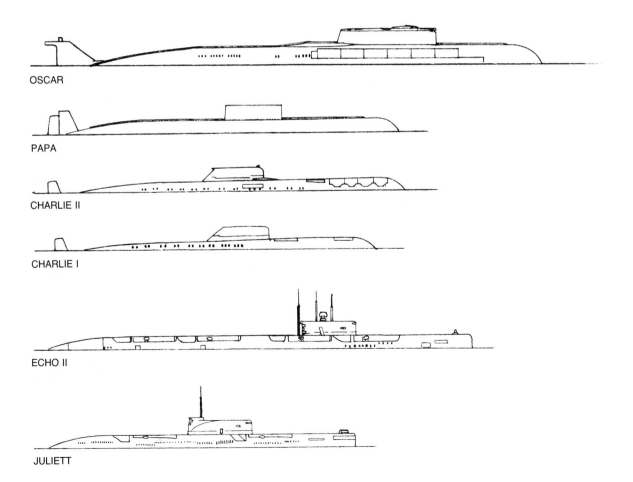

OSCAR

PAPA

CHARLIE II

CHARLIE I

ECHO II

JULIETT

NUCLEAR-PROPELLED GUIDED MISSILE SUBMARINES (SSGN): NEW DESIGN

A new cruise missile submarine (SSGN) intended to carry the SS-N-24 strategic cruise missile is believed to be in the advanced design stage and possibly under construction. The lack of strategic arms agreements on cruise missiles and the Soviet increase in cruise missiles in the Oscar class indicate (along with other factors) that the new SSGN may carry as many as 24 missiles.

A converted Yankee-class SSGN is shown launching two SS-NX-24 missiles in this artist's concept. The drawing shows how the amidships section of the Yankee has been rebuilt to accommodate vertical launch tubes, six per side, angled forward in the manner of the Oscar SSGN configuration.

1 NUCLEAR-PROPELLED GUIDED MISSILE SUBMARINE (SSGN): YANKEE

Builders:	(see Yankee SSBN listing)
Displacement:	
	13,650 tons submerged
Length:	501 ft 10 in (153.0 m) oa
Beam:	39 ft 4 in (12.0 m)
Draft:	29 ft 6 in (9.0 m)
Propulsion:	steam turbines; 50,000 shp; 2 shafts/5-bladed propellers
Reactors:	2 pressurized water
Speed:	
	23 knots submerged
Complement:	
Missiles:	12 SS-N-24 land-attack cruise missiles
ASW weapons:	torpedoes [18]
Torpedoes:	6 21-in (533-mm) torpedo tubes (fwd)
Radars:	
Sonars:	

A single Yankee I SSBN has been converted to a test ship for the SS-N-24 strategic cruise missile. The submarine's 16 SS-N-6 SLBM launch tubes and associated fire-control equipment were deleted and a new amidships section installed between the control spaces and reactor plant. The new section, which lengthens the submarine by some 75 feet, contains 12 tubes for the cruise missile, fitted six per side; the beam appears to have been increased significantly.

The submarine was launched in its new configuration in December 1982 and began launch tests with the SS-N-24 in 1985. The submarine is in the Northern Fleet. No additional conversions of this type are envisioned.

3+ NUCLEAR-PROPELLED GUIDED MISSILE SUBMARINES (SSGN): OSCAR

Name	Launched	Completed
(unit 1)	Apr 1980	1982
(unit 2)	Dec 1982	1983
(unit 3)	1984	
(unit 4)	1986	building

Builders:	Severodvinsk
Displacement:	approx. 11,500 tons surface
	approx. 14,500 tons submerged
Length:	492 ft (150.0 m) oa
Beam:	59 ft (18.0 m)
Draft:	36 ft (11.0 m)
Propulsion:	steam turbines; approx. 90,000 shp; 2 shafts/7-bladed propellers
Reactors:	2 pressurized water
Speed:	
	35 knots submerged (see Engineering notes)
Complement:	
Missiles:	24 SS-N-19 anti-ship
ASW weapons:	torpedoes [18]
	SS-N-15
	SS-N-16
Torpedoes:	... 21-in (533-mm) and/or 26-in (650-mm) torpedo tubes
Radars:	
Sonars:	Shark Gill low/medium frequency

The Oscar is a very large "attack"-type submarine, carrying three times the number of anti-ship missiles in the previous Charlie and Echo II SSGNs. The missiles are launched while the submarine is submerged. The lead ship was laid down in 1978.

An Oscar-class SSGN on the surface, showing the amidship hatches, starboard and port, with each hatch covering two SS-N-19 missile tubes. The device atop the rudder is for streaming a towed sonar array. (1984, Royal Norwegian Air Force)

Additional units of the Oscar class are under construction.

Classification: Soviet PLARK type.

Design: The 24 missile tubes are in two rows of 12, in a fixed position at an angle of approximately 40°. The tubes are covered by six shutters per side, each covering two missile tubes. The missile tubes are fitted between the inner (pressure) and outer (hydrodynamic) hulls. This provides a "stand-off" distance of some 11½ ft (3.5 m) between the hulls, giving the Oscar significant reserve buoyancy and increased protection against conventional torpedoes.

Engineering: Earlier Western estimates credited the Oscar with a submerged speed of some 30 knots. This has been revised upward, a further indication of Soviet emphasis on submarine performance.

Oscar-class SSGN (1984, RNorAF)

1 NUCLEAR-PROPELLED GUIDED MISSILE SUBMARINE (SSGN): PAPA

Name	Launched	Completed
. . . . . .	1968	1970

Builders:	Gor'kiy
Displacement:	6,700 tons surface
	8,000 tons submerged
Length:	357 ft 6 in (109.0 m) oa
Beam:	40 ft (12.2 m)
Draft:	31 ft 2 in (9.5 m)
Propulsion:	steam turbines; 60,000–75,000 shp; 2 shafts/5-bladed propellers
Reactors:	2 pressurized water
Speed:	16 knots surfaced
	39 knots submerged (see Engineering notes)
Complement:	approx. 85
Missiles:	10 SS-N-9 anti-ship (see Missile notes)
ASW weapons:	torpedoes
	SS-N-15
Torpedoes:	6 21-in (533-mm) torpedo tubes (fwd)
Radars:	
Sonars:	low frequency

Only a single Papa-class SSGN has been built, apparently as a prototype for advanced SSGN concepts. The Papa probably made a limited number of deployments and subsequently conducted only local operations. It is in the Northern Fleet.

Classification: Soviet PLARK type.

Engineering: Earlier Western estimates gave the Papa a speed of 35–40 knots. It has been raised to the upper end of that range.

Missiles: Most Western estimates indicate that the Papa carries the SS-N-9 missile; however, this is not certain.

The Papa SSGN; note the circular hull form and short sail structure.

The one-of-a-kind Papa SSGN. She has a distinctive "notched" upper rudder. Apparently some of her features were incorporated in the larger and more-capable Oscar SSGN.

6 NUCLEAR-PROPELLED GUIDED MISSILE SUBMARINES (SSGN): CHARLIE II

Name	Completed
. . . . . .	1973–1982

Builders:	Gor'kiy
Displacement:	4,500 tons surface
	5,400 tons submerged
Length:	334 ft 7 in (102.0 m) oa
Beam:	32 ft 10 in (10.0 m)
Draft:	26 ft 3 in (8.0 m)
Propulsion:	steam turbines; 15,000 shp; 1 shaft/5-bladed propeller
Reactors:	1 pressurized water
Speed:	16 knots surfaced
	23 knots submerged
Complement:	approx. 100
Missiles:	8 SS-N-9 anti-ship
ASW weapons:	torpedoes [12]
	SS-N-15
Torpedoes:	6 21-in (533-mm) torpedo tubes (fwd)
Radars:	Snoop Tray
Sonars:	low frequency

These are improved versions of the original Charlie SSGN, lengthened forward of the sail structure by 26⅓ feet to accommodate improved weapons and electronic capabilities. The Charlie II carries the longer-range SS-N-9. These submarines were built at about half the rate of the Charlie I class—there were only six—an indication that the design was unsatisfactory. No Charlie III class has emerged, although there were some indications that there would be a follow-on sub-type.

All units are in the Northern Fleet.

Classification: Soviet PLARK type.

Engineering: The Charlie class has a single reactor, the only Soviet combat nuclear submarines with a single-reactor plant and a single propeller shaft. Western intelligence originally estimated a slightly higher speed for these submarines (26 knots).

Charlie II SSGN maneuvering alongside a submarine tender.

A Charlie II SSGN. The bulbous bow houses eight tubes for the SS-N-9 anti-ship missile. The Charlie-class submarines are the only Soviet nuclear-propelled combat submarines with one reactor; they have not been as successful as expected.

11 NUCLEAR-PROPELLED GUIDED MISSILE SUBMARINES (SSGN): CHARLIE I

Name	Completed
. . . . . .	1967–1973

Builders:	Gor'kiy
Displacement:	4,000 tons surface
	5,000 tons submerged
Length:	308 ft 4 in (94.0 m) oa
Beam:	32 ft 10 in (10.0 m)
Draft:	26 ft 3 in (8.0 m)
Propulsion:	steam turbines; 15,000 shp; 1 shaft/5-bladed propeller
Reactors:	1 pressurized water
Speed:	16 knots surface
	23 knots submerged
Complement:	approx. 100
Missiles:	8 SS-N-7 anti-ship
ASW weapons:	torpedoes [12]
	SS-N-15
Torpedoes:	6 21-in (533-mm) torpedo tubes (fwd)
Radars:	Snoop Tray
Sonars:	low frequency

These were the first Soviet submarines capable of launching cruise missiles underwater. They have shorter-range missiles than the previous Echo SSGN.

Class: Twelve Charlie I-class SSGNs were built, completed at the average rate of two submarines per year. One unit sank in the Bering Sea, off Kamchatka Peninsula, in June 1983. That submarine has been salvaged but is not believed to have been returned to service.

Charlie I SSGN; the Park Lamp DF loop and the Brick Pulp ECM mast are raised.

Eight units are in the Northern Fleet, three units are in the Pacific Fleet.

Classification: Soviet PLARK type.

Design: The missile tubes are housed in the bow, external to the pressure hull, angled upward, six on each side, with large outer doors. The tubes cannot be reloaded from inside the submarine.

Engineering: These submarines were previously estimated to have a submerged speed of 27 knots. See Charlie II notes.

A Charlie I SSGN in the South China Sea while transiting to the Pacific Fleet. The bow diving planes are retracted into the hull just forward of the sail structure, with the starboard cover plate visible in this view. (1974, U.S. Navy)

Charlie I-class SSGN. (1974)

26(2) NUCLEAR-PROPELLED GUIDED MISSILE SUBMARINES (SSGN): ECHO II

Name	Completed
. . . . . .	1962–1968

Builders:	Komsomol´sk
	Severodvinsk
Displacement:	5,000 tons surface
	6,000 tons submerged
Length:	377 ft 2 in (115.0 m) oa
Beam:	29 ft 6 in (9.0 m)
Draft:	24 ft 7 in (7.5 m)
Propulsion:	steam turbines; 30,000 shp; 2 shafts/4-bladed propellers
Reactors:	2 pressurized water
Speed:	20 knots surface
	23 knots submerged
Complement:	approx. 90
Missiles:	8 SS-N-3a Shaddock anti-ship or 8 SS-N-12 Sandbox anti-ship
ASW weapons:	torpedoes
Torpedoes:	6 21-in (533-mm) torpedo tubes (fwd)
	4 16-in (406-mm) torpedo tubes (aft)
Radars:	Front Door
	Front Piece
	Snoop Slab
Sonars:	Feniks/low frequency

These were the Soviet Navy's primary anti-carrier submarines during the 1960s and 1970s. They are the definitive Shaddock-armed SSGNs, evolving from the Echo I and Juliett SSGN designs. About 15 of these submarines were refitted to fire the improved SS-N-12 by 1986.

The Echo II SSGNs were built in about equal numbers by the Komsomol´sk and Severodvinsk yards. (All of five Echo I-class SSGNs were built at Komsomol´sk.)

The active units are assigned to the Northern and Pacific fleets. Two SSGNs have been decommissioned and are apparently in reserve.

Class: Twenty-nine of these submarines were built. One has been converted to a special-purpose submarine (AGSSN) (see below). The Echo I class was a different design; five SSGNs of the class were subsequently converted to torpedo attack submarines (SSN).

Classification: Soviet PLARK type.

Design: These submarines have their large missile tubes mounted in pairs above the pressure hull. For firing, the submarine surfaces and the paired tubes are elevated. While on the surface, the forward section of the sail structure rotates 180° to reveal the Front-series missile-guidance radars.

Engineering: The reactor plant is similar to that of the Hotel SSBN and November SSN classes.

Echo II SSGN with two pairs of SS-N-3/12 missile tubes in the elevated, firing position. (U.S. Navy)

An Echo II SSGN in the Pacific. The mast at the after end of the sail structure folds back into a deck recess when not in use. (1970, U.S. Navy)

Echo II SSGN with the forward edge of the sail structure fully rotated to expose the Front Door radar. (Ministry of Defence)

A closeup of an Echo II SSGN in the North Atlantic. The broad face of the sail structure covers the Front Door radar used for guiding the SS-N-3/12 anti-ship missiles. (1979, Ministry of Defence)

Echo II-class SSGN.

15(1) GUIDED MISSILE SUBMARINES (SSG): JULIETT CLASS

Name	Completed
. . . . . .	1961–1969

Builders:	Gor´kiy
Displacement:	3,000 tons surface
	3,750 tons submerged
Length:	295 ft 2 in (90.0 m) oa
Beam:	32 ft 10 in (10.0 m)
Draft:	23 ft (7.0 m)
Propulsion:	diesel electric; diesel motors 7,000 hp/electric motors 5,000 shp; 2 shafts
Speed:	16 knots surface
	14 knots submerged
Range:	9,000 n.miles at 7 knots
Complement:	approx. 80
Missiles:	4 SS-N-3a Shaddock anti-ship
ASW weapons:	torpedoes
Torpedoes:	6 21-in (533-mm) torpedo tubes (fwd)
	4 16-in (406-mm) torpedo tubes (aft)
Radars:	Front Door
	Front Piece
	Snoop Slab
Sonars:	medium frequency

These submarines remain in front-line service. Note that their period of construction overlaps that for the nuclear-powered Echo II SSGNs and the improved Charlie SSGNs.

Eleven units are assigned to the Northern Fleet (with some deploying to the Mediterranean) and to the Pacific Fleet, three to the Baltic Fleet, and one to the Black Sea Fleet. One unit was decommissioned in 1984–1985.

Classification: Soviet PLRK type.

Design: The Shaddock missile tubes are paired, above the pressure hull, representating one-half the missile battery of the Echo II. The tubes elevate in pairs for firing. The Front Door/Front Piece guidance radar is built into the forward edge of the sail structure, which opens by rotating 180°.

Juliett-class SSG; the snorkel mast is partially raised; the snorkel exhaust is faired into the after end of the sail structure. The Front Door radar is visible at the forward end of the structure. (1979, Ministry of Defence)

Juliett-class SSG making high speed in rough seas. These submarines have one-half the Shaddock missile battery of an Echo II SSGN; although diesel-electric propelled, the Soviets consider them a highly successful submarine class.

GUIDED MISSILE SUBMARINES (SSG): WHISKEY-CLASS CONVERSIONS

A total of 13 Whiskey-class submarines were converted to guided-missile submarines to carry the SS-N-3 Shaddock missile. The conversions were completed between 1961 and 1964. One single-cylinder and five twin-cylinder conversions were followed by seven definitive "long-bin" conversions (these NATO terms refer to their missile configuration). The long-bin type received four missiles fitted into the sail structure for forward firing at a fixed elevation of about 15°. These submarines were lengthened to 272¼ feet. Additional Whiskey long-bin conversions were planned but not undertaken.

All have been discarded, the last in 1985. See the 3rd edition, pages 103–104, for additional details.

ATTACK SUBMARINES

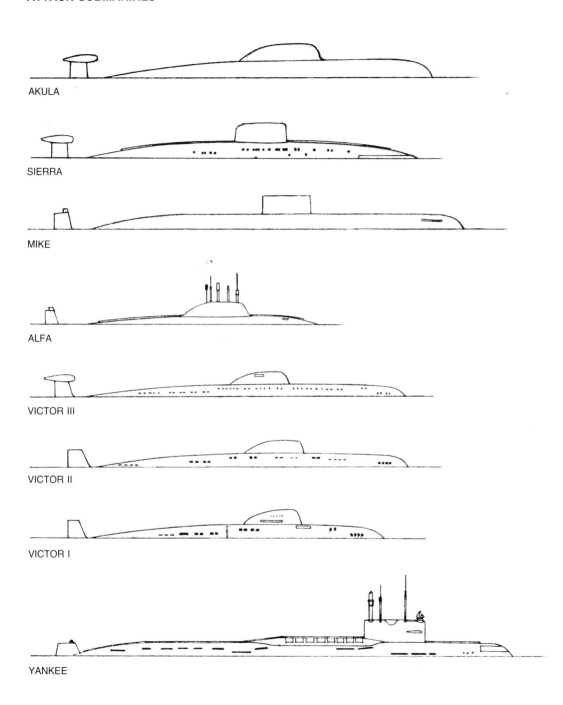

AKULA

SIERRA

MIKE

ALFA

VICTOR III

VICTOR II

VICTOR I

YANKEE

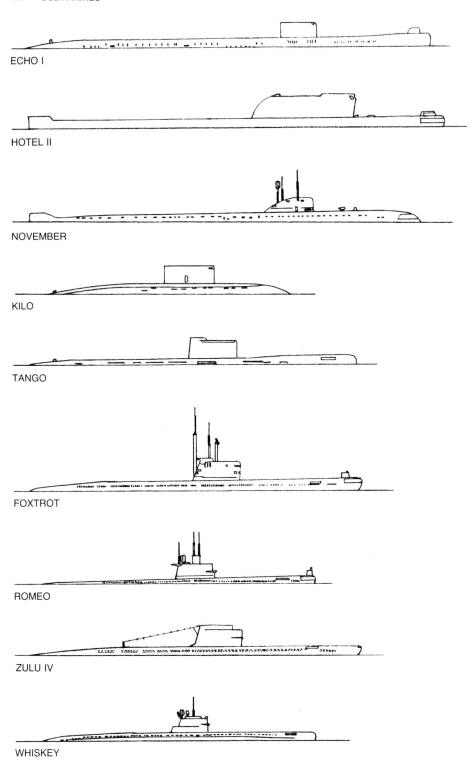

ECHO I

HOTEL II

NOVEMBER

KILO

TANGO

FOXTROT

ROMEO

ZULU IV

WHISKEY

13 NUCLEAR-PROPELLED ATTACK SUBMARINES (SSN/SSXN): YANKEE CLASS

Name	Converted
. . . . . . (1 unit)	1984
. . . . . . (12 units)	converting (?)

Builders:	Komsomol´sk
	Severodvinsk
Displacement:	8,000 tons surface
	9,600 tons submerged
Length:	426 ft 5 in (130.0 m) oa
Beam:	39 ft 4 in (12.0 m)
Draft:	28 ft 10 in (8.8 m)
Propulsion:	steam turbines; 50,000 shp; 2 shafts/5-bladed propellers
Reactors:	2 pressurized water
Speed:	
	27 knots submerged
Complement:	approx. 120
Missiles:	(removed)
ASW weapons:	torpedoes [18]
Torpedoes:	6 21-inch (533-mm) torpedo tubes (fwd)
Radars:	Snoop Tray
Sonars:	low frequency

These are former SLBM submarines with their missile tubes and associated fire-control equipment removed or partially dismantled in accordance with SALT agreements. Only one submarine was identified by the end of 1985 as being fully operational in the SSN configuration. However, other units were reported to be in the process of conversion to SSNs.

Class: A total of 34 Yankee SSBNs were constructed between 1967 and 1974. See the Yankee SSBN listing for additional details. One former Yankee SSBN has been converted to a cruise missile submarine (SSGN) and is listed separately.

1 + NUCLEAR-PROPELLED ATTACK SUBMARINES (SSN): AKULA CLASS

Name	Launched	Completed
(unit 1)	July 1984	1985
. . . . . .		building and planned

Builders:	Komsomol´sk
Displacement:	6,800 tons surface
	8,300 tons submerged
Length:	351 ft (107.0 m) oa
Beam:	39 ft 4 in (12.0 m)
Draft:	
Propulsion:	steam turbines; 1 shaft/7-bladed propeller
Reactors:	2 pressurized water
Speed:	
	30 + knots submerged
Complement:	
Missiles:	possibly SS-N-21 land-attack cruise missile
ASW weapons:	torpedoes
	SS-N-16
Torpedoes:	6 21-inch (533-mm) and/or 26-inch (650-mm) torpedo tubes (fwd)
Radars:	
Sonars:	low frequency
	towed array

This is an attack submarine design, distinguished from the contemporary Sierra SSN by the elongated sail structure. The Akula is slightly larger than the Sierra. The first unit of the Akula class is in the Pacific Fleet.

Design: The Akula is believed to have a titanium hull.

Engineering: There are reported to be advanced quieting techniques in this design.

Name: A Russian submarine named AKULA was completed in 1911 to a then-advanced design; she was lost on a minelaying operation in the Baltic in late 1915.

The prototype Akula SSN off the Siberian coast; the Akula has the longest sail structure of any Soviet attack submarine.

1+ NUCLEAR-PROPELLED ATTACK SUBMARINES (SSN): MIKE CLASS

Name	Launched	Completed
(unit 1)	June 1983	1985
......		building and planned

Builders:	Severodvinsk
Displacement:	7,800 tons surface
	9,700 tons submerged
Length:	400 ft 2 in (122.0 m) oa
Beam:	39 ft 4 in (12.0 m)
Draft:	29 ft 6 in (9.0 m)
Propulsion:	steam turbines; 60,000 shp; 1 shaft/7-bladed propeller
Reactors:	2 liquid metal
Speed:	
	36–38 knots submerged
Complement:	
Missiles:	possibly SS-N-21 land-attack cruise missile
ASW weapons:	torpedoes
	SS-N-15
	SS-N-16
Torpedoes:	... 21-inch (533-mm) and/or 26-inch (650-mm) torpedo tubes (fwd)
Radars:	
Sonars:	Shark Gill/low frequency

The Mike is an apparent follow-on to the Alfa-class SSN, with a titanium hull and an advanced liquid-metal cooled reactor plant. Al-though slower than the Alfa, the Mike is quieter and has more weapons and other capabilities than most previous attack submarines.

This is the world's largest purpose-built attack submarine (compare with the 6,900-ton [submerged displacement] USS LOS ANGELES, now in series production, and the planned 9,150-ton SEAWOLF design).

The lead ship was probably laid down in 1982. It is in the Northern Fleet.

Engineering: The Mike is reported to be significantly quieter than previous Soviet attack submarines, having corrected the high noise levels of the Alfa's propulsion plant.

A drawing of the Mike-class SSN, apparently the successor to the Alfa SSN in terms of advanced hull materials and propulsion plant. The Mike is the world's largest SSN except for the converted Yankees.

The lines of the prototype Sierra-class SSN reveal her origins in the Victor class. The pod atop the rudder contains a towed array sonar for long-range, passive detection. Note the safety track and limber holes. (1984, RNorAF)

1 + NUCLEAR-PROPELLED ATTACK SUBMARINES (SSN): SIERRA CLASS

Name	Launched	Completed
(unit 1)	July 1983	1984
. . . . . .		building and planned

Builders:	Gor´kiy
	United Admiralty, Leningrad
Displacement:	6,000 tons surface
	7,550 tons submerged
Length:	360 ft 10 in (110.0 m) oa
Beam:	39 ft 4 in (12.0 m)
Draft:	
Propulsion:	steam turbines; 1 shaft/6-bladed propeller
Reactors:	2 pressurized water
Speed:	
	approx. 35 knots submerged
Complement:	
Missiles:	possibly SS-N-21 land-attack cruise missile
ASW weapons:	torpedoes
	SS-N-16
Torpedoes:	6 21-in (533-mm) and/or 26-inch (650-mm) torpedo tubes (fwd)
Radars:	
Sonars:	Shark Gill/low frequency
	towed array

This class is apparently the successor to the Victor III class, but it is quieter and has improved sonar, a higher speed, and a greater operating depth. The first unit of the Sierra class was built at Gor´kiy and transferred to the Northern Fleet through the inland river-canal route.

Design: The Sierra is believed to have a titanium hull.

Engineering: Note that the Sierra has a greater beam than the Victor III, indicating a different engineering plant and/or additional machinery-quieting features.

Sierra-class SSN.

The prototype Sierra-class SSN in the Norwegian Sea. (1984, RNorAF)

6 NUCLEAR-PROPELLED ATTACK SUBMARINES (SSN): ALFA CLASS

Name	Completed
. . . . . .	1979–1983 (?)

Builders:	Severodvinsk
	Sudomekh, Leningrad
Displacement:	2,900 tons surface
	3,700 tons submerged
Length:	267 ft (81.4 m) oa
Beam:	31 ft 2 in (9.5 m)
Draft:	23 ft (7.0 m)
Propulsion:	steam turbines driving electric generators; 45,000 shp; 1 shaft/7-bladed propeller
Reactors:	1 liquid metal
Speed:	
	43–45 knots submerged
Complement:	approx. 45
ASW weapons:	torpedoes
	SS-N-15
Torpedoes:	6 21-in (533-mm) torpedo tubes (fwd)
Radars:	Snoop Tray
Sonars:	low frequency

The Alfa is the world's fastest and deepest-diving combat submarine, incorporating a number of innovations, including a high power-to-weight reactor plant using a liquid metal as the heat-exchange medium, a titanium hull, and extensive automation. The Alfa was conceived in the late 1950s (see chapter 10).

The Soviets refer to the Alfa as *zolotaya ryba* (golden fish), apparently because of the high unit cost.

Class: The first Alfa was initially completed at Sudomekh in 1972 and engaged in lengthy trials in the Baltic and Northern Fleet areas. Major problems were encountered and the lead ship was rebuilt at the Sudomekh yard. That unit was scrapped about 1974. Series production began in the mid-1970s, and the second unit was completed in 1979.

Classification: Soviet PLA type. The NATO code name for the class is *Alfa*, not *Alpha*.

Design: The Alfa was the world's first submarine to have a titanium hull. This provided more strength than a conventional hull but was lighter. The engineering spaces, which are highly automated, may be unmanned while the submarine is under way. Western intelligence credits the Alfa with an operating depth of at least 1,970 ft (600 m) and a maximum depth of 2,950 feet (900 m). The U.S. nuclear-propelled research submersible NR-1 has an operating depth of approximately 3,000 feet (915 m), but she is an unarmed research craft with limited mobility and no combat capabilities.

Engineering: The Alfa has an advanced reactor that uses a liquid metal such as sodium rather than pressurized water as the heat-exchange medium for the reactor and steam systems. Acoustic data on the first Alfa SSNs indicated that the radiated noise levels at lesser speeds were generally similar to those of other Soviet SSNs, indicating a net improvement in view of the higher power of the Alfa reactor plant.

The very low manning level in the Alfa suggests a high degree of automation in the propulsion system.

Alfa-class SSN revealing the clean lines, with the sail structure fully faired into the hull for improved underwater performance.

Alfa-class SSN—the world's fastest and deepest-diving combat submarine.

Sail of an Alfa SSN showing (from left) Park Lamp DF loop, HF radio mast, radome mast, search and attack periscopes.

21 NUCLEAR-PROPELLED ATTACK SUBMARINES (SSN): VICTOR III CLASS

Name	Completed
. . . . . .	1978–1986

Builders:	Admiralty, Leningrad
	Komsomol sk
Displacement:	4,800 tons surface
	6,300 tons submerged
Length:	347 ft 8 in (106.0 m) oa
Beam:	32 ft 10 in (10.0 m)
Draft:	23 ft (7.0 m)
Propulsion:	steam turbines; 30,000 shp; 1 shaft/4-bladed propellers (see Engineering notes)
Reactors:	2 pressurized water
Speed:	20 knots
	29 knots submerged
Complement:	approx. 85
ASW weapons:	torpedoes
	SS-N-15
	SS-N-16
Torpedoes:	2 21-inch (533-mm) torpedo tubes (fwd)
	4 26-inch (650-mm) torpedo tubes (fwd)
Radars:	Snoop Tray
Sonars:	low frequency
	towed array

These are a further improvement of the basic Victor SSN, with the additional hull space forward of the sail structure probably intended for an improved weapons capability (i.e., 26-inch torpedoes). The last Victor III was launched in 1985, being replaced on the building ways at the Admiralty shipyard by the Sierra-class SSN.

Classification: Soviet PLA type.

Engineering: Some or all units have tandem, four-bladed propellers mounted on the same shaft. The propellers rotate in the same direction.

Note that the Victor III is slower than the Victor I. The same propulsion plant drives a larger submarine, resulting in a loss of up to three knots.

Operational: A Victor III fouled the towed hydrophone array of the USS McCLOY (FF 1038) off the U.S East Coast in November 1983. The submarine was towed to Cuba and repaired.

Sonar: The Victor III was the first Soviet submarine fitted with a towed-array sonar, streamed from a distinctive pod fitted atop the vertical stabilizer/rudder.

The stern of a Victor III

Victor III SSN adrift off the coast of South Carolina. The submarine was subsequently towed to Cuba for repairs. (1983, U.S. Navy)

7 NUCLEAR-PROPELLED ATTACK SUBMARINES (SSGN): VICTOR II CLASS

Name	Completed
. . . . . .	1972–1978

Builders:	Admiralty, Leningrad
Displacement:	4,500 tons surface
	5,700 tons submerged
Length:	328 ft (100.0 m) oa
Beam:	32 ft 10 in (10.0 m)
Draft:	23 ft (7.0 m)
Propulsion:	steam turbines: 30,000 shp; 1 shaft/5-bladed propeller
Reactors:	2 pressurized water
Speed:	
	30 knots submerged
Complement:	approx. 80
ASW weapons:	torpedoes
	SS-N-15
	SS-N-16
Torpedoes:	6 21-inch (533-mm) torpedo tubes (fwd)
Radar:	Snoop Tray
Sonar:	low frequency

Victor II-class SSN.

These are improved Victor-class SSNs, enlarged to provide additional weapons capability (probably an improved fire-control system and larger weapons).

Classification: Soviet PLA type. This variant was initially given the NATO code name Uniform, changed to Victor II.

Victor II-class SSN in the Barents Sea. (1982, U.S. Navy)

The streamlined sail of a Victor II with open doors and hatches for several raised periscopes and masts. The second mast from the right is a Park Lamp direction-finding loop; DF of communications is an important means of detecting ships at sea as well as a means of collecting technical intelligence.

16 NUCLEAR-PROPELLED ATTACK SUBMARINES (SSN): VICTOR I CLASS

Name	Completed
50 LET SSR	1968–1975
. . . . . . (15 units)	

Builders:	Admiralty, Leningrad
Displacement:	4,300 tons surface
	5,100 tons submerged
Length:	311 ft 7 in (95.0 m) oa
Beam:	32 ft 10 in (10.0 m)
Draft:	23 ft (7.0 m)
Propulsion:	steam turbines; 30,000 shp; 1 shaft/5-bladed propeller (see Engineering notes)
Reactors:	2 pressurized water
Speed:	
	30–32 knots submerged
Complement:	approx. 80
ASW weapons:	torpedoes
	SS-N-15
Torpedoes:	6 21-in (533-mm) torpedo tubes (fwd)
Radar:	Snoop Tray
Sonar:	low frequency

These are advanced attack submarines, built to the tear-drop hull design for high underwater speeds. One unit is named 50 LET SSR (50 Years of the USSR).

Classification: Soviet PLA type.

Engineering: The Victor SSN reactor plant is similar to that fitted in the Yankee-Delta SSBNs.

Two small, two-bladed propellers are fitted on the stern planes for slow-speed operation.

Victor I-class SSN. (1974, U.S. Navy)

3(2) NUCLEAR-PROPELLED ATTACK SUBMARINES (SSN): ECHO I CLASS

Name	Completed	Converted to SSN
. . . . . .	1960–1962	1970–1974

Builders:	Komsomol´sk
Displacement:	4,500 tons surface
	5,500 tons submerged
Length:	360 ft 10 in (110.0 m) oa
Beam:	29 ft 6 in (9.0 m)
Draft:	24 ft 7 in (7.5 m)
Propulsion:	steam turbines; 25,000 shp; 2 shafts/5-bladed propellers
Reactors:	2 pressurized water
Speed:	20 knots surface
	25 knots submerged
Complement:	approx. 75
ASW weapons:	torpedoes
Torpedoes:	6 21-in (533-mm) torpedo tubes (fwd)
	4 16-in (406 mm) torpedo tubes (aft)
Radars:	Snoop Tray
Sonars:	medium frequency

An Echo I-class SSN at sea in the Pacific.

Five Echo I SSGNs were built with six launch tubes for the SS-N-3 Shaddock missile. They lack the Front-series radars and other features of the Juliette SSG and Echo II SSGN classes that would permit them to launch the anti-ship versions of the Shaddock and were thus converted to an attack configuration. Three are assigned to the Pacific Fleet; two units were decommissioned in 1984–1985.

Classification: Soviet PLA type.

Conversion: Conversions to attack configuration began in 1968, with all five units modified at Komsomol´sk.

An Echo I SSN after conversion from a Shaddock missile submarine. In the SSGN configuration, these submarines lacked the Front Door radar of the Echo II and Juliett classes. They are now being retired from the fleet. The radio mast visible here folds back into a deck recess.

12(2) NUCLEAR-PROPELLED ATTACK SUBMARINES (SSN): NOVEMBER CLASS

Name	Completed
LENINSKIY KOMSOMOLETS	1958
LENINETS	1959–1964
. . . . . . (10 units)	

Builders:	Severodvinsk
Displacement:	4,500 tons surface
	5,300 tons submerged
Length:	360 ft 10 in (110.0 m) oa
Beam:	29 ft 6 in (9.0 m)
Draft:	25 ft 3 in (7.7 m)
Propulsion:	steam turbines; 30,000 shp; 2 shafts/4- or 6-bladed propellers
Reactors:	2 pressurized water
Speed:	
	30 knots submerged
Complement:	approx. 80
ASW weapons:	torpedoes [32]
Torpedoes:	8 21-in (533-mm) torpedo tubes (fwd)
	4 16-in (406-mm) torpedo tubes (aft)
Radars:	Snoop Tray
Sonars:	medium frequency

November-class SSN showing bow and sail-mounted sonar antennas. (Soviet Navy)

These were the Soviet Navy's first nuclear submarines. The LENINSKIY KOMSOMOLETS was commissioned on 8 April 1958; she was the first Soviet submarine to reach the geographic North Pole (1962). Two of these submarines may be in reserve.

Class: Fifteen units of this class were built. One submarine of this class sank off the Atlantic coast of Spain in April 1970. (No personnel are believed to have been lost.)

Two additional units have been discarded.

Classification: Soviet PLA type.

Engineering: The November's reactor plant is similar to that of the Echo II SSGN and Hotel SSBN classes.

Sail structure of a November SSN. Only a radome is in the raised position. (1970)

The November-class SSN was the Soviet Navy's first nuclear-propelled submarine, but was constructed almost simultaneously with the Hotel SSBN and Echo SSGN classes.

4 NUCLEAR-PROPELLED ATTACK SUBMARINES (SSXN): HOTEL II CLASS

Name	Completed
. . . . . .	1959–1962

Builders:	Komsomol´sk
	Severodvinsk
Displacement:	5,000 tons surface
	6,000 tons submerged
Length:	377 ft 2 in (115.0 m) oa
Beam:	29 ft 6 in (9.0 m)
Draft:	23 ft (7.0 m)
Propulsion:	steam turbines; 30,000 shp; 2 shafts/6-bladed propellers
Reactors:	2 pressurized water
Speed:	20 knots surface
	25 knots submerged
Complement:	approx. 80
Missiles:	disarmed
ASW weapons:	torpedoes
Torpedoes:	6 21-in (533-mm) torpedo tubes (fwd)
	4 16-in (406-mm) torpedo tubes (aft)
Radars:	Snoop Tray
Sonars:	medium frequency

The Soviet Navy constructed eight Hotel-class SSBNs, with further production being halted because of the changes in strategic forces policy in 1959–1961 and the subsequent development of the more capable Yankee SSBN.

Completion dates for the original eight-ship class are given above; they were converted to the Hotel II configuration in 1962–1967.

Class: One Hotel II has been converted to the Hotel III configuration as test ship for the SS-N-8 missile and at least one to a´ communications submarine (SSQN); these submarines are listed separately in this chapter. Two others were decommissioned in the early 1980s and apparently stricken.

The four units listed here have had their three SS-N-5 missile tubes disabled in compliance with SALT requirements. Their future use is unknown.

One unit was named KRASNOGVARDETS (Red Guardsman).

Classification: Soviet PLARB type.

Conversion: Seven units were originally fitted with the surface-launch SS-N-4 Sark missile (designated Hotel I); they were refitted with the underwater-launch, longer-range SS-N-5 missile. One unit is believed to have been completed as Hotel II.

Engineering: The Hotel-class reactor plant is similar to that fitted in the Echo SSGN and November SSN classes.

ATTACK SUBMARINES (SS): NEW DESIGN

A new diesel-electric-propelled attack submarine (SS) can be expected to enter service by the early 1990s as the Soviet Navy continues to construct and operate large numbers of these craft in addition to providing them to Warsaw Pact and Third World navies. The new submarine will probably be larger than the Kilo class to accommodate ASW missiles—the SS-N-15 and possibly the SS-N-16.

Construction of the long-range Foxtrot and Tango classes have ceased, leaving the medium-range Kilo the only diesel submarine in series production when this edition went to press.

Hotel II-class submarine as an SSBN off the coast of Newfoundland. (1972, Ministry of Defence)

9 + ATTACK SUBMARINES (SS): KILO CLASS

Name	Launched	Completed
. . . . . . (1 unit)	Sep 1980	Apr 1982
. . . . . . (8 units)		1983–1986
. . . . . .		Building and planned

Builders:	Komsomol´sk
	Gor'kiy
	Sudomekh (Admiralty)
Displacement:	2,500 tons surface
	3,000 tons submerged
Length:	229 ft 7 in (70.0 m) oa
Beam:	32 ft 6 in (9.9 m)
Draft:	21 ft 4 in (6.5 m)
Propulsion:	diesel-electric; 1 shaft/6-bladed propeller
Speed:	12 knots surface
	25 knots submerged
Range:	
Complement:	approx. 60
Missiles:	... SA-N-( ) system
ASW weapons:	torpedoes [12]
Torpedoes:	6 21-in (533 mm) torpedo tubes (fwd)
Radars:	Snoop Tray
Sonars:	low frequency

Tango-class submarines moored at an Arctic submarine base. (Sovfoto, Semion Meistermann)

The Kilo is an advanced diesel attack submarine intended for Soviet use and possibly for foreign transfer. The first few units were built at Komsomol'sk.

Classification: Soviet PL type.

Design: The Kilo has a hull form somwhat similar to the U.S. ALBACORE (SS 569)/tear-drop design. The Kilo, however, is significantly slower than its foreign contemporaries.

Missiles: This was one of the first Soviet submarine classes to be fitted with an anti-aircraft missile system. It was fitted in the sail structure.

The Kilo SS is the latest Soviet diesel-electric attack submarine design. (1984, JMSDF)

20 ATTACK SUBMARINES (SS): TANGO CLASS

Name	Completed
. . . . . .	1972–1982

Builders:	Gor´kiy
Displacement:	3,200 tons surface
	3,900 tons submerged
Length:	301 ft 9 in (92.0 m) oa
Beam:	29 ft 6 in (9.0 m)
Draft:	23 ft (7.0 m)
Propulsion:	diesel-electric; diesel engines, 6,000 hp/electric motors 6,000 shp; 3 shafts
Speed:	20 knots surface
	16 knots submerged
Range:	
Complement:	approx. 70
Missiles:	.... SA-N-( ) in one or more units
ASW weapons:	torpedoes
	SS-N-15
Torpedoes:	10 21-in (533-mm) torpedo tubes (6 fwd 4 aft)
Radars:	Snoop Tray
Sonars:	low frequency

The Tango-class submarines are long-range attack craft, the successor to the Foxtrot class in Soviet service.

Classification: Soviet PL type.

Design: These submarines have significantly more pressure-hull volume than the Foxtrot class, with their increased space providing more battery capacity. Submerged endurance (i.e., on battery) is significantly greater than that of the Foxtrot class.

Missiles: One or more Tango-class submarines were fitted with a surface-to-air missile system, at least for evaluation and possibly for service use.

Tango-class SS with masts and periscopes raised.

A Tango-class submarine in the eastern Atlantic. (1981)

APPROX. 50 ATTACK SUBMARINES (SS): FOXTROT CLASS

Name	Completed
CHELYABINSKIY KOMSOMOLETS	
KOMSOMOLETS KAZAKHSTANA	
KUIBISHEVSKIY KOMSOMOLETS	
MAGNITOGORSKIY KOMSOMOLETS	1958–1967
UL'YANOVSKIY KOMSOMOLETS	
VLADIMIRSKIY KOMSOMOLETS	
YAROSLAVSKIY KOMSOMOLETS	
. . . . . . (40 + units)	

Builders:	Sudomekh, Leningrad
Displacement:	1,950 tons surface
	2,400 tons submerged
Length:	300 ft 2 in (91.5 m) oa
Beam:	24 ft 7 in (7.5 m)
Draft:	19 ft 8 in (6.0 m)
Propulsion:	diesel-electric; diesel engines, 6,000 hp/electric motors, 5,300 shp; 3 shafts
Speed:	16 knots surface
	15.5 knots submerged
Range:	11,000 n.miles at 8 knots
Complement:	approx. 75–80
ASW weapons:	torpedoes [22]
Torpedoes:	10 21-in (533-mm) torpedo tubes (6 fwd 4 aft)
Radars:	Snoop Tray
Sonars:	medium frequency

These are highly capable, long-range submarines derived from the Zulu class.

Class: This is the second largest class of diesel submarines built by any navy in the post–World War II period. Sixty-two units are believed to have been built for the Soviet Navy. Several units have operated as oceanographic research ships (see AGSS listing). Some Soviet units have been lost and others stricken.

An additional 17 Foxtrots were built for foreign transfer between 1967 and 1983 (all at the Sudomekh shipyard). These have gone to Cuba (3), India (8), and Libya (6).

Classification: Soviet PL type.

Engineering: Submerged (non-snorkel) endurance is estimated at more than seven days at very slow speed.

Names: Class names that are known honor komsomol (young Communist) groups.

The differences in the hull configuration of the Foxtrot (left) and Tango (right) are evident in this photo showing the undersea craft being serviced by an Oskol-class "floating workshop" (*plavuchaya masterskaya*). This is the PM-24 with twin 25-mm guns aft and a twin 57-mm gun mount forward.

Foxtrot-class SS with periscope, radio mast, and Snoop Slab radar visible. The snorkel exhaust is faired into the after end of the sail structure.

Foxtrot-class SS. (Soviet Navy)

Bow- and sail-mounted sonar of a Foxtrot-class submarine. (1982)

Foxtrot-class SS in the Pacific. These are considered efficient, long-range patrol submarines. (1984, JMSDF)

8 ATTACK SUBMARINES (SS): ROMEO CLASS

Name	Completed
. . . . . .	1958–1962

Builders:	Gor´kiy
Displacement:	1,330 tons surface
	1,700 tons submerged
Length:	252 ft 7 in (77.0 m) oa
Beam:	22 ft (6.7 m)
Draft:	16 ft 1 in (4.9 m)
Propulsion:	diesel-electric; diesel engines, 4,000 hp/electric motors, 3,000 shp; 2 shafts
Speed:	15.5 knots surface
	13 knots submerged
Range:	7,000 n.miles at 5 knots
Complement:	approx. 55

ASW weapons:	torpedoes [14]
Torpedoes:	8 21-in (533-mm) torpedo tubes (6 fwd 2 aft)
Radars:	Snoop Plate
Sonars:	medium frequency

The Romeo is a medium-range submarine, a much-improved successor to the previous Whiskey class.

Class: Twenty submarines of this class were built at Gor´kiy. The completion dates for the entire class are given above. After service in the Soviet Navy, two were transferred to Algeria, two to Bulgaria, six to Egypt, and two to Syria.

Construction of submarines of this design has also been undertaken in both China and North Korea, with two of the Chinese-built craft having been transferred to Egypt in 1982.

Classification: Soviet PL type.

A Romeo-class SS ballasted down. Soviet submarines have a considerable reserve buoyancy and generally ride much higher in the water. There is a large Quad Loop DF antenna fixed on the after end of the sail.

Romeo-class SS.

1(4) ATTACK SUBMARINE (SS): ZULU IV CLASS

Name	Completed
. . . . . .	1952–1955

Builders:	Severodvinsk
	Sudomekh
Displacement:	1,900 tons surface
	2,350 tons submerged
Length:	295 ft 2 in (90.0 m) oa
Beam:	24 ft 7 in (7.5 m)
Draft:	19 ft 8 in (6.0 m)
Propulsion:	diesel-electric; diesel engines, 6,000 hp; electric motors, 5,300 shp; 3 shafts
Speed:	18 knots surface
	16 knots submerged
Range:	9,500 n.miles at 8 knots
Complement:	approx. 70
Guns:	(removed)
ASW weapons:	torpedoes [22]
Torpedoes:	10 21-in (533-mm) torpedo tubes (6 fwd 4 aft)
Radars:	Snoop Plate
Sonars:	medium frequency

The first Soviet long-range submarines of the postwar era, the Zulu also provided the platform for the world's first ballistic-missile submarine. Four additional Zulu-class submarines are believed to be in reserve.

Class: A total of 26 Zulu-class submarines were built. Completion dates for the entire class are given above. Several were converted in the 1950s to ballistic missile submarines, being fitted with two tubes for the SS-N-4 SLBM (redesignated Zulu V); all were subsequently scrapped. Four or five are believed to serve as oceanographic research ships (see below).

Classification: Soviet PL type.

Design: This class incorporates several German design features. The (Zulu I to III configuration of this class had deck guns and no snorkel. All were updated to Zulu IV standards, with guns removed, a snorkel fitted and other features incorporated.)

The Zulu-class submarine bears considerable resemblance to the German Type XXI U-boat that became operational in the closing days of World War II. (1979, Ministry of Defence)

Zulu IV-class SS.

APPROX. 50 (60–70?) ATTACK SUBMARINES (SS): WHISKEY CLASS

Name	Completed
PSKOVSKIY KOMSOMOLETS ······	1951–1957

Builders:	Baltic Shipyard, Leningrad Gor'kiy Komsomol'sk Marti (Nikolayev south)
Displacement:	1,050 tons surface 1,350 tons submerged
Length:	246 ft (75.0 m) oa
Beam:	20 ft 8 in (6.3 m)
Draft:	15 ft 9 in (4.8 m)
Propulsion:	diesel-electric; diesel engines, 4,000 hp/electric motors, 2,500 shp; 2 shafts
Speed:	17 knots surface 13.5 knots submerged
Range:	6,000 n.miles at 5 knots
Complement:	approx. 50–55
Guns:	(removed)
ASW weapons:	torpedoes [12]
Torpedoes:	6 21-in (533-mm) torpedo tubes (4 fwd 2 aft)
Radars:	Snoop Plate
Sonars:	Tamir/medium frequency

This was the first Soviet postwar submarine, built in larger numbers than any other submarine class in peacetime and still widely used. Of the surviving units, some 50 are in various degrees of active status and about 60 to 70 more are believed to be in reserve (in varying degrees of preservation). Some active units are apparently employed in research-experimental roles (see below).

Class: Four Soviet shipyards produced 236 Whiskey-class submarines before the program was abruptly halted. Completion data for the entire class are listed above. Thirteen of these were converted to various missile configurations to carry the SS-N-3 Shaddock missile (SSG); four or five to radar picket configuration (SSR); and two to fisheries research ships (renamed SEVERYANKA and SLAVYANKA). All of these specialized boats have been discarded.

At least 39 Whiskey-class submarines have been transferred to foreign navies: Albania (4), Bulgaria (2), China (6), Cuba (1), Egypt (7), Indonesia (12), North Korea (2), and Poland (5). The single Cuban unit was transferred in 1979 as a non-operational training and battery-charging craft. Additional submarines of this design have been built in China.

Classification: Soviet PL type.

Design: The class was designed during World War II, but some German features were incorporated during postwar redesign. Units built from the Whiskey I, II, and IV designs had light anti-aircraft guns; most were subsequently modified to the definitive Whiskey V configuration.

Figure 12-2 shows the various Whiskey-class conning tower configurations. Note that the Whiskey IV and V as well as the special-purpose types have a distinctive snorkel exhaust at the after end of the conning tower. The one single-cylinder Whiskey SSG had the Shaddock missile tube on the main deck aft of the conning tower.

COASTAL SUBMARINES (SS): QUEBEC CLASS

All 30 of the coastal submarines of the Quebec class built at Sudomekh have been stricken. See 3rd edition (page 116) for details.

Whiskey-class SS.

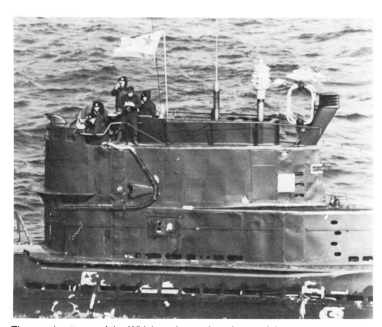

The conning tower of the Whiskey-class submarine: at right are a raised, mast-mounted Stop Light ECM antenna; a fixed Quad Loop DF antenna; and the fixed snorkel exhaust. (1982)

Whiskey-class SS.

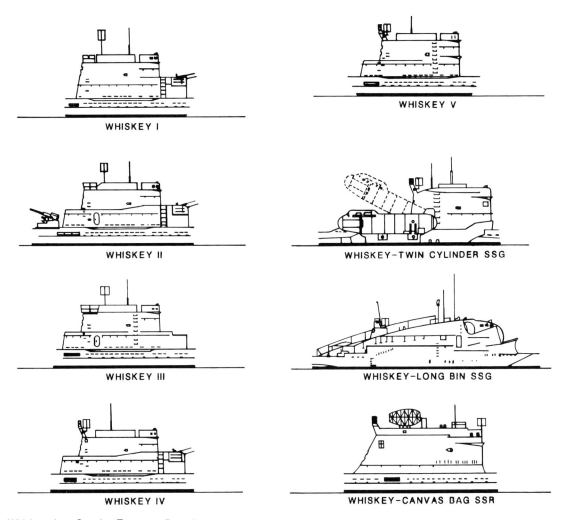

WHISKEY I

WHISKEY II

WHISKEY III

WHISKEY IV

WHISKEY V

WHISKEY-TWIN CYLINDER SSG

WHISKEY-LONG BIN SSG

WHISKEY-CANVAS BAG SSR

Whiskey-class Conning Tower configurations

AUXILIARY SUBMARINES

The Soviet Navy operates about a score of auxiliary and special-purpose submarines.

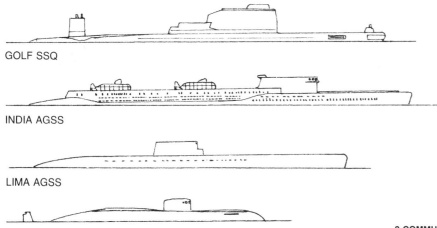

GOLF SSQ

INDIA AGSS

LIMA AGSS

BRAVO SST

1 COMMUNICATIONS SUBMARINE (SSQN): HOTEL CLASS (FORMER SSBN)

One Hotel II-class SSBN has been reconfigured as a communication submarine, similar to three Golf-class SSB conversions.

See Hotel-class SSXN listing for characteristics.

3 COMMUNICATIONS SUBMARINES (SSQ): GOLF CLASS (FORMER SSB)

Three Golf I-class submarines were converted in the 1970s to serve as communications ships. The concept of an underwater command-and-communications ship (for presidential use) was considered for the U.S. nuclear submarine TRITON (SSRN 586) but was never carried out. One modified Golf is assigned to the Northern Fleet and two to the Pacific Fleet.

See Golf-class SSB listing for characteristics.

Golf-class SSQ with Pert Spring antenna raised from the conning tower; several crewmen are sun-bathing.

Golf-class SSQ: the communications mast on the port side of the conning tower folds down into a deck recess; the after mast partially retracts. (1984, JMSDF)

1 NUCLEAR-PROPELLED RESEARCH SUBMARINE (AGSSN): X-RAY

Name	Launched	Completed
. . . . . .	1983	1984

Builders:	Sudomekh
Displacement:	
Length:	206 ft 8 in (63.0 m) oa
Beam:	
Draft:	
Propulsion:	
Reactors:	1
Speed:	
Range:	
Complement:	
Torpedoes:	(probably unarmed)
Radars:	
Sonars:	

This is a small, one-of-a-kind submarine in some respects similar to the U.S. nuclear-propelled submersible NR-1.

1 NUCLEAR-PROPELLED AUXILIARY SUBMARINE (AGSSN): UNIFORM

Name	Launched	Completed
. . . . . .	June 1982	1983

Builders:	Sudomekh, Leningrad
Displacement:	
	2,000 tons submerged
Length:	
Beam:	
Draft:	
Propulsion:	
Reactors:	1
Speed:	
Range:	
Complement:	
Torpedoes:	(probably unarmed)
Radars:	
Sonars:	

The Uniform is a one-of-a-kind research or special-mission submarine.

Design: This is the first Soviet nuclear-propelled submarine with single-hull construction.

2 RESCUE AND SALVAGE SUBMARINES (AGSS): INDIA CLASS

Name	Completed
. . . . . .	1979
. . . . . .	1980

Builders:	Komsomol'sk
Displacement:	3,900 tons surface
	4,000 tons submerged
Length:	347 ft 8 in (106.0 m) oa
Beam:	32 ft 10 in (10.0 m)
Draft:	
Propulsion:	diesel-electric; 2 shafts
Speed:	15 knots surface
	15 knots submerged
Range:	
Complement:	
Torpedoes:	(probably unarmed)
Radars:	
Sonars:	medium frequency

These submarines are specially configured for rescue and salvage operations, being fitted to carry two 36-foot submersibles. One unit is assigned to the Pacific Fleet and one to the Northern Fleet; the latter transited the Arctic route in 1980.

Design: These submarines were designed from the outset for salvage and rescue. Their hulls are configured for high surface speed, probably to permit rapid deployment to operational areas. Two submersibles are carried semi-recessed in tandem deck wells aft of the sail structure. While submerged there is direct access from lower hatches in the submersibles to the carrying submarine (as in the U.S. Navy's DSRV rescue submersibles); this facilitates clandestine and under-ice operations. The submarines can supplant saturation during operations.

It is assumed that these submarines are fitted with bow torpedo tubes.

1 AUXILIARY SUBMARINE (AGSSN): ECHO II CLASS (Former SSGN)

One Echo II-class SSGN has been modified for special operations; the conversion was completed in 1980. Two U.S. nuclear attack submarines were modified for specialized research duties, the SEAWOLF (SSN 575) and HALIBUT (SSGN/SSN 587); the latter has been laid up in reserve.

Stern view of the Northern Fleet's India-class submarine showing the two rescue and salvage submersibles "nested" in the deck. The diving planes are visible. (1982, U.S. Navy)

The Pacific Fleet's India-class submarine in rough seas. Note the bow sonar antenna. (Courtesy *Ships of the World*)

1 AUXILIARY SUBMARINE (AGSS): LIMA

Name	Completed
. . . . . .	1978

Builders:	Sudomekh (Admiralty)
Displacement:	2,000 tons surface
	2,450 tons submerged
Length:	282 ft 1 in (86.0 m) oa
Beam:	31 ft 2 in (9.5 m)
Draft:	24 ft 3 in (7.4 m)
Propulsion:	diesel-electric
Speed:	
Range:	
Complement:	
Torpedoes:	(unarmed)
Radars:	
Sonars:	

The exact purpose and characteristics of this submarine are unknown. The hull length-to-beam ratio is relatively small, there is a large, flat deck area, the sail structure is set well amidships, and there is a fixed radar mast. There are probably thrusters as well.

The submarine is reported to be in the Black Sea.

Few OCEANOGRAPHIC RESEARCH SUBMARINES (AGSS): FOXTROT CLASS

Several Foxtrot-class attack submarines have been employed for oceanographic research operations. When so employed, they carry "star" names. The following have been sighted: GLOBUS, JUPITER, SATURN, SIRIUS, and REGUL.

Few OCEANOGRAPHIC RESEARCH SUBMARINES (AGSS): ZULU IV CLASS

Three or four Zulu IV–class submarines have been converted to oceanographic research ships. The names LIRA, MARS, VEVA, and possibly ORION have been identified with these submarines. At least some if not all have been fitted with thrusters for underwater maneuver and hover, and are fitted for diver lockout operations.

Few RESEARCH SUBMARINES (AGSS): WHISKEY CLASS

Several Whiskey-class submarines are employed in the research role. (The two Whiskey-class submarines converted to fisheries research ships have been discarded.)

A Foxtrot-class submarine employed in research, with the name REGUL on her sail. (1984, JMSDF)

A Zulu IV submarine configured for oceanographic research with the name MARS as she transited the Tsugaru Straits. (1980, courtesy *Ships of the World*)

4 TARGET TRAINING SUBMARINES (SST): BRAVO CLASS

Name	Completed
. . . . . . (1 unit)	1967
. . . . . . (2 units)	1968
. . . . . . (1 unit)	1970

Builders:	Komsomol´sk
Displacement:	2,400 tons surface
	2,900 tons submerged
Length:	239 ft 5 in (73.0 m) oa
Beam:	32 ft 2 in (9.8 m)
Draft:	24 ft 11 in (7.3 m)
Propulsion:	diesel-electric; 1 shaft
Speed:	14 knots surface
	16 knots submerged
Range:	
Complement:	approx. 65
ASW weapons:	torpedoes
Torpedoes:	6 21-in (533-mm) torpedo tubes (fwd)
Radars:	Snoop Tray
Sonars:	

These are specialized target training submarines for ASW forces. They are similar in concept to the USS MARLIN (SST 2) and MACKEREL (SST 1), built in the 1950s. They may also be used to train crews and, in wartime, could be employed operationally.

Design: The submarines are specially configured to serve as "hard" targets for ASW practice torpedoes.

A Bravo-class target and training submarine. The after "hump" is believed to be a padded area for taking hits from practice torpedoes. There is a sonar installation forward, and the submarines are probably armed.

A Bravo-class target and training submarine.

MIDGET SUBMARINES AND SUBMERSIBLES

The Soviet Navy operates several small submarines, apparently for use by *Spetsnaz* special forces and for submarine rescue and salvage activities. The two INDIA-class submarines are each configured to carry two of the latter craft. Other submarines, including the converted Echo II, may be modified for transporting submersibles (as was the USS HALIBUT).

Two types have been identified with the India-class submarines, the 37-foot craft and a 40-foot craft. The submarine rescue ships of the EL´BRUS class can accommodate these craft plus a 45-foot submersible. A 96-foot midget submarine has also been identified in naval operations.

A number of non-naval research craft have been identified, some of which support military programs. These carry the designations ARGUS, ATLANT 2, OKEANOLOG, PISCES, SKAT, MODERN SEVER, SEVER 2, and TINRO 2.

A rescue and salvage submersible being carried by an India-class submarine. These craft are about 40 feet (12.2 m) long.

The mooring tender/lift ship KIL-32 with a salvage submersible on deck. This type of submersible is also carried by the large EL´BRUS-class submarine rescue ships; smaller research submersibles are carried by naval and civilian research ships. (1983, U.S. Navy, PH2 P. Soutar)

13
Aircraft Carriers

In many respects the aircraft carrier has been the major surprise in the post-World War II development of the Soviet Navy. The Soviets in 1986 completed their fourth VSTOL carrier of the Kiev class of 43,000 tons and continued the construction of two nuclear-propelled carriers that will displace an estimated 70,000 tons.

Among the major unknowns in the West concerning the Soviet carrier program are the precise roles intended for these ships as well as the configuration and capabilities of the nuclear ship. The Soviets have not revealed publicly any details of the nuclear carrier. The U.S. government, on the basis of information derived from satellite photography, other intelligence sources, and a carrier flight deck mock-up in the Soviet Union, believes that the ship will eventually have arresting wires (cross-deck pendants) for Conventional Take-Off and Landing (CTOL) aircraft. However, despite early predictions that the ship would have catapults—four were mentioned—it now appears more likely that "ski-ramps" for VSTOL or CTOL aircraft will be fitted, like the ones installed in the British VSTOL carriers of the Invincible class and the Hermes. Catapults may

be fitted to the Soviet ship at a later date. The flight deck mock-up is laid out at the Saki airfield in the Crimea to simulate the carrier. It is some 1,050 feet in length and has arresting wires installed.

The first Soviet nuclear carrier is expected to commence sea trials in 1988–1989. Allowing time for workup with her air group, the ship should be operational by 1990–1991. Because only one building dock—at the Nikolayev south shipyard—can accommodate warships of this size, a second ship is being constructed about four years behind the first. This schedule could give the Soviet Navy three such ships by the late 1990s *if* the required resources are allocated for an aircraft carrier program.

The Kiev-class VSTOL carriers and the Moskva-class cruiser-helicopter carriers are described in this chapter. While the latter ships appear to have been built to counter the U.S. Polaris missile submarines, a task they were incapable of performing, they have been useful in more conventional helicopter carrier and missile-cruiser roles. Both the Kiev and Moskva classes have the armament of contemporary cruisers.

The Kiev, showing how the forward portion of the main deck is devoted to weapons. The angled flight deck markings, with seven helicopter spots, are clearly visible, with two Forgers and five helicopters (four with rotors folded) parked to the right of the safety line. (1985, NATO Standing Naval Force Atlantic, L/A Kev Jeffries)

(2) NUCLEAR-PROPELLED AIRCRAFT CARRIERS

Name	Builder	Laid down	Launched	Completed	Status
. . . . . .	Black Sea Shipyard, Nikolayev (south)	1982	5 Dec 1985	(1988–1989)	Building
. . . . . .	Black Sea Shipyard, Nikolayev (south)	Dec 1985	(1988)		

Displacement:	approx. 70,000 tons
Length:	approx. 1,000 ft (305.0 m) oa
Beam:	
Draft:	
Propulsion:	steam turbines; 4 shafts
Reactors:	probably 4
Speed:	30+ knots
Complement:	
Aircraft:	approx. 60–75
Missiles:	
Guns:	
ASW weapons:	
Guns:	
ASW weapons:	
Torpedoes:	
Radars:	
Sonars:	
EW systems:	

Preparations for the construction of the first ship were initially observed by Western intelligence, apparently by U.S. reconnaissance satellites, late in 1979. This indicates that a decision was taken to construct the ship under the five-year economic-defense plan begun in 1976.

The carriers are being constructed in the same building dock as the KIEV-class carriers. The dock was enlarged after the fourth ship of the earlier class was started, the first nuclear ship was laid down shortly after launching of the BAKU. Completion of the lead ship can be expected before the end of the 1986–1990 five-year plan.

The first ship was launched and the second unit was apparently laid down in December 1985. This ceremony may have been related to the retirement that month of Admiral Gorshkov as CinC of the Soviet Navy.

Aircraft: The estimate of 60–75 fixed-wing aircraft is approximate. It is assumed that existing types will be adopted (see chapter 28) and that all will be stowed in hangars.

Design: The ships are expected to be fitted eventually with catapults and arresting wires for the operation of conventional fixed-wing aircraft. As noted above, initially they may operate a mixture of VSTOL and STOL aircraft plus helicopters.

Engineering: It is anticipated that the ships will have a Combined Nuclear And Steam (CONAS) propulsion plant, probably similar to that of the missile cruiser KIROV.

Names: In 1984 German sources predicted the lead ship would be named SOVETSKIY SOYUZ (Soviet Union); in 1985 unofficial U.S. Navy sources predicted the name would be KREMLIN.

4 AIRCRAFT CARRIERS: "KIEV" CLASS

Name	Builder	Laid down	Launched	Completed	Status
KIEV	Black Sea Shipyard, Nikolayev (south)	Sep 1970	31 Dec 1972	May 1975	**Northern**
MINSK	Black Sea Shipyard, Nikolayev (south)	Dec 1972	May 1975	Feb 1978	**Pacific**
NOVOROSSIYSK	Black Sea Shipyard, Nikolayev (south)	Oct 1975	Dec 1978	Sep 1982	**Pacific**
BAKU	Black Sea Shipyard, Nikolayev (south)	1978	Mar 1982	1986	Trials

Displacement:	36,000 tons standard
	43,000 tons full load (see Design notes)
Length:	818 ft 4 in (249.5 m) wl
	895 ft 5 in (273.0 m) oa
Beam:	107 ft 3 in (32.7 m)
Extreme width:	154 ft 10 in (47.2 m)
Draft:	32 ft 10 in (10.0 m)
Propulsion:	steam turbines; 200,000 shp; 4 shafts
Boilers:	8
Speed:	32 knots
Range:	4,000 n.miles at 31 knots
	13,500 n.miles at 18 knots
Complement:	approx. 1,200 (including air group)
Aircraft:	30 {12 or 13 Yak-38 Forger VSTOL / 14 to 17 Ka-25 Hormone/Ka-27 Helix helicopters
Missiles:	2 twin SA-N-3 Goblet launchers [72]
	2 twin SA-N-4 launchers [40], not fitted in NOVOROSSIYSK and BAKU
	12 verticle SA-N-9 launchers [96] in NOVOROSSIYSK and BAKU
	8 SS-N-12 Sandbox launch tubes [8 + 8 reloads]

Guns:	4 76.2-mm/59-cal AA (2 twin)
	8 30-mm 65-cal close-in (8 multi-barrel)
ASW weapons:	1 twin SUW-N-1 missile launcher
	2 RBU-6000 rocket launchers
	torpedoes
Torpedoes:	10 21-in (533-mm) torpedo tubes (2 × quin)

Radars:	KIEV and MINSK	NOVOROSSIYSK and BAKU
	4 Bass Tilt (fire control)	4 Bass Tilt
	2 Don-2 (navigation)	3 Palm Frond (navigation)
	1 Don Kay (navigation)	
	2 Head Lights (fire control)	2 Head Lights
	2 Owl Screech (fire control)	2 Owl Screech
	2 Pop Group (fire control)	
	1 Trap Door (fire control)	1 Trap Door
	1 Top Sail (3-D air search)	1 Top Sail
	1 Top Steer (3-D air search)	1 Top Steer
	1 Top Knot (air control)	1 Top Knot

Sonars:	low frequency (hull mounted, bistatic)
	medium frequency (variable depth)

EW systems: Bell Clout
                   Rum Tub
                   Side Globe (not fitted in NOVOROSSIYSK and BAKU)
                   Top Hat-A/B

These ships are the first Soviet aircraft carriers to be built, having a full flight deck and a hull designed from the outset as a carrier. Two previous Soviet carrier programs, of the late 1930s and early 1950s, were cancelled early on. Construction of this class was probably approved in the five-year plan that began in 1966.

Aircraft: On her initial (1976) deployment to the Mediterranean the KIEV operated 25 aircraft—9 Yak-36 Forger-A and 1 Yak-36 Forger-B VTOL aircraft plus 14 Ka-25 Hormone-A and 1 Ka-25 Hormone-B helicopters. All could be carried on the hangar deck. Maximum hangar capacity is estimated at 30 to 35 aircraft. (U.S. aircraft carriers stow less than half of their embarked aircraft in the hangar.) The two later ships embark Ka-27 Helix helicopters as well as Hormones.

Classification: The Soviet Navy originally classified the KIEV as a heavy anti-submarine cruiser (*tyazholyi protivolodchyi kreuzer*). However, by the early 1980s the ship was being referred to as a tactical aircraft-carrying cruiser (*takticheskoye avianosnyy kreyser*). Some senior Soviet naval officers referred to the ships as anti-submarine carriers or simply aircraft carriers.

Design: This class has a very large island structure on the starboard side and an angled flight deck, canted at about 4.5° to port from the centerline. No catapults or arresting wires are fitted. Unlike U.S. aircraft carriers, the KIEV has a full missile cruiser's armament of anti-air, anti-ship, and anti-submarine weapons. Most of these are fitted forward, depriving the ship of significant forward flight deck area. Portions of the flight deck are covered with blast-resistant (refractory) tile for VTOL aircraft operation.

The hull design features a large underwater bow "bulb," probably containing a sonar; boat stowage is cut into the after hull. Aft, the ship has a freeboard of some 42 ft 6 in (large carriers have more than 60 ft). The KIEV's stern counter has an opening for Variable-Depth Sonar (VDS) and a reinforced panel to resist exhaust blast as aircraft hover immediately astern while transitioning from conventional to vertical-landing flight configuration.

There are two relatively small aircraft elevators, one alongside the island and one immediately abaft the island; these are approximately 63 ft × 34 ft and 60 ft 8 in × 15 ft 5 in, respectively. There are also three or four weapon elevators that service the flight deck, one forward of the forward aircraft elevator, and two or three on the starboard side, aft of the island. (On some ships the two aftermost weapon elevators have been combined.)

Active fin stabilizers are fitted.

Since publication of the previous (third) edition of this volume in 1983, some Western analysts have increased estimates of the displacement of this ship, earlier thought to be 32,000 tons standard and 37,000–38,000 tons full load. The exact displacement of each ship is still a matter of some speculation.

Electronics: The EW suites of the second pair of ships differ from those of the earlier pair.

Missiles: The KIEV and older KYNDA cruiser classes are the only Soviet classes fitted with reloads for surface-to-surface missiles. The larger SS-N-12 missiles are stowed in a below-deck magazine and carried to the launch tubes by an athwartships elevator. Eight (or possibly more) reloads are stowed in the magazine, giving the ship a total of 16 Sandbox missiles.

Names: These ships are named for major Soviet cities. The fourth ship was originally thought by Western intelligence to be named for the city of Kaharkov, but she went to sea with the name BAKU.

NATO assigned the code name Kurile to this class before the Soviet name KIEV became known. Subsequently the name KIEV was adopted for reporting purposes.

Operational: The KIEV made her first operational deployment to the Mediterranean in July 1976. She transferred to the Northern Fleet that August, stayed with that fleet until late December 1977, then returned to the Mediterranean–Black Sea area. She appears to be permanently based in the Murmansk area but returns to the Nikolayev yards for overhaul/upkeep.

The MINSK transited to the Pacific Fleet in 1979, steaming around the Cape of Good Hope and across the Indian Ocean. Her home port is Vladivostok. She was followed to the Far East by the NOVOROSSIYSK in 1984.

The stern of the NOVOROSSIYSK showing the blast shield for approaching VSTOL aircraft (dark square at left), the doors for the VDS (below Soviet emblem), and opening for stern mooring lines. She has two lowered aircraft elevators; also visible is the (raised) bomb lift, just above the Forgers. She differs from the two earlier ships in several ways, including wind baffles forward (just beyond forward end of parking area) and a larger parking deck abaft the island. (1983, U.S. Navy)

The MINSK at high speed in the Pacific. No aircraft are visible on her flight deck; all of her Forger fighter-attack aircraft and helicopters can be stowed on the hangar deck. Note how the hull carries up to the main (flight) deck and the boat stowage is cut into the hull aft. (1984, Japanese Maritime Self-Defense Force)

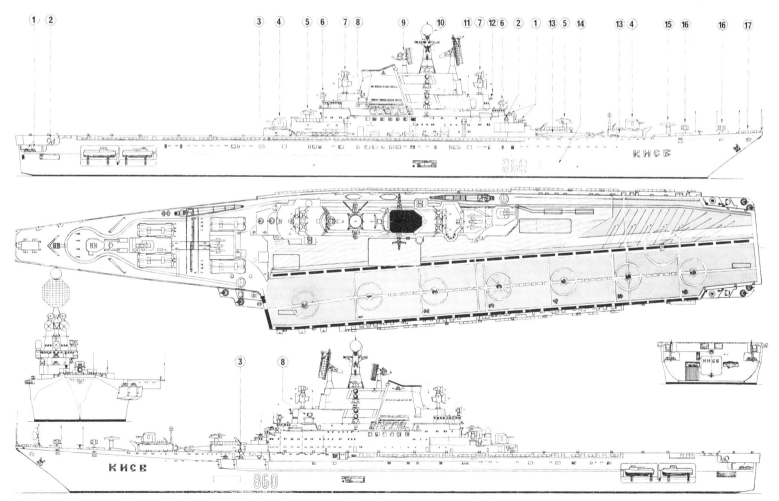

1. 30-mm Gatling gun 2. Bass Tilt radar 3. SA-N-4 launcher (retracted) 4. twin 76.2-mm guns 5. SA-N-3 launchers 6. Owl Screech radar 7. Head Lights radar 8. Pop Group radar 9. Top Steer radar 10. Top Knot radar 11. Top Sail radar 12. Don-2 radar 13. SS-N-12 missile tubes 14. 533-mm torpedo tubes (behind shutters) 15. SUW-N-1 launcher 16. RBU-6000 launchers 17. Trap Door radar (retracted) (M.J. Dodgson)

2 HELICOPTER CARRIERS: "MOSKVA" CLASS

Name	Builder	Laid down	Launched	Completed	Status
MOSKVA	Black Sea Shipyard, Nikolayev (south)	1962	1964	July 1967	**Black Sea**
LENINGRAD	Black Sea Shipyard, Nikolayev (south)	1964	1966	1968	**Black Sea**

Displacement:	14,500 tons standard
	17,000–18,000 tons full load
Length:	619 ft 11 in (189.0 m) oa
Beam:	85 ft 3 in (26.0 m)
Extreme width:	111 ft 10 in (34.1 m)
Draft:	24 ft 11 in (7.6 m)
Propulsion:	steam turbines; 100,000 shp; 2 shafts
Boilers:	4
Speed:	30–31 knots
Range:	4,500 n.miles at 29 knots
	14,000 n.miles at 12 knots
Complement:	approx. 850 (including air group)
Helicopters:	14 Ka-25 Hormone helicopters
Missiles:	2 twin SA-N-3 Goblet launchers [44]
Guns:	4 57-mm/70-cal AA (2 × 2)
ASW weapons:	1 twin SUW-N-1 missile launcher
	2 RBU-6000 rocket launchers
Torpedoes:	(removed)
Radars:	3 Don-2 (navigation)
	2 Head Lights (fire control)
	1 Head Net-C (3-D air search)
	2 Muff Cob (fire control)
	1 Top Sail (3-D air search)
Sonars:	low frequency (hull mounted)
	medium frequency (variable depth)
EW systems:	Bell series
	Side Globe
	Top Hat

These are hybrid helicopter carriers/missile cruisers. They were developed to counter Western strategic missile submarines, but the program was aborted after two ships were built because of the expanding capabilities of missile submarines. Both ships are based in the Black Sea and periodically deploy to the Mediterranean; they have also operated in the Atlantic and the LENINGRAD in the northwest Indian Ocean region.

The MOSKVA was trials ship for the Yak-38 Forger.

Class: Additional ships of this class were probably planned; some Western analysts estimate that there are as many as 12 of the ships.

Classification: Soviet PKR type.

Design: These ships are missile cruisers forward. Aft of the superstructure they have a clear, open flight deck. The superstructure is "stepped" forward to support missile launchers and radars, and has a smooth after face. A small hangar is located between the stack uptakes in the superstructure. Two elevators connect the flight deck to the hangar deck. The flight deck is approximately 282 ft × 112 ft.

The MOSKVA class introduced the SA-N-3 missile system as well as Top Sail and Head Lights radars to Soviet warships.

Names: These ships are named for the country's two traditional capital cities.

Operational: The MOSKVA was modified in the early 1970s for flight tests of the Forger VSTOL aircraft (she has since reverted to her original configuration).

Torpedoes: Two five-tube 21-in rotating banks of torpedo tubes were fitted into the sides of the ships, located immediately aft of the accommodation ladders. They were deleted in the mid-1970s.

A MOSKVA-class carrier. These ships have an unusual hull design, the widest point being aft of amidships. The design was flawed, with the ships riding down by the bow a few meters.

The LENINGRAD with an Mi-8 Hip minesweeping helicopter visible on her flight deck. These ships, primarily ASW cruisers, carry heavy anti-air and ASW batteries forward—weapons and electronics equal to missile cruisers of their time. The SUW-N-1 and SA-N-3 launchers, Head Lights radars, Head Net-C radar, and Top Sail radar are neatly stepped. (French Navy)

A pair of Hormone helicopters with their rotors folded on a MOSKVA-class carrier. The one at right is on a partially lowered elevator. These lifts are too small to accommodate the Hip or Haze helicopters flown by the Soviet Navy.

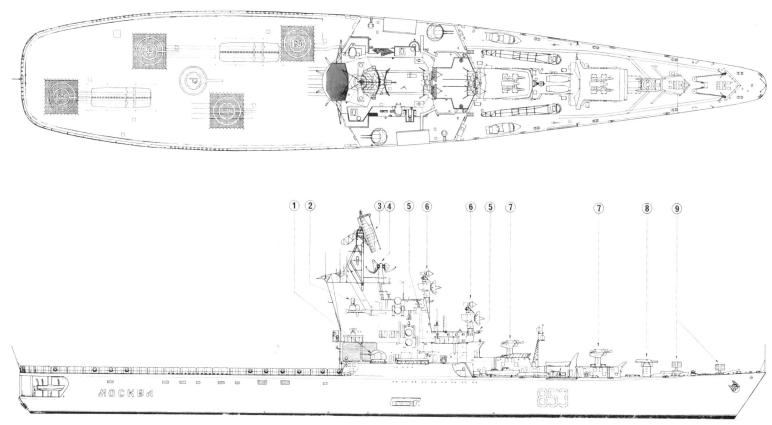

1. twin 57-mm guns 2. Muff Cob radar 3. Top Sail radar 4. Head Net-C radar 5. Don-2 radar 6. Head Lights radar 7. SA-N-3 launcher 8. SUW-N-1 launcher 9. RBU-6000 launcher (M.J. Dodgson)

The aft perspective of the LENINGRAD steaming off Scotland; one of her flight deck hangar doors is open, and the two elevators are lowered. The five helicopter spots have nets rigged to retard helicopter movement during rough-weather landings. The stern VDS is also visible. (1980, Royal Navy)

14
Cruisers

The Soviet Navy has an impressive cruiser construction program, although its future is one of the major questions of Western observers. The Soviet Navy has constructed cruiser-type ships in three of its postwar development phases. During the first phase, the 14 SVERDLOVS were built (completed in the years 1951–1954); they were refinements of the prewar CHAPAYEV design. During the second phase, the Kynda, Kresta I/II, and Kara classes were built (completed in the years 1962–1980). The third phase has seen development of the current KIROV and SLAVA programs.

The KIROVS are the largest surface warships except for aircraft carriers built by any nation since World War II. There will be at least three ships of this class, providing major platforms for anti-aircraft, anti-submarine, and anti-surface roles. The ships have the long-range endurance provided by nuclear propulsion.

The SLAVA represents perhaps the major enigma in Soviet surface-combatant construction. The ship, configured primarily for an anti-ship role, has the heaviest surface-to-surface missile battery of any Soviet warship except for the KIROV and possibly KIEV classes. The SLAVA has half the primary anti-aircraft system of the KIROV (SA-N-6 launchers/ Top Dome radar) and minimal anti-submarine capabilities, and she is gas turbine, not nuclear, propelled. Note that many of her weapons and sensors are from a previous generation, with the SA-N-6/Top Dome and 130-mm guns being the major contemporary weapons. One U.S intelligence officer said, "It was as if the Soviets simply took what sys-

tems were lying around the shipyard and put them into an old hull design." Still, the SLAVA could have a significant impact in many wartime situations.

The SLAVAS were constructed at the Nikolayev north shipyard, which had previously built the seven Kara-class cruisers (completed 1973–1980). The SLAVA could have been considered the successor for series production at that yard. A rate of one ship per year would have been feasible. But the building rate has been much slower, and when this edition went to press, there were no other warships on the building ways at Nikolayev north except for modified Kashin-class destroyers for the Indian Navy.

It is not clear why the SLAVA-class ships are being constructed. Possible answers include: (1) these ships were intended as replacements for the four Kynda-class rocket cruisers, (2) they were intended as an interim design, making use of readily available components, to maintain cruiser production at the Nikolayev north yard pending completion of a new large surface combatant design, or (3) the Soviets simply do not have the resources for large numbers of the SLAVA class in concert with the remainder of their large surface-warship program.

Operational: Fleet assignments for cruisers are listed to the extent the data are available from Soviet and Western sources. However, ships regularly transit between the European fleet areas for exercises and overhauls. Also, the exact status of some SVERDLOV-class ships cannot be ascertained with certainty.

The KIROV at anchor—the largest surface combatant built by any nation since the end of World War II. The KIROVS are multi-purpose ships with high speed and long endurance (1985)

2 + 2 NUCLEAR-PROPELLED BATTLED CRUISERS: "KIROV" CLASS

Name	Builder	Laid down	Launched	Completed	Status
KIROV	Baltic Shipyard, Leningrad	Jun 1973	26 Dec 1977	Sep 1980	**Northern**
FRUNZE	Baltic Shipyard, Leningrad	Jan 1978	23 May 1981	Aug 1984	**Pacific**
. . . . . .	Baltic Shipyard, Leningrad	1983	1985	(1988)	Building
. . . . . .	Baltic Shipyard, Leningrad	1986(?)			Building

Displacement:	24,000 tons standard
	28,000 tons full load
Length:	754 ft 5 in (230.0 m) wl
	813 ft 5 in (248.0 m) oa
Beam:	91 ft 10 in (28.0 m)
Draft:	28 ft 11 in (8.8 m)
Propulsion:	CONAS: steam turbines; 150,000 shp; 2 shafts
Reactors:	2 pressurized water
Boilers:	2
Speed:	32 knots
Range:	virtually unlimited (see Engineering notes)
Complement:	approx. 800
Helicopters:	3 Ka-25 Hormone or Ka-27 Helix
Missiles:	2 twin SA-N-4 launchers [40]
	12 rotary SA-N-6 launchers [96]
	16 vertical SA-N-9 launchers [128] in FRUNZE
	20 SS-N-19 tubes
Guns:	2 100-mm/70-cal DP (2 single) in KIROV
	2 130-mm/70-cal DP (1 twin) in FRUNZE
	8 30-mm/65-cal close-in (8 multi-barrel)
ASW weapons:	2 SS-N-14 Silex launch tubes [8-12] in KIROV
	1 RBU-6000 rocket launcher
	2 RBU-1000 rocket launchers
	torpedoes
Torpedoes:	8 21-in (533-mm) torpedo tubes (2 quad)
Radars:	4 Bass Tilt (fire control)
	2 Eye Bowl (fire control) in KIROV
	1 Kite Screech (fire control)
	3 Palm Fronds (navigation)
	2 Pop Groups (fire control)
	2 Top Dome (fire control)
	1 Top Pair (3-D air search)
	1 Top Steer (3-D air search)
	2 Cross Sword (?) (fire control) in FRUNZE
Sonars:	low frequency (bow mounted)
	low frequency (variable depth)
EW systems:	KIROV FRUNZE
	10 Bell-series 10 Bell-series
	8 Side Globe 8 . . . . . .
	2 Rum Tub

The KIROVs are the largest warships except for aircraft carriers built by any nation since World War II. They have an elegant, streamlined design, reminiscent of earlier battle cruisers. The Soviet ships are significantly larger than their U.S. contemporaries (CGN types) as well as the U.S. strike cruiser (CSGN) proposed in the 1970s but never built. The only larger surface combatants in service with any navy today are the U.S. battleships of the IOWA (BB 61) class.

The KIROV is assigned to the Northern Fleet. The FRUNZE transited to the Far East in 1985. (See Operational notes.)

Aircraft: The ships each carry three helicopters for ASW (Hormone-A in KIROV and Helix-A in FRUNZE) and for over-the-horizon targeting of the SS-N-19 missiles (Hormone-B). (See Design notes.)

Classification: Soviet RKR type. The NATO designation BAL-COM-1 (Baltic Combatant No. 1) was used before the lead ship appeared with the name KIROV.

The term *battle cruiser* has been widely used in the West and seems appropriate in view of the ship's size, hull lines, and firepower.[1]

Design: The KIROVs present an impressive, powerful appearance. The ship is credited with excellent seakeeping capabilities.

The design provides for a long forecastle, with the RBU-6000 and (in the KIROV) SS-N-14 launchers visible, and the large SA-N-6 and SS-N-19 batteries recessed below the main deck. The principal missile batteries are forward, leaving the after portion of the hull available for machinery and the helicopter hangar and large landing area. The ships have large superstructures with numerous radars, EW antennas, and weapons.

The FRUNZE has an enlarged deckhouse forward of the bridge and an after superstructure that has been extended farther aft. She has only a single, 130-mm gun mount. The two small deckhouses adjacent to the KIROV's helicopter deck (each with two CIWS) have been omitted in the FRUNZE. That ship's Gatling guns are farther forward, on the main superstructure.

The helicopters are lowered from the large landing deck to the hangar by an elevator, just forward of the landing area, which fits flush with the deck. The elevator opening is covered by a two-section hatch, with the sections opening outward. This arrangement allows a helicopter to be parked on the lift in the lowered position while the hangar is closed.

There is a hull-mounted sonar and a large VDS is fitted in the stern.

Active fin stabilizers are provided.

Electronics: The EW antennas of the first two ships differ. Both of the KIROV's sonar systems are thought to be the first of their type installed in an operational ship.

These ships have extensive flagship facilities and communications equipment that includes two Punch Bowl satellite communications domes (also found in the SVERDLOV and Don classes, employed as flagships). The KIROV has a pair of distinctive Vee Tube-C antennas for HF radio communications, mounted on a frame at the forward end of the second

---

[1] The term *battle cruiser*, which evolved during the DREADNOUGHT battleship era, denoted a ship with more firepower and speed than a battleship but less armor. The British HOOD (completed 1920) was the last battle cruiser completed by any nation; the Soviets twice began the construction of battle cruisers, the KRONSHTADT and STALINGRAD classes, but none was finished. The U.S. Navy also never completed any battle cruisers, although the "large cruisers" GUAM (CB 1) and ALASKA (CB 2), both completed in 1944, were in some respects conceptually similar to battle cruisers.

radar mast. The FRUNZE does not have this antenna but instead a pair of large, Big Ball radomes for satellite communications abreast the bridge structure.

Engineering: The KIROV class has an innovative Combined Nuclear and Steam (CONAS) propulsion plant. The two reactors are coupled with oil-fired boilers. The reactors generate an estimated 90,000 shp for 24–25 knots. The boilers can provide an estimated 60,000 shp for a maximum speed of 32 knots. (Earlier published Western intelligence estimates listed a maximum speed as high as 34 knots; most sources now agree to a maximum of 32 knots.)

Two arrangements have been suggested for the CONAS plant: the oil-fired boilers are used to boost the heat of the reactor-heated steam en route to the turbines or, more likely, the boilers provide steam to a second set of turbines geared to the same propeller shafts as the nuclear-driven turbines. A 1981 U.S. Navy intelligence estimate noted that "even if the fuel for the superheater were exhausted, ships of this class would still be able to make an estimated 29 knots using only the nuclear plant." Thus, the ships have a virtually unlimited cruising range.

Guns: The 130-mm DP guns in the FRUNZE are similar to those fitted in the cruisers of the SLAVA class and the destroyers of the SOVREMENNYY class.

Missiles: The KIROVs have significant anti-air/surface/submarine capabilities. The FRUNZE has three surface-to-air missile systems, with the SA-N-9 vertical-launch system provided, in part, at the expense of the SS-N-14 ASW missile system fitted in the KIROV. The SA-N-9 provides a short-range capability, primarily as a defense against attacking anti-ship cruise missiles.

The SA-N-6 VLS has eight-round, rotating launchers. Unlike the system in the SLAVA class, the KIROV SA-N-6 system has large cover hatches.

The 20 SS-N-19s represent the heaviest anti-ship missile battery in the warship of any navy. They are fitted in single, fixed launch tubes, angled forward at approximately 45°. These missiles require over-the-horizon targeting from ship-based Hormone-B helicopters or off-board systems. There are Punch Bowl antennas for satellite communications and data transmission.

Only the KIROV has the SS-N-14 ASW system. This is the first reloadable launcher for the SS-N-14 in Soviet ships. An estimated 8 to 12 missiles are carried. The Eye Bowl radar is fitted to the KIROV for SS-N-14 guidance (other Soviet cruisers with that weapon have the Head Lights radar of the SA-N-3 system to guide the ASW weapon).

Names: The KIROV is named for S. M. Kirov (1888–1934), a leading Bolshevik revolutionary. The name was subsequently given to the lead ship of the only heavy cruiser class (7.1-inch gun) built by the Soviets (completed in 1938 and stricken in 1974). M. V. Frunze (1885–1925) was a Bolshevik commander in the Russian Revolution and in 1925 served as People's Commissar for military and naval affairs.

Operational: The KIROV commenced sea trials in the Gulf of Finland on 23 May 1980; she first deployed to the Northern Fleet in September 1980. The FRUNZE began sea trials in November 1983; she deployed to the Northern Fleet in August 1984 and transited to the Far East via the Indian Ocean in October 1985.

Torpedoes: The two banks of four topedo tubes are recessed in the hull with sliding doors. They are located below the after Top Dome antenna.

The FRUNZE with the after Gatling guns moved up to the after superstructure in lieu of the KIROV's fantail position. The ship has a mass of electronic antennas mounted on the superstructure with a pair of Round House TACAN antennas mounted in front of and behind the Top Sail antenna. (Mitsuo Shibata)

The FRUNZE, second of the KIROV class. This ship has a modified armament from the first ship of the class. When this photo was taken, the ship had pennant number 050 on the starboard side and 750 on the port side. (1985, U.S. Navy, PHC John Kristoffersen)

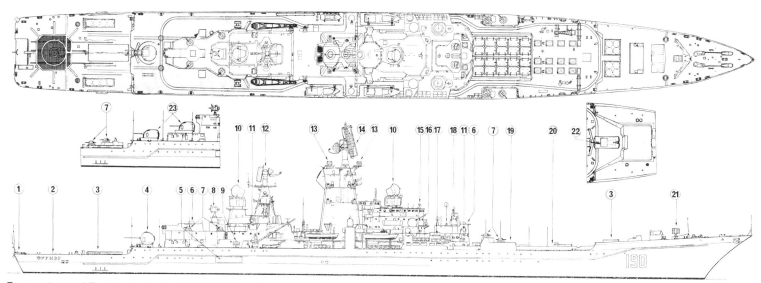

FRUNZE: 1. stern VDs 2. helicopter deck 3. SA-N-9 launchers 4. twin 130-mm gun mount 5. 533-mm torpedo tubes 6. platform for SA-N-9 radar 7. 30-mm Gatling guns 8. Kite Screech radar 9. RBU-1000 rocket launcher 10. Top Dome radar 11. Bass Tilt radar 12. Top Steer radar 13. Round House TACAN 14. Top Pair radar 15. Palm Frond radar 16. Big Ball satellite antenna 17. SA-N-4 launcher (retracted) 18. Pop Group radar 19. SS-N-19 missile tubes 20. SA-N-6 launchers 21. RBU-6000 rocket launchers KIROV inset: 22. SS-N-14 missile launcher 23. 100-mm gun turrets (M.J. Dodgson)

The KIROV's stern shows the initial armament and Gatling gun arrangement of this class. Both configurations have the air control "greenhouse" immediately forward of the large gun mount(s). (Royal Navy)

The stern of the FRUNZE with a Helix helicopter on the elevator. The elevator covers open in two sections. The flight deck has been cleared of the Gatling guns, and the single 130-mm twin mount replaces the two 100-mm single mounts of the KIROV. (Mitsuo Shibata)

2 + 2 GUIDED MISSILE CRUISERS: "SLAVA" CLASS

Name	Builders	Laid down	Launched	Completed	Status
SLAVA	61 Kommuna Shipyard, Nikolayev (north)	1976	1979	1984	**Black Sea**
. . . . . .	61 Kommuna Shipyard, Nikolayev (north)	1978	1981	(1986)	**Black Sea**
. . . . . .	61 Kommuna Shipyard, Nikolayev (north)	1979	1983	(1987)	Building
. . . . . .	61 Kommuna Shipyard, Nikolayev (north)	1985(?)			Building

Displacement:	10,000 tons standard
	12,500 tons full load
Length:	610 ft 1 in (186.0 m) oa
Beam:	66 ft 7 in (20.3 m)
Draft:	26 ft 3 in (8.0 m)
Propulsion:	4 gas turbines; 120,000 shp; 2 shafts
Speed:	32 knots
Range:	2,000 n.miles at 30 knots
	8,800 n.miles at 15 knots
Complement:	approx. 720
Helicopters:	1 Ka-25 Hormone-B
Missiles:	2 twin SA-N-4 launchers [40]
	8 rotary SA-N-6 launchers [64]
	16 SS-N-12 Sandbox
Guns:	2 130-mm/70-cal DP (1 twin)
	6 30-mm/65-cal close-in (6 multi-barrel)
ASW weapons:	2 RBU-6000 rocket launchers
	torpedoes
Torpedoes:	10 21-in (533-mm) torpedo tubes (2 quin)
Radars:	3 Bass Tilt (fire control)
	1 Front Door/Front Piece (fire control)
	1 Kite Screech (fire control)
	3 Palm Frond (navigation)
	2 Pop Group (fire control)
	1 Top Dome (fire control)
	1 Top Pair (3-D air search)
	1 Top Steer (3-D air search)
Sonars:	low frequency (hull mounted)
	medium frequency (variable depth)
EW systems:	. . . Bell-series
	4 Rum Tub
	8 Side Globe

The SLAVAS are primarily anti-ship cruisers, armed with the same anti-ship missiles as the KIEV-class aircraft carriers and the modified Echo II–class submarines. These ships were built at the same time as the larger KIROV class.

Classification: Soviet designation is RKR. The NATO designation was originally BLACK-COM-1 (Black Sea Combatant No. 1) and sub-sequently Krasina, pending public knowledge of the lead ship's actual name.

Design: The basic hull form and machinery arrangement resemble those of the Kara class, the earlier missile cruisers built at the 61 Kommuna Shipyard. The SLAVA has a large, pyramidal mast structure forward with a smaller radar mast amidships, immediately ahead of the twin gas-turbine exhaust stacks. The open space aft of the exhausts are for the SA-N-6 rotary-vertical missile launchers. The after deckhouse, topped by the Top Dome missile control radar, contains the helicopter hangar with the landing area aft. The hangar is a half deck below the flight deck and connected to it by a ramp.

Electronics: There are two Punch Bowl satellite communication antennas. The ship does not appear to have a bow sonar dome.

Engineering: Fitted with a Combination Gas or Gas (COGOG) turbine plant.

Missiles: This is the third class of surface combatants with a heavy battery of anti-ship missiles to be introduced in a three-year period by the Soviet Navy; the others are the KIROV and SOVREMENNYY classes. (All three classes also have a 130-mm gun battery.) A minimal ASW armament is fitted, this being the first Soviet "cruiser" design since the Kresta I that was not provided with the SS-N-14 or FRAS-1 system.

The large SS-N-12 Sandbox missile tubes, an improved version of the SS-N-3 Shaddock, are paired forward, in a fixed position with an elevation of about 15°. A single Hormone-B is embarked for over-the-horizon targeting (which can also be done by off-board sensors).

Names: The name SLAVA is Russian for "glory"; the previous SLAVAS were a pre-dreadnought battleship completed in 1905, which saw major action against German forces in World War I, and a heavy cruiser completed in 1941 as the MOLOTOV but renamed SLAVA in 1958.

Operational: The SLAVA transited from the Black Sea to the Mediterranean for the first time on 15 September 1983.

Torpedoes: The torpedo tubes are fitted in the hull, five per side covered by shutters. They are installed below the Top Dome radar.

The SLAVA underway in the Mediterranean, which will probably be the operating area for most of these ships. The paired SS-N-12 anti-ship missile tubes dominate her design, with the large, open amidships area housing SA-N-6 vertical launch missiles. (1986, U.S. Navy, PH1 Paul Goodrich)

The port quarter of the SLAVA, showing her hangar for a single Hormone-B targeting helicopter and the landing deck. The helicopter transfers directly down an inclined ramp into the hangar, a simplified arrangement in comparison to the Kresta II and KARA designs. (1985)

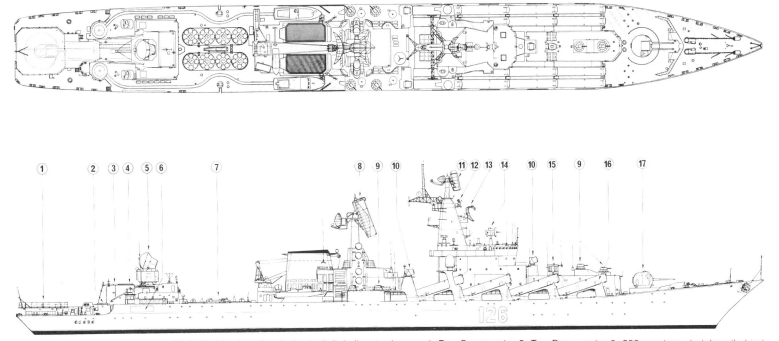

1. helicopter deck (VDS underneath) 2. SA-N-4 launcher (retracted) 3. helicopter hangar 4. Pop Group radar 5. Top Dome radar 6. 533-mm torpedo tubes (behind shutters) 7. SA-N-6 launchers 8. Top Pair radar 9. 30-mm Gatling guns 10. Bass Tilt radar 11. Top Steer radar 12. Palm Frond radar 13. Front Door radar 14. Kite Screech radar 15. RBU-6000 rocket launcher 16. SS-N-12 missile tubes 17. twin 130-mm gun turret (M.J. Dodgson)

The stern of the SLAVA showing, from the left, the SA-N-6 missile launchers, Top Dome missile control radar, helicopter hangar, with covered Pop Group radars, and retracted SA-N-4 launcher structures outboard, and helicopter deck.

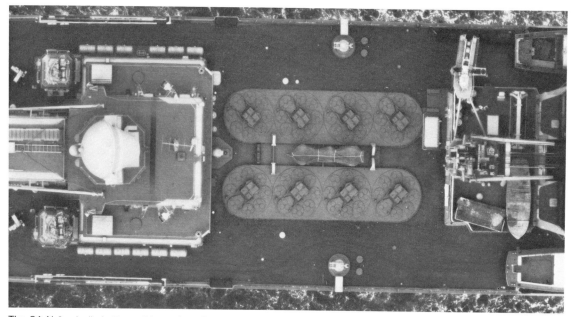

The SA-N-6 missile battery of the cruiser SLAVA, showing the eight VLS launchers, each with eight missile positions; the hatches above each position have three blow-out panels to allow the force of an accidental blast to go up, and not into the ship. (U.S. Navy)

7 GUIDED MISSILE CRUISERS: KARA CLASS

Name	Builder	Laid down	Launched	Completed	Status
NIKOLAYEV	61 Kommuna Shipyard, Leningrad (north)	1969	1971	1973	**Black Sea**
OCHAKOV	61 Kommuna Shipyard, Leningrad (north)	1970	1972	1975	**Black Sea**
KERCH	61 Kommuna Shipyard, Leningrad (north)	1971	1973	1976	**Black Sea**
AZOV	61 Kommuna Shipyard, Leningrad (north)	1972	1974	1977	**Black Sea**
PETROPAVLOVSK	61 Kommuna Shipyard, Leningrad (north)	1973	1975	1978	**Pacific**
TASHKENT	61 Kommuna Shipyard, Leningrad (north)	1975	1976	1979	**Pacific**
TALLINN	61 Kommuna Shipyard, Leningrad (north)	1976	1977	1980	**Pacific**

Displacement:	8,200 tons standard
	9,700 tons full load
Length:	567 ft 5 in (173.0 m) oa
Beam:	61 ft (18.6 m)
Draft:	22 ft (6.7 m)
Propulsion:	4 gas turbines; 120,000 shp; 2 shafts
Speed:	34 knots
Range:	3,000 n.miles at 32 knots
	8,000 n.miles at 15 knots
Complement:	approx. 525
Helicopters:	1 Ka-25 Hormone-A
Missiles:	2 twin SA-N-3 Goblet launchers [72] except 1 launcher in AZOV [36 missiles]
	2 twin SA-N-4 launchers [40]
	. . . rotary SA-N-6 launchers [. . .] in AZOV
Guns:	4 76.2-mm/59-cal AA (2 twin)
	4 30-mm/65-cal close-in (4 multi-barrel)
ASW weapons:	8 SS-N-14 Silex (2 quad)
	2 RBU-6000 rocket launchers
	2 RBU-1000 rocket launchers; deleted from PETROPAVLOVSK
	torpedoes
Torpedoes:	10 21-in (533-mm) torpedo tubes (2 quin)
Radars:	2 Bass Tilt (fire control)
	1 Don-2 or Palm Frond (navigation)
	2 Don-Kay (navigation)
	2 Head Lights (fire control) except 1 in AZOV plus 1 Top Dome
	1 Head Net-C (3-D air search)
	2 Owl Screech (fire control)
	2 Pop Group (fire control)
	1 Top Sail (3-D air search)
Sonars:	low frequency (bow mounted)
	medium frequency (variable depth)
EW systems:	2 Bell Clout
	2 Bell Slam
	2 Bell Tap except 4 Rum Tub in KERCH and PETROPAVLOVSK
	8 Side Globe

These are large, graceful ships, a refinement of the Kresta II design with major anti-air and anti-submarine capabilities. The Azov was an operational trials ship for the SA-N-6/Top Dome air defense system. They were built at almost the same time as the Kresta II class at the Zhdanov shipyard.

Classification: Soviet BPK class.

The PETROPAVLOVSK, with Round House TACAN fitted alongside the hangar in place of the RBU-1000 rocket launchers in other ships of the class. The heavy torpedo battery—ten 533-mm tubes—is evident; U.S. surface combatants carry only 324-mm ''short'' tubes for lightweight, anti-submarine torpedoes. (1984, JMSDF)

Design: These ships are significantly larger than the Kresta II class, have a heavier gun armament, are fitted with extensive command and control facilities, and are all-gas-turbine propelled. Their large superstructure is dominated by the large, square-topped gas-turbine funnel. The helicopter hangar, just forward of the landing area, is partially recessed below the flight deck. To stow the helicopter, the hangar's roof hatch and rear doors open and the helicopter is pushed in and lowered by elevator to the hangar deck.

The PETROPAVLOVSK has a higher hangar structure with two Round House Tactical Air Navigation (TACAN) antennas fitted abreast the hangar (in place of RBU-1000 launchers).

Engineering: When built these were the world's largest warships with all-gas-turbine propulsion. They have subsequently been surpassed in size by the SLAVA and British INVINCIBLE classes.

Missiles: While ostensibly armed with only AAW and ASW missiles, both the SA-N-3 and SS-N-14 have an anti-ship capability.

The AZOV has been fitted as the trials ship for the SA-N-6 vertical-launch AAW system; a launcher has replaced the after SA-N-3 system and the Top Dome missile control radar has been fitted in place of the after Head Lights.

Names: These ships are named for cities of the Soviet Union. All honor port cities except for the TASHKENT, which is named for the capital of the Uzbek republic.

Operational: The AZOV did not deploy out of the Black Sea until 1986. The two other ships in the Black Sea Fleet regularly operate in the Mediterranean.

The Kara-class cruiser TALLINN barely underway in the Pacific. While the KIROV class has the Top Sail radar on the forward superstructure pyramid, the SLAVA and Kara have it mounted farther aft. The TALLINN's pennant number a year later was 547. (1984, JMSDF)

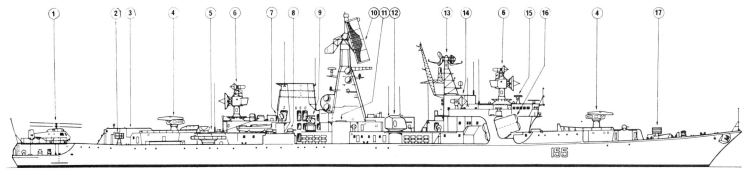

1. helicopter deck 2. RBU-1000 rocket launcher 3. helicopter hangar 4. SA-N-3 launcher 5. 533-mm torpedo tubes 6. Head Lights radar 7. Bass Tilt radar 8. 30-mm Gatling guns 9. Pop Group radar 10. Top Sail radar 11. SA-N-4 launcher (retracted) 12. twin 76.2-mm gun mount 13. Head Net-C radar 14. Owl Screech radar 15. Don Kay radar 16. SS-N-14 missile tubes 17. RBU-6000 rocket launcher (H. Simoni)

The TALLINN at high speed before deploying to the Pacific (carrying pennant number 730). These ships are easily distinguished from other Soviet missile cruisers by their large gas-turbine exhaust funnel. (West German Navy)

The Kara-class missile cruiser TASHKENT in the Far East. These ships have an attractive but unusual design, with the main mast and funnel aft of the midships.

10 GUIDED MISSILE CRUISERS: KRESTA II CLASS

Name	Builder	Laid down	Launched	Completed	Status
KRONSHTADT	Zhdanov Shipyard, Leningrad	1966	1967	Dec 1969	**Northern**
ADMIRAL ISAKOV	Zhdanov Shipyard, Leningrad	1967	1968	Sep 1970	**Northern**
ADMIRAL NAKHIMOV	Zhdanov Shipyard, Leningrad	1968	1969	Aug 1971	**Baltic**
ADMIRAL MAKAROV	Zhdanov Shipyard, Leningrad	1969	1970	Aug 1972	**Northern**
MARSHAL VOROSHILOV	Zhdanov Shipyard, Leningrad	1969	1970	May 1973	**Pacific**
ADMIRAL OKTYABRSKIY	Zhdanov Shipyard, Leningrad	1970	1971	Nov 1973	**Pacific**
ADMIRAL ISACHENKOV	Zhdanov Shipyard, Leningrad	1971	1972	Sep 1974	**Baltic**
MARSHAL TIMOSHENKO	Zhdanov Shipyard, Leningrad	1972	1973	Sep 1975	**Northern**
VASILIY CHAPAYEV	Zhdanov Shipyard, Leningrad	1973	1975	Oct 1976	**Pacific**
ADMIRAL YUMASHEV	Zhdanov Shipyard, Leningrad	1974	1976	Jan 1978	**Northern**

Displacement:	6,200 tons standard
	7,700 tons full load
Length:	521 ft 6 in (159.0 m) oa
Beam:	55 ft 9 in (17.0 m)
Draft:	19 ft 8 in (6.0 m)
Propulsion:	steam turbines; 100,000 shp; 2 shafts
Boilers:	4
Speed:	34 knots
Range:	2,400 n.miles at 32 knots
	10,500 n.miles at 14 knots
Complement:	approx. 380
Helicopters:	1 Ka-25 Hormone-A
Missiles:	2 twin SA-N-3 Goblet launchers [72]
Guns:	4 57-mm/70-cal AA (2 twin)
	4 30-mm/65-cal close-in (4 multi-barrel)
ASW weapons:	8 SS-N-14 Silex (2 quad)
	2 RBU-6000 rocket launchers
	2 RBU-1000 rocket launchers
	torpedoes
Torpedoes:	10 21-in (533-mm) torpedo tubes (2 quin)
Radars:	2 Bass Tilt (fire control) in ADMIRAL MAKAROV and later ships
	1 Don-2 (navigation)
	2 Don-Kay (navigation)
	2 Head Lights (fire control)
	1 Head Net-C (3-D air search)
	2 Muff Cob (fire control)
	1 Top Sail (3-D air search)
Sonars:	medium frequency (bow mounted)
EW systems:	1 Bell Clout
	2 Bell Slam
	2 Bell Tap
	8 Side Globe

These are large ASW/AAW ships, similar to the Kresta I design but with improved surface-to-air missiles and electronics and an SS-N-14 anti-submarine system, which replaces the earlier ship's four SS-N-3 Shaddock anti-ship missiles.

Classification: Soviet BPK type.

Design: These ships have essentially the same hull and arrangement as the interim Kresta I design. Significant changes have been made in missiles and electronics, the most prominent feature being the large Top Sail radar antenna surmounting the superstructure pyramid and the Head Lights fire control radars for the SA-N-3 missile systems. (The SA-N-3 has an anti-ship capability, as does the SS-N-14.) The helicopter is hangared in the same manner as in the Kara class.

The last three ships have an enlarged superstructure with a two-level deckhouse between the mast tower and funnel.

The ships are fitted with fin stabilizers.

Guns: The first three ships do not have the Bass Tilt fire-control directors for the 30-mm Gatling guns. Those ships rely only on optical gun directors for those weapons.

Names: Most of these ships are named for Soviet military and naval commanders. V. I. Chapayev (1887–1919) was a Bolshevik military commander honored by the light cruiser CHAPAYEV (completed in 1949 and discarded in the late 1970s).

The ADMIRAL YUMASHEV showing the four SS-N-14 ASW missile tubes on both sides of the bridge structure. (1981)

The Kresta II-class cruiser ADMIRAL YUMASHEV. This angle makes the ship appear to have a massive, closely spaced superstructure (see drawing). The Kresta II has a similar hull and power plant to the Kresta I, but with improved surface-to-air missiles and electronics. (1985)

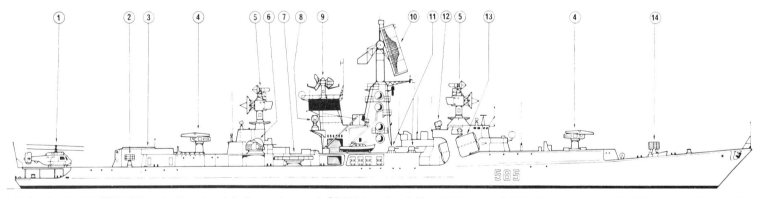

1. helicopter deck 2. RBU-1000 rocket launcher 3. helicopter hangar 4. SA-N-3 launcher 5. Head Lights radar 6. twin 57-mm gun mount 7. 533-mm torpedo tubes 8. Muff Cob radar 9. Head Net-C radar 10. Top Sail radar 11. 30-mm Gatling guns 12. Bass Tilt radar 13. SS-N-14 missile tubes 14. RBU-6000 rocket launcher (H. Simoni)

The stern of the ADMIRAL YUMASHEV. No VDS is fitted below the helicopter deck, as in some Soviet warship classes. (1981)

The open helicopter hangar of the ADMIRAL ISAKOV; the ship's striped windsock is visible. (1975, Royal Navy)

The Kresta I-class cruiser VICE ADMIRAL DROZD, an interim warship design between the Kynda anti-ship cruisers and the Kresta II and Kara anti-submarine ships. Note the level of the fantail helicopter landing deck. (1976)

4 GUIDED MISSILE CRUISERS: KRESTA I CLASS

Name	Shipyard	Laid down	Launched	Completed	Status
ADMIRAL ZOZULYA	Zhdanov Shipyard, Leningrad	Sep 1964	Oct 1965	Mar 1967	**Northern**
VLADIVOSTOK	Zhdanov Shipyard, Leningrad	1965	Aug 1966	Jan 1968	**Pacific**
VITSE ADMIRAL DROZD	Zhdanov Shipyard, Leningrad	1965	Jan 1967	Aug 1968	**Northern**
SEVASTOPOL	Zhdanov Shipyard, Leningrad	1966	June 1967	July 1969	**Pacific**

Displacement:	6,200 tons standard
	7,600 tons full load
Length:	510 ft (155.5 m) oa
Beam:	55 ft 9 in (17.0 m)
Draft:	19 ft 8 in (6.0 m)
Propulsion:	steam turbines; 100,000 shp; 2 shafts
Boilers:	4
Speed:	34 knots
Range:	1,600 n.miles at 34 knots
	7,000 n.miles at 14 knots
Complement:	approx. 380
Helicopters:	1 Ka-25 Hormone-B
Missiles:	2 twin SA-N-1 Goa launchers [44]
	4 SS-N-3b Shaddock (2 twin)
Guns:	4 57-mm/70-cal AA (2 twin)
	4 30-mm/65-cal close-in (4 multi-barrel) in VITSE ADMIRAL DROZD
ASW weapons:	2 RBU-6000 rocket launchers
	2 RBU-1000 rocket launchers
	torpedoes
Torpedoes:	10 21-in (533-mm) torpedo tubes (2 quin)
Radars:	2 Bass Tilt (fire control) in VITSE ADMIRAL DROZD
	1 Big Net (air search)
	1 or 2 Don-2 (navigation) except none in ADMIRAL ZOZULYA
	1 Don-Kay (navigation) in ships with 1 Don-2 and in ADMIRAL ZOZULYA
	1 Head Net-C (3-D air search)
	2 Muff Cob (fire control)
	2 Palm Frond (navigation) in ADMIRAL ZOZULYA
	2 Peel Group (fire control)
	2 Plinth Net (surface search)
	1 Scoop Pair (fire control)
Sonars:	Herkules medium frequency (hull mounted)
EW systems:	1 Bell Clout
	2 Bell-series
	2 Bell Slam
	2 Bell Tap
	8 Side Globe

These ships are an interim design, carrying the Shaddock anti-ship missiles but apparently intended for other weapons systems (see Kresta II listing). The lead ship began trials in the Gulf of Finland in February 1967.

Aircraft: One Hormone-B is embarked to provide over-the-horizon targeting for the Shaddock missiles.

Classification: Originally designated BPK; changed to RKR in 1977–1978, reflecting the primary armament of anti-ship missiles.

Design: These ships are considerably larger than the previous Kynda series. They also have two surface-to-air missile systems and are the first Soviet surface combatants with a helicopter hangar. No mine rails are fitted, as in the previous postwar cruiser and destroyer classes.

Compared with the smaller Kynda-class rocket cruisers (RKRs), the Kresta I design has only one-half the number of Shaddock launch tubes and one-fourth the total number of missiles. The Kresta missile tubes are mounted under cantilever bridge wings; they cannot be trained but are elevated to about 18° for firing.

Modifications: These ships have been modified during their service. The VITSE ADMIRAL DROZD was modified in 1973–1975 with a two-deck structure installed between the bridge and radar pyramid and four 30-mm close-in weapons (Gatling guns) fitted along with the associated Bass Tilt fire control radars. The SEVASTOPOL' received a similar deckhouse in 1980, but Gatling guns and radars have not been observed.

Names: The names of these ships recall two Soviet flag officers and honor two major port cities.

Another view of a Kresta I with the narrow helicopter hangar, designed specifically for the Hormone-B targeting aircraft, evident between the after SA-N-3 launcher and the helicopter landing deck. The 533-mm torpedo tubes, just forward of the 57-mm gun mounts, are covered with canvas. (1971, Canadian Forces)

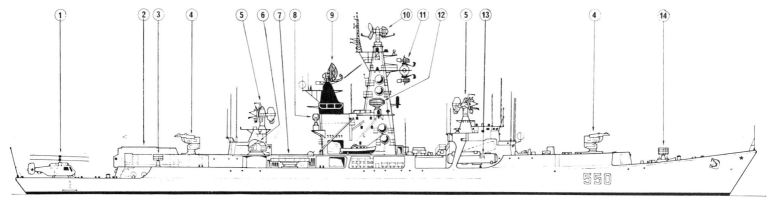

1. helicopter deck 2. helicopter hangar 3. RBU-1000 rocket launcher 4. SA-N-1 launcher 5. Peel Group radar 6. twin 57-mm gun mounts 7. 533-mm torpedo tubes 8. Muff Cob radar 9. Big Net radar 10. Head Net-C radar 11. Scoop Pair radar 12. Plinth Net radar 13. SS-N-3 missile tubes 14. RBU-6000 rocket launcher (H. Simoni)

This dated photo of a Kresta I clearly shows the massive pyramid superstructure, rising several levels above the ship's navigation bridge. The twin SS-N-3 missile tubes are barely visible, in their lowered position outboard of the bridge. (1971, U.S. Navy)

4 GUIDED MISSILE CRUISERS: KYNDA CLASS

Name	Builder	Laid down	Launched	Completed	Status
GROZNYY	Zhdanov Shipyard, Leningrad	Jun 1959	Apr 1961	Jun 1962	**Baltic**
ADMIRAL FOKIN	Zhdanov Shipyard, Leningrad	Aug 1960	May 1962	Aug 1963	**Pacific**
ADMIRAL GOLOVKO	Zhdanov Shipyard, Leningrad	Dec 1960	1962	Jul 1964	**Black Sea**
VARYAG	Zhdanov Shipyard, Leningrad	Sep 1961	Jun 1963	Feb 1965	**Pacific**

Displacement:	4,400 tons standard
	5,500 tons full load
Length:	464 ft 9 in (141.7 m) oa
Beam:	51 ft 10 in (15.8 m)
Draft:	17 ft 5 in (5.3 m)
Propulsion:	steam turbines; 100,000 shp; 2 shafts
Boilers:	4
Speed:	34 knots
Range:	2,000 n.miles at 32 knots
	7,000 n.miles at 14 knots
Complement:	approx. 375
Helicopters:	(landing area only)
Missiles:	1 twin SA-N-1 Goa launcher [24]
	8 SS-N-3b Shaddock tubes [8 + 8 reloads]
Guns:	4 76.2-mm/59-cal AA (2 twin)
	4 30-mm/65-cal close-in (4 multi-barrel) in GROZNYY and VARYAG
ASW weapons:	2 RBU-6000 rocket launchers
	torpedoes
Torpedoes:	6 21-in (533-mm) torpedo tubes (2 triple)
Radars:	2 Bass Tilt (fire control) in GROZNYY and VARYAG
	2 Don-2 (navigation)
	2 Head Net-A in ADMIRAL GOLOVKO; 1 in ADMIRAL FOKIN
	2 Head Net-C in GROZNYY and VARYAG; 1 in ADMIRAL FOKIN
	1 Owl Screech (fire control)
	1 Peel Group (fire control)
	2 Plinth Net (surface search) in GROZNYY and ADMIRAL FOKIN
	2 Scoop Pair (fire control)
Sonars:	Herkules high frequency (hull mounted)
EW systems:	1 Bell Clout
	1 Bell Slam
	1 Bell Tap
	2 Guard Dog
	4 Top Hat

These were among the first of the modern Soviet warships resulting from the defense decisions made in the mid-1950s, after the death of Stalin. Additional ships of this design were probably planned but cancelled, as was a larger Shaddock-armed missile cruiser. The GROZNYY spent most of her career in the Black Sea, returning to the Baltic Fleet in 1982.

Classification: Soviet RKR type. The U.S. Navy originally listed these ships and subsequent Soviet RKR/BPK ships as "guided missile frigates" (DLGs) until the 1975 reclassification of U.S. frigates as destroyers or cruisers. At that time the Soviet RKR/BPK classes were changed to cruisers.

Design: The Kynda-class cruisers are only slightly longer than the Krupnyy and Kildin destroyer classes but have lines more akin to the conventional cruiser hull and significantly more firepower. These ships

introduced the imposing pyramid structure to Soviet ships to support radar and EW antennas. They are the only ships with pyramids and twin funnels.

There are no helicopter hangar or maintenance facilities.

Mine rails are installed in these ships, the last Soviet cruiser type to have them.

Missiles: The large Shaddock tubes are mounted in four-tube banks forward and amidships. The launchers swing outboard and elevate to fire. Eight reload missiles are in magazines in the superstructure, behind the launchers. Reloading the Shaddock tubes is a slow and awkward process.

Modifications: The GROZNYY was fitted with Gatling guns and Bass Tilt radars in 1980, and the VARYAG was similarly modified in 1981.

These ships were built with two Head Net-A radars; some ships were subsequently refitted with Head Net-C. The Plinth Net was added after completion.

Names: Two ships remember Soviet flag officers. The GOLOVKO's eponym, A. G. Golovko, commanded the Northern Fleet from 1940 to 1946 and the Baltic Fleet from 1952 to 1956 and was considered a candidate for head of the Navy when Admiral Gorshkov was appointed in 1956. The GROZNYY and VARIAG are traditional Russian warship names (the first means "terrible," and refers to Ivan the Terrible, the second is a shortened form of "Varangian," or "Norseman").

The after section of a Kynda showing the pyramid masts carrying extensive radar and EW antennas, and the after bank of Shaddock missile tubes. (1976)

The Kynda-class cruiser ADMIRAL GROZNYY, with a built-up amidships structure carrying two 30-mm Gatling guns on each side. The Kyndas were the first oceangoing missile ships of the modern Soviet Navy. (1985)

The balanced arrangement of the Kynda-class design is clearly shown in this view. The helicopter deck is rarely used. (1974)

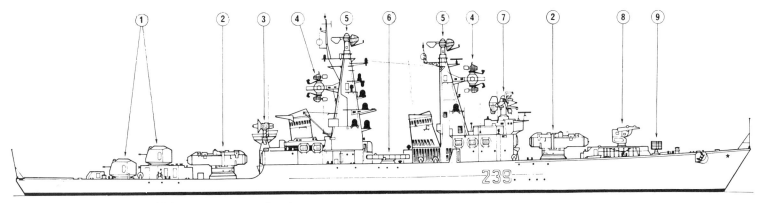

1. twin 76.2-mm gun mounts 2. SS-N-3 missile tubes 3. Owl Screech radar 4. Scoop Pair radar 5. Head Net-A radar 6. 533-mm torpedo tubes 7. Peel Group radar 8. SA-N-1 launcher 9. RBU-6000 rocket launcher (H. Simoni)

2 COMMAND CRUISERS: CONVERTED "SVERDLOV" CLASS

Name	Builder	Laid down	Launched	Completed	Conversion Completed	Status
ADMIRAL SENYAVIN	Baltic Works, Leningrad	May 1951	Sep 1952	July 1954	1972	**Pacific**
ZHDANOV	Baltic Works, Leningrad	Oct 1949	Dec 1950	Jan 1952	1972	**Black Sea**

Displacement:	12,900 tons standard
	17,200 tons full load
Length:	656 ft (200.0 m) wl
	688 ft 10 in (210.0 m) oa
Beam:	70 ft 10 in (21.6 m)
Draft:	23 ft 7 in (7.2 m)
Propulsion:	steam turbines; 110,000 shp; 2 shafts
Boilers:	6
Speed:	32 knots
Range:	2,400 n.miles at 32 knots
	10,000 n.miles at 13.5 knots
Complement:	approx. 1,000
Helicopters:	1 Ka-25 Hormone-C in ADMIRAL SENYAVIN
Missiles:	1 twin SA-N-4 launcher [20]

Guns:	ADMIRAL SENYAVIN	ZHDANOV
	6 152-mm/57-cal SP (2 triple)	9 152-mm/57-call SP (3 triple)
	12 100-mm/50-cal DP (6 twin)	12 100-mm/50-cal DP (6 twin)
	32 37-mm/63-cal AA (16 twin)	16 37-mm/63-cal AA (8 twin)
	16 30-mm/65-cal close-in (8 twin)	8 30-mm/65-cal close-in (4 twin)

ASW weapons:	none
Torpedoes:	(removed)
Mines:	(rails removed)
Radars:	4 Drum Tilt in SENYAVIN, 2 in ZHDANOV
	6 Egg Cup (fire control)
	1 Pop Group (fire control)
	2 Sun Visor-B (fire control)
	2 Top Bow (fire control)
	1 Top Trough (air search)
Sonars:	Tamir-5N high frequency (hull mounted)
EW systems:	None

These ships were standard SVERDLOV-class light cruisers that were extensively converted for the command ship role in 1971–1972. Both ships are in commission. See listing for the SVERDLOV class for additional notes.

Classification: Soviet KU (command ship) type.

Conversion: The different configurations of these ships probably represent the requirements of specific fleet commanders for their respective operating areas. Most obvious, the SENYAVIN has a large helicopter hangar aft (requiring removal of all after 152-mm guns). The after superstructure has been built with the SA-N-4 missile system and 30-mm guns for close-in defense. The ZHDANOV, without a hangar, does have a helicopter landing area aft or an aircraft control position at the after end of the superstructure. Their mine rails and torpedo tubes have been removed.

Electronics: Both ships have been fitted with extensive command and communications facilities. A third mast, aft of the second funnel, carries the distinctive Vee Cone HF communications antennas. A pair of Big Ball communications satellites were fitted on small deckhouses immediately aft of the second funnel in 1979–1981.

Names: The ADMIRAL SENYAVIN honors a family of five distinguished 18th-century Russian naval officers. A. A. Zhdanov (1896–1948) was a leading Soviet official with major responsibilities in the development of the Soviet Navy under Stalin.

The ZHDANOV differs from the ADMIRAL SENYAVIN primarily in retaining one after 152-mm gun turret in place of a helicopter hangar—probably reflecting the fleet commanders' preferences at the time of their conversion. (1982, U.S. Navy)

The command ship cruiser ADMIRAL SENYAVIN, assigned to the Pacific Fleet. There are paired Big Ball satellite antenna domes abaft the second funnel in these ships; a Top Trough air search radar is on the second (tripod) mast and paired Vee Cone HF communication antennas on the third (lattice) mast. (1982)

The ZHDANOV and other SVERDLOVS have a superstructure crowded with secondary gun batteries, life boats and life rafts, and various antennas and fire control directors. The torpedo tubes have been removed from all surviving SVERDLOVS. (1983)

7(2) LIGHT CRUISERS: "SVERDLOV" CLASS

Name	Builder	Laid down	Launched	Completed	Status
SVERDLOV	Baltic Works, Leningrad	July 1949	13 July 1950	1951	Baltic (Reserve)
ALEKSANDR NEVSKI	Marti Shipyard, Leningrad (Admiralty)	Mar 1950	June 1951	1952	**Northern**
ADMIRAL LAZAREV	Baltic Works, Leningrad	May 1950	Oct 1951	Nov 1952	Pacific (Reserve)
ADMIRAL USHAKOV	Baltic Works, Leningrad	July 1950	May 1952	Aug 1953	**Black Sea**
ALEKSANDR SUVOROV	Marti Shipyard, Leningrad (Admiralty)	Oct 1950	June 1952	1953	**Pacific**
MIKHAIL KUTUZOV	Marti Shipyard, Nikolayev (south)	1950	May 1954	1955	**Black Sea**
DMITRIY POZHARSKIY	Baltic Works, Leningrad	Sep 1951	Apr 1953	1953	**Pacific**
OKTOBRASKAYA REVOLUTSIYA	Molotovsk Shipyard, Severodvinsk	1951	1954	Sep 1954	**Baltic**
MURMANSK	Molotovsk Shipyard, Severodvinsk	1952	1955	1955	**Northern**

Displacement:	12,900 tons standard
	17,200 tons full load
Length:	656 ft (200.0 m) wl
	688 ft 10 in (210.0 m) oa
Beam:	70 ft 10 in (21.6 m)
Draft:	23 ft 7 in (7.2 m)
Propulsion:	steam turbines; 110,000 shp; 2 shafts
Boilers:	6
Speed:	32 knots
Range:	2,400 n.miles at 32 knots
	10,000 n.miles at 13.5 knots
Complement:	approx. 1,000
Helicopters:	(no facilities)
Guns:	12 152-mm/57-cal SP (4 triple)
	12 100-mm/50-cal DP (6 twin)
	32 37-mm/63-cal AA (16 twin) except 28 guns in ships with 30-mm guns
	16 30-mm/65-cal close-in (8 twin) in ADMIRAL USHAKOV, ALEXSANDR SUVOROV, OKTYABRSKAYA REVOLUTSIYA
ASW weapons:	none
Torpedoes:	(removed)
Mines:	rails for 140 to 200
Radars:	1 Big Net or Top Trough (air search)
	1 Don-2 or Neptune (navigation)
	4 Drum Tilt (fire control) in ships with 30-mm guns
	8 Egg Cup (fire control); removed from ships with 30-mm guns
	1 High Sieve or Low Sieve (air search)
	1 Knife Rest (air search) in some ships
	1 Slim Net (air search)
	2 Sun Visor-B (fire control)
	2 Top Bow (fire control)
Sonars:	Tamir-5N high frequency (hull mounted)
EW systems:	2 Watch Dog

These are the last conventional, all-gun cruisers in commission with any navy. The only ships in commission with larger guns are the U.S. battleships of the IOWA class, each with nine 16-inch guns.

Seven ships are in various stages of commission, although information on the exact status of the ships varies. Two ships are in reserve. The OKTOBRASKAYA REVOLUTSIYA is listed as a gunnery training ship. The SVERDLOVS periodically serve as fleet flagships. Several of the active ships can be expected to be decommissioned in the near future although probably one will be retained in service in each fleet for at least the remainder of this decade.

Class: Twenty-four of these ships were planned in the post–World War II construction program. Only 20 ships were laid down, with 14 completed between 1951 and 1955 as light cruisers. Three additional hulls were launched but not finished. Five of the completed ships are not listed above:

ORDZONIKIDZE (1951) was transferred to Indonesia in October 1962 and renamed IRIAN. She was scrapped in Taiwan in 1972.

ZHDANOV (1952) and ADMIRAL SENYAVIN (1954) were converted to command ships and are listed separately in this volume.

ADMIRAL NAKHIMOV (1952) was converted to a test ship for surface-to-surface missiles and operated in the Black Sea until scrapped in 1961.

DZERZHINSKIY (1952) had been converted to guided missile configuration with an SA-N-2 Guideline system by 1961. She was not operationally successful. After operating in the Black Sea–Mediterranean area was probably broken up in the early 1980s.

Classification: Soviet KR type.

Design: These are large, graceful-looking ships, with classic World War II-era lines. They reflect the influence of Italian design, with a prominent, free-standing conning tower forward, separate funnels, and two tripod masts immediately forward of the funnels. The long forecastle extends to the after gun turrets. Tracks for between 140 and 200 mines are fitted on the after deck. A stern anchor is fitted in addition to the bow anchors.

Modifications: The radar arrangements on these ships have been changed during their long service lives. Three of these ships have had 30-mm close-in guns (with their associated Drum Tilt radars) fitted on an enlarged superstructure in the area of their forward mast and funnel.

Names: The ships of this class honor Russian naval and military heroes, the port city of Murmansk, and Russian revolutionary Ya.M. Sverdlov (1985–1919). The OKTOBRASKAYA REVOLUTSIYA was originally named MOLOTOVSK; the ship was renamed in 1957 with the political demise of Foreign Minister V. M. Molotov.

Torpedoes: When built these ships had ten 21-inch (533-mm) torpedo tubes, mounted in two banks on the main deck, outboard of the motor launch stowage. The tubes were removed from all ships by the early 1960s.

The ADMIRAL USHAKOV, one of three SVERDLOVS refitted with 30-mm twin rapid-fire guns, four mounts forward and four on the after end of the main superstructure. Their Drum Tilt fire control radars are visible on posts alongside the forward mast. (1980, U.S. Navy)

The SVERDLOV in the Barents Sea. Note the elevated 100-mm dual-purpose guns on the starboard side and the Big Net radar on the second, tripod mast. (1982)

A closeup of the OCTOBER REVOLUTION showing the twin 30-mm guns and Drum Tilt radar directors. (West German Navy)

BATTLE CRUISERS: "STALINGRAD" CLASS

The Soviets began building the STALINGRAD-class battle cruisers after World War II. The information on these ships available in the West is limited and contradictory. The lead ship apparently was laid down at Nikolayev, but reports differ on whether this occurred in early 1949 or 1951. (The earlier date is considered more likely by the author, because of the intensive postwar building effort made by the Soviets; the ship was reported by the same sources as being about 60 percent complete and ready for launching in 1953, when it was cancelled shortly after Stalin's death.) A second ship, which may have been named MOSKVA, is reported to have been laid down at the Baltic Shipyard in Leningrad in October 1952 although the ship reported seen there may have been the remains of the earlier KRONSHTADT (see below); alternative reports contend the MOSKVA was to have been laid down at Nikolayev following the launching of the STALINGRAD. Again, reports vary on the fate of the hulls, some saying one and some saying both were broken up on the building ways; more likely, the STALINGRAD was floated and her hull expended on missile tests.

The STALINGRAD design was probably based on that of the prewar KRONSHTADT class. The older class (never completed) was to have had a standard displacement of 35,240 tons with a full-load displacement of 38,360 tons and an overall length of 813 ft 8 in. Primary armament would have been nine 12-inch/56-cal guns in triple turrets. The STALINGRAD may have been slightly larger; that design was modified at some stage to launch the Kennel surface-to-surface missile (i.e., the initial version of the Kennel AS-1 missile) in place of one (or two?) of the triple 12-inch turrets.

LIGHT CRUISERS: "CHAPAYEV" CLASS

Seven CHAPAYEV-class light cruisers were laid down in 1938–1940. Full-load displacement was 15,000 tons with a main battery of 12 5.9-in guns. All construction stopped when the Soviet Union entered the war in June 1941. Work resumed on five ships after the war, with the CHAPAYEV, CHKALOV, and ZHELEZNIAKOV completed in 1949, the FRUNZE and KUIBISHEV in 1950. All were scrapped from 1962 onward.

HEAVY CRUISERS: "KIROV" CLASS

Six KIROV-class heavy cruisers were laid down in 1935–1939. Full-load displacement was 11,500 tons for the first two ships and 9,790 tons for the later four with a main battery of nine 7.1-inch guns. Four ships were completed in 1938–1941, before the outbreak of war: the KIROV, MAKSIM, GOR'KIY, MOLOTOV (later renamed SLAVA), and VOROSHILOV; two other ships were completed during the war, the KALININ in 1943 and the KAGANOVICH (later PETROPAVLOVSK) in 1944. The ships were broken up after 1956.

15
Destroyers

The Soviet Navy has ended its long hiatus in the construction of "destroyers" with the large and heavily armed SOVREMENNYY and UDALOY classes. Both classes, introduced in 1981, are in series production and represent two distinct warship roles; their basic hull and propulsion systems are quite different, as are their armament and sensors. The SOVREMENNYY is primarily an anti-surface warship with significant anti-air capabilities; the UDALOY is primarily an anti-submarine ship.

The previous destroyer class built in the Soviet Union was the Kashin class. Twenty units were completed for the Soviet Navy from 1963 to 1971. (Subsequent units were built for the Indian Navy; see page 572.) Although there has been an ongoing modernization/conversion program for older destroyers, new construction did not occur until the SOVREMENNYY and UDALOY were laid down in 1976 and 1978, respectively, about a decade after the last Kashin was begun for the Soviet Navy.

Both of the new destroyer classes are the size of some contemporary Soviet and foreign warships classified as cruisers, with the SOVREMENNYY being a continuation of the Zhdanov shipyard's modern "cruiser"

construction line that began with the Kynda class and continued through the Kresta I/II classes. The Zhdanov yard in Leningrad produced 18 ships of these classes between 1962 and 1978 for an average rate of better than one ship per year. The SOVREMENNYY class is being built at Zhdanov at the same rate of one unit per year.

Simultaneously, the slightly larger UDALOY class is being built at two yards, Zhdanov and Yantar/Kaliningrad (Lithuanian SSR). Thus, there is an increase in the warship building rate at Zhdanov while the UDALOY is the largest and most complex warship yet built at the Yantar/Kaliningrad yard in the postwar period. (The Yantar/Kaliningrad yard previously built Krivak-class frigates.) The combined output of the two yards is just over one UDALOY-class destroyer per year. The output rate for these classes could probably be increased slightly. And, of course, there is the possibility that the Nikolayev north shipyard, upon completing the SLAVA cruiser program, could be employed in producing one or both of these destroyer classes. Both ships have significant anti-air capabilities.

The Soviet Navy is currently constructing two classes of destroyers, as large as many ships classified as cruisers in the Soviet and other navies. These destroyers of the UDALOY and SOVREMENNYY classes provide highly capable consorts for the new Soviet aircraft carriers and cruisers. This is the UDALOY-class ASW destroyer ADMIRAL SPIRIDONOV, transiting the East China Sea shortly after completion. The ship has a Top Steer/Top Mesh radar on the second lattice mast. (1985, Japanese Maritime Self-Defense Force)

8+ GUIDED MISSILE DESTROYERS: "UDALOY" CLASS

Name	Builder	Laid down	Launched	Completed
UDALOY	Yantar, Kaliningrad	1978	1980	1981
VITSE ADMIRAL KULAKOV	Zhdanov Shipyard, Leningrad	1978	1982	Apr 1982
MARSHAL VASIL'YEVSKIY	Yantar, Kaliningrad	1979	1981	July 1983
ADMIRAL ZAKHAROV	Zhdanov Shipyard, Leningrad	1979	1982	Sep 1983
ADMIRAL SPIRIDONOV	Yantar, Kaliningrad	1981	1983	1984
ADMIRAL TRIBUTS	Zhdanov Shipyard, Leningrad	1982	1984	1985
MARSHAL SHAPOSHNIKOV	Zhdanov Shipyard, Leningrad	1983	1985	1985
. . . . . .	Yantar, Kaliningrad	1983	1986	1986

Displacement:	6,200–6,700 tons standard
	8,200 tons full load
Length:	492 ft (150.0 m) wl
	531 ft 4 in (162.0 m) oa
Beam:	63 ft 4 in (19.3 m)
Draft:	20 ft 3 in (6.2 m)
Propulsion:	4 gas turbines; 120,000 shp; 2 shafts
Speed:	34 knots
Range:	2,000 n.miles at 33 knots
	5,000 n.miles at 20 knots
Complement:	approx. 300
Helicopters:	2 Ka-27 Helix-A
Missiles:	8 vertical SA-N-9 launchers [64]
Guns:	2 100-mm/70-cal DP (2 single)
	4 30-mm/65-cal close-in (4 multi-barrel)
ASW weapons:	8 SS-N-14 Silex (2 quad)
	2 RBU-6000 rocket launchers
	torpedoes
Torpedoes:	8 21-in (533-mm) torpedo tubes (2 quad)
Mines:	rails fitted
Radars:	2 Bass Tilt (fire control)
	2 Cross Sword (fire control); see notes
	2 Eye Bowl (fire control)
	1 Kite Screech (fire control)
	3 Palm Frond (navigation)
	2 Strut Pair (surface search) in UDALOY and ADMIRAL KULAKOV; 1 in later ships
	1 Top Plate/Top Mesh (air search) in MARSHAL VASIL'YEVSKIY and later ships
Sonars:	low frequency (bow mounted)
	low frequency (variable depth)
EW systems:	2 Bell Shroud
	2 Bell Squat
	(space provided for additional systems)

The UDALOY during an at-sea refueling over her bow. The helicopter deck is fitted with netting to retard helicopters from rolling on deck and has tracks for a mechanical system to pull the helicopters to and from the twin hangars.

These are large anti-submarine destroyers, similar in concept to the USS SPRUANCE (DD 963) class. The UDALOY began trials in the Gulf of Finland in August 1980. Construction of the class continues.

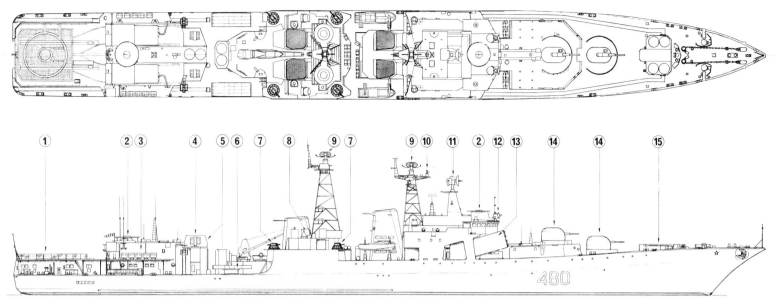

1. helicopter deck (above VDS) 2. SA-N-9 radar platform 3. helicopter hangars 4. RBU-6000 launcher 5. SA-N-9 vertical launchers 6. 533-mm torpedo tubes 7. 30-mm Gatling guns 8. Bass Tilt radar 9. Strut Pair radar 10. Palm Frond radar 11. Kite Screech radar 12. Eye Bowl radars 13. SS-N-14 missile tubes 14. single 100-mm guns 15. SA-N-9 vertical launchers (M.J. Dodgson)

As of early 1986, 3 ships were in the Northern Fleet, 2 in the Baltic, and 1 in the Pacific; 2 other ships apparently were engaged in trials and fitting out.

Classification: Soviet BPK type. Pending disclosure of the lead ship's name, this class was designated BAL-COM-3 (Baltic Combatant No. 3) by NATO intelligence.

Design: These ships have a long, low superstructure with their quad SS-N-14 launchers under a cantilevered extension to the bridge structure, as in the Kresta II and Kara classes. The hangar has separate bays to accommodate two helicopters, which are lowered into them by elevators (this is similar to the arrangement in the Kara and Kresta II classes). There is a control station between the hangar bays and a pair of Round House TACANs. A variable-depth sonar, similar to that of the KIROV class, is fitted in the stern counter.

Electronics: The early ships were completed with empty positions for the Cross Sword radar directors (above the bridge and above the hangars). The ADMIRAL ZAKHAROV was the first ship to have the full SA-9/Cross Sword system installed.

Missiles: Forward of the guns, between the second lattice mast and helicopter hangar, are four vertical launchers for the SA-N-9 system with another battery of four launchers on the forecastle.

The SS-N-14 launchers are fixed in elevation.

Names: UDALOY, a traditional Soviet destroyer name, means "courageous" or "daring." The other ships are named for deceased senior officers of the Army and Navy.

Details of the VITSE ADMIRAL KULAKOV, showing the after pair of gas-turbine exhausts, 30-mm Gatling guns, Bass Tilt fire control radars, and (mounted on mast) two Round House TACAN antennas. A second Strut Pair was fitted to the mast shortly after this photo was taken. There are another pair of Gatling guns forward of the Bass Tilt radars. (1984, U.S. Navy)

The VITSE ADMIRAL KULAKOV, the second UDALOY-class ship, riding at anchor with a Helix ASW helicopter on board and the doors open to the port-side hangar. The below-deck vertical launchers for the SA-N-9 missiles are visible forward of the 100-mm gun mounts; another set of launchers is amidships. She has open pedestals forward and aft for the SA-N-9 related radars. (1984)

The UDALOY in the Barents Sea with her stern VDS housing open. The pedestal for the large SA-N-9 radar above the hangars is empty; note the pair of Round House TACANs atop the second lattice mast. These are primarily ASW ships, similar in concept to the U.S. Navy's SPRUANCE (DD 963) class. (1982)

6+ GUIDED MISSILE DESTROYERS: "SOVREMENNYY" CLASS

Name	Builder	Laid down	Launched	Completed
SOVREMENNYY	Zhdanov Shipyard, Leningrad	1976	Nov 1978	1981
OTCHAYANNYY	Zhdanov Shipyard, Leningrad	1977	Aug 1980	1982
OTLICHNYY	Zhdanov Shipyard, Leningrad	1978	1981	1983
OSOMOTRITEL'NYY	Zhdanov Shipyard, Leningrad	1979	1982	1984
BEZUPRECHNYY	Zhdanov Shipyard, Leningrad	1980	1983	July 1985
. . . . . .	Zhdanov Shipyard, Leningrad	1981	1984	1986

Displacement:	6,300 tons standard
	7,900 tons full load
Length:	475 ft 7 in (145.0 m) wl
	511 ft 8 in (156.0 m) oa
Beam:	55 ft 9 in (17.0 m)
Draft:	20 ft (6.1 m)
Propulsion:	steam turbines; 100,000 shp; 2 shafts
Boilers:	4
Speed:	34 knots
Range:	2,400 n.miles at 32 knots
	10,500 n.miles at 14 knots
Complement:	approx. 380
Helicopters:	1 Ka-25 Hormone-B
Missiles:	2 SA-N-7 launchers [40]
	8 SS-N-22 (2 quad)
Guns:	4 130-mm/70-cal DP guns (2 twin)
	4 30-mm/65-cal close-in (4 multi-barrel)
ASW weapons:	2 RBU-1000 rocket launchers
	torpedoes
Torpedoes:	4 21-in (533-mm) torpedo tubes (2 twin)

Mines:	rails fitted
Radars:	1 Band Stand (fire control)
	2 Bass Tilt (fire control)
	6 Front Dome (fire control)
	1 Kite Screech (fire control)
	3 Palm Frond (navigation)
	1 Top Steer (3-D air search) but Top Steer/Top Plate
	combination in OSOMOTRITEL'NYY and later units
Sonars:	medium frequency (hull mounted)
EW systems:	2 Bell Shroud
	2 Bell Squat
	4 . . . . . .

This destroyer class is intended primarily for anti-ship operations. The ships have a significant anti-air capability but minimal ASW weapons and sensors. With the UDALOY class, they have succeeded the Kresta II cruisers in series production at the Zhdanov yard. The SOVREMENNYY began sea trials in the Gulf of Finland in August 1980. Construction of the class continues.

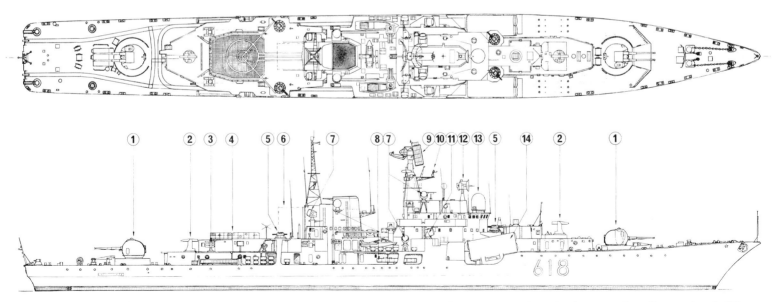

1. twin 130-mm guns 2. SA-N-7 launcher 3. RBU-1000 launcher 4. helicopter deck 5. 30-mm Gatling guns 6. telescoping hangar 7. Front Dome radars 8. 533-mm torpedo tubes 9. Top Steer radar 10. Palm Frond radar 11. Bass Tilt radar 12. Kite Screech radar 13. Band Stand radar 14. SS-N-22 missile tubes (M.J. Dodgson)

As of early 1986, there were 3 ships in the Northern Fleet and 3 in the Baltic Fleet.

Classification: Soviet EM (destroyer) type. These ships were originally designated BAL-COM-2 by Western intelligence.

Design: These ships are similar in size to the UDALOY, but with different hull form, propulsion, weapons, and sensors. The basic hull form and propulsion are similar to those of the Kresta II, built at the same shipyard. The quad surface-to-surface missile launchers are mounted slightly forward of the bridge structure; the main gun armament is divided fore and aft (the UDALOY has guns forward); pressure-fired steam propulsion is provided (vice the UDALOY's gas turbines); and there is a telescoping helicopter hangar adjacent to the landing areas to accommodate a single Ka-25 Hormone-B helicopter for over-the-horizon targeting. This is the first Soviet surface combatant with the landing area amidships instead of at the stern, and the first to use the telescoping hangar.

Minimal ASW armament is fitted and, while the ship does have a bow sonar dome, it is smaller than that provided in the UDALOY and other recent BPK classes. However, like the UDALOY, these ships have mine rails.

Electronics: Two small, spherical radomes are located on platforms on both sides of the single stack. Their exact function is unknown, but they may be associated with over-the-horizon targeting for the SS-N-22 missiles.

Engineering: The use of steam propulsion in the SOVREMMENNYY was somewhat surprising in view of the use of gas turbines in the previous Kara class and the contemporary UDALOY. The estimated range of the two destroyer classes is approximately the same.

Guns: The 130-mm guns are the same type fitted in the KIROV and SLAVA cruiser classes. They are the largest guns installed in any of the world's recent destroyers.

Missiles: The SS-N-22 anti-ship missiles are an improved version of the SS-N-9.

Names: These ships like the Soviet destroyers of the past, have adjectival names; SOVREMENNYY, for example, means "modern."

The OTCHAYANNYY shows the helicopter facilities in the SOVREMENNYY class. The hangar (right) extends on tracks to provide shelter for a single Hormone-B helicopter for missile targeting. Visible are the after SA-N-7 launcher, two RBU-1000 rocket launchers, and two 30-mm rapid-fire Gatling guns. (1983)

The OTCHAYANNYY in the eastern Atlantic. This class differs significantly from the UDALOY ASW ships in basic design, including propulsion, weapons, electronics, and structure arrangement. The single, solid radar mast supports a Top Steer 3-D antenna; above the bridge is the Band Stand radome for the SS-N-22 missile radar.

The SOVREMENNYY-class destroyers are intended for anti-surface and anti-air warfare. The ship's large, 130-mm gun mounts are readily evident, as are the forward SA-N-7 missile launcher (aft of the forward gun mount) and the SS-N-22 quad missile tubes, seen with open covers. (West German Navy)

The SOVREMENNYY-class destroyer OSMOTRITEL'NYY, photographed in the Indian Ocean en route to the Far East, has a Top Steer/Top Plate radar mounted on her forward mast. When this edition went to press, she was the only destroyer identified with this radar. (1984, U.S. Navy, PHC John Kristoffersen)

1 GUIDED MISSILE TRIALS SHIPS: CONVERTED KASHIN CLASS

Name	Completed	Converted
PROVORNYY	1965	1981

Builders:	61 Kommuna Shipyard, Nikolayev (north)
Displacement:	3,750 tons standard
	4,750 tons full load
Length:	472 ft 4 in (144.0 m) oa
Beam:	51 ft 2 in (15.8 m)
Draft:	15 ft 9 in (4.8 m)
Propulsion:	4 gas turbines; 96,000 shp; 2 shafts
Speed:	38 knots
Range:	1,500 n.miles at 35 knots
	4,000 n.miles at 20 knots
Complement:	approx. 300

Helicopters:	landing area aft
Missiles:	1 single SA-N-7 launcher [20]
Guns:	4 76.2-mm/59-cal AA (2 twin)
ASW weapons:	2 RBU-6000 rocket launchers
	2 RBU-1000 rocket launchers
	torpedoes
Torpedoes:	5 21-in (533-mm) torpedo tubes (1 quin)
Mines:	rails removed
Radars:	1 Don-2 (navigation)
	2 Don-Kay (navigation)
	8 Front Dome (fire control)
	1 Heat Net-C (3-D air search)
	2 Owl Screech (fire control)
	1 Top Steer (air search)
Sonars:	medium frequency (hull mounted)
	medium frequency (variable depth)
EW systems:	(deleted except for chaff launchers)

The weapons test ship PROVORNYY, converted from a Kashin-class destroyer for trials of the SA-N-7 missile system and new radar/fire control systems. In this bow-on view the empty SA-N-7 positions forward of the bridge are evident, as is the new pyramid mast between the funnels for the Top Steer radar.

The PROVORNYY was converted from a standard Kashin-class destroyer to a trials ships for the SA-N-7 missile system and its associated radars and fire control system. For additional details see the listing for the Kashin class.

Conversion: Converted in the 1970s, probably at the 61 Kommuna Shipyard in Nikolayev. The ship went to sea in her new configuration in late 1981. The two SA-N-1 missile systems were removed. An SA-N-7 launcher was installed aft; there are spaces for two additional SA-N-7 launchers forward, but they have not been installed.

Like the cruiser AZOV, the trials ship for the SA-N-6/Top Dome system, the PROVORNYY retains major combat capabilities. However, note that the ship's electronic warfare capability has been reduced.

The PROVORNYY with canvas covering the SA-N-7 launcher, fitted aft of the second pair of funnels, in the position previously occupied by the SA-N-1 launcher. Several of the ship's eight Front Dome fire control radars can be seen, e.g., outboard of the after mast and the after funnels.

6 GUIDED MISSILE DESTROYERS: MODIFIED KASHIN CLASS

Name	Builder	Completed	Converted
OGNEVOY	Z	1964	1973
SLAVNYY	Z	1966	1975
STROYNYY	N	1966	1980
SMYSHLENNYY	N	1968	1974
SMEL'YY	N	1970	1974
SDERZHANOYY	N	1973	(see notes)

Builders:	N = 61 Kommuna Shipyard, Nikolayev (north)
	Z = Zhdanov Shipyard, Leningrad
Displacement:	3,950 tons standard
	4,950 tons full load
Length:	478 ft 11 in (146.0 m) oa
Beam:	51 ft 2 in (15.8 m)
Draft:	15 ft 9 in (4.8 m)
Propulsion:	4 gas turbines; 96,000 shp; 2 shafts
Speed:	38 knots
Range:	1,500 n.miles at 35 knots
	4,000 n.miles at 20 knots
Complement:	approx. 300
Helicopters:	landing area aft
Missiles:	2 twin SA-N-1 Goa launchers [36]
	4 SS-N-2c Styx (4 single)
Guns:	4 76.2-mm/59-cal AA (2 twin)
	4 30-mm/65-cal close-in (4 multi-barrel)
ASW weapons:	2 RBU-6000 rocket launchers
	torpedoes
Torpedoes:	5 21-in (533-mm) torpedo tubes (1 quin)

Mines:	rails removed
Radars:	2 Bass Tilt (fire control)
	2 Don-Kay (navigation)
	1 Big Net (3-D air search)
	1 Head Net-C (3-D air search)
	2 Owl Screech (fire control)
	2 Peel Group (fire control)
Sonars:	medium frequency (hull mounted)
	medium frequency (variable depth)
EW systems:	2 Bell Shroud
	2 Bell Squat

These are Kashin-class destroyers modified with improved electronics and four rear-firing, improved Styx missiles. In addition to the SS-N-2c missiles, the SA-N-1 system has an anti-ship capability. See Kashin-class listing for additional details.

Of these 6 ships, 2 are in the Northern Fleet, 3 in the Baltic, and 1 in the Black Sea.

Classification: Soviet BPK type.

Conversion: Conversions were completed between 1973 and 1980; the SDERZHANDOYY was probably completed to this configuration. The hull was lengthened by approximately 6 ft 7 in (2 m), and a stern VDS was installed under the raised helicopter deck. Improved hull-mounted sonar was also fitted. Rapid-fire Gatling guns replaced the two RBU-1000 rocket launchers. Improved air-search radars were provided. The after 76.2-mm gun mount has a severely restricted field of fire.

The modified Kashin-class destroyers have been considerably upgraded during the past two decades, with additional weapons and electronics provided while all of their original weapons have been retained, testimony to the robust character of Soviet ship designs. All Kashins now have the Big Net radar on the second lattice mast. (1984)

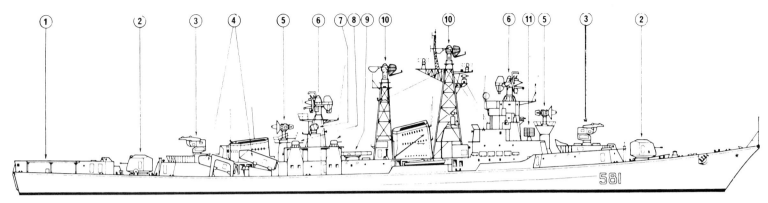

1. helicopter deck (above VDS) 2. twin 76.2-mm guns 3. SA-N-1 launchers 4. SS-N-2c launch tubes 5. Owl Screech radars 6. Peel Group radars 7. Bass Tilt radars 8. 30-mm Gatling guns 9. 533-mm torpedo tubes 10. Head Net-A radars 11. RBU-6000 launchers (H. Simoni)

The SLAVNYY shows the distinctive, slightly angled exhaust stacks of the Kashin class, the world's first oceangoing warship with all-gas-turbine propulsion. The raised helicopter platform, seldom seen occupied, surmounts the VDS installation. (Ministry of Defence)

12 GUIDED MISSILE DESTROYERS: KASHIN CLASS

Name	Builder	Completed
KOMSOMOLETS UKRAINYY	N	Feb 1962
SOOBRAZITEL'NYY	N	Sep 1963
OBRAZTSOVYY	Z	July 1965
ODARENNYY	Z	Sep 1965
STEREGUSHCHIY	Z	Oct 1966
KRASNYY KAVKAZ	N	1967
RESHITELNYY	N	Jan 1968
STROGIY	N	Aug 1968
SMETLIVVY	N	Sep 1969
KRASNYY KRYM	N	Sep 1970
SPOSOBNYY	N	Aug 1971
SKORYY	N	Aug 1972

Builders:	N = 61 Kommuna Shipyard, Nikolayev (north)
	Z = Zhdanov Shipyard, Leningrad
Displacement:	3,750 tons standard
	4,750 tons full load
Length:	472 ft 4 in (144.0 m) oa
Beam:	51 ft 2 in (15.8 m)
Draft:	15 ft 9 in (4.8 m)
Propulsion:	4 gas turbines; 96,000 shp; 2 shafts
Speed:	38 knots
Range:	1,500 n.miles at 35 knots
	4,000 n.miles at 20 knots
Complement:	approx. 280
Helicopters:	landing area aft
Missiles:	2 twin SA-N-1 Goa launchers [36]
Guns:	4 76.2-mm/59-cal AA (2 twin)

ASW weapons:	2 RBU-6000 rocket launchers
	2 RBU-1000 rocket launchers
	torpedoes
Torpedoes:	5 21-in (533-mm) torpedo tubes (1 quin)
Mines:	rails fitted
Radars:	1 Big Net (3-D air search)
	2 or 3 Don-2 or 2 Don-Kay or 2 Palm Frond (navigation)
	1 Head Net-C (3-D air search)
	2 Owl Screech (fire control)
	2 Peel Group (fire control)
Sonars:	medium frequency (hull mounted)
EW systems:	2 Watch Dog

The Kashins were the world's first major warships with all-gas-turbine propulsion. They are multi-purpose destroyers. Of these ships, 1 is in the Northern Fleet, 1 is in the Baltic, 7 in the Black Sea, and 3 in the Pacific.

Class: Twenty ships were built to this class for the Soviet Navy, and subsequently six modified ships (Kashin II) were built for the Indian Navy (completed from 1980 on). One Soviet ship, the OTVAZHNYY, was lost to an internal fire and explosion in the Black Sea on 31 August 1974. According to press reports, at least 200 crewmen were killed.

Six ships have been extensively modified and are listed separately. The PROVORNYY was converted to a test ship for the SA-N-7 missile system.

Classification: Originally ordered as EM (destroyer) type, but completed as BRK (large missile ship) by the Soviets; changed to Soviet BPK in the early 1960s.

The RESHITELNYY, barely underway, with her forward 76.2-mm gun mount and Owl Screech fire control radar trained to starboard. Like most Soviet surface combatants, she has large, 533-mm-diameter torpedo tubes; Western warships now have only smaller, 324-mm ASW tubes. (Ministry of Defence)

Design: These are large, graceful flush-deck destroyers, with a low superstructure topped by four large funnels for gas turbine exhaust, two radar-topped lattice masts, and four smaller radar towers. There is a helicopter landing area aft (with enclosed control station) but no hangar.

Engineering: These ships became operational more than a decade before the first U.S. gas-turbine warships of the SPRUANCE class.

Names: Most Kashin-class ships have adjectival names. The ex-

ceptions are KOMSOMOLETS UKRAINY (Ukrainian Young Communist), KRASNYY KAVKAZ (Red Caucasus), and KRASNYY KRYM (Red Crimea).

Operational: The OBRAZTSOVYY made a port visit to Portsmouth, England, in May 1976, the first Soviet warship to visit Great Britain in two decades. (The previous visit was made by the SVERDLOV-class cruiser ORDZHONIKIDZE, carrying Soviet leaders Bulganin and Khrushchev to Britain in April 1956.)

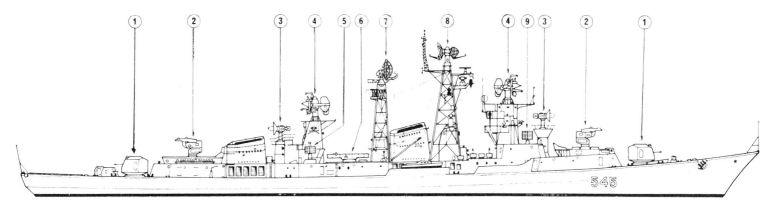

1. twin 76.2-mm AA gun mounts 2. SA-N-1 launchers 3. Owl Screech radars 4. Peel Group radars 5. RBU-1000 rocket launcher 6. 533-mm torpedo tubes 7. Big Net radar 8. Head Net-C radar 9. RBU-6000 rocket launcher (H. Simoni)

The SPOSOBNYY, showing the "balanced" arrangement of primary weapons and radars of the Kashin design. These ships also had a balanced design in terms of AAW/ASW/ASUW capabilities. (1984, JMSDF)

6 (2) GUIDED MISSILE DESTROYERS: KANIN CLASS

Name	Builder	Completed	Converted
GREMYASHCHIY	Z	1959	
ZHGUCHIY	Z	1960	
GORDYY	N	1960	
UPORNYY	K	1960	
DERZKIY	Z	1961	1968–1977
ZORKIY	Z	1961	
BOIKIY	N	1961	
GNEVNYY	N	1961	

Builders:	K = Komsomol'sk
	N = 61 Kommuna, Nikolayev (north)
	Z = Zhdanov Shipyard, Leningrad
Displacement:	3,700 tons standard
	4,750 tons full load
Length:	455 ft 11 in (139.0 m) oa
Beam:	49 ft 2 in (15.0 m)
Draft:	16 ft 5 in (5.0 m)
Propulsion:	steam turbines; 80,000 shp; 2 shafts
Boilers:	4
Speed:	34 knots
Range:	1,000 n.miles at 30 knots
	4,500 n.miles at 18 knots
Complement:	approx. 300
Helicopters:	landing deck
Missiles:	1 twin SA-N-1 Goa launcher [16]
Guns:	8 57-mm/70-cal AA (2 quad)
	8 30-mm/65-cal close-in (4 twin)
ASW weapons:	3 RBU-6000 rocket launchers
	torpedoes
Torpedoes:	10 21-in (533-mm) torpedo tubes (2 quin)
Radars:	2 Don-Kay (navigation)
	2 Drum Tilt (fire control)
	1 Hawk Screech (fire control)
	1 Head Net-C (3-D air search)
	1 Peel Group (fire control)
Sonars:	medium frequency (bow mounted)
EW systems:	2 Bell series
	4 Top Hat

These are AAW/ASW destroyers converted from surface-to-surface missiles ships. Six ships are active: 4 are in the Northern Fleet and 2 in the Pacific Fleet. Two others were decommissioned in 1984–1985.

Classification: Soviet BPK type.

Conversion: These ships are converted Krupnyy-class missile destroyers (with two SS-N-1 launchers), which in turn are modified Kotlin-class destroyers. For their present configuration, the forward SS-N-1 launcher was replaced by a second quad 57-mm mount and an RBU-6000; the after SS-N-1 launcher and quad 57-mm gun mount were deleted and the after section of the ship reconfigured for the SA-N-1 system and a larger helicopter deck. The superstructure was modified, and additional electronics and twin 30-mm guns were fitted, the latter in place of two amidships 57-mm mounts. (Gun armament for the Krupnyy configuration is 16 57-mm weapons.) Torpedo armament increased (from six tubes), and electronic equipment was upgraded. The conversions were completed between 1968 and 1977.

All these ships were converted at Zhdanov except for the GNEVNYY and GORDYY, converted at Vladivostok.

Guns: These ships and the single unmodified Kildin (NEUDERZHIMYY) have the lightest gun armament (in terms of caliber) of any destroyers operated by major navies.

Names: These ships have adjectival names.

Operational: In May 1975 the BOIKIY and ZHGUCHY visited the port of Boston, Massachusetts, to celebrate the 30th anniversary of the end of World War II. They were the first Soviet warships to visit the United States since the end of the war.

A Kanin underway in the Pacific. The Soviets retain a large number of these and older destroyers that have limited effectiveness against Western forces. They are being succeeded by newer ships, but still could be effective in certain combat scenarios, especially in the Third World. (1984, JMSDF)

The Kanin-class destroyerr GREMYASHIY; this view shows the ship's general layout, although her forward quad 57-mm gun mount, torpedo tubes, and amidships RBU-6000 rocket launchers are under protective canvas. These ships have the smallest caliber guns of any destroyers, although they have been fitted with four 30-mm Gatling guns. (1982, U.S. Navy)

3 GUIDED MISSILE DESTROYERS: MODIFIED KILDIN CLASS

Name	Builder	Completed	Converted
BEDOVYY	N	1958	
NEULOVIMYY	Z	1958	} 1973–1975
PROZORLIVYY	Z	1959	

Builders:	N = 61 Kommuna, Nikolayev (north)
	Z = Zhdanov Shipyard, Leningrad
Displacement:	2,800 tons standard
	3,700 tons full load
Length:	414 ft 11 in (126.5 m) oa
Beam:	42 ft 8 in (13.0 m)
Draft:	15 ft 5 in (4.7 m)
Propulsion:	steam turbines; 72,000 shp; 2 shafts
Boilers:	4
Speed:	36 knots
Range:	1,000 n.miles at 32 knots
	3,600 n.miles at 18 knots
Complement:	approx. 300
Helicopters:	(no facilities)
Missiles:	4 SS-N-2c Styx launchers (4 single)
	4 76.2-mm/59-cal AA (2 twin)
	16 57-mm/70-cal AA (4 quad) except in BEDOVYY, which has 16
	45-mm/85-cal AA (4 quad)

ASW weapons:	2 RBU-2500 rocket launchers
	torpedoes
Torpedoes:	4 21-in (533-mm) torpedo tubes (2 twin)
Radars:	1 Don-2 (navigation)
	2 Hawk Screech (fire control)
	1 Head Net-C (3-D air search) except Strut Pair in BEDOVYY
	1 Owl Screech (fire control)
Sonars:	1 Herkules or Pegasus medium frequency (hull mounted)
EW systems:	2 Watch Dog

The three modified Kildin-class ships have had their single SS-N-1 (aft) launcher replaced by twin 76.2-mm gun mounts and four SS-N-2c anti-ship missiles. The PROZORLIVYY is in the Baltic Fleet, and the two other ships of this class are in the Black Sea.

Class: Four ships were converted during construction from Kotlin-class destroyers to the world's first missile destroyers. Subsequently, three ships were modified; their SS-N-1 launchers were removed and they rejoined the fleet in 1973–1975. The fourth Kildin, the NEUDER-ZHIMYY, was not converted (see below).

Classification: Soviet BRK type.

Conversion: All three ships were converted at Nikolayev north.

This stern angle of the PROZORLIVYY shows clearly the ship's twin 76.2-mm gun battery and aft-firing Styx missiles, added after removal of the ships bulky, ineffective SS-N-1 missile launcher. Like the Kanin class, these ships were extensively modified to provide a more effective combat capability. (West German Navy)

Another modified Kildin, with the hull lines and basic arrangement common to the Kildin, Kanin, Krupnyy, and Kotlin classes. Note the quad 57-mm gun mounts fitted amidships as well as forward, and two RBU-2500 rocket launchers installed on the forecastle. (West German Navy)

1 GUIDED MISSILE DESTROYER: KILDIN CLASS

Name	Completed
NEUDERZHIMYY	1959

Builder:	Komsomol'sk

The NEUDERZHIMYY is in essentially her original configuration, with a single SS-N-1 missile launcher aft supplemented by 16 57-mm AA guns. Basic characteristics are the same as those of the modified Kildin class.

The ship is in the Pacific Fleet and is unlikely to be modified because of her age.

The NEUDERZHIMYY is the last Soviet warship to carry the SS-N-1 anti-ship missile; it is unlikely that her missile system remains operational. She will probably not be modernized and should be discarded in the near future.

7 (1) GUIDED MISSILE DESTROYERS: SAM KOTLIN CLASS

Name	Builder	Completed	Converted
SKROMNYY	Z	1955	1969
NESOKRUSHIMYY*	Z	1956	1967
NAKHODCHIVYY	Z	1957	1968
VOZBUZHDENNYY*	K	1957	1970
SKRYTNYY*	Z	1957	1971
NASTOYCHIVYY	Z	1958	1970
SOZNATEL'NYY*	Z	1958	1972
BRAVYY	N	1961–1962	(see notes)

Builders:	K = Komsomol'sk
	N = 61 Kommuna, Nikolayev (north)
	Z = Zhdanov Shipyard, Leningrad
Displacement:	2,700 tons standard
	3,600 tons full load
Length:	414 ft 11 in (126.5 m) oa
Beam:	42 ft 8 in (13.0 m)
Draft:	15 ft 1 in (4.6 m)
Propulsion:	steam turbines; 72,000 shp; 2 shafts
Boilers:	4
Speed:	36 knots
Range:	1,000 n.miles at 34 knots
	3,600 n.miles at 18 knots
Complement:	
Helicopters:	(no facilities)
Missiles:	1 SA-N-1 Goa launcher [16]
Guns:	2 130-mm/58-cal DP (1 twin)
	4 45-mm/85-cal AA (1 quad) except BRAVYY 12 45-mm (3 quad)
	8 30-mm/65-cal close-in (4 twin) in 4 ships*
ASW weapons:	2 RBU-6000 rocket launchers (2 RBU-2500 in BRAVYY, SKROMNYY)
	torpedoes

Torpedoes:	5 21-in (533-mm) torpedo tubes (1 quin)
Mines:	rails removed
Radars:	1 or 2 Don-2 (navigation)
	2 Drum Tilt in 4 ships*
	1 Egg Cup (fire control) (deleted in NASTOCHIVYY)
	1 Hawk Screech (fire control)
	1 Head Net-C (3-D air search)
	1 Peel Group (fire control)
	1 Sun Visor-B (fire control)
Sonars:	Herkules or Pegasus high frequency (hull mounted)
EW systems:	2 Watch Dog

These anti-aircraft ships have heavier gun batteries than the later Kildin-class ships. One ship serves in the Northern Fleet, 1 in the Baltic Fleet, 3 in the Black Sea Fleet, and 2 in the Pacific Fleet; 1 ship is believed to be in reserve.

Class: Nine ships were converted from standard Kotlin-class destroyers to this SAM configuration. The SPRAVEDLIVYY was transferred to Poland in 1970.

Classification: Soviet EM type.

Conversion: The Kotlins' after twin 130-mm gun mount and half of the torpedo battery were removed. An SA-N-1 missile system and associated radars were fitted, as well as improved electronics and ASW weapons. Details of the ships differ.

The BRAVYY was completed as the trials ship for the SA-N-1. She initially had only four 45-mm AA guns and no torpedo tubes; her armament was increased in the mid-1960s.

The BRAVYY was the first of the SAM Kotlin conversions, distinguished by the unique shape of her second funnel. Amidship 45-mm guns are provided with RBU-2500 rocket launchers forward of the bridge (alongside the forward 45-mm mount). All have five 533-mm torpedo tubes. (1975, U.S. Navy)

A SAM Kotlin with RBU-6000 rocket launchers forward of bridge and Head Net-C radar, but no amidships 45-mm gun mounts or 30-mm Gatling guns. The details of these eight ships now differ considerably. There is a Wasp Head gun director with Sun Visor-B radar atop the bridge. (West German Navy)

17 DESTROYERS: KOTLIN CLASS

Name	Builder	Completed
SPESHNYY	Z	1955
BYVALYY*	N	1956
BURLIVYY*	N	1956
MOSKOVSKIY KOMSOMOLETS*	Z	1956
SPOKOYNYY	Z	1956
SVEDUSHCHIY*	Z	1956
VDOKHNOVENNYY*	K	1956
VYZYVAYUSHCHIY*	K	1956
VLIYATELNYY	K	1956
BLAGORODNYY*	N	1957
BLESTYASHCHIY*	N	1957
SVETLYY	Z	1957
VESKIY	K	1957
NAPORISTIY*	N	1958
DALNYVOSTOCHNYY KOMSOMOLETS	K	1958
PLAMENNYY*	N	1958
VYDERZHANNYY*	K	1958

Builders:	K = Komsomol'sk
	N = 61 Kommuna, Nikolayev (north)
	Z = Zhdanov Shipyard, Leningrad
Displacement:	2,600 tons standard
	3,500 tons full load
Length:	414 ft 11 in (126.5 m) oa
Beam:	42 ft 8 in (13.0 m)
Draft:	15 ft 1 in (4.6 m)
Propulsion:	steam turbines; 72,000 shp; 2 shafts
Boilers:	4
Speed:	36 knots
Range:	1,000 n.miles at 34 knots
	3,600 n.miles at 18 knots
Complement:	approx. 335
Helicopters:	no facilities except landing deck in SVETLYY
Missiles:	none

Guns:	4 130-mm/58-cal DP (2 twin)	
	16 45-mm/85-cal AA (4 quad)	
	4 25-mm/60-cal AA (2 twin) except 8 guns (4 twin) in modified ships*	
ASW weapons:	unmodified ships	modified ships*
	6 BMB-2 depth-charge projectors	2 RBU-600 rocket launchers except 2 RBU-6000 launchers in MOSKOVSKIY KOMSOMOLETS
	2 depth-charge racks	
	torpedoes	torpedoes
Torpedoes:	unmodified ships	modified ships*
	10 21-inch (533-mm) torpedo tubes (2 quin)	5 21-inch (533-mm) torpedo tubes (1 quin)
Mines:	rails fitted for approx. 70 mines	
Radars:	2 Don-2 or 1 Neptune (navigation)	
	2 Egg Cup (fire control)	
	2 Hawk Screech (fire control)	
	1 Post Lamp or Top Bow (fire control)	
	1 Sun Visor (fire control)	
Sonars:	Herkules high frequency (hull mounted)	
	medium frequency (variable depth) in MOSKOVSKIY KOMSOMOLETS	
EW systems:	2 Watch Dog	

These are graceful flush-deck destroyers. Eleven ships (indicated by asterisk) were modified and are considered a sub-class. Other Kotlins have been partially and fully converted to missile configurations (see below). The seventeen ships listed here are believed to be in active service.

Class: Twenty-seven Kotlin-class ships of a planned 36 were completed between 1954 and 1961. Nine of these ships were subsequently converted to the SAM Kotlin configuration (armed with the SA-N-1). Four of the Kotlin hulls were completed as Kildin (SS-N-1) missile destroyers, and eight new ships of this basic design were built as Krupnyy (SS-N-1) missile destroyers. The latter ships were later converted again, to the Kanin configuration (SA-N-1 system).

Classification: Soviet EM type.

Design: These were the world's last destroyers to be built to classic World War II destroyer lines, mounting heavy DP and light AA gun batteries, with a large torpedo battery, high speed, and minimal ASW weapons and sensors.

Engineering: These were the first of the Soviet Navy's high-speed surface combatants.

Modification: Eleven ships were modified between 1960 and 1962, having their after bank of torpedo tubes replaced by a deckhouse and their ASW weapons improved. The MOSKOVSKIY KOMSOMOLETS was further modified, being fitted with two RBU-6000 launchers forward and, in 1978, a variable-depth sonar. The SVETLYY has been fitted with a helicopter platform aft.

Names: Most of these ships have adjectival names, with two ships being named for city *komsomols*. The Western class name Kotlin was bestowed when the ships were first seen off Kotlin Island (Kronshtadt) in the Gulf of Riga.

A detailed view of the MOSKOVSKIY KOMSOMOLETS, showing the variable-depth sonar installation. The after 130-mm twin mount is at near full elevation as is the after 45-mm quad mount; the Square Head EW antenna and Slim Net radar are visible on the after mast.

A Kotlin with the RBU-600 launchers forward of the bridge and mine rails clearly visible.

The standard Kotlin configuration provided a balanced armament arrangement. The 25-mm guns are fitted alongside the second funnel. The fantail is crowded with depth-charge projectors and racks. The mine rails, common to all Soviet surface combatants of the period, are not visible in this dated photo, retained here because of its clarity for detail. (1974, U.S. Navy)

The modified Kotlin-class destroyer MOSKOVSKIY KOMSOMOLETS, fitted with two RBU-6000 launchers forward; she has two 25-mm mounts on each side amidships, and is provided with a VDS installation aft, the only Kotlin so fitted.

2 (18) DESTROYERS: "SKORYY" CLASS

Name	Builder	Completed
BEZUDERZHNYY	N	1949
OGNENNYY*	M	1949
OSTOROZHNY*	M	1949
OTVETSTVENNYY	M	1949
OZHESTOCHENNYY	M	1953
OZHIVLENNY	M	1953
SERDITY	Z	1949
SMOTRYASHCHY	Z	1949
SOLIDNY	Z	1951
SOKRUSHITELNYY	Z	1951
SOVERSHENNYY	Z	1951
STATNYY	Z	1951
STEPENNYY	Z	1952
STOYKIY*	Z	1949
STREMITELNYY	Z	1950
SUROVYY	Z	1949
SVOBODNYY*	Z	1950
VDUMCHIVYY	K	1953
VNIMATELNYY	K	1953
VRAZUMITELNYY	K	1953

Builders:	K = Komsomol'sk
	M = Molotovsk/Severodvinsk
	N = 61 Kommuna, Nikolayev (north)
	Z = Zhdanov Shipyard, Leningrad
Displacement:	2,600 tons standard
	3,130 tons full load
Length:	397 ft 6 in (121.2 m) oa
Beam:	39 ft 4 in (12.0 m)
Draft:	14 ft 9 in (4.5 m)
Propulsion:	steam turbines; 60,000 shp; 2 shafts
Boilers:	4
Speed:	34 knots
Range:	850 n.miles at 30 knots
	3,00 n.miles at 18 knots

Complement:	approx. 220	
Helicopters:	no facilities	
Guns:	unmodified ships	modified ships*
	4 130-mm/50-cal SP (2 twin)	4 130-mm/50-cal SP (2 twin)
	2 85-mm/50-cal AA (1 twin)	5 57-mm/70-cal AA (5 single)
	7 or 8 37-mm/63-cal AA	
	(7 single or 4 twin)	
	4 or 6 20-mm AA (2 or 3 twin)	
	(see notes)	
ASW weapons:	unmodified ships	modified ships*
	2 depth-charge projectors	2 RBU-2500 rocket launchers
	2 depth-charge racks	2 depth-charge racks
	torpedoes	torpedoes
Torpedoes:	unmodified ships	modified ships*
	10 21-in (533-mm) torpedo	5 21-in (533-mm) torpedo tubes
	tubes (2 quin)	(1 quin)
Mines:	rails fitted for approx. 50 mines	
Radars:	unmodified ships	modified ships*
	1 Cross Bird (air search)	
	1 or 2 Don-2 (navigation)	1 or 2 Don-2
	1 Half Bow or Post Lamp or	2 Hawk Screech (fire control)
	Top Bow (fire control)	1 Slim Net (air search)
	1 High Sieve (air search)	
Sonars:	1 Pegas high frequency	
EW systems:	2 Watch Dog	

These were the first Soviet destroyers constructed after World War II. Most if not all are laid up in reserve, with some being periodically employed for training duties.

Class: Seventy-two destroyers of this class were built; of these, after being in Soviet service, 6 were transferred to Egypt, 7 to Indonesia, and 2 to Poland.

Classification: Soviet EM type.

Design: This design was derived from the prewar OGNEVOYY class (the first ship of that class was laid down in 1939 but not completed until 1943). The SKORYY design incorporated some features of German

A modified SKORYY-class destroyer. The eight modified ships can be easily identified by their second lattice mast carrying a Slim Net radar. Canvas-covered RBU-2500 rocket launchers are forward of the bridge.

ships, and had better seakeeping, more torpedo armament, and more AA guns than the OGNEVOYY class.

Guns: In the early 1970s those ships with eight 37-mm weapons were provided with 25-mm AA guns. The main battery lacks sufficient elevation for dual-purpose use.

Modification: A modernization program was begun in 1958, but in the event only eight ships were updated, probably because of the expense and because yard capacity was needed for new construction. Principal changes were the upgrading of radar, the construction of a deckhouse in place of the forward torpedo bank, and the installation of modern 57-mm guns in place of earlier AA armament.

Names: These ships have adjectival names. The lead ship SKORYY ("speedy") has been stricken, and that name is now carried by a Kashin-class destroyer.

A "broken-deck" SKORYY, the first Soviet destroyer class completed after World War II although of earlier design. Note the large Four Eyes optical fire control director atop the bridge (removed from modified ships); there is a smaller Cylinder Head director aft. These directors survive only in SKORYY-class ships. (Skyfotos)

DESTROYER: TALLINN CLASS

The single destroyer of the Tallinn class, the NASTOYCHIVYY, later renamed NEUSTRASHIMY, was completed in 1955 and discarded in the 1970s. She was modeled after the Soviet destroyer TASHKENT, built in Italy before World War II. The NASTOYCHIVYY carried four 130-mm guns and ten torpedo tubes on a full-load displacement of 4,400 tons, and had an overall length of 426 feet and a maximum speed of 38 knots.

Additional ships of this class were apparently planned but not built.

16
Frigates

The Soviet Navy employs frigate-type ships for conventional frigate roles—mainly anti-submarine warfare—but also for coastal defense and patrol duties. The term frigate is used here in the contemporary Western context.

The ships in this chapter have the classification patrol ship (SKR—*Storozhevoy Korabl'* or small ASW ship (MPK—*Malyy Protivolodochnyy Korabl'*); they are roughly equivalent in size and capability to Western small ASW frigates and corvettes; Western intelligence generally lists all but the Krivaks as light frigates (i.e., FFL).

The employment of the Soviet SKR and MPK ship types, however, is quite different from that of Western frigates and corvettes, which are primarily *escort* ships. Rather, the Soviet patrol or ASW ships are intended to *patrol* or to *guard* an area. They can be employed as escort ships, but lack the endurance and some capabilities (e.g., helicopters) to undertake escort operations in the Western sense of the role.

Additional frigate-type ships are operated by the KGB Maritime Border Troops (see chapter 25).

No frigates are currently believed to be under construction for the Soviet Navy. However, in view of the large number of outdated Rigas still in service and the age of the Petya and Mirka classes, new construction of the Koni class or, more likely, an improved design can be expected in the near future for Soviet use.

The Krivaks are the only Soviet frigates that compare to Western warships in this category. Production of Krivaks for the Soviet Navy has ceased after 32 ships; the Krivak III is being built for the KGB Maritime Border Troops. The Bezzavetnyy shows off the design's clipper bow and low, attractive superstructure lines. (1984, U.S. Navy)

51+ LIGHT ANTI-SUBMARINE FRIGATES: GRISHA I/III/IV/V CLASSES

Name	Completed
Grisha I	
. . . . . (16 units)	1968–1974
Grisha III	
KOMSOMOLETS BASHKIRIY	
KOMSOMOLETS GRUZIN	1975–. . . .
ORLOVSKIY KOMSOMOLETS	
. . . . . . (30 units)	
Grisha IV	
. . . . . . (1 unit)	
Grisha V	
. . . . . . (1 + units)	

Builders:	Khabarovsk (Grisha III)
	Zelenodolsk (Grisha I/III)
Displacement:	950 tons standard
	1,200 tons full load
Length:	234 ft 10 in (71.6 m) oa
Beam:	32 ft 2 in (9.8 m)
Draft:	12 ft 2 in (3.7 m)
Propulsion:	CODAG: 4 diesels (M503); 16,000 hp +
	1 gas turbine; 15,000 shp = 31,000 hp;
	3 shafts
Speed:	30 knots
Range:	450 n.miles at 27 knots
	4,500 n.miles at 10 knots
Complement:	approx. 60
Helicopters:	no facilities
Missiles:	1 twin SA-N-4 launcher [20]
Guns:	Grisha I
	2 57-mm/80-cal AA (1 twin)
	Grisha III
	2 57-mm/80-cal AA (1 twin)
	1 30-mm/65-cal close-in (multibarrel)
	Grisha IV
	1 76.2-mm/59-cal AA
	1 30-mm/65-cal close-in (multibarrel)
ASW weapons:	2 RBU-6000 rocket launchers except 1 in Grisha IV
	2 depth-charge racks (see notes)
	torpedoes
Torpedoes:	4 21-in (533-mm) torpedo tubes (2 twin)
Mines:	rails for 18 mines
Radars:	Grisha I
	1 Don-2 (navigation)
	1 Muff Cob (fire control)
	1 Pop Group (fire control)
	1 Strut Curve (air search)
	Grisha III
	1 Don-2 (navigation)
	1 Bass Tilt (fire control)
	1 Pop Group (fire control)
	1 Strut Curve (air search)
	Grisha IV
	1 Don-2 (navigation)
	1 Bass Tilt (fire control)
	1 Pop Group (fire control)
	1 Strut Pair (air search)
Sonars:	medium frequency (hull mounted)
	high frequency (dipping)
EW systems:	2 Watch Dog

These are small ASW frigates. The principal differences are the addition of a 30-mm Gatling gun in the Grisha III with the associated Bass Tilt radar. The Grisha IV has a 76.2-mm gun aft and a heavier radar, requiring the deletion of one RBU as a partial weight compensation. Seven similar ships of the Grisha II class were built for the KGB Maritime Border Troops (see chapter 25). A Grisha V series is reported to be under construction.

Classification: The Grisha I and III series are Soviet MPK type, having been briefly typed SPK when they first appeared. Western intelligence designates the Grishas and other Soviet light frigates as well as other small combatants with personal nicknames, with Grisha translating to "Greg."

Design: The Grisha variants have a heavy ASW armament coupled with a heavy self-defense armament.

Racks for 12 depth charges can be fitted to the after end of the mine rails.

These ships have a layout similar to the larger Koni class, but with only two "steps" forward on the superstructure. The Grishas also have a solid mast structure similar to the Koni in contrast to the lattice masts of the earlier Mirkas and Petyas.

Operational: The Grisha's variable-depth sonar cannot be used while the ship is under way. Thus, Grishas normally perform ASW searches in pairs, alternating in the sprint and drift (sonar search) modes.

Stern view of the Grisha III showing her offset Bass Tilt radar for twin 57-mm AA gun mount and, above it, the single 30-mm Gatling gun. The stern openings are for mine rails or depth-charge racks, both of which are important for coastal operations.

A Grisha I at high speed in rough seas. These light frigates are well suited for coastal patrol/ASW operations in the many seas that border the Soviet Union. Even these relatively small (and heavily armed) ships have 533-mm torpedo tubes. (Royal Navy, courtesy *Ships of the World*)

At slower speed a Grisha III shows the built-up after structure of the class that supports a Bass Tilt fire control radar and the 30-mm Gatling gun. These ships continue in production for the Navy (production of the Grisha II class for the KGB has ceased). This unit was photographed in the Sea of Japan in 1983.

45 LIGHT ANTI-SUBMARINE FRIGATES: PETYA I/II CLASSES

Name	Completed
. . . . . (7) Petya I	
. . . . . (11) Mod. Petya I	} 1961–1964
. . . . . (26) Petya II	
. . . . . (1) Mod. Petya II	} 1964–1969

Builders:	Khabarovsk (Petya I/II)
	Yantar/Kaliningrad (Petya I/II)
Displacement:	950 tons standard
	1,150 tons full load
Length:	268 ft 4 in (81.8 m) oa
Beam:	30 ft 2 in (9.2 m)
Draft:	9 ft 2 in (2.8 m)
Propulsion:	CODAG: 1 diesel 6,000 hp + 2 gas turbines 30,000 shp = 36,000 hp; 3 shafts
Speed:	30 knots
Range:	450 n.miles at 29 knots
	1,800 n.miles at 16 knots
Complement:	approx. 90
Helicopters:	no facilities
Guns:	4 76.2-mm/59-cal AA (2 twin); reduced to 2 guns in a few modified ships
ASW weapons:	4 RBU-2500 rocket launchers in Petya I
	2 RBU-6000 rocket launchers in Petya II
	2 depth-charge racks; 1 in modified Petya I and removed from modified Petya II
	torpedoes
Torpedoes:	5 16-in (406-mm) torpedo tubes (1 quin) in Petya I
	10 16-in (406-mm) torpedo tubes (2 quin) in Petya II
Mines:	rails for 22 mines; removed from modified Petya I
Radars:	1 Don-2 (navigation)
	1 Hawk Screech (fire control)
	1 Slim Net (air search) in some Petya I
	1 Strut Curve (air search) in Petya II and some Petya I
Sonars:	Herkules high frequency (hull-mounted)
	high frequency (dipping) in modified Petya I
	medium frequency (variable-depth) in 11 modified Petya I
EW systems:	2 Watch Dog

The Petya is a light frigate that was produced in larger numbers than the similar Mirka class, indicating a more successful design. The Petyas have been built and modified to several different configurations.

Class: Forty-five Petyas were built for the Soviet Navy—18 of the Petya I type and 27 of the Petya II type. Modified export versions were constructed for Ethiopia (1), India (10), Syria (2), and Vietnam (4).

Classification: Originally designated as the PLK type, these were the first Soviet ships to have the designation "anti-submarine ship." They were changed to "medium" ASW ship (SKR) in 1964. The NATO *Petya* translates in Russian to "Peter."

Conversions: Several Petya Is have been employed in experimental roles. About 1966 one was fitted with the SUW-N-1 ASW rocket launcher in place of the forward 76.2-mm gun mount; in 1967 one ship tested the variable-depth sonar for the MOSKVA-class helicopter ships; and another ship was modified by 1969 to test towed sonar arrays (a large deckhouse was installed aft).

Beginning in 1973, 11 of the Petya I type were modified with a large poop deck aft to carry variable-depth sonar. The two after RBU-2500 launchers as well as minelaying capabilities were deleted, as was one depth-charge rack.

One Petya II was modified with a deckhouse aft, the purpose of which is not clear; that modification retains the mine rails.

Design: These ships have a large hull-mounted sonar, with a dome that projects almost four feet beneath the keel; the drag created by this reduces the ships' potential speed by approximately six knots.

Electronics: The dipping sonar is similar to that fitted in the Ka-25 Hormone-A helicopters.

Engineering: These were the first large Soviet warships to have gas-turbine propulsion. The diesel drives the centerline propeller.

Missiles: One Petya had been fitted with a twin SUW-N-1 ASW missile launcher on her bow in the mid-1970s, apparently as a trials ship.

Modification: The ten "modified" ships have a raised stern deckhouse enclosing a large variable-depth sonar. Some ships with this arrangement have their after 76.2-mm twin mount removed as well as their mine rails.

One unit has been fitted with a large VDS but no raised stern; one ship has a deckhouse abaft the stack with a complex towing and cable-handling array; and one ship has a small, box-like structure at her stern.

Torpedoes: The second bank of ASW torpedo tubes was fitted on the stern of these ships, replacing the two after RBU-2500s of the Petya I design.

A Petya I refitted with three 533-mm torpedo tubes amidships. There are RBU-2500 launchers forward of the bridge and, on the stern; twin 76.2-mm gun mounts forward and aft; and mine rails. (1979)

A Petya II with RBU-6000 rocket launchers (canvas covered) and two banks of five 406-mm torpedo tubes. No reloads are carried for these or the 533-mm tubes in Soviet warships.

Modified Petya I with what is probably a VDS installation on the stern. The after 76.2-mm gun mount has been removed. The RBU-2500 rocket launchers are forward of the bridge, adjacent to the twin 76.2-mm gun mount.

Modified Petya I with deck structure aft to house the VDS. There are several variants of the Petya. They can be easily distinguished from the Mirka classes by the position of the mast (i.e., "attached" to the deck structure while the Mirka mast is "freestanding"). (1985, JMSDF)

18 LIGHT ANTI-SUBMARINE FRIGATES: MIRKA I/II CLASSES

Name	Completed
. . . . . . (9) Mirka I	1964–1965
. . . . . . (9) Mirka II	1965–1966

Builders:	Yantar/Kaliningrad
Displacement:	950 tons standard
	1,150 tons full load
Length:	270 ft 3 in (82.4 m) oa
Beam:	30 ft 2 in (9.2 m)
Draft:	9 ft 6 in (2.9 m)
Propulsion:	2 gas turbines 30,000 shp + 2 diesels 12,000 hp = 42,000 hp;
	2 shafts
Speed:	34 knots
Range:	500 n.miles at 30 knots
	4,800 n.miles at 10 knots
Complement:	approx. 90
Helicopters:	no facilities
Guns:	4 76.2-mm/59-cal AA (2 twin)
ASW weapons:	4 RBU-6000 rocket launchers in Mirka I
	2 RBU-6000 rocket launchers in Mirka II
	1 depth-charge rack in Mirka I
	torpedoes
Torpedoes:	5 16-in (406-mm) torpedo tubes (1 quin) in Mirka I
	10 16-in (406-mm) torpedo tubes (2 quin) in Mirka II
Mines:	no rails fitted
Radars:	1 Don-2 (navigation)
	1 Hawk Screech (fire control)
	1 Slim Net (air search) except Strut Curve in later Mirka II units
Sonars:	1 Herkules or Pegas high frequency (hull-mounted)
	1 high frequency (dipping) in Mirka II
EW systems:	2 Watch Dog

A small number of these light frigates were built simultaneously with the larger Petya program, being "sandwiched" between the Petya I and II series at the Kaliningrad yard. Nine ships are of the Mirka II configuration with a helicopter-type dipping sonar installed in a new stern structure.

Classification: Originally classified by the Soviet Navy as PLK; changed to SKR in 1964 (see notes under Petya class). NATO name *Mirka* translates to the Russian nickname for Vladimir.

Design: These ships are generally similar to the Petya series, but have a different propulsion arrangement (see Engineering notes).

The two classes can be readily distinguished by the Petya's mast being adjacent to the bridge structure and the Mirka's mast standing separate amidships. The Petya has a short, squat funnel amidships, while the Mirka has large air intakes at the stern and exhaust ports in the stern transom. (The stern configuration necessary for the machinery arrangement prevents these ships from having depth-charge racks or mine rails.)

Electronics: The dipping sonar is similar to that in the Hormone-A helicopter.

Engineering: Two shafts, each driven by gas turbine and diesel compared to the triple-shaft Petya. In these ships the turbines were placed all the way aft, preventing the fitting of mine rails or VDS. The propellers are mounted in tunnels, with the gas turbines powering compressors that inject air into the tunnels to provide a pump-jet action.

Operational: All Mirkas are assigned to the Baltic and Black Sea fleets and apparently have not undertaken the long deployments that Petyas have made.

A Mirka I with only one bank of 406-mm torpedo tubes (between mast and after gun mount) and with a second pair of RBU-6000 launchers aft. The Watch Dog EW antennas are mounted halfway on the lattice mast. (Royal Navy)

Mirka II light frigates. These ships—like the Petyas—have more ASW weapons than the later Koni class. Note the large air intakes for the gas turbines fitted on the stern. (West German Navy)

A Mirka II at rest. The port-side RBU-6000 launcher is in the vertical, reloading position. After firing, the rockets are automatically reloaded from twin magazines in the superstructure. (Royal Navy)

35 (10) FRIGATES: RIGA CLASS

Name	Builder	Completed
. . . . . . (22 units)	various	1955–1956
ARKHANGEL'SKIY KOMSOMOLETS	YK	1957
ASTRAKHAN'SKIY KOMSOMOLETS	YK	1957
BARS	YK	1957
BARSUK	YK	1957
BOBR	N	1957
BUYVOL	N	1957
BYK	N	1957
GEPARD	K	1957
GIENA	YK	1958
GRUZIY KOMSOMOLETS	YK	1958
KOBCHIK	YK	1958
KRASNODARSKIY KOMSOMOLETS	YK	1958
KUNITSA	N	1958
LEOPARD	N	1958
LEV	N	1958
LISA	K	1958
LITVIY KOMSOMOLETS	YK	1959
MEDVED	YK	1959
PANTERA	YK	1959
RYS ROSOMAKHA	YK	1959
SHAKAL	YK	1959
TIGR	YK	1959
TURMAN	N	1959
VOLK	N	1959
VORON	N	1959
YAGUAR	K	1959

Builders:	K = Komsomol'sk
	N = Nikolayev (north)
	YK = Yantar/Kaliningrad
Displacement:	1,260 tons standard
	1,480 tons full load
Length:	298 ft 6 in (91.0 m) oa
Beam:	33 ft 6 in (10.2 m)
Draft:	10 ft 6 in (3.2 m)
Propulsion:	steam turbines; 20,000 shp; 2 shafts
Boilers:	2
Speed:	30 knots
Range:	550 n.miles at 28 knots
	2,000 n.miles at 13 knots
Complement:	approx. 170
Helicopters:	no facilities
Guns:	3 100-mm/56-cal DP (3 single)
	4 37-mm/63-cal AA (2 twin)
	4 25-mm/60-cal AA (2 twin) in most active ships
ASW weapons:	2 RBU-2500 rocket launchers; deleted in 1 ship (with Bell-series EW system)
	2 depth-charge racks
	torpedoes
Torpedoes:	2 or 3 21-in (533-mm) torpedo tubes (1 twin or triple)
Mines:	rails for 28 mines
Radars:	1 Don-2 or Neptune (navigation)
	1 Hawk Screech (fire control) in 1 ship
	1 Slim Net (air search)
	1 Sun Visor-B (fire control)
Sonars:	Herkules or Pegas high frequency (hull-mounted)
EW systems:	2 Watch Dog
	2 Bell series in 1 ship

An estimated 66 Rigas were built, 58 for the Soviet Navy plus eight ships going directly to foreign navies. About 35 ships remain in active service with another 10 laid up in reserve. The lead ship of the class was completed in 1954.

Class: Ships of this class have been transferred to Bulgaria (2), East Germany (5), Finland (2), and Indonesia (8).[1] Eight additional ships are believed to have been built specifically for foreign use, the other transfers being ex-Soviet ships for a class total of 66 units. A modified Riga design was constructed in China.

Classification: Soviet SKR type. *Riga* is a NATO code name.

Design: The Rigas are an improved and *smaller* development of the previous Kola class.

Electronics: One ship has been modified with Bell Series EW system installed on a short mast fitted aft. Another ship has a Hawk Screech radar/director forward and the Sun Visor radar/director mounted aft.

Modernization: Most—but probably not all ships—have had an ASW refit. Original ASW armament consisted of 1 MBU-600 hedgehog, 4 BMB-2 depth-charge mortars, plus depth-charge racks, mines, and torpedoes. The original gun armament consisted of the 100-mm and 37-mm guns.

[1] One of the East German ships was gutted by fire shortly after transfer and never entered operational service.

Stern quarter of a Riga refueling on a calm sea in the western Pacific. The after 100-mm gun is trained forward, revealing the open-mount configuration. Also shown are the Watch Dog and Square Head antennas fitted outboard of the mast. She was refueling from a SVERDLOV when snapped. (1970, U.S. Navy)

A Riga under tow in the Northern Dvina River at Arkhangel'sk. The ship's superstructure is dominated by the Wasp Head gunfire control director with its small Sun Visor-B radar. The port-side RBU-2500 rocket launcher is visible adjacent to the No. 2 gun mount; there is a deck structure abaft the funnel (no torpedo tubes). (1985, L. & L. Van Ginderen collection)

This overhead view of a Riga-class frigate in the Mediterranean details the ship's arrangement, including a pair of 533-mm torpedo tubes abaft the funnel. This unit has a modified bridge structure, the Wasp Head director mounted aft, and a Hawk Screech GFS/radar atop the bridge. (1975, U.S. Navy)

FRIGATES: KOLA CLASS

All earlier Kola-class frigates have been stricken. Eight ships were completed in 1951–1952, being based partially on German designs of World War II. Each ship, displacing 1,500 tons full load, carried four 100-mm guns and three torpedo tubes, plus lesser guns and ASW weapons. All were stricken by the late 1970s.

17
Corvettes

The Soviet Navy operates approximately 130 corvette-type warships. These ships are employed mainly in the regional seas surrounding the Soviet Union and tend to be specialized for the anti-submarine or anti-ship role. The U.S. Navy does not operate corvette-type ships, although this type of ship is common in several European NATO navies. The U.S. Coast Guard cutters of the BEAR (WMEC 901) class are of corvette size, but lack the combat capabilities (including speed) to effectively perform wartime tasks.

A sleek-looking Tarantul missile corvette in the Baltic Sea. Note the over-under Styx missile tubes and paired Gatling guns aft; new electronics suite. The Soviets continue to emphasize the development and construction of corvettes and small combatants as well as warships. (West German Navy)

12+ GUIDED MISSILE CORVETTES: TARANTUL I/II/III CLASSES

Name	Completed
. . . . . . (2) Tarantul I	1979–1980
. . . . . . (10+) Tarantul II	1981–
. . . . . . (1) Tarantul III	

Builders:	Petrovskiy, Leningrad
	Srednyy Neva, Kolpina
Displacement:	480 tons standard
	540 tons full load
Length:	172 ft 2 in (52.5 m) wl
	185 ft 4 in (56.5 m) oa
Beam:	34 ft 5 in (10.5 m)
Draft:	8 ft 3 in (2.5 m)
Propulsion:	CODAG: 2 gas turbines; 24,000 shp + 2 diesels; approx 12,000 hp; 2 shafts
Speed:	36 knots
Range:	2,000 n.miles at 20 knots
	400 n.miles at 36 knots
Complement:	approx. 40
Missiles:	Tarantul I/II 4 SS-N-2c Styx anti-ship (2 twin)
	Tarantul III 4 SS-N-22 anti-ship (2 twin)
	1 quad SA-N-5 Grail launcher [16]
Guns:	1 76.2-mm/59-cal AA
	2 30-mm/65-cal close-in (2 multibarrel)
ASW weapons:	none
Torpedoes:	none
Mines:	none
Radars:	1 Band Stand (fire control) in Tarantul II/III
	1 Bass Tilt (fire control)
	1 Kivach (surface search)
	1 Light Bulb (targeting) in Tarantul II/III
	1 Plank Shave (targeting)
Sonars:	none

These missile corvettes are smaller and less capable than the previous Nanuchka class, except that the Tarantuls are several knots faster. They are more likely considered as successors to the Osa class, but it is unlikely that they can be built in sufficient numbers for even a partial replacement program.

The two Tarantul I units retained in the Soviet Navy were built at the Petrovskiy yard; the Tarantul IIs are being built at two shipyards. Additional units of the Tarantul I class have been built for export, all at the Volodarskiy shipyard, Rybinsk (see Class notes). The Tarantul II differs only in electronic equipment.

Class: Tarantul I units have been transferred to East Germany (1) and Poland (3).

Design: The Tarantul has the small hull and basic arrangement as the Pauk class, but with a different propulsion system.

A Tarantul II-class corvette armed with SS-N-22 missiles can be easily distinguished by the ship's Band Stand radar and probable data link antenna atop the mast. The newer small combatants are receiving larger, 76.2-mm guns in place of the 57-mm guns of their predecessors. (Royal Danish Navy)

24 + GUIDED MISSILE CORVETTES: NANUCHKA I/III CLASSES

Name	Name	Completed
Nanuchka I		
BURUN	SHTORM	
GRAD	TAYFUN	
MOLNIYA	TSIKLON	1969–1976
MUSSON	ZARNITSA	
RADUGA	ZUB'	
SHKVAL	. . . . . . (6 units)	
Nanuchka III		
. . . . . . (7 + units)		1977–

Builders:	Petrovskiy, Leningrad
	. . . . . . , Vladivostok
Displacement:	770 tons full load
Length:	194 ft 6 in (59.3 m) oa
Beam:	41 ft 4 in (12.6 m)
Draft:	7 ft 10 in (2.4 m)
Propulsion:	3 diesels (M504); 30,000 hp; 3 shafts (see Engineering notes)
Speed:	32 knots
Range:	2,500 n.miles at 12 knots
	900 n.miles at 30 knots
Complement:	approx. 60
Missiles:	6 SS-N-9 Siren anti-ship (2 triple)
	1 SA-N-4 anti-aircraft [20]
Guns:	Nanuchka I 2 57-mm/80-cal AA (1 twin)
	Nanuchka III 1 76.2-mm/59-cal AA
	1 30-mm/65-cal close-in (multibarrel)
ASW weapons:	none
Torpedoes:	none

Mines:	none
Radars:	1 Band Stand (fire control)
	1 Bass Tilt (fire control) in Nanuchka III
	1 Muff Cob (fire control) in Nanuchka I
	1 Peel Pair (air search)
	1 Pop Group (fire control) in Nanuchka I
Sonars:	none

These are heavily armed coastal missile ships. They provide more gun and anti-air defense capabilities than previous Soviet missile craft. Construction of the Nanuchka III class, with improved gun/fire control systems, continues as well as the export variant.

Class: The Nanuchka II is an export version similar to the Nanuchka I, but with four SS-N-2c Styx missiles in place of the SS-N-9 system; also, the foreign Nanuchkas have the Square Tie radar within the Band Stand radome. Ships of this class have been transferred to Algeria (3), India (3), and Libya (4).

Classification: Soviet MRK type. The NATO designation *Nanuchka* is a child's name in Russian.

Design: The Nanuchka III class has a larger gun battery than the previous units plus the installation of a Gatling gun (also aft); the superstructure is enlarged, with the bridge higher.

These ships are reported to be poor sea boats.

Engineering: Early units have M503 diesels with 24,000 hp and a speed of 30 knots.

Name: The known names are Russian words for meteorological phenomena.

A Nanuchka III in the Baltic Sea, showing the 76.2-mm gun fitted aft, with a Gatling gun stepped above it. These small combatants have a relatively large array of electronic equipment. A Nanuchka with the forward SA-N-4 launcher raised is shown in chapter 30 of this edition. (West Germany Navy)

The Nanuchka is impressive for the firepower and electronic equipment fitted in a small hull. This is a Nanuchka I; the construction of the Nanuchka III variant continues. (West German Navy)

A Pacific Fleet Nanuchka I with a different radar arrangement than the later Nanuchka series as well as a twin 57-mm gun aft and no Gatling gun. This unit was photographed by a P-2J Neptune off the coast of Japan. (1985, Japanese Maritime Self-Defense Force)

14 + ANTI-SUBMARINE CORVETTES: PAUK CLASS

Name	Completed
Komsomolets Gruzin	
Odesskiy Komsomolets	1980–
. . . . . . (12 units)	

Builders:	(USSR)
Displacement:	480 tons standard
	580 tons full load
Length:	191 ft 11 in (58.5 m) oa
Beam:	30 ft 10 in (9.4 m)
Draft:	8 ft 2 in (2.5 m)
Propulsion:	2 diesels (M504); 20,000 hp; 2 shafts
Speed:	28–32 knots
Range:	
Complement:	approx. 40
Missiles:	1 quad SA-N-5 Grail launcher [16]
Guns:	1 76.2-mm/59-cal AA
	1 30-mm/65-cal close-in (multibarrel)
ASW weapons:	2 RBU-1200 rocket launchers
	2 depth-charge racks
	torpedoes
Torpedoes:	4 16-in (406-mm) torpedo tubes (4 single)
Mines:	none
Radars:	1 Bass Tilt (fire control)
	1 Spin Trough (air search)
	1 . . . . . . (search)
Sonars:	medium frequency (hull-mounted)
	medium frequency (dipping)

This class has the same hull as the Tarantul missile corvettes, but with ASW weapons and sensors and all diesel propulsion. The lead ship is reported to have entered the Baltic for trials in early 1979. These ships are apparently the successor to the Poti class. Some Pauk-class ships are operated by the KGB (included in above total).

Classification: Soviet MPK type and, probably, PSKR in KGB service.

Design: A circular housing for a dipping sonar is fitted in the stern, on the starboard side.

Some later units have the pilothouse one deck higher.

The VDS housing on the Pauk projects two meters aft of the hull, as shown in this view. (1982)

The position of the mast in the Pauk class gives the illusion that the superstructure is farther aft than it is; the torpedo tubes are covered with canvas in this view, and the stern VDS housing is clearly seen.

The Pauk is an ASW corvette, with same hull and general arrangement as the Tarantul missile corvettes. There are RBU-1200 rocket launchers (forward) and 406-mm torpedo tubes on both sides, partially hidden by the superstructure. There are life raft canisters aft. (West Germany Navy)

Approx. 60 ANTI-SUBMARINE CORVETTES: POTI CLASS

Name	Completed
. . . . . .	1961–1967

Builders:	Kamysh-Burun
	Khabarovsk
	Zelenodolsk
Displacement:	500 tons standard
	580 tons full load
Length:	194 ft 10 in (59.4 m) oa
Beam:	25 ft 11 in (7.9 m)
Draft:	6 ft 7 in (2.0 m)
Propulsion:	CODAG: 2 diesels (M503A) 8,000 hp + 2 gas turbines 40,000 shp; 2 shafts
Speed:	38 knots
Range:	500 n.miles at 37 knots
	4,500 n.miles at 10 knots
Complement:	approx. 40
Missiles:	none
Guns:	2 57-mm/80-cal AA (1 twin); see notes
ASW weapons:	2 RBU-6000 rocket launchers
	torpedoes

Torpedoes:	2 or 4 16-in (406-mm) torpedo tubes (2 or 4 single)
Mines:	none
Radars:	1 Don-2 (navigation)
	1 Muff Cob (fire control)
	1 Strut Curve (air search)
Sonars:	Herkules high frequency (hull-mounted)
	high frequency (dipping sonar)
EW systems:	2 Watch Dog

About 70 of these ASW ships were built for the Soviet Navy with most remaining in service.

Class: Three of these ships were transferred to Bulgaria and three to Romania.

Classification: Soviet MPK type.

Design: The early ships were built with an open 57-mm/70-cal twin mount, two RBU-2500 rocket launchers, and two torpedo tubes. Most have been upgraded to the configuration shown above, with most ships built with the remote (director)-controlled, automatic 57-mm gun mount. The fixed torpedo tubes are angled out some 15° from the centerline.

Electronics: The dipping sonar, installed beginning in the mid-1970s, is the same used in the Ka-25 Hormone-A helicopter.

The Poti is a coastal ASW corvette, similar to the Mirka light frigate from a technology viewpoint. The four fixed, 406-mm torpedo tubes are outboard of the (elevated) 57-mm gun mount. The large RBU-6000 rocket launchers dominate the forward portion of the ship.

At rest, a Poti showing the gas turbine air intakes and the (closed) gas turbine exhausts built into the stern counter. (West German Navy)

17 PATROL CORVETTES: T-58 CLASS (Ex-Minesweepers)

Name	Name	Completed
KALININGRAD KOMSOMOLETS	PRIMORSKIY KOMSOMOLETS	
KOMOSOMOLETS LATVIY	SOVIETSKIY POGRANICHNIK	1957–1961
MALAKHIT	. . . . . . (11 units)	
PAVLIN VINOGRADEV		

Builders:	(USSR)
Displacement:	725 tons standard
	860 tons full load
Length:	229 ft 7 in (70.0 m) oa
Beam:	29 ft 10 in (9.1 m)
Draft:	8 ft 2 in (2.5 m)
Propulsion:	2 diesels; 4,000 hp; 2 shafts
Speed:	18 knots
Range:	2,500 n.miles at 13.5 knots
Complement:	
Missiles:	none
Guns:	4 57-mm/70-cal AA (2 twin)

ASW weapons:	2 RBU-1200 rocket launchers
	2 depth-charge racks
Torpedoes:	none
Mines:	rails for 18 mines
Radars:	1 Don-2 (navigation)
	1 Muff Cob (fire control)
	1 Spin Trough (air search)
Sonars:	high frequency (hull-mounted)
EW systems:	2 Watch Dog

These are former T-58 minesweepers reclassified in 1978 as patrol ships with some operated by the KGB Maritime Border Troops. A few have been further modified to carry the Big Net radar and serve as picket ships (see below).

Class: One unit of this configuration has been transferred to Guinea and one to Yemen.

Classification: Soviet SKR type in naval service and PSKR in KGB service.

A T-58 patrol corvette, one of many fleet minesweepers of steel construction that are used by the Navy and KGB for patrol duties. Others have been modified for radar picket and auxiliary roles, with some having kept watch on Western warships while serving in an AGI role. (1978)

3 + RADAR PICKET SHIPS: T-58 CLASS (Ex-Minesweepers)

Name	Completed	Conversion Completed
. . . . . .	1957–1961	1979–1983

Builders:	(USSR)
Displacement:	760 tons standard
	880 tons full load
Length:	229 ft 6 in (70.0 m) oa
Beam:	29 ft 10 in (9.1 m)
Draft:	8 ft 2 in (2.5 m)
Propulsion:	2 diesels; 4,000 hp; 2 shafts
Speed:	17 knots
Range:	2,500 n.miles at 13.5 knots
Complement:	approx. 100
Missiles:	2 quad SA-N-5 Grail launchers [16]
Guns:	2 57-mm/70-cal AA (1 twin)
	4 30-mm/65-cal AA (2 twin)
ASW weapons:	2 depth-charge racks
Torpedoes:	none
Mines:	none
Radars:	1 Big Net (air search)
	1 Muff Cob (fire control)
	1 Spin Trough (air search)
	1 Strut Curve (air search)
Sonars:	high frequency (hull-mounted)

Three T-58 fleet minesweepers previously converted to radar picket ships have been further modified to carry the Big Net radar. The reference work *Combat Fleets* notes, "Considering the small number converted, the age of the hulls, and the pace of the program, these ships are probably intended for a specialized range security role, rather than as classical 'radar pickets.' "

Classification: Soviet KVN type.

RADAR PICKET SHIPS: T-43 CLASS (Ex-Minesweepers)

The several T-43 minesweepers converted to radar picket ships are believed to have been discarded. See the 3rd edition (page 198) for details.

A T-58 radar picket ship, fitted with a new deck structure aft and a Big Net radar antenna atop a squat lattice mast. While the open-mount 57-mm guns are retained forward, two twin 30-mm rapid-fire gun mounts are installed aft. (Royal Danish Navy)

18
Missile, Patrol, and Torpedo Craft

These are for coastal defense. The primary production craft when this edition went to press was the Matka, which in some respects could be considered the successor to the widely used Osa missile craft. The rate of production, however, is far too small to replace the Osa force, while the Matka carries only two anti-ship missiles (albeit with a large gun armament) compared to four Styx in the slightly smaller Osa. The larger, one-of-a-kind Sarancha—armed with four SS-N-9 Siren anti-ship missiles—has not been a success; that ship also may have been intended as an Osa successor.

Rather, the coastal defense role apparently is viewed by the Soviets as requiring larger, corvette-type ships (armed with anti-ship missiles) as well as land-based aircraft, as the seaward frontiers of the Soviet Union are pushed farther out.

In addition to the units listed here, a large number of patrol craft are operated by the KGB Maritime Border Troops. These include the Mu-ravey, Stenka, and Zhuk classes; all of the Pchela and Poluchat I classes operated by the KGB have probably been discarded; see chapter 25.

MISSILE BOATS

16 HYDROFOIL GUIDED MISSILE BOATS: MATKA CLASS

Completed:	1978–1981
Builders:	Izhora, Kalpino
Displacement:	225 tons standard
	260 tons full load
Length:	131 ft 2 in (40.0 m) oa
Beam:	24 ft 11 in (7.6 m) hull
	39 ft 4 in (12.0 m) over foils
Draft:	6 ft 11 in (2.1 m) hull-borne
	10 ft 6 in (3.2 m) foil-borne
Propulsion:	3 diesels (M504); 15,000 hp; 3 shafts
Speed:	40 knots foil-borne
Range:	400 n.miles at 36 knots
	650 n.miles at 25 knots
Complement:	approx. 30
Missiles:	2 SS-N-2c Styx anti-ship (2 single)
Guns:	1 76.2-mm/59-cal AA
	1 30-mm/65-cal close-in (multibarrel)
ASW weapons:	none
Torpedoes:	none
Mines:	none
Radars:	1 Bass Tilt (fire control)
	1 Cheese Cake (search)
	1 Plank Shave (targeting)
Sonars:	none

Control of regional seas is important to Soviet defense planners, and the Matka is one of the latest ships for this role, armed with two Styx missiles. Note the relatively large, 76.2-mm gun forward; a Gatling gun is fitted aft. (Royal Danish Navy)

The Matka is a missile-armed version of the Turya-class hydrofoil torpedo boat, with a larger superstructure (to accommodate a more complex missile system) and different gun arrangement.

The termination of the program after only 16 craft indicates that it was not a successful program. The lead Matka was launched in 1976 and completed in 1978, although the search and targeting radars were not provided until 1980.

Classification: Soviet TKA type.

Design: This class is derived from the Osa, with the same hull and propulsion plant, the hydrofoils having been fitted forward. At high speeds the craft's stern planes on the water surface.

A Matka at high speed, providing a clear view of the Plank Shave radar mounted on the lattice mast. The ribbed Styx missile tubes are fitted aft. (West German Navy)

A Matka prior to installation of the Plank Shave radar; the Bass Tilt and Cheese Cake radars are mounted atop the bridge structure. (Courtesy *Ships of the World*)

1 HYDROFOIL GUIDED MISSILE BOAT: SARANCHA CLASS

Completed:	1977
Builders:	Petrovskiy, Leningrad
Displacement:	320 tons full load
Length:	148 ft 3 in (45.2 m) hull
	175 ft 10 in (53.6 m) over foils
	166 ft (50.6 m) foil-borne
Beam:	36 ft 1 in (11.0 m) hull
	102 ft 8 in (31.3 m) over foils
Draft:	8 ft 6 in (2.6 m) hull-borne
	23 ft 11 in (7.3 m) foil-borne
Propulsion:	2 gas turbines; 30,000 shp; 4 shafts
Speed:	60 knots
Range:	
Complement:	
Missiles:	4 SS-N-9 Siren anti-ship (2 twin)
	1 twin SA-N-4 launcher [20]
Guns:	1 30-mm/65-cal close-in (multibarrel)
ASW weapons:	none
Torpedoes:	none
Mines:	none
Radars:	1 Band Stand (fire control)
	1 Bass Tilt (fire control)
	1 Pop Group (fire control)
Sonars:	none

Only a single unit of this highly complex design has been constructed.

Engineering: Two propellers are fitted to each of two pods mounted on the after foils.

A Sarancha at high speed on foils, showing the craft's gas-turbine air intakes and twin exhausts.

Another view of a Sarancha on foils; note the stepped bottom of the ship's hydroplane hull.

Approx. 30 GUIDED MISSILE BOATS: OSA II CLASS

Completed:	1966–1969
Builders:	Petrovskiy, Leningrad
	and other yards
Displacement:	215 tons standard
	245 tons full load
Length:	126 ft 7 in (38.6 m) oa
Beam:	25 ft (7.6 m)
Draft:	6 ft 7 in (2.0 m)
Propulsion:	3 diesels (M504); 15,000 hp; 3 shafts
Speed:	35 knots
Range:	500 n.miles at 34 knots
	750 n. miles at 25 knots
Complement:	approx. 30
Missiles:	4 SS-N-2b/c Styx anti-ship (4 single)
	1 SA-N-5 launcher (hand-held) in some units
Guns:	4 30-mm/65-cal close-in (2 twin)
ASW weapons:	none
Torpedoes:	none
Mines:	none
Radars:	1 Drum Tilt (fire control)
	1 Square Tie (targeting)
Sonars:	none

The Osa II is an improved version of the basic Osa I design, carrying the more capable SS-N-2c missile.

Class: About 115 units of this type were built; 92 boats were transferred to Warsaw Pact and Third World navies—Algeria, Angola, Bulgaria, Cuba, Ethiopia, Finland, India, Iraq, Libya, Somalia, Syria, Vietnam, North Yemen, and South Yemen. Bulgaria is the only Warsaw Pact nation to operate this class, one unit having been transferred in 1978 and one in 1982.

Classification: Soviet RKA type.

Design: These craft can be distinguished from the Osa I type by the later craft's circular missile tubes with rib-like rings. At least one unit has been observed with a deckhouse between the bridge and Drum Tilt radar. See Osa I listing for additional notes.

Names: Soviet names believed to apply to this class are: AMURSKIY KOMSOMOLETS, BRESTSKIY KOM., KALININGRADSKIY KOM., KIROVSKIY KOM., and TAMBOVSKIY KOM.

Operational: Iraq has used Osa missile boats in combat against Iran during the war that began on 20 September 1980, with at least four Iraqi Osa IIs being lost. (Also see Osa I notes.)

The Osa II has four Styx missiles in ribbed canisters; there are twin 30-mm gun mounts forward and aft, and a bridge structure that reveals the motor torpedo boat origins of the craft. Details of their structure differ.

Approx. 60 GUIDED MISSILE BOATS: OSA I CLASS

Completed:	1959–1966
Builders:	Petrovskiy, Leningrad
	and other yards
Displacement:	185 tons standard
	215 tons full load
Length:	126 ft 7 in (38.6 m) oa
Beam:	25 ft (7.6 m)
Draft:	5 ft 11 in (1.8 m)
Propulsion:	3 diesels (M503A); 12,000 hp; 3 shafts
Speed:	36 knots
Range:	500 n.miles at 34 knots
	750 n.miles at 25 knots
Complement:	approx. 30
Missiles:	4 SS-N-2a/b Styx anti-ship (4 single)
	1 SA-N-5 launcher (hand held) in some units
Guns:	4 30-mm/65-cal close-in (2 twin)
ASW weapons:	none
Torpedoes:	none
Mines:	none
Radars:	1 Drum Tilt (fire control)
	1 Square Tie (targeting)
Sonars:	none

These are steel-hulled missile boats, developed to succeed the wood-hulled Komar class that carried two Styx missiles. This class introduced

the twin 30-mm rapid-fire, remote-control gun mountings now common to several Soviet ship classes.

Class: An estimated 175 units of this type were built in the Soviet Union plus up to 100 more being built in China. Ninety-three of the Soviet-built units have been transferred to Warsaw Pact and Third World navies—Algeria, Bulgaria, China, Cuba, Egypt, East Germany, India, Iraq, North Korea, Poland, Romania, Syria, and Yugoslavia. (China received four units about 1960, sans radars, for use as construction prototypes.)

Some of the earlier Osas have been discarded from Soviet service, with a number being converted to target craft.

Classification: Soviet RKA type. The NATO name Osa is Russian for "Wasp" (Komar was "Mosquito").

Design: The Osa has an all-welded-steel hull with a superstructure of fabricated steel and aluminum alloy. A "citadel" control station is provided for operation in a CBR environment. These craft have four Styx missile launchers, twice the number in the preceding Komar class. The launchers are fixed, with the two after launchers, elevated to approximately 15°, firing over the forward launchers, elevated to about 12°. The mounting arrangement of the Drum Tilt gunfire control radar varies.

The Matka, Mol, Stenka, and Turya classes have the basic Osa hull and propulsion plant (the Mol being a torpedo boat developed for export).

Names: Soviet names associated with this class include KOMSO-MOLETS TATARIY and KRONSHTADTSKIY KOMSOMOLETS.

Operational: Indian Osas sank a Pakistani destroyer in the 1971 war between those two nations, as well as merchant ships. Egypt and Syria used Osa I missile craft against Israel in 1973 and sustained heavy losses while inflicting no damage on Israeli missile boats.

Osa I, showing the large missile canisters for the early Styx missiles, with a different wing arrangement than in the Osa II ships that have ribbed missile canisters. The gun and electronic systems are the same in the two variants. (1984, U.S. Navy, PH2 D. Beech)

GUIDED MISSILE BOATS: KOMAR CLASS

All wood-hulled missile boats of the Komar class have been discarded from Soviet service. These were the world's first guided missile boats. About 100 units were completed from 1959 onward. They were built on the same hull as the P-6 torpedo boat with some 75 having been transferred to Third World navies. Another 40-odd units were built in China.

These boats each carried two SS-N-2 Styx missiles. Some units survive in target and other auxiliary roles, and a few are still operational in other navies.

A pair of Egyptian missile boats sank the Israeli destroyer ELATH with three missile hits on 21 October 1967; the Egyptian boats were in the shelter of Alexandria harbor when they fired their missiles.

PATROL BOATS

1 HYDROFOIL PATROL BOAT: BABOCHKA CLASS

Completed:	1976
Builders:	(USSR)
Displacement:	400 tons full load
Length:	164 ft (50.0 m) oa
Beam:	27 ft 9 in (8.5 m) hull
	42 ft 8 in (13.0 m) over foils
Draft:	
Propulsion:	CODOG: 2 diesels + 3 gas turbines =
	approx. 30,000 shp; 3 shafts
Speed:	45+ knots
Range:	
Complement:	
Missiles:	none
Guns:	2 30-mm/65-cal close-in (2 multibarrel)
ASW weapons:	torpedoes
Torpedoes:	8 16-in (406-mm) torpedo tubes (2 quad)
Mines:	none
Radars:	1 Bass Tilt (fire control)
	1 Don-2 (navigation)
	1 Peel Cone (search)
Sonars:	none

This is a prototype-evaluation ASW patrol craft with only one unit being built. The Muravey-class hydrofoil patrol boats are operated by the KGB (see chapter 25).

Design: There are fixed, fully submerged foils forward and aft. The torpedo tubes are stacked two above two, in two quad launchers on the bow, angled out to both sides.

1 PATROL GUNBOAT: SLEPEN CLASS

Completed:	~1969
Builders:	Petrovskiy, Leningrad
Displacement:	205 tons standard
	230 tons full load
Length:	126 ft 7 in (38.6 m) oa
Beam:	24 ft 11 in (7.6 m)
Draft:	6 ft 3 in (1.9 m)
Propulsion:	3 diesels (M504); 15,000 hp; 3 shafts
Speed:	36 knots
Range:	500 n.miles at 34 knots
	750 n.miles at 25 knots
Complement:	approx. 30
Missiles:	none
Guns:	1 76.2-mm/59-cal AA
	1 30-mm/65-cal close-in (multibarrel)
ASW weapons:	none
Torpedoes:	none
Mines:	none
Radars:	1 Bass Tilt (fire control)
	1 Don-2 (navigation)
Sonars:	none

This is the Soviet Navy's only high-speed gunboat. The craft may be employed as a trials ship for small combatant systems.

Design: Similar to the Matka design, but without the hydrofoils or missiles.

Guns: As built, the ship had a twin 57-mm gun mount forward; replaced by the single 76.2-mm gun in 1975.

ANTI-SUBMARINE PATROL BOATS: S.O.-1 CLASS

All of these coastal ASW craft have been discarded from Soviet service, the last in the early 1980s. Just over 100 units of this class were built for the Soviet Navy and KGB Maritime Border Troops with additional units built for export. Many remain in foreign navies.

The one-of-a-kind Babochka; note the supports for the forward hydrofoils and the after gas-turbine housing. One of the ship's Gatling guns and the 406-mm torpedo tubes are fitted on the forecastle; the second gun mount is aft of the lattice mast. (1978)

TORPEDO BOATS

31 HYDROFOIL TORPEDO BOATS: TURYA CLASS

Completed:	1974–1979
Builders:	Srednly Neva, Kolpino
	Ulis, Vladivostok
Displacement:	215 tons standard
	250 tons full load
Length:	127 ft 11 in (39.0 m) oa
Beam:	24 ft 11 in (7.6 m)
	41 ft (12.5 m) over foils
Draft:	6 ft 7 in (2.0 m) hull-borne
	13 ft 2 in (4.0 m) over foils
Propulsion:	3 diesels (M504); 15,000 hp; 3 shafts
Speed:	40 knots
Range:	420 n.miles at 38 knots
	650 n.miles at 25 knots
Complement:	approx. 25
Missiles:	none
Guns:	2 57-mm/80-cal AA (1 twin)
	2 25-mm/60-cal AA (1 twin)
ASW weapons:	torpedoes
Torpedoes:	4 21-in (533-mm) torpedo tubes (4 single)
Mines:	none
Radars:	1 Muff Cob (fire control)
	1 Pot Drum (fire control)
Sonars:	high frequency (dipping sonar)

These are high-speed coastal ASW and torpedo attack craft.

Class: Nine units of this class have been transferred to Cuba (without dipping sonar); other units have gone to Kampuchea (Cambodia) and Vietnam.

Classification: Soviet TK type.

Design: The Turya uses a modified Osa II hull and propulsion plant. The forward foils are fixed, and at high speed the craft's stern planes on the water. The stern is trimmed by an adjustable flap with twin supports protruding from the stern transom. Later units are reported to have semi-retractable foils to facilitate berthing.

Electronics: The Ka-25 Hormone-A helicopter dipping sonar is fitted on the starboard quarter. (Not provided in units transferred to Cuba.)

A pair of Turyas on a merchant ship show the torpedo crafts' general arrangement; the torpedo tubes, in pairs on each side, are covered with canvas as are the Muff Cob fire control radars. (U.S. Navy)

A Turya torpedo craft at high speed on her displacement hull. Again, the Soviet trend toward large guns in small ships is shown by the twin 57-mm, automatic mount aft and a twin 25-mm gun forward. (1975, Sovfoto)

A port bow view of a Turya showing the forward 25-mm gun mount and torpedo tubes; the after 57-mm guns are elevated; visible forward are the supports for the ship's forward foils.

TORPEDO BOATS

All older Soviet torpedo boats have been discarded. The last of the approximately 80 Shershen-class boats were transferred or otherwise disposed of in the early 1980s. They continue in service with several foreign navies and have been built in Yugoslavia under license.

RIVERINE CRAFT

The Soviet Navy operates riverine patrol craft on the Amur, Danube, and Ussuri rivers. In addition to the craft described below, the Pivyaka

The SSV-10, flagship of the Danube flotilla. There are a pair of 45-mm saluting guns abreast the stack. (1972)

and Vosh classes have been reported; no details are available for these craft.

Riverine craft perform routine peacetime patrols and in wartime would support ground operations (with their main guns and rocket launchers using army ammunition).

1 RIVERINE FLAGSHIP: SSV-10

Completed:	
Builders:	(USSR)
Displacement:	360 tons full load
Length:	160 ft 9 in (49.0 m) oa
Beam:	
Draft:	
Propulsion:	diesels; 2 shafts
Speed:	12 knots
Range:	
Complement:	
Missiles:	none
Guns:	
ASW weapons:	none
Torpedoes:	none
Mines:	none
Radars:	...... (navigation)
Sonars:	none

This ship serves as flagship of the Danube riverine flotilla. Now designated SSV-10 (formerly PS-10). SSV indicates a communications vessel.

15+ RIVERINE MONITORS: YAZ CLASS

Completed:	1981–
Builders:	Khabarovsk
Displacement:	400 tons full load
Length:	196 ft 11 in (60.0 m) oa
Beam:	
Draft:	
Propulsion:	diesels; 2 shafts
Speed:	15 knots
Range:	
Complement:	
Missiles:	none
Guns:	2 100-mm or 120-mm tank guns (2 single)
	2 30-mm/65-cal close-in (1 twin)
ASW weapons:	none
Torpedoes:	none
Mines:	none
Radars:	1 Bass Tilt (fire control)
	1 Kivach or Spin Trough (navigation)
Sonars:	none

These are riverine monitors employed on the Amur River in Siberia. From at least World War II riverine gunboats built by the Soviets have mounted tank guns.

A Yaz-class river monitor, with her tank-turret guns fitted forward and aft.

A Shmel-class river monitor with a tank-mounted 76.2-mm gun forward. Note the multi-barrel rocket launcher amidships and twin 25-mm guns aft. (1980)

Approx. 80 RIVERINE GUNBOATS: SHMEL CLASS

Completed:	1967–1974
Builders:	(USSR)
Displacement:	60 tons full load
Length:	92 ft 10 in (28.3 m) oa
Beam:	15 ft 1 in (4.6 m)
Draft:	3 ft (0.9 m)
Propulsion:	2 diesels (M50F-4); 2,400 hp; 2 shafts
Speed:	22 knots
Range:	240 n.miles at 20 knots
	600 n.miles at 10 knots
Complement:	approx. 15
Missiles:	1 18-tube 122-mm rocket launcher in some units
Guns:	1 76.2-mm/48-cal SP
	2 25-mm/60-cal AA machine guns (1 twin)
	5 7.62-mm machine guns (5 single; see notes)
ASW weapons:	none
Torpedoes:	none
Mines:	8 mines can be carried
Radars:	none
Sonars:	none

These are heavily armed river craft, similar in concept to the French and U.S. riverine monitors of the Indochina-Vietnam wars. The craft patrol the several Soviet rivers that border on foreign states.

Class: Eighty-five units were built. Four units were transferred to Kampuchea (Cambodia) in 1984–1985.

Classification: Soviet AKA type.

Design: These are very shallow-draft craft. The 76.2-mm weapon is mounted in a PT-76 tank turret with one 7.62-mm MG coaxially mounted. The other 7.62-mm MGs are hand held and fired through ports in the open-top deckhouse. The rocket launcher—mounted aft of the deckhouse—is deleted in some units.

A Shmel river patrol boat with a tank-turret 76.2-mm gun forward and an open-mount, twin 25-mm gun aft.

Close-up of a Shmel river patrol boat with a multiple-tube rocket launcher amidships.

19
Mine Warfare Ships and Craft

The Soviet Navy maintains the world's largest mine warfare forces, with a larger mine stockpile, a greater minelaying capability, and at least quantitatively a much more capable mine countermeasures capability than any other nation.

In addition to the three minelayers listed below, several Soviet surface combatant classes are configured to lay mines as are Soviet bomber and maritime patrol aircraft. Essentially all Soviet combat submarines can also lay mines.

The large force of surface mine countermeasures craft—mine hunters and minesweepers—are supplemented by specialized minesweeping helicopters of the Mi-8 Hip and Mi-14 Haze types (see chapter 26). Note that most Soviet minesweepers have defensive guns and an ASW capability, permitting them to serve as escorts even with sweep gear installed.[1] Some can also carry a few mines, for laying practice mines or for defensive minelaying.

Several Polnocny-class landing ships are fitted for clearing mines and explosives from landing areas (see chapter 20).

These are minelaying and support ships. They can lay mines, tend defensive anti-submarine nets, support minesweepers, and serve as command/control ships for mine operations. They are believed to be the only specialized minelayers now in service with any major navy.

Classification: Soviet ZM type. NATO code names for Soviet mine warfare ships and craft are Russian names for children, as *Alesha*, *Natya*, and *Yurka* ("Georgie").

Design: Mine rails are fitted on two decks, with a stern ramp over which mines can be laid or large objects hauled aboard. The lead ship has a crane fitted forward and two booms amidships; the two others have a kingpost and booms forward.

3 MINELAYERS: ALESHA CLASS

Name	Completed
PRIPET'	
VYCHEGDA	1967–1969
. . . . . .	

Builders:	(USSR)
Displacement:	2,900 tons standard
	3,500 tons full load
Length:	318 ft 2 in (97.0 m) oa
Beam:	45 ft 11 in (14.0 m)
Draft:	17 ft 9 in (5.4 m)
Propulsion:	4 diesels; 8,000 hp; 2 shafts
Speed:	17 knots
Range:	4,000 n.miles at 16 knots
	8,500 n.miles at 8 knots
Complement:	approx. 190
Helicopters:	no facilities
Guns:	4 57-mm/70-cal AA (1 quad)
ASW weapons:	none
Mines:	rails for approx. 300
Radars:	1 Don-2 (navigation)
	1 Muff Cob (fire control)
	1 Strut Curve (air search)
Sonars:	none:

[1] In World War II the U.S. Navy built 58 "submarine chaser sweepers" (PCS), but these were 136-footers with sweep gear removed and ASW weapons fitted in their place.

Stern view of an Alesha-class minelayer.

The Pacific Fleet's minelayer/support ship VYCHEGDA in the Tsushima Strait. The three Soviet ships of this class are the only minelayers now serving in any of the major navies. The mine rails can be seen on the after decks. A number of Soviet surface warships and virtually all submarines can also lay mines as can bomber-type aircraft. (1985, Japanese Maritime Self-Defense Force)

Few MINE HUNTERS: NATYA II CLASS

Completed	1981
Builders:	Srednly Neva, Kolpino
Displacement:	650 tons standard
	750 tons full load
Length:	200 ft 1 in (61.0 m) oa
Beam:	32 ft 2 in (9.8 m)
Draft:	9 ft 10 in (3.0 m)
Propulsion:	2 diesels; 5,000 hp; 2 shafts
Speed:	18 knots
Range:	1,800 n.miles at 16 knots
	5,200 n.miles at 10 knots
Complement:	
Missiles:	2 quad SA-N-5 Grail launchers [16]
Guns:	4 30-mm/65-cal close-in (2 twin)
ASW weapons:	none
Mines:	none
Radars:	1 Don-2 (navigation)
	1 Drum Tilt (fire control)
Sonars:	minehunting high frequency

A Natya-class fleet minesweeper with the newer-style davits on her fantail for handling sweep gear. The twin 30-mm gun mounts forward and aft, and twin 25-mm guns abaft the funnel, are typical of the arming of Soviet minesweepers for self-defense and their use in patrol or AGI roles. (1983)

These are mine hunter versions of the Natya-class fleet minesweepers. They can be distinguished from the minesweeper variant by the long deckhouse aft in place of the sweep gear and the deletion of ASW armament and 25-mm guns. Construction continues.

Classification: Soviet MT type.

35 FLEET MINESWEEPERS: NATYA I CLASS

Name	Name	Name
ADMIRAL PERSHIN	MASHINIST	SIGNAL'SHCHIK
DIZELIST	MINER	SNAYPER
ELEKTRIK	MOTORIST	TURBINIST
KONTRA ADMIRAL	PULEMETCHIK	VSEVOLOD
HOROSHKIN	RADIST	VISHNEVSKIY
KURSKIY KOMSOMOLETS	RULEVOY	ZENITCHIK
(ex-NOVODCHIK)		. . . . . . (19 units)

Completed:	1970–1982
Builders:	Srednly Neva, Kolpino
Displacement:	650 tons standard
	750 tons full load
Length:	200 ft 1 in (61.0 m) oa
Beam:	32 ft 2 in (9.8 m)
Draft:	9 ft 10 in (3.0 m)
Propulsion:	2 diesels; 5,000 hp; 2 shafts
Speed:	18 knots
Range:	1,800 n.miles at 16 knots
	5,200 n.miles at 10 knots
Complement:	approx. 60
Missiles:	2 quad SA-N-5 Grail launchers [16] in some units
Guns:	4 30-mm/65-cal close-in (2 twin)
	4 25-mm/60-cal AA (2 twin)
ASW weapons:	2 RBU-1200 rocket launchers
Mines:	can carry 10 mines
Radars:	1 or 2 Don-2 (navigation)
	1 Drum Tilt (fire control)
Sonars:	Tamir minehunting high frequency

These are fleet minesweepers with a limited ASW capability and self-defense armament, permitting them to serve as anti-submarine escorts. Production continues of export units.

Class: At least ten ships of this class have been built for India, five for Libya, and one for Syria; the Syrian unit, transferred in 1985, had no ASW or minesweeping gear installed.

Classification: Soviet MT type.

Design: These ships have aluminum-alloy hulls. Early ships have fixed davits aft for handling sweeping gear; the davits are articulated in later units. There is a stern ramp to facilitate handling sweep gear. The twin 25-mm guns are "hidden" in the topside clutter, with one mount on the port side just forward of the funnel and the other on the starboard side, abaft the funnel and just behind the launch.

40 FLEET MINESWEEPERS: YURKA CLASS

Name	Name	Name
GAFEL'	SEMEN ROSHAL	. . . . . . (35+ units)
KOMSOMOLETS BYELORUSSIY	YERGENIY MIKONOR	

Completed:	1962–1970(?)
Builders:	(USSR)
Displacement:	400 tons standard
	460 tons full load
Length:	170 ft 7 in (52.0 m) oa
Beam:	30 ft 6 in (9.3 m)
Draft:	6 ft 7 in (2.0 m)
Propulsion:	2 diesels; 4,000 hp; 2 shafts
Speed:	16 knots
Range:	2,000 n.miles at 14 knots
	3,200 n.miles at 10 knots
Complement:	approx. 45
Missiles:	2 quad SA-N-5 Grail launchers [16] in some units
Guns:	4 30-mm/65-cal close-in (2 twin)
ASW weapons:	none
Mines:	can carry 20 mines
Radars:	1 or 2 Don-2 (navigation)
	1 Drum Tilt (fire control)
Sonars:	Tamir minehunting high frequency

Natya I showing the stern ramp and davits for handling sweep gear. While the U.S. Navy constructed no mine countermeasure craft in the 1960s and 1970s, the development and construction of minesweepers continued unabated in the Soviet Navy. (1977)

A Yurka fleet minesweeper in the Baltic. (1982, West German Navy)

These are smaller than the later Natya-class minesweepers, without the later ships' ASW weapons.

Class: Four ships of this class have been transferred to Egypt and one unit to Vietnam.

Classification: Soviet MT type.

Design: Aluminum-alloy hulls. This is a similar design to the Natya class, but without the stern ramp. The Yurka's broad funnel indicates a side-by-side arrangement of the diesel engines. When viewed from the side, the classes are easily distinguished by the Natya's larger funnel.

The Yurka fleet minesweeper has an unusual funnel configuration, but otherwise is typical of the large number of Soviet fleet minesweepers in service.

Approx. 30 FLEET MINESWEEPERS: T-43 CLASS

Name	Name
ASTRAKHANSKIY KOMSOMOLETS	MEHADIY AZIZBAKOV
IVAN FIOLETOV	NIKOLAY MARKIN
KONTRA ADMIRAL YUROKOVSKIY	SAKHALINSKIY KOMSOMOLETS
KOMSOMOLETS KALMYKIY	STEPHAN SAUMYAN
LAMINE SADJIKABA	. . . . . . (20 + units)

Completed:	1949–1957
Builders:	(USSR)
Displacement:	500 tons standard
	early units 570 tons full load
	later units 590 tons full load
Length:	early units 190 ft 3 in (58.0 m) oa
	later units 196 ft 10 in (60.0 m) oa
Beam:	28 ft 2 in (8.6 m)
Draft:	7 ft 7 in (2.3 m)
Propulsion:	2 diesels (9D); 2,200 hp; 2 shafts
Speed:	14 knots
Range:	2,000 n.miles at 14 knots
	3,200 n.miles at 10 knots
Complement:	approx. 65

Guns:	4 37-mm/60-cal AA (2 twin)
	4 25-mm/60-cal AA (2 twin) in larger units
ASW weapons:	2 depth-charge mortars
Mines:	can carry 16 mines
Radars:	1 Ball End (fire control)
	1 Don-2 (navigation) or Spin Trough (search)
Sonars:	Tamir high-frequency

The T-43 class was the Soviet Navy's first postwar minesweeper design. After serving as minesweepers, many units were modified for auxiliary roles as well as for radar picket ships (see chapter 17). Several T-43s have gone to other navies and several are operated by the KGB Maritime Border Troops as patrol ships (see chapter 25). The remaining units in Soviet service will be discarded in the near future.

Class: More than 200 ships of this class were built. Ships of this class have been transferred to Albania, Algeria, Bulgaria, China, Egypt, Indonesia, Iraq, Poland, and Syria.

Classification: Soviet designation is MT.

Design: These are steel-hulled ships. The early ships had a shorter hull and a "flat face" bridge structure; later units were two meters longer with a stepped bridge and a broader stern.

A T-43 fleet minesweeper, one of a large number of these ships, several of which have been converted to patrol, AGI, radar picket, and auxiliary roles. This unit is a Polish-built T-43 of the Polish Navy. (West German Navy)

1 AUXILIARY MINESWEEPER: BALTIKA CLASS (former fishing boat)

Completed:	1978
Builders:	Leninskaya Kuznitsa, Kiev
Displacement:	210 tons full load
Length:	83 ft (25.3 m) oa
Beam:	22 ft 4 in (6.8 m)
Draft:	8 ft 2 in (2.5 m)
Propulsion:	1 diesel; 300 hp; 1 shaft
Speed:	9.5 knots
Range:	
Complement:	approx. 10
Guns:	none
ASW weapons:	none
Mines:	none
Radars:	
Sonars:	

This is a stern-haul purse-seiner acquired about 1980–1981 and adapted for minesweeping to evaluate the feasibility of wartime conversion of fishing craft for this role. Additional ships may be involved.

During the Falklands War of 1982 the Royal Navy acquired five trawlers for mine countermeasures, although they were not used in that role. In the early 1980s the U.S. Navy initiated the Craft Of Opportunity Program (COOP) to develop the methods and equipment for employing fishing craft and naval seamanship training craft (YP) in the minecountermeasure role.

45 COASTAL MINESWEEPERS: SONYA CLASS

Name	Name
KOLOMENSKIY KOMSOMOLETS	SEVASTOPOL'SKIY KOMSOMOLETS
KOMSOMOLETS KIRGIZIY	(ex-KOMSOMOL'SKIY
ORENBURGSKIY KOMSOMOLETS	TELEGRAF)
	. . . . . . (41 units)

Completed:	1973–
Builders:	(USSR)
Displacement:	380 tons standard
	450 tons full load
Length:	160 ft 1 in (48.8 m) oa
Beam:	28 ft 10 in (8.8 m)
Draft:	6 ft 11 in (2.1 m)
Propulsion:	2 diesels; 2,400 hp; 2 shafts
Speed:	15 knots
Range:	1,600 n.miles at 14 knots
	3,000 n.miles at 10 knots
Complement:	approx. 40
Missiles:	1 quad SA-N-5 Grail in some units
Guns:	2 30-mm/65-cal close-in (1 twin)
	2 25-mm/60-cal AA (1 twin)
ASW weapons:	none
Mines:	none
Radars:	1 Spin Trough (search)
Sonars:	

These are modern coastal minesweepers with wooden hulls sheathed in fiberglass. Three units have been transferred to Cuba.

Classification: Soviet BT type.

A Pacific Fleet Sonya under tow. The Soviets regularly tow their smaller combatants, apparently to conserve engines. Again, these relatively small ships are heavily armed, with a twin 30-mm gun mount forward and twin 25-mm gun mount amidships (under canvas). (1985, JMSDF)

Another Pacific Fleet Sonya, this unit also under tow. (1985, JMSDF)

3 COASTAL MINESWEEPERS: ZHENYA CLASS

Completed:	1967–1972
Builders:	(USSR)
Displacement:	220 tons standard
	300 tons full load
Length:	139 ft 1 in (42.4 m) oa
Beam:	25 ft 11 in (7.9 m)
Draft:	5 ft 11 in (1.8 m)
Propulsion:	2 diesels; 2,400 hp; 2 shafts
Speed:	16 knots
Range:	1,400 n.miles at 14 knots
	2,400 n.miles at 10 knots
Complement:	approx. 40
Guns:	2 30-mm/65-cal close-in (1 twin)
ASW weapons:	none
Mines:	none
Radars:	1 Spin Trough (search)
Sonars:	

These were prototypes for an advanced coastal minesweeper but series construction was deferred, apparently in favor of the larger Sonya design.

Classification: Soviet BT type.

Design: Glass-reinforced plastic hulls.

Zhenya-class coastal minesweeper.

Approx. 70 COASTAL MINESWEEPERS: VANYA I/II CLASSES

Completed:	1960–1973
Builders:	(USSR)
Displacement:	200 tons standard
	Vanya I 250 tons full load
	Vanya II 260 tons full load
Length:	Vanya I 131 ft 10 in (40.2 m) oa
	Vanya II 135 ft 2 in (41.2 m)
Beam:	25 ft 11 in (7.9 m)
Draft:	5 ft 7 in (1.7 m)
Propulsion:	2 diesels; 2,200 hp; 2 shafts
Speed:	14 knots
Range:	1,400 n.miles at 14 knots
	2,400 n.miles at 10 knots
Complement:	approx. 30
Guns:	2 30-mm/65-cal close-in (1 twin) (see Modification notes)
ASW weapons:	none
Mines:	can carry 12 mines
Radars:	1 Don-2 (navigation)
Sonars:	

A large class of coastal minesweepers, at least one of which has been reconfigured as a minehunter (see below).

Class: Four of these units were transferred to Bulgaria and two to Syria.

Classification: Soviet BT type.

Design: Wooden-hulled ships. The few modified or Vanya II type are slightly larger, having a larger fantail work area; they can be identified by the larger diesel generator exhaust pipe amidships.

Modification: At least one unit was refitted (or possibly completed) as a minehunter in 1974. That unit has two 25-mm guns (single mounts) in place of the 30-mm mount, a Don-Kay radar in place of the Don-2, a small mast fitted amidships, sweep gear removed, and other changes.

Vanya-class coastal minesweeper.

Vanya-class coastal minesweeper.

COASTAL MINESWEEPERS: SASHA CLASS

The last of this class of coastal sweepers was discarded in the early 1980s. The steel-hulled craft were also employed as patrol boats.

Approx. 40 INSHORE MINESWEEPERS: YEVGENYA CLASS

Completed:	1970–
Builders:	Srednly Neva, Kolpino
Displacement:	80 tons standard
	90 tons full load
Length:	85 ft 11 in (26.2 m) oa
Beam:	20 ft (6.1 m)
Draft:	4 ft 11 in (1.5 m)
Propulsion:	2 diesels; 600 hp; 2 shafts
Speed:	11 knots
Range:	300 n.miles at 10 knots
Complement:	approx. 10
Guns:	2 14.5-mm machine guns (1 twin)
ASW weapons:	none
Mines:	none
Radars:	1 Spin Trough (search)
Sonars:	

These are fiberglass-hulled craft, several of which have been transferred abroad.

Class: Units of this type have been transferred to Bulgaria, Cuba, India, Iraq, and North Yemen. Some export versions have a twin 25-mm AA gun mount.

Classification: Soviet RT type.

Yevgenya-class inshore minesweeper. (West German Navy)

3 SPECIAL MINESWEEPERS: ANDRYUSHA CLASS

Completed:	1975–1976
Builders:	(USSR)
Displacement:	320 tons standard
	360 tons full load
Length:	156 ft 9 in (47.8 m) oa
Beam:	27 ft 11 in (8.5 m)
Draft:	9 ft 11 in (3.0 m)
Propulsion:	2 diesels; 2,200 hp; 2 shafts
Speed:	15 knots
Range:	
Complement:	approx. 40
Guns:	none
ASW weapons:	none
Mines:	none
Radars:	1 Spin Trough (search)
Sonars:	

These minesweepers have non-magnetic wooden or fiberglass hulls with large cable ducts along their sides, indicating a probable magnetic-sweep capability.

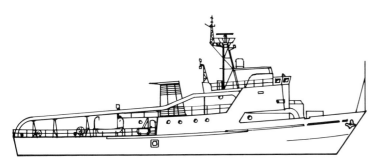

Andryusha-class special minesweeper.

4 MINESWEEPING BOATS: OLYA CLASS

Completed:	1976–
Builders:	(USSR)
Displacement:	44 tons standard
	50 tons full load
Length:	80 ft 8 in (24.6 m) oa
Beam:	13 ft 9 in (4.2 m)
Draft:	3 ft 3 in (1.0 m)
Propulsion:	2 diesels; 600 hp; 2 shafts
Speed:	18 knots
Range:	
Complement:	approx. 15
Guns:	2 25-mm/60-cal AA (1 twin)
ASW weapons:	none
Mines:	none
Radars:	1 Spin Trough (search)
Sonars:	none

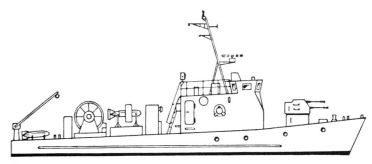

Olya-class minesweeping boat.

Approx. 25 MINESWEEPING BOATS: K-8 CLASS

Completed:	1953–1959
Builders:	Polnocny, Gdansk (Poland)
Displacement:	19.4 tons standard
	26 tons full load
Length:	55 ft 5 in (16.9 m) oa
Beam:	10 ft 6 in (3.2 m)
Draft:	2 ft 7 in (0.8 m)
Propulsion:	2 diesels (3D6); 300 hp; 2 shafts
Speed:	12 knots
Range:	300 n.miles at 9 knots
Complement:	approx. 6
Guns:	2 14.5-mm machine guns (1 twin)
ASW weapons:	none
Mines:	none
Radars:	none
Sonars:	none

Outdated, wooden-hulled sweeps that tow sweep gear, but with no handling facilities. They are being replaced by the Yevgenya class. A large number served in the Polish Navy.

K-8-class minesweeping boat.

11 MINESWEEPING DRONES: ILYUSHA CLASS

Completed:	1970–
Builders:	(USSR)
Displacement:	80 tons standard
	85 tons full load
Length:	85 ft 11 in (26.2 m) oa
Beam:	19 ft (5.8 m)
Draft:	4 ft 11 in (1.5 m)
Propulsion:	1 diesel; 450 hp; 1 shaft
Speed:	12 knots
Range:	
Complement:	(see notes)
Guns:	none
ASW weapons:	none
Mines:	none
Radars:	1 Spin Trough (search)
Sonars:	none

These are radio-controlled minesweeping craft, similar to the MSD-type operated by the U.S. Navy in the Vietnam War. They can be manned for self-transit for short distances.

Ilyusha-class minesweeping drone. (1977)

Few TOWED MINESWEEPING CRAFT

These craft are towed by minesweepers or minehunters; they have reels and winches to deploy magnetic sweep arrays or explosive line charges. They are transported on board ship.

20
Amphibious Warfare Ships

The number of amphibious ships in the Soviet Navy has been declining slightly, with no new ship construction reported when this edition went to press. Particularly significant was the halt in construction of the ROGOV class after only two ships were built. Soviet amphibious capabilities for short-range operations are being increased, however, through the acquisition of large air-cushion landing craft (see chapter 21). Reports persist of a new LST-type ship, probably to be built in Poland.

Troop capacity: The troop capacity listed for amphibious ships is the number for which berths are provided; a larger number could be carried in all classes of amphibious ships for short transits.

The IVAN ROGOV and her sister ship ALEKSANDR NIKOLAYEV are the largest amphibious ships yet built for the Soviet Navy. The ROGOV, shown here in the Baltic, has a variety of Naval Infantry vehicles parked forward and a pair of Hormone-C helicopters aft. An internal docking well can carry amphibious personnel carriers, conventional landing craft, or air-cushion landing craft. (1982, West German Navy)

2 HELICOPTER/DOCK LANDING SHIPS: "IVAN ROGOV" CLASS

Name	Launched	Completed
IVAN ROGOV	1976	1978
ALEKSANDR NIKOLAYEV		Nov 1982

Builders:	Kaliningrad
Displacement:	11,000 tons standard
	13,000 tons full load
Length:	518 ft 3 in (158.0 m) oa
Beam:	78 ft 9 in (24.0 m)
Draft:	26 ft 11 in (8.2 m)
Propulsion:	2 gas turbines; 50,000 shp; 2 shafts
Speed:	23 knots
Range:	8,000 n.miles at 20 knots
	12,500 n.miles at 14 knots
Complement:	approx. 200
Troops:	approx. 550
Helicopters:	4 Ka-25 Hormone-C
Missiles/rockets:	1 twin SA-N-4 launcher [20]
	2 quad SA-N-5 Grail launchers in NIKOLAYEV
	1 40-tube 122-mm barrage rocket launcher
Guns:	2 76.2-mm/59-cal AA (1 twin)
	4 30-mm close-in (4 multibarrel)

Radars:	2 Bass Tilt (fire control)
	2 Don-Kay (navigation) in ROGOV
	1 Head Net-C (air search)
	1 Owl Screech (fire control)
	1 Palm Frond (navigation) in NIKOLAYEV
	1 Pop Group (fire control)
EW systems:	2 Bell Shroud (3 in NIKOLAYEV)
	2 Bell Squat

These are the largest and most versatile amphibious ships yet constructed for the Soviet Navy. Each ship can embark a Naval Infantry battalion, including its vehicles and equipment. They are also the only amphibious ships with a helicopter facility.

Class: Only two ships have been built. Although more ships were predicted by some Western analysts, they have not appeared.

The IVAN ROGOV has bow doors faired into her hull and an internal ramp for unloading vehicles onto the beach. The four-level structure forward of the bridge mounts a 122-mm rocket launcher for shore bombardment.

The IVAN ROGOV with a Hormone-C parked on her flight deck and the doors open for access to her helicopter hangar/drive-through to the forward helicopter deck/parking area. Note the large stern gate that opens to the docking well, and stern anchor for retracting the ship after being beached. (1980, Royal Navy)

Classification: Soviet BDK type.

Design: These are multi-role amphibious ships, having bow vehicle ramps; a floodable docking well for landing craft and amphibious tractors; and a helicopter hangar with two landing decks (forward and abaft the superstructure). The hangar can accommodate four Hormone helicopters; they can be moved through the superstructure and down a ramp to the forward landing area. The funnel uptakes are split to provide the helicopter pass through. The float-in docking well can hold three Lebed air-cushion landing craft.

The ship has a flat bottom and large tank deck with bow doors to permit the unloading of amphibious vehicles into the water or across the beach. Ten light or medium tanks plus 30 armored personnel carriers can be transported.

The barrage rocket launcher is mounted atop a four-level structure offset to starboard, forward of the main superstructure. The four Gatling guns are mounted alongside the pylon mast. There is a four-level "stack" of canisters containing life rafts arranged outboard of the rocket-launcher structure.

Names: Ivan Rogov was a political officer and Chief of the Main Political Directorate of the Soviet Navy during World War II; Aleksandr Nikolayev was the chief political officer of the Northern Fleet during World War II.

Operational: The lead ship was transferred to the Pacific Fleet in 1979 (with the aircraft carrier MINSK); she returned to the Baltic in the fall of 1981 for the *Zapad* amphibious exercises. The NIKOLAYEV transferred to the Pacific Fleet in late 1983.

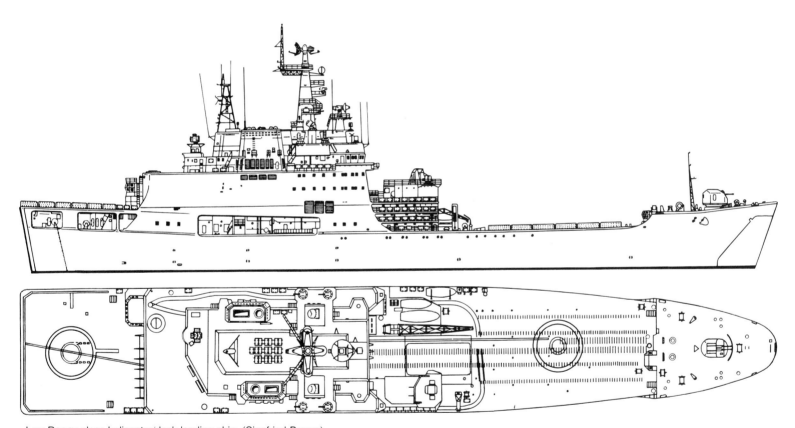

IVAN ROGOV-class helicopter/dock landing ship. (Siegfried Breyer)

19 TANK LANDING SHIPS: ROPUCHA CLASS

Completed:	1975–1978 (11 units)
	1982–1985 (8 units
Builders:	Polnocny, Gdansk (Poland)
Displacement:	2,200 tons standard
	3,200 tons full load
Length:	370 ft 8 in (113.0 m) oa
Beam:	45 ft 11 in (14.0 m)
Draft:	9 ft 6 in (2.9 m)
Propulsion:	2 diesels; 10,000 hp; 2 shafts
Speed:	18 knots
Range:	3,500 n.miles at 16 knots
	6,000 n.miles at 12 knots
Complement:	approx. 70
Troops:	approx. 230
Helicopters:	no facilities
Missiles/rockets:	4 quad SA-N-5 Grail launchers [32] in some ships
Guns:	4 57-mm/80-cal AA (2 twin)
Radars:	1 Don-2 (navigation)
	1 Muff Cob (fire control)
	1 Strut Curve (air search)

These ships are smaller than the previous, Soviet-built Alligator class. Of the 19 ships in Soviet service, 5 are in the Northern Fleet, 6 in the Baltic Fleet, and 8 in the Pacific Fleet.

Class: One ship of this class was transferred to South Yemen in 1980. No ships of this type are in Polish service. The East German Frosch class has some similarities, although it is a significantly smaller design.

Classification: Soviet BDK type.

Design: The Ropucha class has traditional LST lines with superstructure aft 2nd bow and stern ramps for unloading vehicles. Cargo capacity is 450 tons with a usable deck space of 600 m². Up to 25 armored personnel carriers can be embarked. The superstructure is big and boxy, with large, side-by-side funnels. The Ropucha class, as well as the Polnocny class, has a long sliding hatch cover above the bow section to permit vehicles and cargo to be lowered into the tank deck by dockside cranes.

Several ships have been fitted with Grail short-range missiles. There are provisions for two barrage rocket launchers on the forecastle, but they have not been installed.

Ropucha-class tank landing ship. (1982, U.S. Navy)

A Polish-built Ropucha-class landing ship. The Polish Polnocny shipyard at Gdansk has built most of the Soviet Navy's amphibious ships, as well as many noncombatant ships for the Red fleet. The Polish Navy does not operate this LST class. (1979)

14 TANK LANDING SHIPS: ALLIGATOR CLASS

Name	Name	Name
ALEKSANDR TORTSEV	KRYMSKIY	SERGEI LAZO
DONETSKIY SHAKHTER	KOMSOMOLETS	TOMSKIY KOMSOMOLETS
ILYA AZAROV	NIKOLAY FIL'CHENKOV	VORONEZHSKIY KOMSOMOLETS
KOMSOMOLETS	NIKOLAY VILKOV	50 LET SHEFSTVA V.L.K.S.M.
KARELIYY	NIKOLAY OBYEKOV	
KRASNAYA PRESNYA	PETR IL'ICHYEV	

Completed:	1964–1977
Builders:	Kaliningrad
Displacement:	3,400 tons standard
	4,700 tons full load
Length:	370 ft (112.8 m) oa
Beam:	50 ft 2 in (15.3 m)
Draft:	14 ft 5 in (4.4 m)
Propulsion:	2 diesels; 8,000 hp; 2 shafts
Speed:	18 knots
Range:	9,000 n.miles at 16 knots
	14,000 n.miles at 10 knots
Complement:	approx. 75
Troops:	approx. 300
Helicopters:	no facilities
Missiles/rockets:	1 40-tube 122-mm barrage rocket launcher in most ships
	3 quad SA-N-5 Grail launchers [24] in some ships

Guns:	2 57-mm/70-cal AA (1 twin)
	4 25-mm/60-cal AA (2 twin) in FIL'CHENKOV and VILKOV
Radars:	2 Don-2 (navigation) and/or Spin Trough (search)

Built on traditional LST lines, these ships are less attractive than the later Ropucha class, but have a significantly larger cargo capacity. Two ships are assigned to the Northern Fleet, 2 to the Baltic Fleet, 5 to the Black Sea Fleet, and 5 to the Pacific Fleet.

Classification: Soviet BDK type.

Design: The Alligator class has a superstructure-aft configuration with bow and stern ramps for unloading vehicles. The arrangement of individual ships differs; early units have three cranes—one 15-ton capacity, two 5-ton capacity; later ships have one crane. There are two to four large hatches above the tank deck to permit vehicles and cargo to be lowered by shipboard or dockside cranes. Later ships have an enclosed bridge and a rocket launcher forward, and the last two ships have 25-mm guns aft.

About 25 to 30 tanks or armored personnel carrriers or 1,500 tons of cargo can be carried; only about 600 tons can be carried for beaching operations.

An Alligator-class LST with a 122-mm rocket launcher for shore bombardment fitted on a small structure on the forecastle. (West German Navy)

The Alligator-class LSTs resemble superstructure-aft cargo ships rather than amphibious ships. They do, however, have vehicle parking areas and bow doors with a ramp for unloading onto beaches. In this view the Voronezhskiy Komsomolets has her stern ramp lowered; it can be used to unload amphibious personnel carriers into the water. (1984, U.S. Navy)

39 MEDIUM LANDING SHIPS: POLNOCNY A/B/C CLASSES

(7 units) Polnocny A Class

Completed:	1963–1967(?)
Builders:	Polnocny, Gdansk (Poland)
Displacement:	770 tons full load
Length:	239 ft 5 in (73.0 m) oa
Beam:	28 ft 2 in (8.6 m)
Draft:	6 ft 3 in (1.9 m)
Propulsion:	2 diesels; 5,000 hp; 2 shafts
Speed:	19 knots
Range:	900 n.miles at 18 knots
	1,500 n.miles at 14 knots
Complement:	approx. 35
Troops:	approx. 100
Helicopters:	no facilities
Missiles/rockets:	2 18-tube 140-mm barrage rocket launchers
	2 or 4 quad SA-N-5 Grail launchers [16–32] in most ships
Guns:	2 30-mm/65-cal close-in (1 twin)
	or 2 14.5-mm machine guns (1 twin)
Radars:	1 Spin Trough (search)

(23 units) Polnocny B Class

Completed:	1968–1970
Builders:	Polnocny, Gdansk (Poland)
Displacement:	800 tons full load
Length:	242 ft 9 in (74.0 m) oa
Beam:	28 ft 2 in (8.6 m)
Draft:	6 ft 7 in (2.0 m)
Propulsion:	2 diesels; 5,000 hp; 2 shafts
Speed:	18 knots
Range:	900 n.miles at 18 knots
	1,500 n.miles at 14 knots
Complement:	approx. 40
Troops:	approx. 100
Helicopters:	no facilities
Missiles/rockets:	2 18-tube 140-mm barrage rocket launchers
	4 quad SA-N-5 Grail launchers [32]
Guns:	2 or 4 30-mm/65-cal close-in (1 or 2 twin)
Radars:	1 Drum Tilt (fire control)
	1 Spin Trough (search)

(9 units) Polnocny C Class

Completed:	1970–1973
Builders:	Polnocny, Gdansk (Poland)
Displacement:	1,150 tons full load
Length:	266 ft 8 in (81.3 m) oa
Beam:	33 ft 2 in (10.1 m)
Draft:	6 ft 11 in (2.1 m)
Propulsion:	2 diesels; 5,000 hp; 2 shafts
Speed:	18 knots
Range:	1,800 n.miles at 18 knots
	3,000 n.miles at 14 knots
Complement:	approx. 40
Troops:	approx. 180
Helicopters:	no facilities
Missiles/rockets:	2 18-tube 140-mm barrage rocket launchers
	4 quad SA-N-5 Grail launchers [32]
Guns:	4 30-mm/65-cal close-in (2 twin)
Radars:	1 Drum Tilt (fire control)
	1 Spin Trough (search)

This is the largest series of landing ships in service with any navy. The Polnocny LSM series consists of three principal variants, the design being enlarged and improved during the construction period. Most of the Soviet units are of the B variant.

Class: Thirty-one ships of this type have been transferred since 1966 to Angola (3 B class), Cuba (2 B), Egypt (3 A), Ethiopia (2 B), India (2A + 4 C), Iraq (4 C), Libya (3 C), Somalia (1 A), Vietnam (3 B), and South Yemen (4 B). Some of the transferred ships have a platform for light helicopters installed immediately forward of the superstructure. Another 23 ships of this design were built at Polnocny for the Polish Navy (completed 1964–1971). Thus, a total of 94 units of all variants have been constructed.

Classification: Soviet SDK type. The NATO code name is derived from the Polnocny yard that constructed all of these ships. Initially NATO designated the Polnocny classes with Roman numerals; subsequently changed to the current A-B-C scheme.

Design: The Polnocnys have a conventional landing ship appearance with bow doors. The A class has a convex bow form while the later series have a concave bow. Superstructure and mast details differ among classes and individual ships. Cargo capacity is about 180 tons in the A and B classes and 250 tons in the C class. The earlier ships can carry 6 to 8 armored personnel carriers and the C class about eight. There are minor differences within the sub-classes.

Minesweeping: Some Polnocny A ships are fitted with long troughs along the sides and carry two self-propelled devices for laying line charges on racks at the stern (see photo). These devices are used to clear minefields and obstructions off landing beaches.

A stern quarter view of a Polnocny-C; blast shields are fitted behind the rocket launchers, and life-raft canisters are mounted on the forward deck.

A Polnocny-A LSM with a pair of unmanned minesweeping vehicles mounted on chutes on the fantail and explosive-charge cables fitted along the sides of the ship. (1984, Japanese Maritime Self-Defense Force)

Polnocny-B LSM showing the small, tall funnel of this variant of the Polish-built landing ships. Also visible are the 140-mm rocket launchers on the forward deck.

Polnocny-C LSM with the light lattice mast and built-up amidships structure of this variant.

16 UTILITY LANDING SHIPS: VYDRA CLASS

Completed:	1967–1969
Builders:	
Displacement:	425 tons standard
	600 tons full load
Length:	180 ft 1 in (54.9 m) oa
Beam:	24 ft 1 in (7.6 m)
Draft:	6 ft 7 in (2.0 m)
Propulsion:	2 diesels; 800 hp; 2 shafts
Speed:	12 knots
Range:	1,900 n.miles at 12 knots
	2,700 n.miles at 10 knots
Complement:	approx. 20
Troops:	approx. 100
Helicopters:	no facilities
Missiles/rockets:	none
Guns:	none
Radars:	1 Spin Trough (search)

These are utility landing ships with an open tank deck. Cargo capacity is approximately 250 tons.

An estimated 56 of these ships were built. Units of this type have been transferred to Bulgaria and Egypt.

Classification: Soviet DK type.

Vydra-class utility landing ship. (Royal Danish Navy)

MEDIUM LANDING SHIPS: MP 4 CLASS

All ships of the MP 4 class have been discarded from the amphibious role. Some MP-series ships continue to serve in auxiliary roles.

One MP 4 landing ship was transferred to Egypt and one to Indonesia.

21
Landing Craft

Some 70 air-cushion landing craft are currently in Soviet service with construction continuing on several classes.

1+ AIR-CUSHION LANDING CRAFT: POMORNIK CLASS

Completed:	1986–
Builders:	(USSR)
Displacement:	360 tons full load
Length:	193 ft 6 in (59.0 m) oa
Beam:	72 ft 2 in (22.0 m)
Draft:	
Propulsion:	gas turbines; 3 aircraft-type propellers (tractor) + lift fans
Speed:	approx. 55 knots on air cushion
Range:	
Complement:	
Troops:	200+
Missiles:	SA-N-5 launchers (?)
Guns:	2 30-mm/65-cal close-in (multibarrel)
Radars:	1 Band Stand (fire control)
	1 Bass Tilt (fire control)
	1 . . . . . . (navigation)

The Pomornik is the largest Soviet air-cushion vehicle. Note the distinctive superstructure.

Cargo capacity is rated at three medium tanks.

20+ AIR-CUSHION LANDING CRAFT: LEBED CLASS

Completed:	1976–
Builders:	(USSR)
Displacement:	85 tons full load
Length:	81 ft 4 in (24.8 m) oa
Beam:	35 ft 5 in (10.8 m)
Draft:	
Propulsion:	3 gas turbines; 2 aircraft-type propellers (tractor) + lift fans
Speed:	70 knots on air cushion
Range:	100 n.miles at 65 knots
	250 n.miles at 60 knots
Complement:	
Troops:	approx. 120
Missiles:	none
Guns:	1 30-mm/65-cal close in (multibarrel)
Radars:	

These landing craft are the type seen aboard the amphibious ship Ivan Rogov. They can carry two PT-76 amphibious tanks or troops or some 45 tons of cargo. Their control cabin is offset to starboard with the Gatling gun mounted on top.

The first large air-cushion landing craft of the Pomornik class, seen in the Baltic. Note the massive superstructure and the exhausts of the turbojet engines. (West German Navy)

The Soviet Union has led in the development of air-cushion landing craft, as this large Lebed moving at high speed in the Baltic Sea. There is a 30-mm Gatling gun forward on the starboard side with the control cabin/cockpit on the port side. The (closed) bow ramp is visible as are the large shrouded propellers and rudders. (Royal Danish Navy)

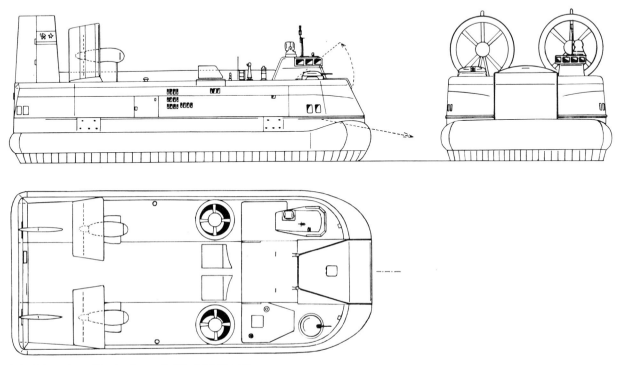

Lebed-class air-cushion landing craft. (Siegfried Breyer)

1 + AIR-CUSHION LANDING CRAFT: TSAPLYA CLASS

Completed:	1982–
Builders:	(USSR)
Displacement:	90 tons full load
Length:	
Beam:	
Draft:	
Propulsion:	gas turbines
Speed:	
Range:	
Complement:	
Troops:	approx. 160 (see notes)
Missiles:	
Guns:	

This class can reportedly carry one amphibious tank plus 80 troops, or 160 troops, or 25 tons of cargo.

2 + AIR-CUSHION LANDING CRAFT: UTENOK CLASS

Completed:	1982–
Builders:	Feodosiya
Displacement:	
Length:	86 ft 3 in (26.3 m) oa
Beam:	42 ft 8 in (13.0 m)
Draft:	
Propulsion:	gas turbines
Speed:	
Range:	
Complement:	
Troops:	
Missiles:	
Guns:	4 30-mm/65-cal close-in (2 twin)

Cargo capacity is one tank.

17 + AIR-CUSHION LANDING CRAFT: AIST CLASS

Completed:	1971–
Builders:	Dekabristov, Leningrad
Displacement:	250 tons full load
Length:	155 ft 2 in (47.3 m) oa
Beam:	57 ft 1 in (17.4 m)
Draft:	1 ft (0.3 m)
Propulsion:	2 gas turbines (NK-12MV); 4 aircraft-type propellers (2 pusher/2 tractor) + 2 lift fans
Speed:	80 knots on air cushion
Range:	100 n.miles at 65 knots
	350 n.miles at 60 knots
Complement:	
Troops:	approx. 220
Missiles:	2 quad SA-N-5 Grail launchers in later units
Guns:	4 30-mm/65-cal close in (2 twin)
Radars:	1 Drum Tilt (fire control)
	1 Spin Trough (search)

These are the world's second largest military air-cushion vehicles. They carry four PT-76 amphibious tanks or two medium tanks plus 220 troops or cargo. Bow and stern ramps are fitted to the "drive-through" cargo space. The 30-mm gun mounts are forward (only one mount was provided on the prototype).

Classification: Soviet DKVP type.

Aist-class air-cushion landing craft. (Siegfried Breyer)

An Aist ACV landing craft afloat on its air cushion. The 30-mm guns are under canvas.

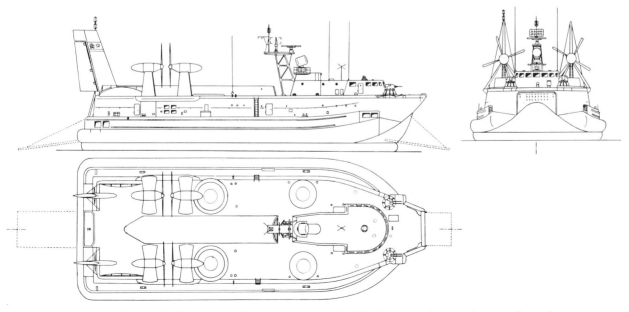

An Aist ACV landing craft in the Baltic, showing the usual arrangement of two tractor and two pusher propeller pods, mounted forward of the twin rudders; the vertical propeller wells are visible amidships. Two twin 30-mm gun mounts are fitted forward of the control cabin/cockpit. (1978, West German Navy)

30 AIR CUSHION LANDING CRAFT: GUS CLASS

Completed:	1970–1974
Builders:	(USSR)
Displacement:	27 tons full load
Length:	69 ft 10 in (21.3 m) oa
Beam:	23 ft 3 in (7.1 m)
Draft:	8 in (0.2 m)
Propulsion:	3 gas turbines; 2,340 shp; 2 aircraft-type propellers (tractor) + 1 lift fan
Speed:	60 knots
Range:	185 n.miles at 50 knots
	200 n.miles at 43 knots
Complement:	
Troops:	approx. 25
Missiles:	none
Guns:	none
Radars:	. . . . . . (navigation)

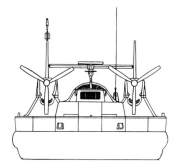

These were the first naval air-cushion landing craft to be produced in significant numbers. They cannot carry vehicles. There is a training version with two control cabins.

The Gus is a naval version of the civilian Skate air-cushion vehicle. The Soviet Union operates the world's largest fleet of commercial air-cushion vehicles.

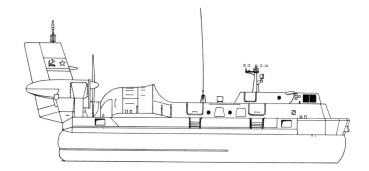

A Gus ACV landing craft at high speed, probably in the Leningrad area.

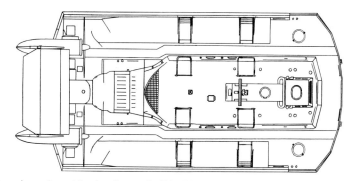

Gus-class air-cushion landing craft. (Siegfried Breyer)

16 LANDING CRAFT: ONDATRA CLASS

Completed:	1978–
Builders:	(USSR)
Displacement:	90 tons standard
	140 tons full load
Length:	79 ft 5 in (24.2 m) oa
Beam:	19 ft 8 in (6.0 m)
Draft:	4 ft 11 in (1.5 m)
Propulsion:	2 diesels; 600 hp; 2 shafts
Speed:	10 knots
Range:	
Complement:	4
Guns:	none

Small personnel/vehicle landing craft. One is normally embarked in the IVAN ROGOV-class ships for use as a tug for the Lebed air-cushion vehicles. A ROGOV can carry six of these craft in the docking well.

Several LANDING CRAFT: T-4 CLASS

Completed:	1954–1974
Builders:	(USSR)
Displacement:	70 tons full load
Length:	62 ft 4 in (19.0 m) oa
Beam:	14 ft 1 in (4.3 m)
Draft:	3 ft 3 in (1.0 m)
Propulsion:	2 diesels; 600 hp; 2 shafts
Speed:	10 knots
Range:	
Complement:	5
Guns:	none

Small landing craft, some fitted with bow ramps to permit loading light and medium tanks.

The T-4 landing craft, of the type shown in this dated photo carrying a PT-76 amphibious tank, is still widely used by the Soviet Navy. It is similar to the LCMs of Western navies. (Sovfoto)

22
Naval Auxiliaries

The ships described in this chapter are all manned by naval personnel except for the hospital ships of the Oʙ' class. These have civilian crews, but carry naval medical personnel.

The icebreakers, supply ships, and armed tugs operated by the KGB Maritime Border Troops are listed in chapter 25.

Auxiliary ships in this chapter are listed in the following order:

Submarine Support Ships	Hospital Ships
Repair Ships	Training Ships
Salvage and Rescue Ships	Experimental and Trials Ships
Heavy Lift Ships	Generator Ships
Cable Ships	Degaussing and Deperming Ships
Missile Transports	Noise Measurement Ships
Oilers and Tankers	Icebreakers
Special-Purpose Tankers	Fleet Tugs
Water Tankers	Service Craft and Target Craft
Cargo and Supply Ships	

Western intelligence in early 1986 credited the Soviet Navy with operating some 775 auxiliary ships in the following categories:

- 40 tankers (point-to-point carriers)
- 20 oilers (underway replenishment)
- 20 other replenishment (stores ships, water carriers)
- 70 tenders and support ships (including munition carriers)
- 145 tug, salvage, and submarine rescue ships
- 480 other auxiliaries (including AGIs, research, surveying, cargo, and miscellaneous ships)

These figures do not include "sealift" ships employed to carry troops and equipment; this capability is provided by the Soviet merchant fleet. The Soviet merchant and scientific fleets also carry out other military-related missions.

SUBMARINE SUPPORT SHIPS

These ships are similar to Western submarine tenders and depot ships. They provide specialized services to submarines in Soviet base areas and, on occasion, in remote areas. In addition, the Ugra and Don classes provide extensive command and control facilities for fleet or task force commanders.

The large submarine salvage and rescue ships of the Eʟ'ʙʀus class may also have some submarine support capabilities (see page 281).

The Soviet Navy operates a large force of fleet auxiliaries. Here, at an open anchorage in the Mediterranean, are the water carrier MANYCH and the large underway replenishment ship BEREZINA. The BEREZINA is smaller than her U.S. Navy contemporaries of the AOE/AOR types, while the MANYCH has no counterpart in the U.S. Navy. Note the Ka-25 Hormone-C on the BEREZINA'S flight deck; another is in the hangar. She is heavily armed—the only Soviet oiler now fitted with weapons. (The MANYCH beached her weapons.)

6 SUBMARINE SUPPORT SHIPS: UGRA CLASS

Name	Name	Name	Completed
Ivan Kolyshkin	Ivan Vakhrameev	Volga	
Ivan Kucherenko	Tobol	. . . . . .	} 1963–1972

Builders:	Black Sea, Nikolayev
Displacement:	6,750 tons standard
	9,600 tons full load
Length:	475 ft 7 in (145.0 m) oa
Beam:	58 ft (17.7 m)
Draft:	21 ft (6.4 m)
Propulsion:	4 diesels; 8,000 hp; 2 shafts
Speed:	17 knots
Range:	21,000 n.miles at 10 knots
Complement:	approx. 450
Helicopters:	landing deck; hangar facilities for 1 Ka-25 Hormone-C in Ivan Kolyshkin
Missiles:	2 quad SA-N-5 Grail [16]
Guns:	8 57-mm/80-cal AA (4 twin)
Radars:	1 to 3 Don-2 (navigation)
	2 Muff Cob (fire control)
	1 Strut Curve (air search)
EW systems:	4 Watch Dog

These are enlarged versions of the previous Don-class submarine support ships. All have some flagship capabilities (see Design notes).

Class: Two ships of this class are employed as training ships and are listed separately (see page 000). One Ugra-class submarine tender was transferred to India in 1968; her armament and radars were changed before transfer, possibly to simplify maintenance by the Indian Navy.

Classification: Soviet PB type.

Design: These ships are larger than the previous Don class, with a larger forward superstructure and a shorter funnel. The ships have extensive workshops and can provide submarines with food, diesel fuel, fresh water, and torpedoes. They are fitted with one 10-ton-capacity and two 6-ton-capacity cranes. Extensive modifications have changed the appearance of these ships from their original configuration and from each other.

The Ivan Kolyshkin has been fitted with a helicopter hangar; she retains the after twin 57-mm gun mounts outboard of the hangar. The others have had the after superstructure built up; the Ivan Kucherenko and Volga have large lattice masts aft mounting Vee Cone communications antennas.

The submarine tender Ivan Kolyshkin is the only Ugra-class ship with a helicopter hangar. The configurations of the several Ugra and Don submarine tenders vary considerably. Two other Ugras serve the Navy as training ships. (1978, French Navy)

The IVAN KUCHERENKO in Western Pacific waters, with her Vee Cone HF antenna visible on the after mast. Note her heavy armament of eight 57-mm anti-aircraft guns; she has a small helicopter deck aft. (1984, Japanese Maritime Self-Defense Force)

6 SUBMARINE SUPPORT SHIPS: DON CLASS

Name	Name	Name	Completed
DMITRIY GALKIN	KAMCHATSKIY KOMSOMOLETS	MAGOMED GADZIEV	1958–1961
FYODOR VIDYAEV	MAGADANSKIY KOMSOMOLETS	VIKTOR KOTEL'NIKOV	

Builders:	Black Sea, Nikolayev
Displacement:	6,730 tons standard
	9,000 tons full load
Length:	459 ft 2 in (140.0 m) oa
Beam:	58 ft (17.7 m)
Draft:	21 ft (6.4 m)
Propulsion:	4 diesels; 8,000 hp; 2 shafts
Speed:	17 knots
Range:	21,000 n.miles at 10 knots
Complement:	approx. 450
Helicopters:	landing deck in MAGADANSKIY KOMSOMOLETS and VIKTOR KOTEL'NIKOV
Missiles:	none
Guns:	4 100-mm/56-cal DP (4 single) except 2 guns in VIKTOR KOTEL'NIKOV; none in MAGADANSKIY KOMSOMOLETS
	8 57-mm/70-cal AA (4 twin)
	8 25-mm/60-cal AA (4 twin) in FYODOR VIDYAEV
Radars:	1 or 2 Don-2 (navigation)
	2 Hawk Screech (fire control) except removed from DMITRIY GALKIN and FYODOR VIDYAEV
	1 Slim Net (air search)
	1 Sun Visor-B (fire control) except none in MAGADANSKIY KOMSO-MOLETS
EW systems:	2 Watch Dog

The Don-class ships were the Soviet Navy's first modern submarine tenders comparable to their Western counterparts.

Class: An additional ship of this class was transferred to Indonesia in 1962.

A Don-class submarine tender with a Foxtrot diesel submarine alongside. Note the heavy gun armament of 100-mm and 57-mm guns. U.S. fleet auxiliaries generally have only close-in or point-defense gun and missile systems.

Classification: Soviet PB type.

Design: These are large submarine support ships and flagships. Details differ. Most ships retain the Wasp Head fire-control director (with Sun Visor radar) atop the forward superstructure. The MAGADANSKIY KOMSOMOLETS was completed with a helicopter platform and without 100-mm guns. The VIKTOR KOTEL'NIKOV had her two after 100-mm gun mounts replaced by a helicopter platform.

At least two ships, the DMITRIY GALKIN and FYODOR VIDYAEV, have had Vee Cone antennas fitted to their after lattice masts, while the VIKTOR KOTEL'NIKOV has a pair of Big Ball satellite communication antennas (no Vee Cone). The ships with the Vee Cone have their Slim Net antenna on a lattice mast adjacent to the bridge structure.

The ships have a bow hook with a 100-ton lift capacity plus one 10-ton, two 5-ton, and two 1-ton cranes.

The VIKTOR KOTEL'NIKOV, modified to serve as a flagship in addition to tending submarines. Note her Big Ball satellite communication antennas adjacent to the lattice mast and large helicopter deck. (1984)

The KAMCHATSKIY KOMSOMOLETS retains the basic Don-class armament, with single 100-mm and twin 57-mm guns forward and aft. There is a Wasp Head fire control director with Sun Visor-B radar atop the bridge. She lacks the flagship features of other Don-class ships. (1984, JMSDF)

6 SUBMARINE SUPPORT SHIPS: "ATREK" CLASS

Name	Name	Name	Completed
ATREK	BAKHMUT	EVGENIY OSIPOV	1955–1957
AYAT	DVINA	MURMAT	

Builders:	Neptun, Rostock (East Germany)
Displacement:	3,400 tons standard
	5,385 tons full load
Length:	335 ft 10 in (102.4 m) oa
Beam:	47 ft 3 in (14.4 m)
Draft:	18 ft (5.5 m)
Propulsion:	1 triple-expansion reciprocating plus low-pressure turbine; 2,400 hp; 1 shaft
Boilers:	2
Speed:	13 knots
Range:	6,900 n.miles at 13 knots
Complement:	
Helicopters:	no facilities
Missiles:	none
Guns:	see notes
Radars:	1 Don-2 or Neptune (navigation)

These ships were converted from KOLOMNA-class cargo ships to submarine tenders during their construction. They no longer deploy out of coastal waters, and some may be in a reduced commission status if not laid up.

Class: Originally eight ships were in this class.
Classification: Soviet PB type.
Design: Fitted with two 5-ton cranes forward.
Guns: Details of current armament are not available. At least into the 1970s the BAKHMUT carried six 37-mm AA guns in twin mounts (two forward, just behind cranes, and one aft on a small deckhouse). A second ship similarly armed was believed to have a quad 45- or 57-mm AA gun mount on the bow.

The ATREK-class submarine tender BAKHUMT riding at anchor in 1975. She and her sister ships were begun as merchant ships, but completed to this configuration to support submarines. All later Soviet submarine tenders were built for that role. Lost in the topside clutter, the ship has two pairs of 37-mm guns just behind the forward mast, and a third pair on the after deckhouse.

REPAIR SHIPS

. . . REPAIR SHIPS: NEW CONSTRUCTION

A new series of repair ships for the Soviet Navy is reported under construction at the Wisla Shipyard in Gdansk, Poland.

2 REPAIR SHIPS: MALINA CLASS

Name	Completed
PM-63	1984
PM-74	1985

Builders:	Black Sea, Nikolayev
Displacement:	10,000 tons full load
Length:	459 ft 1 in (140.0 m) oa
Beam:	72 ft 2 in (22.0 m)
Draft:	16 ft 5 in (5.0 m)
Propulsion:	4 gas turbines; 60,000 shp; 2 shafts
Speed:	17 knots
Range:	
Complement:	approx. 260
Helicopters:	
Missiles:	none
Guns:	none
Radars:	2 Palm Frond (navigation)

The Malina-class ships are the largest repair/tender-type ships in the Soviet Navy. Note the square funnel, typical of gas-turbine-propelled ships. (1984, U.S. Navy)

These are significantly larger than the previous Soviet naval repair ships. They have facilities for supporting nuclear-propelled surface ships and submarines.

Classification: Soviet PM type.

The Malina-class repair ship PM-74 in the East China Sea. The container-like structures forward (fore and aft of the cranes) are probably for handling nuclear cores when supporting nuclear-propelled submarines. (1985, JMSDF)

24 REPAIR SHIPS: AMUR CLASS

Name	Name	Name	Completed
PM-5	PM-52	PM-129	
PM-9	PM-56	PM-138	
PM-10	PM-64	PM-139	
PM-15	PM-73	PM-140	1969–1978
PM-34	PM-75	PM-156	1981–1983
PM-37	PM-81	PM-161	
PM-40	PM-82	PM-163	
PM-49	PM-94	PM-164	

Builders:	Adolf Warski, Szczecin (Poland)
Displacement:	4,000 tons standard
	5,490 tons full load
Length:	399 ft 2 in (121.7 m) oa
Beam:	55 ft 9 in (17.0 m)
Draft:	16 ft 9 in (5.1 m)
Propulsion:	2 diesels; 4,000 hp; 1 shaft
Speed:	12 knots
Range:	13,200 n.miles at 8 knots
Complement:	approx. 210
Helicopters:	no facilities
Missiles:	none
Guns:	none
Radars:	1 Don-2 (navigation)

Amur-class repair ship PM-5. (1983)

These are enlarged Oskol-class repair ships.

Classification: Soviet PM type.

Design: These ships perform maintenance and repairs on surface ships and submarines. They have workshops and stock spare parts. Three cranes are fitted. Accommodations are provided for 200 crewmen of ships under repair.

The Amur-class repair ship PM-82 shows the unusual lines typical of Soviet auxiliaries of this type. There are two light cranes forward and one aft; no armament is fitted. (1984)

12 REPAIR SHIPS: OSKOL CLASS

Name	Name	Name	Completed
PM-2	PM-26	PM-68	
PM-20	PM-28	PM-146	1964–1967
PM-21	PM-51	PM-148	
PM-24	PM-62	PM-477	

Builders:	Adolf Warski, Szczecin (Poland)
Displacement:	2,500 tons standard
	3,000 tons full load
Length:	299 ft 9 in (91.4 m) oa
Beam:	40 ft (12.2 m)
Draft:	13 ft 1 in (4.0 m)
Propulsion:	2 diesels; 4,000 hp; 1 shaft
Speed:	12 knots
Range:	9,000 n.miles at 8 knots
Complement:	approx. 60
Helicopters:	no facilities
Missiles:	none
Guns:	4 25-mm/60-cal AA (2 twin) in PM-24
	2 12.7-mm machine guns (1 twin) in some ships
Radars:	1 or 2 Don-2 (navigation)

These are small repair ships with limited capabilities. Each ship has one or two 3.4-ton-capacity cranes.

Classification: Soviet PM type.

Design: Details differ; the last three ships are flush-decked with higher bridges; known as Oskol III type. The Oskols differ in basic configuration from the Amurs by a deck structure forward and the absence of a crane aft.

Guns: Only a few are armed; the PM-24 had a twin 57-mm gun mount removed from the bow in the early 1980s (no fire-control radar); she is known as Oskol II type.

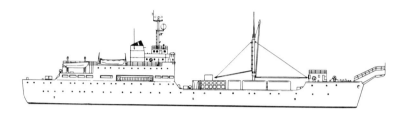

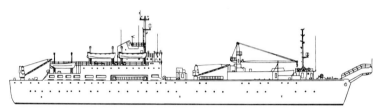

Drawings of the rarely photographed Dnepr I (top) and Dnepr II repair ships. The principal differences in the two types are the flush deck of the Dnepr II and their crane arrangements. (Siegfried Breyer)

The Oskol-class repair ship PM-24 (lower) and the Lama-class missile carrier GENERAL RYABIKOV. The Oskol has twin 25-mm guns aft; the Lama a twin 57-mm mount forward. (1984)

5 REPAIR SHIPS: DNEPR CLASS

Name	Name	Name	Completed
PM-17	PM-30	PM-135	} 1960–1964
PM-22	PM-130		

Builders:	Black Sea, Nikolayev
Displacement:	4,500 tons standard
	5,300 tons full load
Length:	371 ft 8 in (113.3 m) oa
Beam:	54 ft 2 in (16.5 m)
Draft:	14 ft 5 in (4.4 m)
Propulsion:	1 diesel; 2,000 hp; 1 shaft
Speed:	11 knots
Range:	6,000 n.miles at 8 knots
Complement:	approx. 420
Helicopters:	no facilities
Missiles:	none
Guns:	none
Radars:	1 Don-2 (navigation)

These repair ships have a distinctive, 150-ton-capacity bow hoist in addition to smaller cranes. They are primarily intended to support submarines.

Classification: Soviet PM type.

Design: Details and equipment varies. The last two ships are flush-decked (Dnepr II type).

Guns: These ships are designed to be armed with a 57-mm AA twin gun mount. It was installed on some ships when completed; subsequently removed.

SALVAGE AND RESCUE SHIPS

In addition to the salvage ships listed below, the Navy operates a number of buoy and mooring tenders and lift ships that can be used for salvage operations.

Smaller salvage and fire-fighting tugs are listed later in this chapter.

2 SALVAGE AND RESCUE SHIPS: "EL'BRUS" CLASS

Name	Completed
EL'BRUS	1981
. . . . . .	1984

Builders:	61 Kommuna, Nikolayev
Displacement:	20,000 tons full load
Length:	574 ft (175.0 m) oa
Beam:	82 ft (25.0 m)
Draft:	24 ft 7 in (7.5 m)
Propulsion:	4 diesels; 2 shafts
Speed:	17 knots
Range:	
Complement:	approx. 400
Helicopters:	1 Ka-25 Hormone-C
Missiles:	none
Guns:	none (see notes)
Radars:	1 Don-2 (navigation)
	2 Don-Kay (navigation)

The EL'BRUS-class ships are the world's largest submarine salvage and rescue ships, almost five times the displacement of the U.S. Navy's largest ships of this type, the PIGEON (ASR 21) and ORTOLAN (ASR 22).

The large salvage and rescue ship EL BRUS underway in the North Atlantic. There is a large gantry crane amidships for handling submersibles. Western navies have no ships of this type. (1982, U.S. Navy)

The EL'BRUS began her first deployment from the Black Sea into the Mediterranean in late December 1981.

Classification: Soviet SS type.

Design: The EL'BRUS has a massive superstructure and a helicopter platform aft. A hangar is provided, the "drawbridge" door forming a ramp down to the platform. There is a gantry-crane arrangement amidships for lowering submersibles over the side. The ships have extensive mooring, diving, and fire-fighting equipment and are capable of sustained operations in remote areas.

At least two and possibly four rescue submersibles are carried, similar to the same type carried on board the India-class submarines. In the EL'BRUS, the submersibles are carried in a hangar abaft the funnel, with rails provided for moving them forward to where extending gantry cranes (port and starboard) can lower them to the water.

Guns: The ship has provisions for mounting four 30-mm guns of either the twin-barrel or multibarrel (Gatling) type.

Names: EL'BRUS is named for the highest peak in Europe, in the Caucasus Mountains.

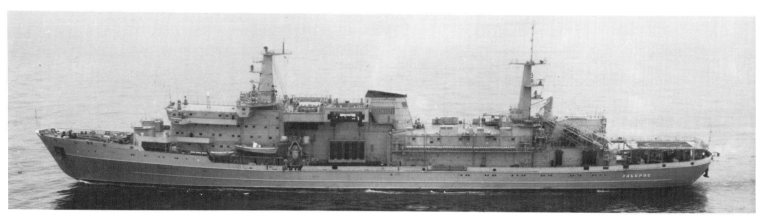

In this view the EL'BRUS has a diving chamber beneath the gantry crane.

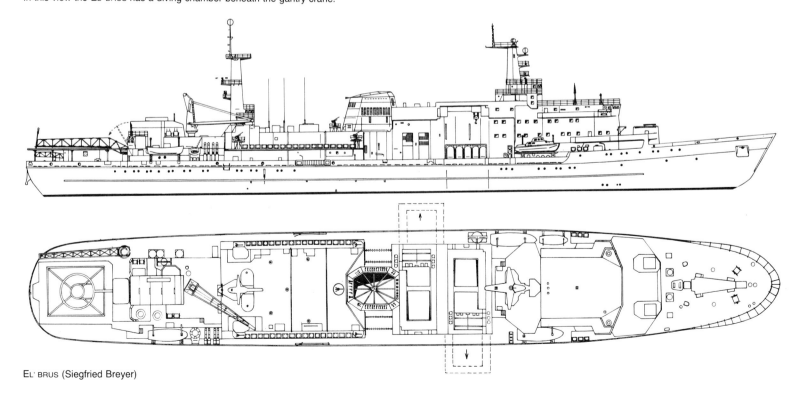

EL'BRUS (Siegfried Breyer)

3 SALVAGE AND RESCUE SHIPS: "PIONEER MOSKVYY" CLASS

Name	Conversion Completed
MIKHAIL RUDNITSKIY	1979
GIORGIY KOZMIN	1980
GIORGIY TITOV	1983

Builders:	Vyborg
Displacement:	10,700 tons full load
Length:	430 ft (130.3 m)
Beam:	57 ft 1 in (17.3 m)
Draft:	24 ft 1 in (7.3 m)
Propulsion:	1 diesel (B&W 5DKRN 62/140−3); 6,100 hp; 1 shaft
Speed:	15.5 knots
Range:	12,000 n.miles at 15.5 knots
Complement:	approx. 120
Helicopters:	no facilities
Missiles:	none
Guns:	none
Radars:	2 Don-2 (navigation)

These are cargo ships converted for salvage operations. A salvage submersible can be carried.

Class: From 1973 onward, 27 ships of this class were delivered for Soviet merchant and naval use, plus two ships for the East German merchant service. The class is a variation of the SESTRORETSK-class cellular container ships.

A fourth Navy ship, the SAYANIY, is a research ship (see chapter 23).

Design: These are large, superstructure-aft ships, with two large kingposts and two 40-ton-capacity and two 20-ton-capacity booms. Four holds are provided. For the salvage role, deckhouses have been built over the aftermost hold and over the forward hold in some ships; details differ. Bow and stern thrusters have been fitted and deep-mooring gear is provided.

Names: These ships are named for pioneers in submersible development. (All of the Soviet merchant ships of this class have "pioneer" names.)

The GIORGIY KOZMIN is one of three large salvage ships converted while under construction as merchant ships. This ship participated in the 1983 search for the wreckage of Korean Air lines flight 007 that was shot down by a Soviet fighter. (1979)

3 SALVAGE SHIPS: INGUL CLASS

Name	Completed
MASHUK	1974
PAMIR	1975
ALATAU	1984

Builders:	Admiralty, Leningrad
Displacement:	3,200 tons standard
	4,050 tons full load
Length:	304 ft 5 in (92.8 m) oa
Beam:	50 ft 6 in (15.4 m)
Draft:	19 ft (5.8 m)
Propulsion:	2 diesels (58D-4R); 9,000 hp; 2 shafts
Speed:	20 knots
Range:	9,000 n.miles at 19 knots
Complement:	approx. 120
Helicopters:	no facilities
Missiles:	none
Guns:	none (see notes)
Radars:	2 Don-2 (navigation)

These are powerful salvage tugs, fitted with submarine rescue, diving, salvage, and fire-fighting equipment. Two sister ships serve in the Soviet merchant fleet, the YAGUAR and BARS. These ships should not be confused with two (smaller) intelligence collection ships of the PAMIR class.

Design: The hull has a bulbous bow with thrusters fitted for precise maneuvering. Note the high horsepower of these ships.

Classification: Soviet SS type.

Guns: These ships have provisions for mounting one 57-mm AA twin gun mount and two 25-mm AA twin gun mounts.

Names: Confusion should be avoided with the INGUL-class cable ships.

A large salvage/rescue tug of the INGUL class underway some 200 miles east of Japan. At the time the ship had an Echo-II-class SSGN in tow and was en route to the submarine base at Petropavlovsk. (1986, JMSDF)

1 SUBMARINE RESCUE SHIP: NEPA CLASS

Name	Completed
KARPATY	1970

Builders:	Black Sea, Nikolayev
Displacement:	9,800 tons full load
Length:	424 ft 9 in (129.5 m) oa
Beam:	63 ft (19.2 m)
Draft:	21 ft (6.4 m)
Propulsion:	4 diesels; 8,000 hp; 2 shafts
Speed:	16 knots
Range:	8,000 n.miles at 14 knots
Complement:	approx. 270
Helicopters:	no facilities
Missiles:	none
Guns:	none
Radars:	2 Don-2 (navigation)

The KARPATY is a large, one-of-a-kind submarine rescue ship. She has a 600-ton lift device mounted on her stern plus submarine rescue, fire-fighting, diving, and salvage equipment.

Classification: Soviet SS type.

The KARPATY is a large, one-of-a-kind auxiliary fitted for submarine rescue and salvage. She has an unusual stern lift device; a submarine rescue chamber is held by davits on the port side.

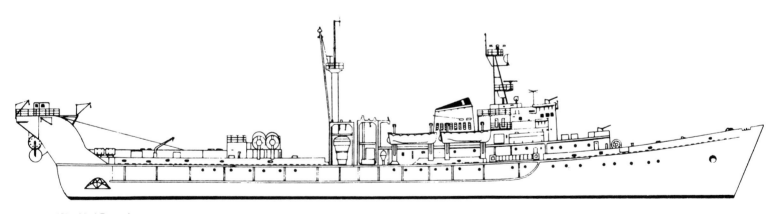

KARPATY (Siegfried Breyer)

8 SUBMARINE RESCUE SHIPS: PRUT CLASS

Name	Name	Name	Completed
ALTAY	ZHIGULI	SS-26	
BESHTAU	SS-21	SS-83	1961–1968
VLADIMIR TREFOLEV	SS-23		

Builders:	61 Kommunar, Nikolayev
Displacement:	2,800 tons standard
	3,300 tons full load
Length:	295 ft 10 in (90.2 m) oa
Beam:	46 ft 11 in (14.3 m)
Draft:	18 ft (5.5 m)
Propulsion:	4 diesels; 8,000 hp; 2 shafts
Speed:	20 knots
Range:	10,000 n.miles at 16 knots
Complement:	approx. 120
Helicopters:	no facilities
Missiles:	none
Guns:	none (see notes)
Radars:	1 or 2 Don-2 (navigation)

These are large tug-type ships fitted for submarine rescue and diving operations. The mast arrangement differs.

Class: The SS-44 of this class was lost in the 1970s.

Classification: Soviet SS type.

Guns: These ships have provisions for a single 57-mm AA quad mounting and Muff Cob radar; one ship was armed in this manner.

A Prut-class submarine rescue ship at anchor.

The Prut-class submarine rescue ship SS-28, one of a large class of these ships that are similar to the (smaller) U.S. Navy ASRs of World War II construction. A diving bell and submarine rescue chamber are fitted on the port side; mooring buoys are behind the after mast. (1979, Royal Navy)

2 SALVAGE TUGS: PAMIR CLASS

Name	Completed
AGATAN	1958
ALDAN	1958

Builders:	Gävle (Sweden)
Displacement:	1,445 tons standard
	2,240 tons full load
Length:	255 ft 10 in (78.0 m) oa
Beam:	42 ft (12.8 m)
Draft:	13 ft 2 in (4.0 m)
Propulsion:	2 diesels (MAN G10V); 4,200 hp; 2 shafts
Speed:	17.5 knots
Range:	15,200 n.miles at 17.5 knots
	21,800 n.miles at 12 knots
Complement:	
Helicopters:	no facilities
Missiles:	none
Guns:	none
Radars:	2 Don-2 (navigation)

These are salvage tugs fitted for diving, salvage, and fire-fighting. Two sister ships serve in the Soviet Navy as intelligence collectors (AGI).

Classification: Soviet SS type.

One of the Pamir-class salvage tugs underway; these ships should not be confused with the larger salvage tug with the name PAMIR.

11 SUBMARINE RESCUE SHIPS: T-58 CLASS (ex-minesweepers)

Name	Name	Name	Completed
KAZBEK	ZANGEZUR	SS-47	
KHIBINY	SS-30	SS-50	
VALDAY	SS-35	SS-51	late 1950s
POLKOVO	SS-40		

Builders:	(USSR)
Displacement:	815 tons standard
	930 tons full load
Length:	235 ft 2 in (71.7 m) oa
Beam:	31 ft 6 in (9.6 m)
Draft:	8 ft 10 in (2.7 m)
Propulsion:	2 diesels; 4,000 hp; 2 shafts
Speed:	17 knots
Range:	2,500 n.miles at 12 knots
Complement:	approx. 60
Helicopters:	no facilities
Missiles:	none
Guns:	none (see notes)
Radars:	1 or 2 Don-2 (navigation)
	1 Spin Trough (search) in some units
Sonars:	Tamir high frequency

These ships were modified while under construction as mine-sweepers and were completed as submarine rescue ships. A rescue chamber is carried on the port side; also fitted with diving equipment.

Class: One ship of this type was transferred to India (1971). Several Soviet ships have been stricken, including the GIDROLOG that also operated in the intelligence-collection role. No ships of this class remain in the minesweeping role.

Classification: Soviet SS type.

Guns: In the minesweeping configuration two 57-mm AA twin mounts could be fitted as well as associated Ball End or Muff Cob radars. The rescue ships are not believed to have ever carried armament.

The T-58-class minesweepers converted to submarine rescue ships have a rescue chamber on the port side and lifting gear aft. (The U.S. Navy's first submarine rescue ships were converted World War I-built "Bird"-class minesweepers.) (1978)

HEAVY LIFT SHIPS

These ships plant and maintain navigation buoys and undertake salvage tasks. The Soviet Navy's hydrographic ships, listed in chapter 23, also plant and maintain buoys.

10 LIFT SHIPS: SURA CLASS

Name	Name	Name	Completed
KIL-1	KIL-23	KIL-32	
KIL-2	KIL-27	KIL-33	1965–1972
KIL-21	KIL-29		1976–1978
KIL-22	KIL-31		

Builders:	Neptun, Rostock (East Germany)
Displacement:	2,370 tons standard
	3,150 tons full load
Length:	223 ft (68.0 m) wl (see notes)
	285 ft 4 in (87.0 m) oa
Beam:	48 ft 6 in (14.8 m)
Draft:	16 ft 5 in (5.0 m)
Propulsion:	diesel-electric: 4 diesels (Karl Liebknecht); 2,240 hp; 4 generators connected to 2 electric motors; 2 shafts
Speed:	13 knots
Range:	4,000 n.miles at 10 knots
Complement:	
Helicopters:	no facilities
Missiles:	none
Guns:	none
Radars:	2 Don-2 (navigation)

These are heavy lift ships used for handling buoys and other lift functions. The lifting rig projects over the stern and has a 60-ton capacity. A smaller crane and lifting boom are fitted amidships. The ships have a cargo hold that can accommodate 890 tons, in addition to buoys or other material stowed on deck. The ships also have a very large fuel capacity for transfer to other ships.

Additional ships of this type are operated by the Soviet merchant marine.

Classification: Soviet KIL type.

Engineering: The propulsion machinery is forward in these ships, hence the use of the diesel-electric plant to alleviate the need for very long propeller shafts.

The Sura-class heavy lift ship KIL-32 with a submersible on deck. These ships are employed in a variety of support roles. (1983)

The KIL-2, showing the "tunnel" into the superstructure. These ships have a large, open working deck with a variety of lift gear. (1982, L. & L. Van Ginderen)

10 HEAVY LIFT SHIPS: NEPTUN CLASS

Name	Name	Name	Completed
KIL-3	KIL-12	KIL-17	
KIL-5	KIL-14	KIL-18	1957–1960
KIL-6	KIL-15		
KIL-9	KIL-16		

Builders:	Neptun, Rostock (East Germany)
Displacement:	700 tons standard
	1,240 tons full load
Length:	152 ft 6 in (46.5 m) wl (see notes)
	188 ft (57.3 m) oa
Beam:	37 ft 5 in (11.4 m)
Draft:	11 ft 2 in (3.4 m)
Propulsion:	2 triple-expansion reciprocating engines; 1,000 hp; 2 shafts
Boilers:	2
Speed:	12 knots
Range:	1,000 n.miles at 11 knots
Complement:	approx. 40
Helicopters:	no facilities
Missiles:	none
Guns:	none
Radars:	

These small lift ships are being retired, with four units believed to have been discarded in 1983. There is an 80-ton-capacity bow lift for hauling buoys and for salvage operations.

Classification: Soviet KIL type.

Engineering: All were originally coal burners; some have been converted to oil.

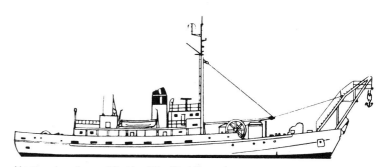

Neptun-class heavy lift ship. (Siegfried Breyer)

CABLE SHIPS

Cable ships lay and tend underwater cables for communications purposes and support sea-floor hydrophone arrays. They are supplemented in these roles by several civilian-operated cable ships (see chapter 24).

5 CABLE SHIPS: "EMBA" CLASS

Name	Completed
EMBA	1980
NEPRYADVA	1981
SETUN	1981
. . . . . . (2 units)	Building

Builders: Wärtsilä, Turku (Finland)
Displacement: 2,050 tons full load
Length: 224 ft 8 in (68.5 m) wl (see notes)
               248 ft 11 in (75.9 m), except last two ships 282 ft 5 in (86.1m) oa

Beam: 41 ft 4 in (12.6 m)
Draft: 10 ft 2 in (3.1 m)
Propulsion: 2 diesels (Wärtsilä Vasa 6R22); 41,360 hp; 1 shaft
Speed: 11 knots
Range:
Complement: approx. 40
Helicopters: no facilities
Missiles: none
Guns: none
Radars: 1 . . . . . . (navigation)

These are coastal cable ships. Cable sheave and lift devices overhang the bow, and there is a crane forward. Last two ships ordered in 1985 from Wärtsilä at Helsinki.

Classification: Soviet KS type.

Engineering: Fitted with two propeller pods on the rudder and with a bow thruster for precise station keeping during cable laying/repair operations.

One of the new EMBA-class cable ships, the SETUN is one of several Soviet ships employed in the laying and maintenance of seafloor communications cables and acoustic detection arrays. (1981, Wärtsilä)

8 CABLE SHIPS: KLAZMA CLASS

Name	Completed
DONETS	1969
INGUL	1962
INGURI	1978
KATYN	1973
TAVDA	1977
TSNA	1968
YANA	1963
ZEYA	1970

Builders:	Wärtsilä, Turku (Finland)
Displacement:	6,920 tons full load except INGUL and YANA 6,810 tons; KATYN 7,885 tons
Length:	393 ft 7 in (120.0 m) wl (see notes) 427 ft 9 in (130.4 m) oa
Beam:	52 ft 6 in (16.0 m)
Draft:	18 ft 10 in (5.75 m)
Propulsion:	diesel-electric: 5 diesels (Wärtsilä 624TS); 5,000 hp; 5 generators connected to 2 electric motors; 2 shafts (see notes)
Speed:	14 knots
Range:	12,000 n.miles at 12 knots
Complement:	approx. 110
Helicopters:	no facilities
Missiles:	none
Guns:	none
Radars:	1 . . . . . . (navigation)

These are large cable ships, fitted with British-built cable equipment. Cable sheaves and handling gear project over both bow and stern. Details vary.

Classification: Soviet KS type.

Engineering: The first two ships completed, INGUL and YANA, have four 2,436-hp diesels; they have a longer forecastle. A 550-hp active rudder and 650-hp bow thruster are fitted to these ships for precise station keeping while handling cables.

The INGURI, one of the large Klazma-class cable ships. Note her bow and stern cable sheaves; these ships have large cable holds and facilities for splicing and repairing cables and other seafloor equipment. (Royal Danish Navy)

1 CABLE SHIP: "TELNOVSK" CLASS

Name	Completed
KS-7	1950s

Builders:	Budapest (Hungary)
Displacement:	1,700 tons full load
Length:	239 ft 5 in (73.0 m) oa
Beam:	32 ft 10 in (10.0 m)
Draft:	13 ft 9 in (4.2 m)
Propulsion:	1 diesel (Karl Liebknecht); 800 hp; 1 shaft
Speed:	11 knots
Range:	3,300 n.miles at 10 knots
Complement:	
Helicopters:	no facilities
Missiles:	none
Guns:	none
Radars:	

This is a small cable layer converted from a cargo ship. Cable sheave and handling gear project over the bow.

Class: About 100 of these ships were built by the same shipyard, most being delivered to the Soviet Union. The Soviet Navy currently operates three cargo ships and five as survey ships derived from this class, in addition to this unit.

Classification: Soviet KS type.

The KS-7 is a converted TELNOVSK-class cargo ship. She operates in the Pacific.

MISSILE TRANSPORTS

3 MISSILE TRANSPORTS: "AMGA" CLASS

Name	Completed
AMGA	1973
VETLUGA	1976
DAUGAVA	1981

Builders:	(USSR)
Displacement:	4,500 tons standard
	5,500 tons full load except DAUGAVA 6,200 tons
Length:	AMGA 339 ft 10 in (103.6 m) oa
	VETLUGA 359 ft 6 in (109.6 m) oa
	DAUGAVA 371 ft (113.1 m) oa
Beam:	58 ft 5 in (17.7 m)
Draft:	14 ft 6 in (4.4 m)
Propulsion:	2 diesels; 4,000 hp; 2 shafts
Speed:	16 knots
Range:	4,500 n.miles at 14 knots
Complement:	approx. 200
Helicopters:	none
Missiles:	none
Guns:	4 25-mm/60-cal AA (2 twin)
Radars:	1 Don-2 (navigation)

These ships transport ballistic missiles for SSBNs.

Design: Improved versions of the previous Lama class, this design provides for lighter armament. Propulsion machinery, accommodations, and controls are aft with missile stowage forward. Their hulls are ice-strengthened. A 55-ton-capacity crane is fitted.

The AMGA shows the unusual configuration of Soviet missile transports. The heavy crane lifts ballistic missiles and lowers them into SSBN missile tubes.

2 MISSILE TENDERS 5 MISSILE TRANSPORTS } LAMA CLASS			
Name	Name	Name	Completed
GENERAL RIYABAKOV	PM-93	PB-625	
VORONEZH (PM-872)	PM-131		} 1963–1979
PM-44	PM-150		

Builders:	Black Sea, Nikolayev
Displacement:	4,500 tons full load
Length:	370 ft (112.8 m) oa
Beam:	48 ft 10 in (14.9 m)
Draft:	14 ft 5 in (4.4 m)
Propulsion:	2 diesels; 4,000 hp; 2 shafts
Speed:	14 knots
Range:	6,000 n.miles at 10 knots
Complement:	approx. 250
Helicopters:	no facilities
Missiles:	2 or 4 quad SA-N-5 Grail launchers [16-32]
Guns:	4 or 8 57-mm/70-cal AA (1 quad or 2 or 4 twin) except VORONEZH 2 57-mm/80-cal AA (1 twin)
	4 25-mm/60-cal AA guns (2 twin) in VORONEZH and 1 other unit
Radars:	1 Don-2 (navigation)
	1 Slim Net or Strut Curve (air search)
	1 or 2 Hawk Screech or 2 Muff Cob except none in VORONEZH and 1 other unit

These ships carry cruise missiles for surface ships and submarines. Details with respect to weapons and radars differ for all ships. The VORONEZH and one other unit are modified to rearm and support missile corvettes and missile boats; they have larger magazines with smaller cranes.

Classification: Soviet PM type except GENERAL RIYABAKOV and PB 625 are designated PB.

Design: The design provides for machinery, accommodations, and controls aft with missile stowage forward. Five ships have 20-ton-capacity cranes and the VORONEZH and one other unit have two 10-ton-capacity cranes.

An early Lama-class missile transport, the PM-93 has a small superstructure. Guns vary; this unit has a quad 57-mm mount forward (and a Muff Cob radar atop the bridge); some ships have a second quad 57-mm aft of the funnel.

A large-superstructure type or modified Lama; she has twin 57-mm gun mounts fore and aft, and paired 25-mm guns on bridge wings. No fire control radars are evident. (1982, U.S. Navy)

2 MISSILE TRANSPORTS } **MODIFIED "ANDIZHAN" CLASS**
3 CARGO SHIPS

Name	(Type)	Completed
ONDA	(Cargo)	
POSET	(Cargo)	
YEMETSK	(Cargo)	1958–1960
VENTA (ex-LAKHTA)	(Missile)	
VILYUY (ex-POSYET)	(Missile)	

Builders:	Neptun, Rostock (East Germany)
Displacement:	4,500 tons standard
	6,740 tons full load
Tonnage:	4,375 DWT
Length:	341 ft 2 in (104.0 m) oa
Beam:	47 ft 3 in (14.4 m)
Draft:	21 ft 8 in (6.6 m)
Propulsion:	1 diesel (MAN); 3,250 hp; 1 shaft
Speed:	13.5 knots
Range:	6,000 n.miles at 13.5 knots

Complement:	approx. 100
Helicopters:	landing platform in some ships
Missiles:	none
Guns:	none
Radars:	2 Don-2 (navigation)

These ships are former merchant ships converted in the 1970s, two to transport missiles and three to naval cargo ships.

Class: These are former ANDIZHAN/KOVEL-class dry cargo ships, almost 50 of which were built by the Neptun yard, most for Soviet merchant service, including three as training ships. Three other ships were completed as naval oceanographic ships (POLYUS class).

Classification: The missile transports are Soviet VTR type.

Design: In the missile transports a single heavy-lift crane is fitted forward and a pole mast aft in place of the original A-frame cranes. Their forward holds can carry 10 SS-N-9 missiles and 20 SA-N-1 or SA-N-3 missiles. Cargo capacity is 3,950 tons.

The VILYUY, a missile transport variation of the ANDIZHAN-class cargo ships in naval service. She has a missile-handling crane and four missile hatches forward, with smaller cranes and a helicopter landing deck aft. (1981)

The ONDA retains the basic configuration of the ANDIZHAN class, with cargo-handling booms fitted to A-frame masts forward and aft. The position of the mast atop the bridge varies in these ships.

2 MISSILE TRANSPORTS
3 CARGO SHIPS } **MP 6 CLASS (Former Landing Ships)**

Name	(Type)	Completed
BIRA	(Cargo)	
BUREYA	(Missile)	
IRGIZ	(Cargo)	1958–1960
KHOPER	(Missile)	
VOLOGDA	(Cargo)	

Builders:	(Hungary)
Displacement:	2,100 tons full load
Length:	245 ft (74.7 m) oa
Beam:	37 ft (11.3 m)
Draft:	14 ft 5 in (4.4 m)
Propulsion:	1 diesel; 1,000 hp; 1 shaft
Speed:	10.5 knots
Range:	3,300 n.miles at 9 knots

Complement:	
Helicopters:	no facilities
Missiles:	none
Guns:	see notes
Radars:	1 Don-2 (navigation)

These are former MP 6-class landing ships, two of which have been modified to transport missiles and three to naval cargo ships. They resemble small coastal freighters with their superstructure aft. The missile transports carry SS-N-5 ballistic missiles for Golf-class SSBs; they have a large crane.

Class: About ten landing ships of this design were built.

Classification: All believed to be Soviet VTR type.

Guns: No armament is fitted; there are provisions for six 37-mm/60-cal AA guns (3 twin mounts).

Modification: Their bow doors have been welded shut and bow ramps removed about 1960 to permit use as cargo ships.

The BIRA is a former MP 6-class landing ship employed as a naval cargo ship. There are two A-frame masts fitted with cargo booms.

The BUREYA retains the forward A-frame mast of the cargo configuration, with missile crane and three missile holds forward of the superstructure.

2 MISSILE TRANSPORTS: CONVERTED CARGO SHIPS

Name	Completed
INDIRKA FORT SHEVERENKO	mid–1950s

Builders:	(USSR)
Displacement:	1,200 tons full load
Length:	188 ft 11 in (57.6 m) oa
Beam:	29 ft 6 in (9.0 m)
Draft:	14 ft 1 in (4.3 m)
Propulsion:	1 diesel (6DR30/40); 600 hp; 1 shaft
Speed:	11 knots
Range:	2,500 n.miles at 10.5 knots
Complement:	
Helicopters:	no facilities
Missiles:	none
Guns:	none
Radars:	1 Don-2 (navigation)

These are small, superstructure-aft cargo ships of the Melitopol class that were converted in the late 1970s to carry missiles. Cargo booms have been deleted.

Three sister ships serve as naval hydrographic survey ships.

10 MISSILE AND TORPEDO TRANSPORTS: MUNA CLASS

Name	Name	Name	Completed
VTR-81	VTR-85	VTR-93	
VTR-82	VTR-91	VTR-94	1960s
VTR-83	VTR-92	VTR-148	
VTR-84			

Builders:	Nakhodka
Displacement:	680 tons full load
Length:	167 ft 3 in (51.0 m) oa
Beam:	27 ft 11 in (8.5 m)
Draft:	8 ft 10 in (2.7 m)
Propulsion:	1 diesel; 600 hp; 1 shaft
Speed:	11 knots
Range:	
Complement:	approx. 40
Helicopters:	no facilities
Missiles:	none
Guns:	none
Radars:	1 or 2 Spin Trough (search)

These are small, superstructure-aft, torpedo and missile transports. Cargo arrangements differ for specialized weapon-carrying roles.

Classification: They have the designation MBSS—*Morskaya Barzha Samokhodnaya Sukhogruznaya* (seagoing self-propelled dry-cargo lighters) when in Soviet home waters, and VTR when deployed.

Muna-class torpedo transport.

OILERS AND TANKERS

All of these ships are employed to carry fuels for Soviet naval forces. The terms "oiler" and "tanker" in the Western vernacular refer to ships that perform at-sea replenishment and point-to-point fuel transport, respectively. The ships listed here have the Soviet designations of military tanker (VT) except for the one-of-a-kind BEREZINA, which is a military transport (VTR). The latter designation is used for a number of naval dry-cargo ships as well as other auxiliaries.

The Soviet Navy has long used merchant tankers for at-sea replenishment and continues to do so on a large scale. Until the mid-1960s even naval fuel ships refueled warships while dead in the water or over-the-bow while being towed. Subsequently, several new classes were acquired in the 1960s and 1970s with an alongside Underway Replenishment (UNREP) capability, while older ships were refitted with a limited alongside capability.

The relatively high acquisition rate of naval fueling ships in the 1960s and 1970s abruptly halted in early 1979 when the last of four DUBNA-class ships were acquired. Only one ship of the large BEREZINA-class UNREP ship has been built. (She is the only Soviet ship comparable to the U.S. Navy's large AOE/AOR ships.) Subsequently, two oilers under construction in Finland were acquired from the merchant construction program in 1983.

(The acquisition of civilian tankers for the Soviet merchant and fishing fleets continues at a high rate.)

2 REPLENISHMENT OILERS: "KALININGRAD" CLASS

Name	Completed
VYAZ'MA (ex-KATUN)	1983
ARGUN (ex-KALLARERE)	1983

Builders:	Rauma-Repola, Rauma (Finland)
Displacement:	8,700 tons full load
Tonnage:	5,873 DWT
Length:	378 ft 10 in (115.5 m) oa
Beam:	55 ft 9 in (17.0 m)
Draft:	23 ft (7.0 m)
Propulsion:	1 diesel (Bryansk/Burmeister & Wain); 3,500 hp; 1 shaft
Speed:	14 knots
Range:	5,000 n.miles at 14 knots
Complement:	approx. 30
Helicopters:	no facilities
Missiles:	none
Guns:	none
Radars:	2 Okean-A/B (navigation)

These ships were acquired for naval use shortly after completion as merchant tankers in 1982 (merchant names are shown in parentheses).

Class: These were the last of 25 tankers of this design that were launched through 1983 by the Rauma-Repola shipyard for the Soviet fishing fleet.

1 REPLENISHMENT OILER: "BEREZINA" CLASS

Name	Completed
BEREZINA	1978

Builders:	61 Kommuna, Nikolayev
Displacement:	36,000 tons full load
Length:	695 ft 4 in (212.0 m) oa
Beam:	85 ft 3 in (26.0 m)
Draft:	36 ft 1 in (11.0 m)
Propulsion:	2 diesels; 54,000 hp; 2 shafts
Speed:	22 knots
Range:	12,000 n.miles at 18 knots
Complement:	approx. 600
Helicopters:	2 Ka-25 Hormone-C
Missiles:	1 twin SA-N-4 launcher [20]
Guns:	4 57-mm/80-cal AA (2 twin)
	4 30-mm close-in (4 multibarrel)
ASW weapons:	2 RBU-1000 rocket launchers
Radars:	2 Bass Tilt (fire control)
	1 Don-2 (navigation)
	2 Don-Kay (navigation)
	1 Muff Cob (fire control)
	1 Pop Group (fire control)
	1 Strut Curve (air search)
Sonars:	. . . . . . (hull-mounted)

This is the Soviet Navy's largest and most capable underway replenishment ship. Only one unit has been built. The BEREZINA made her first operational deployment from the Black Sea into the Mediterranean in December 1978. She operates mainly in the Black Sea.

Classification: Soviet VTR type.

Design: BEREZINA was designed from the outset for the underway replenishment of petroleum, munitions, and stores. The ship can carry an estimated 16,000 tons of fuels, 500 tons of fresh water, and 2,000 to 3,000 tons of munitions and provisions. The ship can transfer fuel stores to ships on either side and fuel over the stern. Special provisions are provided for replenishing submarines. There are four 10-ton capacity cranes for loading stores and servicing ships alongside.

Of special significance is the ship's heavy armament, which includes ASW weapons. She is currently the only armed Soviet replenishment ship. Note that the ship has sonar fitted (as well as ASW weapons), probably the only naval auxiliary of any nation with this capability except for training ships. Two chaff launchers are also provided.

Name: Berezina is a major river in Belorussia and the scene of a major battle during Napoleon's retreat from Moscow in 1812.

The BEREZINA, at anchor, shows considerable similarity to the U.S. Navy's AOE replenishment ships. In the event, only one of this type was built, and her success is questionable. She has a significant gun, missile, and ASW rocket armament. (Courtesy *Joint Services Recognition Journal*)

4 REPLENISHMENT OILERS: "DUBNA" CLASS

Name	Completed
DUBNA	1974
IKRUT	1975
PECHENGA	1978
SVENTA	1979

Builders:	Rauma-Repola, Rauma (Finland)
Displacement:	4,300 tons light
	11,100 tons full load
Tonnage:	6,500 DWT
Length:	426 ft 9 in (130.1 m) oa
Beam:	65 ft 7 in (20.0 m)
Draft:	23 ft 8 in (7.2 m)
Propulsion:	1 diesel (Russkiy 8DRPH); 6,000 hp; 1 shaft
Speed:	16 knots

Range:	8,000 n.miles at 15 knots
Complement:	approx. 60
Helicopters:	no facilities
Missiles:	none
Guns:	none
Radars:	2 Don-2 (navigation)

These are small replenishment ships with at least the first two units, the DUBNA and IKRUT, having initially been employed to support the Soviet fishing fleet as well as naval forces.

Class: Only these four units were built to this specific design.

Classification: Soviet VT type.

Design: These ships can transfer fuel and dry stores to ships on either side and over the stern.

Electronics: The commercial Okean radars originally fitted were replaced in the early 1980s by naval sets.

DUBNA-class replenishment oiler IKRUT (1984, JMSDF)

6 REPLENISHMENT OILERS: "BORIS CHILIKIN" CLASS

Name	Name	Name	Completed
BORIS BUTOMA BORIS CHILIKIN	DNESTR GENRIKH GASANOV	IVAN BUBNOV VLADIMIR KOLYACHITSKIY	} 1967–1978

Builders:	Baltic, Leningrad
Displacement:	8,750 tons light
	24,500 tons full load
Length:	532 ft 4 in (162.3 m) oa
Beam:	70 ft 2 in (21.4 m)
Draft:	37 ft 9 in (11.5 m)
Propulsion:	1 diesel (Bryansk/Burmeister & Wain or Cegielski/Sulzer); 9,600 hp; 1 shaft
Speed:	16.5 knots
Range:	10,000 n.miles at 16.5 knots
Complement:	
Helicopters:	no facilities
Missiles:	none

Guns:	removed
Radars:	2 Don-Kay (navigation)

These are naval versions of the VELIKIY OKTYABR-class merchant tankers. The merchant ships are 16,540 DWT.

Class: Twelve ships of this class were built for Soviet merchant service.

Classification: Soviet VT type.

Design: Cargo capacity is 13,500 tons of fuels and fresh water, 400 tons of munitions, and 800 tons of stores and provisions. There are provisions in these ships for transferring fuels to ships on either side and astern; the early units could transfer provisions on both sides, but the later ships only to starboard.

Four ships were completed with four 57-mm/80-cal AA guns in twin mounts forward as well as Muff Cob fire-control radar and Strut Curve air-search radar; subsequently removed. The IVAN BUBNOV and GENRIKH GASANOV were completed in merchant configuration without guns or naval radars.

The BORIS BUTOMA has been disarmed, but remains in naval service. Note the differing mast arrangements. (1984, JMSDF)

5 REPLENISHMENT OILERS: ALTAY CLASS

Name	Name	Name	Completed
ILIM IZHORA	KOLA YEGORLIK	YEL'NYA	} 1968–1973

Builders:	Rauma-Repola, Rauma (Finland)
Displacement:	approx. 2,200 tons light
	7,230 tons full load
Tonnage:	5,045 DWT
Length:	348 ft (106.1 m) oa
Beam:	50 ft 6 in (15.4 m)
Draft:	22 ft (6.7 m)
Propulsion:	1 diesel (Bryansk/Burmeister & Wain-550 VTBN-110); 3,250 hp; 1 shaft
Speed:	14 knots

Range:	5,000 n.miles at 13 knots
	8,600 n.miles at 12 knots
Complement:	approx. 60
Helicopters:	no facilities
Missiles:	none
Guns:	none
Radars:	2 Don-2 (navigation)

Converted merchant tankers fitted for underway replenishment.

Class: Some 60 ships of this type have been built, most for service with the Soviet fishing and merchant fleets, with most deliveries between 1968 and 1973.

Classification: Soviet VT type.

Design: These ships can refuel one ship at a time from either side plus astern refueling. Their masts and details differ.

The Altay-class oiler Ilim, photographed in the central Pacific with a Soviet carrier task force, is typical of the small Soviet replenishment ships. Numerous ships of this class serve the Soviet merchant and fishing fleets. (1985, U.S. Navy)

3 TANKERS: "OLEKHMA" AND "PEVEK" CLASSES

Name	Completed
Zolotoi Rog	1960
Olekhma	1964
Iman	1966

Builders:	Rauma-Repola, Rauma (Finland)
Displacement:	Rog 7,280 tons full load
	others 7,380 tons full load
Tonnage:	Rog 4,320 DWT
	others 4,400 DWT
Length:	Rog 344 ft 9 in (105.1 m) oa
	others 345 ft 9 in (105.4 m) oa
Beam:	48 ft 6 in (14.8 m)
Draft:	22 ft 4 in (6.8 m)
Propulsion:	1 diesel (Burmeister & Wain); 2,900 hp; 1 shaft
Speed:	13.5 knots
Range:	10,000 n.miles at 13.5 knots
Complement:	approx. 40

Helicopters:	no facilities
Missiles:	none
Guns:	none
Radars:	1 Don-2 (navigation)

Fifty tankers of this basic design were built for the Soviet Union, two in Sweden and the remainder in Finland. The Zolotoi Rog belongs to the Lokbatan or Pevek series (delivered 1956–1960) and the two other ships to the Aksay or Olekhma series (1961–1967).

Class: Most ships of these series remain in Soviet merchant service; two ex-Soviet ships were transferred to China and one to Indonesia.

Classification: Soviet VT type.

Design: The design has a traditional three-island superstructure arrangement (all later Soviet naval fuel ships of merchant design have a structure-aft configuration). The Olekhma was modernized in 1978 and has an A-frame abaft the bridge to permit fueling of a ship alongside; all can refuel over the stern while under way.

The Olekhma has the traditional tanker configuration, with bridge amidships and machinery/funnel aft. An A-frame replenishment mast is fitted abaft the bridge.

1 TANKER: "SOFIA" CLASS

Name	Completed
AKHTUBA (ex-HANOI)	1963

Builders:	Admiralty, Leningrad
Displacement:	62,600 tons full load
Tonnage:	49,385 DWT
Length:	756 ft (230.5 m) oa
Beam:	101 ft 8 in (31.0 m)
Draft:	38 ft 8 in (11.8 m)
Propulsion:	2 steam turbines (Kirov); 19,000 shp; 1 shaft
Boilers:	2
Speed:	17 knots
Range:	21,000 n.miles at 17 knots
Complement:	approx. 70

Helicopters:	no facilities
Missiles:	none
Guns:	none
Radars:	

The AKHTUBA is the largest ship in service with the Soviet Navy.

Class: Twenty-two SOFIA-class tankers were delivered between 1963 and 1970, with one entering naval service.

Classification: Soviet VT type.

Design: This is the third largest merchant tanker design built in the Soviet Union (the KRYM class at 150,500 DWT and POBYEDA class at 67,980 DWT are larger). The AKHTUBA's cargo capacity is 44,500 tons of fuels. She can refuel only over the stern and is used mainly to transfer fuel to oilers and tankers.

The SOFIA-class tanker AKHTUBA is the largest ship in the Soviet Navy, pending completion of the nuclear-propelled aircraft carriers and missile range instrumentation ships now under construction. (1973, Royal Air Force)

6 TANKERS: UDA CLASS

Name	Name	Name	Completed
DUNAY	LENA	TEREK	} 1962–1964
KOIDA	SHEKSNA	VISHERA	

Builders:	Vyborg
Displacement:	7,100 tons full load
Length:	400 ft 2 in (122.0 m) oa
Beam:	51 ft 10 in (15.8 m)
Draft:	20 ft 8 in (6.3 m)
Propulsion:	2 diesels; 8,000 hp; 2 shafts
Speed:	17 knots
Range:	4,000 n.miles at 17 knots
Complement:	approx. 85

Helicopters:	no facilities
Missiles:	none
Guns:	see notes
Radars:	1 or 2 Don/Don-2 (navigation)

These are small tankers built specifically for naval service.

Class: Three ships of this type were transferred to Indonesia.

Classification: Soviet VT type.

Design: There are provisions in each ship for fitting eight 57-mm/70-cal AA guns in quad mounts (plus one Strut Curve and two Muff Cob radars). At least one ship was observed in the Baltic in 1962 with armament, possibly for evaluation.

The LENA and VISHERA have a second A-frame, providing two amidships refueling positions.

Uda-class tanker SHEKSNA, with a single amidships replenishment mast; some ships have two, while the KOIDA has none. (1983)

4 TANKERS: "KONDA" CLASS

Name	Name	Name	Completed
KONDA	SOYANA	YAKHROMA	} 1954–1965
ROSSOCH'			

Builders:	Turku (Sweden)
Displacement:	1,980 tons full load
Tonnage:	1,265 DWT
Length:	226 ft 4 in (69.0 m) oa
Beam:	32 ft 10 in (10.0 m)
Draft:	14 ft 1 in (4.3 m)

Propulsion:	1 diesel; 1,600 hp; 1 shaft
Speed:	12 knots
Range:	2,500 n.miles at 10 knots
Complement:	approx. 25
Helicopters:	no facilities
Missiles:	none
Guns:	none
Radars:	1 or 2 Don-2 (navigation) and/or Spin Trough (search)

These are small naval tankers.
Classification: Their naval designation is VT.
Design: Cargo capacity is approximately 1,100 tons of fuels.

The KONDA-class tanker YAKHROMA. (1982, U.S. Navy)

13 TANKERS: "KHOBI" CLASS

Name	Name	Name	Completed
CHEREMSHAN	METAN	SOS'VA	
ORSHA	SASHA	SYSOLA	
INDIGA	SEIMA	TARTU	1950s
KHOBI	SHELON'	TUNGUSKA	
LOVAT'			

Builders:	(USSR)
Displacement:	1,525 tons full load
Length:	203 ft 4 in (62.0 m) oa
Beam:	32 ft 10 in (10.0 m)
Draft:	14 ft 5 in (4.4 m)
Propulsion:	2 diesels; 1,600 hp; 2 shafts
Speed:	12 knots
Range:	2,500 n.miles at 12.5 knots
Complement:	approx. 30
Helicopters:	no facilities
Missiles:	none
Guns:	none
Radars:	1 Don-2 (navigation)
	1 Spin Trough (search)

These are small tankers, similar to U.S. Navy gasoline tankers (AOG). They will probably be discarded in the near future.

Class: Ships of this type have been transferred to Albania and Indonesia. At least five other units have already been stricken from Soviet naval service.

Classification: Soviet VT type.

Design: Cargo capacity is approximately 1,500 tons of fuel. They generally refuel naval units over the bow.

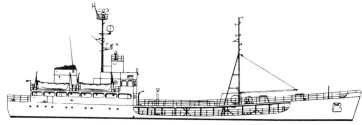

KHOBI-class tanker. (Siegfried Breyer)

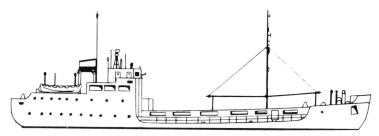

NERCHA-class tanker. (Siegfried Breyer)

3 TANKERS: "NERCHA" CLASS

Name	Name	Name	Completed
KLYAZMA	NARVA	NERCHA	1952–1955

Builders:	Crichton-Vulcan or Valmet, Abo (Finland)
Displacement:	1,800 tons full load
Tonnage:	1,300 DWT
Length:	208 ft 3 in (63.5 m) oa
Beam:	32 ft 10 in (10.0 m)
Draft:	14 ft 9 in (4.5 m)
Propulsion:	1 diesel; 1,000 hp; 1 shaft
Speed:	11 knots
Range:	2,000 n.miles at 10 knots
Complement:	approx. 25
Helicopters:	no facilities
Missiles:	none
Guns:	none
Radars:	1 Don series (navigation)

Small tankers. Several similar ships are in Soviet merchant service. They refuel over the stern.

Classification: Soviet naval designation is VT.

3 TANKERS: "KAZBEK" CLASS

Name	Name	Name	Completed
ALATYR'	DESNA	VOLKHOV	early 1950s

Builders:	Kherson
Displacement:	16,250 tons full load
Tonnage:	11,800 DWT
Length:	477 ft 3 in (145.5 m) oa
Beam:	63 ft (19.2 m)
Draft:	27 ft 11 in (8.5 m)
Propulsion:	2 diesels (Russkiy); 4,000 hp; 2 shafts
Speed:	14 knots
Range:	18,000 n.miles at 14 knots
Complement:	approx. 45
Helicopters:	no facilities
Missiles:	none
Guns:	none
Radars:	2 Don-2 (navigation)

About 50 of these tankers were built at Kherson and the Admiralty yard in Leningrad between 1951 and 1958. Many remain in merchant service, and these are used periodically to refuel naval ships.

Classification: Soviet VTR type.

Design: These ships are similar in design to the United States T-2 type of the late 1930s. Kingposts and an A-frame are fitted to the naval units to carry refueling hoses. They can carry about 11,000 tons of fuel.

The KAZBEK-class tanker ALATYR riding high. (1984)

1 TANKER: "POLYARNIK"

Name	Completed
POLYARNIK (ex-KARNTEN, ex-TANKBOOT I)	1942

Builders:	C. av den Giessen, Krimpen (Netherlands)
Displacement:	12,500 tons full load
Tonnage:	6,640 DWT
Length:	433 ft 3 in (132.1 m) oa
Beam:	53 ft 1 in (16.2 m)
Draft:	24 ft 11 in (7.6 m)
Propulsion:	2 diesels (Werkspoor); 7,000 hp; 2 shaft
Speed:	17 knots
Range:	
Complement:	approx. 55

Helicopters:	no facilities
Missiles:	none
Guns:	none
Radars:	

This ship was laid down for the Dutch Navy in December 1939 and taken over by German troops while still under contruction in 1941; she was launched on 3 May 1941 and commissioned by the German Navy on 27 December 1941. The ship was taken over by the Soviets in December 1945. Still in active service, the POLYARNIK serves in the Pacific Fleet.

Classification: Soviet VT type.

Design: Cargo capacity is 5,600 tons of fuels; she also carries dry stores and provisions.

The POLYARNIK, the oldest tanker in Soviet naval service, has had an unusual career.

SPECIAL-PURPOSE TANKERS

1 NUCLEAR WASTE TANKER: "URAL"

Name	Completed
URAL	1969

Builders:	(USSR)
Displacement:	2,600 tons full load
Length:	295 ft 2 in (90.0 m) oa
Beam:	32 ft 10 in (10.0 m)
Draft:	12 ft 2 in (3.7 m)
Propulsion:	2 diesels; 1,200 hp; 1 shaft
Speed:	12 knots
Range:	3,000 n.miles at 9 knots
Complement:	
Helicopters:	no facilities
Missiles:	none
Guns:	none
Radars:	1 Spin Trough (search)

The URAL is a small, superstructure-aft tanker employed to carry nuclear waste. She has a high freeboard and a travelling crane.

Classification: Soviet TNT type.

6 SPECIAL CARGO TANKERS: LUZA CLASS

Name	Name	Name	Completed
ALAMBAY	BARGUZIN	KANA	
ARAGUVY	DON	SELENGA	} 1960s

Builders:	
Displacement:	1,900 tons full load
Length:	205 ft (62.5 m) oa
Beam:	35 ft 1 in (10.7 m)
Draft:	14 ft 1 in (4.3 m)
Propulsion:	1 diesel; 1,000 hp; 1 shaft

Speed:	12 knots
Range:	2,000 n.miles at 11 knots
Complement:	
Helicopters:	no facilities
Missiles:	none
Guns:	(see notes)
Radars:	1 Don-2 (navigation)

These small tankers are used to transport volatile liquids, probably fuels for Soviet SLBMs. Some units have a 12.7-mm MG twin mount.

Class: Three ships were apparently stricken from naval service in the early 1980s.

Classification: Soviet TNT type.

5 NUCLEAR WASTE TANKERS: VALA CLASS

Name	Name	Name	Completed
TNT-11	TNT-19	. . . . . .	} 1960s
TNT-12	TNT-29		

Builders:	
Displacement:	3,100 tons full load
Length:	250 ft (76.2 m) oa
Beam:	41 ft (12.5 m)
Draft:	16 ft 5 in (5.0 m)
Propulsion:	1 diesel; 1,000 hp; 1 shaft
Speed:	14 knots
Range:	2,000 n.miles at 11 knots
Complement:	
Helicopters:	no facilities
Missiles:	none
Guns:	none
Radars:	1 . . . . . . (navigation)

This class of small tankers carries radioactive waste.

Classification: Soviet TNT type.

The special-purpose tanker BARGUZIN of the Luza class. (1982)

WATER TANKERS

Soviet water tankers provide water to submarines and surface ships for crew consumption and (in surface ships) for use in boilers.

2 WATER TANKERS: "MANYCH" CLASS

Name	Completed
MANYCH	1971
TAYGIL	1977

Builders:	Vyborg
Displacement:	7,800 tons full load
Length:	379 ft 10 in (115.8 m) oa
Beam:	51 ft 10 in (15.8 m)
Draft:	22 ft (6.7 m)
Propulsion:	2 diesels; 9,000 hp; 2 shafts
Speed:	18 knots
Range:	7,500 n.miles at 16 knots
	11,500 n.miles at 12 knots
Complement:	approx. 90
Helicopters:	no facilities
Missiles:	none
Guns:	(see notes)
Radars:	2 Don-Kay (navigation)

These ships were built to serve as naval replenishment ships to provide diesel fuel and stores to submarines. However, the design was not operationally successful and they became water tankers.

Classification: Soviet MVT type.

Guns: The MANYCH was completed as an oiler with four 57-mm AA guns in twin mounts supported by two Muff Cob radars. Her armament was removed in 1975.

14 WATER TANKERS: VODA CLASS

Name	Name	Name	Completed
ABAKAN	MVT-16	MVT-24	
SURA	MVT-17	MVT-134	
MVT-6	MVT-18	MVT-138	1950s
MVT-9	MVT-20	MVT-428	
MVT-10	MVT-21		

Builders:	
Displacement:	2,100 tons standard
	3,100 tons full load
Length:	267 ft 4 in (81.5 m) oa
Beam:	37 ft 9 in (11.5 m)
Draft:	14 ft 1 in (4.3 m)
Propulsion:	2 diesels; 1,600 hp; 2 shafts
Speed:	12 knots
Range:	3,000 n.miles at 10 knots
Complement:	approx. 40
Helicopters:	no facilities
Missiles:	none
Guns:	none
Radars:	1 Don-2 (navigation)

These ships are water distilling and transport ships.

Classification: Soviet MVT type.

The MANYCH-class water tanker TAYGIL.

TRANSPORTS

The Soviet merchant fleet operates the world's largest fleet of passenger ships, which would become available for naval service in wartime.

1 NAVAL TRANSPORT: "MIKHAIL KALININ" CLASS

Name	Completed
KUBAN (ex-NADEZHDA KRUPSKAYA)	1963

Builders:	Mathias Thesen, Wismar (East Germany)
Displacement:	6,400 tons full load
Length:	400 ft 10 in (122.2 m) oa
Beam:	52 ft 6 in (16.0 m)
Draft:	16 ft 9 in (5.1 m)
Propulsion:	2 diesels (MAN); 8,000 hp; 2 shafts
Speed:	18 knots
Range:	8,100 n.miles at 17 knots
Complement:	
Passengers:	340
Helicopters:	no facilities
Missiles:	none
Guns:	none
Radars:	2 Don-2 (navigation)

This former passenger cruise liner is employed to transport naval personnel in the Mediterranean.

Class: Nineteen ships of this class were delivered between 1958 and 1964, with the above ship being taken into naval service in 1976.

Design: The ship carries 1,000 tons of cargo, with cranes installed forward and aft.

CARGO AND SUPPLY SHIPS

In addition to the cargo ships listed here, several are included above in the missile transport listings; also, the KGB Maritime Border Troops operate several cargo ships (see chapter 25).

1 CARGO SHIP: "NEON ANTONOV" CLASS

Name	Completed
IRBIT	late 1970s

Builders:	(USSR)
Displacement:	5,200 tons full load
Length:	311 ft 11 in (95.1 m) oa
Beam:	48 ft 3 in (14.7 m)
Draft:	21 ft 4 in (6.5 m)
Propulsion:	1 diesel; 1 shaft
Speed:	16 knots
Range:	
Complement:	
Helicopters:	no facilities
Guns:	see notes
Radars:	2 Palm Frond (navigation)

The IRBIT is the only Navy subordinated ship of the class; the remaining units are operated by the KGB Maritime Border Troops (see chapter 25).

Guns: There are positions in the KGB ships for two 14.5-mm twin machine-gun mounts and two SA-N-5/SA-7 Grail missile launchers.

4 CARGO SHIPS: "YUNIY PARTIZAN" CLASS

Name	Completed
TURGAY	1975
PECHORA	1976
PINEGA	1976
UFA	1978

Builders:	Santierul, Turnu-Severin (Romania)
Displacement:	3,947 tons full load
Tonnage:	2,150 DWT
Length:	291 ft 1 in (88.75 m) oa
Beam:	42 ft (12.8 m)
Draft:	17 ft 1 in (5.2 m)
Propulsion:	1 diesel (Cegielski/Sulzer); 2,080 hp; 1 shaft
Speed:	13 knots
Range:	4,000 n.miles at 12 knots
Complement:	approx. 25
Helicopters:	no facilities
Missiles:	none
Guns:	none
Radars:	1 Don-2 (navigation)

These are small coastal container ships.

Class: Twenty ships of this design were built for Soviet merchant service plus several units for Cuba and Romania.

Design: Cargo capacity in merchant service is 58 standard freight containers. These are superstructure-aft ships with three 10-ton-capacity cranes, one of which can be rigged to lift up to 28 tons.

1 CARGO SHIP: "AMGUEMA" CLASS

Name	Completed
YAUZA	1975

Builders:	(USSR)
Displacement:	15,100 tons full load
Tonnage:	9,045 DWT
Length:	436 ft 7 in (133.1 m) oa
Beam:	62 ft (18.9 m)
Draft:	29 ft 10 in (9.1 m)
Propulsion:	diesel-electric: 4 diesels with 4 generators; 7,200 hp; 1 shaft
Speed:	15 knots
Range:	approx. 10,000 n.miles at 15 knots
Complement:	
Helicopters:	no facilities
Missiles:	none
Guns:	none
Radars:	2 Don-2 (navigation)

One of a class of about 15 cargo ships designed for polar operations. One ship, the MIKHAIL SOMOV, is a naval research and supply ship.

Design: Cargo capacity is 6,600 tons. The ship has a limited ice-breaking capability, recessed anchors, and other features for ice/cold-weather operations.

AMGUEMA-class cargo ship YAUZA; note the icebreaking bow configuration and cargo booms (in vertical stowed position).

6 SUPPLY SHIPS: MAYAK CLASS

Name	Name	Name	Conversion Completed
BULZULUK	LAMA	NEMAN	} 1971–1976
ISHIM	MIUS	RIONI	

Builders:	Dnepr, Kiev
Displacement:	1,050 tons full load
Length:	180 ft 2 in (54.6 m)
Beam:	30 ft 8 in (9.3 m)
Draft:	11 ft 11 in (3.6 m)
Propulsion:	1 diesel; 800 hp; 1 shaft
Speed:	11 knots
Range:	9,400 n.miles at 11 knots
Complement:	approx. 30
Helicopters:	no facilities
Missiles:	none
Guns:	none
Radars:	2 Spin Trough (search)

One of the ubiquitous Mayak-class trawlers, shown here in the supply-ship configuration. This is the NEMAN. (1983)

These are converted Mayak-class side trawlers. They have been modified to carry provisions for naval ships. A large number of these craft were completed from 1962 onward, with several others having been converted to naval intelligence ships (AGI); see chapter 23.

Classification: Soviet VTR type.

Design: Small, superstructure-aft ships, built to trawl over the starboard side and fitted with freezer holds.

8 SUPPLY SHIPS: "VYTEGRALES" CLASS

Name	Name	Completed
Apsheron (ex-Tosnales)	Donbass (ex-Kirishi)	
Baskunchak (ex-Vostok-4)	Sevan (ex-Vyborgles)	1964–1966
Dauriya (ex-Suzdal)	Taman' (ex-Vostok-3)	
Dikson (ex-Vagales)	Yamal (ex-Svirles)	

Builders:	Zhdanov, Leningrad
Displacement:	9,650 tons full load
Length:	399 ft 10 in (121.9 m) oa
Beam:	54 ft 9 in (16.7 m)
Draft:	24 ft (7.3 m)
Propulsion:	1 diesel (Burmeister & Wain 950 VTBF 110); 5,200 hp; 1 shaft
Speed:	16 knots
Range:	7,400 n.miles at 14.5 knots
Complement:	approx. 90
Helicopters:	landing platform
Missiles:	none
Guns:	none
Radars:	2 Don-2 (navigation)
	1 Big Net (air search) in Donbass

These are converted merchant timber carriers. They were originally converted to an SESS configuration with the addition of special communications and radar equipment plus a helicopter platform aft. They have subsequently been employed as fleet supply ships, although they have been reported to continue to support space-related activities.

Class: About 20 additional ships of this class remain in merchant service, some of which have been modified to carry containers.

Another seven ships of this type were converted to civilian satellite tracking ships (under the aegis of the Soviet Academy of Sciences); see chapter 24.

Classification: Soviet VTR type.

9 CARGO SHIPS: "KEYLA" CLASS

Name	Name	Name	Completed
Mezen'	Ritsa	Unzha	
Onega	Teriberka	Ussuri	1960–1966
Ponoy	Tuloma	Yeruslan	

Builders:	Hungary
Displacement:	2,000 tons full load
Tonnage:	1,280 DWT
Length:	257 ft 6 in (78.5 m) oa
Beam:	34 ft 6 in (10.5 m)
Draft:	15 ft 1 in (4.6 m)
Propulsion:	1 diesel; 1,000 hp; 1 shaft
Speed:	11.5 knots
Range:	4,000 n.miles at 11 knots
Complement:	approx. 25
Helicopters:	no facilities
Missiles:	none
Guns:	none
Radars:	1 Don-2 (navigation) or Spin Trough (search)

Small cargo ships. The Ritsa has special communications equipment installed (deckhouse fitted over after hatch).

Classification: Soviet VTR type.

Design: Cargo capacity is 1,100 tons.

The Vytegrales-class cargo ship Taman' with a Hormone-C helicopter on her fantail. The mast arrangements in these ships vary; they formerly carried a variety of antennas for the ships' SESS role.

KEYLA-class cargo ship.

1 CARGO SHIP: "CHULYM" CLASS

Name	Completed
SEVERODONETSK	1950s

Builders:	Szczecin (Poland)
Displacement:	5,500 tons full load
Tonnage:	3,200 DWT
Length:	334 ft 3 in (101.9 m) oa
Beam:	47 ft 11 in (14.6 m)
Draft:	19 ft 8 in (6.0 m)
Propulsion:	compound reciprocating with auxiliary turbine; 1,650 hp; 1 shaft
Boilers:	2
Speed:	12 knots
Range:	5,000 n.miles at 11.5 knots
Complement:	approx. 40
Helicopters:	no facilities
Missiles:	none
Guns:	none
Radars:	1 Don-2 (navigation)

This is a small, amidships-superstructure cargo ship.

Class: Forty-one ships of this class were built at Szczecin. A few others remain in Soviet merchant service while others may be operational in other communist merchant fleets.

Three naval cargo ships of this class apparently were discarded in the early 1980s.

Classification: Soviet VTR type.

Design: Cargo capacity 2,240 tons.

CARGO SHIPS: "KOLOMNA" CLASS

Two naval cargo ships of the KOLOMNA class were discarded in the early 1980s, the KRASNOARMEYSK and MEGRA. The SVANETIYA was converted to an experimental ship and is listed separately in this chapter.

Six KOLOMNA-class cargo ships completed as submarine tenders are also listed in this chapter while the MIKHAIL LOMONOSOV serves as a civilian research ship (see chapter 24).

1 CARGO SHIP: "DONBASS" CLASS

Name	Completed
SVIR	1955

Builders:	Szczecin (Poland)
Displacement:	7,200 tons full load
Tonnage:	4,865 DWT
Length:	354 ft 11 in (108.2 m) oa
Beam:	47 ft 11 in (14.6 m)
Draft:	23 ft 7 in (7.2 m)
Propulsion:	compound reciprocating with low-pressure turbine; 2,300 hp; 1 shaft
Boilers:	2
Speed:	12 knots
Range:	9,800 n.miles at 12 knots
Complement:	
Helicopters:	no facilities
Missiles:	none
Guns:	none
Radars:	1 Neptune (navigation)

The SVIR is the only ship of this large class in Soviet naval service.

Class: The DONBASS-class ships were designed as colliers, with many serving as general (tramp) cargo ships in the Soviet merchant marine and several foreign merchant fleets; some served the Soviet fishing industry as fish carriers.

Classification: Soviet VTR type.

Engineering: Originally a coal-burning ship; converted to oil.

CARGO SHIPS: "TELNOVSK" CLASS

The three naval cargo ships of the TELNOVSK class were being retired when this edition went to press: the BUREVESTNIK, LAG, and MANOMETER; see 3rd edition (page 256) for details.

The KS-7 of this class is a cable ship and is listed earlier in this chapter; several other units serve the Soviet Navy as survey ships (see chapter 24).

HOSPITAL SHIPS

2 HOSPITAL SHIPS: "OB'" CLASS

Name	Completed
OB'	1980
YENESEY	1981

Builders:	Adolph Warski, Szczecin (Poland)
Displacement:	11,000 tons full load
Length:	505 ft 2 in (154.0 m) oa
Beam:	67 ft 3 in (20.5 m)
Draft:	17 ft 1 in (5.2 m)
Propulsion:	2 diesels; 2 shafts
Speed:	20 knots
Range:	
Complement:	approx. 80 (civilian)

Medical staff:	approx. 200
Helicopters:	1 Ka-25 Hormone-C
Missiles:	none
Guns:	none
Radars:	3 Don-2 (navigation)

These are purpose-built hospital ships. The ships are civilian-manned but carry naval medical staffs. The commanding officers are believed to be Navy captains 3rd rank, with the medical staffs commanded by lieutenant colonels of the Naval Medical Service.

The OB' is assigned to the Pacific Fleet and the YENESEY to the Black Sea Fleet.

Design: The ships have seven operating rooms and 100 beds. A hangar is provided for a single helicopter for casualty evacuation.

Engineering: A bow thruster is provided.

The YENESEY at high speed; these ships have 100 ward beds for patients and seven operating rooms. A Hormone C helicopter is on the fantail. (1984, U.S. Navy)

This view of the YENESEY clearly shows the helicopter deck and hangar. The YENESEY and OB' have civilian crews and naval medical personnel assigned.

TRAINING SHIPS

These ships primarily serve the Navy's higher naval schools (i.e., naval academies). The armament of the SMOL'NY class permits those ships to be employed in limited combat roles.

3 TRAINING SHIPS: "SMOL'NY" CLASS

Name	Name	Name	Completed
KHASAN	PEREKOP	SMOL'NY	1976–1978

Builders:	Adolf Warski, Szczecin (Poland)
Displacement:	8,500 tons full load
Length:	452 ft 8 in (138.0 m) oa
Beam:	59 ft (18.0 m)
Draft:	20 ft 4 in (6.2 m)
Propulsion:	4 diesels; 16,000 hp; 2 shafts
Speed:	20 knots
Range:	12,000 n.miles at 15 knots
Complement:	approx. 210
Students:	approx. 275
Helicopters:	no facilities
Missiles:	none
Guns:	4 76.2-mm/59-cal AA (2 twin)
	4 30-mm/65-cal close-in (2 twin)
ASW weapons:	2 RBU-2500 rocket launchers
Radars:	2 Don-2 (navigation) except 3 in PEREKOP
	1 Don-Kay in PEREKOP
	1 Drum Tilt (fire control)
	1 Head Net-C (air search)
	1 Owl Screech (fire control)
Sonars:	medium frequency (hull-mounted)
EW systems:	2 Watch Dog

These are large, graceful training ships, of a type not employed by Western navies.

Classification: Soviet US type.

(2) SAIL TRAINING SHIPS: NEW CONSTRUCTION

Completed:	
Builders:	Lenin Shipyard, Gdansk (Poland)
Displacement:	2,385 tons full load
Length:	345 ft 9 in (105.4 m) oa
Beam:	46 ft (14.0 m)
Draft:	19 ft 8 in (6.0 m)
Propulsion:	auxiliary diesel (Sulzer/Cegielski 20/24); 1,500 hp; 1 shaft
Speed:	12 knots on diesel
Range:	
Complement:	
Missiles:	none
Guns:	none
Radars:	

These are three-masted sail training ships reported to be under construction for use by the Soviet Navy; however, their final disposition is not clear. Soviet merchant and fisheries officers are already trained under sail (see chapter 24).

The ships' waterline length is 260 1/2 feet.

The SMOL'NY and her sister ships provide at-sea training for Soviet naval personnel in a specialized school ship with modern weapon systems. (1977, Royal Air Force)

2 TRAINING SHIPS: "WODNIK" CLASS

Name	Name	Completed
LUGA	OKA	1977

Builders:	Polnocny, Gdansk (Poland)
Displacement:	1,500 tons standard
	1,800 tons full load
Length:	236 ft 2 in (72.0 m) oa
Beam:	39 ft 4 in (12.0 m)
Draft:	13 ft 9 in (4.2 m)
Propulsion:	2 diesels (Zgoda-Sulzer 6TD48); 3,600 hp; 2 shafts
Speed:	16.5 knots
Range:	7,500 n.miles at 11 knots
Complement:	approx. 60
Students:	approx. 90
Helicopters:	no facilities
Missiles:	none
Guns:	none
Radars:	3 Don-2 (navigation)

Navigation training ships. Two similar ships serve in the Polish Navy and one in the East German Navy.

Classification: Soviet US type.

Design: The WODNIK design is based on the Moma class.

2 TRAINING SHIPS: UGRA CLASS

Name	Completed
BORODINO	1970
GANGUT	1971

Builders:	Black Sea, Nikolayev
Displacement:	6,750 tons standard
	9,650 tons full load
Length:	475 ft 7 in (145.0 m) oa
Beam:	58 ft 1 in (17.7 m)
Draft:	21 ft (6.4 m)
Propulsion:	4 diesels; 8,000 hp; 2 shafts
Speed:	17 knots
Range:	21,000 n.miles at 10 knots
Complement:	approx. 300
Students:	approx. 400
Helicopters:	no facilities
Missiles:	none
Guns:	8 57-mm/80-cal AA (4 twin)
	4 Don-2 (navigation)
	2 Muff Cob (fire control)
	1 Strut Curve (air search)
EW systems:	2 Watch Dog

These ships were built with classrooms and training facilities in place of the workshops and storerooms of the Ugra-class submarine tenders.

Classification: Soviet US type.

Design: The ships' superstructures have been built up aft in comparison with the submarine tenders. They retain cranes forward and amidships.

1+ ASW TRAINING SHIPS: MAYAK CLASS

Builders:	(USSR)
Displacement:	1,050 tons full load
Length:	177 ft 9 in (54.2 m) oa
Beam:	30 ft 6 in (9.3 m)
Draft:	11 ft 10 in (3.6 m)
Propulsion:	1 diesel (Karl Liebnecht 8NVD48); 800 hp; 1 shaft
Speed:	11 knots
Range:	9,400 n.miles at 11 knots
Complement:	approx. 60 (including students)
Helicopters:	no facilities
Missiles:	none
Guns:	2 25-mm AA (1 twin)
ASW weapons:	4 RBU-1200 rocket launchers
	4 16-inch (406-mm) torpedo tubes (4 single)
	2 depth-charge racks
Radars:	1 Spin Trough (search)
Sonars:	high frequency (hull-mounted)

One unit of the Mayak class was modified with ASW weapons and sensors for specialized training. Converted in the early 1980s. Additional conversions may be forthcoming.

Classification: Soviet US type.

The GANGUT is similar to the submarine tenders of the Ugra class, but has a large "school house" amidships. (1981, Giorgio Arra)

EXPERIMENTAL AND TRIALS SHIPS

The shipbuilding research ship IZUMRUD, constructed specifically for the Ministry of Shipbuilding to test ship structures and materials as well as other ship components, is listed under civilian auxiliary ships (chapter 24).

1 EXPERIMENTAL SHIP: "PIONEER MOSKVYY" CLASS

Name	Conversion Completed
SAYANIY	1984

Builders:	Vyborg
Displacement:	10,700 tons full load

Length:	430 ft (130.3 m) oa
Beam:	57 ft 1 in (17.3 m)
Draft:	24 ft 1 in (7.3 m)
Propulsion:	1 diesel (B&W 5DKRN 62/140-3); 6,100 hp; 1 shaft
Speed:	15.5 knots
Range:	12,000 n.miles at 15.5 knots
Complement:	approx. 120
Helicopters:	no facilities
Missiles:	none
Guns:	none
Radars:	2 Don-2 (navigation)

The SAYANIY is a converted cargo ship. Three sister ships were converted to submarine rescue and salvage ships (see page 283).

The experimental ship SAYANIY. Deckhouses have been erected over most of her cargo spaces. (1984, JMSDF)

5 TORPEDO TRIALS SHIPS: POTOK CLASS

Name	Name	Name	Completed
OS-100	OS-145	. . . . . .	1978–
OS-138	OS-225		

Builders:	
Displacement:	750 tons standard
	860 tons full load
Length:	232 ft 11 in (71.0 m) oa
Beam:	29 ft 10 in (9.1 m)
Draft:	8 ft 2 in (2.5 m)
Propulsion:	2 diesels; 4,000 hp; 2 shafts
Speed:	18 knots
Range:	5,000 n.miles at 12 knots
Complement:	
Helicopters:	no facilities
Missiles:	none
Guns:	none
ASW weapons:	1 21-inch (533-mm) torpedo tube
	1 16-inch (406-mm) torpedo tube
Radars:	1 Don-2 (navigation)

These are torpedo trials and recovery ships. They are probably replacements for the modified T-43 minesweepers previously employed in this role. A crane is provided aft for torpedo recovery.

Classification: Soviet OS type.

A former T-43 minesweeper employed in a research role.

1 + TRIALS SHIPS: AL'PINIST CLASS

Name
OS-104

Builders:	Yaroslavl
Displacement:	1,200 tons full load
Length:	176 ft 2 in (53.7 m) oa
Beam:	34 ft 5 in (10.5 m)
Draft:	14 ft 1 in (4.3 m)
Propulsion:	1 diesel (8NVD48-2U); 1,320 hp; 1 shaft
Speed:	13 knots
Range:	7,600 n.miles at 13 knots
Complement:	
Helicopters:	no facilities
Missiles:	none
Guns:	none
Radars:	1 Don-2 (navigation)
	1 . . . . . . (navigation)

This unit is a modified stern trawler; there is a two-level deckhouse built on the starboard side, aft of the bridge.

The OS-104 has been identified in the Pacific. Additional units are believed being converted. Additional units of this type serve in the AGI role (see page 327).

1 or 2 TRIALS SHIPS: DALDYN CLASS

Builders:	
Displacement:	360 tons full load
Length:	104 ft (31.7 m) oa
Beam:	23 ft 7 in (7.2 m)
Draft:	9 ft 2 in (2.8 m)
Propulsion:	1 diesel (8NVD 36U); 300 hp; 1 shaft
Speed:	9 knots
Range:	
Complement:	approx. 15
Helicopters:	no facilities
Missiles:	none
Guns:	none
Radars:	1 Spin Trough (search)

Modified seiners of the Kareliya class, used for experimental work.

Few EXPERIMENTAL SHIPS: T-43 CLASS (Former Minesweepers)

Former minesweepers of the T-43 class employed in various experimental roles with the OS classification. See chapter 18 for class data.

1 EXPERIMENTAL SHIP: "KOLOMNA" CLASS

Name	Completed
SVANETIYA	early 1950s

Builders:	Neptun, Rostock (East Germany)
Displacement:	6,700 tons full load
Tonnage:	4,355 DWT
Length:	335 ft 6 in (102.3 m) oa
Beam:	47 ft 3 in (14.4 m)
Draft:	21 ft 8 in (6.6 m)
Propulsion:	1 triple-expansion compound plus low-pressure turbine; 2,400 hp; 1 shaft
Boilers:	2
Speed:	13 knots
Range:	6,900 n.miles at 13 knots
Complement:	approx. 45
Helicopters:	none
Missiles:	none
Guns:	none
Radars:	1 Don-2 (navigation)
	1 Neptune (navigation)

Former merchant ship, initially taken over by the Navy for cargo work and lately employed in an experimental role.

Class: Some 30 ships of this class were built by the Neptun yard for the Soviet Union, several of which saw service as naval cargo ships. Six sister ships serve as submarine tenders (ATREK class) and another is a naval research ship (MIKHAIL LOMONOSOV). See 3rd edition (page 255) for notes as cargo ships.

Classification: Soviet OS type.

Design: The KOLOMNA configuration has an amidships superstructure with two cargo hatches forward and two aft, each pair served by kingpost cranes. The SVANETIYA has several boats stowed on deck.

The SVANETIYA underway clearly reveals her origins as a KOLOMNA-class cargo ship.

ELECTRIC GENERATOR SHIPS

4 ELECTRIC GENERATOR SHIPS: TOMBA CLASS

Name	Name	Name	Completed
ENS-244	ENS-348	ENS-357	} 1974–1976
ENS-254			

Builders:	Adolf Warski, Szczecin (Poland)
Displacement:	4,400 tons standard
	5,800 tons full load
Length:	351 ft (107.0 m) oa
Beam:	55 ft 9 in (17.0 m)
Draft:	16 ft 5 in (5.0 m)
Propulsion:	1 diesel; 4,500 hp; 1 shaft
Speed:	14 knots
Range:	7,000 n.miles at 12 knots
Complement:	approx. 50
Helicopters:	no facilities
Missiles:	none
Guns:	none
Radars:	1 Don-2 (navigation)

These ships provide electric power for naval activities in remote areas.

Classification: Soviet ENS type.

DEGAUSSING/DEPERMING SHIPS

9+ DEPERMING SHIPS: PELYM CLASS

Name	Name	Completed
SR-180	SR-409	
SR-191	. . . . . . (5+ units)	} 1971–
SR-241		

Builders:	(USSR)
Displacement:	1,300 tons full load
Length:	214 ft 10 in (65.5 m) oa
Beam:	38 ft (11.6 m)
Draft:	11 ft 2 in (3.4 m)
Propulsion:	2 diesels; 2 shafts
Speed:	16 knots
Range:	4,500 n.miles at 12 knots
Complement:	approx. 70
Helicopters:	no facilities
Missiles:	none
Guns:	none
Radars:	1 Don-2 (navigation)

These are built-for-the purpose degaussing/deperming ships.

Class: One unit was transferred to Cuba in 1982.

Classification: Soviet SR type.

PELYM-class deperming ship SR-191. (1983)

The Tomba-class power generator ship ENS-357. These ships can provide electric power in remote areas. (1980, L. & L. Van Ginderen)

PELYM-class deperming ship SR-241. (Royal Danish Navy)

Few DEPERMING SHIPS: KHABAROV CLASS

Completed:	1950s
Builders:	(USSR)
Displacement:	650 tons full load
Length:	152 ft 2 in (46.4 m) oa
Beam:	26 ft 3 in (8.0 m)
Draft:	10 ft 10 in (3.3 m)
Propulsion:	1 diesel; 600 hp; 1 shaft
Speed:	10 knots
Range:	1,600 n.miles at 8 knots

Complement:	
Helicopters:	no facilities
Missiles:	none
Guns:	none
Radars:	

Small, steel-hulled cargo ships converted to the deperming role. A large deckhouse covers the forward hold area.

Classification: Soviet SR type.

Khabarov-class cargo ship. Several of these ships have been converted to deperming ships and other auxiliary roles.

Approx. 20 DEPERMING SHIPS: SEKSTAN CLASS

Completed:	1949–1955
Builders:	(Finland)
Displacement:	400 tons full load
Length:	134 ft 6 in (41.0 m) oa
Beam:	30 ft 6 in (9.3 m)
Draft:	13 ft 9 in (4.2 m)
Propulsion:	1 diesel; 400 hp; 1 shaft
Speed:	11 knots
Range:	1,200 n.miles at 10.5 knots
Complement:	approx. 25
Helicopters:	no facilities
Missiles:	none
Guns:	none

Small, wooden-hulled ships, built as war reparations for Finland's support of Germany in World War II. Cargo ships and a coastal survey ship were built to the same design for Soviet use; all discarded.

Sekstan-class ship; few of these Finnish-built ships survive.

1 + (?) DEPERMING SHIPS: "KORALL" CLASS

Completed:	early 1950s
Builders:	Laivateollisuus, Turku (Finland)
Displacement:	approx. 600 tons full load
Length:	139 ft 5 in (42.5 m) wl
Beam:	29 ft 6 in (9.0 m)
Draft:	10 ft 2 in (3.1 m)
Propulsion:	1 diesel (Halberstadt 6NVD36); 300 hp; 1 shaft
Speed:	8 knots
Range:	4,000 n.miles at 8 knots
Complement:	
Helicopters:	no facilities
Missiles:	none
Guns:	none

Former three-masted schooner; wooden-hulled. One or more of these ships have been demasted and modified for the deperming role. The

ZARYA of this type serves as a civilian-manned research ship (see chapter 24).

NOISE-MEASUREMENT SHIPS

5 + NOISE-MEASUREMENT SHIPS: ONEGA CLASS

Name	Name	Name	Completed
GKS-52	GKS-224	SFP-95	
GKS-83	GKS-286		1973–

Builders:	
Displacement:	1,925 tons full load
Length:	265 ft 8 in (81.0 m) oa
Beam:	36 ft 1 in (11.0 m)
Draft:	13 ft 9 in (4.2 m)
Propulsion:	1 gas turbine; 15,000 hp; 1 shaft
Speed:	20 knots
Range:	
Complement:	approx. 45
Helicopters:	landing area
Missiles:	none
Guns:	none
Radars:	1 Don-2 (navigation)

These ships provide noise-measurement data on surface ships and submarines.

Classification: Soviet GKS type, except one ship listed as SFP, an unknown type designation.

19 NOISE-MEASUREMENT SHIPS: T-43 CLASS (Former Minesweepers)

Name	Name	Name	Completed
GKS-11	GKS-18	GKS-25	
GKS-12	GKS-19	GKS-26	
GKS-13	GKS-20	GKS-42	
GKS-14	GKS-21	GKS-45	1950s
GKS-15	GKS-22	GKS-46	
GKS-16	GKS-23		
GKS-17	GKS-24		

Builders:	(USSR)
Displacement:	500 tons standard
	570 tons full load
Length:	190 ft 3 in (58.0 m) oa
Beam:	28 ft 2 in (8.6 m)
Draft:	7 ft 6 in (2.3 m)
Propulsion:	2 diesels (9D); 2,200 hp; 2 shafts
Speed:	14 knots
Range:	
Complement:	approx. 75
Helicopters:	no facilities
Missiles:	none
Guns:	none
Radars:	1 Neptune (navigation) or Spin Trough (search)

These are former minesweepers, modified to lay bottom-mounted hydrophones to monitor surface ship and submarine noises.

Classification: Soviet GKS type.

The converted T-43 minesweeper GKS-14 noise-measurement ship.

These are former armed icebreakers operated by the KGB that have been transferred to the Navy. Their guns and Owl Screech and Strut Curve radars were deleted, and they have been painted black. They are similar to the Navy and civilian icebreakers of the DOBRYNYA NIKITICH class. See chapter 25 for details of KGB configuration.

The ships have a helicopter deck, but no hangar.

The former KGB patrol icebreaker IVAN SUSANIN, unarmed, in naval service. (1983)

ICEBREAKERS

These are Navy-manned icebreakers. A few are armed. Additional icebreakers are operated by civilian government agencies (see chapter 24), and armed icebreakers are employed in the patrol role by the KGB Maritime Border Troops (see chapter 25).

2 SUPPORT ICEBREAKERS: "IVAN SUSANIN" CLASS

Name	Completed
IVAN SUSANIN	1974
RUSLAN	1981

Builders:	Admiralty, Leningrad
Displacement:	3,400 tons full load
Length:	222 ft 1 in (67.7 m) oa
Beam:	60 ft (18.3 m)
Draft:	21 ft (6.4 m)
Propulsion:	3 diesels (13D100); 5,400 hp; 3 generators connected to electric motors; 2 shafts
Speed:	14.5 knots
Range:	5,500 n.miles at 12 knots
	13,000 n.miles at 9.5 knots
Complement:	approx. 140
Helicopters:	landing area
Guns:	removed
Radars:	2 Don-Kay (navigation)

7 SUPPORT ICEBREAKERS: "DOBRYNYA NIKITICH" CLASS

Name	Name	Name	Completed
BURAN	PERESVET	SADKO	
DOBRYNYA NIKITICH	PURGA	VYUGA	1959–1974
IL'YA MUROMETS			

Builders:	Admiralty, Leningrad
Displacement:	2,940 tons full load
Length:	222 ft 1 in (67.7 m) oa
Beam:	60 ft (18.3 m)
Draft:	20 ft (6.1 m)
Propulsion:	3 diesels (13D100); 5,400 hp; 3 generators connected to electric motors; 3 shafts (1 forward); see notes
Speed:	14.5 knots
Range:	5,500 n.miles at 12 knots
	13,000 n.miles at 9.5 knots
Complement:	approx. 100
Helicopters:	no facilities
Missiles:	none
Guns:	2 57-mm/70-cal AA (1 twin) in 4 ships
	2 25-mm/60-cal AA (1 twin) in 4 ships
Radars:	1 or 2 Don-2 (navigation)

These are Navy-manned icebreakers, at least four of which are armed.

Class: Thirty ships of this design are believed to have been built, with five operated by the KGB Maritime Border Troops as patrol icebreakers (see chapter 25), one Navy-manned unit being employed as a research ship (see chapter 23), and the remainder being civilian-manned—14 as icebreakers and one polar research ship (see chapter 24). The KGB ships are armed and have a helicopter hangar and landing deck.

Classification: Soviet LDK type.

Design: These are small, efficient icebreakers. They are rigged for ocean towing. Later units do not have a bow propeller, but retain the same horsepower rating.

Names: Il'ya Muromets (Russian Knight) was a Russian folk hero and the name given by Igor Sikorsky to the world's first four-engine aircraft, which he built in Russia in 1914. The name PURGA is assigned to a civilian tug and is the former name of a KGB icebreaker.

The DOBRYNYA NIKITICH, lead ship of a large series of Soviet icebreakers operated by the Navy, KGB, and a civilian institute. All of the KGB ships—which differ slightly—are armed. (1978, Royal Air Force)

FLEET, SALVAGE, AND FIRE-FIGHTING TUGS

This section lists Soviet naval MB, SB, and PZHS types of tugs. The larger tug-type ships especially fitted for salvage and rescue operations are listed earlier in this chapter. The large SB-series tugs can support divers. The KGB Maritime Border Troops operate several armed tugs in the patrol role (see chapter 25).

4+ SALVAGE TUGS: SLIVA CLASS

Name	Completed
SB-406	1984
SB-408	1984
SB-921	1985
SB-922	1985

Builders:	Rauma-Repola, Rauma (Finland)
Displacement:	3,300 tons full load
Tonnage:	810 DWT
Length:	220 ft 5 in (67.2 m) oa

Beam:	50 ft 6 in (15.4 m)
Draft:	16 ft 9 in (5.1 m)
Propulsion:	2 diesels (SEMT-Pielstick/Russkiy 6 PC 2.5 L400); 7,800 hp; 2 shafts
Speed:	16 knots
Range:	
Complement:	approx. 45 + 10 salvage crew
Guns:	none
Radars:	2 . . . . . . (navigation)

These are ice-strengthened salvage tugs. The type is operated only by the Soviet Navy. They have accommodations for 10 salvage specialists in addition to crew. Five-ton-capacity crane is fitted to each ship. Additional ships are planned.

Classification: Soviet SB type.

Engineering: A bow thruster is fitted for precise maneuvering.

The SB-406 testing her fire cannon during trials. Note the twin funnel configuration. (1984, Rauma-Repola)

2 TUG/SUPPLY SHIPS: NEFTEGAZ CLASS

Name	Completed
ALEKSEY KORTUNOV	1983
ILGA	1983

Builders:	Adolf Warski, Szczecin (Poland)
Displacement:	2,800 tons full load
Tonnage:	1,396 DWT
Length:	211 ft 3 in (64.4 m) oa
Beam:	45 ft 3 in (13.8 m)
Draft:	17 ft 8 in (5.4 m)
Propulsion:	2 diesels (Zgoda/Sulzer); 9,000 hp; 2 shafts
Speed:	15 knots
Range:	
Complement:	approx. 25
Guns:	none
Radars:	2 . . . . . . (navigation)

Some 60 of these ships have been built for the tug and offshore oilfield supply role. Two of the early units were taken over by the Navy.

Design: Up to 600 tons of cargo can be carried on the after deck.

Engineering: A bow thruster is fitted.

A civilian Neftegaz-class tug/supply ship, also with a twin-funnel configuration, but with a large cargo deck area aft. (1984)

13 OCEANGOING TUGS: GORYN CLASS

Name	Name	Name	Completed
MB-105 (BAYKALSK)	MB-31	MB-38	
MB-18 (BEREZINSK)	MB-32	MB-61	1977–1978
MB-119 (BILBINO)	MB-35	SB-523 (ex-MB-64)	1982–1983
SPASTEL'NOYE BUKSIR (SB-365, ex-MB-29)	MB-36	SB-524 (ex-MB-108)	
MB-30			

Builders:	Rauma-Repola, Rauma (Finland)
Displacement:	2,240 tons standard
	2,600 tons full load
Tonnage:	600 DWT
Length:	208 ft 3 in (63.5 m) oa
Beam:	46 ft 11 in (14.3 m)
Draft:	16 ft 9 in (5.1 m)
Propulsion:	1 diesel (Russkiy 67N); 3,500 hp; 1 shaft
Speed:	13.5 knots
Range:	
Complement:	approx. 40
Guns:	none
Radars:	2 Don-2 (navigation)

These are oceangoing tugs with a salvage and fire-fighting capability. The MB-15, -18, -105, and -119 were built in 1977–1978; the others in 1982–1983.

Class: All ships of this class are believed to have been built for naval service. The BOLSHEVETSK was lost off Japan in February 1979.

Classification: Soviet MB type except for three units rated as SB (salvage tugs).

Names: Three MB types were formally assigned names.

11 OCEANGOING TUGS: SORUM CLASS

Name	Name	Name	Completed
MB-6	MB-58	MB-148	
MB-25	MB-112	MB-304	1974–
MB-26	MB-115	MB-307	
MB-28	MB-119		

Builders:	Yaroslavskiy (USSR)
Displacement:	1,210 tons standard
	1,655 tons full load
Tonnage:	440 DWT
Length:	191 ft 3 in (58.3 m) oa
Beam:	41 ft 4 in (12.6 m)
Draft:	15 ft 1 in (4.6 m)
Propulsion:	diesel-electric: 2 diesels (5-2D42); 1,500 hp; 1 shaft
Speed:	14 knots
Range:	6,700 n.miles at 13 knots
Complement:	approx. 35
Guns:	none
Radars:	2 Don-2 (navigation)

Several additional tugs of this class are operated by the KGB Maritime Border Troops as armed patrol tugs (see chapter 25). In addition, several are operated as salvage tugs by the Ministry of Fisheries (PURGA class) while others have been transferred to Bulgaria and Poland.

Classification: Naval units are designated MB.

The Goryn-class oceangoing tug MB-18. (1984, JMSDF)

The Sorum-class oceangoing tug MB-25. (1984, JMSDF)

11 SEAGOING FIRE-FIGHTING TUGS: KATUN CLASS

Name	Name	Name	Completed
PZHS-64	PZHS-123	PZHS-282	
PZHS-96	PZHS-124	...... (4 units)	1970–
PZHS-98	PZHS-209		

Builders:	(USSR)
Displacement:	1,016 tons full load
Length:	Katun I 205 ft 4 in (62.6 m) oa
	Katun II 215 ft 2 in (65.6 m) oa
Beam:	33 ft 6 in (10.2 m)
Draft:	11 ft 10 in (3.6 m)
Propulsion:	2 diesels (40DM); 4,000 hp; 2 shafts
Speed:	17 knots
Range:	2,200 n.miles at 16 knots
Complement:	approx. 30
Guns:	none
Radars:	1 Don-2 (navigation)

These ships are oceangoing fire-fighting and decontamination tugs. The Admiralty yard has built additional ships of this type for civilian use.

Classification: Original Soviet PDS type (fire-fighting and decontamination ship); subsequently changed to PZHS (fire-fighting ship).

Design: The later ships are slightly longer and have an additional bridge level; they are Katun II.

40+ OCEANGOING TUGS: OKHTENSKIY CLASS

Completed:	1958–early 1960s
Builders:	Petrozavod, Leningrad
Displacement:	700 tons standard
	925 tons full load
Length:	155 ft 2 in (47.3 m) oa
Beam:	33 ft 9 in (10.3 m)
Draft:	18 ft (5.5 m)
Propulsion:	2 diesels; 1,500 hp; 1 shaft
Speed:	13 knots

The Okhtenskiy-class oceangoing tug SB-28 (with two boats carried). She was towing a Sonya-class minesweeper when the photo was taken in the Western Pacific. (1985, JMSDF)

Range:	5,800 n.miles at 13 knots
	7,800 n.miles at 7 knots
Complement:	approx. 40
Guns:	none
Radars:	1 or 2 Don-2 (navigation) or Spin Trough (search)

Several additional tugs of this type are armed and employed as patrol craft by the KGB Maritime Border Troops.

Class: Sixty-three tugs of this class were built. A few were operated as civilian tugs.

Classification: All are MB or SB, the latter with an additional boat and other salvage gear provided in some units.

2 SALVAGE TUGS: "OREL" CLASS

Name	Name	Completed
SB-38	SB-43	late 1950s

Builders:	Valmet, Turku (Finland)
Displacement:	1,200 tons standard
	1,760 tons full load
Length:	201 ft (61.3 m) oa
Beam:	39 ft (11.9 m)
Draft:	14 ft 9 in (4.5 m)
Propulsion:	1 diesel (MAN G5Z52/70); 1,700 hp; 1 shaft
Speed:	15 knots
Range:	13,000 n.miles at 13.5 knots
Complement:	approx. 35
Guns:	none
Radars:	1 Don-2 or Don (navigation)

The OREL class consisted of about 25 large tugs built in Tarku for the Soviet Navy and fishing fleet. Several naval units have been discarded. They are fitted for salvage.

Classification: Soviet SB type.

9 OCEANGOING TUGS: ROSLAVL CLASS

Name	Name	Name	Completed
MB-69	MB-145	SB-46	
MB-94	MB-146	...... (2 units)	1950s
MB-134	MB-147		

Builders:	(USSR)
Displacement:	750 tons full load
Length:	147 ft (44.5 m) oa
Beam:	31 ft 2 in (9.5 m)
Draft:	11 ft 6 in (3.5 m)
Propulsion:	diesel-electric; 1,200 hp; 2 shafts
Speed:	11 knots
Range:	6,000 n.miles at 11 knots
Complement:	approx. 30
Guns:	none
Radars:	

Small tug types, slowly being discarded.

Classification: Soviet MB type except that one unit is listed as salvage tug (SB).

The Roslavl-class oceangoing tug MB-94.

Shelon-class torpedo retriever recovering a torpedo in the Barents Sea. (1982, U.S. Navy)

SERVICE AND TARGET CRAFT

The Soviet Navy operates a large number of self-propelled and towed service craft. Only the larger self-propelled units are listed here.

TORPEDO RETRIEVERS: SHELON CLASS

Displacement:	270 tons full load
Length:	134 ft 6 in (41.0 m) oa
Beam:	19 ft 8 in (6.0 m)
Draft:	
Propulsion:	2 diesels; 2 shafts
Speed:	24 knots
Range:	
Complement:	approx. 40
Radars:	1 Spin Trough (search)
Sonars:	1 high-frequency (dipping)

These are torpedo recovery craft, with a boom aft and stern ramp. Several are in service, the first being completed in 1978. They can be armed with a twin 25-mm or 30-mm AA mount forward.

TORPEDO RETRIEVERS: POLUCHAT I CLASS

Displacement:	90 tons full load
Length:	97 ft 1 in (29.6 m) oa
Beam:	20 ft (6.1 m)
Draft:	6 ft 3 in (1.9 m)
Propulsion:	2 diesels (M50); 2,400 hp; 2 shafts
Speed:	18 knots
Range:	450 n.miles at 17 knots
	900 n.miles at 10 knots
Complement:	approx. 20
Radars:	1 Spin Trough (search)

A large number of these craft have been built, with more than 40 remaining in the Soviet Navy as torpedo recovery craft. Additional units were employed as patrol craft; all of these have been discarded from Soviet service although many are in foreign navies and coast guards.

Classification: Soviet TL type.

Shelon-class torpedo retriever. (1982)

Poluchat I-class torpedo retriever.

DIVING TENDERS: YELVA CLASS

Displacement:	295 tons full load
Length:	134 ft 2 in (40.9 m) oa
Beam:	26 ft 3 in (8.0 m)
Draft:	6 ft 11 in (2.1 m)
Propulsion:	2 diesels (3D12A); 600 hp; 2 shafts
Speed:	12.5 knots
Range:	
Complement:	approx. 30
Radars:	1 Spin Trough (search)

These diving ships can simultaneously support several divers working to depths up to 200 feet. Several are in Soviet service, and several units have gone to other countries.

A decompression chamber is fitted.

DIVING TENDERS: NYRYAT I CLASS

Displacement:	120 tons full load
Length:	95 ft 2 in (29.0 m) oa
Beam:	16 ft 5 in (5.0 m)
Draft:	5 ft 7 in (1.7 m)
Propulsion:	1 diesel; 450 hp; 1 shaft
Speed:	12 knots
Range:	1,600 n.miles at 10 knots
Complement:	approx. 15
Radars:	1 Spin Trough (search)

Several of these craft are in service, built from the late 1950s. They were built after the tenders designated Nyryat II. Some have been transferred to other navies.

Classification: Soviet VM type.

DIVING TENDERS: NYRYAT II CLASS

Displacement:	50 tons full load
Length:	69 ft (21.0 m) oa
Beam:	14 ft 9 in (4.5 m)
Draft:	
Propulsion:	1 diesel (3D6); 150 hp; 1 shaft
Speed:	9 knots
Range:	
Complement:	approx. 10
Radars:	1 Spin Trough (search)

TARGET CONTROL BOATS: OSA CLASS

A large number of target control craft were built with the hulls and propulsion plants of the Osa missile boats. They carry the Square Tie radar and have large radio antenna arrays.

Classification: Soviet KT type.

TARGET CRAFT: MODIFIED OSA CLASS

Several Osa missile craft have been modified to serve as radio-controlled targets. They have radar reflectors fitted to large lattice masts, and heat generators with two large funnels are provided.

A few older Komar craft may also survive as target craft (with radar reflectors only).

TARGET BARGES

A number of non-self-propelled (towed) target barges are also employed for gun and missile-firing tests and training.

Modified Osa-class missile boat configured as a radio-controlled target. She is fitted with "furnaces" to produce infrared signatures and radar reflectors.

A target barge fitted for use as a target for infrared and radar homing missiles. (Royal Danish Navy)

23
Research and Intelligence Ships

INTELLIGENCE COLLECTION SHIPS

Most of the Soviet Navy's intelligence-collection ships (designated AGI by Western navies) are based on trawler designs, probably because of the designs' availability, good seakeeping qualities, long endurance, and insulated fish-storage holds that provide space for electronic equipment bays. The largest of the AGI classes—the Bal'zam class—appears to have been designed from the outset specifically for intelligence collection and processing activities. These are also the only AGI class built with armament.

None of these ships are disguised as civilian fishing craft. All are Navy manned, readily identifiable by their electronic antennas, and some are armed. Soviet fishing craft as well as merchant ships, however, undoubtedly collect intelligence as opportunities permit.

Other Soviet naval ships—submarines, surface combatants, the Alesha-class minelayers, minesweepers, and various auxiliary ships—also perform intelligence-collection missions on a regular basis.

Classification: These ships generally have the Soviet classification of GS (hydrographic vessel) or SSV (communications vessel); see chapter 3.

Missiles: In addition to the weapons listed here, many AGIs have been observed with shoulder-fired SA-7 Grail missile launchers (the same missile as fired from the SA-N-5 launcher).

The Soviet Navy operates the world's largest fleets of research and intelligence ships. Their functions, which often overlap, support a variety of naval and maritime activities. There are some 75 specialized intelligence collection ships (AGI) in service, including the large SSV-493, shown here off the U.S. Trident submarine base at Bangor, Washington. This number can be expected to decline as older units are retired. (1984, U.S. Navy)

4+ INTELLIGENCE COLLECTION SHIPS: AL'PINIST CLASS

Name	Name	Name	Completed
GS-7	GS-19	GS-39	} 1981–
GS-8			

Builders:	Yaroslavl
Displacement:	1,200 tons full load
Tonnage:	322 DWT
Length:	176 ft 2 in (53.7 m) oa
Beam:	34 ft 5 in (10.5 m)
Draft:	14 ft 1 in (4.3 m)
Propulsion:	1 diesel (8NVD48-2U); 1,320 hp; 1 shaft
Speed:	13 knots
Range:	7,600 n.miles at 13 knots
Complement:	
Missiles:	none
Guns:	none
Radars:	1 Don-2

These are modified stern trawlers. Fitted with a bow thruster. Additional units are probably undergoing conversion to the AGI configuration to replace some of the older ships employed in this role.

Class: Several hundred stern trawlers of this type were built for the Soviet fishing fleet. Three units have been converted to civilian research ships for operation by the Ministry of Fisheries, and at least one serves as a naval trials ship.

The GS-8, with electronic intercept antennas fitted to the after mast. Note the trawler-type stern.

The Al'pinist-class AGIs represent a return to relatively small trawler hulls for this role, following the large Bal'zam and Primor'ye classes. Here the GS-8 operates some 250 miles off the Japanese island of Chichi Jima. (1985, Japanese Maritime Self-Defense Force)

4+ INTELLIGENCE COLLECTION SHIPS: BAL'ZAM CLASS

Name	Name	Name	Completed
SSV-80	SSV-493	SSV-...	} 1980–
SSV-443	SSV-516		

Builders:	Kaliningrad
Displacement:	5,000 tons full load
Length:	346 ft (105.5 m) oa
Beam:	50 ft 10 in (15.5 m)
Draft:	19 ft (5.8 m)
Propulsion:	2 diesels; 9,000 hp; 2 shafts
Speed:	22 knots
Range:	
Complement:	approx. 200
Missiles:	2 quad SA-N-5 Grail launchers [16]
Guns:	1 30-mm close-in (multibarrel)
Radars:	2 Don-Kay (navigation)

This is the largest AGI in Soviet service. Additional units are believed to be under construction.

Design: The Bal'zam class appears to have been designed specifically for the intelligence-collection role. There are significant at-sea replenishment facilities to permit them to provide supplies and fuel to other ships at sea. No radar FCS is provided for the Gatling gun; only an optical system.

Classification: Soviet SSV type.

The Bal'zam class represents the largest AGI design yet built. The 30-mm Gatling gun is fitted forward of the bridge; SA-N-5/SA-7 missiles are also provided. (1983, U.S. Navy)

Another Bal'zam-class AGI, probably the SSV-516. The Western press often depicts AGIs as disguised fishing trawlers. This is no longer correct, especially when one considers these large ships.

6 INTELLIGENCE COLLECTION SHIPS: "PRIMOR'YE" CLASS

Name		Name		Completed
SSV-454	ZABAYKAL'YE	SSV-590	KRYM	
SSV-465	PRIMOR'YE	SSV-591	KAVKAZ	1970–
SSV-501	ZAPOROZH'YE	SSV-502	ZAKARPATIYE	

Builders:	(USSR)
Displacement:	2,600 tons standard
	3,700 tons full load
Length:	277 ft 10 in (84.7 m) oa
Beam:	45 ft 11 in (14.0 m)
Draft:	18 ft (5.5 m)
Propulsion:	2 diesel (Russkiy); 2,000 hp; 1 shaft
Speed:	13 knots
Range:	12,000 n.miles at 13 knots
	18,000 n.miles at 12 knots
Complement:	approx. 160
Missiles:	none
Guns:	none
Radars:	2 Don-Kay (navigation)

These AGIs have large, distinctive "box" deckhouses forward and aft on their superstructure to house electronic equipment.

Design: These ships are based on a highly successful, Soviet-built series of stern trawler-factory ships. More than 200 units of this design have been built as the MAYAKOVSKIY class, with several being modified to civilian research ships (see chapter 24).

In their AGI configuration the ships have a distinctive superstructure with three antenna masts, while some ships retain the trawler kingpost aft (i.e., a total of four masts).

Names: Names were removed from the ships in 1979–1981.

The ZAPOROZH'YE operating west of the Azore Islands. She has a Pert Spring antenna atop the bridge and a different intercept antenna atop the kingpost than is fitted in the PRIMOR'YE. (1982, U.S. Navy)

The ZAKARPATIYE has a five-mast configuration, the third mast being a "Christmas tree," laden with electronic intercept antennas. (1985, U.S. Navy)

The PRIMOR'YE-class AGIs have widely differing mast and antenna arrangements. This is the KAVKAZ off Portsmouth, New Hampshire, a major U.S. submarine operating area. A Pert Spring-type antenna is fitted atop the kingpost. (1984, U.S. Navy)

The PRIMOR'YE reveals still another class configuration, with a stub mast atop the second deckhouse and no kingpost aft. The windows of the two deckhouse "boxes" are open—an unusual view. (1982, U.S. Navy)

9 INTELLIGENCE COLLECTION SHIPS: MOMA CLASS

Name		Name		Completed
GS-117	IL'MEN	SSV-514	SELIGR	
SSV-501	VEGA	SSV-...	EKVATOR	
SSV-506	NAKHODKA	SSV-...	KIL'DIN	1968–1974
SSV-509	PELORUS	SSV-...	YUPITER	
SSV-512	ARKHIPELAG			

Builders:	Polnocny, Gdansk (Poland)
Displacement:	1,260 tons standard
	1,540 tons full load
Length:	240 ft 5 in (73.3 m) oa
Beam:	35 ft 5 in (10.8 m)
Draft:	12 ft 6 in (3.8 m)
Propulsion:	2 diesels (Zgoda/Sulzer 6TD48); 3,600 hp; 2 shafts
Speed:	17 knots
Range:	8,000 n.miles at 11 knots
Complement:	approx. 100
Missiles:	2 quad SA-N-5 Grail launchers (16) in some ships
Guns:	none
Radars:	2 Don-2 (navigation)

These ships are converted survey ships/buoy tenders, with about 40 ships having been built to this design. The SELIGR was assigned to monitor the initial missile launch tests from the first U.S. Trident submarine, the OHIO (SSBN 726) off the Florida coast in January 1982.

Class: A number of these ships serve the Soviet Navy as hydrographic survey ships (see below).

Classification: Eight ships are designated SSV with the IL'MEN designated GS.

Design: The ships vary considerably in details. Some retain their buoy-handling cranes forward; others have a low deckhouse of varying length between the forward mast and superstructure; forward mast positions (in some ships) vary in height and configuration. There is a deck area aft of the funnel and boat davits for carrying vans with electronic equipment.

The Moma-class AGI ARKHIPELAG has a large deckhouse forward of the bridge in place of the crane normally fitted in these ships. An antenna-bearing mast is fitted forward.

This variation of the Moma-class AGIs, the SSV-472, has a low deckhouse forward. (1982, U.S. Navy)

A Moma-class AGI reveals the large antenna array of these converted survey ships/buoy tenders.

8 INTELLIGENCE COLLECTION SHIPS: MAYAK CLASS

Name		Name	Completed
GS-239		KHERSONES	
GS-242		KURS	1967–1970
GS-536	GIRORULEVOY	KURSOGRAF	
ANEROYD		LADOGA	

Builders:	(USSR)
Displacement:	1,050 tons full load
Length:	177 ft 9 in (54.2 m) oa
Beam:	30 ft 6 in (9.3 m)
Draft:	11 ft 10 in (3.6 m)
Propulsion:	1 diesel (8NVD48); 800 hp; 1 shaft
Speed:	11 knots
Range:	9,400 n.miles at 11 knots
	11,000 n.miles at 7.5 knots
Complement:	approx. 60
Missiles:	none
Guns:	4 14.5-mm machine guns (2 twin) in KURSOGRAF
Radars:	1 or 2 Don-2 (navigation) and/or Spin Trough (search)

These ships are former side trawlers that have been converted to the AGI configuration. More than 100 Mayak-class ships were built in the 1960s, several being converted to auxiliary ships (see chapter 22).

Classification: Soviet naval GS type.

Design: Details vary: the GIRORULEVOY has a flat-topped randome fitted above the bridge; the KHERSONES has a wider main deckhouse; the LADOGA has a separate structure forward of the bridge and a third lattice mast; and the KURS a tall deckhouse on the stern. The deckhouse forward of the bridge varies in length, and mast configurations vary. The KURSOGRAF was fitted with two 14.5-mm MG twin mounts in 1980; they have since been removed.

Name: Mayak is the NATO class name for this design. The Soviet ship named MAYAK is a naval hydrographic survey ship of the Melitopol class.

The Mayak-class AGI KURSOGRAF has a deckhouse forward as well as a short lattice mast atop the bridge, distinguishing the ship from others of the class. These ships have a small deckhouse on the fantail.

Mayak-class AGI GIRORULEVOY, with lengthened deckhouse forward of bridge and antenna housing atop bridge. (1983, U.S. Navy)

Mayak-class AGI ANEROYD. (1984, JMSDF)

4 INTELLIGENCE COLLECTION SHIPS: MIRNYY CLASS

Name	Name	Name	Completed
BAKAN LOTSMAN	VAL	VERTIKAL	} 1962–1964

Builders:	61 Kommuna, Nikolayev
Displacement:	850 tons standard
	1,300 tons full load
Length:	208 ft 7 in (63.6 m) oa
Beam:	31 ft 2 in (9.5 m)
Draft:	14 ft 9 in (4.5 m)
Propulsion:	4 diesels; 4,000 hp; electric drive; 1 shaft
Speed:	17.5 knots
Range:	8,700 n.miles at 11 knots
Complement:	approx. 60
Missiles:	none
Guns:	none
Radars:	2 Don-2 (navigation)
	1 Spin Trough (search) in some ships

These ships are converted whale hunter/catcher ships, easily identified by their high, "notched" bows (for harpoon gun). Details vary. New deckhouses were fitted between the superstructure and forward mast in the early 1970s to provide additional working spaces.

Mirnyy-class AGI.

Mirnyy-class AGI BAKAN. (1974, U.S. Navy)

3 INTELLIGENCE COLLECTION SHIPS: "NIKOLAY ZUBOV" CLASS

Name		Name		Completed
SSV-468	GAVRIL SARYCHEV	SSV-503	KHARITON LAPTEV	} 1963–1968
SSV-469	SEMYEN CHELYUSHKIN			

Builders:	Adolf Warski, Szczecin (Poland)
Displacement:	2,200 tons standard
	3,100 tons full load
Length:	297 ft (90.0 m)
Beam:	42 ft 11 in (13.0 m)
Draft:	15 ft 6 in (4.7 m)
Propulsion:	2 diesels (Zgoda 8TD48); 4,800 hp; 2 shafts
Speed:	16.5 knots
Range:	11,000 n.miles at 14 knots
Complement:	approx. 100
Missiles:	see notes
Guns:	none
Radars:	2 Don-2 (navigation)

These are former oceanographic ships (completion dates above); converted to AGIs. Positions for three quad SA-N-5 Grail launchers [24 missiles] have been provided in all three ships.

Class: Eight additional ships of this class serve as naval oceanographic research ships.

Design: The GAVRIL SARYCHEV has been extensively reconstructed with her forecastle deck extended to the stern and an additional level added to her superstructure. The others have a small raised platform aft, which is not a helicopter deck.

The NIKOLAY ZUBOV-class ships serve in the oceanographic research as well as AGI roles. This is the SEMYEN CHELYUSHKIN, configured for the latter role. The identifying features of this class include the bipod masts and enclosed crow's nest forward. (1983, U.S. Navy)

15 INTELLIGENCE COLLECTION SHIPS: OKEAN CLASS

Name	Name	Name	Completed
ALIDADA	EKHOLOT	REDUKTO	
AMPERMETR	GIDROFON	REPITER	
BAROGRAF	KRENOMETR	TEODOLIT	1962–1967
BAROMETR	LINZA	TRAVERS	
DEFLEKTOR	LOTLIN' (GS-319)	ZOND	

Builders:	(East Germany)
Displacement:	760 tons full load
Length:	166 ft 8 in (50.8 m) oa
Beam:	29 ft 2 in (8.9 m)
Draft:	12 ft 2 in (3.7 m)
Propulsion:	1 diesel; 540 hp; 1 shaft
Speed:	11 knots

Range:	7,900 n.miles at 11 knots
Complement:	approx. 60
Missiles:	see notes
Guns:	4 14.5-mm machine guns (2 twin) in BAROGRAF
Radars:	1 or 2 Don-2 (navigation)

This is the largest and hence probably most observed class of AGIs. They are converted side trawlers. Details differ. They retain their trawler arrangement of a tripod mast well forward and a pole mast well aft.

There are provisions in most ships for two quad SA-N-5 Grail launchers [16 missiles]. One ship has been fitted with machine guns.

Classification: Soviet GS type.

Names: Okean is the NATO class name. A Moma-class hydrographic survey ship carries the Soviet name OKEAN (listed in this chapter).

Okean-class AGI.

Okean-class AGI DEFLEKTOR (with extended deckhouse).

2 INTELLIGENCE COLLECTION SHIPS: DNEPR CLASS

Name	Name	Completed
IZERMETEL'	PROTRAKTOR	1959

Builders:	Ishikawajima, Tokyo
Displacement:	750 tons full load
Length:	173 ft 11 in (52.7 m)
Beam:	29 ft 8 in (9.0 m)
Draft:	11 ft 7 in (3.5 m)
Propulsion:	2 diesel (Burmeister & Wain); 1,210 hp; 1 shaft
Speed:	14 knots
Range:	7,500 n.miles at 13 knots
Complement:	
Missiles:	none
Guns:	2 14.5-mm machine guns (1 twin)
Radars:	

These AGIs were built as tuna-fishing research ships. Their conversion to intelligence ships included adding a small deckhouse abaft the funnel. They have not been observed at sea in the last few years and may have been stricken.

Dnepr-class AGI. (1982)

2 INTELLIGENCE COLLECTION SHIPS: "PAMIR" CLASS

Name		Completed	Conversion Completed
SSV-477	PELENG (ex-PAMIR)	1958	. . .
SSV-480	GIDROGRAF (ex-ARBAN)	1958	1967

Builders:	Gävle (Sweden)
Displacement:	1,443 tons standard
	2,300 tons full load
Length:	255 ft 10 in (78.0 m) oa
Beam:	42 ft (12.8 m)
Draft:	13 ft 2 in (4.0 m)
Propulsion:	2 diesels (MAN G10V 40/60); 4,200 hp; 2 shafts
Speed:	17.5 knots
Range:	15,200 n.miles at 17.5 knots
	21,800 n.miles at 12 knots
Complement:	approx. 120
Missiles:	none (see notes)
Guns:	none
Radars:	2 Don-2 (navigation)

These ships are converted salvage tugs (with two ships remaining in that role; see chapter 22). In the AGI configuration their superstructures have been enlarged and antennas fitted. There are positions in these ships for three quad SA-N-5 Grail launchers [24 missiles].

PAMIR-class AGI GIDROGRAF; this photo clearly reveals the ship's origins of a long-range salvage tug.

PAMIR-class AGI PELENG; note that the after pair of boat davits are empty, with canister-stowed life rafts taking the place of two boats.

OCEANOGRAPHIC RESEARCH SHIPS

The Soviet Navy operates more oceanographic and hydrographic research ships than the rest of the world's nations combined. In addition, there are a large number of civilian research ships (see chapter 24).

18 OCEANOGRAPHIC RESEARCH SHIPS: "YUG" CLASS

Name	Name	Name	Completed
BRIZ	PEGAS	STVOR	
GALS	PERSEY	TAYGA	
GIDROLOG	PLUTON	VIZIR	1978–1983
GORIZONT	SENEZH	YUG	
NIKOLAY MATUSEVICH	STRELETS	ZODIAK	
DONUZLAY	MANGYSHLAK	MARSHAL GELOVANI	

Builders:	Polnocny, Gdansk (Poland)
Displacement:	2,500 tons full load
Length:	270 ft 7 in (82.5 m) oa
Beam:	44 ft 3 in (13.5 m)
Draft:	13 ft 2 in (4.0 m)
Propulsion:	2 diesels (Zgoda/Sulzer STD48); 4,400 hp; 2 shafts
Speed:	15.5 knots
Range:	11,000 n.miles at 12 knots
Complement:	approx. 45 + 20 scientists
Helicopters:	no facilities
Missiles:	none
Guns:	see notes
Radars:	2 Don-2 (navigation)

YUG-class research ship PLUTON.

These ships were built specifically for the oceanographic research role with facilities for hydrographic surveys. They have provisions for the installation of three 25-mm AA twin gun mounts.

Classification: Soviet EHOS type.

Design: These ships are fitted with two 100-kw electric motors for quiet, slow-speed operations and a 300-hp bow thruster for precise station keeping. They have two 5-ton-capacity booms. Six laboratories.

The YUG-class oceanographic research ships are typical of the large number of medium-size scientific ships being produced for the Soviet fleets. While purpose built, these ships have many trawler features. These are Navy-manned ships. (1984, JMSDF)

6 OCEANOGRAPHIC RESEARCH SHIPS: "AKADEMIK KRYLOV" CLASS

Name	Name	Completed
ADMIRAL VLADIMIRSKY	LEONID DEMIN	
AKADEMIK KRYLOV	LEONID SOBELYEV	1974–1979
IVAN KRUZHENSTERN	MIKHAIL KRUSKIY	

Builders:	Adolf Warski, Szczecin (Poland)
Displacement:	6,600 tons standard
	9,200 tons full load
Length:	482 ft 2 in (147.0 m) oa except LEONID DEMIN and MIKHAIL KRUSKIY
	485 ft 5 in (148.0 m) oa
Beam:	61 ft (18.6 m)
Draft:	20 ft 8 in (6.3 m)
Propulsion:	4 diesels; 16,000 hp; 2 shafts
Speed:	20.4 knots
Range:	23,000 n.miles at 15 knots
Complement:	approx. 90
Helicopters:	1 utility helicopter
Missiles:	none
Guns:	none
Radars:	3 Don-2 (navigation)

The AKADEMIK KRYLOV-class ships are among the few of this type with a helicopter hangar and landing deck. This is one of the last two ships, with a pointed stern.

These ships are the largest oceanographic research ships in Soviet service.

Classification: Soviet EHOS type.

Design: This class has graceful, liner-like lines with a crane on the long forecastle. There are 20 to 26 laboratories in each ship. There is a helicopter hangar and flight deck aft. The last two ships, the DEMIN (1978) and KRUSKIY (1979), have pointed sterns, slightly increasing their length.

The LEONID SOBELYEV is one of the large, graceful research ships that operate on many of the world's seas. Like most of the Soviet research fleet, the AKADEMIK KRYLOV class was built in Poland. (1985, L. & L. Van Ginderen)

1 OCEANOGRAPHIC RESEARCH SHIP: "DOBRYNYA NIKITICH" CLASS

Name	Completed
Vladimir Kavrayskiy	1973

Builders:	Admiralty, Leningrad
Displacement:	3,900 tons full load
Length:	229 ft 7 in (70.0 m) oa
Beam:	59 ft (18.0 m)
Draft:	21 ft (6.4 m)
Propulsion:	3 diesels (13D100) driving 3 generators connected to electric motors; 5,400 hp; 2 shafts
Speed:	15.5 knots
Range:	5,500 n.miles at 12.5 knots
	13,000 n.miles at 9.5 knots
Complement:	
Helicopters:	landing deck
Missiles:	none
Guns:	none
Radars:	2 Don-2 (navigation)

This ship is a Navy-manned icebreaker extensively modified for polar research. Sister ships serve with the KGB, Navy, and civilian agencies.

Design: The ship has a helicopter deck aft but no hangar; a helicopter control station is prominent at the after end of the superstructure. She is fitted with nine laboratories and has one 8-ton crane and two 3-ton booms.

4 OCEANOGRAPHIC RESEARCH SHIPS: "AKADEMIK KURCHATOV" CLASS

Name	Name	Completed
Abkhaziya	Bashkiriya	1972–1973
Adzhariya	Moldaviya	

Builders:	Mathias Thesen, Wismar (East Germany)
Displacement:	5,460 tons standard
	7,500 tons full load
Length:	409 ft (124.7 m) oa
Beam:	55 ft 9 in (17.0 m)
Draft:	21 ft (6.4 m)
Propulsion:	2 diesels (Halberstadt-MAN K6Z 57/80); 8,000 hp; 2 shafts
Speed:	21 knots
Range:	20,000 n.miles at 16 knots
Complement:	approx. 85
Helicopters:	1 utility helicopter
Missiles:	none
Guns:	none
Radars:	3 Don-2 (navigation)

These are Navy-manned research ships, similar to seven ships operated by the Academy of Science (see chapter 24).

Classification: Soviet EHOS type.

Design: Built with graceful, liner lines, these ships have a helicopter deck and telescoping hangar. There are 27 laboratories and extensive communications equipment (including Vee Cone antennas). Two 190-hp bow thrusters are fitted along with a 300-hp active rudder for precise station keeping.

Akademik Kurchatov-class research ship Abkhaziya; note Vee Cone HF antennas on mast abaft funnel.

The BASHKIRIYA of the AKADEMIK KURCHATOV class in heavy seas off Japan. These ships also have passenger-ship lines with a full helicopter capability. (1984, JMSDF)

8 OCEANOGRAPHIC RESEARCH SHIPS: "NIKOLAY ZUBOV" CLASS

Name	Name	Completed
ALEKSEY CHIRIKOV	FYDOR LITKE	
ANDREY VIL'KITSKIY	NIKOLAY ZUBOV	1964–1968
BORIS DAVYDOV	SEMEN DEZHNEV	
FADDEY BELLINGSGAUZEN	VASILIY GOLOVNIN	

Builders:	Adolf Warski, Szczecin (Poland)
Displacement:	2,200 tons standard
	3,020 tons full load
Length:	295 ft 2 in (90.0 m) oa
Beam:	42 ft 8 in (13.0 m)
Draft:	15 ft 5 in (4.7 m)
Propulsion:	2 diesels (Zgoda/Sulzer 8TD48); 4,800 hp; 2 shafts
Speed:	16.5 knots
Range:	11,000 n.miles at 14 knots
Complement:	approx. 50
Helicopters:	no facilities
Missiles:	none
Guns:	none
Radars:	2 Don-2 (navigation)

Eight of these ships are configured for oceanographic research, and three, listed separately, are AGIs. The lead ship, the NIKOLAY ZUBOV, was placed in commission on 1 April 1964.

Classification: Soviet EHOS type.

Design: These ships are designed for polar operations. They have two 7-ton and two 5-ton booms; fitted with nine laboratories. Details of the ships vary. The ZUBOV and possibly others have more elaborate communications equipment, including Vee Cone antennas.

NIKOLAY ZUBOV-class oceanographic research ship FADDEY BELLINGSGAUZEN. (1983, John Jedrlinic)

NIKOLAY ZUBOV-class oceanographic research ship SEMEN DEZHNEV. (1983, U.S. Navy)

3 OCEANOGRAPHIC RESEARCH SHIPS: "POLYUS" CLASS

Name	Completed
POLYUS	1962
BALKHASH	1964
BAYKAL	1964

Builders:	Neptun, Rostock (East Germany)
Displacement:	4,560 tons standard
	6,900 tons full load
Length:	366 ft (111.6 m) oa
Beam:	47 ft 3 in (14.4 m)
Draft:	20 ft 8 in (6.3 m)
Propulsion:	4 diesels driving 4 generators connected to 2 electric motors;
	4,000 hp; 1 shaft
Speed:	13.5 knots
Range:	25,000 n.miles at 12 knots
Complement:	

Helicopters:	no facilities
Missiles:	none
Guns:	none
Radars:	2 Don-2 (navigation) except 2 Palm Frond in BALKHASH

There ships were built on ANDIZHAN/KOVEL cargo hulls for the oceanographic research role.

Class: About 50 ships of this class were built for merchant use, including these research ships and other converted to missile test support ships; three ships serve as merchant cadet-training ships.

Classification: Soviet EHOS type.

Design: Details and masts vary (the POLYUS has her bridge mast aft of the funnel, others are forward, and the POLYUS has a pole mast forward while the others have goalposts). The ships have an active rudder and bow thruster for station keeping. There are 17 laboratories.

POLYUS-class oceanographic research ship BALKHASH.

1 OCEANOGRAPHIC RESEARCH SHIP: "NEVEL'SKOY"

Name	Completed
NEVEL'SKOY	1961

Builders:	Nikolayev
Displacement:	2,350 tons full load
Length:	274 ft 10 in (83.8 m) oa
Beam:	49 ft 10 in (15.2 m)
Draft:	12 ft 6 in (3.8 m)
Propulsion:	2 diesels; 4,000 hp; 2 shafts
Speed:	17 knots
Range:	10,000 n.miles at 11 knots
Complement:	approx. 45
Helicopters:	no facilities
Missiles:	none
Guns:	none
Radars:	2 Don-2 (navigation)

A one-of-a-kind ship, probably the prototype for the NIKOLAY ZUBOV class.

Classification: Soviet EHOS type.

The oceanographic research ship NEVEL'SKOY has the same basic arrangement as the NIKOLAY ZUBOV class, but with a much smaller bridge structure.

HYDROGRAPHIC SURVEY SHIPS

These ships conduct hydrographic surveys and service the extensive Soviet coastal waterways—surveying and marking channels, planting and retrieving buoys, etc. These ships are operated by the Navy's Hydrographic Service.

22 HYDROGRAPHIC SURVEY SHIPS: FENIK CLASS

Name	Name	Name	Completed
GS-44	GS-280	GS-400	
GS-47	GS-297	GS-401	
GS-86	GS-301	GS-402	
GS-87	GS-388	GS-403	1979–1981
GS-260	GS-392	GS-404	
GS-270	GS-397	GS-405	
GS-272	GS-398		
GS-278	GS-399		

Builders:	Polnocny, Gdansk (Poland)
Displacement:	1,200 tons full load
Length:	201 ft 1 in (61.3 m) oa
Beam:	38 ft 8 in (11.8 m)
Draft:	10 ft 9 in (3.3 m)
Propulsion:	2 diesels (Cegielski/Sulzer); 1,920 hp; 2 shafts (see notes)
Speed:	13 knots
Range:	3,000 n.miles at 13 knots
Complement:	approx. 30
Helicopters	no facilities
Missiles:	none
Guns:	none
Radars:	2 Don-2 (navigation)

These ships are employed for hydrographic surveys as well as buoy tending.

Class: One ship of this type has been provided to East Germany and four to Poland.

Design: A 7-ton-capacity crane is located forward, with a work area for handling buoys.

Engineering: The ships have two 75-kilowatt electric motors for quiet operation during surveys; they can reach six knots on these motors. A bow thruster is provided.

This Fenik-class hydrographic survey ship is typical of the large number of Soviet ships that conduct such surveys and maintain marker buoys and other navigational aids in Soviet waters. (1984, JMSDF)

Fenik-class hydrographic survey ship GS-404.

14 HYDROGRAPHIC SURVEY SHIPS: BIYA CLASS

Name	Name	Name	Completed
GS-182	GS-204	GS-269	
GS-193	GS-206	GS-271	
GS-194	GS-208	GS-273	1972–1976
GS-198	GS-210	GS-275	
GS-202	GS-214		

Builders:	Polnocny, Gdansk (Poland)
Displacement:	750 tons full load
Length:	180 ft 5 in (55.0 m) oa
Beam:	30 ft 2 in (9.2 m)
Draft:	8 ft 6 in (2.6 m)
Propulsion:	2 diesels; 1,200 hp; 2 shafts
Speed:	13 knots
Range:	4,700 n.miles at 11 knots
Complement:	approx. 25
Helicopters:	no facilities
Missiles:	none
Guns:	none
Radars:	1 Don-2 (navigation)

Small hydrographic survey and buoy tending ships.
Class: One ship transferred to Cuba and one to Guinea-Bissau.
Design: Fitted with 5-ton-capacity crane.

10 HYDROGRAPHIC SURVEY SHIPS: KAMENKA CLASS

Name	Name	Name	Completed
GS-66	GS-107	GS-203	
GS-74	GS-108 (ex-VERNIER)	GS-207	1968–1972
GS-82	GS-114 (ex-BEL'BEK)	GS-211	
GS-103			

Builders:	Polnocny, Gdansk (Poland)
Displacement:	703 tons full load
Length:	175 ft 6 in (53.5 m) oa
Beam:	29 ft 10 in (9.1 m)
Draft:	8 ft 6 in (2.6 m)
Propulsion:	2 diesels; 1,765 hp; 2 shafts
Speed:	13.7 knots
Range:	4,000 n.miles at 10 knots
Complement	approx. 40
Helicopters:	no facilities
Missiles:	none
Guns:	none
Radars:	1 Don-2 (navigation)

These ships are similar to the Biya class, but have more buoy-handling capability. Fitted with 5-ton-capacity crane.

Class: One ship of this class was transferred from the Soviet Navy to Cape Verde; another ship serves with the East German Navy.

Kamenka-class hydrographic survey ship GS-108.

Kamenka-class hydrographic survey ship.

18 HYDROGRAPHIC SURVEY SHIPS
1 OCEANOGRAPHIC RESEARCH SHIP } MOMA CLASS

Name	Name	Name	Completed
AL'TAYR	CHELEKEN	OKEAN	
ANADYR'	EL'TON	RYBACHIY (ex-ODOGRAF)	
ANDROMEDA	KOLGUEV		
ANTARES	KRIL'ON	SEVER	1967–1974
ANTARTIKA	LIMAN	TAYMYR	
ARTIKA	MARS	ZAPOLAR'E	
ASKOL'D	MORZHOVETS		

Builders:	Polnocny, Gdansk (Poland)
Displacement:	1,260 tons standard
	1,540 tons full load
Length:	240 ft 5 in (73.3 m) oa
Beam:	35 ft 5 in (10.8 m)
Draft:	12 ft 6 in (3.8 m)
Propulsion:	2 diesels (Zgoda/Sulzer 6TD46); 3,600 hp; 2 shafts
Speed:	17 knots
Range:	8,700 n.miles at 11 knots
Complement:	approx. 55
Helicopters:	no facilities
Missiles:	2 quad SA-N-5 Grail launchers [32] in RYBACHIY
Guns:	4 12.7-mm machine guns (2 twin) in RYBACHIY
Radars:	2 Don-2 (navigation)

These are large hydrographic survey and research ships, which also tend buoys.

Class: Nine ships of this class serve in the AGI role with the Soviet Navy. Others have been built at the Polnocny shipyard for the Bulgarian, Polish, and Yugoslav navies.

Design: There are large work areas forward and aft, with a 7-ton-capacity crane forward. Four laboratories are provided.

The RYBACHIY has a deckhouse forward (no crane) and has been armed. She is reported to be involved in oceanographic research.

Moma-class oceanographic research ship RYBACHIY, with deckhouse forward (no crane). (1982, U.S. Navy)

15 HYDROGRAPHIC SURVEY SHIPS: SAMARA CLASS

Name	Name	Name	Completed
AZIMUT	GRADUS	TURA (ex-GLOBUS)	
DEVIATOR	KOMPAS	VAYGACH	
GIGROMETR	PAMYAT' MERKURIYA	VOSTOK	1962–1964
GLUBOMETR	RUMB (GS-118)	GS-275 (ex-YUG)	
GORIZONT	TROPIK	ZENIT	

Builders:	Polnocny, Gdansk (Poland)
Displacement:	1,050 tons standard
	1,276 tons full load
Length:	193 ft 6 in (59.0 m) oa
Beam:	34 ft 1 in (10.4 m)
Draft:	12 ft 6 in (3.8 m)
Propulsion:	2 diesels (Zgoda 5TD48); 3,000 hp; 2 shafts
Speed:	15.5 knots
Range:	6,200 n.miles at 11 knots
Complement:	approx. 45
Helicopters:	no facilities
Missiles:	none
Guns:	none
Radars:	2 Don-2 (navigation)

Hydrographic research ships and buoy tenders. The TURA is employed in a training role. The DEVIATOR has served as an AGI.

Design: The ships are fitted with a 7-ton-capacity crane. The TURA has a large deckhouse forward (crane removed); she can accommodate a total of 120 men.

Moma-class AGI TAYMYR in the Sea of Japan during the KAL 007 search. (1983, U.S. Navy)

Samara-class hydrographic survey ship VAYGACH; note added deckhouse between crane and bridge. (1982, U.S. Navy)

3 HYDROGRAPHIC SURVEY SHIPS: MELITOPOL CLASS

Name	Name	Name	Completed
MAYAK	NIVILER	PRIZMA	1952–1955

Builders:	(USSR)
Displacement:	1,200 tons full load
Tonnage:	776 DWT
Length:	188 ft 11 in (57.6 m) oa

Melitopol-class hydrographic survey ship.

Beam:	29 ft 6 in (9.0 m)
Draft:	14 ft 1 in (4.3 m)
Propulsion:	1 diesel (6DR 30/40); 600 hp; 1 shaft
Speed:	11 knots
Range:	2,500 n.miles at 10.5 knots
Complement:	
Helicopters:	no facilities
Missiles:	none
Guns:	none
Radars:	1 Don (navigation)

These are the only Soviet-built ships employed as naval hydrographic survey ships. They were converted from small cargo ships.

HYDROGRAPHIC SURVEY SHIPS: TELNOVSK CLASS

All ships of this class are believed to have been discarded. See 3rd edition (page 305).

INSHORE SURVEY CRAFT

Several INSHORE SURVEY CRAFT: GPB-480 CLASS

Completed:	1960s
Builders:	(USSR)
Displacement:	120 tons full load
Length:	95 ft 2 in (29.0 m) oa
Beam:	16 ft 5 in (5.0 m)
Draft:	55 ft 9 in (1.7 m)
Propulsion:	1 diesel; 450 hp; 1 shaft
Speed:	12 knots
Range:	1,600 n.miles at 10 knots
Complement:	approx. 15
Guns:	none
Radars:	1 Spin Trough (search)

These craft have the same hull and propulsion plant as the Nyryat I-class diving tenders. Two 1½-ton booms are fitted.
Classification: Soviet GPB type.

Several INSHORE SURVEY BOATS: GPB-710 CLASS

Builders:	(USSR)
Displacement:	7 tons full load
Length:	36 ft 1 in (11.0 m) oa
Beam:	9 ft 10 in (3.0 m)
Draft:	2 ft 3 in (0.7 m)
Propulsion:	diesel
Speed:	10 knots
Range:	150 n.miles at 10 knots
Complement:	
Guns:	none
Radars:	

These boats are carried on board larger oceanographic and hydrographic survey ships.

MISSILE RANGE INSTRUMENTATION SHIPS

These Navy-manned ships support the Soviet test firings of long-range ballistic missiles (ICBMs and SLBMs) and can additionally support military space activities. The civilian-manned Space Event Support Ships (SESS), described in chapter 24, do not normally provide range instrumentation for missiles.

(1) MISSILE RANGE INSTRUMENTATION SHIP (NUCLEAR-PROPELLED)

Name	Launched	Completed
. . . . . .	1983	Building

Builders:	Baltic Shipyard, Leningrad
Displacement:	
Length:	approx. 850 ft (259.15 m) oa
Beam:	
Draft:	
Propulsion:	steam turbines; 2 shafts
Reactors:	2
Speed:	
Range:	
Complement:	
Helicopters:	
Missiles:	
Guns:	
Radars:	

This will be the world's largest scientific ship when completed.

1 + 1 MISSILE RANGE INSTRUMENTATION SHIPS: "MARSHAL NEDELIN" CLASS

Name	Completed
MARSHAL NEDELIN	1983
. . . . . .	Building

Builders:	Admiralty (Leningrad)
Displacement:	24,000 tons full load
Length:	698 ft 8 in (213.0 m) oa
Beam:	88 ft 11 in (27.1 m)
Draft:	25 ft 3 in (7.7 m)
Propulsion:	diesel; 2 shafts
Speed:	
Range:	
Complement:	
Helicopters:	2 to 4 Ka-25 Hormone-C/Ka-27 Helix
Missiles:	
Guns:	(see notes)
Radars:	

These are the largest Navy-operated scientific ships pending completion of the nuclear-propelled unit. The NEDELIN transferred to the Far East in 1984.

Names: Chief Marshal of Artillery M.I. Nedelin was the first commander in chief of the Soviet Strategic Rocket Forces, assuming the post in 1959. He was killed in October of the following year in the accidental explosion of an ICBM.

These ships have foundations for the installation of six 30-mm Gatling guns and three associated Bass Tilt radar directors.

The MARSHAL NEDELIN, the first of a new class of missile range instrumentation ships operated by tne Soviet Navy. The massive ship also serves as a sea-based terminal for Soviet spacecraft data and communication links, and could provide naval command ship facilities.

2 MISSILE RANGE INSTRUMENTATION SHIPS: DESNA CLASS

Name	Completed
CHAZHMA (ex-DANGERA)	1963
CHUMIKAN (ex-DOLGESCHTCHEL'YE)	1963

Builders:	Warnow, Warnemünde (East Germany)
Displacement:	13,500 tons full load
Length:	458 ft 11 in (139.9 m) oa
Beam:	59 ft (18.0 m)
Draft:	25 ft 11 in (7.9 m)
Propulsion:	1 diesel (MAN); 5,400 hp; 1 shaft
Speed:	15 knots
Range:	12,000 n.miles at 13 knots
Complement:	
Helicopters:	1 or 2 Ka-25 Hormone-C
Missiles:	none
Guns:	none
Radars:	2 Don-2 (navigation)
	1 Head Net-B (air search)
	1 Ship Globe (tracking)
EW systems:	2 Watch Dog

These are missile range instrumentation ships converted from DZHANKOY-class ore/coal carriers. Both ships operate in the Pacific.

Class: The Warnow yard delivered 15 merchant ships of the DZHANKOY design (9,750 DWT) to the Soviet merchant fleet between 1960 and 1962.

Classification: Soviet OS type.

Design: These ships have a distinctive arrangement, with two island superstructure groupings. Three large missile tracking directors are mounted forward with the Ship Globe radome mounted above the forward island structure. The after structure consists of the funnel, with a faired-in mast mounting two Vee Cone communication antennas, and a helicopter hangar on each side of the funnel. There is a large helicopter landing area aft.

(The merchant ships of the DZHANKOY type are superstructure-aft ships.)

Electronics: These are the only ships fitted with the Head Net-B radar.

One of the DESNA-class missile range instrumentation ships. There are three missile trackers forward of the bridge. The short stack is surmounted by a mast carrying Vee Cone HF antennas. The Navy-manned missile/space support ships have helicopter facilities; the civilian SESS do not.

4 MISSILE RANGE INSTRUMENTATION SHIPS: "SIBIR'" CLASS

Name	Name	Completed
CHUKOTA	SIBIR'	}1958
SAKHALIN	SPASSK (ex-SUCHAN)	

Builders:	Adolf Warski, Szczecin (Poland)
Displacement:	7,800 tons full load
Length:	354 ft 11 in (108.2 m) oa
Beam:	47 ft 11 in (14.6 m)
Draft:	23 ft 7 in (7.2 m)
Propulsion:	compound piston with low-pressure turbine; 2,500 hp; 1 shaft
Boilers:	2
Speed:	11.5 knots
Range:	11,800 n.miles at 12 knots
Helicopters:	1 Ka-25 Hormone-C (no hangar)
Missiles:	none
Guns:	none
Radars:	1 Big Net or Head Net-C (3-D air search)
	2 Don-2 (navigation)

These ships were converted during construction from DONBASS-class cargo ships. They were Polish built but completed in Leningrad; all converted about 1960 to the missile range instrumentation role. All four ships operate in the Pacific.

Class: More than 40 DONBASS-class cargo ships (approx. 4,900 DWT) were delivered to the Soviet merchant fleet between 1952 and 1958, plus units delivered to other communist fleets.

Classification: Soviet OS type.

Design: The CHUKOTA is flush-decked; the others have a well deck forward. They have an impressive appearance, with large antenna-bearing kingposts forward and aft of the central superstructure. Two or three missile tracking directors are mounted forward of the bridge. A large helicopter platform is fitted aft. One utility helicopter is normally embarked, although the ships do not have a hangar.

The SIBIR'-class missile range instrumentation ships are easily distinguished by the large after kingpost carrying the Big Net or Head Net-C radar antenna and by the helicopter platform (but no hangar). Both ships shown here have a Hormone-C on deck.

SIBIR'-class missile range instrumentation ship CHUKOTA. (1981, U. S. Navy)

24
Civilian Auxiliary Ships

The Soviet Union's civilian research fleet continues to expand at a remarkable rate. During the past decade (through the end of 1985) the fleet has increased by more than 50 ships. This is in addition to Navy-manned units and the civilian-manned Space Event Support Ships (SESS), which perform "maritime" research, and naval research ships. While some of the new civilian ships are replacing older units, there is still a significant rate of growth.

Although the entire Soviet Merchant Marine is available to support the nation's military establishment, the Space Event Support Ships (SESS),

research ships, icebreakers, and some of the training ships appear to provide regular support to naval activities.

In addition to the civilian research ships listed here, there are more than 50 fisheries research ships in service under the aegis of the Ministry of Fisheries (see chapter 32).

These ships are civilian-manned. None of them is armed although the nuclear-propelled icebreakers of the ARKTIKA class were armed during sea trials, and there are mounting fixtures for weapons in the YUG-class research ships and possibly some other classes.

A large number of Soviet civilian-manned ships provide support to naval research, training, and auxiliary activities. The major civilian specialized ships (i.e., non-cargo and non-passenger) are listed here. The close association of the Navy with other maritime activities is demonstrated with the civilian nuclear icebreaker ROSSIYA; here the ship is shown with Top Plate radar, Drum Tilt FCS (forward of bridge), and a 76.2-mm gun mount on the bow for sea trials. Her "wartime" outfit also includes 30-mm Gatling guns. (1985)

SPACE EVENT SUPPORT SHIPS

These ships support civilian and military space activities as well as upper-atmosphere research and communications research programs. All operate under the direction of the Academy of Sciences.

Beyond their primary research activities, these ships are well suited to the collateral activities of intelligence collection and military communications relay.

4 SPACE CONTROL-MONITORING SHIPS: "KOSMONAUT PAVEL BELYAYEV" CLASS

Name	Completed	Conversion Completed
KOSMONAUT PAVEL BELYAYEV (ex-VYTEGRALES)	1963	1977
KOSMONAUT VLADILAV VOLKOV (ex-YENISEILES)	1964	1977
KOSMONAUT GEORGIY DOBROVOSLKIY (ex-SEMYON KOSINOV)	1968	1978
KOSMONAUT VIKTOR PATSAYEV (ex-NAZAR GUBIN)	1968	1978

Builders:	Zhdanov, Leningrad
Displacement:	9,000 tons full load
Tonnage:	2,010 DWT
Length:	399 ft 6 in (121.8 m) oa
Beam:	54 ft 11 in (16.75 m)
Draft:	23 ft 11 in (7.3 m)
Propulsion:	1 diesel (Bryansk/Burmeister & Wain 950 VTBF 110); 5,200 hp; 1 shaft
Speed:	14.5 knots
Range:	
Complement:	approx. 90
Helicopters:	no facilities
Radars:	1 Don-2 (navigation)
	1 Kite Screech (tracking)
	1 Okean (navigation)

These ships were converted from VYTEGRALES-class cargo/timber carriers. Their conversion permitted two ships, the BEZHITSA and RISTNA, temporarily employed in this role, to return to merchant cargo service.

Class: The Zhdanov yard produced 36 timber carriers of this type for the Soviet merchant fleet, of which eight were transferred to the Soviet Navy for conversion to auxiliary roles, and another eight were converted to the SESS role (BELYAYEV and BOROVICHI classes). A design derived from the VYTEGRALES class has been built at the Vyborg yard; the Navy's PIONEER MOSKVYY salvage ships are from the latter group.

Electronics: A Quad Spring communication antenna array is fitted amidships in addition to smaller satellite communication antennas.

Names: Civilian scientific ships are named for Soviet kosmonauts/astronauts and scientists. Yuri Gagarin was the first man to fly in space; he was killed in an airplane crash in 1968. Sergei Korolev was the foremost Soviet designer of guided and ballistic missiles and spacecraft; he died in 1966.

SESS KOSMONAUT VIKTOR PATSAYEV. (1983, L. & L. Van Ginderen)

The SESS Kosmonaut Viktor Patsayev at Rotterdam (with the Dutch flag flying from the foremast). There is a large, four-element tracking antenna amidships as well as three of the smaller Quad Ring telemetry antennas, two mounted atop the bridge and one abaft the funnel; numerous communications antennas are also fitted. (1984, L. & L. Van Ginderen)

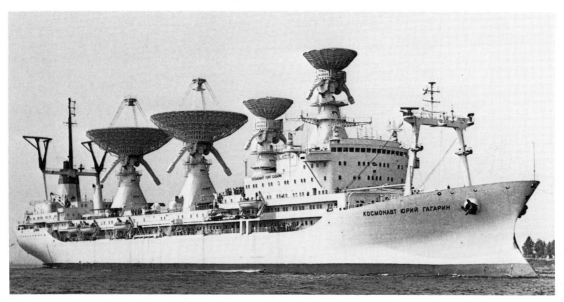

The SESS Kosmonaut Yuri Gagarin with four massive tracking antennas atop the superstructure and two pairs of Vee Cone HF antennas fitted aft. (1982, L. & L. Van Ginderen)

1 SPACE CONTROL-MONITORING SHIP: "KOSMONAUT YURI GAGARIN"

Name	Completed
KOSMONAUT YURI GAGARIN	Dec 1971

Builders:	Baltic, Leningrad
Displacement:	53,500 tons standard
Tonnage:	31,300 DWT
Length:	760 ft (231.7 m) oa
Beam:	102 ft (31.1 m)
Draft:	32 ft 10 in (10.0 m)
Propulsion:	2 steam turbines (Kirov) with electric drive; 19,000 shp, 1 shaft
Boilers:	2
Speed:	17.7 knots
Range:	24,000 n.miles at 17.7 knots
Complement:	approx. 160 + 180 scientists-technicians
Helicopters:	no facilities
Radars:	1 Don-Kay (navigation)
	1 Okean (navigation)

The GAGARIN is the world's largest ship fitted for scientific activities and the largest ship in service with turbo-electric propulsion. The ship was built for scientific purposes with a SOFIYA-class tanker hull and propulsion plant.

Class: Twenty-two tankers of the SOFIYA class were built at two Soviet yards; one serves as a naval tanker (AKHTUBA).

Design: The ship has a large bulbous bow and is fitted with bow and stern thrusters. Recreation facilities include three swimming pools and a theater seating 300 persons plus a sports hall.

Electronics: The ship's tracking-communications equipment includes Quad Ring, Ship Bowl, Ship Shell, and Vee Tube antennas. (Two pair of the last—HF antennas—are rigged outboard of the ship's funnel.)

SESS KOSMONAUT YURI GAGARIN. (1983)

1 SPACE CONTROL-MONITORING SHIP: "AKADEMIK SERGEI KOROLEV"

Name	Completed
AKADEMIK SERGEI KOROLEV	Dec 1970

Builders:	Black Sea Shipyard, Nikolayev
Displacement:	17,115 tons standard
	21,250 tons full load
Tonnage:	7,067 DWT
Length:	596 ft 8 in (181.9 m) oa
Beam:	82 ft (25.0 m)
Draft:	25 ft 11 in (7.9 m)
Propulsion:	1 diesel (Bryansk/Burmeister & Wain); 12,000 hp; 1 shaft

Speed:	17.5 knots
Range:	22,500 n.miles at 16 knots
Complement:	approx. 190 + 170 scientist-technicians
Helicopters:	no facilities
Radars:	2 Don-Kay (navigation)

Although smaller than the GAGARIN, this is still a large and imposing SESS. The KOROLEV was built from the keel up for this role.

Electronics: Tracking and communications equipment includes Quad Ring, Ship Bowl, Ship Globe, and Vee Tube antennas (with the last, in pairs, angled out from the funnel).

The SESS AKADEMIK SERGEI KOROLEV has Quad Ring antennas atop the bridge as well as another antenna housed in a radome. There are two large tracking antennas amidships and aft, with paired Vee Tube antennas mounted on a kingpost-like structure just forward of the funnel.

1 SPACE CONTROL-MONITORING SHIP: "KOSMONAUT VLADIMIR KOMAROV"

Name	Completed
KOSMONAUT VLADIMIR KOMAROV (ex-GENICHESK)	1966

Builders:	Kherson
Displacement:	11,090 tons standard
	17,500 tons full load
Tonnage:	7,065 DWT
Length:	510 ft 8 in (155.7 m) oa
Beam:	76 ft 5 in (23.3 m)
Draft:	28 ft 2 in (8.6 m)
Propulsion:	1 diesel (Bryansk/Burmeister & Wain); 9,000 hp; 1 shaft
Speed:	17.5 knots
Range:	16,700 n.miles at 17.5 knots

Complement:	approx. 115 + 125 scientists-technicians
Helicopters:	no facilities
Radars:	2 Don-Kay (navigation)

The KOMAROV was converted during construction from a POLTAVA-class dry cargo ship, with her conversion being completed in Leningrad.

Class: In addition to the KOMAROV, between 1962 and 1967 two Soviet yards produced 20 of the POLTAVA-class general cargo ships for the Soviet merchant fleet, plus another 31 ships for West Germany, Hungary, Iraq, India, Kuwait, and Pakistan.

Electronics: Tracking and communications antennas include 2 Quad Ring, 2 Ship Globe, and 1 Ship Wheel, plus 2 Vee Cone HF antennas at the masthead.

The SESS KOSMONAUT VLADIMIR KOMAROV provides a sleek appearance with three tracking antennas fitted within radomes and the paired Vee Cone HF antennas on separate, tandem masts. The second mast is faired into the funnel. There are two Quad Rings and another antenna forward. (1984)

4 SPACE CONTROL-MONITORING SHIPS: "BOROVICHI" CLASS

Name	Completed	Name	Completed
BOROVICHI	1965	MORZHOVETS	1966
KEGOSTROV	1966	NEVEL	1966

Builders:	Zhdanov, Leningrad
Displacement:	7,600 tons full load
Tonnage:	1,834 DWT
Length:	399 ft 11 in (121.9 m) oa
Beam:	54 ft 11 in (16.75 m)
Draft:	15 ft 5 in (4.7 m)
Propulsion:	1 diesel (Bryansk/Burmeister & Wain 950 VTBF 110); 5,200 hp; 1 shaft
Speed:	15.5 knots
Range:	7,400 n.miles at 15 knots
Complement:	approx. 80
Helicopters:	no facilities
Radars:	2 Don-2 (navigation)

These ships were laid down as VYTEGRALES-type cargo ships, but were completed to an SESS configuration. These ships differ in config-uration from the BELYAYEV class, which were converted after service as cargo ships (see above for class notes).

SESS MORZHOVETS. (1984)

The KEGOTROV is typical of the second class of space event support ships converted from VYTEGRALES-class cargo ships. Their tracking and communications capabilities appear to be less than any other dedicated SESS class. (1986, L. & L. Van Ginderen *collection*)

RESEARCH SHIPS

(2) HYDROGRAPHIC RESEARCH SHIPS: NEW CONSTRUCTION

Builders:	Rauma-Repola, Rauma (Finland)
Displacement:	
Tonnage:	920 GRT
Length:	163 ft 4 in (49.8 m) oa
Beam:	34 ft 5 1/2 in (10.5 m)
Draft:	6 ft 7 in (2.0 m)
Propulsion:	2 diesels; electric drive; 1,114 hp; 2 rudder-propellers (see notes)
Speed:	11 knots
Range:	
Complement:	approx. 30
Helicopters:	no facilities
Radars:	

Both ships ordered 28 February 1985.

Engineering: Propulsion and station keeping are achieved through the use of two (shrouded) rudder-propellers.

1+1 RESEARCH SHIPS: NEW CONSTRUCTION

Name	Completed
. . . . . .	1986
. . . . . .	Building

Builders:	Hollming, Rauma (Finland)
Displacement:	approx. 6,000 tons full load
Tonnage:	
Length:	approx. 393 ft 7 in (120.0 m) oa
Beam:	59 ft 8 1/2 in (18.2 m)
Draft:	19 ft 4 in (5.9 m)
Propulsion:	2 diesels (SEMT-Pielstick/Russkiy 6PC2.5 L400); 7,000 hp; 2 shafts

Speed:	15 knots
Range:	
Complement:	
Helicopters:	no facilities
Radars:	

These are large research ships ordered on 13 May 1985; to complete 1986–1987. These will be the largest civilian research ships completed for the Soviet Union in two decades (not including SESS).

2 SEAFLOOR RESEARCH SHIPS: "BAVENIT" CLASS

Name	Completed
BAVENIT	Building
. . . . . .	Building

Builders:	Hollming, Rauma (Finland)
Displacement:	5,300 tons full load
Tonnage:	
Length:	281 ft 5 in (85.8 m) oa
Beam:	55 ft 1 in (16.8 m)
Draft:	18 ft 4 in (5.6 m)
Propulsion:	4 diesels (Russkiy EG-74); electric drive; 1,700 hp; 2 rudder-propellers
Speed:	13 knots
Range:	8,000 n.miles at 12 knots
Complement:	approx. 65
Helicopters:	no facilities
Radars:	2 . . . (navigation)

These are seafloor research ships, fitted for drilling at depths to 300 meters. A 35-ton derrick is fitted amidships to support the drilling operations, and a large A-frame gantry is fitted at the stern. Operated by the Institute of Thermal Physics of the Far Eastern Academy of Sciences. Two 1,360-hp bow thrusters are provided.

4+ GEOPHYSICAL RESEARCH SHIPS: "AKADEMIK FERSMAN" CLASS

Name	Completed
AKADEMIK FERSMAN	1985
AKADEMIK SHATSKIY	1985
. . . . . .	1986
. . . . . .	1986

Builders:	Szczecin (Poland)
Displacement:	approx. 3,300 tons full load
Tonnage:	
Length:	268 ft 6 in (81.85 m) oa
Beam:	48 ft 6 in (14.8 m)
Draft:	16 ft 5 in (5.0 m)
Propulsion:	1 diesel (Zgoda-Sulzer 6 ZL 40/48); 4,200 hp; 1 shaft
Speed:	14.5 knots
Range:	
Complement:	approx. 60
Helicopters:	no facilities
Radars:	2 . . . (navigation)

Research ships intended to support offshore gas and oil exploration and exploitation. The lead ship was launched on 24 January 1985. Several additional units are under construction.

The ships have extensive laboratory facilities and two have a six-kilometer seismic sonar array. Fitted with bow thruster.

2 HYDROGRAPHIC RESEARCH SHIPS: NEW CONSTRUCTION

Name	Completed
GS-525	Nov 1985
GS-526	Dec 1985

Builders:	Rauma-Repola, Rauma (Finland)
Displacement:	450 tons full load
Tonnage:	
Length:	105 ft 11 in (32.3 m) oa
Beam:	31 ft 6 in (9.6 m)
Draft:	8 ft 6 in (2.6 m)
Propulsion:	2 diesels (Baikal 300); 600 hp; 2 shafts
Speed:	10 knots
Range:	
Complement:	
Helicopters:	no facilities
Radars:	

These are small, echo-sweeping craft.

6 GEOPHYSICAL/HYDROGRAPHIC RESEARCH SHIPS: "AKADEMIK BORIS PETROV" CLASS

Name	Launched	Completed
AKADEMIK BORIS PETROV	7 July 1983	29 June 1984
AKADEMIK M.A. LAVRENT'YEV	28 Oct 1983	12 Oct 1984
AKADEMIK NIKOLAI STRAKHOV	3 Feb 1984	14 May 1985
AKADEMIK OPARIN	1 Feb 1985	29 Nov 1985
. . . . . .	1985	1986
. . . . . .	1986	1986

Builders:	Hollming, Rauma (Finland)
Displacement:	2,550 tons full load

Tonnage:	
Length:	247 ft 8 in (75.5 m) oa
Beam:	48 ft 3 in (14.7 m)
Draft:	14 ft 9 in (4.5 m)
Propulsion:	1 diesel (SEMT-Pielstick/Russkiy 6PC2.5 L400); 3,500 hp; 1 shaft
Speed:	15.25 knots
Range:	15,000 n.miles at 14.75 knots
Complement:	approx. 75
Helicopters:	no facilities
Radars:	1 Okean (navigation)
	1 . . . (navigation)

Intended for geophysical and hydrographic surveys, these ships were ordered on 17 June 1982 (three ships) and 28 June 1984 (three ships). A bow thruster is fitted for station keeping and precise maneuvering.

1 GEOLOGICAL RESEARCH SHIP: "GEOLOG PRIMOR'YE"

Name	Completed
GEOLOG PRIMOR'YE	Oct 1983

Builders:	Vladivostok
Displacement:	
Tonnage:	2,000 DWT
Length:	281 ft 5 in (85.8 m) oa
Beam:	55 ft 1 in (16.8 m) each hull
Draft:	18 ft 4 in (5.6 m)
Propulsion:	2 diesels; 2 shafts
Speed:	9 knots
Range:	
Complement:	
Helicopters:	no facilities
Radars:	

The GEOLOG PRIMOR'YE is a catamaran research ship employed to search for seafloor mineral resources. The ship is fitted with two 1,150-hp bow thrusters.

10+4 RESEARCH SHIPS: "AKADEMIK SHULEYKIN" CLASS

Name	Completed	Name	Completed
AKADEMIK SHOKALSKIY	1982	AKADEMIK GOLITSIN	1984
AKADEMIK SHULEYKIN	1982	PROFESSOR POLSHAOV	1984
PROFESSOR PAVEL MOLCHANOV	1982	GEOLOG DIMITRIY NALYVKIN	1985
PROFESSOR KHROMOV	1983	AKADEMIK ALEKSANDR SIDORENKO	1984
PROFESSOR MULTANOVSKIY	1983	. . . . (4 units)	Building
AKADEMIK GAMBURTSHEV	1984		

Builders:	Laivateollisuus, Turku (Finland)
Displacement:	2,140 tons full load
Tonnage:	620 DWT
Length:	234 ft 10 in (71.6 m) oa
Beam:	42 ft (12.8 m)
Draft:	15 ft 9 in (4.8 m)
Propulsion:	2 diesels (Gorkiy G-74); 3,060 hp; 2 shafts
Speed:	12 knots
Range:	14,000 n.miles at 12 knots
Complement:	approx. 40 + 38 scientists-technicians
Helicopters:	no facilities
Radars:	2 Okean (navigation)

These are medium-size research ships, the first five being operated by the Academy of Sciences and the second five by the Ministry of Geology. At least four additional ships of this class are under construction.

Design: Funnel-aft design especially fitted for cold-weather operations. Bow thrusters are provided.

1 RESEARCH SHIP: "AKADEMIK ALEKSEY KRYLOV"

Name	Completed
AKADEMIK ALEKSEY KRYLOV	1981

Builders:	Okean Shipyard, Nikolayev
Displacement:	9,920 tons full load
Tonnage:	1,930 DWT
Length:	409 ft (124.7 m) oa
Beam:	57 ft 4 in (17.5 m)
Draft:	23 ft 9 in (7.2 m)
Propulsion:	2 diesels (58D-6R); 9,000 hp; 2 shafts
Speed:	16 knots
Range:	10,000 n.miles at 16 knots
Complement:	approx. 130
Helicopters:	no facilities
Radars:	1 Don-2 (navigation)
	1 Okean (navigation)

This is a large scientific research ship. A research submersible is hangared on the port side, with an internal gantry crane for lowering and raising the craft. Bow and stern thrusters are fitted for station keeping and precise maneuvering. The ship operates in the Pacific.

The PROFESSOR MULTANOVSKIY is one of a large class of medium-size research ships in Soviet scientific work. There are cranes and lift devices for handling research equipment forward and aft.

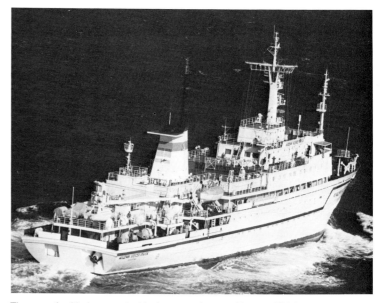

The one-of-a-kind research ship AKADEMIK ALEKSEY KRYLOV. This large ship carries a submersible (port side). (1983)

Research ship AKADEMIK SHULEYKIN. (1983, U.S. Navy)

3 HYDROGRAPHIC-METEOROLOGICAL RESEARCH SHIPS: "VITYAZ'" CLASS

Name	Completed
VITYAZ'	1981
AKADEMIK ALEKSANDR NESMEYANOV	1982
AKADEMIK ALEKSANDR VINOGRADOV	1983

Builders:	Adolf Warski, Szczecin (Poland)
Displacement:	5,700 tons full load
Tonnage:	1,790 DWT
Length:	363 ft 9 in (110.9 m) oa
Beam:	54 ft 5 in (16.6 m)
Draft:	18 ft 8 in (5.7 m)
Propulsion:	2 diesels (Zgoda/Sulzer); 6,400 hp; 2 shafts
Speed:	16 knots
Range:	16,000 n.miles at 16 knots
Complement:	approx. 16 + 65 scientists-technicians
Helicopters:	no facilities
Radars:	1 Don-2 (navigation)
	1 Okean (navigation)

Seabed research ships operated by the Academy of Sciences.

Design: These ships are of the Polish B-86 design. They are fitted with 20 to 26 laboratories and have provisions for deep-sea "saturation" diving to depths of 850 feet.

They each can also carry a manned research submersible of the Argus type.

1 OCEANOGRAPHIC RESEARCH SHIP: "AKADEMIK MSTISLAV KELDYSH"

Name	Completed
AKADEMIK MSTISLAV KELDYSH	1980

Builders:	Hollming, Rauma (Finland)
Displacement:	approx. 6,500 tons full load
Tonnage:	1,500 DWT
Length:	400 ft 10 in (122.2 m) oa
Beam:	58 ft 5 in (17.8 m)
Draft:	17 ft 9 in (5.4 m)
Propulsion:	4 diesels (Wartisla/Vasa 824B); 5,820 hp; 2 shafts

Speed:	16 knots
Range:	20,000 n.miles at 16 knots
Complement:	approx. 50 + 80 scientists-technicians
Helicopters:	no facilities
Radars:	

This is the world's largest oceanographic research ship. The ship is operated by the Academy of Sciences.

Design: Fitted with a bow thrusters and a stern propulsor. There are 18 laboratories plus space for support vans. A Pisces-type submersible is carried.

1 RESEARCH ICEBREAKER: "DOBRYNYA NIKITICH" CLASS

Name	Completed
OTTO SCHMIDT	1979

Builders:	Admiralty, Leningrad
Displacement:	3,650 tons full load
Tonnage:	1,095 DWT
Length:	239 ft 5 in (73.0 m) oa
Beam:	59 ft (18.0 m)
Draft:	21 ft (6.4 m)
Propulsion:	3 diesels (13D100); 5,400 hp; 3 generators connected to electric motors; 2 shafts
Speed:	14.5 knots
Range:	5,500 n.miles at 12 knots
	13,000 n.miles at 9.4 knots
Complement:	approx. 50 + 30 scientists-technicians
Helicopters:	no facilities
Radars:	

The ship is operated by the Arctic Research Institute of the Academy of Sciences. There are 14 laboratories.

Class: Thirty units of this basic design have been built, also being operated by the Navy (see chapters 22 and 23) and the KGB Maritime Border Troops (chapter 25). See page 320 for class notes.

Design: Details vary from other ships of this class.

The research ship AKADEMIK ALEKSANDR NESMEYANOV shows the twin-funnel configuration of the Polish B-86 trawler design. (1983, L. & L. Van Ginderen)

Research ship AKADEMIK MSTISLAV KELDYSH. (1982, U.S. Navy)

1 SEISMIC RESEARCH SHIP: "SHELF II"

Name	Completed	Converted
SHELF II (ex-LONGVA)	1962	1977

Builders:	A.M. Liasen, Alesund (Norway)
Displacement:	approx. 1,400 tons full load
Length:	206 ft 8 in (63.0 m) oa
Beam:	32 ft 10 in (10.0 m)
Draft:	13 ft 9 in (4.2 m)
Propulsion:	1 diesel ((Humboldt-Klockner-Deutz); 1,500 hp; 1 shaft
Speed:	13 knots
Range:	
Complement	approx. 50
Helicopters:	no facilities
Radars:	3 ...... (navigation)

This ship is especially configured for seismic research to support oil exploration. The ship was purchased in 1977. Fitted with passive stabilization tanks and bow thruster.

1 SEAFLOOR RESEARCH SHIP: "SHELF I"

Name	Completed
SHELF I	1976

Builders:	(USSR)
Displacement:	
Tonnage:	193 DWT
Length:	205 ft 4 in (62.6 m) oa
Beam:	34 ft 5 in (10.5 m)
Draft:	10 ft 2 in (3.1 m)
Propulsion:	2 diesels; 2 shafts
Speed:	
Range:	
Complement:	
Helicopters:	
Radars:	

Specialized ship for developing seafloor mining techniques; capable of supporting operations to a depth of 325 feet.

1 POLAR RESEARCH AND LOGISTICS SHIP: "MIKHAIL SOMOV"

Name	Launched	Completed
MIKHAIL SOMOV	Mar 1975	1975

Builders:	Kherson
Displacement:	5,000 tons standard
	14,000 tons full load
Tonnage:	8,445 DWT
Length:	436 ft 7 in (133.1 m) oa
Beam:	61 ft 8 in (18.8 m)
Draft:	30 ft 2 in (9.2 m)
Propulsion:	2 diesels driving generator connected to 1 electric motor; 7,150 hp; 2 shaft
Speed:	20 knots
Range:	10,000 n.miles at 16.5 knots
Complement:	approx. 100
Helicopters:	landing area (see notes)
Radars:	2 Don-2 (navigation)

The SOMOV was converted from an AMGUEMA-class cargo ship. The ship is operated by the Arctic and Antarctic Research Institute as a research and logistic support ship, primarily to support Soviet operations in the Antarctic. An Mi-8 Hip helicopter was embarked in the ship during her 1985 Antarctic cruise.

Design: The ship has an icebreaking bow and other features for cold-weather operations; a raised helicopter platform is provided at the stern. The ship has four cargo holds.

The research ship MIKHAIL SOMOV has an icebreaking bow and other features for polar operations. A Hip utility helicopter is on the fantail landing deck. (1981, L. & L. Van Ginderen)

18 HYDROGRAPHIC-METEOROLOGICAL RESEARCH SHIPS: "VALERIAN URYVAYEV" CLASS

Name	Completed	Name	Completed
POISK	1974	DALNIYE ZELYENTSY	1978
VALERIAN URYVAYEV	1974	VYACHESLAV FROLOV	1978
MORSKOY GEOFIZIK	1975	LEV TITOV	1980
VSEVLOD BERYOZKIN	1975	VEKTOR	1980
YAKOV GAKKEL	1975	MODUL	1981
VULKANOLOG	1976	ELM	1982
ISKATEL	1977	PROFESSOR FEDYINSKIY	1982
ISSLEDOVATEL	1977	CHAYVO	1983
RUDOLF SAMOYLOVICH	1977	GEOFIZIK	1983

Builders:	Khabarovsk
Displacement:	1,050 tons full load
Tonnage:	350 DWT
Length:	179 ft 9 in (54.8 m) oa
Beam:	31 ft 2 in (9.5 m)
Draft:	13 ft 9 in (4.2 m)
Propulsion:	1 diesel (Karl Liebknecht); 880 hp in early ships; 1,320 hp in later ships; 1 shaft
Speed:	11.5 knots in early ships
	12.5 knots in later ships
Range:	10,000 n.miles at 11 knots
Complement:	approx. 40 + 12 scientists-technicians
Helicopters:	no facilities
Radars:	1 Don-2 (navigation)
	1 Okean (navigation)
	1 End Tray (research) in some ships

These are small, funnel-aft research ships operated by various scientific and research agencies.

Design: Details differ. Eight laboratories are provided. Fitted with a bow thruster for precision station keeping.

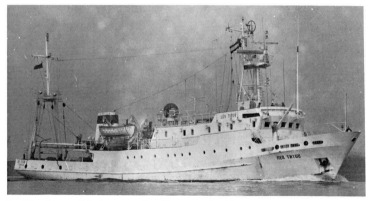

Besides the world's largest scientific research ships, the Soviet Union also operates a number of small research ships, such as the LEV TITOV, shown here. (1983, L. & L. Van Ginderen)

Research ship VULKANOLOG. (1986, L. & L. Van Ginderen)

19 HYDROGRAPHIC RESEARCH SHIPS: "DMITRIY OVTSYN" CLASS

Name	Completed	Name	Completed
10 First Group		**9 Second Group**	
DMITRIY LAPTEV	1970	FEDOR MATISEN	1976
DMITRIY OVTSYN	1970	PROFESSOR BOGOROV	1976
DMITRIY STERLIGOV	1971	PROFESSOR KURENTSOV	1976
STEPAN MALYGIN	1971	PROFESSOR VODYANITSKIY	1976
EDUARD TOLL	1972	GEORGIY MAKSIMOV	1977
NIKOLAY KOLOMEYTSYEV	1972	IVAN KIREYEV	1977
VALERIAN ALBANOV	1972	PAVEL BASHMAKOV	1977
VLADIMIR SUKHOTSKIY	1973	YAKOV SMIRNITSKIY	1977
NIKOLAY YEVGENOV	1974	PROFESSOR SHTOKMAN	1979
SERGEY KRAVKOV	1974		

Builders:	Laivateollisuus, Abo and Turku (Finland)
Displacement:	1,600 tons full load
Tonnage:	295 DWT
Length:	225 ft 4 in (68.7 m) oa
Beam:	39 ft (11.9 m)
Draft:	13 ft 5 in (4.1 m)
Propulsion:	1 diesel (Humboldt-Klockner-Deutz); 2,200 hp; 1 shaft
Speed:	13.75 knots
Range:	9,700 n.miles at 13.5 knots
Complement:	approx. 40
Helicopters:	no facilities
Radars:	1 or 2 Don, Don-2, or Okean

Medium-size research ships with minor differences that lead to their consideration as two groups. Fourteen of the ships operate for the Merchant Fleet for hydrographic and seismic surveys; the others for the Academy of Sciences.

Design: The class has a funnel-aft configuration. The first group has one cargo hold and an 8-ton-capacity crane; the second group has two cargo holds, two 3-ton-capacity cranes. Bow thrusters are fitted.

The four ships with Professor names have no crow's nest and no boats alongside the funnel.

Research ship PROFESSOR VODYANITSKIY. (1984, L. & L. Van Ginderen)

3 HYDROGRAPHIC-METEOROLOGICAL RESEARCH SHIPS: MODIFIED "PASSAT" CLASS

Name	Completed
ERNST KRENKEL (ex-VIKHR)	1971
GEORGIY USHAKOV (ex-SHKVAL)	1971
VIKTOR BUGAEV (ex-PORYV)	1971

Builders:	Adolf Warski, Szczecin (Poland)
Displacement:	4,200 tons full load
Tonnage:	1,450 DWT
Length:	328 ft 4 in (100.1 m) oa
Beam:	48 ft 6 in (14.8 m)
Draft:	16 ft 9 in (5.1 m)
Propulsion:	2 diesels (Cegielski or Zgoda/Sulzer); 4,800 hp; 2 shafts
Speed:	16 knots
Range:	15,000 n.miles at 16 knots
Complement:	approx. 110 + 60 scientists-technicians
Helicopters:	no facilities
Radars:	2 Don-2 (navigation)

Modified PASSAT-class ships; derived from the Polish B-88 design.

6 HYDROGRAPHIC-METEOROLOGICAL RESEARCH SHIPS: "PASSAT" CLASS

Name	Completed	Name	Completed
MUSSON	1968	OKEAN	1969
PASSAT	1968	PRIBOY	1969
VOLNA	1968	PRILIV	1970

Builders:	Adolf Warski, Szczecin (Poland)
Displacement:	4,145 tons full load
Tonnage:	1,170 DWT
Length:	317 ft 10 in (96.9 m) oa
Beam:	45 ft 3 in (13.8 m)
Draft:	17 ft 5 in (5.3 m)
Propulsion:	2 diesels (Sulzer or Zgoda/Sulzer); 4,800 hp; 2 shafts
Speed:	16 knots
Range:	
Complement:	approx. 50–55 + 50–60 scientists-technicians
Helicopters:	no facilities
Radars:	2 Don-2 (navigation) 1 End Tray (tracking)

These ships are of the Polish B-88 design with 23 laboratories provided. They are assigned to the Hydrometeorological Institute.

The research ship GEORGIY USHAKOV, modified from the Polish B-88 design. Polish shipyards have produced much of the large Soviet research fleet. (1983, L. & L. Van Ginderen)

The research ship PASSAT is slightly smaller than the later, modified PASSAT class, and has a different bridge structure. (1983, U.S. Navy)

7 OCEANOGRAPHIC RESEARCH SHIPS: "AKADEMIK KURCHATOV" CLASS

Name	Completed	Name	Completed
AKADEMIK KURCHATOV	1966	PROFESSOR ZUBOV	1967
AKADEMIK KOROLEV	1967	DMITRIY MENDELEYEV	1968
AKADEMIK SHIRSHOV	1967	AKADEMIK VERNADSKIY	1968
PROFESSOR VIZE	1967		

Builders:	Mathias Thiesen, Wismar (East Germany)
Displacement:	6,986 tons full load
Tonnage:	1,986 DWT
Length:	407 ft 5 in (124.2 m) oa
Beam:	23 ft (17.0 m)
Draft:	20 ft (6.1 m)
Propulsion:	2 diesels (Halberstadt/MAN K6Z 57/60); 8,000 hp; 2 shafts
Speed:	18.25 knots
Range:	20,000 n.miles at 16 knots
Complement:	approx. 85 + 80 scientists-technicians
Helicopters:	1 utility helicopter
Radars:	2 Don-2 (navigation except 1 Don-2 and 1 Okean in KOROLEV and MENDELEYEV)
	1 End Tray (tracking)

Large research ships, similar to four ships operated by the Soviet Navy (see chapter 23). The KURCHATOV, MENDELEYEV, and VERNADSKIY are assigned to the Institute of Oceanology; the four other ships are assigned to the Hydrometeorological Institute.

Design: This class has graceful, liner-like lines. There are 27 laboratories. The ships are fitted with two 190-hp bow thrusters and an active 300-hp rudder for precise station keeping. The ships have a cargo hold with two 8-ton cranes and lesser ones.

Electronics: Antennas vary, with the SHIRSHOV having two domes for satellite communication antennas abaft the funnel. Vee Bar HF antennas are fitted to the masts of the weather (Hydromet) ships.

1 GEOLOGICAL RESEARCH SHIP: "SEVER"

Name	Completed
SEVER	1967

Builders:	Black Sea Shipyard, Nikolayev
Displacement:	1,780 tons full load
Tonnage:	706 DWT
Length:	232 ft 11 in (71.0 m) oa
Beam:	43 ft (13.1 m)
Draft:	16 ft 5 in (5.0 m)
Propulsion:	3 diesels with generator connected to electric motor; 3,000 hp; 1 shaft
Speed:	13.25 knots
Range:	11,000 n.miles at 13 knots
Complement:	approx. 50
Helicopters:	no facilities
Radars:	1 Don-2 (navigation)

The SEVER was built as the prototype for a stern trawler, but was an unsuccessful design. Operated in the research role (in the Black Sea) by the Ministry of Geophysics.

Design: The ship has four holds and two 3-ton-capacity derricks.

The AKADEMIK SHIRSHOV has two satellite communication domes amidships, the only ship of the class believed to have this gear. Note the position of the Vee Bar HF antennas. (1983, L. & L. Van Ginderen)

The AKADEMIK KURCHATOV shows another class configuration, with neither the Vee Bar nor satellite communication antennas. Nets enclose a ball court aft of the bipod mast. (1984, U.S. Navy)

The research ship AKADEMIK VERNADSKIY has civilian- and Navy-manned sister ships. The Navy ships have a helicopter landing deck and telescoping hangar.

1 OCEANOGRAPHIC RESEARCH SHIP: "AKADEMIK PETROVSKIY"

Name	Completed
AKADEMIK PETROVSKIY (ex-MOSKOVSKIY UNIVERSITET)	1966

Builders:	Khabarovsk
Displacement:	922 tons full load
Length:	177 ft 6 in (54.1 m) oa
Beam:	30 ft 6 in (9.3 m)
Draft:	12 ft 2 in (3.7 m)
Propulsion:	1 diesel; 780 hp; 1 shaft
Speed:	11 knots
Range:	10,000 n.miles at 11 knots
Complement:	approx. 40 + 10 scientists
Helicopters:	no facilities
Radars:	1 Don-2 (navigation)
	1 Spin Trough (search)

Converted trawler operated by the Moscow State University on a variety of ocean study programs. Modernized and renamed in 1970.

Class: Several ships of this and similar Mayak classes serve as fisheries research ships.

The AKADEMIK PETROVSKIY is one of the smaller Soviet research ships; similar units serve in the fisheries research role. (Courtesy *Flottes de Combat*)

2 RESEARCH SHIPS: "TROPIK" CLASS

Name	Completed
PEGAS	1963
KALLISTO	1964

Builders:	Volks, Stralsund (East Germany)
Displacement:	approx. 3,000 tons full load
Tonnage:	988 DWT
Length:	261 ft 9 in (79.8 m) oa
Beam:	43 ft 4 in (13.2 m)
Draft:	17 ft 1 in (5.2 m)
Propulsion:	2 diesels (Karl Liebknecht); 1,660 hp; 1 shaft
Speed:	11.75 knots
Range:	
Complement:	approx. 40 + 30 scientists-technicians
Helicopters:	no facilities
Radars:	2 Don-2 (navigation)

These are converted stern-trawler factory ships of the TROPIK class. The PEGAS operates for the Academy of Sciences and the KALLISTO for the Oceanographic Science Research Institute.

Class: About 90 ships of this class were built for the Soviet Union between 1962 and 1966, of which nine have been converted to the fishery research role. Most remain in service. Others have been transferred to other nations (the prototype TROPIK went to Ghana).

Research ship KALLISTO. (1983, L. & L. Van Ginderen)

2 RESEARCH SHIPS: "BOLOGUE" CLASS

Name	Completed
AKADEMIK ARCHANGELSKIY	1963
YURIY GODIN	1963

Builders:	Leninskaya Kuznitsa, Kiev
Displacement:	580 tons full load
Length:	143 ft (43.6 m) oa
Beam:	24 ft 11 in (7.6 m)
Draft:	9 ft 10 in (3.0 m)
Propulsion:	1 diesel (Karl Liebknecht); 450 hp; 1 shaft
Speed:	10 knots
Range:	
Complement:	approx. 35 + 15 scientists-technicians
Helicopters:	no facilities
Radars:	1 Spin Trough (search)

Converted BOLOGUE-class side trawlers. The ARCHANGELSKIY is operated by the Ministry of Geology and the GODIN by the Geophysics Institute.

4 RESEARCH SHIPS: "AYU-DAG" CLASS

Name	Completed
Ayu-Dag	1961
Ay-Petri	1962
Professor Kolesnikov (ex-Aytodor)	1962
Pitsunda	1963

Builders:	Georgi Dimitrov shipyard, Varna (Bulgaria)
Displacement:	approx. 1,000 tons full load
Tonnage:	176 DWT
Length:	209 ft 3 in (63.8 m) oa
Beam:	30 ft 6 in (9.3 m)
Draft:	9 ft 10 in (3.0 m)
Propulsion:	2 diesels (Karl Liebknecht); 830 hp; 2 shafts
Speed:	13 knots
Range:	
Complement:	
Helicopters:	no facilities
Radars:	

These ships were built as Black Sea passenger ferries, but converted to environmental-geological research ships. They have a limited research capability.

2 HYDROACOUSTIC RESEARCH SHIPS: "PETR LEBEDEV" CLASS

Name	Completed	Converted
Petr Lebedev (ex-Chapayev)	1957	1960
Sergey Vavilov (ex-Furmanov)	1957	1960

Builders:	Crichton-Vulcan, Turku (Finland)
Displacement:	4,800 tons full load
Tonnage:	1,675 DWT
Length:	302 ft 5 in (92.2 m) oa
Beam:	45 ft 11 in (14.0 m)
Draft:	18 ft 8 in (5.7 m)
Propulsion:	1 diesel (Sulzer 6TD 56); 2,400 hp; 1 shaft
Speed:	13.5 knots
Range:	6,000 n.miles at 13.5 knots
Complement:	approx. 90
Helicopters:	no facilities
Radars:	1 Don (navigation)
	1 Don-2 (navigation)

Former cargo ships, rebuilt in 1960 as research ships. They are assigned to the Hydroacoustics Institute and operate together.

Class: These ships were the first two of 13 cargo ships of the Fryazino class delivered to the Soviet merchant fleet from 1957 through 1960.

The Ayu-Dag was built as a Black Sea passenger ferry; subsequently converted to a limited-capability research ship. (1983, L. & L. Van Ginderen)

Research ship Sergei Vavilov. (1983, U.S. Navy)

The PETR LEBEDEV, one of the older Soviet research ships, has an unusual two-funnel configuration. (1985, Royal Netherlands Navy)

1 RESEARCH SHIP: "MAYAKOVSKIY" CLASS

Name	Completed
ALEXANDR IVANOVICH VOYEYKOV	1959

Builders:	Black Sea Shipyard, Nikolayev
Displacement:	approx. 3,600 tons full load
Tonnage:	1,287 DWT
Length:	277 ft 11 in (84.7 m) oa
Beam:	45 ft 11 in (14.0 m)
Draft:	18 ft 8 in (5.7 m)
Propulsion:	2 diesels (Russkiy); 2,000 hp; 1 shaft
Speed:	13 knots
Range:	18,000 n.miles at 12 knots
Complement:	approx. 55 + 35 scientists-technicians
Helicopters:	no facilities
Radars:	2 Don-2 (navigation)
	1 End Tray (tracking)

This is one of at least 15 ships of this class of stern trawler-factory ships converted to research configurations. All of the others are fisheries research ships, subordinate to the Ministry of Fisheries.

Class: An estimated 227 ships of this class were built at two Soviet yards, including three completed for Bulgaria. They were completed between 1958 and 1969.

The PRIMOR'YE-class AGIs have the same hull and propulsion plant.

Design: The stern ramp has been plated over.

1 SEISMIC RESEARCH SHIP: CONVERTED TUG

Name	Completed
VLADIMIR OBRUCHEV	1959

Builders:	Galati, Romania
Displacement:	900 tons full load
Length:	149 ft 11 in (45.7 m) oa
Beam:	31 ft 2 in (9.5 m)
Draft:	12 ft 9 in (3.9 m)
Propulsion:	2 diesels; 1,200 hp; 1 shaft
Speed:	11 knots
Range:	
Complement:	approx. 35 + 10 scientists
Helicopters:	no facilities
Radars:	2 Don-2 (navigation)

Former commercial tug modified for seismic research; operated by the Ministry of Geology.

Two converted Roslavl-class tugs have been discarded.

1 OCEANOGRAPHIC RESEARCH SHIP: "MIKHAIL LOMONOSOV"

Name	Completed
MIKHAIL LOMONOSOV	1957

Builders:	Neptun, Rostock (East Germany)
Displacement:	5,960 tons full load
Tonnage:	2,452 DWT
Length:	335 ft 10 in (102.4 m) oa
Beam:	47 ft 3 in (14.4 m)
Draft:	19 ft 8 in (6.0 m)
Propulsion:	1 triple-expansion compound plus low-pressure turbine; 2,400 hp; 1 shaft
Boilers:	2
Speed:	13.5 knots
Range:	11,000 n.miles at 13.5 knots
Complement:	approx. 80 + 55 scientists-technicians
Helicopters:	no facilities
Radars:	2 Don-2 (navigation)

Converted during construction from a KOLOMNA-class cargo ship. Operated by the Ukraine Institute of Oceanology.

Class: Some 30 ships of this class were built by the Neptun yard for the Soviet Union, several of which saw service as naval cargo ships. Six sister ships serve as submarine tenders (ATREK class) and one is an experimental ship (see chapter 22)

Design: Fitted with 16 laboratories. Two holds are provided.

1 NONMAGNETIC SAILING SCHOONER: "ZARYA" CLASS

Name	Completed
ZARYA	1956

Builders:	Laivateollisuus, Turku (Finland)
Displacement:	approx. 600 tons full load
Tonnage:	78 DWT
Length:	172 ft 2 in (52.5 m) oa
	139 ft 5 in (42.5 m) wl
Beam:	29 ft 6 in (9.0 m)
Draft:	10 ft 2 in (3.1 m)
Propulsion:	1 diesel (Halberstadt 6NVD36); 300 hp; 1 shaft
Speed:	6.5 knots with sails
	8 knots with auxiliary engine
Complement:	approx. 35 + 10 scientists
Radars:	1 Spin Trough (search)

The ZARYA is a three-masted schooner with a wooden hull and minimum built-in iron and steel; brass and copper-bronze alloys were used where possible. The ship is employed by the Institute of Terrestrial Magnetism, Academy of Sciences, in surveys of the earth's magnetic field.

Class: One of a class of sailing schooners built as war reparations by Finland for the Soviet Union after World War II. A few remain as naval deperming ships (these are dismasted; see chapter 22).

The ZARYA after undergoing an extensive refit at Antwerp. Note the Spin Trough radar fitted to the mizzen mast. (1983, L. & L. Van Ginderen)

COASTAL RESEARCH CRAFT

23 COASTAL OCEANOGRAPHIC CRAFT: "AGAT" CLASS

Name	Name	Name	Completed
AGAT	ILMENIT	RUTIL	
AKVANAVT	KARTESH	SHELF	
BERILL	KVARTS	TANTAL	
BOREY	METAN	TOPAZ	1969–1979
BRIG	MONATSIT	TSIRKON	
GEOTERMIK	MORION	URAN	
GIDROLOG	PLUTON	YANTAR	
GRANAT	RADON		

Builders:	
Displacement:	350 tons full load
Tonnage:	35 DWT
Length:	111 ft 6 in (34.0 m) oa
Beam:	23 ft 3 in (7.1 m)
Draft:	8 ft 6 in (2.6 m)
Propulsion:	1 diesel (Karl Liebnecht); 300 hp; 1 shaft
Speed:	9.5 knots
Range:	1,600 n.miles at 9 knots
Complement:	
Radars:	1 . . . . . . (navigation)

These are small oceanographic craft, converted from MANEVRENNYY-class seiner fishing craft. These craft are operated by the Academy of Sciences, including the Hydrometeorological Institute, and the Ministry of Geology.

The research ship SHELF at Gdynia. (1983, L. & L. Van Ginderen)

1 COASTAL RESEARCH SHIP: GONETS CLASS

Name	Completed
AKADEMIK A. KOVALEVSKIY	1949

Builders:	Elbe (shipyard), Wolgast (East Germany)
Tonnage:	48 DWT
Length:	(38.5 m) oa
Beam:	(7.2 m)
Draft:	(2.9 m)
Propulsion:	1 diesel (Karl Liebknecht); 300 hp; 1 shaft
Speed:	8 knots
Radars:	1 Spin Trough (search)

Modified side-trawler, operated by the Academy of Sciences.

EXPERIMENTAL AND TRIALS SHIPS

1 SHIPBUILDING RESEARCH SHIP: "IZUMRUD"

Name	Completed
IZUMRUD	1979

Builders:	Black Sea Shipyard, Nikolayev
Displacement:	5,170 tons full load
	2,640 DWT
Length:	326 ft (99.4 m) oa
Beam:	45 ft 11 in. (14.0 m)
Draft:	17 ft 9 in (5.4 m)
Propulsion:	4 diesels; 4,000 hp; with generators connected to 4 electric motors; 1 shaft
Speed:	14 knots
Range:	
Complement:	approx. 110 (civilian) + 40 scientists-technicians
Helicopters:	no facilities
Missiles:	none
Guns:	none
Radars:	1 Don-2 (navigation
	1 Low Sieve (search)
	1 Okean (navigation)

The IZUMRUD was constructed specifically for the Ministry of Shipbuilding to test ship structures and materials as well as other ship components. The ship is civilian manned, is operated by the Krylov Institute of Shipbuilding in Leningrad; she operates in the Black Sea.

Design: The ship is based on the TAVRIYA-class passenger cargo design. She has one cargo hold forward with a 3¼-ton crane.

Names: A Grisha II operated by the KGB Maritime Border Troops is also named IZUMRUD.

The IZUMRUD is a unique shipbuilding research ship, designed and built specifically to test ship components.

ICEBREAKERS

There are several river and inland icebreakers in service in addition to the oceangoing ships listed here. Other oceangoing icebreakers are operated by the Navy and by the KGB Maritime Border Troops.[1]

Most of these ships are fitted for ocean towing.

(2) NUCLEAR-PROPELLED ICEBREAKERS: TAIMYR CLASS

Builders:	Wärtsilä, Helsinki (Finland)
Displacement:	
Length:	approx. 459 ft (140.0 m) oa
Beam:	91 ft 10 in (28.0 m)
Draft:	26 ft (7.9 m)
Propulsion:	steam turbines; 52,000 shp driving electric generators
Reactors:	2 pressurized water
Speed:	
Range:	
Complement:	
Helicopters:	
Radars:	

A new class of nuclear icebreakers is planned for construction by the Wärtsilä yard for Soviet use; the reactor plants are expected to be installed at the Baltic Shipyard in Leningrad. These are to be shallow-draft ships, to be completed in 1988 and 1989.

[1] A recent discussion of Soviet icebreakers is provided in Commander Lawson W. Brigham, USCG, "New Developments in Soviet Nuclear Arctic Ships," Naval Institute *Proceedings,* (December 1985), pp. 131–33.

An artist's concept of the TAIMYR-class nuclear-propelled icebreakers. These will be the first Soviet nuclear ships built outside of the Soviet Union, although the actual reactor plants will be installed at the Baltic shipyard. (Wärtsilä)

3 ICEBREAKERS: "MUDYUG" CLASS

Name	Completed
MUDYUG	Sep 1982
MAGADAN	Dec 1982
DIKSON	Mar 1983

Builders:	Wärtsilä, Helsinki (Finland)
Displacement:	5,560 tons
Tonnage:	1,257 DWT
Length:	290 ft 7 in (88.6 m) oa
Beam:	69 ft 6 in (21.2 m)
Draft:	19 ft 8 in (6.0 m)
Propulsion:	4 diesels (Wärtsilä Vasa 8R32) driving generators connected to electric motors; 12,400 hp; 2 shafts
Speed:	16.5 knots
Range:	
Complement:	
Helicopters:	no facilities
Radars:	

This class resembles a scaled-down SOROKIN icebreaker design (e.g., superstructure block is four levels plus bridge). No helicopter deck is provided.

The MUDYUG is one of the smaller Soviet icebreakers. The large icebreaking fleet permits year-round use of Soviet naval bases and commercial ports, as well as transits of the Arctic route between European Russia and the Far East. (1983, L. & L. Van Ginderen)

Icebreaker MUDYUG. (Wärtsilä)

4 ICEBREAKERS: "KAPITAN SOROKIN" CLASS

Name	Completed	Name	Completed
KAPITAN SOROKIN	1977	KAPITAN DRANITSYN	1980
KAPITAN NIKOLAYEV	1978	KAPITAN KLEBNIKOV	1981

Builders:	Wärtsilä, Helsinki (Finland)
Displacement:	10,440 tons standard
	14,655 tons full load
Tonnage:	4,225 DWT
Length:	432 ft 8 in (131.9 m) oa
Beam:	86 ft 11 in (26.5 m)
Draft:	27 ft 11 in (8.5 m)
Propulsion:	6 diesels (Wärtsilä/Sulzer 9ZL 40/48), 24,840 hp driving 6 generators connected to 3 electric motors; 20,000 hp; 3 shafts
Speed:	18.75 knots
Range:	10,700 n.miles at 16 knots

Icebreaker KAPITAN DRANITSYN. (Wärtsilä)

Icebreaker KAPITAN NIKOLAYEV. (Wärtsilä)

Complement:	approx. 75
Helicopters:	landing area
Radars:	

These ships have a massive superstructure block; the first two units have five levels plus the bridge, the two later units have six levels plus the bridge. These are considered shallow-draft icebreakers.

3 + 1 NUCLEAR-PROPELLED ICEBREAKERS: "ARKTIKA" CLASS

Name	Launched	Completed
LEONID BREZHNEV (ex- ARKTIKA)	Oct 1973	1 May 1975
SIBIR'	23 Feb 1976	1977
ROSSIYA	7 Nov 1983	Nov 1985
. . . . . .		Building

Builders:	Baltic Shipyard, Leningrad
Displacement:	20,480 tons standard
	23,460 tons full load
Tonnage:	4,096 DWT
Length:	492 ft (150.0 m) oa
Beam:	98 ft 5 in (30.0 m)
Draft:	36 ft 1 in (11.0 m)
Propulsion:	2 steam turbines (Kirov), 75,000 shp driving 2 generators connected to electric motors; 3 shafts
Reactors:	2 pressurized water
Speed:	20.5 knots
Complement:	approx. 160
Helicopters:	1 Ka-32 Helix
Radars:	1 Don-2 (navigation)
	1 Okean (navigation)
	1 Head Net-C (search) except Top Plate in ROSSIYA

These are the world's largest and most powerful icebreakers. The lead ship was originally named ARKTIKA; renamed LEONID BREZHNEV in 1982. The ship began sea trials on 3 November 1974; the SIBIR' began sea trials on 22 October 1977; and the ROSSIYA in 1984.

The ARKTIKA was the first surface ship to reach the geographic North Pole, doing so on 17 August 1977. (The U.S. Coast Guard icebreaker WESTWIND/WAGB 281 came within 375 n.miles of the North Pole in 1979.) The ARKTIKA spent 15 hours at the North Pole; her round trip from Murmansk took 13 days.

Armament: The ARKTIKA was armed during her initial sea trials, carrying 8 76.2-mm AA guns (4 twin) and 4 30-mm Gatling guns (4 multibarrel), with 2 Hawk Screech and 2 Drum Tilt radar/GFCS plus an air-search radar. All were removed before the ship departed the Baltic. Other ships of the class have carried guns and fire-control radars on trials. Thus, the ships are designed to be armed for wartime when they would come under Navy operational control. (See page 348.)

Class: The ARKTIKA was laid down in 1971. The fourth ship of the class was laid down in November 1983.

Design: The design provides for a large helicopter deck aft and a helicopter hangar capable of accommodating one helicopter for ice reconnaissance.

Engineering: Service speed is reported as 18 knots.

The nuclear-propelled icebreaker SIBIR' at sea; the naval guns and radars that were installed for sea trials have been deleted in service. Note the nuclear symbol on the side of the hull, beneath the bridge. (Royal Danish Navy)

3 ICEBREAKERS: "YERMAK" CLASS

Name	Completed
YERMAK	Apr 1974
ADMIRAL MAKAROV	June 1975
KRASIN	Feb 1976

Builders:	Wärtsilä, Helsinki (Finland)
Displacement:	13,280 tons standard
	20,241 tons full load
Tonnage:	7,441 DWT
Length:	445 ft 5 in (135.8 m) oa
Beam:	85 ft 3 in (26.0 m)
Draft:	36 ft 1 in (11.0 m)
Propulsion:	9 diesels (Wärtsilä/Sulzer 12ZH40/48), 41,400 hp driving 9 generators connected to 3 electric motors; 36,000 hp; 3 shafts
Speed:	19.5 knots
Range:	29,300 n.miles at 15 knots
Complement:	approx. 145
Helicopters:	1 utility helicopter
Radars:	

These ships are improved and enlarged versions of the MOSKVA class. They have a helicopter hangar and landing platform. There are spare accommodations for 28 passengers.

Icebreaker ADMIRAL MAKAROV. (Wärtsilä)

14 ICEBREAKERS: "DOBRYNYA NIKITICH" CLASS

Name	Completed	Name	Completed
VASILIY PRONCHISHCHEV	1961	SEMEN CHELYUSKIN	1965
AFANASIY NIKITIN	1962	YURIY LISYANSKIY	1965
KHARITON LAPTEV	1962	PETR PAKHTUSOV	1966
VASILIY POYARKOV	1963	GEORGIY SEDOV	1967
YEFOFEY KHARBAROV	1963	FEODOR LITKE	1970
IVAN KRUZENSHTERN	1964	IVAN MOSKVITIN	1971
VLADIMIR RUSANOV	1964	SEMEN DEZHNEV	1971

Builders:	Admiralty, Leningrad
Displacement:	2,675–2,940 tons full load
Length:	222 ft 1 in (67.7 m) oa
Beam:	60 ft (18.3 m)
Draft:	20 ft (6.1 m)
Propulsion:	3 diesels (13D100) driving 3 generators connected to electric motors; 5,400 hp; 3 shafts (1 forward)
Speed:	14.5 knots
Range:	5,500 n.miles at 12 knots
	13,000 n.miles at 9.5 knots
Complement:	approx. 40
Helicopters:	no facilities
Radars:	1 or 2 Don-2 (navigation)

These are relatively small but highly useful icebreakers.

Class: See listing for Navy ships of this class (chapter 22) for details. One additional ship of this design built at the Admiralty shipyard was delivered to East Germany in 1968.

Names: The early ships were originally named LEDOKIL (*icebreaker*) with a numeral suffix.

The DOBRYNYA NIKITICH-class icebreaker YURIY LISYANSKIY represents the largest class of Soviet icebreakers, with units of this general design in service with the Navy and KGB as well as civilian merchant and research fleets. (1984, L. & L. Van Ginderen)

5 ICEBREAKERS: "MOSKVA" CLASS

Name	Completed	Name	Completed
MOSKVA	1960	MURMANSK	1968
LENINGRAD	1961	VLADIVOSTOK	1968
KIEV	1965		

Builders:	Wärtsilä, Helsinki (Finland)
Displacement:	13,290 tons standard
	15,360 tons full load
Tonnage:	4,221 DWT
Length:	400 ft 6 in (122.1 m) oa
Beam:	80 ft 4 in (24.5 m)
Draft:	34 ft 5 in (10.5 m)
Propulsion:	8 diesels (Wärtsilä/Sulzer 9MH51), driving 8 generators connected to 4 electric motors; 26,300 hp; 3 shafts
Speed:	18.25 knots
Range:	20,000 n.miles at 14 knots
Complement:	approx. 115
Helicopters:	2 utility helicopters
Radars:	

These ships have a helicopter hangar and landing platform.

The MOSKVA-class icebreaker KIEV. (Wärtsilä)

1 NUCLEAR-PROPELLED ICEBREAKER: "LENIN"

Name	Launched	Completed
LENIN	5 December 1957	September 1959

Builders:	Admiralty, Leningrad
Displacement:	15,940 tons standard
	19,240 tons full load
Tonnage:	3,849 DWT
Length:	439 ft 6 in (134.0 m) oa
Beam:	87 ft 11 in (26.8 m)
Draft:	34 ft 5 in (10.5 m)
Propulsion:	4 steam turbines (Kirov), 44,000 shp driving 4 generators connected to 3 electric motors (Elektrosila); 39,200 hp; 3 shafts
Reactors:	2 pressurized water
Speed:	19.7 knots
Complement:	approx. 150
Helicopters:	1 utility helicopter
Radars:	

The LENIN was the world's first nuclear-propelled surface ship. The ship's keel was laid down on 25 August 1956; the ship left the Admiralty shipyard for the first time on 12 September 1959 and anchored in the Neva River until beginning sea trials on 15 September 1959.

Design: A helicopter hangar and flight deck are provided.

Engineering: The ship was built with three reactors, with two being sufficient to propel the ship at full speed and a third available for maintenance and research.

The LENIN suffered a major nuclear radiation accident in 1966 or 1967, with some reports citing a "reactor meltdown." Up to 30 crewmen died as a result of radiation poisoning, and others suffered injuries. The ship lay abandoned for more than a year, after which she was towed to a shipyard in the Arctic and rebuilt. A two-reactor plant was installed and the ship returned to service.

Service speed is 18 knots.

3 ICEBREAKERS: "KAPITAN BELOUSOV" CLASS

Name	Completed
KAPITAN BELOUSOV	1954
KAPITAN VORONIN	1955
KAPITAN MELEKHOV	1956

Builders:	Wärtsilä, Helsinki (Finland)
Displacement:	5,360 tons full load
Tonnage:	1,308–1,423 DWT
Length:	272 ft 11 in (83.2 m) oa
Beam:	63 ft 8 in (19.4 m)
Draft:	23 ft (7.0 m)
Propulsion:	6 diesels (Wärtsilä Polar), 10,500 hp driving 6 generators connected to electric motors; 4 shafts (2 forward and 2 aft)
Speed:	16.5 knots
Range:	10,000 n.miles at 14.8 knots
Complement:	approx. 120
Helicopters:	no facilities
Radars:	

These were the first icebreakers built for the Soviet Union after World War II. One additional icebreaker of this class was built for Sweden and one for Finland.

The pioneer nuclear surface ship LENIN has returned to service after having her damaged nuclear plant replaced. Here, crusted with ice, the ship works to free a merchant ship trapped in the Arctic. (Courtesy *Ships of the World*)

The KAPITAN MELEKHOV was one of the first icebreakers built for the Soviet Union after World War II. Except for the DOBRYNYA NIKITICH designs and the nuclear-propelled ships, all Soviet icebreakers have been built in Finland. (Royal Danish Navy)

The cargo-training ship VASILIY KALASHNIKOV is typical of the merchant marine cadet training ships. These ships carry small amounts of cargo on their training cruises. (1984, L. & L. Van Ginderen)

TRAINING SHIPS

The following ships provide at-sea instruction for Soviet Merchant Marine personnel, mainly in engineering, seamanship, and cargo handling. Some of these ships have been identified with naval personnel. There are also several smaller ships as well as a number of fisheries training ships.

The EQUATOR, built in 1935, is believed to have been discarded; see 3rd edition (page 325).

5 CADET TRAINING SHIPS: MODIFIED "BALTISKY" CLASS

Name	Completed	Name	Completed
PAVEL YABLOCHKOV	1980	VASILIY KALASHNIKOV	1981
ALEKSANDR POPOV	1981	IVAN POLZUNOV	1981
IVAN KULIBIN	1981		

Builders:	Laivateollisuus, Abo and Turku (Finland)
Displacement:	
Tonnage:	1,987 DWT
Length:	311 ft 7 in (95.0 m) oa
Beam:	43 ft 3 in (13.2 m)
Draft:	13 ft 1 in (4.0 m)
Propulsion:	2 diesels (Karl Liebknecht); 1,740 hp; 2 shafts
Speed:	12.5 knots
Range:	
Complement:	
Helicopters:	no facilities
Radars:	

These ships have duplicated navigating bridges.

Class: Four additional ships of this type are sea-river cargo ships, placed in Soviet merchant service between 1978 and 1980.

9 CADET TRAINING SHIPS: PROFESSOR CLASS

Name	Completed	Name	Completed
PROFESSOR KUDREVICH	1970	PROFESSOR MINYAYEV	1972
PROFESSOR SHCHYOGOLEV	1970	PROFESSOR UKHOV	1972
PROFESSOR ANICHKOV	1971	PROFESSOR KHLYUSTIN	1973
PROFESSOR RYBALTOVSKIY	1971	PROFESSOR PAVLENKO	1973
PROFESSOR YUSHCHENKO	1971		

Builders:	Stocznia, Szczecin (Poland)
Displacement:	
Tonnage:	5,385–5,457 DWT
Length:	403 ft 1 in (122.9 m) oa
Beam:	55 ft 9 in (17.0 m)
Draft:	23 ft 11 in (7.3 m)
Propulsion:	2 diesels (Cegielski/Burmeister & Wain); 4,900 hp; 1 shaft except KHLYUSTIN and PAVLENKO have Sulzer diesels; 5,500 hp
Speed:	15.25 knots except KHLYUSTIN and PAVLENKO 15.75 knots
Range:	
Complement:	
Helicopters:	no facilities
Radars:	

The PROFESSOR UKHOV is one of four ships of this class assigned to the Leningrad Higher Marine Engineering School. Extensive classroom facilities are provided in these ships.

Merchant marine training ship PROFESSOR YUSHCHENKO. (1984, L. & L. Van Ginderen)

These are Polish B-80 ships employed in cadet training. Details vary. A similar ship was built for Bulgaria, two for Poland, and one for Romania.

3 CADET TRAINING SHIPS: MODIFIED "KOVEL" CLASS

Name	Completed
GORIZONT	1961
ZENIT	1961
MERIDIAN	1962

Builders:	Neptun, Rostock (East Germany)
Displacement:	
Tonnage:	3,083 DWT
Length:	344 ft 1 in (104.9 m) oa
Beam:	47 ft 3 in (14.4 m)
Draft:	20 ft 4 in (6.2 m)
Propulsion:	2 diesels (Gorlitzer); 3,250 hp; 1 shaft
Speed:	13.5 knots
Range:	
Complement:	. . . + 140 cadets
Helicopters:	no facilities
Radars:	

These ships were completed as cadet training ships, being converted during construction from KOVEL-class dry cargo ships. (Three other ships of this class are civilian research ships.)

The GORIZONT was one of three ships completed specifically for the training of merchant marine cadets, the first Soviet ships of this type not converted from existing hulls. (1985, L. & L. Van Ginderen *collection*)

1 CADET TRAINING SHIP: "SAYMA" CLASS

Name	Completed
LAYNE (ex-YUNGA, ex-SULAK)	1969

Builders:	Baku
Displacement:	
Tonnage:	301 DWT
Length:	225 ft 4 in (68.7 m) oa
Beam:	31 ft 6 in (9.6 m)
Draft:	8 ft 6 in (2.6 m)
Propulsion:	2 diesels (Karl Liebknecht); 800 hp; 1 shaft
Speed:	11.25 knots
Range:	
Complement:	
Helicopters:	no facilities
Radars:	

One of a pair of small passenger ships.

1 CADET TRAINING SHIP: "JAN KREUKS" CLASS

Name	Completed
VOLODYA DUBININ	1954

Builders:	Gheorghiu Dej, Budapest (Hungary)
Displacement:	
Tonnage:	294 DWT
Length:	230 ft 3 in (70.2 m) oa
Beam:	32 ft 10 in (10.0 m)
Draft:	12 ft 5 in (3.8 m)
Propulsion:	2 diesels (Ganz); 1,000 hp; 2 shafts
Speed:	9.5 knots
Range:	
Complement:	
Helicopters:	no facilities
Radars:	

This ship apparently was a modified version of the JAN KREUKS class.

Class: More than 100 general-cargo ships of this design were built for the Soviet Union between 1948 and 1959, with additional ships being built by Hungarian yards for other countries. Several remain in service with the Soviet merchant fleet.

1 SAIL TRAINING BARK: "TOVARISHCH"

Name	Completed
TOVARISHCH (ex-German GORCH FOCK)	1933

Builders:	Blohm & Voss, Hamburg (Germany)
Displacement:	1,350 tons standard
	1,500 tons full load
Length:	269 ft 6 in (81.7 m) oa
Beam:	39 ft 4 in (11.9 m)
Draft:	17 ft (5.2 m)
Propulsion:	1 auxiliary diesel; 520 hp; 1 shaft
Speed:	8 knots on diesel
Range:	
Complement:	approx. 50 + 120 cadets
Radars:	

The ship was built as the training ship GORCH FOCK for the German Navy, one of four similar sail training vessels (the MIRCEA built for Romania and the HORST WESSEL and ALBERT LEO SCHLAGETER for Germany). The GORCH FOCK served as a naval training ship until scuttled on 1 May 1945 near Stralsund. The ship was salvaged by Soviet forces in 1948 and placed in service in 1951 as the TOVARISHCH.

The sail-training bark TOVARISHCH in the Mediterranean, underway on her auxiliary diesel engine. (1975, U.S. Navy)

She is home-ported in Kherson as a training ship for the Soviet merchant marine.

(The HORST WESSEL now serves as the U.S. Coast Guard training ship EAGLE/WIX 327, and the ex-ALFRED LEO SCHLAGETER, after briefly being held by the U.S. Navy, serves in the Portuguese Navy. The TOVARISHCH and KRUZENSHTERN participated in Operation Sail during the American Bicentennial celebrations, visiting U.S. ports in July 1976.)

1 SAIL TRAINING BARK: "KRUZENSHTERN"

Name	Completed
KRUZENSHTERN (ex-German PADUA)	1926

Builders:	Tecklenborg, Wesermunde (Germany)
Displacement:	3,065 tons standard
	3,570 tons full load
Length:	372 ft 11 in (113.7 m) oa
Beam:	45 ft 7 in (13.9 m)
Draft:	25 ft 5 in (7.75 m)
Propulsion:	2 auxiliary diesels; 1,600 hp; 1 shaft
Speed:	
Range:	
Complement:	approx. 70 + 200 cadets

The ship was the last cargo-carrying, four-masted bark to be built. Named PADUA, she sailed for the Hamburg firm of L. Laeisz until being laid up in 1932. She sailed again briefly before World War II and was taken over by the Soviet Union in 1945 and subsequently employed as a sail training ship.

She is home-ported in Riga as a training ship for the fishing industry.

1 SAIL TRAINING BARK: "SEDOV"

Name	Completed
SEDOV (ex-German KOMMODORE JOHNSEN, ex-MAGDALENE VINNEN)	1922

Builders:	Germania, Kiel (Germany)
Displacement:	3,065 tons standard
	3,570 tons full load
Length:	385 ft 1 in (117.4 m) oa
Beam:	47 ft 7 in (14.5 m)
Draft:	23 ft 11 in (7.3 m)
Propulsion:	2 auxiliary diesels; 1 shaft
Speed:	
Range:	
Complement:	.... + 130 cadets

This is a four-masted bark built as a training ship for the North German Lloyd line. She was acquired by the Soviet Union in 1945 and employed as a sail training ship. She was laid up from 1967 to January 1981; subsequently employed as a merchant marine and fisheries training ship.

Home-ported in Riga.

Sail-training bark KRUZENSHTERN. (1985, L. & L. Van Ginderen *collection*).

25

KGB Maritime Border Troops

The Maritime Border Troops (*Morskaya Pogranichnaya Okhrama—MPO*) of the KGB are responsible for the coastal security of the Soviet Union—protecting that nation's maritime borders against penetration by foreign agents or paramilitary forces, and preventing Soviet citizens from leaving by water without proper authorization. The Border Troops have an army- style organization with Vice Admiral N.N. Dalmatov holding the position of a deputy commander for maritime forces. His staff maintains close liaison with naval headquarters, and there are obviously joint seamanship training and ship-procurement programs. Approximately 12,000 personnel are currently assigned to the Maritime Border Troops.

Maritime Border Troops have Navy-style uniforms, the officers having green shoulder boards bearing their insignia of rank, and enlisted men wearing green cap ribbons inscribed with the words "Naval Forces of the Border Troops."

SHIPS AND CRAFT

The KGB operates about 200 combat ships, patrol craft, and armed auxiliaries plus about a dozen supply ships. In general, the KGB ships are similar to those of the Soviet Navy, but with a reduction in anti-air and anti-submarine capabilities in favor of a heavier gun armament.

The exact numbers and types of ships and craft assigned to the Maritime Border Troops is not publicly known.

The KGB ships have a significant combat capability. In wartime they would undoubtedly be used to supplement naval forces in combat operations (much the same as the U.S. Coast Guard operates under U.S. Navy control in wartime).

The ship classes are arranged by (1) category (warship or auxiliary), (2) type (frigate, corvette, etc.), and (3) completion of lead ship of the class. Classifications of KGB ships are listed in chapter 3.

AIRCRAFT

The KGB operates a large number of light fixed-wing aircraft and helicopters. Apparently several Ka-27 Helix and possibly Ka-25 Hormone-C utility helicopters are flown by the Maritime Border Troops and are based on board the Krivak III-class frigates and armed icebreakers.

COMBAT SHIPS

3 + GUIDED MISSILE FRIGATES: KRIVAK III CLASS

Name	Completed
MENZHINSKIY	Aug 1984
DZERZHINSKIY	Aug 1985
. . . . . .	1986
. . . . . .	Building

Builders:	Kamysh-Burun, Kerch'
Displacement:	3,900 tons full load
Length:	377 ft 2 in (115.0 m) wl
	405 ft 1 in (123 .5 m) oa
Beam:	46 ft 3 in (14.1 m)
Draft:	14 ft 9 in (4.6 m)
Propulsion:	2 gas turbines (24,200 hp) + 2 boost gas turbines (24,600 hp); total output 48,800 shp; 2 shafts
Speed:	32 knots
Range:	700 n.miles at 30 knots
	3,900 n.miles at 20 knots
Complement:	approx. 200
Helicopters:	1 Ka-27 Helix
Missiles:	1 twin SA-N-4 launcher [20]
Guns:	1 100-mm/70-cal DP
	2 30-mm close-in (2 multibarrel)
ASW weapons:	2 RBU-6000 rocket launchers
	torpedoes
Torpedoes:	8 21-in (533-mm) torpedo tubes (2 quad)
Mines:	rails for 20 mines
Radars:	1 Bass Tilt (fire control)
	1 Don-2 (navigation)
	1 Don-Kay (navigation)
	1 Head Net-C (3-D air search)
	1 Kite Screech (fire control)
	1 Palm Frond (navigation)
	1 Pop Group (fire control)
Sonars:	medium frequency (bow-mounted)
	medium frequency (variable-depth)
EW systems:	2 Bell Shroud
	2 Bell Squat

The MENZHINSKIY, the lead ship of the Krivak III class, upon arrival in the Far East. The frigate has significantly greater combat capabilities than U.S. Coast Guard cutters, which have a similar function of coastal patrol and police work as well as taking on combat roles in wartime. (1984, Japanese Maritime Self-Defense Force)

These ships are an adaption of the Krivak I/II-class ASW ships built for the Soviet Navy. They are the largest combat ships operated by the Maritime Border Troops. The first two Krivak IIIs are in the Far East, having transferred there shortly after their completion, with the MEN-ZHINSKIY arriving at Nachodka on 22 October 1985.

The Krivak III is the smallest Soviet combatant ship to regularly embark a helicopter. While both AAW and ASW armament have been reduced, these ships still have significant capabilities in both areas. Note that no surface-to-surface weapons are fitted except for the 100-mm gun, an adequate weapon for coastal guard and patrol duties.

Class: Construction of the Krivak III class continues for the Maritime Border Troops. Some Western sources estimate about 12 ships of this type will be constructed for the KGB.

Naval construction of the Krivak I/II ceased after 32 units were built; see chapter 16. The Kamysh-Burun shipyard also built ships of the Krivak I class (with other naval Krivaks built at shipyards in Kaliningrad and Leningrad).

Classification: Soviet classification is PSKR.

Design: These ships are a modification of the Krivak I/II classes of Navy ASW ships. The principal changes made for the KGB service are a single-barrel 100-mm DP gun forward in place of the previous SS-N-14 ASW missile launcher and a raised helicopter platform aft in place of the second SA-N-4 missile launcher and after 76.2- or 100-mm gun mounts. Also, two 30-mm Gatling guns are mounted on top of the helicopter hangar (these weapons are not found in the Krivak I/II).

Two motor launches are carried compared to one in the Krivak I/II ships; they are fitted to port and starboard, abreast of the single funnel.

Names: The lead ship is named for Viacheslav Rudolfovich Men-zhinskiy, head of the OGPU (predecessor to the KGB) from 1926 until his death in 1934. Feliks Dzerzhinski organized and headed the Soviet *Cheka* or secret police from 1917 to 1921; this was the precursor of the OGPU and the KGB. Previously a SVERDLOV-class cruiser carried his name as well as a T-58-class corvette operated by the KGB.

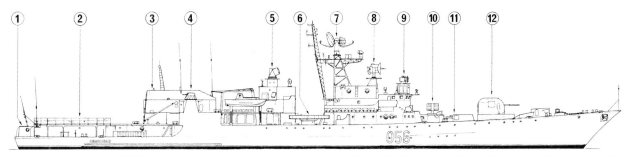

1. Variable-depth sonar (VDS) 2. helicopter deck 3. helicopter hangar 4. 30-mm Gatling guns 5. Bass Tilt radar 6. 533-mm torpedo tubes 7. Head Net-C radar 8. Kite Screech radar 9. Pop Group radar 10. RBU-6000 rocket launchers 11. SA-N-4 missile launcher (retracted) 12. 100-mm gun (M.J. Dodgson)

9 ANTI-SUBMARINE FRIGATES: GRISHA II CLASS

Name	Completed
AMETIST	
BRILLIANT	
IZUMRUD	
RUBIN	1974–(. . .)
SAFFIR	
ZHEMCHUG	
. . . . . . (3 units)	

Builders:	Zelenodolsk
Displacement:	950 tons standard
	1,200 tons full load
Length:	234 ft 10 in (71.6 m) oa
Beam:	32 ft 2 in (9.8 m)
Draft:	12 ft 2 in (3.7 m)
Propulsion:	4 diesels. 16,000 hp/l gas turbine, 1 gas turbine 15,000 shp; =
	31,000 hp; 3 shafts
Speed:	30 knots
Range:	450 n.miles at 27 knots
	4,500 n.miles at 10 knots
Complement:	approx. 60
Helicopters:	no facilities
Missiles:	none

Guns:	4 57-mm/80-cal AA (2 twin)
ASW weapons:	2 RBU-6000 rocket launchers
	2 depth-charge racks (see notes)
	torpedoes
Torpedoes:	4 21-in (533-mm) torpedo tubes (2 twin)
Mines:	rails for 18 mines (see notes)
Radars:	1 Don-2 (navigation)
	1 Muff Cob (fire control)
	1 Strut Curve (air search)
Sonars:	medium frequency (hull-mounted)
EW systems:	2 Watch Dog

These are small ASW frigates with minor differences in armament (see below). The similar Grisha I/III/IV/V classes are operated by the Navy. A few of these ships may also be KGB subordinated.

The Navy ships are similar except for an SA-N-4 launcher and associated Pop Group radar/FCS forward (in place of a twin 57-mm gun mount). See chapter 16 for additional details.

Armament: Racks for 12 depth charges can be fitted to the after end of the mine rails.

Classification: The Soviet classification for the Grisha II is PSKR.

Engineering: CODAG propulsion plant.

Grisha II-class anti-submarine frigate.

The KGB-operated Grisha II has a twin 57-mm mount forward (trained on camera!) in place of the SA-N-4 missile launcher in Navy units. The after twin 57-mm mount is trained to starboard.

Few PATROL CORVETTES: PAUK CLASS

Completed:	1980–
Builders:	USSR
Displacement:	480 tons standard
	580 tons full load
Length:	191 ft 11 in (58.5 m) oa
Beam:	30 ft 10 in (9.4 m)
Draft:	8 ft 2 in (2.5 m)
Propulsion:	2 diesels (M504); 20,000 hp; 2 shafts
Speed:	28–32 knots
Range:	
Complement:	approx. 40
Missiles:	1 quad SA-N-5 Grail launcher [16]
Guns:	1 76.2-mm/59-cal AA
	1 30-mm/65-cal close-in (multibarrel)
ASW weapons:	2 RBU-1200 rocket launchers
	2 depth-charge racks
	torpedoes
Torpedoes:	4 16-in (406-mm) torpedo tubes (4 single)
Mines:	none
Radars:	1 Bass Tilt (fire control)
	1 Spin Trough (air search)
	1 . . . . . . (search)
Sonars:	medium frequency (hull-mounted)
	medium-frequency (dipping)

A few Pauk-class ASW corvettes are reported to be in service with the KGB Maritime Border Troops; most of the class serve with the Soviet Navy. (See Navy listing for details.)

Classification: Soviet PSKR type in KGB service.

Design: A circular housing for the dipping sonar is fitted in the stern, on the starboard side. Some later units have the pilothouse one deck higher.

Pauk-class patrol corvette. (West German Navy)

Few PATROL CORVETTES: T-58 CLASS (Ex-Minesweepers)

Completed:	1957–1961
Builders:	(USSR)
Displacement:	725 tons standard
	860 tons full load
Length:	229 ft 7 in (70.0 m) oa
Beam:	29 ft 10 in (9.1 m)
Draft:	8 ft 2 in (2.5 m)
Propulsion:	2 diesels; 4,000 hp; 2 shafts
Speed:	18 knots
Range:	2,500 n.miles at 13.5 knots
Complement:	
Missiles:	none
Guns:	4 57-mm/70-cal AA (2 twin)
ASW weapons:	2 RBU-1200 rocket launchers
	2 depth-charge racks
Torpedoes:	none
Mines:	rails for 18 mines
Radars:	1 Don-2 (navigation)
	1 Muff Cob (fire control) ·
	1 Spin Trough (air search)
Sonars:	high frequency (hull-mounted)
EW systems:	2 Watch Dog

These are former T-58 minesweepers reclassified in 1978 as patrol ships; some are operated by the KGB Maritime Border Troops. (See chapter 17.)

Classification: The KGB units are Soviet PSKR type.

11 PATROL CORVETTES: T-43 CLASS (Ex-Minesweepers)

Completed:	1947–1957
Builders:	(USSR)
Displacement:	500 tons standard
	570 tons full load
Length:	190 ft 3 in (58.0 m) oa
Beam:	28 ft 2 in (8.6 m)
Draft:	7 ft 7 in (2.3 m)
Propulsion:	2 diesels (9D); 2,200 hp; 2 shafts
Speed:	14 knots
Range:	2,000 n.miles at 14 knots
	3,200 n.miles at 10 knots
Complement:	approx. 65
Guns:	4 37-mm/60-cal AA (2 twin) or 2 45-mm/85-cal AA (2 single)
ASW weapons:	2 depth-charge mortars
Mines:	can carry 16 mines
Radars:	1 Ball End (fire control)
	1 Don-2 (navigation) or Spin Trough (search)
Sonars:	Tamir high-frequency

These are former minesweepers, changed to patrol ships in the 1970s and transferred to the KGB. More than 200 of these units were built, several of which continue in naval service as corvettes as well as in specialized auxiliary roles.

Classification: KGB designation is PSKR.

T-58-class patrol corvette. (1978)

T-43-class minesweeper; canvas covers the forward and after 37-mm gun mounts and various deck gear. Only a few of the once-numerous T-43s remain in Soviet service. (U.S. Navy)

PATROL CRAFT

4+ HYDROFOIL PATROL CRAFT: MURAVEY CLASS

Completed:	1982–
Builders:	(USSR)
Displacement:	230 tons full load
Length:	126 ft 7 in (38.6 m) oa
Beam:	24 ft 11 in (7.6 m)
Draft:	
Propulsion:	
Speed:	
Range:	
Complement:	
Missiles:	none
Guns:	1 76.2-mm/59-cal AA
	1 30-mm/65-cal close-in (multibarrel)
ASW weapons:	torpedoes
Torpedoes:	4 16-in (406-mm) torpedo tubes
Mines:	none
Radars:	
Sonars:	

This is a new patrol boat design. These craft are reported to be operated by the KGB.

30+ PATROL CRAFT: ZHUK CLASS

Completed:	1975–
Builders:	
Displacement:	48 tons standard
	60 tons full load
Length:	78 ft 9 in (24.0 m) oa
Beam:	16 ft 5 in (5.0 m)
Draft:	5 ft 11 in (1.8 m)
Propulsion:	2 diesels (M50); 2,400 hp; 2 shafts
Speed:	34 knots
Range:	700 n.miles at 28 knots
	1,100 n.miles at 15 knots
Complement:	approx. 15
Missiles:	none
Guns:	2 or 4 14.5-mm machine guns (1 or 2 twin)
ASW weapons:	none
Torpedoes:	none
Mines:	none
Radars:	1 Spin Trough (search)
Sonars:	none

These patrol craft have been built in large numbers for Soviet and foreign use. Most and possibly all of the Soviet units are manned by KGB Border Troops.

Class: Some 60 units of this class have been transferred to at least 16 other nations (see appendix D).

Guns: One MG mount is fitted aft; units with two gun mounts have one forward of the bridge.

Approx. 100 PATROL CRAFT: STENKA CLASS

Completed:	1967–(. . .)
Builders:	Petrovskiy, Leningrad
	. . . . . . (?)
Displacement:	170 tons standard
	210 tons full load
Length:	129 ft 7 in (39.5 m) oa
Beam:	24 ft 11 in (7.6 m)
Draft:	5 ft 11 in (1.8 m)
Propulsion:	3 diesels (M503A); 12,000 hp; 3 shafts
Speed:	36 knots
Range:	550 n.miles at 34 knots
	750 n.miles at 25 knots
Complement:	approx. 20-25
Missiles:	none
Guns:	4 30-mm/65-cal close-in (2 twin)
ASW weapons:	2 depth-charge racks
	torpedoes
Torpedoes:	4 16-in (406-mm) torpedo tubes (4 single)
Mines:	none
Radars:	1 Pot Drum or . . . . . . (search)
	1 Drum Tilt (fire control)
Sonars:	high-frequency dipping sonar

These are graceful patrol craft operated by the KGB Border Troops.

Class: The modification of the Stenka for foreign use has been designated as the Mol class; these have been transferred to Ethiopia (2), Somalia (4), Sri Lanka (1), and South Yemen (2). Some of these units have their torpedo tubes deleted.

Classification: Soviet PSKR type.

Design: These are derivatives of the Osa design. The torpedo tubes are deleted in some units and a new search-navigation radar is fitted in recent units in place of the Pot Drum. Twelve depth charges are carried.

Electronics: Fitted with a Hormone-A helicopter dipping sonar.

Stenka-class patrol craft off Nakhodka. (Kohji Ishiwata)

Stenka-class patrol craft at Yalta; note the torpedo tubes and depth-charge racks aft. (1983, L. & L. Van Ginderen)

PATROL CRAFT: PCHELA AND POLUCHAT I CLASSES

All units of these classes, operated by the KGB, have been discarded, the last in the early 1980s. See 3rd edition (pages 207 and 209).

Patrol craft of the POLUCHAT I class have been transferred to Angola, Guinea, Iraq, Mozambique, Somalia, and South Yemen.

ARMED AUXILIARIES

5 PATROL ICEBREAKERS: "IVAN SUSANIN" CLASS

Name	Completed
AYSBERG	
DUNAY	
IMENI XXV SEZDA K.P.S.S.	1975–1981
IMENI XXVI SEZDA K.P.S.S.	
NEVA	

Builders:	Admiralty, Leningrad
Displacement:	3,400 tons full load
Length:	222 ft 1 in (67.7 m) oa
Beam:	60 ft (18.3 m)
Draft:	21 ft (6.4 m)
Propulsion:	3 diesels (13D100); 5,400 hp; 3 generators connected to electric motors; 2 shafts
Speed:	14.5 knots
Range:	5,500 n.miles at 12 knots
	13,000 n.miles at 9.5 knots
Complement:	approx. 140
Helicopters:	landing area
Guns:	2 76.2-mm/59-cal AA (1 twin)
	2 30-mm/65-cal close-in (2 multibarrel)
Radars:	2 Don-Kay (navigation)
	1 Owl Screech (fire control)
	1 Strut Curve (search)

These are armed icebreakers, of the same design as the Navy and civilian DOBRYNYA NIKITICH class. A total of 30 of these ships are in Soviet service as icebreakers and polar research ships.

Classification: The KGB units are PSKR type.

Design: These ships differ from the Navy units primarily with their helicopter platform (no hangar) and heavy gun armament. There are no Bass Tilt directors for the 30-mm Gatling guns, only optical sights. The DUNAY and NEVA have been observed with positions for hand-held SA-N-5/SA-7 Grail missile launchers.

Operational: All of these ships are in the Pacific.

IVAN SUSANIN-class patrol icebreaker IMENI XXV SEZDA K.P.S.S. The twin 76.2-mm mount is forward, and the two Gatling guns are at the after end of the superstructure.

1 PATROL ICEBREAKER: Ex-"PURGA"

Name	Completed
. . . . . . (ex-PURGA)	1955

Builders:	Sudomekh, Leningrad
Displacement:	4,500 tons full load
Length:	319 ft 10 in (97.5 m) oa
Beam:	49 ft 10 in (15.2 m)
Draft:	21 ft (6.4 m)
Propulsion:	4 diesels with electric drive; 8,000 hp; 2 shafts
Speed:	16 knots
Range:	
Complement:	approx. 250
Helicopters:	no facilities
Guns:	4 100-mm/56-cal DP (4 single)
ASW weapons:	none
Torpedoes:	none
Mines:	rails for approx. 50-60 mines
Radars:	2 Don-2 (navigation)
	1 High Sieve (air search)
	1 Strut Curve (search)
	1 Sun Visor-B (fire control)
Sonars:	none
EW systems:	2 Watch Dog

The PURGA was laid down prior to World War II, probably in 1939, apparently as a combination gunboat-icebreaker in view of her heavy armament (see below). She was launched in 1951 or 1952. Only one ship of this design was built.

Reportedly, she was employed as a training ship as well as a patrol ship and icebreaker. She operates in the Pacific.

Armament: As completed, the ship additionally mounted eight 37-mm AA guns in twin mounts amidships; they were removed during a 1958–1960 overhaul. The ship was also built with four depth-charge projectors.

Like most Soviet naval ships completed in the 1950s, she has mine rails.

A Wasp Head fire-control director with the Sun Visor-B radar is fitted atop the bridge.

Name: The name PURGA is also assigned to a civilian salvage tug.

Operational: The ship was apparently laid up during the 1970s.

12 ARMED TUGS: SORUM CLASS

Name	Name	Name	Completed
AMUR	KARELIYA	SAKHALIN	
BREST	LADOGA	YAN BERZIN'	1974–(?)
CHUKOTA	PRIMORSK	ZABAYKALYE	
KAMCHATKA	PRIMOR'YE	. . . . . .	

Builders:	Yaroslavl
Displacement:	1,210 tons standard
	1,655 tons full load
Length:	191 ft 3 in (58.3 m) oa
Beam:	41 ft 4 in (12.6 m)
Draft:	15 ft 1 in (4.6 m)
Propulsion:	2 diesels (5-2D42) with electric; drive; 1,500 hp; 1 shaft
Speed:	14 knots
Range:	6,700 n. miles at 13 knots
Complement:	approx. 35
Guns:	4 30-mm/65-cal close-in (2 twin)
Radars:	2 Don-2 (navigation)

These are of the same class widely used by the Soviet Navy and civilian towing and salvage fleets. The KGB units have side-by-side 30-mm twin mounts installed forward of the bridge.

Classification: The KGB units are PSKR type.

Sorum-class patrol tug.

The former PURGA in the Far East. (1983, U.S. Navy)

Few ARMED TUGS: OKHTENSKIY CLASS

Completed:	1958–early 1960s
Builders:	Petrozavod, Leningrad
Displacement:	700 tons standard
	950 tons full load
Length:	155 ft 2 in (47.3 m) oa
Beam:	33 ft 9 in (10.3 m)
Draft:	
Propulsion:	2 diesels; 1,500 hp; 1 shaft
Speed:	13 knots
Range:	7,800 n.miles at 7 knots
Complement:	approx. 40
Helicopters:	no facilities
Guns:	2 57-mm/70-cal AA (1 twin)
Radars:	1 or 2 Don-2 (navigation) or Spin Trough (search)

Standard Soviet tug design, with a few units armed and operated by the KGB. A total of 63 units were built for Soviet naval and civilian service.

SUPPLY SHIPS

7+ SUPPLY SHIPS: "NEON ANTONOV" CLASS

Name	Name	Name	Completed
Ivan Antonov	Mikhail Konovalov	Nikolay Starshinkov	
Ivan Asdnev	Neon Antonov	. . . . . . (?)	1978–
Ivan Lednev	Nikolay Sipyagin		

Builders:	(USSR)
Displacement:	5,200 tons full load
Length:	311 ft 11 in (95.1 m) oa
Beam:	48 ft 3 in (14.7 m)
Draft:	21 ft 4 in (6.5 m)

Propulsion:	1 diesel; 1 shaft
Speed:	16 knots
Range:	
Complement:	
Helicopters:	no facilities
Guns:	see notes
Radars:	2 Palm Frond (navigation)

These are specialized supply ships employed to support KGB Maritime Border Troops in remote locations. One ship of this class is operated by the Navy, the Irbit (see chapter 22). Small landing craft are carried.

Guns: There are positions for two 14.5-mm twin machine gun mounts and two SA-N-5/SA-7 Grail missile launchers.

5 SUPPLY SHIPS: KHABAROVSK CLASS

Completed:	1950s
Builders:	(USSR)
Displacement:	650 tons full load
Tonnage:	400 DWT
Length:	152 ft 2 in (46.4 m) oa
Beam:	26 ft 3 in (8.0 m)
Draft:	10 ft 6 in (3.2 m)
Propulsion:	1 diesel; 600 hp; 1 shaft
Speed:	10 knots
Range:	1,600 n.miles at 8 knots
Complement:	approx. 30
Helicopters:	no facilities
Missiles:	none
Guns:	2 14.5-mm machine guns (1 twin) in some ships
Radars:	1 Neptune or Don (navigation)

These are small, superstructure-aft cargo ships operated by the KGB in the Pacific. Several others have been discarded as ships of the Antonov class enter service.

Mikhail Konovalov. (1983)

26
Naval Aircraft

This chapter describes the principal aircraft flown by Soviet Naval Aviation (SNA). Details on the strength, structure, and operations of SNA are found in chapter 8 of this volume. The aircraft described in this chapter are listed in table 26-1 in their respective order; aircraft are listed in this chapter by type and then by date of entering service.

Designations. Contemporary Soviet aircraft are given designations in two schemes: The first uses a NATO code name that indicates the aircraft type and the specific aircraft, and the other scheme indicates the Soviet method of identifying the aircraft design bureau and sequence of the aircraft.

The NATO scheme now in use was adopted in 1954, the name assignments being made by the Air Standards Coordinating Committee.

The aircraft code name indicates the basic type, with the following categories being applicable to SNA aircraft:

- B = Bomber (one-syllable names for propeller and two-syllable names for jet aircraft)
- C = Cargo
- F = Fighter
- H = Helicopter
- M = Miscellaneous fixed-wing (including maritime patrol aircraft)

Suffix letters are appended to the NATO code names to indicate variants of a basic aircraft, as Bear-D; the use of these suffix letters with Soviet designations, as Tu-20D, is incorrect.

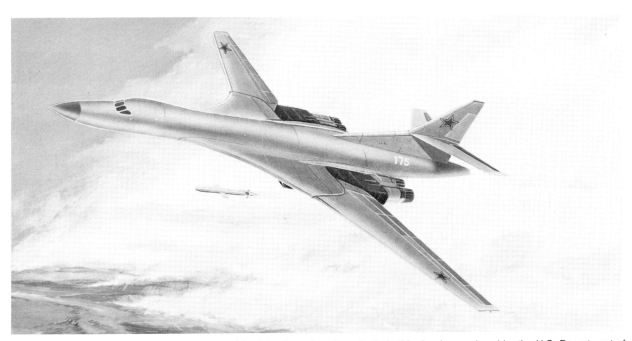

A Blackjack is depicted launching a long-range AS-15 land-attack cruise missile in this drawing produced by the U.S. Department of Defense. The progression from Badger to Backfire to Blackjack and their associated anti-ship missiles has increased the threat to Western warships and merchant shipping from Soviet Naval Aviation. Similarly, the KIEV and later carriers present an increased naval air threat away from Soviet territory.

TABLE 26-1. SOVIET NAVAL AIRCRAFT

Soviet Designations	NATO Name	Status*		Naval roles
Bomber/Strike types				
Tu-...	Blackjack	development		bomber/missile strike
Tu-22M/Tu-26	Backfire	SAF	SNA	bomber/missile strike
Tu-22	Blinder	SAF	SNA	bomber; photo reconnaissance
Tu-20/95/142	Bear	SAF	SNA	reconnaissance/targeting; ASW
Tu-16	Badger	SAF	SNA	bomber/missile strike; ELINT/reconnaissance; ECM; tanker
Fighter/Attack types				
Su-17	Flanker	SAF	possibly SNA	fighter
MiG-29	Fulcrum	SAF	possibly SNA	fighter
Su-25	Frogfoot	SAF	possibly SNA	ground attack
Yak-38	Forger	—	SNA	fighter/attack
Su-20	Fitter-C	SAF	SNA	fighter/attack
Maritime Patrol types				
Il-38	May	—	SNA	maritime patrol/ASW
Be-12	Mail	—	SNA	maritime patrol/ASW
Cargo types				
Il-20	Coot-C	—	SNA	ELINT/reconnaissance
An-12	Cub	SAF	SNA	ELINT/reconnaissance; ASW test bed
Helicopters				
Ka-27	Helix	—	SNA	ASW; utility
Mi-14	Haze	—	SNA	ASW; mine countermeasures
Mi-8	Hip	SAF	SNA	transport
Ka-25	Hormone	—	SNA	ASW; targeting; utility

*SAF = Soviet Air Forces; SNA = Soviet Naval Aviation.

Soviet design bureau designations applicable to naval aircraft are based on the following code, derived from the names of the founders of the specific bureaus; the following are those currently used by naval aircraft:

An = Antonov
Be = Beriev
Il = Ilyushin
Ka = Kamov
Mi = Mil'
Su = Sukhoi
Tu = Tupolev
Yak = Yakovlev

This basic scheme was adopted by the Soviet government in 1940 (although aircraft designs supervised by Andrei N. Tupolev carried the bureau prefix ANT until 1947). The numbers used in conjunction with these bureau designations indicate the sequence of the aircraft, with two numerical series in use for some aircraft, one indicating the bureau design (e.g., Tu-95) and one the military designation (Tu-20).

Suffix letters are used with these bureau designations, the most common ones being *bis* for later variants; M for *Modifikatsirovanny* (modification); MP for *Morskoy Pulubnyi* (maritime carrier-based); R for

Razvedchik (reconnaissance); and U for *Uchebno* (instructional—for trainer version).

Characteristics.[1] The performance, dimensions, and weight data provided here are approximate, based on the best available public sources. Combat radius indicates the aircraft's radius, carrying weapons, with a majority of the flight to and from the target at optimum speed and altitude, with a low-level, high-speed "dash" to and from the target, except that missile-launching aircraft will release their weapons at a medium altitude (approximately 20,000 ft/6,100 m).

Special abbreviations used in this chapter are IGE = In Ground Effect, OGE = Out of Ground Effect, and T/O = Take Off.

BOMBER/STRIKE AIRCRAFT

Tu- . . . Blackjack

The Blackjack is a new Soviet bomber-type aircraft expected to enter operational service by 1988 with the Soviet Air Forces and SNA.

The aircraft is larger than the U.S. B-1 strategic bomber. The Blackjack has variable-geometry wings that extend for cruise flight, landing, and takeoff, and sweep back for high-speed flight; four engines are fitted in the wing roots. The estimated dimensions of the Blackjack indicate that up to 12 of the AS-15 land-attack cruise missiles could be carried internally; the design of the variable-geometry wings probably prevents weapons from being carried on wing pylons.

Status: The Blackjack is believed to have been initially photographed by U.S. reconnaissance satellites in November 1981, parked at Ramenskoye next to two Tu-144 supersonic transports. The plane was reported in flight testing when this edition went to press. Series production is expected to take place at a new complex built at Kazan.

Crew	
Engines:	4 Koliesov turbofan with afterburner
Weights:	empty approx. 143,000 lbs (65,000 kg)
	maximum T/O approx. 397,000 lbs (180,450 kg)
Dimensions:	span approx. 174 ft (53.0 m) fully extended
	span approx. 95 ft (28.9 m) fully swept
	length approx. 188 ft 8 in (57.5 m)
Speed:	maximum approx. 1,375 mph (2,200 km/h)
Ceiling:	
Range:	combat radius approx. 4,525 miles (7,300 km)
Armament:	anti-ship or land-attack cruise missiles
Radar:	

Tu-22M Backfire

The Backfire is a long-range, high-performance bomber flown by Soviet strategic aviation and Soviet Naval Aviation. (In the former service the Backfire appears to be assigned to the theater strike role, and is not intended for strategic attacks against the United States.) SNA employs the Backfire in the anti-ship missile role.

[1] More detailed descriptions of contemporary Soviet aircraft will be found in the monthly journal *Air International* and the annual *Jane's All the World's Aircraft*. The most comprehensive compendium of information on Soviet naval aircraft up to its publication date is Bill Gunston, *Aircraft of the Soviet Union* (London: Osprey, 1983).

Backfire-B with variable-geometry wings swept back for high-speed flight. The fixed, nose-mounted refueling probe has been removed in accordance with Soviet-U.S. agreements to deter use of the Backfire as a strategic bomber, although the probes can be installed within a matter of hours.

The prototype Backfire-A aircraft underwent extensive redesign to produce the definitive -B version. In particular, the wings and landing gear were thoroughly changed. The Backfire is a variable-geometry aircraft; the outer wing sections extending for takeoff, landing, and cruise flight and sweep back for high-speed flight. Two large turbofan engines are buried in the wing roots. The huge tail fin is fitted with fuel tanks and ECM equipment as well as the tail-gun mounting. A fixed refueling probe can be installed in the nose. A twin 23-mm, remote-control gun mounting is provided in the tail. Offensive ordnance consists of one AS-4 or possibly AS-6 missile semi-recessed under the fuselage or two missiles carried on pylons under the forward portion of the very long engine housings. The aircraft also carries ECM pods and possibly decoys. An internal weapons bay is provided for carrying bombs, but cannot be used when a missile is fitted in the semi-recessed configuration.

There has been considerable debate over the Backfire's range. Previously the U.S. Defense Intelligence Agency (DIA) estimated the aircraft's unrefueled range at 3,100 miles (5,000 km), while the U.S. Central Intelligence Agency (CIA) estimate was 2,300 miles (3,700 km). During 1985 the DIA revised its estimates downward, although there still is no agreement among analysts. Their current estimates are given below.

Designation: During SALT negotiations the Soviets used the designation Tu-22M, the M suffix indicating that the Backfire evolved from an extensive modification of the Tu-22 Blinder (see below). The designation Tu-26 has been used for the Backfire in the Western press, while Tu-136 may have been the design bureau designation. The Backfire-A was a pre-production development aircraft with different wing and landing-gear arrangements, and other changes from the production -B model.

Status: Flight tests began in 1969 with a least two prototypes. Up to 12 Backfire-A models were built and formed a transition/training unit. The Backfire-B entered SNA service in 1974, shortly after becoming operational with Soviet strategic aviation. Since the start of production, Backfires have been assigned to the two Soviet air services in approximately equal numbers, with some 280 built by early 1986; the current production rate is at least 30 aircraft per year. An improved Backfire-C is now being delivered to SNA, believed to have an improved weapons delivery capability.

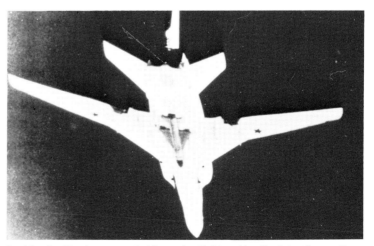

Backfire-B with wings extended for cruise flight and landing/takeoff operations; an AS-4 Kitchen missile is fitted on the fuselage centerline.

BACKFIRE-B

Crew:	4
Engines:	2 Kuznetsov NK-144 derivative turbofan with afterburner; approx. 44,090 lbst (19,840 kgst) each
Weights:	empty 110,000 lbs (49,500 kg) maximum T/O 270,000 lbs (121,500 kg)
Dimensions:	span 113 ft (34.45 m) fully extended span 85 ft 11 in (26.2 m) fully swept length 139 ft 5 in (42.2 m) height 33 ft (10.06 m)
Speed:	cruise approx. 500 mph (800 km/h) maximum 1,250 mph (2,000 km/h) at 36,080 ft (11,000 m) (Mach 1.8); 650 mph (1,050 km/h) at sea level
Ceiling:	service 55,760 ft (17,000 m)
Range:	CIA estimate 4,050 miles (6,460 km) DIA estimate 6,450 miles (10,320 km) CIA estimated combat radius 2,100–2,475 miles (3,360–3,960 km) DIA estimated combat radius 2,480 miles (4,000 km) (range is extended in Backfire-C)
Armament:	2 AS-4 Kitchen air-to-surface missiles; also AS-9 anti-radar missile or 26,400 lbs (12,000 kg) ordnance in weapons bay 2 23-mm cannon (remote-control tail turret)
Radar:	Down Beat (bombnav) Fan Tail (gunfire control)

Tu-22 Blinder

The Tu-22 Blinder was the first supersonic bomber to enter Soviet service. The twin-turbojet aircraft is in service with Soviet strategic aviation and SNA. However, it has been less than fully successful and did not enter large-scale production to replace the Badger, as once planned. The Blinder was the last bomber-type aircraft to be produced in the Soviet Union until the debute of the Tu-22M Backfire. In SNA service the Blinder is used to deliver free-fall bombs, with a few aircraft configured for reconnaissance and training.

The Blinder is a swept-wing aircraft with two turbojet engines mounted in pods at the base of the tail fin. Most aircraft have a partially retractable in-flight refueling probe in the nose, a nose radome, and tandem seating for the crew of three. External fuel tanks are faired into the trailing edges of the wings. The Blinder-A carries bombs internally in two weapon bays; the Blinder-B (Air Forces) can carry an AS-4 Kitchen missile. Defensive armament consists of a remote-control, single NR-23 23-mm tail gun. The Blinder-D trainer has a raised rear cockpit with dual controls for an instructor (replacing the radar observer's position). The aircraft has a supersonic dash capability.

Designation: The Tupolev design-bureau designation for the aircraft was Tu-105, the military designation being Tu-22. The Blinder was apparently developed as a supersonic bomber to be competitive with the Myasishchev M-52 Bounder, which did not enter squadron service.

Status: The Blinder entered service in 1962, and missile-armed aircraft became operational in the Soviet Air Forces from about 1967; less than 200 aircraft were built before the production ended in 1969. Some 50 Blinder-A bombers are in SNA service, plus a few Blinder-C reconnaissance and Blinder-D training aircraft. Blinders have been transferred to Iraq and Libya. Only a few Blinder-C reconnaissance aircraft have

been identified; they have six cameras fitted in the weapons bay plus various electronic gear (details vary).

Naval variants:

Blinder-A	bomber aircraft carrying gravity bombs.
Blinder-C	photo reconnaissance aircraft.
Blinder-D	trainer aircraft with modified cockpit (Tu-22U).

Crew	3
Engines:	2 Kolesov VD-7 turbojet with afterburner; approx. 30,800 lbst (14,000 kgst) each
Weights:	empty 88,000 lbs (40,000 kg) maximum T/O 184,580 lbs (83,900 kg)
Dimensions:	span 89 ft 3 in (27.7 m) length 132 ft 11 in (40.53 m) height 35 ft (10.67 m)
Speed:	cruise 560 mph (900 km/h) at 36,080 ft (11,000 m) (Mach 0.85) maximum 920 mph (1,475 km/h) at 36,080 ft (11,000 m) (Mach 1.5)
Ceiling:	service 60,000 ft (18,300 m)
Range:	4,030 miles (6,500 km) all subsonic combat radius 1,800-mile (2,900 km) on hi-lo-hi mission
Armament:	1 23-mm NR-23 cannon 17,600 lbs (8,000 kg) bombs
Radar:	Down Beat (bombnav) Bee Hind (gunfire control)

Tu-20/95/142 Bear

The Tu-20 Bear was developed as a strategic bomber and has been in Soviet first-line service for almost three decades. It continues in operation with Soviet strategic aviation and SNA, in the latter air arm being flown in the reconnaissance–ship targeting and ASW roles. The Bear-F (Navy) and Bear-H (Air Forces) remain in production, with earlier Bear-B/C aircraft being converted to the Bear-G configuration (Air Forces). The Bear is the largest aircraft flown by the Soviet Navy.[2]

The only turboprop-propelled strategic bomber to achieve operational service with any air force, the Bear is a large, swept-wing aircraft with four turboprop engines turning contra-rotating, four-bladed propellers. The plane's long range can be further extended through in-flight refueling; a fixed receiving probe is fitted in the nose. Defensive armament can consist of one 23-mm fixed cannon in the nose and up to three 23-mm twin gun mounts (dorsal, ventral, and tail). The Bear-D is a naval reconnaissance and targeting version; it carries no offensive weapons, and is fitted with the Big Bulge surface-search radar and a Video Data Link (VDL) for transmitting target data to missile-launching units. The Bear-F ASW variant carries expendable sonobuoys as well as radar for detecting submarines, and can attack with a large payload of homing torpedoes and depth bombs. Some Bear-D aircraft have been observed with the tail turret replaced by an extended tailcone, possibly housing a trailing antenna for low-frequency communications (a Magnetic Anomaly Detection [MAD] antenna is normally fitted to the tail of the Bear-F variant).

[2] For a recent commentary and pictorial on the Bear see Norman Polmar, "The Ubiquitous Bear," Naval Institute *Proceedings* (December 1985), pp. 54–59.

Blinder-A, showing the aircraft's sleek but unsuccessful design. Naval Blinders carry only free-fall bombs; those assigned to the Air Forces carry air-to-surface missiles.

Blinder-C reconnaissance aircraft in a "dirty" configuration—with flaps and wheels down—coming in for a landing. The aircraft has photographic and probably electronic reconnaissance gear.

A Bear-F releases a sonobuoy (seen between starboard engines); the after weapons bay is open; the modified Wet Eye radar is just forward of the weapons bays; there is no radome in the chin position. The Bear has been in production longer than any other combat aircraft in history.

The Bear-D is distinguished by the Big Bulge-A surface-search radar in the ventral position and a smaller radome in the chin position. All naval Bears have the fixed refueling probe and, apparently, twin 23-mm guns in the dorsal, ventral, and tail positions.

Bear-F anti-submarine aircraft with open weapons bay (the Bear-D does not carry weapons). The Bear-F has larger engine nacelles than the Bear-D; there are blade antennas atop the fuselage and a MAD antenna mounted on top of the tail.

Designation: Tu-95 is the Tupolev design bureau designation, which is sometimes used (incorrectly) in the West to indicate military versions of the aircraft, which the Soviets at least initially designated Tu-20. The Bear-F and possibly Bear-H have the bureau designation Tu-142. The Bear's engines, wing, tail assembly, and other components were used for the Tu-114 *Rossiya* (NATO Cleat) civilian airliner, the world's largest civil passenger aircraft prior to the Boeing 747. The Bear also was the basis for the Tu-114D Moss, a Soviet AWACS (Airborne Warning And Control System) aircraft.

Status: First flight 1954; the aircraft entered service with strategic aviation in 1955, with SNA receiving its first Bear-D in the mid-1960s and the Bear-F in 1970. Approximately 250 to 300 Bear bomber aircraft were built into the mid-1960s, with production of the Bear-D and then -F models following. Subsequently, production of the Bear-H (to carry the AS-15 strategic cruise missile) began in the early 1980s, with older bombers being converted to the Bear-G to carry the AS-4 missile. The aircraft remains in service with Soviet strategic aviation as a bomber, while SNA flies some 45 Bear-D reconnaissance-targeting aircraft and some 55 Bear-F ASW aircraft, with the latter aircraft still being produced. Reportedly, India plans to purchase six to eight Bear-F for the maritime patrol role. Soviet naval Bears are assigned to the Northern and Pacific fleets.

(Soviet strategic aviation flies the A/B/C/E/G/H variants, the Bear-E being a reconnaissance aircraft; the Bear-A has an unrefueled combat *radius* estimated at 3,360 miles/5,425 km with a 25,000-lb/11,350-kg bomb load or 4,500 miles/7,240 km with an 1,000-lb/5,000-kg load; the Bear-B/C aircraft carry the AS-3 Kangaroo missile.)

Naval variants:

Bear-D	reconnaissance/anti-ship targeting aircraft; Big Bulge-A radar.
Bear-F	reconnaissance/ASW aircraft; enlarged engine nacelles; Wet Eye radar; IOC 1970.

Crew:	
Engines:	4 Kuznetsov NK-12MV turboprop; 12,000 shp each
Weights:	empty approx. 165,000 lbs (75,000 kg)
	Bear-D maximum T/O 356,000 lbs (160,200 kg)
	Bear-F maximum T/O 413,600 lbs (188,000 kg)
Dimensions:	Bear-D span 159 ft 1 in (48.5 m)
	Bear-F span 167 ft 1 in (51.2m)
	Bear-D length 155 ft 10 in (47.5 m)
	Bear-F length 162 ft 4 in (49.5 m)
	Bear-D height 38 ft 8½ in (11.8 m)
	Bear-F height 39 ft 8 in (12.1 m)
Speed:	cruise 465 mph (750 km/h)
	maximum 575 mph (925 km/h)
Ceiling:	service 41,000 ft (12,500 m)
Range:	7,750 + mi (12,500 + km)
	Bear-F combat radius 3,100 miles (5,000 km)
Armament:	up to 7 23-mm NR-23 cannon
	17,600 + lbs (8,000 + kg) torpedoes, depth bombs in Bear-F
Radar:	Big Bulge-A (surface search) in Bear-D
	Wet Eye (surface search) in Bear-F
	. . . . . . (gunfire control)

Tu-16 Badger

The Tu-16 Badger is a turbojet-powered medium bomber that has been in wide use by the Soviet Union for three decades. It serves in the conventional bomber, anti-ship missile, reconnaissance, ELINT, ECM, and tanker roles with Soviet strategic aviation and SNA.

The Badger has a swept-wing configuration with two large turbojet engines housed in nacelles faired into the fuselage at the wing roots. The engines have been updated during the aircraft's long production run, culminating in the engines listed below. When employed in the tanker role, the Badger has fuel tanks fitted in the weapons bay and trails a drogue from the starboard wing-tip; the receiving probe is fitted in the port wing-tip of Badgers. The -A variant carries gravity bombs in an internal weapons bay; the -C and -G strike aircraft carry air-to-surface missiles under the fuselage or on wing pylons. Most aircraft have two 23-mm cannon in dorsal, ventral, and tail mounts, and bombers not having a large radome can mount a seventh cannon fixed on the starboard side of the nose.

Designation: The Tupolev bureau's design designation for the Badger was Tu-88; the Tu-98 Backfin was a Badger airframe flown in 1955 in the research role; and the Tu-104 Camel was a civilian airliner derived from the Badger.

Status: First flight late 1952; production began the following year with squadron delivery to the Air Forces from 1954−1955 and deliveries to the Navy beginning in the late 1950s (with many Air Forces aircraft transferred to SNA). Approximately 2,000 Badgers were built in the Soviet Union through the mid-1960s and more than 80 more were produced in China. SNA currently flies some 275 Badgers in the missile-strike role; 80 Badger-A aircraft serve in the tanker role; perhaps another 80 Badgers fly in reconnaissance, ELINT, and ECM roles; and a few Badgers in conventional bomber and trainer configurations.

Badgers have been transferred to China, Egypt, Indonesia, Iraq, and Libya.

Naval variants:

Badger-A	bomber, tanker, trainer; flown by SNA and strategic aviation; can carry 8,360 lbs (3,800 kg) bombs with 2,975 n.mile (4,800 km) radius; IOC 1954−1955.
Badger-C	missile strike; 2 AS-2 Kipper or 2 AS-5 Kelt missiles; Puff Ball radar with AS-2; Shorthorn radar with AS-5; IOC 1960.
Badger-D	electronic reconnaissance; Puff Ball and Short Horn radars.
Badger-E	photo reconnaissance; cameras in weapons bay.
Badger-F	electronic and photo reconnaissance.
Badger-G	missile strike; 2 AS-5 Kelt or 2 AS-6 Kingfish missiles; combat radius 1,985+ n.mile (3,200+ km); Shorthorn radar; IOC 1965.
Badger-H	EW/strike escort aircraft.
Badger-J	EW/strike escort aircraft
Badger-K	ELINT/electronic reconnaissance aircraft.

Crew:	6
Engines:	2 Mikulin AM-3M turbojets; 20,950 lbst (9,425 kg) each in later aircraft
Weights:	empty 81,840 lbs (37,200 kg)
	maximum T/O 158,456 lbs (72,000 kg)
Dimensions:	span 108 ft (32.93 m)
	length 114 ft 2 in (34.8 m)
	height 35 ft 5 in (10.8 m)
Speed:	cruise 530 mph (850 km/h) (Mach 0.8)
	maximum 615 mph (990 km/h) (Mach 0.9)
Ceiling:	service 40,350 ft (12,300 m)
Range:	4,000 mi (6,400 km)
	combat radius 1,920 mi (3,100 km)
Armament:	19,800 lbs (9,000 kg) in weapons bay in Badger-A
	2 AS-2 Kelt or AS-5 Kelt missiles in Badger-C
	2 AS-5 Kelt or 2 AS-6 Kingfish missiles in Badger-G; also AS-9 anti-radar missile
	up to 7 23-mm cannon
Radar:	see above for bombnav radars
	Bee Hind (gunfire control)

Badger-G naval strike aircraft with AS-5 Kelt missiles on wing pylons, outboard of the landing gear. The bomber/strike variants have Plexiglas noses; the other variants differ in nose configurations. A 23-mm cannon is fitted on the starboard side of the fuselage.

The Badger-E photo aircraft is similar to the bomber/strike versions, but with cameras fitted in the weapons bays. The dorsal and tail 23-mm gun positions are visible; another twin mounting is in the ventral position. The housings outboard of the engine nacelles are for the four-wheel bogies.

The Badger-D electronic reconnaissance aircraft has the Short Horn radar in the nose and the Puff Ball radar in the chin position; there is a Towel Rail HF antenna blade above the cockpit and four small electronic "blisters" under the fuselage. (U.S. Navy)

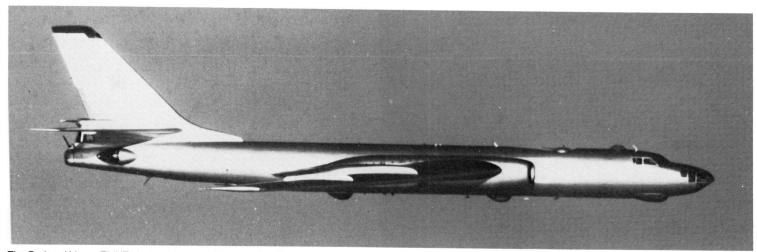

The Badger-K is an ELINT/electronic reconnaissance aircraft with a bomber-type nose configuration, with two electronic blisters in the ventral positions. Soviet Naval Aviation flies more Badgers than any other aircraft type. (U.S. Navy)

A Badger-A tanker (lower aircraft) refuels another Badger. SNA and the Soviet Air Forces fly Badgers in the tanker role; the Air Forces also fly Mya-4 Bison and Il-76 Candid tankers.

FIGHTER/ATTACK AIRCRAFT

The U.S. intelligence community has identified the Su-27 Flanker and MiG-29 Fulcrum as the most likely candidates to operate in the fighter/attack role from the nuclear-propelled aircraft carriers now under construction in the Soviet Union. In addition, the Su-25 Frogfoot has been named along with the Flanker and Fulcrum as having been observed in airfield tests of carrier operating techniques.

Su-27 Flanker

This is a new air-intercept fighter assigned to the Soviet Air Defense Forces; the Flanker has a look-down/shoot-down capability and is capable of all-weather operation. The aircraft is highly maneuverable and believed to be comparable in capability to the U.S. F-15 Eagle. A ground-attack version is also being produced.

The Flanker originally flew with a variable-geometry wing, but is also being manufactured with a fixed-wing. The aircraft has the same track-while-scan radar as the MiG-29 Fulcrum and is reported to carry up to eight AA-10 missiles in the fighter role or 13,200 lbs (6,000 kg) of other ordnance in the attack role. The twin-engine aircraft is credited with a speed of Mach 2.3 at altitude and 1.1 at sea level.

Status: The Flanker entered operational service in 1984–1985.

MiG-29 Fulcrum

This is an advanced air-intercept fighter assigned to the Air Defense Forces; it is also being produced in a ground-attack configuration for the Air Forces. The Fulcrum has been described by *Jane's All the World's Aircraft* as "First of a completely new generation of Soviet fighters to enter service. . . ." The Fulcrum is about the same size as the U.S. F-16.

In the air-intercept role the aircraft carries six AA-8 or AA-9 missiles; the air-to-ground version can deliver up to 8,800 lbs (3,960 kg) of ordnance and has a twin-barrel 23-mm cannon with a rate of fire of 3,000 rounds-per-minute.

Status: The aircraft entered squadron service in 1984.

Su-25 Frogfoot

The Frogfoot is a subsonic ground-attack aircraft, intended to attack tanks and defend ground positions. It is similar in concept to the U.S. A-10 Thunderbolt close-air-support aircraft (although its configuration is closer to the unsuccessful Northrop A-9 competitive prototype). The Frogfoot has seen extensive combat in the anti-guerrilla operations in Afghanistan.

An estimated 8,800 pounds of air-to-ground ordnance can be carried, including an anti-tank cannon.

Status: The Frogfoot is believed to have become operational in 1982.

Yak-38MP Forger

The Forger is a VSTOL aircraft developed for operation from the KIEV-class aircraft carriers. The plane serves in the fighter/attack roles.

The Forger has a lift-plus-lift-cruise configuration, using two forward lift engines that are mounted vertically and an aft-mounted vectored thrust engine for both vertical lift and propulsion. This configuration enhances VTOL payload compared to the British-U.S. Harrier VSTOL aircraft, the Forger having a 64 percent VTOL payload advantage over the AV-8A Harrier and 25 percent over the AV-8B. The Soviet plane initially was seen flying only in the VTOL mode, but now operates as a VSTOL aircraft as well. The Forger has a swept-wing configuration with the outer panels folding upward for shipboard handling. The wing area is relatively small (approximately 199 ft²/18.5m²). The single-seat -A version is the standard, with one or two -B versions embarked in carriers as an operational (combat) trainer. Four wing pylons can accommodate a variety of weapons or fuel tanks; in the interceptor role the aircraft generally carries two Aphid air-to-air missiles and two external fuel tanks.

(Steps in the Forger development included the MiG-21PFM Fishbed-G lift-engine test bed, a high-performance fighter with two lift engines buried in its fuselage, and the Yakovlev Freehand, a VSTOL technology demonstration aircraft, with twin engines with vectorable nozzles. The Freehand, first seen publicly in 1967, is believed to have flown VTOL sea trials on the helicopter carrier MOSKVA.)

Designation: The Forger was initially identified by Western intelligence as Yak-36; subsequently identified about 1984 as the Yak-38, with the suffix MP for *Morskoy Pulubnyi*.

Status: First deployed on board the KIEV in 1976 and subsequently in the other ships of the class. Flown only by Soviet Naval Aviation.

Forgers on the deck of a KIEV-class VSTOL carrier with wings folded for stowage. The intakes are open for the vertical-lift engines and AA-8 Aphid air-to-air missiles are visible under the wings.

A Forger-A with landing gear extended and intake open for verrtical-lift engines (behind cockpit). The Forger has been only a limited success and the Indian Navy, which uses considerable Soviet equipment, opted instead for the Anglo-American Harrier VSTOL aircraft for carrier operations. (West German Navy)

A Forger approaching the carrier KIEV during operations in the Mediterranean. The naval ensign is on both sides of the fuselage, on the engine air intakes.

One two-seat Forger-B is generally embarked in each of the KIEV-class carriers. This aircraft is larger in most dimensions than the single-seat Forger-A. (Courtesy *Air International*)

Crew:	1 in Forger-A; 2 in Forger-B
Engines:	1 Lyul'ka AL-21 turbojet cruise engine; approx. 17,600 lbst (8,000 kgst)
	2 Kolesov turbojet lift engines; approx. 7,700 lbst (3,500 kgst) each
Weights:	maximum T/O 25,740 lbs (11,700 kg)
Dimensions:	span 24 ft (7.32 m)
	Forger-A length 50 ft 10 in (15.5 m)
	Forger-B length 58 ft (17.68 m)
	height 14 ft 4 in (4.37 m)
Speed:	maximum 625 mph (1,010 km/h) at 36,000 ft (11,000 m) (Mach 0.95); 610 mph (980 km/h) at sea level (Mach 0.8)
Ceiling:	39,360 ft (12,000 m)
Range:	radius as deck-launched interceptor 115 mi (185 km) with 75 minutes on station
	strike radius 150 mi (240 km) with approx. 6,600 lbs (3,000 kg) weapons (lo-lo-lo mission); 230 mi (370 km) with same payload (hi-lo-hi mission)
Armament:	approx. 6,600 lbs (2,970 kg) external stores (bombs, rockets, missiles, gun pods, including AA-8 Aphid air-to-air or SA-7 Kerry air-to-surface missiles)
Radar:	(small ranging radar)

Su-20 Fitter-C

This is a ground-support fighter with variable-sweep wings that evolved from the Su-7 fixed-wing strike fighter. The Fitter is the Navy's only land-based fighter, with regiments in both the Baltic and Pacific fleets. These were the first land-based fighter aircraft to be flown by SNA since about 1960.

The Fitter-C is a swept-wing, varible-geometry aircraft, with a streamlined configuration based on a single, high-powered AL-21F engine. The outer wing sections, fitted with slats and trailing-edge flaps, are used primarily to aid STOL takeoff and landing. The aircraft suffers from limited internal fuel and is generally seen with two large drop tanks (294 gallons each) on twin fuselage pylons. The Fitter-C has an advanced weapon-aiming system with six or eight pylons for more than 7,000 lbs (3,150 kg) of weapons and drop tanks; two 30-mm cannon are in the wing roots.

Status: A modified Su-7 served as a test bed for the variable-geometry aircraft, and was first observed publicly in 1967 (code named Fitter-B). The definitive Su-20 Fitter-C was first seen in 1970. Fitters are flown by the Soviet Air Forces and SNA as well as by the air forces of Egypt, Libya, Peru, Poland, and Syria.

Crew:	1
Engines:	1 Lyul'ka AL-21F turbojet with afterburner; 24,200 lbst (11,000 kgst)
Weights:	empty 22,000 lbs (10,000 kg)
	maximum T/O 38,940 lbs (17,700 (17,700 kg)
Dimensions:	span 45 ft 11 in (14.0 m) fully extended
	span 34 ft 9 in (10.6 m) fully swept
	length 61 ft 6 in (18.75 m) over nose probe
	height 15 ft 7 in (4.75 m)
Speed:	maximum 1,333 mph (2,133 km/h) at 36,000 ft (11,000 m) Mach 2.0); 790 mph (1,246 km/h) at sea level (clean) (Mach 1.05); maximum with external stores approx. 590 mph (685 km/h) (Mach 0.8) at sea level
Ceiling:	55,760 ft (17,000 m)

Range: strike radius 390 mi (625 km) with 4,400 lbs (2,000 kg) external stores (hi-lo-hi mission); 225 mi (360 km) with same load (lo-lo-lo mission)

Armament: 2 30-mm NR-30 cannon

7,000 lbs (3,150 kg) external stores (bombs, rockets, missiles, including AA-2 Atoll air-to-air missiles; AS-9 anti-radar missiles; and probably AS-7 Kerry air-to-surface missiles)

Radar: High Fix (air intercept)

Fitter-C making a landing approach. These fighter-attack aircraft were the first land-based fighter planes operated by SNA since about 1960; up to that time SNA had a large fighter for the defense of naval bases and to support coastal operations.

Fitter fighter-attack aircraft with two drop tanks under the wings and a pair of air-to-air missiles mounted on wing-root pylons. Two fuselage attachment points are also visible on this aircraft. (U.S. Navy)

The May land-based patrol/anti-submarine aircraft was produced in only limited numbers and has not enjoyed the wide use of that of its Western counterparts, especially the Lockheed P-3 Orion series. Note the four turboprop engines and the long MAD "stinger" in the tail.

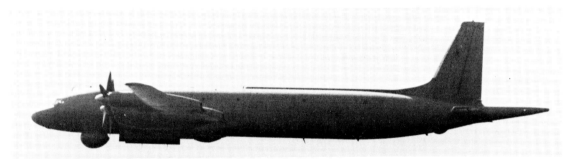

A May with its weapons bay open and the Wet Eye radar clearly visible forward. The aircraft was lengthened from the Il-18 Coot design to provide space for the weapons bay. (U.S. Navy)

MARITIME PATROL AIRCRAFT

Il-38 May

Generally resembling the U.S. P-3 Orion patrol aircraft in appearance and role, the May is believed to be the first Soviet land-based aircraft designed from the outset for the maritime patrol/ASW mission. The aircraft was adopted from Il-18 Coot transport (much the same as the Orion was adapted from the commercial Lockheed Electra).

The May is a large, low-wing aircraft with four turboprop engines. The fuselage is lengthened from the original Il-18 design, and the wings have been strengthened and mounted farther forward. A radome is fitted under the forward fuselage, a Magnetic Anomaly Detector (MAD) antenna boom extends from the tail, and there is an internal weapons bay for torpedoes, mines, and depth bombs. Expendable sonobuoys and non-acoustic sensors are also carried, and the plane has a computerized tactical evaluation system. No defensive armament is fitted. Endurance is about 12 hours at cruise speed.

(The Il-20 Coot ELINT aircraft are variants of the original passenger configuration and not of the Il-38 May.)

Status: The aircraft apparently flew in prototype form in 1967–1968, and entered squadron service in 1970. Several aircraft have been transferred to India. Some Mays were flown with Egyptian markings until 1972, but were subsequently removed from Egypt.

Crew:	12
Engines:	4 Ivchyenko AI-20M turboprop; 4,200 shp + 495 lbst (223 kgst) each
Weights:	empty 79,200 lbs (36,000 kg)
	maximum T/O 139,700 lbs (63,500 kg)

Dimensions:	span 122 ft 8 in (37.4 m)
	length 129 ft 10 ½ in (39.6 m) over MAD boom
	height 33 ft 4 in (10.16 m)
Speed:	cruise 250 mph (400 km/h)
	maximum 370 mph (600 km/h)
Ceiling:	
Range:	4,465 mi (7,200 km)
Armament:	ASW torpedoes and depth bombs; mines
Radar:	Wet Eye (surface search)

Be-12 Mail

The Mail is one of the two flying boats remaining in first-line naval service, the other being the Japanese PS-1 *Shin Mewa*. SNA flies about 95 of these amphibians for maritime patrol, ASW, and search-and-rescue operations. The Soviet designation for this aircraft is also M-12 and its popular Russian name is *Tchaika* (seagull).

This is the last aircraft in a long line of Beriev flying boats produced in the Soviet Union. The Mail has distinctive gull-shaped wings, twin tail, and other features seen by the earlier, piston-engine Be-6 Madge.[3] The Mail has an elongated radome protruding from a glazed nose, and a Magnetic Anomaly Detector (MAD) boom mounted in the tail. The twin turboprop engines are mounted high on the wings. The main landing gear and tail wheel retract fully into the boat hull. Torpedoes, mines, and depth bombs can be carried on a pylon under each wing and in an internal weapons bay fitted in the after section of the hull. Expendable sonobuoys can also be carried.

[3] The principal intermediate design between the Be-6 and Be-12 was the swept-wing, turbojet Be-10 Mallow, which, like its contemporary U.S. P6M Seamaster, did not enter operational service. China continues to fly a few Be-6 flying boats.

The Mail continues in first-line Soviet service after the retirement of the last flying boats from the U.S. Navy. The gull-winged aircraft has a distinctive twin-tail configuration, with an elongated nose radome and a MAD antenna in the tail. (West German Navy)

Status: First flight in 1960. Operational only in SNA, although they were flown with Egyptian markings prior to 1973.

Crew:	5
Engines:	2 Ivchyenko AL-20D turboprop; 4,190 ehp each
Weights:	empty 47,850 lbs (21,700 kg)
	maximum T/O 64,790 lbs (29,450 kg)
Dimensions:	span 97 ft 5 ½ in (29.71 m)
	length 98 ft 11 ½ in (30.17 m)
	height 22 ft 11 ½ in (7.0 m) on undercarriage
Speed:	cruise 200 mph (320 km/h)
	maximum 380 mph (610 km/h)
Ceiling:	37,000 ft (11,280 m)
Range:	2,480 mi (4,000 km)
Armament:	ASW torpedoes and depth bombs; mines
Radar:	(surface search)

A Mail on the beach with landing gear extended. There is an internal, fuselage weapons bay, and weapons can be carried on wing pylons.

Maintenance personnel check a Mail's turboprop engines prior to a flight.

CARGO AIRCRAFT

The aircraft listed below are those cargo-type aircraft known to be employed by SNA for ELINT, reconnaissance, and research purposes. Several other aircraft of this category are flown by SNA in the cargo-utility roles.

Il-20 Coot-A

The Coot-A is a naval ELINT aircraft derived from the basic Il-18, a turboprop-powered transport that was in wide use during the 1960s and early 1970s with *Aeroflot*, the Soviet national airline, on both domestic and international routes. In the late-1970s a modified version of the Coot was observed flying in the ELINT role, being designated Coot-A by NATO.

The aircraft is a low-wing, four-turboprop aircraft of conventional design. The improved Il-18D civilian variant carries up to 122 passengers. Several aircraft have been configured for research projects, with I1-18D aircraft configured for polar research operating in the Antarctic and from Arctic drift stations. The Coot-A ELINT version has a large, side-looking radar beneath the forward fuselage in a "canoe" housing estimated to be 10.25 m long and 1.15 m in diameter; other antennas are faired into the fuselage, including a large "hump" on the left forward side of the fuselage (approximately 4.4 m long and 0.88 m in diameter).

Status: In operational service as a civilian airliner and, in limited numbers, as a research and ELINT aircraft. The first flight took place in July 1957, with estimates of total production ranging from 600 to 900 aircraft. The ELINT versions are probably conversions of civilian or military passenger aircraft; the first Coot-A was observed in early 1978. While being phased out of *Aeroflot*, it is still flown by several Eastern European nations as well as by China, North Korea, and Vietnam.

Coot-A, showing under-fuselage SLAR canoe, electronic blisters under fuselage, and on the starboard side, forward of the wing. There is a large nose radome.

Coot-A ELINT aircraft overflying a NATO exercise. Unlike the Il-38 May, the Coot-A is virtually unchanged from the civilian Il-18 airliner except for numerous "black boxes" inside and external antennas, including the large SLAR (Side-Looking Aircraft Radar) fitted in the under-fuselage "canoe." (Royal Navy)

Il-18D/E (TRANSPORT)

Crew	5 + 122 passengers
Engines:	4 Ivchyenko AI-20M turboprop; 4,250-ehp each
Weights:	empty 77,000 lbs (35,000 kg)
	maximum T/O 140,800 lbs (64,000 kg)
Dimensions:	span 122 ft 9 in (37.4 m)
	length 117 ft 9 in (35.9 m)
	height 33 ft 4 in (10.17 m)
Speed:	cruise 390 mph (625 km/h)
	max. cruise 420 mph (675 km/h)
Ceiling:	26,250–32,800 ft (8,000–10,000 m)
Range:	2,480 mi (4,000 km) with 29,700-lb (13,500-kg) payload; 4,030 mi (6,500 km) with 14,300 lbs (6,500 kg)
Armament:	nil
Radar:	(navigation)

An-12 Cub

The An-12 Cub is a cargo/transport aircraft, one of the most important aircraft of this category in Soviet military and civilian operation. Several planes have been configured for the ECM and ELINT roles, and more recently, the Cub has been observed as an ASW systems test bed. The Soviet designation for the basic cargo/transport aircraft is An-12BP.

The Cub evolved as a militarized version of the An-10 Cat transport. The aircraft has a high-wing configuration to provide clear cargo space and has four turboprop engines. Similarly, the main landing gear is housed in pods on the fuselage to avoid cutting into floor space. The sharply upswept rear fuselage incorporates an underside rear-loading ramp. A tail-gun position for twin 23-mm turret is provided in most aircraft (some with civil markings), although there is no fire-control radar. In the cargo role, up to 44,090 lbs (20,015 kg) of material can be lifted. A variety of military electronic configurations of the Cub have been observed since 1970. The Cub-B designation covers ECM aircraft, with antenna domes faired into the fuselage and tail (no tail turret); Cub-C is used for ELINT configurations, with ventral antenna housings and other features indicating the capability of "ferreting" electronic intelligence. In the early 1980s a Cub was identified in the ASW role, apparently as a systems test bed.

Status: First flight 1955; the flight of the military An-12PB variant took place in 1958. About 850 aircraft produced. In the cargo/transport role the Cub is widely used by the Soviet Air Forces as well as those of other Warsaw Pact and Third World air arms. Some aircraft—civilian and military—fly with *Aeroflot* markings.

Transfers (Cub-C): Egypt.

CUB-A (TRANSPORT)

Crew:	6 (including tail gunner) + 100 troops
Engines:	4 Ivchyenko AI-20K turboprop; 4,000-shp each
Weights:	empty 61,600 lbs (28,000 kg)
	maximum T/O 134,200 lbs (61,000 kg)
Dimensions:	span 124 ft 8 in (38.0 m)
	length 108 ft 7 in (33.1 m)
	height 34 ft 6½ in (10.53 m)
Speed:	cruise 360 mph (580 km/h)
	maximum cruise 415 mph (670 km/h)
Ceiling:	33,450 ft (10,200 m)
Range:	2,230 mi (3,600 km) with 22,000 lbs (10,000 kg) payload
Armament:	2 × 23-mm NR-23 cannon in some aircraft (tail turret)
Radar:	Toad Stool (navigation radar)

Cub-C ELINT aircraft with Egyptian markings. The plane has a Toadstool navigation radar in the chin position, several antenna arrays under the fuselage, and a large tail fairing that contains several electronic antennas. The two smaller "pods" on the side of the forward fuselage are air scoops for equipment cooling systems.

This EW-configured Cub (with civilian, *Aeroflot* markings) has large electronic blisters in the "cheek" position (forward of the wings), fitted on the after loading ramp, and under the tail-gun position.

Also flying the *Aeroflot* markings, this Cub was configured as a test bed for advanced airborne ASW systems with extended nose and tail fairings. (Tail-gun positions are provided in civilian Cub aircraft; a twin 23-mm mounting is fitted in some military transports.)

HELICOPTERS

The length is the overall length of the fuselage, excluding main and tail rotor blades.

Ka-27 Helix

This Kamov-designed Helix is the successor to the Ka-25 Hormone as a ship-based ASW helicopter.[4]

The Helix is similar in appearance to the Hormone, having the familiar contra-rotating rotors of all Kamov helicopters of the past 40 years. The Helix is larger and the empennage has a horizontal stabilizer with twin fins (the Hormone has three fins). The helicopter's ASW systems include radar, dipping sonar, and sonobuoys, with an internal weapons bay for torpedoes and depth charges. Maximum endurance is 4½ hours. The Helix-B is a troop carrier, the Helix-C is civilian, and the Helix-D is a utility/search-and-rescue variant. (See photo page 452.)

Designation: The civil version is designated Ka-32; a Ka-32S version, with more comprehensive avionics, is being developed for use on the larger civilian icebreakers.

Status: The Helix became operational in 1980 and was first observed at sea on board the ASW destroyer UDALOY in September 1981. (Two helicopters were embarked, one in standard Soviet naval markings and one in *Aeroflot* colors.) Eighteen Helix ASW helicopters have been ordered by the Indian Navy.

[4] A recent review of the Helix is found in John W.R. Taylor, "Ka-27/32 Helix helicopters in close up," *Jane's Defence Weekly* (21 December 1985), pp. 1356–1358.

Crew:	4–5
Engines:	2 Isotov TV3-117 turboshaft; 2,225 shp each
Weights:	normal T/O 24,200 lbs (11,000 kg)
	maximum T/O 27,720 lbs (12,600 kg)
Dimensions:	length 36 ft 1 in (11.0 m)
	rotor diameter 54 ft 11 in (16.75 m)
Speed:	cruise 143 mph (230 km/h)
	maximum 161 mph (260 km/h)
Ceiling:	19,680 ft (6,000 m)
Range:	combat radius 185 mi (300 km)
Armament:	ASW torpedoes and depth bombs
Radar:	(surface search)

Helix-D search-and-rescue helicopter fitted with a rescue hoist above the (port) door opening. (U.S. Navy)

Helix on the deck of the ASW destroyer UDALOY. Like the U.S. SPRUANCE (DD 963)-class destroyers, these ships can each embark two helicopters. The new U.S. ARLEIGH A. BURKE (DDG 51)-class ships will not have hangar facilities.

The Helix-A ASW helicopter generally resembles its progenitor, the Ka-25 Hormone. The newer helicopter is significantly larger and more capable; it can be identified by the shape of the chin-position radome and the twin tail fins. The Kamov design bureau has specialized in contra-rotating main rotors, alleviating the need for a tail boom-and-rotor configuration. (U.S. Navy)

Mi-14 Haze

This is a land-based ASW and mine-countermeasures helicopter, developed as a replacement for the less-capable and outdated ASW configuration of the Mi-4 Hound. The Haze is too large for the elevators of the helicopter ships of the MOSKVA class or aircraft carriers of the KIEV class.

The Haze is an ASW derivative of the Mi-8 helicopter (see below), using the power plant and dynamic components of the Hip-C. The two helicopters differ primarily in the fuselage configuration and equipment. The ASW configuration has an amphibious hull with stabilizing sponsons on each side that house the main wheels of the tricycle undercarriage. A surface-search radar is fitted in the "chin" position, with the dome projecting beneath the hull. The Haze also has towed MAD gear, expendable sonobuoys, and a dipping sonar, and can carry ASW homing torpedoes. A mine countermeasures version that tows a "sled" is designated Haze-B.

Unlike Western navies, the Soviet Navy has a large number of land-based ASW helicopters of the Haze-A type. The Haze is derived from the Mi-8 Hip, with a "boat hull"; a radome is fitted in the chin position with a streamed MAD detector stowed abaft the fuselage; sonobuoys and dipping sonar are also carried. (U.S. Navy, PH2 Paul Soutar)

Haze-A ASW helicopter in flight, showing details of fuselage and the small, stabilizing float under the tail boom. The helicopter—like the Helix and Hormone—has an internal weapons bay. (U.S. Navy, PH2 D. Beech)

Status: The first flight of the Haze occurred about 1973 and it entered service with SNA in 1975. These helicopters have also been transferred to Bulgaria, Cuba, East Germany, Libya, Poland, and Romania.

Crew:	approx. 6
Engines:	2 Isotov TV2-117A turboshaft; 1,500 shp each
Weights:	loaded approx. 23,900 lbs (10,900 kg)
Dimensions:	length approx. 59 ft (18.0 m)
	rotor diameter 69 ft 10 in (21.29 m)
Speed:	maximum 161 mph (260 km/h)
Ceiling:	
Range	combat radius 155 mi (250 km)
Armament:	ASW torpedoes and depth bombs
Radar:	. . . . . . (surface search)

Mi-8 Hip

The Hip is the primary transport helicopter of the Soviet armed forces and has been flown by about 30 other nations. SNA has employed the Hip as a land-based transport and in the minesweeping role. The helicopter carrier LENINGRAD has operated the Hip in mine-clearing operations. The helicopter, however, is too large for the ship's twin elevators and remains on the flight deck when embarked.

The basic Hip design has a five-blade main rotor and a three-blade tail rotor of all-metal construction driven by two turboshaft engines. The fuselage is an all-metal, semi-monocoque pod with the tail boom mounting the smaller rotor on the starboard side of a small vertical stabilizer.

The Hip is widely flown in the Soviet armed forces in the troop transport, gunship, and EW roles. It is flown by SNA in the transport and mine countermeasures roles.

A fixed tricycle landing gear is fitted. There are clamshell doors at the rear of the cabin. Up to 8,820 lbs (4,000 kg) of cargo can be carried internally. External fuel tanks can be fitted.

Status: The Hip-C is the production version, the A/B having been prototypes; the E/F models are assault helicopter/gunships fitted with anti-tank missiles. The first flight of the Mi-8 occurred in 1962, and it was introduced into Soviet military service in 1967.

HIP-C

Crew:	2 + 26 troops
Engines:	2 Isotov TV2-117A turboshaft; 1,700 shp each
Weights:	empty 15,972 lbs (7,260 kg)
	loaded 26,400 lbs (12,000 kg)
Dimensions:	length 59 ft 7 in (18.17 m)
	rotor diameter 69 ft 10 in (21.29 m)
Speed:	cruise 111.5 mph (180 km/h)
	maximum 155 mph (250 km/h)
Ceiling:	hover OGE 2,625 ft (800 m)
	hover IGE 6,232 ft (1,900 m)
	service 14,760 ft (4,500 m)
Range:	combat radius 185 miles (300 km)
Armament:	none
Radar:	none

Ka-26 Hormone

The Hormone is the principal Soviet ship-based ASW and missile-targeting helicopter, being found on board the KIEV and MOSKVA carriers, as well as in various cruiser classes and auxiliary ships. There are two principal versions, the -A for anti-submarine operations and the -B for missile targeting. The -C model is flown in the utility and rescue roles.

The Ka-20 Harp was the prototype for the Hormone; the earlier aircraft was publicly seen for the first time in July 1961, flying at a Soviet aviation display with two dummy missiles fitted on its fuselage. The Hormone has a distinctive configuration with a compact fuselage, two contra-rotating rotors driven by twin turboshaft engines, a short tail boom supporting a multi-fin empennage, and a quadricycle landing gear. The rotor arrangement alleviates the need for a tail boom to facilitate ship-

board handling; the main rotors also fold. Some helicopters have inflatable flotation bags attached to the landing gear in the event the helicopter has come down at sea.

The Hormone-A ASW configuration has the Puff Ball surface-search radar, expendable sonar buoys, dipping sonar that can be lowered while the helicopter is hovering, and an internal weapons bay for ASW homing torpedoes or depth bombs. An electro-optical sensor has been seen on some helicopters. The Hormone-B is fitted with the larger Big Bulge-B radar for surface surveillance and can transmit targeting data via VDL to surface ships and submarines armed with anti-ship missiles. The Hormone-C is a utility/passenger variant that can carry 12 passengers. None has been observed armed with air-to-surface missiles, as indicated in a demonstration flight by the Ka-20 prototype.

(The helicopter is used as a civilian flying crane in the Ka-25K version; the following characteristics are primarily for the civil version.)

Status: The Hormone entered operational service in 1967, going to sea that year in the MOSKVA and Kresta II cruiser classes. Hormone-A helicopters have been transferred to India and Yugoslavia.

Crew:	4–5
Engines:	2 Glushenkov GTD-3F turboshaft; 900 shp each
Weights:	empty 10,485 lbs (4,765 kg)
	loaded 16,500 lbs (7,500 kg)
Dimensions:	length 32 ft (9.75 m)
	rotor diameter 51 ft 6 in (15.7 m)
Speed:	cruise 120 mph (193 km/h)
	maximum 136 mph (220 km/h)
Ceiling:	service 11,480 ft (3,500 m)
Range:	combat radius 155 mi (250 km)
Armament:	ASW torpedoes and depth bombs
Radar:	Puff Ball (surface search) in Hormone-A
	Big Bulge-B (surface search) in Hormone-B

Hormone-B targeting helicopter on the deck of a KIEV-class carrier. It has the Big Bulge-B surface-search radar and VDL for transmitting target data to missile shooters.

Hormone-A ASW helicopter over the Sea of Japan. The ASW version has radar, sonobuoys, MAD, and electronic detection devices, and can carry torpedoes or depth bombs in an internal weapons bay. There are fuselage fittings for sonobuoy canisters and other gear. (U.S. Navy)

Hormone-A helicopter landing on the carrier MINSK, with sonobuoys fitted, shows the twin-turbine engine configuration with contra-rotating rotors.

The development of aircraft carriers is forcing the Soviet Union to develop a new generation of naval aircraft and to modify existing designs for shipboard use. The new "flattops" will operate higher performance planes than the helicopters and VSTOL planes seen here on the MINSK. (JMSDF)

27
Naval Weapons

Sailors work on one of the forward 30-mm Gatling guns of the cruiser SLAVA. At left are the ship's RBU-6000 ASW rocket launchers; at top and bottom are SS-N-12 Sandbox missile tubes. (U.S. Navy, Lt. Comdr. Lyle Gordon)

ANTI-SUBMARINE WEAPONS

The following anti-submarine weapons are believed to be in current use by the Soviet Navy. The weapons are arranged by launch platform. Anti-submarine missiles, mines, and torpedoes are discussed in subsequent sections of this chapter.

Air Launched. Soviet fixed-wing ASW aircraft carry depth bombs, torpedoes, mines; helicopters carry torpedoes and depth bombs.

Surface Launched. The older Soviet ASW ships and some smaller craft carry depth charges, generally launched from rails over the stern. Most Soviet surface combatants and ASW craft have torpedo tubes that can launch ASW torpedoes, while mine rails are also fitted in most cruisers and destroyers, including ships of the new UDALOY and SOV-REMENNYY classes.

The large ASW ships completed from 1970 onward (Krivak, Kresta II, Kara, KIROV classes) have SS-N-14 launchers for rocket-propelled torpedoes. These are similar in concept to the French Malafon and Anglo-Australian Ikara torpedo-carrying missiles. The aircraft carriers of the MOSKVA and KIEV classes do not have the SS-N-14, instead mounting the SUW-N-1 missile launcher that fires the FRAS-1, a nu-clear-only, ballistic weapon.

(The SS-N-14 and SUW-N-1/FRAS-1 are described in this chapter under the listing for Missiles.)

Soviet frigates and larger warships (including aircraft carriers) are fitted with multiple rocket launchers; these weapons have the Soviet designation RBU for *Raketnaya Bombometnaya Ustanovka.*[1] All are multibarrel rocket launchers developed from the ahead-firing "hedge-hog" weapons of World War II. They can fire high-explosive charges with either depth or influence fuzing. Most can be trained in azimuth and elevation. The charges are immune to torpedo countermeasures, and if influence fuzing is used, they will not affect sonar performance as they will not detonate unless they make contact with a submarine's magnetic signature.

The following are Soviet RBU designations. Characteristics are approximate.

RBU-6000

Twelve-barrel launcher arranged in a horseshoe and fired in paired sequence; can be trained and elevated. Elevates to vertical position for rapid, automatic reloading. Formerly given the NATO designation MBU-2500-A.

[1] The underway replenishment ship BEREZINA is fitted with two RBU-1000 launchers.

The fantail of a Koni-class ASW frigate shows the ship's mine rails, with depth-charge racks bolted to them. Torpedo decoy and minesweeping gear are also on the fantail, abaft the twin 76.2-mm guns.

RBU-6000 rocket launcher.

The RBU-6000 rocket launchers on the cruiser TALLINN are maintained in the ship's home port. At left a sailor cleans out barrels through the muzzle; right, a sailor and junior officer work on the other launcher. Note the blast shield between the launchers. A Kara is at left and a Kynda at right. (Sovfoto, Sergei Kozlov)

Maximum range:	6,560 yds (6,000 m)	
Barrel length:	5 ft 3 in (1.6 m)	
Projectile diameter:	250 mm	
Projectile weight:		
Warhead weight:	46 lbs (21 kg)	
IOC:	1962	
Platforms:	*carriers*	KIEV, MOSKVA
	cruisers	Kara, KIROV, Kresta I/II, Kynda
	destroyers	Kanin, Kashin, Kotlin, SAM Kotlin, UDALOY
	frigates	Grisha, Krivak, Petya, Mirka III
	corvettes	Poti

RBU-2500

Sixteen-barrel launcher arranged in two rows of eight; can be trained and elevated. Manual reloading. Formerly designated MBU-2500.

Maximum range:	2,730 yds (2,500 m)	
Barrel length:	5 ft 3 in (1.6 m)	
Projectile diameter:	250 mm	
Projectile weight:		
Warhead weight:	46 lbs (21 kg)	
IOC:	1957	
Platforms:	*destroyers*	Kildin, Kotlin, SAM Kotlin, Mod. SKORYY
	frigates	Riga, Petya I
	auxiliaries	SMOL'NY

RBU-2500 rocket launcher

RBU-1000 rocket launcher

RBU-1200

Five barrels, with three mounted over two; tubes elevate, but do not train. Manual reloading. Formerly designated MBU-1800.

Maximum range:	1,310 yds (1,200 m)	
Barrel length:	4 ft 7 in (1.4 m)	
Projectile diameter:	250 mm	
Projectile weight:	154 lbs (70 kg)	
Warhead weight:	75 lbs (34 kg)	
IOC:	1958	
Platforms:	*corvettes*	Pauk, T-58
	minesweepers	Natya

RBU-1000

Six barrels in two vertical rows of three; can be trained and elevated. Automatic reloading. Formerly designated MBU-4500.

Maximum range:	1,095 yds (1,000 m)	
Barrel length:	5 ft 11 in (1.8 m)	
Projectile diameter:	300 mm	
Projectile weight:	198 lbs (90 kg)	
Warhead weight:	121 lbs (55 kg)	
IOC:	1962	
Platforms:	*cruisers*	Kara, Kresta I/II
	destroyers	Kashin, SOVREMENNYY
	auxiliaries	BEREZINA

RBU-600

Two rows of three barrels in the horizontal position; rockets are fired in salvo only. Manual reloading.

Maximum range:	655 yds (600 m)	
Barrel length:	4 ft 11 in (1.5 m)	
Projectile diameter:	300 mm	
Projectile weight:	198 lbs (90 kg)	
Warhead weight:	121 lbs (55 kg)	
IOC:	1960	
Platforms:	*destroyers*	Kotlin

Submarine Launched. Soviet submarines all have 533-mm (21-inch) bow torpedo tubes that can launch ASW homing torpedoes. The later attack submarines can launch nuclear SS-N-15 missiles from these tubes.

Several later submarine classes have 650-mm (26-inch) bow torpedo tubes for launching large-diameter torpedoes and the SS-N-16 torpedo-carrying missile (see below).

Several older submarine classes have stern 533-mm or 406-mm (16-inch) torpedo tubes, the latter for ASW torpedoes only.

Most Soviet submarines can also carry tube-launched mines, normally in the ratio of two mines per torpedo space.

NAVAL GUNS

152-mm/57-caliber limited DP (triple)[2]

These are the largest naval guns in service today with any navy except for the 16-inch (406-mm) guns in the U.S. Iowa (BB 61)-class battleships. The 152-mm guns are of prewar design and are fitted in triple mounts in the Sverdlov-class cruisers, including the two command ship conversions. The barrels within the turrets can be individually elevated. They have a limited anti-aircraft capability with barrage fire.

Nuclear shells were developed for this gun and may still be in service.

Muzzle velocity:	915 m/sec
Rate of fire:	4 to 5 rounds per minute per barrel
Maximum range:	29,700 yds (27,000 m)
Effective range:	19,800 yds (18,000 m)
Elevation:	−5° to +50°
Projectile weight:	110 lbs (50 kg)
Fire-control radar:	Egg Cup-A, Top Bow
Platforms:	*cruisers* Adm. Senyavin, Sverdlov

130-mm/70-caliber DP (twin)

These are fully automatic guns of recent design. They have water cooling. Note that the range of the gun exceeds that of the earlier 152-mm weapon.

Muzzle velocity:	
Rate of fire:	65 rounds per minute per barrel
Maximum range:	30,600 yds (28,000 m)
Effective range:	
Elevation:	−15° to +85°
Projectile weight:	
Fire-control radar:	Kite Screech
Platforms:	*cruisers* Frunze, Slava
	destroyers Sovremennyy

[2] Gun barrel length is determined by multiplying the inner diameter of the barrel by the caliber. Thus, the 152-mm/57 gun has a length of 8,664 mm or approximately 28.9 ft.

Twin 130-mm forward turret of the guided missile cruiser Slava.

130-mm/58-caliber DP (twin)

Developed as the main battery for destroyers, these are semi-automatic guns introduced into service about 1953.

Muzzle velocity:	900 m/sec
Rate of fire:	10 rounds per minute per barrel
Maximum range:	anti-surface 30,600 yds (28,000 m)
	anti-air 14,200 yds (13,000 m)
Effective range:	anti-surface 17,500–19,675 yds (16,000–18,000 m)
Elevation:	−5° to +80°
Projectile weight:	59 lbs (27 kg)
Fire-control radar:	Wasp Head director with Sun Visor-B; Egg Cup-B
Platforms:	*destroyers* Kotlin, SAM Kotlin

Triple 152-mm turrets on Sverdlov-class cruiser Aleksandr Suvorov; the second mount has an Egg Cup-A radar. (U.S. Navy)

SAM Kotlin-class destroyer NAKHODCHIVYY showing, from right, the twin 130-mm gun mount, quad 45-mm gun mount, and two RBU-6000 rocket launchers. A Wasp Head fire control director with Sun Visor-B radar is mounted atop the bridge.

130-mm/50-caliber SP (twin)

These are semi-automatic guns of 1930s design deployed as the main battery for destroyers. They have insufficient elevation for dual-purpose use.

Muzzle velocity:	875 m/sec
Rate of fire:	10 rounds per minute per barrel
Maximum range:	26,240 yds (24,000 m)
Effective range:	15,300–16,400 yds (14,000–15,000 m)
Elevation:	−5° to +45°
Projectile weight:	59 lbs (27 kg)
Fire-control radar:	Four Eyes director with Top Bow or Post Lamp
Platforms:	*destroyers* SKORYY

100-mm/70-caliber DP (single)

Rapid-fire, water-cooled gun fitted in Soviet warships from mid-1970s.

Muzzle velocity:		
Rate of fire:	80 rounds per minute	
Maximum range:	16,400 yds (15,000 m)	
Effective range:	8,750 yds (8,000 m)	
Elevation:		
Projectile weight:		
Fire-control radar:	Kite Screech	
Platforms:	*cruisers*	KIROV
	destroyers	UDALOY
	frigates	Krivak II/III

Single 100-mm/70 gun mount on destroyer UDALOY.

100-mm/50-caliber DP (twin)

Secondary gun battery in SVERDLOV-class cruisers. Available from the late 1940s onward.

Muzzle velocity:	900 m/sec
Rate of fire:	15 rounds per minute per barrel
Maximum range:	anti-surface 21,870 yds (20,000 m)
	anti-air 16,400 yds (15,000 m)
Effective range:	anti-surface 10,930–13,120 yds (10,000–12,000 m)
	anti-air 8,750–9,840 yds (8,000–9,000 m)
Elevation:	−15° to +85°
Projectile weight:	35 lbs (16 kg)
Fire control radar:	Round Top director with Sun Visor-B and /or Top Bow or Post Lamp; Egg Cup-B
Platforms:	*cruisers* ADM. SENYAVIN, SVERDLOV

Twin 100-mm/50 gun mount on cruiser SVERDLOV. (U.S. Navy)

100-mm/56-caliber SP (single)

Dual-purpose gun fitted in shields rather than fully enclosed mounts. Elevation limits their anti-aircraft effectiveness. They were developed in the 1930s and updated for installation from the later 1940s.

Muzzle velocity:	850 m/sec
Rate of fire:	15 rounds per minute
Maximum range:	17,500 yds (16,000 m)
Effective range:	10,930 yds (10,000 m)
Elevation:	−5° to +40°
Projectile weight:	30 lbs (13.5 kg)
Fire control radar:	Wasp Head director with Sun Visor-B; Top Bow
Platforms:	*frigates* Riga
	tenders Don

85-mm/50-caliber AA (twin)

Obsolescent anti-aircraft weapon available from about 1943.

Muzzle velocity:	850 m/sec
Rate of fire:	10 rounds per minute per barrel
Maximum range:	anti-surface 16,400 yds (15,000 m)
Effective range:	anti-surface 8,750–9,840 yds (8,000–9,000 m)
	anti-air 6,560 yds (6,000 m)
Elevation:	−5° to +70°
Projectile weight:	26 lbs (12 kg)
Fire control radar:	Cylinder Head director (no radar)
Platforms:	*destroyers* SKORYY

Single 100-mm/56 gun mount on Riga-class frigate with Wasp Head/Sun Visor-B at right. (U.S. Navy)

76.2-mm/59-caliber AA (twin)

Rapid-fire gun mounting in Soviet surface warships and auxiliary ships. Fitted in ships completed from the early 1960s.

Muzzle velocity:	900 m/sec
Rate of fire:	45 rounds per minute per barrel
Maximum range:	anti-air 10,930 yds (10,000 m)
Effective range:	anti-air 6,560–7,650 yds (6,000–7,000 m)
Elevation:	0° to +80°
Projectile weight:	35 lbs (16 kg)
Fire control radar:	Hawk Screech or Owl Screech
Platforms:	*carriers* KIEV
	cruisers Kara, Kynda
	destroyers Kashin
	frigates Koni, Krivak I, Mirka, Petya
	auxiliaries IVAN SUSANIN, SMOL'NY

Twin 76.2-mm/59 gun mount on Kara-class cruiser. (Royal Air Force)

76.2-mm/59-caliber DP (single)

Fully automatic gun installed in corvettes and small combatants from the late 1970s onward.

Muzzle velocity:	
Rate of fire:	120 rounds per minute
Maximum range:	anti-surface 15,300 yds (14,000 m)
	anti-air 10,930 yds (10,000 m)
Effective range:	anti-air 6,560–7,650 yds (6,000–7,000 m)
Elevation:	(?) to +85°
Projectile weight:	35 lbs (16 kg)
Fire control radar:	Bass Tilt
Platforms:	*corvettes* Nanuchka III, Pauk, Tarantul, Poti
	small combatants Matka, Muravey, Slepen

Single 76.2-mm/59 gun mount on Pauk-class corvette.

57-mm/80-caliber AA (twin)

This is a fully automatic weapon installed in a variety of ships of various sizes. The barrels are water-cooled. In service from the early 1960s.

Muzzle velocity:	1,000 m/sec
Rate of fire:	110 to 120 rounds per minute per barrel
Maximum range:	anti-surface 13,120 lbs (12,000 m)
	anti-air 7,325 yds (6,700 m)
Effective range:	anti-air 5,470–6,560 yds (5,000–6,000 m)
Elevation:	(?) to +85°
Projectile weight:	6 lbs (2.8 kg)
Fire control radar:	Bass Tilt or Muff Cob
Platforms:	*carriers* MOSKVA
	cruisers Kresta, I,II
	frigates Grisha
	corvettes Nanuchka I, Poti
	small combatants Turya
	amphibious Ropucha
	auxiliaries BEREZINA, BORIS CHILIKIN, MANYCH, Ugra

Twin 57-mm/80 gun mount and Muff Cob radar in Nanuchka II-class missile corvette. (U.S. Navy)

57-mm/70-caliber AA (single, twin, quad)

This is a widely used weapon, installed in a variety of ships since the 1950s.

Muzzle velocity:	900 to 1,000 m/sec
Rate of fire:	120 rounds per minute per barrel
Maximum range:	anti-surface 9,840 yds (9,000 m)
	anti-air 6,560 yds (6,000 m)
Effective range:	anti-surface 8,750 yds (8,000 m)
	anti-air 4,920 yds (4,500 m)
Elevation:	0° to +90°
Projectile weight:	6 lbs (2.8 kg)
Fire control radar:	Hawk Screech or Muff Cob
Platforms:	*destroyers* Kanin, Kildin, Mod. SKORYY
	corvettes T-58
	minelayers Alesha
	minesweepers Sasha, T-58
	amphibious Alligator
	auxiliaries Don, Lama

Quad 57-mm/70 gun mounts on Kildin-class destroyer. (U.S. Navy)

45-mm/85-caliber AA (single, quad)

This semi-automatic weapon is mounted principally in destroyers.

Muzzle velocity:	900 m/sec
Rate of fire:	75 rounds per minute per barrel
Maximum range:	anti-surface 9,840 yds (9,000 m)
	anti-air 7,650 yds (7,000 m)
Effective range:	anti-surface 4,375 yds (4,000 m)
	anti-air 4,150 yds (3,800 m)
Elevation:	0° to +90°
Projectile weight:	4.8 lbs (2.2 kg)
Fire control radar:	Hawk Screech (in destroyers)
Platforms:	*destroyers* Kildin (1 unit), Kotlin, SAM Kotlin
	minesweepers Sasha (single mounting)

Quad 45-mm/85 gun mount on Kotlin-class destroyer. (U.S. Navy)

37-mm/60-caliber AA (twin)

Muzzle velocity:	900 m/sec
Rate of fire:	160 rounds per minute per barrel
Maximum range:	anti-surface 10,170 yds (9,300 m)
	anti-air 6,125 yds (5,600 m)
Effective range:	anti-surface 4,375 yds (4,000 m)
	anti-air 3,280 yds (3,000 m)
Elevation:	0° to +80°
Projectile weight:	1.5 lbs (0.7 kg)
Fire control radar:	none
Platforms:	*cruisers* Adm. Senyavin, Sverdlov
	destroyers Skoryy
	frigates Riga
	minesweepers T-43

30-mm/65-caliber close-in (multibarrel)

This is a close-in weapon intended to defeat incoming anti-ship missiles. The gun was introduced to Soviet ships in the late 1960s. The mounting has six 30-mm barrels within a larger, rotating cylinder. It is similar in concept to the U.S. Navy's 20-mm/76-caliber Mk 15 Phalanx Close-In Weapon System (CIWS). The Soviet weapon was originally reported to have a 23-mm barrel diameter. The Soviet designation is AK-630 (NATO designation is ADMG-630).

Twin 37-mm/60 gun mount.

Muzzle velocity:	
Rate of fire:	3,000 rounds per minute per mount
Maximum range:	
Effective Range:	
Elevation:	
Projectile weight:	
Fire control radar:	Bass Tilt (or remote visual director only in some ships)
Platforms:	*carriers* Kiev
	cruisers Kara, Kirov, Adm. Senyavin, Kresta I/II,
	Kynda
	destroyers Kashin, Sovremennyy, Udaloy
	frigates Grisha III
	corvettes Nanuchka III, Pauk, Tarantul
	small combatants Babochka, Matka, Sarancha, Slepen
	amphibious Ivan Rogov
	landing craft Lebed
	auxiliaries Bal'zam, Berezina, Ivan Susanin

Grisha III-class frigate with 30-mm Gatling gun and twin 57-mm/80 gun mount; note the water-cooling hoses on the 57-mm gun barrels.

Gatling gun 30-mm mount.

30-mm/65-caliber AA (twin)

These are fully automatic, close-in defense weapons introduced in the Soviet Navy about 1960. The theoretical rate of fire is reported at 1,050 rounds per minute per barrel, but 200–240 rounds is the maximum realistic firing rate. There is a backup optical director. Soviet designation is AK-230.

Velocity:	1,000 m/sec
Rate of fire:	approx. 1,000 rounds peer barrel per minute
Maximum range:	anti-surface 4,375 yds (4,000 m)
	anti-air 5,465 yds (5,000 m)
Effective range:	anti-surface 2,735 yds (2,500 m)
	anti-air 2,735–3,280 yds (2,500 to 3,000 m)
Elevation:	(?) to +85°
Projectile weight:	1.2 lbs (0.54 kg)
Fire control radar:	Drum Tilt (or optical director)
Platforms:	*carriers* ADM. SENYAVIN, SVERDLOV
	destroyers Kanin, SAM Kotlin
	frigates Koni
	small combatants Osa, Shershen, Stenka
	minesweepers various classes
	amphibious Polnocny
	landing craft Aist
	auxiliaries various classes

Twin 30-mm/65 gun mount on SAM Kotlin-class destroyer SKRYTNYY with Drum Tilt radar at left. (U.S. Navy)

25-mm/60-caliber AA (twin)

Muzzle velocity:	900 m/sec
Rate of fire:	150–200 rounds per minute per barrel
Maximum range:	anti-surface 4,375 yds (4,000 m)
Effective range:	anti-surface 2,515 yds (2,300 m)
	anti-air 3,280 yds (3,000 m)
Elevation:	(?) to +85°
Projectile weight:	0.75 lbs (0.34 kg)
Fire control radar:	none
Platforms	various ships and small craft

NAVAL MINES

The Soviet Navy is estimated to maintain a stock of between 350,000 and 400,000 naval mines, several times the number available to the U.S. Navy. Many of these mines date to World War II; however, most are newer weapons. Among the newer mines are several deep-water types, apparently capable of being planted in depths of at least 3,000 feet (915 m). These mines are fitted with passive acoustic detection and, like the U.S. Navy's Mk-60 CAPTOR mine, release an anti-submarine weapon that homes on submarine targets.

Analyses of Soviet literature indicate that the Soviet Navy has developed influence mines of all types, homing mines, rising mines, and remotely controlled mines. Minelaying is exercised by naval aircraft, surface ships, and submarines. Many classes of cruisers, destroyers, and frigates as well as small combatants have mine rails, while most submarines can carry mines in place of torpedoes at the ratio of one or two mines per torpedo, depending upon the type of mine.

The relative distances at which the Soviets can sow mines was addressed by the NATO Supreme Allied Commander Atlantic as:

> . . . they pose distinct threats to our reinforcement and resupply [of Europe]. Their mining of the entrances to the Norwegian Sea, although the depth of water sometimes does not accommodate all of the mines that they are capable of laying, will pose threats to our naval combatants passing into the Norwegian Sea as they attempt to contain the Soviet northern fleet and the Warsaw Pact navies in that area of the world.[3]

The Soviets have provided relatively modern mines to other nations, as evidenced by the planting of Soviet mines in the Gulf of Suez and Red Sea during July 1985 by a Libyan merchant ship. Eighteen merchant ships of various flags were damaged between 9 July and 20 September. Following a multi-nation sweeping operation, a single bottom-laid mine of recent Soviet manufacture (1981) was recovered from a depth of 150 feet (46 m). The canister-shaped weapon was 10 feet (3 m) long and 21 inches (533 mm) in diameter, and held only a fraction of its warhead capacity estimated at 1,500 pounds of high explosives. (The reduced charge led British naval analysts to conclude that the effort was intended only to scare shippers, and not to sink ships.[4]

The intense Soviet interest in mine warfare is also demonstrated by the Navy's large coastal and oceangoing mine countermeasures forces; see chapter 19.

[3] Admiral Wesley L. McDonald, USN, testimony before the Committee on Armed Services, U.S. Senate, 27 February 1985.

[4] See Dr. Scott C. Truver, "Mines of August: an International Whodunit." Naval Institute Proceedings (Naval Review, May 1985), pp. 94-117.

TABLE 27-1.   SOVIET MINES

Designation	Type	Firing Mechanism	Laying Platform	Depth Maximum
*M 09/39	moored	influence	ship	110 ft
*M 12	moored	contact	ship	147 ft
*M 16	moored	contact	ship	366 ft
*M 26	moored	contact	ship	139 ft
*M 31	moored	contact	aircraft	
*KB 1	moored	contact	ship	160 ft
MAG	moored	contact	ship	457 ft
AMG-1	moored	contact	aircraft	100 ft
PLT	moored	contact	submarine	137 ft
*PLT-G	moored	contact	submarine	
PLT-3	moored	contact	submarine	128 ft
*PL-150	moored	contact	submarine	
*R	moored	contact	ship	35 ft
*R-1	moored	contact	ship	35 ft
MYaM	moored	contact	ship	60 ft
YaRM	moored	contact	ship	
YaM	moored	contact	ship	
Unkown	moored	contact antenna	ship	2,000 ft
MZh-26	moored	obstacle	ship	
*KRAB	moored	influence	ship	272 ft
MKB	moored	influence	ship	
MKB-3	moored	influence	ship	
UEP	moored	influence	submarine	490 ft
PDM-1M	bottom	contact	ship	
PDM-2	bottom	contact	ship	
*MIRAB	bottom	influence	ship	10 ft
KMD-500	bottom	multiple	ship	70 ft
KMD II-500	bottom	multiple	ship	
KMD-IV-500	bottom	multiple	ship	
KMD 1000	bottom	multiple	ship	200 ft
KMD II-1000	bottom	multiple	ship	
KMD IV-1000	bottom	multiple	ship	
AMD 500	bottom	multiple	aircraft	70 ft
AMD II-500	bottom	multiple	aircraft	
AMD IV-500	bottom	multiple	aircraft	
AMD-1000	bottom	multiple	aircraft	200 ft
AMD II-1000	bottom	multiple	aircraft	
AMD IV-1000	bottom	multiple	aircraft	
MKD	bottom	multiple	ship/aircraft	
99501	bottom	multiple	ship/submarine	<50 ft
Unknown	bottom	multiple	submarine	1,400 ft
Cluster Bay	rising	acoustic	submarine	910 ft
Cluster Gulf	rising	acoustic	submarine	910 ft
Unknown	mobile	influence	submarine	70 ft
BPM	limpet	time delay	swimmers	
BPM2	limpet	time delay	swimmers	
VZD-1M	limpet	time delay	swimmers	
Turtle	limpet	time delay	swimmers	

* Obsolete, but believed to remain in the Soviet Navy inventory.

Source: Dr. Milan Vego, "The Soviet View of Mine Warfare," Navy International (March 1986), pp. 176–80; and research by Dr. Vego and Mr. Jeff Bray.

MISSILES

The missiles in use with the Soviet Navy are described below. Some of the air-launched missiles are also used by Soviet strategic aviation. All weapons in the naval missile designation scheme are listed to provide continuity.

The rate of modernization of Soviet naval forces is indicated by the early 1986 statement of the U.S. Secretary of Defense that estimated the Soviets were producing 700 sea-launched cruise missiles and 100 submarine-launched ballistic missiles per year.

Designations. Soviet missiles are given designations in two NATO schemes, one of which assigns an alphanumeric serial and the other a code name. The serial number indicates the launch platform and target with the following primary designations:

    AS = Air-to-Surface
    SA = Surface-to-Air
    SS = Surface-to-Surface (also underwater-to-surface)
    SSC = Surface-to-Surface Coastal
    SUW = Surface-to-Underwater (Weapon)

The additional letter N is added to the designation of all missiles except air-launched weapons to indicate naval use; NX is used to indicate naval missiles under development.

The NATO code names, which are not assigned to all missiles, indicate the launch platform and target:

    G = surface-to-air
    K = air-to-surface
    S = surface-to-surface (also underwater-to-surface)

Soviet strategic aviation also has the AS-3, -4, -5, -15, and possibly -6 missiles, mainly for use against ground targets, but with the AS-4 and possibly some others having a secondary capability against surface ships.

Characteristics: Characteristics are approximate, based mainly on published U.S. Department of Defense estimates.

AIR-TO-SURFACE MISSILES

AS-1 Kennel

This was probably the first fully operational Soviet air-to-surface missile, designated "Komet" in Soviet service. Development started in 1946 or possibly earlier. It was developed initially for use with the Tu-4 Bull, a Soviet copy of the Boeing B-29 Superfortress. Admiral Gorshkov has implied that the missile was developed for use aboard surface ships, but limitations of the engine dictated that it could be used only from aircraft.[5] The land-launched SSC-2b Samlet, which has been phased out of the Soviet armed forces, was a variant of this weapon.

[5] Admiral Gorshkov, *The Sea Power of the State*, p. 204.

Three missile systems are fitted in the cruiser SLAVA—there are 12 tubes for the SS-N-12 anti-ship missile dominating the forward end of the ship; eight vertical-launch magazines for the SA-N-6 anti-air missile are aft of the large funnel structure; and a circular magazine-launcher housing for the short-range SA-N-4 missile are adjacent to the helicopter hangar. (U.S. Navy)

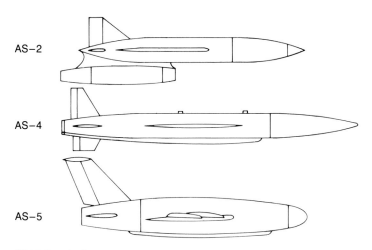

AS-series missiles.

AS-4 Kitchen missile.

AS-2 Kipper

Anti-ship missile being phased out of Soviet service in favor of the AS-5.

Weight:	9,240 lbs (4,200 kg)
Length:	31 ft 1 in (9.5 m)
Span:	16 ft 1 in (4.9 m)
Propulsion:	turbojet
Range:	100+ n.miles (185+ km)
Guidance:	active radar homing
Warhead:	nuclear or conventional (2,200 lbs/1,000 kg)
Platforms:	Badger-C/G
IOC:	1961

AS-3 Kangaroo

This is a strategic-attack missile fitted with a nuclear warhead carried by the Bear-B/C bombers of Soviet strategic aviation. Range is estimated at more than 199 n.miles (370 km). The Bear-B/C aircraft are being reconfigured to the Bear-G variant to carry the AS-4 missile.

AS-4 Kitchen

The AS-4 was developed as a stand-off, anti-ship missile for the Bear and Blinder bombers, being first seen in 1961 on the Blinder-B of the strategic air arm. It has subsequently been adopted for the Backfire-B. (SNA Blinders and Bears do not carry missiles.) The ventral fin of the AS-4 folds to starboard while carried aboard the launching aircraft. After launch from medium altitude (approximately 20,000 ft/6,100 m), the missile climbs steeply to achieve a high cruise altitude and speeds estimated at between Mach 2.5 to 3.5, and then dives steeply at its target.

Weight:	14,300 lbs (6,500 kg)
Length:	37 ft 1 in (11.3 m)
Span:	11 ft (3.35 m)
Propulsion:	turbojet
Range:	148-250 n.miles (275-465 km)
Guidance:	inertial and terminal (1) active radar or (2) anti-radar homing

Warhead:	nuclear or conventional (2,200 lbs/1,000 kg)
Platforms:	Backfire-B
IOC:	1967

AS-5 Kelt

Improved anti-ship missile.

Weight:	10,340 lbs (4,700 kg)
Length:	31 ft (9.45 m)
Span:	15 ft 1 in (4.6 m)
Propulsion:	liquid-fuel rocket
Range:	100+ n.miles (185+ km)
Guidance:	inertial and terminal (1) active radar or (2) anti-radar homing
Warhead:	nuclear or conventional (2,200 lbs/1,000 kg)
Platforms:	Badger-C/G
IOC:	1965-1966

AS-6 Kingfish

This is an advanced anti-ship missile, believed to have been developed for use from the Backfire bomber. However, up to press time of this edition the AS-6 has been observed only on Badger aircraft. A flight profile similar to the AS-4 is estimated with maximum speed of Mach 2.5 to 3.5.

Weight:	10,780 lbs (4,900 kg)
Length:	34 ft 5½ in (10.5)
Span:	8ft 2½ in (2.5 m)
Propulsion:	turbojet
Range:	148-250 n.miles (275-465 km)
Guidance:	inertial and terminal (1) active radar or (2) anti-radar homing
Warhead:	nuclear or conventional
Platforms:	Backfire-B/C (?)
	Badger-C/G
IOC:	1970

AS-6 Kingfish missile on Badger-C aircraft; note the centerline missile position for an AS-4 Kipper. (Courtesy *Joint Services Recognition Journal*)

AS-7 Kerry

Tactical missile that can be carried by naval Fitter and Forger fighter-attack aircraft. Speed is approximately Mach 1.

Weight:	
Length:	11 ft 6 in (3.5 m)
Span:	
Diameter:	
Propulsion:	solid-propellant rocket
Range:	approx. 7 n.miles (13 km)
Guidance:	radio command and radar homing
Warhead:	conventional (220 lbs/100 kg)
Platforms:	Fitter
	Forger
IOC:	late 1970s

AS-9

High-speed, Mach 3 attack missile for use against radar installations.

Weight:	
Length:	
Span:	
Diameter:	
Propulsion:	turbojet
Range:	
Guidance:	anti-radar homing
Warhead:	330 lbs (150 kg)
Platforms:	Backfire
	Badger
	Fitter-C
IOC:	late 1970s

SURFACE-TO-AIR MISSILES

SA-N-1 Goa

This was the first surface-to-air missile to be installed in Soviet warships and is considered effective at low to medium altitudes as well as in the surface-to-surface mode. It is fired from twin-arm launchers in destroyers and cruisers. The missiles load with the launcher at 90° elevation from a below-deck magazine. The four square-shaped tail fins are folded until the missile leaves the launcher. The missile system is derived from the land-based SA-3 system, which became operational in 1964. Maximum speed is approximately Mach 2.0. The Peel Group fire-control radar is used with the SA-N-1.

Weight:	880 lbs (400 kg)	
Length:	21 ft 8 in (6.6 m)	
Span:	4 ft 11 in (1.5 m)	
Diameter:	missile 18.1 in (460 mm)	
	booster 27.6 in (701 mm)	
Propulsion:	solid-fuel rocket with tandem solid-fuel boosters	
Range:	approx. 17 n.miles (31.5 km)	
Guidance:	radio command	
Warhead:	conventional (132 lbs/60 kg); some sources cite a possible nuclear warhead alternative	
Platforms:	*cruisers*	Kresta I, Kynda
	destroyers	Kanin, Kashin, SAM Kotlin
IOC:	1961	

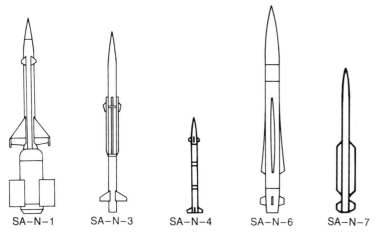

SA-N-series missiles.

SA-N-1 Goa missile in flight.

SA-N-1 Goa missile launcher on a Kashin-class missile destroyer.

SA-N-2 Guideline

The SA-N-2 was adopted from the widely used land-based SA-2 missile system and is considered a medium-altitude weapon. Only one cruiser, the DZERZHINSKIY of the SVERDLOV class, was fitted with the sea-based version, indicating a lack of success in the naval version. The ship has been discarded (see page 192).

SA-N-3 Goblet

This missile system went to sea in the second generation of warships developed during the Gorshkov regime, beginning with the MOSKVA-class helicopter carrier-cruisers and Kresta II cruisers. It is a low- to medium-altitude missile with improved capabilities over the SA-N-1, which it succeeds. The missile is also capable of use in the anti-ship role. Like most other Soviet naval surface-to-air missiles, it is derived from a land-based system, the SA-6 Gainful, which became operational in 1967. Maximum speed is approximately Mach 2.5. It is employed with the Head Lights fire-control radar.

Weight:	1,210 lbs (550 kg)
Length:	20 ft 4 in (6.2 m)
Span:	4 ft 11 in (1.5 m)
Diameter:	13.2 in (335 mm)
Propulsion:	ramjet with solid-fuel booster
Range:	approx. 29.5 n.miles (55 km)
Guidance:	semi-active homing
Warhead:	nuclear or conventional (176 lbs/80 kg)
Platforms:	*carriers* MOSKVA, KIEV
	cruisers Kresta II, Kara
IOC:	1967

SA-N-3 Goblet missile launcher on Kara-class cruiser. (Royal Air Force)

SA-N-4 Gecko

The SA-N-4 system has a fully retractable, twin-arm launcher for point-defense of large ships as well as small combatants. The SA-N-4 uses the Pop Group missile-control radar, which is similar to the radar associated with the land-based SA-8 surface-to-air missile.

Weight:	approx. 418 lbs (190 kg)
Length:	10 ft 6 in (3.2 m)
Span:	2 ft 1 in (0.64 m)
Diameter:	8.25 in (210 mm)
Propulsion:	solid-fuel rocket
Range:	approx. 8 n.miles (15 m)
Guidance:	semi-active homing
Warhead:	conventional (110 lbs/50 kg)

Platforms:		
	carriers	KIEV (2 ships)
	cruisers	ADM. SENYAVIN, KIROV, Kara
	frigates	Krivak, Koni, Grisha
	corvettes	Nanuchka
	small combatants	Nanuchka, Grisha, Sarancha
	amphibious ships	IVAN ROGOV
	auxiliary ships	BEREZINA
IOC:	1969	

SA-N-5

This is a ship-borne form of the shoulder-launched SA-7 Grail missile and is fitted in various small combatants and amphibious and auxiliary ships. It is fired from a four-missile launch rack or a single, shoulder-held launch tube.

Weight:	20.3 lbs (9.2 kg)
Length:	2 ft 5 in (0.76 m)
Span:	(small canard stabilizing fins)
Diameter:	2.75 in (699 mm)
Propulsion:	solid-fuel rocket
Range:	5.4 n.miles (10 km)
Guidance:	infrared homing
Warhead:	conventional (5.5 lbs/2.5 kg)

Platforms:		
	corvettes	Pauk, Tarantul
	small combatants	Osa
	amphibious ships	Polnocny, Ropocha
	auxiliary ships	various AGIs
IOC:	1974	

SA-N-4 missile launcher on Krivak I-class frigate.

SA-7 Grail missile launcher (held by Polish Marine).

SA-N-6

This is an advanced surface-to-air missile with anti-cruise missile capabilities. The SA-N-6 is vertically launched from a below-deck rotary magazine, with six missiles per launcher. Guidance provides for track-via-missile with the in-flight missile providing radar data to the launching ship. Initially fitted in one Kara-class cruiser and subsequently in cruisers of the KIROV and SLAVA classes, which have Top Dome radar. It appears to be adapted from the SA-10 missile. Some reports credit the SA-N-6 with a nuclear capability; probably has anti-ship capability.

Weight:	
Length:	22 ft 11 1/2 in (7 m)
Span:	
Propulsion:	solid-fuel rocket
Range:	29.6 + n.miles (55 + m)
Guidance:	command track-via-missile
Warhead:	conventional and nuclear(?)
Platforms:	*cruisers* Kara (1 ship), KIROV, SLAVA
IOC:	1981

SA-N-7

This is a shipboard version of the land-based SA-11 missile; it went to sea in 1981 in the Kashin-class destroyer PROVORNYY and subsequently in the new SOVREMENNYY-class destroyers. Estimated to be able to engage targets up to 46,000 feet (14,025 m). The PROVORNYY was extensively modified with eight Front Dome tracker/illuminators for the SA-N-7, but there is only one single-arm launcher, installed aft. (There appear to be provisions forward for two more launchers.) The SOVREMENNYY-class ships have two launchers and six directors. Mach 3 speed.

Weight:	
Length:	
Span:	
Diameter:	
Propulsion:	solid-fuel rocket
Range:	approx. 15 n.miles (28 m)
Guidance:	radio command + semiactive radar and infrared homing
Warhead:	conventional
Platforms:	*destroyers* Kashin (1 unit), SOVREMENNYY
IOC:	1981

Forward deck of the battle cruiser KIROV showing, from left, the reloadable SS-N-14 Silex ASW missile launcher, hatches for the SA-N-6 VLS, and hatches for the SS-N-19 VLS.

The destroyer SOVREMENNYY showing, from left, twin 130-mm gun turret, SA-N-7 missile launcher, and quad SS-N-22 missile tubes.

SA-N-8

Apparently an early designation for the SA-N-9 system.

SA-N-9

Advanced vertical-launch, short-range missile; reportedly capable of engaging attacking anti-ship cruise missiles. Estimated to be able to engage aircraft up to 40,000–60,000 feet (12,200–18,300 m). The SA-N-9 system is fitted in the two later ships of the KIEV class in place of the SA-N-4 launchers, and in the second and later ships of the KIROV class in place of the SS-N-14 ASW missile system. In the UDALOY-class destroyers, the SA-N-9 is the primary surface-to-air missile.

Weight:
Length:
Span:
Diameter:
Propulsion:
Range: approx. 8 n.miles (15 km)
Guidance:
Warhead:
Platforms: *carriers*   KIEV (2 ships)
                cruisers   KIROV
                destroyers UDALOY
IOC: 1981–1982

Hatches for SA-N-9 VLS system on destroyer UDALOY; there are eight missile tubes under each circular hatch cover.

SA-N-(. . .)

The Soviet Navy is believed to have developed at least two surface-to-air missile systems for use from submarines. A probable mockup of this weapon was observed in a Tango-class SS in the Adriatic Sea in the early 1980s. The Kilo is reported to have been fitted with such a weapon system.

A fully submerged submarine can detect aircraft with a towed passive sonar array.

Britain has developed a submarine anti-aircraft missile system with the Blowpipe missile, the launcher extending from the sail and out of the water for firing. The U.S. Navy has looked at several submarine-launched missile concepts, one dubbed "Subwinder" (based on the Sidewinder missile) and, more recently, the SIAM (Self-Initiating Anti-aircraft Missile); neither Britain nor the United States has plans to deploy such missiles.

SURFACE-TO-SURFACE COASTAL MISSILES

SSC-1 Sepal

Land-based, anti-ship missile in service with the Navy's Coastal Missile-Artillery Force. This is a land-launched version of the SS-N-3 Shaddock missile (see below for description). The SSC-1b has a range of some 250 n.miles (350 km); it can carry a conventional and probably a nuclear warhead.

The launcher is fitted to an eight-wheel vehicle.

SSC-2 Samlet

The Samlet was a ground-launched missile developed from the AS-1 air-launched cruise missile. It previously was used by Soviet, East German, and Yugoslav coastal defense forces, and the SSC-2b is believed still in use with Polish, Romanian, and Bulgarian forces. Range was estimated at 60–90 n.miles (110–165 km).

SSC-3 Styx

This is an adaption of the SS-N-2 Styx anti-ship missile, fitted in twin launchers on eight-wheel vehicles. The range is believed on the order of 43–48.5 n.miles (80–90 km). The missile is in service with East German and Yugoslav forces.

SSC-X-4

This is a ground-launched variant of the SS-N-21 and AS-15 cruise missiles, launched by attack submarines and Bear-H aircraft, respectively. The SSC-X-4 variant is in development and is expected to become operational in 1986–1987. See SS-N-21 for data.

SSC-X-(. . .)

A ground-launched variant of the SS-NX-24 submarine-launched missile is believed to be in development.

SS-N-1 Scrubber/Strela

The Scrubber was the first surface-to-surface missile to be deployed by the Soviet Navy, going to sea from 1959 in four destroyers of the Kildin class (1 launcher) and from 1960 in eight destroyers of the Krupnyy (2 launchers) class. The missile had a maximum range of approximately 100 n.miles (185 km); the missile had several limitations and was awkward to handle on board ship. By the late 1960s the ships were being discarded or converted. Scrubber was the NATO code name, but American intelligence agencies generally used the name Strela.

SS-N-2a/b Styx

The Styx was developed to provide an anti-ship missile capability for small combat craft in the coastal defense role. It is a subsonic missile that has undergone several development stages. Soviet doctrine appears to call for launching the SS-N-2a/b versions at a range of some 10 to 13 n.miles (18 to 24 km), or about one-half of their maximum range. Maximum speed is approximately Mach 0.9. The Square Tie radar is used to detect targets. Once launched, there is no data link to the SS-N-2a/b version; the missile's terminal radar seeker is automatically switched on some five miles from the estimated target position; the missile will home on the largest target in a group of ships.

The SS-N-2a was first deployed on Soviet Komar-class missile boats and subsequently in the Osa I. The -2b version, which has folding wings, was initially used in the Osa II. Including Third World sales, the Styx was the world's most widely used anti-ship missile before the French Exocet became operational in 1973 and the U.S. Harpoon in 1977. The Styx gained international attention after Egyptian Komar boats, from the safety of Alexandria harbor, sank the Israeli destroyer ELATH steaming 12 miles offshore on 21 October 1967. The weapon was subsequently used by the Indian Navy to sink a number of Pakistani ships in the 1971 Indo-Pakistani conflict, including the destroyer KHAIBER.

Weight:	approx. 5,500 lbs (2,500 kg)
Length:	19 ft (5.8 m)
Span:	9 ft 2 in (2.8 m)
Diameter:	29.5 in (750 mm)
Propulsion:	turbojet with solid-fuel booster
Range:	SS-N-2a approx. 25 n.miles (46 km)
	SS-N-2b approx. 27 n.miles (50 km)
Guidance:	active radar homing
Warhead:	conventional (1,100 lbs/500 kg)
Platforms:	*small combatants* Osa
IOC:	SS-N-2a 1958
	SS-N-2b 1964

SS–N–2a

SS–N–3c

SS–N–7

SS–N–9

SS–N–12

SS–N–14

SS–N–19

SS–N–21

SS–N–24

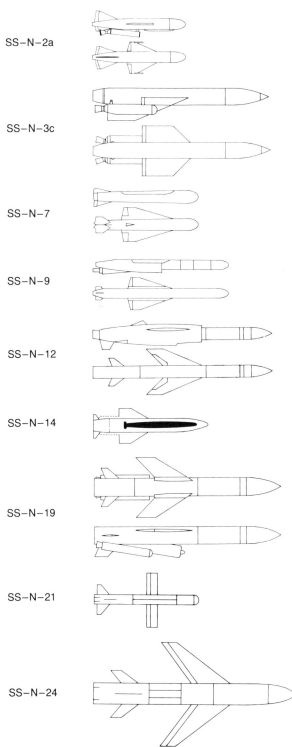

SS-N-series missiles.

SS-N-2 Styx missile.

SS-N-2 Styx being loaded on missile boat.

SS-N-3b Shaddock missile tubes on Kresta I-class cruiser.

SS-N-2c Styx

This is an improved version of the Styx, having initially been designated SS-N-11 when first observed by Western intelligence. (The missile has also been fitted in Soviet-built Koni-class frigates transferred to Yugoslavia.)

Weight:
Length: 19 ft (5.8 m)
Span: 9 ft 2 in (2.8 m)
Diameter: 31 in (788 mm)
Propulsion: turbojet with solid-fuel booster
Range: 45 n.miles (83 km)
Guidance: (1) active radar or (2) infrared homing
Warhead: conventional (1,100 lbs/500 kg)
Platforms: *destroyers*   mod. Kashin, Kildin
                  small combatants Matka, Tarantul, in Nanuchkas for foreign transfer
IOC: 1967

SS-N-3 Shaddock

The Shaddock is a large, air-breathing cruise missile originally developed for the strategic attack role in the SS-N-3c variant (a contemporary of the U.S. Regulus missile, which was operational from 1954, on a limited basis, to 1964). When submarine-launched, it is fired from the surface. The land-launched SSC-1 Sepal missile is similar. The SS-N-3b was also assigned the NATO code name Sepal, but all ship-launched versions are generally referred to as Shaddock. The SS-N-12 is an improved version and has replaced the SS-N-3 in some Echo II submarines. (The five Echo I SSGNs that originally carried the SS-N-3 have been converted to attack submarines, and the earlier Whiskey SSG conversions have been discarded.) The Scoop Pair radar is used for fire control in surface ships and the Front Door or Front Piece radar in submarines.

The missile requires mid-course guidance for over-the-horizon use. This is sent as a radar picture via Video Data Link (VDL) from the targeting ship or aircraft to the launching ship and then relayed—with target indicated—to the missile in flight. The launching submarine is thus required to remain on the surface after launch, possibly for as long as 25 minutes when firing against targets at a range of some 250 n.miles.

Weight: 11,880 lbs (5,400 kg)
Length: SS-N-3c 38 ft 6 in (11.75 m)
                  SS-N-3a/b 33 ft 6 in (10.2 m)
Span: 16 ft 5 in (5 m)
Diameter: approx. 38 1/2 in (975 mm)
Propulsion: turbojet + 2 solid-fuel boosters
Range: SS-N-3c 400+ n.miles (740+ km)
                  SS-N-3a/b 250 n.miles (463 km)
Guidance: SS-N-3a/b inertial with mid-course command; active radar homing for terminal phase
                  SS-N-3c inertial
Warhead: nuclear or conventional (2,200 lbs/1,000 kg)
Platforms: SS-N-3a *submarines* Juliett, Echo II
                  SS-N-3b *cruisers*   Kynda, Kresta I
                  SS-N-3c *submarines* Juliett, Echo II
IOC: SS-N-3a 1962
                  SS-N-3b 1962
                  SS-N-3c 1960

SS-N-7 Siren

The SS-N-7 was the Soviet Navy's first underwater-launched, anti-ship cruise missile. Maximum speed is approximately Mach 0.9. It has been succeeded in later, Charlie II-class SSGNs by the SS-N-9, which has about double the earlier missile's range.

Weight: 6,380 lbs (2,900 kg)
Length: 22 ft 11 1/2 in (7 m)
Span:
Diameter:
Propulsion: solid-fuel rocket
Range: 35 n.miles (64 km)
Guidance: (1) active radar or (2) anti-radar homing
Warhead: nuclear or conventional (1,100 lbs/500 kg)
Platforms: *submarines* Charlie I
IOC: 1968

SS-N-9

This is a supersonic anti-ship missile, launched initially from surface ships and subsequently fitted in the Charlie II-class SSGNs for underwater launch. It is also believed to be carried by the one-of-a-kind Papa SSGN. Maximum speed is approximately Mach 0.9. The Band Stand radar is used on surface ships for search and fire control. The Nanuchka-class missile corvettes transferred to other nations have the SS-N-2c missile in place of the SS-N-9.

Weight:	7,260 lbs (3,300 kg)
Length:	29 ft (8.84 m)
Span:	
Propulsion:	solid-fuel rocket
Range:	60 n.miles (111 km)
Guidance:	inertial and (1) active radar or (2) anti-radar homing
Warhead:	nuclear or conventional (1,100 lbs/500 kg)
Platforms:	*small combatants* Nanuchka I/III, Sarancha
	submarines Charlie II, Papa
IOC:	1969

SS-N-10

The SS-N-14 anti-submarine missile was originally assigned this designation.

SS-N-11

This designation was initially assigned to an improved version of the Styx, which was subsequently redesignated SS-N-2c.

SS-N-12 Sandbox

An advanced version of the SS-N-3 Shaddock anti-ship missile, being capable of supersonic speed. It is fitted in surface ships and modified Echo II-class SSGNs. It is used with the Trap Door radar in the KIEV-class carriers and the Front Door/Front Piece radar of the Echo II and SLAVA classes.

Weight:	
Length:	38 ft 4 1/2 in (11.7 m)
Span:	
Propulsion:	turbojet
Range:	300 n.miles (555 km)
Guidance:	radio command and (1) active radar or (2) anti-radar homing
Warhead:	nuclear or conventional (2,200 lbs/1,000 kg)
Platforms:	*carriers* KIEV
	cruisers SLAVA
	submarines mod. Echo II
IOC:	1973

VSTOL carrier MINSK showing, from left, 76.2-mm gun mount flanked by SS-N-12 Sandbox missile tubes; elevators for raising SS-N-14s from missile magazine; and SA-N-3 launcher flanked by SS-N-12 tubes. (U.S. Navy)

SS-N-12 Sandbox missile tubes on cruiser SLAVA.

SS-N-14 Silex

This is a rocket-propelled anti-submarine weapon, carrying a homing torpedo out to the first sonar convergence zone. Water entry is slowed by a parachute. Minimum effective range is estimated at 4 n.miles (7.4 km). It could probably be employed against surface ships as well. Of the five warship classes armed with the missile, only the nuclear-powered KIROV has an on-board reload capability. A pair of quad launchers—two tubes above two—are fitted in cruisers and destroyers; the Krivak-class frigate has a single, four-tube launcher of a different type. The Head Lights or Eye Bowl radar is used for in-flight guidance.

(Note that only the lead ship of the KIROV class has the SS-N-14.)

The SS-N-14 was initially evaluated by Western intelligence as an anti-ship weapon and designated SS-N-10.

SS-N-14 Silex missile launchers on destroyer UDALOY; two Eye Bowl guidance radars are mounted above the bridge.

Weight:	
Length:	approx. 25 ft (7.6 m)
Span:	
Propulsion:	solid-fuel rocket
Range:	30 n.miles (55 km)
Guidance:	command radio and inertial
Warhead:	acoustic ASW homing torpedo (conventional)
Platforms:	*cruisers* Kara, KIROV (1 ship), Kresta II
	destroyers UDALOY
	frigates Krivak I, II
IOC:	1969

SS-N-15

An ASW weapon similar to the U.S. Navy's SUBROC (Submarine Rocket), the SS-N-15 is fired from standard submarine torpedo tubes and carries a nuclear warhead. The weapon is fired with range and bearing probably derived from the launching submarine's active sonar.

Weight:	
Length:	
Span:	
Diameter:	21 in (533 mm) (maximum)
Propulsion:	solid-fuel rocket
Range:	20 n.miles (37 km)
Guidance:	inertial
Warhead:	nuclear
Platforms:	*submarines* Akula, Alfa, Mike, Sierra, Tango, Victor
IOC:	1972

SS-N-16

A further development of the SS-N-15, this missile carries an anti-submarine homing torpedo in lieu of the nuclear warhead. A parachute lowers the torpedo into the water, and a protective nosecap separates upon water entry; when the torpedo reaches a prescribed depth, a programmed search maneuver is begun, with the torpedo homing on any target detected during the search. The weapon is launched from tubes larger than the standard 533-mm torpedo tubes.

Weight:	
Length:	
Span:	
Diameter:	26 in (650-mm)(?)
Propulsion:	solid-fuel rocket
Range:	30–50 n.miles (55–92 km)
Guidance:	inertial (to torpedo release point)
Warhead:	ASW homing torpedo (conventional)
Platforms:	*submarines* Victor II/III
	possibly Akula, Mike, Sierra, Oscar
IOC:	1972

SS-N-19

This is an improved long-range, anti-ship cruise missile that evolved from the SS-N-3/12 designs. The high speed of the SS-N-19 (Mach 1+) alleviates the need for mid-course guidance because of the limited distance that the target ship could travel during the missile's time of flight. It is carried in the large KIROV-class nuclear cruisers and submerged-launched from the large Oscar-class SSGNs.

Weight:	
Length:	
Span:	
Propulsion:	turbojet
Range:	300 n.miles (555 km)
Guidance:	inertial with anti-radar homing
Warhead:	conventional or nuclear
Platforms:	*cruisers* KIROV
	submarines Oscar
IOC:	1981

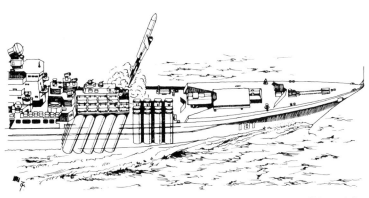

SS-N-19 missile being fired from battle cruiser KIROV. (Courtesy *Ships of the World*)

SS-N-21

This is an advanced land-attack cruise missile believed to be launched from standard Soviet submarine torpedo tubes, much like the U.S. Navy Tomahawk Land-Attack Missile (TLAM); the similarity of design to the U.S. weapon has led to the Soviet weapon's being called "Tomahawk-ski" by Western intelligence. Speed is estimated at Mach 0.7. The air-launched version of this missile is the AS-15, and there is a ground-launched version designated SSC-X-4.

Launch trials for the SS-NX-21 were conducted from a modified Victor III-class SSN; that submarine was distinguished by a long cylinder fitted on the deck immediately forward of the sail structure.

Weight:	
Length:	approx. 21 ft (6.4 m)
Span:	
Diameter:	
Propulsion:	turbofan
Range:	approx. 1,200 n.mi (1,670 km)
Guidance:	inertial; probably with Terrain Contour Matching (TERCOM) homing
Warhead:	nuclear
Platforms:	*submarines* SSN type
IOC:	1986

SS-N-22

This anti-ship missile is an improved version of the SS-N-9 anti-ship cruise missile. It is carried in quad launchers in the SOVREMENNYY class and in twin launchers in the Tarantul III class. Speed is estimated at Mach 2.5.

Weight:	
Length:	approx. 30 ft(9.15m)
Span:	
Propulsion:	solid-fuel rocket
Range:	approx. 60 n.miles (110 km)
Guidance:	mid-course guidance with active radar homing
Warhead:	conventional or nuclear
Platforms:	*destroyers* SOVREMENNYY
	corvettes Tarantul III
IOC:	1981

SS-NX-24

Advanced, submarine-launched, land-attack cruise missile of much larger dimensions than the SS-N-21. The missile has a supersonic speed, possibly in the region of Mach 2. It underwent launch trials from a former Yankee-class SSBN specifically converted for this role.

It is not clear if additional Yankee-class submarines will be converted to fire the missile. A new SSGN class is believed under construction. A ground-launched version is reported in development for coastal defense. The missile carries a large nuclear warhead. Length is approximately 41 feet (12.5m).

IOC: 1986–1987 (est.)

SUBMARINE-LAUNCHED BALLISTIC MISSILES

The Soviet Navy has an estimated 944 SLBMs in 62 modern SSBNs; in addition, there are 13 diesel-electric Golf-class SSBs in service, carrying 39 SLBMs for the theater strike role. Three older SSB/SSBNs are employed as launch trial ships for SLBMs. The estimated Soviet SLBM strength as of mid-1986 is shown in Table 27-1.

All Soviet SLBMs have liquid-propellant rocket motors, except for the SS-N-17 and SS-N-20, which have solid-propellant motors (as do all Western SLBMs.)

TABLE 27-2. SOVIET SUBMARINE-LAUNCHED BALLISTIC MISSILES

Submarines	Missiles	MIRV Warhead	Notes
4 SSBN Typhoon	20 SS-N-20	yes	
2 SSBN Delta IV	16 SS-N-23	yes	
14 SSBN Delta III	16 SS-N-18	yes	
4 SSBN Delta II	16 SS-N-8	no	
18 SSBN Delta I	12 SS-N-8	no	
1 SSBN Yankee II	12 SS-N-17	no	
19 SSBN Yankee I	16 SS-N-6	no	
1 SSBN Hotel III	3 SS-N-8	no	trials ship
1 SSB Golf V	1 SS-N-20	yes	trials ship
1 SSB Golf III	6 SS-N-8	no	trials ship
13 SSB Golf II	3 SS-N-5	no	diesel-propelled submarine

SS-N-4 Sark

The SS-N-4 was the Soviet Navy's first operational SLBM, being a surface-launch weapon originally fitted in the Zulu V, Golf I, and Hotel I classes. The Zulu V craft (2 missiles) were discarded, while 13 of the Golf class and all 8 of the nuclear-powered Hotel class were converted to fire the SS-N-5 missile (3 missiles per submarine). Range was approx. 350 n.miles (650 km).

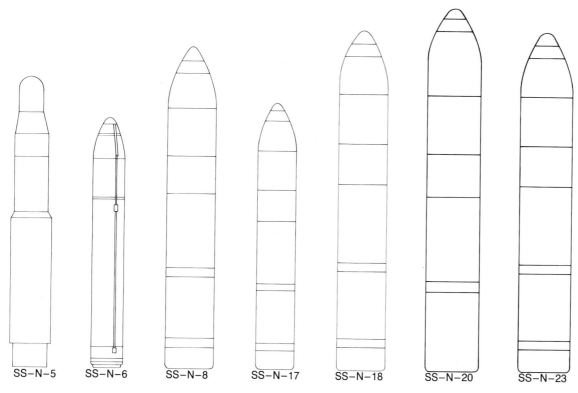

SS-N-5   SS-N-6   SS-N-8   SS-N-17   SS-N-18   SS-N-20   SS-N-23

SS-N-series missiles.

SS-N-5 Serb

The SS-N-5 was an improved SLBM, featuring underwater launch and a greater range compared to the previous SS-N-4. It replaced the SS-N-4 in 13 of the Golf-class submarines and all eight of the Hotel-class SSBNs (3 missiles per submarine); all of the latter have been discarded or converted. The missile range is believed to have been increased during service life from approximately 700 n.miles (1,300 km) to the distance indicated below.

Weight:	36,300 lbs (16,500 kg)
Length:	42 ft 8 in (13 m)
Span:	(ballistic)
Diameter:	47 1/2 in (1.2 m)
Propulsion:	liquid-fuel rocket
Range:	900 n.miles (1,650 km)
Guidance:	inertial
Warhead:	nuclear (1 RV approx. 800 KT)
Platforms:	*submarines* Golf II
IOC:	1963

SS-N-6

This strategic missile was deployed in the Yankee-class submarines, the first modern Soviet SSBN design. It is a single-stage, liquid-fuel, underwater-launch missile. All Yankee SSBNs originally carried the SS-N-6; one has subsequently been rearmed with the SS-N-17, and some have had their missile tube sections removed in accordance with the SALT I agreement. A single Golf-class SSB was fitted as trials ship for the SS-N-6. The SS-N-6 initially had a range of 1,300 n.miles (2,395 km).

The SLBM given the NATO code name Sawfly was apparently a competitive prototype to the SS-N-6 and not the same missile.

Weight:	41,580 lbs (18,900 kg)
Length:	32 ft 10 in (10 m)
Span:	(ballistic)
Diameter:	71 in (1.8 m)
Propulsion:	liquid-fuel rocket
Range:	Mod 1 1,300 n.miles (2,400 km)
	Mod 2 1,600 n.miles (2,950 km)
	Mod 3 1,600 n.miles (2,950 km)
Guidance:	inertial
Warhead:	nuclear (approx. 1 MT; 1 RV in Mod 1 and 2; 2 MRV in Mod 3)
Platforms:	*submarines* Yankee I, Golf IV
IOC:	Mod 2/3 1972–1973

SS-N-8

This SLBM was developed for the Delta-class strategic-missile submarines. It is the first Soviet two-stage submarine missile, being significantly larger than the SS-N-6, used in the previous Yankee-class SSBNs, indicating that it was developed from the SS-N-4/5 SLBM series. One Golf-class SSB and one Hotel-class SSBN were modified as trials ships for the SS-N-8.

Weight:	66,000 lbs (30,000 kg)
Length:	42 ft 8 in (13 m)
Span:	(ballistic)
Diameter:	
Propulsion:	liquid-fuel rocket

Range:	Mod 1 4,240 n.miles (7,800 km)
	Mod 2 4,950 n.miles (9,100 km)
Guidance:	inertial
Warhead:	nuclear (1 RV approx. 0.8-1.5 MT)
Platforms:	*submarines* Delta III, Golf III, Hotel III
IOC:	Mod 1 1973
	Mod 2 1977

SS-NX-13

This is a submarine-launched, *tactical* ballistic missile developed for the anti-carrier role. Development began in the early 1960s, with subsequent flight tests being conducted until November 1973. The missile was not deployed.

The SS-NX-13 apparently was developed for launching from the Yankee-class SSBNs, probably with satellite targeting at launch and a terminal radar-homing system. Range was approximately 370 n.miles (685 km) with a terminal maneuvering capability of some 30 n.miles (55 km). A nuclear warhead would have been employed with the operational missile.

Some Western analysts believe that the missile may also have been intended in a later version for the anti-SSBN role, had long-range targeting capabilities been available.

SS-N-17 Snipe

A single Yankee-class SSBN has been fitted with the SS-N-17 missile. This missile was the first Soviet solid-propellant SLBM and the first to employ a Post Boost Vehicle (PBV) or "bus" to aim the single re-entry vehicle. It is credited with greater accuracy than previous Soviet SLBMs, but has not been deployed beyond replacing the SS-N-6 in a single submarine. Flight testing began in 1975.

(Note that the Yankee II carries 12 SS-N-17 missiles compared to 16 of the SS-N-6 missiles in the basic Yankee class.)

Weight:	
Length:	34 ft 9 in (10.6 m)
Span:	(ballistic)
Diameter:	
Propulsion:	solid-fuel rocket
Range:	2,100 + n.miles (3,900 + km)
Guidance:	inertial
Warhead:	nuclear (1 RV approx. 1 MT)
Platforms:	*submarines* Yankee II
IOC:	1977

SS-N-18 Stingray

One variant of the SS-N-18 is the first Soviet SLBM to have a MIRV warhead (initially two re-entry vehicles). This is a two-stage weapon. Flight testing began in 1975.

The Soviet designation for this missile is RSM-50. The CEP has been estimated in the Western press at 0.76 n.miles for the MIRV version.

Weight:	74,800 lbs (34,000 kg)
Length:	44 ft 7 in (13.6 m)
Span:	(ballistic)
Diameter:	
Propulsion:	liquid-fuel rocket

Range:	Mod 1 3,530 n.miles (6,500 km)
	Mod 2 4,350 n.miles (8,000 km)
	Mod 3 3,530 n.miles (6,500 km)
Guidance:	inertial
Warhead:	nuclear (approx. 450 KT for single warhead, approx. 200 KT for each multiple warhead; Mod 1 3 MIRV; Mod 2 1 RV; Mod 3 7 RV)
Platforms:	*submarines* Delta III
IOC:	1978

SS-N-20 Sturgeon

The largest Soviet SLBM yet produced, the three-stage SS-N-20 was developed for the Typhoon-class SSBN, the largest submarine yet constructed by any nation. The missile is presumed to have a greater payload and more accuracy than any previous Soviet SLBM, and is the first solid-propellant SLBM to be produced in quantity. The missile was reported to have experienced significant development problems. One Golf-class submarine was modified to serve as trials ship for the missile.

Weight:	132,000 lbs (60,000 kg)
Length:	approx. 49 ft 2 1/2 in (15 m)
Span:	(ballistic)
Diameter:	
Propulsion:	solid-fuel rocket
Range:	4,500 n.miles (8,300 km)
Guidance:	inertial
Warhead:	nuclear (6-9 MIRV)
Platforms:	*submarines* Typhoon, Golf V
IOC:	1983

SS-N-23 Skiff

Submarine-launched ballistic missile developed for the Delta IV-class submarines. This is a three-stage missile. The missile is believed to have more accuracy and throw-weight than the SS-N-18, and may replace that missile in the Delta III-class SSBNs.

Weight:	approx. 88,000 lbs (40,000 kg)
Length:	approx. 44 ft 7 in (13.6 m)
Span:	(ballistic)
Diameter:	
Propulsion:	liquid-fuel rocket
Range:	4,500 n.miles (8,300 km)
Guidance:	
Warhead:	nuclear (7 MIRV)
Platforms:	*submarines* Delta IV
IOC:	1986

SURFACE-TO-UNDERWATER MISSILES

SUW-N-1

This is a short-range ASW missile system found on the two Soviet carrier classes built to date, apparently in place of the SS-N-14 found in other modern Soviet warships. However, this is a ballistic weapon with a shorter range, and carries only a nuclear warhead. The projectile itself is designated FRAS-1, for Free Rocket Anti-Submarine. The SUW-N-1 is a twin-arm launcher similar in design to the SA-N-1/3 launchers. The rocket was developed from the FROG-7 artillery rocket (Free Rocket Over Ground) and is unguided after being launched on a ballistic trajectory.

Weight:	
Length:	
Span:	(ballistic)
Propulsion:	solid-fuel rocket
Range:	16 n.miles (29.6 km)
Guidance:	unguided (inertial)
Warhead:	nuclear
Platforms:	*carriers* KIEV, MOSKVA
IOC:	1967

FRAS-1 missile on SUW-N-1 launcher on MOSKVA-class helicopter cruiser.

NUCLEAR WEAPONS

The Soviet Navy has a large number and variety of nuclear weapons available. Such weapons have been in the Soviet Fleet since the 1950s when nuclear torpedoes were deployed, which were, according to Western intelligence sources, intended for "strategic" attacks against Western coastal cities.

Subsequently, the Soviets have deployed nuclear weapons at sea and in naval aircraft for the anti-air, anti-submarine, anti-surface, and land-attack roles. The reported detection of torpedoes with nuclear warheads in the Whiskey-class submarine that ran aground in Swedish waters in October 1981 tends to indicate the proliferation of these weapons in the fleet. That Whiskey SS was at least 25 years old, operating in waters close to the Soviet Union, in a non-crisis period, and on an intelligence-collection mission against a neutral nation.

Although there have been periodic reports of Soviet naval mines with nuclear charges, there has been no official (Western) confirmation of such weapons. Further, from a tactical viewpoint such weapons are hardly practical.

Naval weapon systems indicated to have a nuclear capability are listed in table 27-3 with current U.S. nuclear-capable naval systems indicated for comparative purposes.

TORPEDOES

The Soviet Navy employs primarily torpedoes of 533-mm (21-inch) and 406-mm (16-inch) diameter. Most recently, a torpedo with a diameter estimated at 650-mm (26-inch) has entered service.[5]

650-mm torpedoes

These torpedoes are believed to have entered service in the early 1980s, being carried by Soviet SSN/SSGN-type submarines. The torpedo is approximately 30 feet (9.1 m) long with an advanced closed-cycle thermal propulsion system; public estimates of performance are 50 knots for up to 27 n.miles (50 km) or 30 knots for up to 54 n.miles (100 km). Warhead size is estimated at about 2,000 pounds (900 kg); guidance is believed to be wake homing.

Submarine classes that are believed to have 650-mm torpedo tubes are the Oscar SSGN, and the Akula, Mike, Sierra, and Victor II/III SSN types.

This is the world's largest torpedo, carrying the heaviest explosive charge of any torpedo in service, and some models may be fitted with a nuclear warhead.

533-mm torpedoes

These torpedoes are launched from trainable tubes in surface warships and fixed tubes in submarines for use against surface and submarine targets. These torpedoes are approximately 21 feet long (6.4 m). Propulsion is provided by steam or electric motors (batteries) with speeds from 28 up to approximately 45 knots and effective ranges from 2 miles

[5] In this century the only torpedoes to enter service with a larger diameter than 553 mm were the German Type H-8 (23.6 in/600 mm) and British Mk I (24.5 in/622 mm) of World War I, and the famed Japanese Type-93 "Long Lance" (24 in/610 mm) of World War II.

TABLE 27-3. SOVIET NAVAL NUCLEAR WEAPONS

Launch Platform	Weapon	Role	U.S. Naval System
Surface Ships	SA-N-1 (?)	anti-aircraft/anti-ship	Terrier BTN*
	SA-N-3	anti-aircraft/anti-ship	Standard-ER/SM-2†
	SA-N-6 (?)	anti-aircraft/anti-ship	
	SS-N-3b	anti-ship	
	SS-N-9	anti-ship	
	SS-N-12	anti-ship	
	SS-N-19	anti-ship	
	SS-N-22	anti-ship	
	152-mm gun	anti-ship	
	torpedoes (?)	anti-ship/ASW	
	SUW-N-1/	anti-submarine	ASROC, Sea
	FRAS-1		Lance†
Attack Submarines	torpedoes	anti-ship/ASW	
	SS-N-3	anti-ship	
	SS-N-3c	land-attack	
	SS-N-7	anti-ship	
	SS-N-9	anti-ship	
	SS-N-12	anti-ship/land-attack	
	SS-N-15	anti-submarine	SUBROC§
	SS-N-21	land-attack†	TLAM‡
	SS-N-24	land-attack	
Strategic Submarines	SS-N-5	theater strike	
	SS-N-6	strategic-theatre strike	
	SS-N-8	strategic	Poseidon C-3
	SS-N-17	strategic	
	SS-N-18	strategic	
	SS-N-20	strategic	
	SS-N-23	strategic	Trident C-4
Aircraft	bombs	anti-ship/land-attack	B-57, B-61 / B-61
	depth bomb	ASW	B-57
	AS-2	anti-ship	
	AS-4	anti-ship	
	AS-5	anti-ship	
	AS-6	anti-ship	
Coastal Defense	SSC-1	anti-ship	
	SSC-X-4	anti-ship§	

*BTN = Beam-riding, Terrier, Nuclear.
†In development.
‡TLAM (N) = Tomahawk Land-Attack Missile (Nuclear).
§SUBROC = Submarine Rocket (limited availability; being phased out of service; to be succeeded from about 1990 by the ASW Stand-Off Weapon (SOW).

Three 533-mm (21 inch) torpedoes are partially exposed in the starboard band of torpedo tubes of a Krivak I-class frigate. Frigates and larger Soviet warships have 533-mm torpedo tubes while U.S. and NATO surface ships have only "short" tubes for Mk-44 and Mk-46 324-mm (12.75-inch) ASW torpedoes.

(3.2 km) up to possibly 10 miles (16 km). Guidance is both pre-set (straight-running) and acoustic homing.

Warheads are both high-explosive and nuclear, the torpedoes having been the first Soviet naval weapon with a nuclear capability.[6] The Soviet Type 53-VA torpedo, which has been exported to Warsaw Pact and Third World nations for use with Soviet-built small combatants, has a high-explosive warhead of 1,250 lbs (562.5 kg) with an electromagnetic exploder.

[6] The U.S. Navy's only nuclear torpedo was the Mk-45 ASTOR (Anti-submarine Torpedo), in service in attack and strategic missile submarines from 1958 to 1977.

406-mm torpedoes

These are anti-submarine weapons that are launched from small ASW ships and craft, and from stern tubes in submarines. They are also dropped from ASW fixed-wing aircraft and helicopters with a parachute fitted to slow water entry. These torpedoes apparently have electric (battery) propulsion, acoustic homing guidance, and high-explosive warheads.

28
Naval Electronics

The antenna array of Kara-class missile cruiser TALLINN is indicative of the Soviet Navy's emphasis on electronics.

This chapter describes those Soviet naval electronic systems that have been publicly identified by Soviet or Western sources.

Designations. All of the systems listed in this chapter are identified by their NATO code names. Most aircraft and all shipboard radars and Electronic Warfare (EW) systems are identified by two one-syllable words. The words generally indicate the physical characteristics of the radar, except that the term "screech" in fire-control radars is believed to be derived from the distinctive, screech-like signal emitted by the radar. In turn, bird names are used to differentiate screech-series radars (i.e., Hawk, Kite, Owl).

The basic words used in radar and EW antenna designations are:

(1) Position: Front, head, high, side, tilt, and top.

(2) Shape: Ball, band stand, bar, bell, big, bowl, brick, bulge, cobb, cone, dome, drum, eye, fan, globe, hat, head, high, house, light, mushroom (one word), palm frond, park lamp, peel (as orange peel), pole, post, pot, puff ball, round, rum tub, sail, scoop, short horn, shroud, slab, slim, spring, square, squat, stop light, tail, tee (shaped as the letter "T"), toadstool (one word), tray, and tube.

(3) Construction: Cage, curve, mesh, net, plate, plinth, round, strut, and tilt.

(4) Multiple antennas: Group and pair.

There are several exceptions to this designation scheme. The radar names Neptune and Okean ("ocean") are Soviet names, and not NATO. "Guard" names are used for some Electronic Countermeasure (ECM)/Electronic Surveillance Measures (ESM) systems, e.g., Guard Dog and Watch Dog.

Suffix letters are assigned to major variations, as Big Bulge-A/B and Head Net-A/B/C.

ELECTRONIC WARFARE

Soviet combat aircraft, surface ships, and submarines have electronic warfare equipment to (1) detect threats, (2) collect Electronic Intelligence (ELINT), (3) Identification of Friend or Foe (IFF), and (4) detect and counter threats (ESM/ECM). Few details of these systems are available for publication.

The following are the identified EW systems fitted in Soviet surface ships and submarines. IFF sets are noted. (In addition, surface ships as well as some aircraft have chaff and decoy launchers.)

Surface Ships:

Bell Clout	Cage Pot	Side Globe
Bell Shroud	Dead Duck (IFF)	Square Head (IFF)
Bell Slam	Guard Dog	Top Head
Bell Squat	High Pole-A/B (IFF)	Watch Dog
Bell Tap	Rum Tub	

Submarines:

Brick Pulp	Park Lamp
Brick Split	Stop Light

The heavy electronic antenna array of the battle cruiser KIROV shows a "stack" of four large Side Globe EW radomes mounted on the side of the ship's "mack" (mast-stack). Just above the Side Globes (right and left) are circular Rum Tub EW radomes, and above those (right and left) are Round House helicopter TACAN/control antennas. Between the Round House antennas is a Palm Frond surface-search radar, with a Top Pair 3-D radar mounted on top of the mack. (U.S. Navy)

AIRCRAFT RADARS

Only aircraft of the types operated by the Soviet Navy are listed below.

Bee Hind

Tail-warning radar generally fitted to bomber aircraft. I-band.

aircraft   Badger
Bear
Blinder

Big Bulge

Surface-search and targeting radar; used with data link to transmit radar picture of target ships to missile-launching aircraft or submarines. Range against surface ships from medium altitudes is estimated at some 230 n.miles (423 km). I/J-band.

The Big Bulge-A is fitted in a large, under-fuselage radome on Bear-D aircraft and Big Bulge-B in a chin mounting on the Hormone-B helicopter.

aircraft   Bear-D
Hormone-B

Down Beat

Bombing/navigation radar for search and targeting with AS-4 and probably later air-to-surface missiles. Range is approximately 175 n.miles (322 km). I-band.

aircraft   Backfire-B

Box Tail

Tail-warning radar. I-band.

aircraft   Bear-D/F

Fan Tail

Gunfire control radar for remote-controlled tail gun turret.

aircraft   Backfire-B

High Fix

Range-only air-intercept radar in fighter-type aircraft. Range approximately 5 n.miles (9 km). I-band.

aircraft   Fitter-C

Jay Bird

Range-only air intercept radar fitted in several fighter aircraft. Associated with AA-2/3/4/7/8 and AS-7 missiles. Relatively short range. I/J-band.

aircraft   Fitter-C

Box Tail radar on a Bear-D reconnaissance/targeting aircraft. (U.S. Air Force)

Mushroom

Bomb/nav radar used in several bomber and EW/ECM aircraft. Range is approximately 175 n.miles (322 km). Radome is located under forward fuselage. I-band.

aircraft   Badger
Bear-D

Puff Ball

Bomb/nav radar used in Badger aircraft for targeting AS-2/5/6 missiles (although some carrying AS-5 missile may have the Short Horn radar). Also fitted in Badger and Bison reconnaissance/EW aircraft, and employed as surface-search radar for Hormone-A ASW helicopter. Range is approximately 175 n.miles (322 km). I-band.

aircraft   Badger-C and later models
Hormone-A

Short Horn

Bomb/nav radar used in earlier bomber-type aircraft and in some updated aircraft. Reportedly associated with AS-5/6 missiles. Range approximately 115 n.miles (212 km). J-band (14–15 GHz).

aircraft   Badger-A/C/G

Short Horn and Puff Ball radars on Badger aircraft.

Toadstool

Navigation radar. I-band.

aircraft   Cub

Wet Eye

Surface-search radar, apparently with sufficient target definition for locating raised submarine periscopes and snorkel masts. J-band.

aircraft   Bear-F
            May

Wet Eye radar (right) on May aircraft.

SHIP AND SUBMARINE RADARS

Ball End

Navigation radar found in several ship types. I-band.

Band Stand

Search and missile tracking and control radar for SS-N-9 and SS-N-22 anti-ship missiles. The radar is mounted in a large radome. The Nanuchka II-class missile corvettes transferred to Third World navies have the SS-N-2 Styx vice SS-N-9 missile, and their Band Stand radome contains a Square Tie radar. Range 25–35 n.miles (46–64.5 km). G/H-band.

destroyers	SOVREMENNYY
corvettes	Nanuchka I/II, Tarantul II
small combatants	Sarancha

Bass Tilt

Primarily the fire-control radar for 30-mm close-in (multibarrel) gun; in the smaller combat craft the Bass Tilt is also used to control the 76.2-mm guns, and in the Grisha III the 57-mm guns. The Bass Tilt is similar to the Drum Tilt and Muff Cobb fire-control radars. Range 10–12 n.miles (18–22 km). H-band.

carriers	KIEV
cruisers	Kara, Kresta II
destroyers	mod. Kildin
frigates	Grisha III
corvettes	Nanuchka III
small combatants	Babochka, Matka, Slepen
amphibious ships	IVAN ROGOV
auxiliaries	various classes

Big Net

Long-range, three-dimensional air-surveillance radar, generally found in ships with the SA-N-1 missile (was also fitted in the cruiser DZERZHINSKIY with the SA-N-2 system.) The antenna has an elliptical parabolic form with an offset-fed reflector providing a narrow azimuth beam; the feedhorn is curved and underslung, with twin balancing vanes. First seen at sea in the missile range ship SIBIR' in the early 1960s. The Big Net antenna is mounted back-to-back with the Top Sail to form Top Pair. Capable of detecting aircraft at high altitudes out to some 200 n.miles (370 km) and medium-altitude targets at over 85 n.miles (156.5 km). C-band.

cruisers	Kresta I, SVERDLOV (some ships)
destroyers	Kashin
radar pickets	T-43, T-58
auxiliaries	SIBIR'

Boat Sail

Long-range search radar that was fitted in Whiskey-class submarines modified to radar pickets (NATO code name Canvas Bag, derived from the covering sometimes seen on the folded Boat Sail radar). E/F-band. All radar picket submarines have been discarded.

Superstructure of Kresta II-class missile cruiser showing, from left, Head Lights, Muff Cob (on funnel), Head Net-C (atop funnel), Top Sail, Bass Tilt (above SS-N-14 launcher), and Head Lights radars.

Head Net-C (left) and Big Net radar antennas on Kashin-class destroyer.

Bow series

Target-designation radar found in older surface warships. Half Bow is associated with torpedoes; Top Bow is used for 152-mm gun control. Long Bow range is 10 n.miles (18.5 km). I/J-band.

cruisers   SVERDLOV
destroyers   Kildin, SKORYY

Cheese Cake

Missile targeting radar for SS-N-2c Styx missiles. Installed from late 1970s. Range 17–25 n.miles (31–46 km). I-band.

Ships: *small combatants* Matka

Cross Bird

Long-range air-search radar developed from British World War II-era radar designated Type 291. Fitted in early postwar Soviet warships. The Soviet designation is GUIS-2. An improved version was the (now-deleted) Sea Gull (GUIS-2M). A-band.

destroyers   SKORYY

Cross Sword

Fire control radar for SA-N-9 surface-to-air missiles in new Soviet destroyers. Several of the early UDALOY-class ships deployed without the radar or with only one installation; two are standard for the ships, one atop the bridge and one between the twin helicopter hangars.

Apparently other radars perform the Cross Sword function in the later KIROV-class cruisers and KIEV-class aircraft carriers that have the SA-N-9 missile.

destroyers   UDALOY

Don series

These are primarily navigation radars, but probably have a target-designation function as well. They are installed in a variety of naval ship types; the Palm Frond radar is being installed in their place in newer Soviet ships. They are horizontally polarized I-band radars. Range is approximately 25 n.miles (46 km). Series includes Don and Don-2 (9250–9500 MHz) and Don-Kay (9350–9500 MHz).

Drum Tilt

Acquisition and tracking radar for twin 25-mm and 30-mm AA guns. First of the weapon-control radar antennas with drum shape. The distinctive plastic radome is tilted about 25°, enclosing a circular parabolic reflector. Range approximately 22 n.miles (40.5 km). H/I-bands.

cruisers	ADM. SENYAVIN, SVERDLOV
destroyers	Kanin, SAM Kotlin
frigates	Koni
small combatants	various classes
amphibious	Polnocny
landing craft	Aist
auxiliaries	SMOL'NYY

Egg Cup

Modified Skin Head radar used for gunfire spotting for 130-mm and 152-mm guns. Provides range-only data. Range 12–15 n.miles (22–27.5 km). E-band.

cruisers	SVERDLOV
destroyers	Kotlin, SAM Kotlin

Eye Bowl

Fire-control radar for the SS-N-14 ASW missile in ships without the larger Head Lights radar. Fitted in pairs. Only the lead ship of the KIROV-class battle cruisers has the SS-N-14 Eye Bowl installation. Range 10–12 n.miles (18.5–22 km). F-band.

cruisers	KIROV (1 unit)
destroyers	UDALOY
frigates	Krivak I/II

Front series

Front Door and Front Piece are submarine sail-mounted radars for mid-course guidance of the SS-N-3a Shaddock and SS-N-12 Sandbox anti-ship missiles. The forward edge of the submarine's sail structure swings open for radar operation. The SLAVA-class cruisers, with the SS-N-12 missile, have a Front Door/Front Piece radar mounted on the pyramid structure. F-band. Also see Trap Door.

submarines	Echo II, Juliett
cruisers	SLAVA

Front Dome

Multiple radome antenna system for target illumination and missile tracking of SA-N-7 system. The radomes resemble Bass Tilt gunfire control radars, but are fixed. The test ship PROVORNYY has eight domes, and the SOVREMENNYY-class ships each have six. H/I-band.

destroyers	Kashin (1 unit), SOVREMENNYY

Drum Tilt radar on Koni-class frigate.

Front Door/Front Piece radars exposed on the front of the sail structure of an Echo II-class cruise missile submarine.

Hawk Screech

Fire-control radar for 45-mm, 57-mm, 76.2-mm, and 100-mm anti-air-craft guns in older destroyers and smaller ships. The circular dish antenna with feedhorn is supported by four legs with a large box housing for transmitter and receiver aft of antenna. Associated with backup optical directors. Similar to the Owl Screech radar. Range 8–12 n.miles (15–22 km). I-band.

destroyers   Kanin, Mod. Kildin, Kotlin, SAM Kotlin
frigates   Koni, Mirka, Petya, Riga (1 ship)
auxiliaries   various classes

Head Lights series

Fire-control radar for the SA-N-3 missile system and SS-N-14 ASW missile. The antenna consists of two large (almost 4-meter diameter) dishes—somewhat resembling headlights—with two smaller dishes above. The main dishes are balanced by vanes at their rear. A smaller dish may provide command signals to the missile. The entire array can elevate and rotate 360°. Head Lights-A is fitted in carriers and Head Lights-B in cruisers. The -C model has also been identified. Range 40 n.miles (74 km). D/F/G/H-bands.

carriers   Kɪᴇᴠ, Mᴏsᴋᴠᴀ
cruisers   Kara, Kresta II

Head Net-A

Air-search radar with two identical sets mounted in some ships. Antennas consist of large, elliptical paraboloid reflectors of open construction, illuminated by a feed horn carried by a boom projecting from under the scanner's lower edge; fitted with large balancing vanes. The radar is also known as Strand. Maximum range is 120 n.miles (221 km); reportedly capable of detecting aircraft at medium-altitudes out to 70 n.miles (129 km). C-band (500–1,000 MHz). Most, if not all, have been deleted from Kashin-class ships.

cruisers   Kynda (some ships)
destroyers   Kashin

Head Net-B

Air/surface-search radar consisting of a back-to-back installation of two Head Net-A reflectors with one angled 15° in elevation to provide both high and low coverage. First seen on a Krupnyy-class destroyer in 1965. E/F-band.

auxiliaries   Dᴇsɴᴀ

Hawk Screech radar on Koni-class frigate.

Head Net-A radar on Kashin-class destroyer.

Head Net-C

Back-to-back installation of two Head Net-A antennas with one angled 30° in elevation for simultaneous use as air-search and height-finding radar. First observed in 1963, Head Net-C is widely used on missile-armed ships, in company with Top Sail on larger units. The back-to-back arrangement of the radar antennas provides the advantages of reducing structural interference to radar emissions, improving data rates, and possibly making track transfer from two- to three-dimensional radars faster and more accurate through common stabilization. Range is approximately 60–70 n.miles (111–129 km). E/F-band.

carriers   MOSKVA
cruisers   Kara, Kresta I/II, Kynda (some ships)
destroyers   Kanin, Kashin, Mod. Kildin, SAM Kotlin
frigates   Krivak
amphibious   IVAN ROGOV
auxiliaries   several classes

High Sieve

Air- and surface-search radar. Range 25 n.miles (46 km). I-band.

cruisers   SVERDLOV
destroyers   SKORYY

Kite Screech

Fire control radar for 100-mm and new 130-mm guns. Range 10–12 n.miles (18–22 km). I/J-band.

cruisers   KIROV, SLAVA
destroyers   SOVREMENNYY, UDALOY
frigates   Krivak II/III

Kivach

Late-model navigation radar in Tarantul-class corvettes and possibly other small combatants.

Knife Rest

Early-warning/surveillance radar with Yagi-array (directional) antennas; previously fitted in SVERDLOV-class cruisers and T-43 radar picket corvettes.

Low Sieve

Surface-search radar in order cruisers. Being phased out. I-band.

cruisers   SVERDLOV

Head Net-C radar on Krivak II with Palm Frond radar and (right) Eye Bowl radar directors for SS-N-14 ASW missile.

Kite Screech radar on UDALOY-class destroyer.

Muff Cobb

Fire-control radar for twin 57-mm automatic gun mounts. Similar to Drum Tilt with improved stabilization. H-band.

carriers	MOSKVA
cruisers	Kresta I/II
frigates	Grisha I
corvettes	Nanuchka I, Poti, T-58
small combatants	various classes
amphibious	Ropucha
auxiliaries	BEREZINA, Lama, Manych, Ugra

Neptune

Navigation radar found in older ships. Range 20–25 n.miles (37–46 km). I-band.

cruisers	SVERDLOV
destroyers	Kotlin

Okean

Search and navigation radar in auxiliary ships.

Owl Screech

Improved version of Hawk Screech fire-control radar for 76.2-mm guns. Range 15–18 n.miles (27.5-33 km). I-band.

carriers	KIEV
cruisers	Kara, Kynda
destroyers	Kashin, Mod. Kildin
frigates	Krivak I
amphibious	IVAN ROGOV
auxiliaries	IVAN SUSANIN, SMOLN'Y

Palm Frond

Improved small search-navigation radar mounted in a variety of ship types; replacing the Don-series radars. Range 25 n.miles (46 km). A-band.

Peel Cone

Small radar that first appeared on the Babochka-type patrol boat in 1978.

Peel Group

Fire-control radar for SA-N-1 missile system. This is an awkward-looking grouping that consists of four radars with elliptical and solid reflectors; two large and two small antennas are mounted in the horizontal and vertical positions to provide tracking (I-band) and missile guidance (E-band). Range 35–40 n.miles (64.5–74 km).

cruisers	Kresta I, Kynda
destroyers	Kashin, SAM Kotlin, Kanin

Peel Pair

Small surface-search and navigation radar.

corvettes	Nanuchka

Peel Group (left) and Owl Screech radars on Kashin-class destroyer.

Peel Group radar (rear aspect) on Kashin-class destroyer.

Plank Sheave

Improved air- and surface-search radar for smaller ships.

corvettes   Pauk

Plate Steer

Phased-array, three-dimensional air-search radar consisting of a Top Steer antenna mounted back-to-back with a Top Plate. Fitted in the fourth and later ships of the SOVREMENNYY class (beginning with the OSMOTRITELNYY completed in 1984). Previously referred to as Top Steer/Top Plate.

destroyers   SOVREMENNYY (later ships)

Plinth Net

Medium-range search radar, apparently associated with the SS-N-3b Shaddock missile system.

cruisers   Kresta I, Kynda

Pop Group

Fire-control radar for SA-N-4 low-altitude missile system. There are three co-located antennas, similar to the SA-8 Land Roll radar. The Pop Group may be a monopole, frequency-hopping system that can be operated at different frequencies. Range 35–40 n.miles (64.5–74 km). F/H/I-bands.

carriers	KIEV
cruisers	ADM. SENYAVIN, Kara, KIROV, SLAVA
frigates	Grisha, Koni, Krivak
corvettes	Nanuchka
small combatants	Sarancha
amphibious	IVAN ROGOV
auxiliaries	BEREZINA

Post Lamp

Torpedo fire-control radar. Range 15–20 n.miles (27.5–37 km). I-band.

destroyers   Kotlin, SKORYY

Plank Sheave radar on Pauk-class corvette.

Pop Group radar on Koni-class frigate.

Pot Drum

Surface-search and torpedo fire-control radar for small combatants housed in drum-shaped radome with a diameter of about 1.5 meters. The radar is identical to the Square Tie in Osa missile boats. The Soviet designation for this radar is *Baklan*. Range 18–20 n.miles (33–37 km). I-band.

small combatant   Stenka

Punch Bowl

Mast-mounted submarine radome.

Round House

Tactical Aircraft Control And Navigation (TACAN)-type radar; for all-weather control and homing of aircraft. Fitted in ships with multi-helicopter capability.

cruisers	Kara (1 ship), KIROV
destroyers	UDALOY

Scoop Pair

Fire-control radar for mid-course guidance of the SS-N-3b Shaddock missile in surface ships. The "pair" consists of top-and-bottom antennas, each with a double feedhorn. Also see Front series. I-band.

cruisers   Kresta I, Kynda

Sheet Bend

Small navigation radar found on coastal and river craft.

Pot Drum radar on Shershen-class torpedo boat. (West German Navy)

Ship Globe

Large tracking radar for use with long-range missile tests and satellites. The parabolic reflector is about 16 meters in diameter. In use on missile range and space event support ships.

Slim Net

High-definition air- and surface-search radar. It replaced the Hair Net on cruisers and destroyers. Slim Net has a distinctive open, lattice-type antenna with multi-leg feedhorn and two large balancing vanes. Maximum range over 175 n.miles (322 km), but realistic effective range against aircraft at medium altitude is 25–30 n.miles (46–64.5 km). E-band.

destroyers Kildin, Kotlin
frigates Petya, Riga
auxiliaries several classes

Snoop series

Mast-mounted, surface-search radars found in various nuclear and conventional submarines. The identified types are Snoop Pair, Snoop Plate, Snoop Slab, and Snoop Tray. I-band.

Spin Trough

Search and navigation radar installed as an alternative to Don-series radars in older surface ships and small craft. I-band.

Spoon Rest

An early-warning radar, apparently developed as a successor to Knife Rest. The naval version is adapted from the land-based P-12 (Soviet designation), which is used with the SA-2 missile. The Spoon Rest antenna consists of six vertical pairs of Yagi antennas. Maximum range is credited at about 150 n.miles (276 km).

cruisers SVERDLOV

Square Tie

Search radar and target designation radar in small combatants for SS-N-2 Styx missile. Detection range for a destroyer up to 25 n.miles (46 km) and another missile boat at perhaps 10 n.miles (18.5 km).

small combatants Osa

Strand

See Head Net-A.

Strut Curve

Small air- and surface-search radar fitted in smaller warships and auxiliaries. Open, lattice-type elliptical paraboloid reflector with horn feed from a boom projecting from the lower edge of the scanner. Maximum range is 150 n.miles (276 km), but realistically about 60 n.miles (111 km) against aircraft at medium altitudes. No balancing vanes are fitted. F-band (3,000–4,000 MHz).

frigates Grisha, Koni, Mirka, Petya
corvettes Poti, T-58
minelayers Alesha
amphibious Ropucha
small combatants various classes
auxiliaries various classes

Strut Curve radar on Koni-class frigate.

Strut Pair

Air-search radar with antenna formed by two Strut Curve antennas mounted back-to-back.

destroyers   Kashin (1 unit), Kildin (1 unit), UDALOY

Sun Visor

Gunfire-control radar with solid parabolic antenna fitted to Wasp Head fire-control directors in older ships (completed from 1953 onward) for use with 130-mm and 100-mm guns. Sun Visor-B version fitted from 1956. Range 15 n.miles (27.5 km). H/I-band.

cruisers   SVERDLOV
destroyers   Kotlin, SAM Kotlin
frigates   Riga
auxiliaries Don, ex-PURGA (KGB patrol icebreaker)

Top Bow

Fire-control radar associated with 152-mm guns.

cruisers   SVERDLOV

Top Dome

Missile guidance radar for SA-N-6 consisting of 4-meter hemispheric radome, fixed in elevation and mechanically steered in azimuth. It is installed with a series of smaller radomes, apparently for tracking multiple targets. Range 40 n.miles (74 km). I or J-band.

cruisers   Kara (1 ship), KIROV, SLAVA

Top Knot

Spherical aircraft navigation/control (TACAN) radar.

carriers   KIEV

Strut Pair radar on UDALOY-class destroyer (flanked by Round House TACAN antennas).

Guided missile cruiser SLAVA showing, at left, SA-N-6 VLS system and Top Dome missile control radar.

VSTOL carrier MINSK with (from left) Top Steer 3-D radar, Top Knot TACAN antenna (above Rum Tub and Side Globe EW antennas), and Top Sail 3-D radar antenna.

Top Pair

Long-range, three-dimensional surveillance radar. See Top Sail listing.

cruisers   KIROV

Top Plate

Air/surface-search radar fitted to the UDALOY-class destroyers in place of one of the two Strut Pair radars beginning with the third ship of the class (the MARSHAL VASIL'YEVSKIY completed in 1983). The antenna has a flat ("solid") plate mounted in front of a "mesh" antenna plate.

destroyers   UDALOY (later ships)
icebreakers   ARKTICA (some ships)

Top Sail

Long-range, three-dimensional air-search and early-warning radar fitted in major warships. The antenna consists of a large scanner that has a cylindrical cross section with the axis tilted back about 20° from the vertical. The reflector is illuminated by a linear radiating element located parallel to the cylindrical axis. It uses frequency scan in elevation. Two large balancing vanes are fitted. The Top Sail is used in conjunction with the Head Net-C search and Head Lights missile control radars. Top Sail is mounted back-to-back with Big Net to form the Top Pair radar. C-band.

carriers   KIEV, MOSKVA
cruisers   Kara, Kresta II, SLAVA

Top Steer

Medium-size, three-dimensional air-search radar, somewhat similar in appearance to the larger Top Sail. The larger antenna is fitted back-to-back with the Strut Pair radar antenna with a common feed. The Top Steer uses frequency scan in elevation. Range 150 n.miles (276 km). F-band.

carriers   KIEV
destroyers   Kashin (1 unit), SOVREMENNYY

Top Trough

Surveillance radar in older surface combatants. The bar-like antenna has a slotted waveguide that feeds a curved reflector. It is used for target discrimination for 100-mm and 152-mm guns. The radar was installed in the 1970s. C-band.

cruisers   SVERDLOV

Trap Door

Radar for mid-course guidance of the SS-N-12 anti-ship missile. The Front-series radars in submarines and the cruiser SLAVA are similar. In the KIEV-class VSTOL carriers the antenna retracts into the forecastle when not in use.

carriers   KIEV

Top Steer radar on battle cruiser KIROV (with Vee Tube-C HF antennas at right).

Top Trough radar on SVERDLOV-class light cruiser. (Giorgio Arra)

SONARS

The initial postwar surface ships mostly had the Tamir-5 series of high-frequency, hull-mounted sonars. They were succeeded by the Pegas-2 series from the mid-1950s, and the Herkules series from the late 1950s. The contemporary submarines were fitted with the Tamir-5L sonar. Subsequently, a variety of improved sonars were developed for the Soviet warships that began joining the fleet in the 1960s. Submarines were fitted with active-passive Herkules and passive Fenks sonars.

In particular, by the 1960s there was an effort to reduce frequencies, and during the past two decades they have been reduced from the 20–30 KHz range to about 2–15 KHz. Variable-Depth Sonars (VDS), dipping sonars (from helicopters and surface ships), and directional systems have been introduced.

Most significant, starting with the Victor III-class SSN, first introduced in 1978, the Soviets have deployed towed passive sonar arrays. Such systems appear to have narrow-band processors, greatly enhancing their capability. Other submarine classes have now been fitted with towed arrays.

The Soviet Navy also employs moored, sea-floor acoustic systems in coastal and regional seas. These do not appear to have the range or capability of the U.S. Navy's SOSUS.[1]

---

[1] The U.S. Navy's Sound Surveillance System (SOSUS) has large sea-floor arrays in several Atlantic and Pacific areas. Their existence was publicly acknowledged for the first time in the late 1960s by the U.S. Secretary of Defense.

Trap Door radar in retracted position (at bow) of VSTOL carrier MINSK with RBU-6000 ASW rocket launcher at right.

Herkules and Feniks sonar installation on a Foxtrot-class attack submarine.

Details of official NATO or Soviet designations for recent Soviet sonars are limited as is information on their performance.

Soviet ASW fixed-wing aircraft and helicopters carry air-dropped, expendable sonobuoys.

High-frequency/keel-mounted (Herkules or Pegas)

destroyers	Kildin, Kotlin, SKORYY
frigates	Mirka, Petya, Riga

Medium-frequency/keel- or bow-mounted

cruisers	Kresta II
destroyers	Kanin
frigates	Grisha, Krivak

Medium-frequency/VDS

carriers	KIEV, MOSKVA
cruisers	Kara
destroyers	mod. Kashin
frigates	Krivak

Low-frequency/keel- or bow-mounted

carriers	KIEV, MOSKVA
cruisers	KIROV
destroyers	UDALOY

Low-frequency/VDS

Reported to operate between 3 and 5 kHz.

cruisers	KIROV
destroyers	UDALOY

Helicopter dipping

helicopters	Haze-A, Helix, Hormone-A
frigates	Mirka, Petya
small combatants	Pchela, Poti, Stenka, Turya

Helix-A ASW helicopter lowering a dipping sonar.

Variable-depth sonar of battle cruiser FRUNZE.

29
Bases and Ports

The Soviet Union is constructing underground berths for submarines on the Kola Peninsula, as shown in this artist's concept of a submarine base complex. At left is a Typhoon-class SSBN with a Delta IV-class SSBN entering an underground "submarine pen" and an Oscar SSGN leaving a tunnel. Thirteen other submarines are portrayed in this drawing with one, lower right, in a floating dry dock. Secretary of the Navy John F. Lehman has called the Kola Peninsula the "most valuable piece of real estate on earth," because of the massive Soviet base structure there.

The Soviet Union has a longer coastline than any other nation—half again as long as that of the United States:[1]

Region	Length (n.miles)
Arctic	8,166
Baltic	988
Black Sea	867
Pacific	6,075
Total	16,096

During the past 15 years there has been a massive effort to enlarge the commercial port capacity and increase cargo-handling facilities. In an extensive containerization program, container ships have been constructed in large numbers (see chapter 31), ports have been built or refitted to handle containerized cargo, and a special rail service has been established to speed containers across the Soviet Union.

The Soviet port expansion has also included facilities for handling coal, ore, lumber, and petroleum products more rapidly. And since the Soviet Union has become a petroleum exporter (although most through pipelines to Eastern Europe), this includes provisions for handling large tankers.

Naval base facilities have also been expanded, primarily to service the increasing number of nuclear-propelled submarines and the larger surface warships of the Soviet fleet, especially the KIROV-class nuclear battle cruisers and the KIEV-class aircraft carriers. In order to dry-dock the latter ships in the Northern Fleet (Arctic) and Pacific Fleet base areas, the Soviets have purchased large floating dry docks. A Swedish-built large floating dry dock was provided for the naval base at Murmansk and a Japanese-built floating dock for the base at Vladivostok, both capable of accommodating a KIEV-class aircraft carrier. Most recently, a third large floating dry dock for carriers, built in Yugoslavia, was delivered to the Black Sea.

The following are the major Soviet bases and ports, listed by geographic area.

[1] By comparison, the U.S. coastline totals 10,985 n.miles, of which 6,544 are in Alaska.

ARCTIC COAST

Arkhangel'sk (Archangel), the oldest seaport of the country, is a major port, provincial capital, and the largest city on the Soviet Arctic coast. When Peter I became tsar in 1682, it was Russia's only outlet to the sea.

The port is on the frigid Arctic coast and is blocked by ice for up to 190 days per year. The extensive use of icebreakers, however, keeps the port open to commercial shipping almost continuously. During the past few years the port's facilities—along 32 miles (51 km) of waterways—have been greatly enlarged, and container and fuel-handling facilities have been added. On the delta of the Dvina River as it enters the White Sea, Arkhangel'sk can be reached by ship from Leningrad via the lake-canal route between Leningrad and the White Sea. The White Sea Canal (formerly the Stalin Canal), is iced over five or six months of the year, as is the White Sea itself. The canal is 140 miles (224 km) long and was built in just 20 months in the early 1930s as Stalin's first major slave-labor project.[2]

About 25 miles (40 km) west of Arkhangel'sk is the major shipyard complex of Severodvinsk, which was known as Molotovsk until 1957.[3] A railway line ties the two cities together and links them with the main rail systems to the south. Severodvinsk was founded in the late 1930s as Stalin sought to develop naval support facilities in the Arctic. Today Severodvinsk rivals Arkhangel'sk in size. It has a small port, but its principal importance is as a naval shipbuilding and industrial center.

Northwest of Severodvinsk-Arkhangel'sk on the Kola Peninsula are the sprawling port of Murmansk and the satellite ports of Pechenga and Polyarnyy. About 155 miles (248 km) of the Kola coast east of the border with Norway, including Murmansk, are free of ice year around, kept open by the warm waters of the Gulf Stream, which carries warm water northward from the Gulf of Mexico, a distance of 6,000 miles (9,600 km).

[2] Several hundred thousand slave laborers died in constructing the canal. A graphic description of their efforts and privations in building this inland waterway is given in Aleksandr I. Solzhenitsyn, *The Gulag Archipelago—Two* (New York: Harper & Row, 1975), pp. 86–100.

[3] See chapter 30 for descriptions of specific Soviet shipyards.

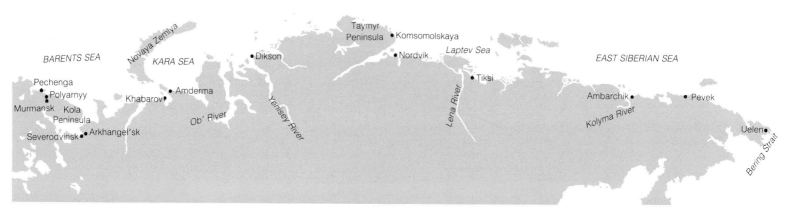

Arctic coast of the USSR

While there was interest in developing Murmansk as a port by Russian traders and whalers in the eighteenth century, there was little progress until World War I. The tsarist government wanted a port with access to the sea for the Allies, as the Baltic and Black Sea ports were vulnerable to German and Turkish interdiction. By September 1916 a railroad to the port was complete and it was formally established to receive transports with military supplies for the Russian armies. American and British troops landed at Murmansk in the Russian Civil War, and it again became known to Americans in World War II because of the "Murmansk Run" for Allied merchant ships carrying war supplies to the Soviet Union. (Arkhangel'sk was also a key port for the Murmansk Run.)

Murmansk is some 125 miles (200 km) north of the Arctic Circle—the world's largest city north of the circle. Its current population exceeds 400,000, and is experiencing a relatively rapid rate of growth. The port is the western terminus for the commercial Northern Sea Route. It was recently modernized to handle freight containers and is a focal point of the fishing and fish-processing industries; it has two building yards for commercial ships, and has maritime schools with intermediate and higher curricula. The town of Severomorsk (formerly Vayenga), about ten miles (16 km) northeast of Murmansk, is headquarters for the Northern Fleet. The Severomorsk base complex has extensive support facilities for warships, including ammunition depots. (There was a disastrous explosion at a principal depot in 1984; see page 19.)

There are reports that by 1984 the Soviets had completed the construction of four large, underwater "tunnels" for strategic-missile submarines in the Severomorsk area. The tunnels are said to be large enough to accommodate the Typhoon-class SSBNs, apparently giving them protection from nuclear attack when they are undergoing maintenance or are being rearmed. The exact location of the tunnels has not been publicly identified, and some sources indicate that the tunnels may be at nearby Saya Guba, which appears to have submarine support facilities.

A 900-mile (1,440-km) rail line connects Murmansk with Leningrad, with goods being transferred at the port of Leningrad for the North Sea Route. From Murmansk, ships also sail westward, to Europe and the Americas, especially during the winter months when the eastern Baltic is partially blocked by ice.

The port of Polyarnyy (formerly Aleksandrovsk), north of Murmansk at the mouth of the Tuloma River, is a major base for Northern Fleet surface ships and submarines. This was the principal base for the Northern Fleet during World War II. Pechenga, formerly Finnish Petsamo, is both a naval and fishing port. It is northwest of Murmansk and only 18 miles (29 km) from the Norwegian border. Farther south on the peninsula is the port of Gremikha (near Iokanga), which has been described as a base for the new Typhoon-class SSBNs. There are many other bases on the Kola Peninsula, which is estimated to have as many as 40 military airfields as well as bases for two army motorized rifle divisions and the Northern Fleet's Naval Infantry brigade.

There are a number of smaller but still significant ports along the Arctic coast. Several are transshipment points for the intensive river traffic that plies the long Siberian rivers. South of the Novaya Zemlya islands in the Kara Sea are the ports of Khabarovo and Amderma on the Yugorskiy Peninsula. These ports are used to ship coal from mines on the mainland, and have provided logistic support for the huge slave-labor camp established on Novaya Zemlya in the 1930s and later for the early Soviet ICBM emplacements on those islands.

Farther east are the important ports of Dikson at the mouth of the Yenisey River, Komsomolskaya on Pravda island off the northern coast of the Taymyr Peninsula, Nordvik on Khatanga Bay, Tiksi at the delta of the Lena River, Ambarchik near the mouth of the Kolyma River, Pevek at Chaunskaya Bay, and Ulen on the Bering Strait, at the eastern tip of Siberia.

BALTIC SEA COAST

Leningrad is the second largest city of the Soviet Union (population over 4 million) and the shipping and shipbuilding center of the Soviet Baltic coast.[4] The city boasts five major shipyards, several lesser yards, and a large commercial port. Located at the eastern end of the Gulf of Finland, the city is built on the delta of the Neva River, and is laced with rivers and canals. The city is also the Baltic entrance to the lake-canal route to the White Sea.

The Gulf of Finland is iced over about half the year; but here too the use of modern icebreakers significantly extends the shipping season and provides continuous access for naval units.

Leningrad's large commercial port is on the southern side of the city. Although there are a large number of naval shipyards and training activities in the city, the Baltic Fleet headquarters is not at Leningrad nor are many warships based there. However, there are always naval units there for trials, training, and overhaul.

Some 15 miles (24 km) west of Leningrad in the Gulf of Finland is Kotlin Island. In its old port city of Kronstadt are a commercial port, a naval base, and a major ship repair yard. Oranienbaum, south of Kronshtadt on the mainland, is believed to be a base for light naval forces.

Farther west, at the southern entrance to the Gulf, is the port of Tallinn (formerly Reval), capital of the Estonian Soviet Socialist Republic (SSR). Estonia, Latvia, and Lithuania comprise the Baltic states. They were Russian from the time of Peter I until World War I, then independent from 1918–1920 to 1939, when, at the outset of World War II, they were seized by Soviet troops and incorporated into the Soviet Union. (During World War II they were overrun by German forces.)

At Tallinn are naval and commercial ports that are ice-free most of the year, and numerous warships up to cruiser size are home-ported there. Nearby are air bases and army installations. There has been a recent addition of commercial port facilities at Tallinn, primarily for refrigerated goods and agricultural products. The first phase of construction was to complete in late 1986, with further expansion planned.

Almost directly south of Tallinn on the Gulf of Riga is the city of Riga, capital of the Latvian SSR and a major sea port. Riga's history as a port dates more than one thousand years, when it was a crossroads for trade between Scandinavian tribes and Greece. Actually situated on the Daugava River, Riga has several shipyards, and extensive con-

---

[4] The city was founded as St. Petersburg by Tsar Peter the Great; it was changed to Petrograd in 1914 and to Leningrad upon Lenin's death in 1924.

Riga—one of Europe's oldest ports—is typical of the older ports of the Soviet Union that have been expanded and modernized. The increase in Soviet shipping has demanded the development of newer ports as well as expanding the existing ones. (Sovfoto, Yury Belinsky)

Leningrad is the center of naval and maritime activity. Sometimes called the Venice of Russia because of the numerous branches of the Neva River and associated canals, there are naval and maritime activities scattered throughout the city. In this view from the Neva are the Nakhimov secondary naval training school and the cruiser AVRORA, which has been preserved as a museum since 1948. (C.P. Lemieux)

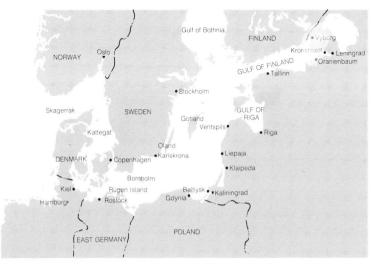

Baltic Sea

tainer-handling facilities have been added. A Soviet naval base has been reported under development in the area.

West of Riga is the newer commercial port of Ventspils (formerly Windau), at the mouth of the Venta River. This port has several times the cargo-handling capacity of Riga, and a new oil export facility can accommodate supertankers of more than 100,000 deadweight tons. American firms have assisted in the construction of a large loading complex for ammonia and other chemicals at the port. While the Gulf of Riga is iced over 80 to 90 days per year, Ventspils is almost always ice-free.

The next significant Baltic port is Lepaia (formerly Libau), on a narrow sandspit between the Baltic and Lake Libau. Protected naval and commercial harbors are located there.

Klaipeda (formerly Memel) in the Lithuanian SSR at the mouth of the Memel River is the republic's capital city. It has long been a ship-building center and has commercial and naval harbors and a petroleum-loading port.

The adjacent cities of Baltiysk (formerly Pillau) and Kaliningrad (Kön-igsberg) are of major importance to Soviet naval operations in the Baltic.

Both are located in what formerly was East Prussia which, after being overrun by Soviet troops in World War II, was incorporated into the Soviet Union after the war.

Baltiysk is headquarters for the Baltic Fleet and the home port for many of the fleet's major warships. There is also a fishing port. And, being near the Polish border, it also hosts a flotilla of KGB Maritime Border Troops. Kaliningrad, on the Pregel River, is connected to Baltiysk by canal. It is a major commercial port and contains a large shipyard. A number of naval activities are located in the area, in part because these are the westernmost ports of the Soviet Union.

BLACK SEA COAST

The Black Sea is a major trading and shipbuilding region of the Soviet Union. The newest of the major ports is Ust'-Dunaysk at the western end of the sea, near Vilkovo, which lies at the northernmost mouth of the Danube River. The port was developed in the late 1970s to handle bulk cargo carriers and barge-carrying ships of the international association Interlikhter (whose members are Bulgaria, Czechoslovakia, Hungary, and the Soviet Union).

Odessa is probably the nation's largest port, handling over 20 million tons of cargo annually, almost twice the amount handled by Leningrad. Unlike most Soviet ports, Odessa is not located on a river but on the Black Sea coast a few miles east of the mouth of the Dniester River. One of Russia's oldest cities, Odessa is also a major passenger/tourist terminal in an area of historical and cultural importance. Odessa's commercial port has more than five miles (eight km) of quays, with facilities for handling specialized cargoes such as grain and sugar. Two large, new ports are being built near Odessa because that port area is surrounded by the city proper and cannot be expanded. In addition, Odessa city officials fear that dust and air pollution from the ships and dry cargoes may affect the tourist trade and damage historic structures.

Twelve miles (19 km) southwest of Odessa is the new commercial port of Il'ichevsk, whose construction began in the late 1950s. It has specialized facilities for handling containers and grain, as well as iron ore and coal. Nearby Yuzhnyy (South Port) is also being developed as a major port; the first ship to depart the port, the ammonia tanker BALDURY, sailed in August 1978. Pipelines running from a large mineral fertilizer plant in Odessa directly to the harbor permit the loading of

Il'ichevsk, near Odessa on the Black Sea, is one of the newer Soviet merchant ports, with a still newer port being developed at nearby Yuzhnyy. This photo shows part of the container handling facility at Il'ichevsk, a reflection of the massive Soviet program to handle and transport containerized cargo. (Sovfoto, I. Pavlenko)

Black Sea

flow goods and materials from ports on the Black and Caspian seas as well as from the inland ports of European Russia.

After Rostov, Zhdanov (formerly Mariupol), on the western coast of the Sea of Azov, is the second major port of that sea. It is an industrial city, being a major steel center. Also shipped through Zhdanov's commercial port are grain, coal, and petroleum.

Novorossiysk, on the Black Sea to the east of the Kerch' Strait, is another major industrial city with a commercial port and a naval harbor for light forces. There are repair yards in the area, but no significant shipbuilding facility.

Lesser ports along the northern coast of the Black Sea include Kamysh-Burun and Tuapse, which are naval and commercial ports; Kerch', location of a major shipyard; Ochamchire, a commercial port and possibly a submarine facility; Poti, at the mouth of the Rioni River, with both commercial and naval sections to its port, destroyers being based there; and Batumi, near the Turkish border and starting point of the Trans-Caucasian Railway. Batumi is also the coastal terminal for the oil pipeline from Baku and handles commercial ships and naval ships up to frigates.

PACIFIC COAST

Vladivostok—"Ruler of the East"—is the major Soviet port complex on the Pacific coast. Located at the southern end of the Muraiev Peninsula, Vladivostok is at the head of Golden Horn Bay, an arm of Peter the Great Bay. Its hills and bays have led some visitors to call Vladivostok the "San Francisco of the Far East." The city was the original eastern port terminus of the Trans-Siberian Railway. Vladivostok is only ten miles (16 km) from the Chinese border, making it extremely vulnerable to an attack by China; it is less than 100 miles (160 km) from North Korea. (American and Japanese troops landed at Vladivostok in 1918, during the Russian Civil War; the troops were not withdrawn until 1922.)

Today Vladivostok is the largest city in the Soviet Far East with a population of over 600,000. The city houses the headquarters of the Pacific Fleet and is home port for much of the fleet's surface and submarine forces, including two KIEV-class aircraft carriers. Naval installations include logistic and training centers for the fleet, some located on adjacent Russian Island, which is connected to Vladivostok by several sea-floor tunnels. A submarine school is also reported on Russian Island. Other military bases in Peter the Great Bay include Novgoradsky, Possiet, Shkotovo, and Tynkin. Accordingly, Vladivostok is closed to most foreign ships. Westerners did obtain a look at the city in November 1974 when President Ford and Party Secretary Brezhnev held a summit meeting there with considerable press coverage.

There is a major fishing base and fish-processing complex at Vladivostok as well as shipyards and repair facilities. A new fishing port at Troitsa, on Peter the Great Bay near Vladivostok, was begun in the late 1970s.

Sixty miles (96 km) east of Vladivostok lies Nakhodka on the Gulf of Amerika, formerly Wrangel Bay. This is the principal commercial port of Siberia. Named "the find" because of its excellent location, the port's development as a major shipping center began in 1960, and operation of the Soviet Union's first mechanized container-handling facility began there in late 1973. Within a few months it was handling 1,000 freight

ammonia into specialized tankers. Container, lumber, coal, and ore loading complexes have also been developed, with a goal of handling some 25 million tons of cargo per year. Eventually the Yuzhnyy port should be about as large as Odessa and Il'ichevsk combined.

These ports and others along this portion of the Black Sea coast are frozen for about three months of the year, but channels are kept open for ship traffic.

The largest shipbuilding and industrial center and a major port of the Black Sea is Nikolayev. Located at the junction of the Bug and Ingul rivers, the city has two major and several lesser shipyards and ship-repair facilities. The commercial port has more than two miles (3.2 km) of quays.

A short distance to the east is Kherson on the Dnepr River, about 20 miles (32 km) from where that long and important waterway enters the Black Sea. There are several maritime industries and a major shipyard in the city in addition to a large commercial port.

Historic Sevastopol' on the Crimean Peninsula is headquarters for the Black Sea Fleet and the main base area for naval units that operate in the Black Sea and Mediterranean. Small craft and submarines are based in Sevastopol' and its southeastern suburb of Balaklava. Several small shipyards, as well as extensive naval storage and other support facilities, are located in and around Sevastopol'. Also in the Crimea is the smaller port of Feodosiya, used by submarines and escorts. Most of the Black Sea Fleet's air bases are located in the Crimea.

Northeast of the Crimea is the Sea of Azov, entered through the narrow Kerch' Straight between the Kerch' and Taman peninsulas. Most of the Sea of Azov is frozen from the end of November until mid-April. About 180 miles (288 km) northeast of the Kerch' Straight and 30 miles (48 km) north of where the Don River enters the Sea of Azov is the port of Rostov. Rostov is the meeting point for cargo from the Don and Volga rivers, which are connected by canal. Through these rivers and canals

Vladivostok is often compared to San Francisco—a major port on a beautiful bay with numerous hills. It is the largest city in the Far East, surrounded by several other ports and naval facilities.

Ice is a major problem at most Soviet ports in the Arctic, Baltic, and Far East regions for much of the year. The use of a large number of powerful icebreakers, however, has overcome this limitation. Here a Krivak II-class frigate and Manych-class water carrier proceed through ice-strewn Far Eastern waters. (Japanese Maritime Self-Defense Force)

containers per day as the Siberian transfer point for the trans-Soviet express container run. Nakhodka is also being developed as a major passenger and fishing port.

However, Nakhodka cannot handle the increasing volume of foreign and domestic trade. Thus, only nine miles (14 km) away, also on the Gulf of Amerika, Vostochnyy has been under development as a major port since 1970. The port was designed in conjunction with the new Siberian railway, the Baykal-Amur Mainline (BAM), which stretches from the Lena River to the Pacific coast.

Within a decade of the start of construction of Vostochnyy, some two million tons of cargo per year were being handled. A local press report in 1984 declared that the port could handle more than 200,000 standard cargo containers per year. Soviet officials plan for Vostochnyy to have an "eventual" capacity of handling 30 to 40 million tons of cargo annually over its planned 66 wharves, making it the largest port in the Soviet Union. Called the "Japanese port" because of Japanese technical assistance and credits used in its development, Vostochnyy loads large amounts of Siberian timber being shipped to Japan. It also has extensive container and coal-handling facilities, with the first container ship sailing from Vostochnyy in May 1976.

Farther up the coast, on the Tatar Strait, is Sovetskaya Gavan', formerly Imperatorhafen, and above that the port of Nikolayevsk at the mouth of the Amur River, just below the Sea of Okhotsk. Sovetskaya Gavan' is a commercial port, handling mostly timber, and is also one of the three most important naval bases of the Pacific Fleet (the others being Vladivostok and Petropavlovsk). A submarine base and school are also reported to be located there, and the port serves as a base for warships up to destroyer size. Nikolayevsk is a fishing center.

To the north, Anadyr', at the mouth of Anadyr' River, is important as a coal port and for Arctic shipping. Major improvements were made at

the commercial port in the late 1970s. Light naval forces are believed to be based there. Neither Anadyr', Magadan on the Sea of Okhotsk, nor Petropavlovsk on the Kamchatka Peninsula are connected to railway lines; rather, they are totally dependent upon sea and air transport. Magadan is a base for submarines and light forces.

Petropavlovsk is a domestic commercial shipping and fishing port, but adjacent Talinskaia Bay is the principal base for submarines of the Pacific Fleet, with two shipyards located there. "Petro" has the advantage of having direct access to the Pacific; ships or submarines leaving the port do not have to pass through narrow straits to get to the sea as is necessary with the other major Pacific Fleet bases. However, as said above, the naval and civilian populations of the peninsula (there are 220,000 inhabitants in the city), as well as the troops stationed in the area, must be supplied entirely by sea and air.

The lack of overland communications has forced the Soviets to employ seafloor cables for communications between Kamchatka and the mainland. (The message traffic on these cables has been intercepted by U.S. submarines operating in the Sea of Okhotsk in a program known as Ivy Bells.)[5]

The Kamchatka Peninsula and the Soviet-controlled Kuril islands form a protective barrier for the Sea of Okhotsk. The Soviets have tried hard through both legal arguments and practice to make the Sea of Okhotsk an "inland sea," forbidden to foreign military and commercial shipping.

On Sakhalin Island, held by Japan from 1905 to 1945 and taken over by the Soviets at the end of World War II, are the naval bases of Korsakov (formerly Otomari) and Aleksandorsk. Another port was developed at Kholmsk in the 1970s for handling cargo and supporting fish-factory ships, and Vostochnyy at the northern end of Sakhalin is a commercial port that began container operations in 1976.

Most Far Eastern ports are iced over for up to half the year. At Vladivostok, the southernmost port, snow lies on the ground for more than three months of the year, and Peter the Great Bay is greatly hampered by ice during much of the winter. The entire Sea of Okhotsk is covered by thin ice from October to June. Again, the large fleet of Soviet coastal and oceangoing icebreakers keep the Far Eastern ports operating around the year.

To support the large military deployments in Siberia, and to counter American, Japanese, and Chinese forces, the coastal areas also contain a large number of air and ground bases.

INLAND PORTS

Inland from the Pacific coast on the Amur River are the shipbuilding centers of Komsomol'sk and Khabarovsk. The latter is one of the largest cities in Siberia. Both have major military and commercial industries and are rail and river transportation crossroads. Their waterfronts are frozen over from November through June.

Pacific coast of the USSR

---

[5] The Soviets learned of this U.S. intercept operation from National Security Agency analyst-turned-traitor Ronald Pelton, probably as early as January 1980; Pelton was arrested in late 1985.

Kronshtadt in the Gulf of Finland is one of the Soviet Navy's largest overhaul and repair bases. Here the cruiser Oktyabrskaya Revolutsiya is covered with scaffolding during an overhaul; a pair of Riga-class frigates are nearby in this 1986 photograph. (Courtesy Hyman Grotkin)

The Soviet Union has several major inland river and canal routes, some of which provide passage for small and some even medium-size ships between the Arctic, Baltic, and Black Sea ports. In Siberia the long Lena, Ob', and Yenisey rivers all are navigable for more than 2,000 miles (3,200 km). They permit river craft to carry raw materials north to the Arctic coast, where they can be transshipped to seagoing cargo ships, and can also carry cargoes from European Russia back down the rivers to Siberian cities and towns. Major ports along these rivers include Narym, Tomsk, Turukhansk, Verkholensk, Yakutsk, and Yeniseysk.

In European Russia the Volga River runs some 2,300 miles (3,680 km), and most of it, from north of Moscow south to the Caspian Sea, is navigable. The Volga-Don Canal, completed in 1952, links the Volga to the Don River and the Sea of Azov and hence to the Black Sea. There are numerous ports along this route. Among the more significant ones are Gor'kiy, with its submarine and river craft building yards, Kazan', Volgograd (formerly Stalingrad and before that Tsaritsyn), and Astrakhan, near the Volga's entrance into the Caspian Sea.

On the inland Caspian Sea, Baku is the largest city and chief port. Smaller port facilities are found at Astrakhan, Guryev, and Krasnovodsk. These ports played a major role in the transshipment of U.S. war material sent to the Soviet Union through Iran during World War II.

In addition to coastal trade, the ports support offshore drilling in the Caspian Sea.

30
Shipbuilding and Shipyards

Shipbuilding is a major factor in the development and future capabilities of the Soviet Navy.[1] While shipbuilding in the West and Far East has suffered a severe depression in the 1980s, the shipyards of the Soviet Union continue to produce large numbers of modern naval and merchant ships, as well as smaller numbers of fishing and specialized research ships. Soviet yards also build a large number of ships for foreign merchant and fishing fleets as well as for foreign navies (see appendix D).

In many respects the Soviet shipbuilding industry is the world's largest. There are more than 20 major shipyards in the Soviet Union, a major yard being one that has more than 2,000 full-time employees.[2] The largest yards are mainly used for the construction of large ships, while hundreds of other yards build and maintain smaller ships of the naval, merchant, fishing, research, and river fleets. Of the major yards that construct ships, three build only warships—Severodvinsk (submarines), Kaliningrad (destroyers and amphibious ships), and Petrovskiy (small combatants), plus the Sudomekh portion of the Leningrad Admiralty Association (submarines; see below).

There are several hundred smaller shipyards that build and repair naval and commercial ships, including the large number of craft that operate on rivers, lakes, and inland seas. Collectively, these large and small yards comprise the world's largest shipbuilding and repair industry, ably supported by an infrastructure of machinery and equipment firms, research institutes, and design bureaus.

The Soviet shipbuilding capabilities are complemented by those of several Eastern European nations, principally Finland, East Germany, and Poland. Their major yards provide up to 70 percent of their annual ship production to the Soviet Union. All three nations are currently benefiting from the Soviet five-year (1986–1990) plan for building a total of 2–6 million deadweight tons of merchant shipping in their yards as well as in Soviet shipyards. This is especially important for these nations in view of the depression in shipbuilding outside of the Soviet bloc. (Polish and East Germany yards also build naval auxiliaries as well as trawlers and fishing support ships for the Soviet Union.)

The Soviet Union also buys a small number of ships, generally of specialized designs, from Western nations. This practice, however, is limited because hard currencies are normally needed to procure products in the West.

History. The first known effort at shipbuilding by the Muscovite (Moscow) government came in 1570 when Tsar Ivan IV ordered vessels built on the Arctic coast. When Peter I became tsar in 1682, the port of Arkhangel'sk (Archangel) on the Arctic coast was Russia's only outlet to the sea. Barges and small ships were constructed there for coastal and river trade. At Peter's direction small seagoing ships were constructed there from 1693; the first built was his 12-gun "yacht" named ST. PETER, which Peter himself launched the following year.[3]

The next Russian shipbuilding effort, in support of Peter's quest to take the enclosed Sea of Azov from the Turks, was much more ambitious. Peter chose the town of Voronezh, at the junction of the Voronezh and Don rivers, some 300 miles (480 km) below Moscow and 500 miles (800 km) above the Sea of Azov, as the site for his new shipyards. River barges were already being built there, and the site was chosen also because of the availability of timber and the distance from Tatar tribes that could threaten the yard.

Peter obtained almost 28,000 local laborers for this effort; he brought Russian and foreign artisans from Arkhangel'sk, appealed to Venice to send him shipbuilding experts, and had a galley newly arrived at Arkhangel'sk from Holland cut into sections and transported to Moscow to serve as a model for his new ships. Smaller craft were built inland in pieces and dragged on sledges to Voronezh for final assembly. Peter, with no technical training in shipbuilding; took personal charge of the effort at Voronezh; at times he worked as an apprentice on the ships. By the summer of 1696 the Voronezh yards had produced 28 galleys and several hundred barges. Simultaneous with this effort, the Admiralty Court—Russia's first permanent shipyard—was begun at Voronezh.

With these Voronezh-built ships, manned mostly by Greeks and com-

---

[1] This chapter is based in part on Joel Bloom, "Technical Assessment of Current Soviet Shipbuilding Capabilities" (Suitland, Md.: Naval Intelligence Support Center, 24 February 1975), published in hearings before the Committee on Appropriations, House of Representatives, in 1975, and updated for this edition by Dr. Boris S. Butman, "Soviet Shipbuilding and Ship Repair" (Arlington, Va.: Spectrum Associates, January 1986). Also see David R. Jones, ed., *The Military-Naval Encyclopedia of Russia and the Soviet Union*, vol. 3 (Gulf Breeze, Fla.: Academic International Press, 1981), pp. 74–139, 158–241; and Ulrich-Joachim Schulz-Torge, "Soviet Naval Industry," *Naval Forces*, no. VI, 1984, pp. 58–65.

[2] By this criterion the United States has 16 major shipyards—eight government-owned naval shipyards and eight private yards.

[3] An interesting account of Peter's early days at Arkhangel'sk and his naval interests is found in Robert K. Massie, *Peter the Great* (New York: Alfred A. Knopf, 1981).

The Soviet shipbuilding industry is large and highly diversified, constructing a variety of ship types of varying degrees of complexity. Although the industry is inefficient by Western standards, it appears to meet Soviet requirements for producing and maintaining the nation's large naval, research, merchant, and fishing fleets. (Sovfoto)

manded by a Swiss officer, Peter was able to gain control of the Sea of Azov and hence an outlet to the Black Sea through the Kerch' Strait. And since the waters of the Sea of Azov were open to navigation more of the year than those of the frigid Arctic coast, Peter ordered a large fleet constructed there. (After Peter's defeat by the Turks at Pruth in 1711, all shipbuilding ceased on the Don River, and his fleets on the Sea of Azov and the Black Sea were disbanded.)

In addition to the importation of Western European workers and ships, Peter sent some 50 Russians, mostly sons of nobles, to England, Holland, and Venice to study shipbuilding, seamanship, and navigation. In the following years more Russians were sent abroad to study naval and maritime matters, and the most distinguished student would be Peter himself.

Peter departed Russia for the West in the spring of 1697. Working under the alias Peter Mikhailoff, but readily known to all, Peter actually studied and labored in shipyards in England and Holland. (More formal visits were made to other countries.) One workman at the Royal Dockyard at Deptford alleged, "The Tzar of Muscovy worked with his own hands as hard as any man in the yard."[4] After these visits to Western Europe, Peter enlisted some 700 English officers and artisans to help him build a fleet, mainly for the Baltic, where he planned a campaign against the Swedes.

In 1703 Peter, in his quest for "warm water ports" for trade with the West, began building small ships at Olonets and other places on Lake Ladoga for his campaign to capture the Neva and a foothold on the Baltic from the Swedes. Lake Ladoga—east of the Gulf of Finland, the easternmost arm of the Baltic Sea—is Europe's largest lake.[5] By May he was able to sail a force of 18 boats with 400 soldiers on the lake to do battle with the Swedes.

That month his boats and more troops were able to wrest the mouth of the Neva River from Swedish control. There he established a settlement, which he named St. Petersburg (now Leningrad), as a port for trade with the West as an alternative to the large, difficult route to Arkhangel'sk.

In October of 1704, because of storms on the lake and problems in navigating the fast-flowing Neva, Peter decided to establish the Admiralty shipyard on the left bank of the Neva, across the river and downstream from the new Peter and Paul Fortress (Petropavlovsk), whose guns could help protect the new yard. The yard's offices soon became headquarters for the Russian fleet. Above the yard rose a tall wooden spire, topped by a weathervane in the shape of a ship. Through rebuilding, the central spire was retained and is today a dominant feature of the Leningrad skyline. The building of scaffolds began immediately, while the yard was expanded and fortified. The first ships were laid down in 1705, and the first warship, an 18-gun coastal gunboat, the ARCKE DES VERBONDES (Ark of the Covenant), was launched on 26 April 1706. More ships followed, often with Peter working on them. (As late

as 1714 the tsar worked in the yard in various roles, using his alias Peter Mikhailoff.) As other Russian yards were given the name "admiralty," from 1723 the original yard was called the Main Admiralty.

On a nearby island formed where the Moika River flows into the Neva, from 1709 there were timber storage sheds and other ancillary functions for the Admiralty yard. This area was known as Galley Court, and by 1713 small ships were being built there; a major thoroughfare was then built to connect the new yard to the Admiralty yard. The thoroughfare was originally named Galernaya Street (now Krasnaya), and the yard was soon called Galerniy Island, although at times the area was also called Admiralty Island. When the old Admiralty yard ceased to construct ships, the Galerniy facility became known as the New Admiralty yard.

During Peter's reign other yards were begun in his new capital city, including one on the eastern end of Kotlin Island in the Gulf of Finland, a short distance off St. Petersburg. Originally called Kronshlot and later Kronshtadt, this yard had a dry dock for repairs as early as 1705 and began building ships in 1716.

At the time of Peter's death in 1725, his Baltic Fleet consisted of 48 ships of the line and almost 800 minor warships, crewed by 28,000 sailors. Most of this fleet had been built in Russian yards. St. Petersburg has continued as the center of Russian shipbuilding. A major characteristic of Peter's shipbuilding industry has survived into the Soviet era: the acquisition of foreign ships, components, and technologies.

The shipbuilding industry continued to develop and spread as Peter's successors pushed Russian borders to the Black Sea and the Pacific coasts. In 1780 a Russian city was established at Sevastopol' near the southern end of the Crimean Peninsula, the site of settlements since a Greek colony was founded in the late 6th century B.C. A naval base and shipyard were started in 1784, and Sevastopol' became the main base and shipyard for the Russian fleet on the Black Sea. The base declined after the Crimean War (1854–1856). Subsequently, the government yard that had been started in 1798 at Nikolayev near the mouth of the Bug River became the major Russian shipbuilding center of the Black Sea. This naval (southern) yard at Nikolayev was followed by a private (northern) shipyard, with the former facility also being taken over by a private firm in 1911.

In the Far East a primitive yard was started in 1714 at Okhotsk, on the sea of that name, with Swedish prisoners of war serving as laborers. This yard became the base of the Siberian naval flotilla. Okhotsk was followed by yards at Petropavlovsk on barren Kamchatka Peninsula, at Nikolayevsk near the mouth of the Amur River, and, finally, at Vladivostok. The last was established as a Russian military post in 1806 with a shipyard dating from 1869. Two years later Vladivostok became the principal base of the Siberian flotilla and has grown steadily; today it is the largest city on the Soviet Pacific coast.

Indigenous construction and foreign purchases resulted in a Russian fleet at the beginning of the twentieth century that stood third in strength, after Britain and France, and ahead of those of Germany, Italy, Japan, and the United States. The scale of the Soviet shipbuilding industry could be seen in the 18 battleships launched between 1900 and 1917 at six Russian yards—three in St. Petersburg and three on the Black

---

[4] Nathan Dews, *The History of Deptford* (London: Conway Maritime Press, 1971 [a new impression of the 1884 edition]), p. 183.

[5] The lake is connected to the Gulf of Finland by the Neva River, which is 45 miles (72 km) long.

Sea. (Five more battleships were launched in 1915–1916, but were not completed.)

Russian warships produced in this period were equal to and some even superior to comparable naval ships of other maritime powers. However, the Russians continued to be heavily dependent upon other nations for design talent and, to a lesser extent, shipbuilding. Battleship construction at the New Admiralty yard in St. Petersburg and at the Nikolayev northern yard were under the technical management of John Brown and Company, and at the southern Nikolayev yard construction was under Vickers, both British firms. There was also strong Italian influence; for example, the largest ships built in tsarist Russia—the four 23,360-ton battleships of the PETROPAVLOVSK class laid down in 1909—were based on the designs of Italy's Vittorio Cuniberti, pioneer in the development of all-big-gun battleships.

Major naval ships were also built in foreign yards in this period, among them the battleship TSESSAREVITCH, launched in France in 1901, and the battleship RETVIZAN, launched in the United States in 1900 (built by the William Cramp Shipyard in Philadelphia). Similarly, in the early 1900s the Russian Navy bought American-built submarines of both the Lake and Holland designs, and three German submarines completed about 1907. When the First World War began, two light cruisers were under construction for the Russians in German shipyards. Lesser naval units were built for the Russian fleet in these countries as well as in Belgium, Denmark, and Sweden.

(Commercial shipbuilding was largely ignored in this period, with only eight merchant ships being built in Russian yards from 1905 to 1917.)

The chaos of the Russian Revolution and Civil War brought shipbuilding to a virtual halt. The new Communist government did put emphasis on merchant ship construction from the mid-1920s, and four yards were reopened in an effort to enhance domestic transportation and foreign trade. Four timber carriers and a tanker were laid down in 1925 at the Baltic yard and the Northern (now Zhdanov) yard in Leningrad, at the Nikolayev complex, and at the Sevastopol' navy yard. At about the same time, the first ship design bureau—Balt Ship Project—was created in Leningrad to produce advanced ship designs. This is considered to be the start of the Soviet shipbuilding industry.

Limited efforts were also undertaken to rebuild the naval fleet, mostly modernizing the existing, tsarist-era warships. The first five-year economic plan (1929–1933) envisioned the construction of 216 merchant ships, but only a few of them were actually completed. The principal naval units built under the first five-year plan were the six DEKABRIST-class submarines, completed 1930–1931, three being built at the Ordzhonikidze (Baltic) yard in Leningrad and three at the Marti south (now Black Sea) yard in Nikolayev.

Between the world wars there was a particularly strong Italian influence on Soviet naval ship design, and in the 1930s there was a remarkable American-Soviet liaison as designs and components were sought in the United States for aircraft carriers and battleships. The latter would have been the largest such ships afloat, with some of the battleship designs providing for a partial aircraft flight deck. Nothing resulted from these efforts, however, mostly because of foot-dragging by U.S. naval officers. Just before World War II erupted there was an

increase in German technical assistance to the Soviet Navy, cumulating in the sale of the unfinished German heavy cruiser LÜTZOW to the Soviets in 1940.[6]

During World War II there was an influx of U.S. and British naval ships of various types into the Soviet fleets, and after the war German and Italian warships were transferred to the Soviet Navy. These ships and their systems provided a technical base for the postwar Soviet warship development. After the war the rehabilitation of shipyards and their supporting industries was given very high priority by Stalin. The contemporary Soviet fleet is in large part the result of this immediate postwar effort.

The current shipyards date from three periods: the tsarist era, the Stalin era, and the Khrushchev period. Particularly significant are the shipyards built under Stalin's regime (1922–1953). His drive to industrialize the country led to the construction of seven major and many lesser yards. Large yards were built on all Soviet coasts as well as on inland waterways. The Arctic and Pacific yards were intended to increase the independence of those flotillas (now fleets). Stalin's approach to shipbuilding established the scheme of simultaneous construction of classes in two or more fleet areas.

During World War II the Soviets established two major inland yards at Gor'kiy and Zelenodol'sk on the Volga River. These yards, as well as Severodvinsk on the Arctic coast, make use of the large Soviet river and canal complex to move ships and material. This move was in part to replace the yards in the Baltic and Black Sea war zones.

In the Khrushchev period (1953–1964) several yards were shifted from naval to merchant construction, and five new major yards were established, all but one of them intended for commercial shipbuilding. Also in the Khrushchev period the first nuclear-propelled surface ship was built, and the Severodvinsk yard on the White Sea began building nuclear submarines. The first, a November-class SSN, was completed in 1958. Two years later the Komsomol'sk yard in the Far East completed its first nuclear submarine. The Admiralty yard in Leningrad built the nuclear-propelled icebreaker LENIN, which first got under way in September 1959, predating the American nuclear-propelled merchant ship SAVANNAH and the nuclear missile cruiser LONG BEACH (CGN 9).

The Krasnoye Sormovo yard at Gor'kiy, one of the major inland shipyards, became the third nuclear submarine yard, completing its first such craft in 1967. Several years after building the LENIN, the Admiralty yard began constructing nuclear-propelled submarines, with its first completion also in 1967. The adjacent Sudomekh yard completed the first of the advanced Alfa-class nuclear submarines about 1967, bringing to five the number of nuclear submarine construction yards.

During the 1970s and into the 1980s these five submarine yards—counting the two components of the Leningrad Admiralty Association

---

[6] The LÜTZOW was a sister ship to the better-known PRINZ EUGEN, which had a standard displacement of 14,800 tons and mounted eight 8-inch guns. The LÜTZOW was never completed, but served as a floating gun battery (renamed TALLINN in 1942 and PETROPAVLOVSK in 1944). The unfinished SEYDLITZ of the same class was taken over by the Soviets after the war (renamed POLTAVA), but she too was never finished. Both ships are believed to have been scrapped about 1950.

as two yards—were producing annually about eight nuclear submarines plus several diesel-electric boats. This was double the U.S. nuclear submarine construction rates (with no U.S. diesel boats being built).[7] The five Soviet yards have an estimated capability of producing more than 20 nuclear submarines per year. Although the Admiralty yard had built the first nuclear icebreaker, beginning in the 1970s the Baltic shipyard in Leningrad began building nuclear-propelled surface ships—the Arktika-class icebreakers and the Kirov-class battle cruisers.

On 1 January 1972 the Admiralty and Sudomekh yards were merged into the Leningrad Admiralty Association. This was part of an industry-wide effort to improve planning while reducing centralized control and cutting administrative personnel at the yards. Several such associations were formed, generally by merging one very large shipyard with one or more nearby small yards, and assigning supporting shops and factories to them as well as related engineering institutes.

Major examples of this affiliation program are the Leningrad Admiralty, the 61 Years of Komsomol Association in Kherson, and the Astrakhan Shipbuilding Association. (In this chapter the Admiralty and Sudomekh yards are described in separate listings.)

ORGANIZATION AND FACILITIES

The several hundred shipbuilding and ship repair yards in the Soviet Union are under the cognizance of the Ministry of Ship Production and the four operating ministries—Navy (a component of the Ministry of Defense), Merchant Marine, Fishing Fleet, and River Fleet.

The Ministry of Ship Production directs the activities of more than 30 of the largest shipyards in the country. These yards primarily construct the naval ships and the large, complex merchant ships as well as various research ships. Created in 1939, the Ministry of Ship Production is one of the defense industry ministries. (The others are the Ministries of Defense, Aviation, Communications Equipment, Electronics, Radio, General Machine Building, Machine Building, and Medium Machine Building, the last a euphemism for nuclear weapons and power reactors. These are directed by civilian ministers.

The four ship operating ministries—Navy, merchant, fishing, river—each operate additional yards that build, repair, and overhaul ships for their own use.

All of these yards participate in a centralized planning scheme with 5-, 10-, and 20-year programs. These long-term programs facilitate the procurement of large classes or series of ships with significant savings in labor, resources, and maintenance. Further, all yards employ uniform and mandatory procedures for calculating costs, with standardized practices and techniques used whenever possible.

Aside from shipyards, the Soviet shipbuilding industry also has an extensive array of design bureaus and research and design institutions. These, too, are subordinate to the various ministries. These institutions exist at several levels: at the highest level are the institutes and laboratories of the Academy of Sciences, several of which specialize in ship-related fields such as Arctic studies, metallurgy, physics, fluid mechanics, nuclear technologies. Several of these institutes and laboratories are assigned specialized research ships.

At the next level are the central scientific and research institutes of the Ministry of Ship Production that specialize in various ship technologies, materials, standardization, and economics. The largest and most prestigious of these is the Krylov Institute in Leningrad, described by the U.S. Navy as "the world's foremost shipbuilding research and development center."[8] The Krylov Institute operates several research ships, including the unique systems/materials test ship Izumrud. The Institute is believed to have a staff of approximately 5,000 personnel, including 1,700 scientists and engineers.

The Merchant Marine, Fishing Fleet, and River Fleet ministries each have their own research institutes that specialize in such areas as ship maintenance and repair, transport automation, and fleet operations. Moreover, a number of the naval and maritime higher schools and academies have research centers that conduct similar research and study efforts; most of these centers tend to specialize in specific maritime areas. In all, there are an estimated 75 design bureaus and ship-related research institutes and centers supporting the various "fleet" ministries.

As in other "hardware" industries, the leading technical institutes produce tables and codes that serve as baseline documents for all ship construction, naval and commercial. These also contribute to standardization in design and components and permit the rapid introduction of advanced designs and construction technologies.

Only a few of the yards still use inclined building ways. The larger ships are built in graving docks, the largest dock being at Nikolayev Black Sea (south) yard, where the Kiev-class carriers were built and the nuclear-propelled carriers are under construction. Production lines with horizontal assembly positions for modules and indirect launching are used at most yards. All of these practices increase efficiency and speed ship production. At the same time, the Soviets pursue the use of computer-driven cutting and fabrication equipment, laser metal cutting, and semi-automatic or automatic welding. The construction of the titanium-hull Alfa SSN demonstrated a capability to work this advanced metal in large sections, which does not now exist in the West. Another feature of Soviet shipyards is the extensive use of covered building halls, especially in the Arctic region, which permit year-round construction to take place. All submarine building ways are covered, a practice that provides a high degree of protection from U.S. reconnaissance satellites.

The quality of Soviet shipyard work can be gauged, in part, by the sales of naval units and merchant ships to other countries. Such traditional seafaring nations as Great Britain, Norway, and Sweden were among the customers for Soviet-built merchant ships during the growth period of the 1970s. Reports concerning the quality of warships built for other navies have been mixed; some clients have liked their ships and others have been disappointed, complained to the Soviets, and in

[7] The two U.S. submarine yards engaged in nuclear submarine construction did produce eight units in 1981—one Trident SSBN and seven SSNs, this output brought about because of previous program delays and larger authorizations in the 1970s. The General Dynamics/Electric Boat yard and Newport News yard have a combined construction capability of about two Trident SSBNs and five SSNs per year.

[8] Bloom, p. 14. Alexei N. Krylov was the principal designer of Russian battleships of the Sevastopol' and Sovietskiy Soyuz classes during the Stalin period.

some instances have turned to the West after sampling Soviet products. (Soviet financial terms and weapons transfer policies in many instances compensate for questionable or poor quality of goods.) Some Soviet ships have had major problems that could be attributed to their construction. A large fish-factory ship built at the Admiralty yard in Leningrad required more than a year of additional work after her sea trials; the poor workmanship was cited in the Soviet press.

The following shipyard problems can also be cited:

> . . . a shortage of modern equipment in many areas of ship production, weak technologies discipline, and low quality of work. Being technically and financially unable to rapidly improve the overall technology level of the entire shipbuilding industry, the Soviets concentrate their efforts on certain important areas and have achieved significant results, especially in welding and cutting of titanium and aluminum alloys, nonmetallic joining materials, and robotics.[9]

ENGINEERS, MANAGERS, AND WORKERS

There are some 215,000 shipyard workers in the Soviet Union according to Western intelligence estimates:[10]

Arctic coast yards	50,000
Baltic coast yards	54,000
Black Sea yards	63,000
Pacific coast yards	30,000
Inland yards	18,000

Many Western sources, however, consider these numbers too low. The numbers do not include naval personnel who are assigned to ships and shipyards and participate in ship repair and maintenance. In addition, many thousands more men and women are employed in the associated ship design bureaus and research institutes.

"The Soviet shipbuilding industry has a corps of well-trained and efficient workers at all skill levels. Training continues after the worker joins a shipyard, as night school and correspondence school courses are offered in most disciplines," according to a U.S. Navy report.[11] The industry has a large and multi-layered, nation-wide infrastructure that hires, trains and educates, and pays employees of the shipyards and the related design bureaus and research institutes. One expert estimates that every year between 7,000 and 9,000 engineers with bachelor's or master's degrees enter shipbuilding and ship repair activities or the bureaus and institutes associated with them.

These men and women are educated at a reported 29 colleges and universities that offer 5- to 6-year engineering programs in ship-related fields, and at about 60 colleges and technical schools that offer a variety of related 2- to 4-year programs. This results in a very high educational level of the professional staff.

Compensation is based on nationwide work rates and norms. The importance of shipbuilding and ship repair, however, has led to a very high degree of flexibility in pay rates within the industry. For example,

[9] Butman, "Soviet Shipbuilding," p. 8-1.
[10] Bloom, "Technical Assessment of Soviet Shipbuilding," p. 14.
[11] Ibid, p. 14.

there are extensive bonuses, overtime and regional incentive payments, and fixed long-term allowances for work in the Arctic and Far Eastern areas. The total bonuses can add 40 to 70 percent to a worker's take-home pay. Beyond ruble compensation, most shipyards provide housing and social amenities for their workers. The scope of this effort may be seen by the Nikolayev and Kherson shipyards (and possibly others) having civil construction capabilities even greater than those of the local government-owned city construction organizations.

The standards and norms existing throughout the shipbuilding and repair industry, the long-range planning processes, and the restrictions on labor mobility in the Soviet Union result in a high degree of employment stability, which, in turn, contributes to an increasingly competent shipyard work force.

There are, however, major problems in the work force. In some respects the worst problem in the shipbuilding industry—as in most levels of the Soviet society—is alcoholism. This is a particular problem in shipyards, where there are many spaces in which to drink unseen. A lesser problem at some yards is a shortage of housing, primarily for the newer workers.

ARCTIC SHIPYARDS

Severodvinsk (Shipyard No. 402)

The Severodvinsk yard is the world's northernmost major shipbuilding facility and ranks as the world's largest submarine construction yard. The yard was originally known as the Molotovsk yard for V.M. Molotov, a leading politician under Stalin; the name was changed in 1957 after Molotov fell from favor in the post-Stalin era.

The yard is located on the Dvina Gulf, about 30 miles (48 km) across the delta of the Northern Dvina River from the city of Arkhangel'sk. The

This is the huge, covered battleship construction hall at Severodvinsk, intended for side-by-side construction of two battleships. This photo was taken in 1944 when the components of two SOVIETSKIY SOYUZ-class dreadnoughts were still in place. The structure and a still larger enclosed dock at Severodvinsk are now used to construct SSBNs. The yard may be the world's largest. (U.S. Navy)

gulf opens onto the White Sea. The yard is connected to Leningrad by the White Sea–Baltic Canal system (completed in 1933 and expanded in the 1970s) as well as by rail lines

History. The decision to build the yard was made in 1932–1933 to help make the Northern Fleet independent of the Baltic shipyards. Its location would reduce the vulnerability to enemy attack in time of war. Stalin envisioned the yard becoming the largest in the world, capable of building ships up to battleship size; the eventual work force when the yard was planned was to be 35,000–40,000.

As estimated 120,000 political and criminal prisoners were brought to the Severodvinsk area in the 1930s to construct the shipyard. The main building dock, under cover to permit work to be carried on year round, is some 1,100 feet (335 m) long and 452 feet (137 m) wide having been intended for side-by-side construction of two SOVIETSKIY SOYUZ-class battleships. Two of these large ships were laid down at Severodvinsk in 1940, but all work on capital ships in the Soviet Union ceased that October and they were never finished. Components and materials for these ships had been brought to the yard from Leningrad and Nikolayev. During World War II the yard had a peak work force of only about 5,000 and built destroyers and S-class submarines, with most of the former being completed after the war.

Subsequently, the yard began construction of the SVERDLOV-class light cruisers and the SKORYY-class destroyers. More significant, the Severodvinsk yard prepared to construct advanced submarines and in 1953 completed the first of eight Zulu-class diesel attack units. It then began producing the Golf-class ballistic-missile submarines and two nuclear classes, the November SSN and the Hotel SSBN.

Some commercial work was done at the yard into the 1950s.

Since the mid-1950s Severodvinsk has constructed only nuclear-propelled submarines. These have been the November, Alfa, and Mike SSNs; the Echo II and Oscar SSGNs; and the Yankee, Delta, and Typhoon SSBNs. Construction of the Alfa and Mike classes, with titanium hulls and advanced nuclear power plants, demonstrates the high-technology level of the yard.

The original battleship building hall, which was used for building Yankee-class SSBNs, has been supplemented by an even larger submarine construction hall, in which the Oscar and Typhoon classes are being built. A third large submarine construction hall has also been erected. These halls are covered and heated, and all permit horizontal construction. In the late 1960s, Admiral H.G. Rickover, while head of the U.S. nuclear propulsion program, said that Severodvinsk had "several times the area and facilities of all of the U.S. submarine yards combined."[12] Although possibly exaggerated, the statement is indicative of the size of the yard.

There are several other ship repair and maintenance facilities in the Arctic. There are submarine support facilities at Polyarnyy as well as

at Severomorsk, both north of Murmansk. Also north of Murmansk, in the Kola Bight, is the Rosta naval dockyard, a major refit facility. An 80,000-ton-capacity Swedish-built floating dry dock is reported to be there to provide docking for the KIEV-class aircraft carrier assigned to the Northern fleet.

At Murmansk there are two large ship repair yards for the merchant and fishing fleets.

The smaller Krasnaya Kuznitsa and Arkhangel'sk ship repair yards are located in Arkhangel'sk and perform commercial work. They have built small coastal and inland craft and floating dry docks, with the latter yard also building small air-cushion vehicles. They are primarily repair yards.

BALTIC SHIPYARDS

Admiralty (Shipyard No. 194)

Admiralty is one of four major shipyards in Leningrad, which is in most respects the shipbuilding center of the Soviet Union. Recent programs have consisted of merchant and fisheries support ships, naval auxiliaries, and nuclear-propelled submarines. Since 1972 the Admiralty and adjacent Sudomekh yards have been consolidated into a single administrative entity, the Leningrad Admiralty Association.

The Admiralty yard is located on Galerniy Island, at the intersection of the Great Neva and Fontanka rivers. The Sudomekh yard is adjacent to the northeast, separated from Admiralty by the small Moika River, and the Baltic shipyard is across the Neva on Vasilevsky Island.

History. Tsar Paul I established the New Admiralty yard on the left bank of the Neva River at St. Petersburg (now Leningrad) in 1800, as

Leningrad

Leningrad has been a shipbuilding center since the time of Peter the Great. This view of the Petrovskiy shipyard shows a Nanuchka-class missile corvette and other small combatants being fitted out (note the mast of another Nanuchka behind the building at right). (N. Polmar)

the Main Admiralty was unsuitable for continued expansion because of the city growing up around it. Battleships were begun at the New Admiralty in the early 1800s when the facility became one of the major Russian yards.

In 1908 the New Admiralty yard was merged with the Galerniy Island yard that had been building naval ships since 1713. (Galerniy had been called the Société Franco-Russe yard from about 1884.) Among the more famous ships built at the yard were the first Russian steamship, the ELIZAVETA, and the historic cruiser AVRORA. After the Revolution of 1917 the yard was renamed Marti, for the French sailor-revolutionary André Marti. Also, from 1921 to 1926, as the Soviets sought to reha-

bilitate the shipbuilding industry, the yard was administratively merged with the Baltic shipyard. The name subsequently was changed back to Admiralty.

Between the world wars Shch-class submarines and then the large K class were built at the yard. Large surface warship construction began in 1938 with the keel-laying for a CHAPAYEV-class light cruiser (not completed until 1949). The following year the keel was laid for the lead ship of the KRONSHTADT-class battle cruisers (that were never finished).

Virtually all ship work halted at the Leningrad yards during World War II while for over three years the city was besieged by German forces. After the war, in addition to completing the light cruiser ZHELEZ-

NIAKOV, the yard geared up to participate in the SVERDLOV cruiser program; however, only three of these ships were completed before the yard ceased building surface warships. Similarly, plans to produce the STALINGRAD-class battle cruisers at the yard were halted.

From the mid-1950s onward the Admiralty yard specialized in non-naval construction—merchant ships, icebreakers (including the nuclear-propelled LENIN, launched in 1957), large rescue and salvage ships, fish-factory ships, and floating dry docks. Several of these ships were completed for naval service. Currently the yard is building the huge MARSHAL NEDELIN-class space event support ships.

No additional nuclear surface ships were produced at Admiralty yard for a decade after the LENIN. The subsequent Soviet nuclear icebreakers were built at the nearby Baltic shipyard. Rather, Admiralty became the fourth Soviet yard to produce nuclear-propelled submarines, with the first two Victor SSNs being launched in 1967. Construction of the Victor II/III classes followed; the follow-on Sierra SSN is also being built at Admiralty.

Baltic (Shipyard No. 189)

The large Baltic or *Baltiyskiy* shipyard produces mainly merchant ships, the notable exceptions being the large ARKTIKA nuclear icebreakers and the KIROV nuclear battle cruisers. The yard is at the lower end of Leningrad's large Vasilevsky Island, near the mouth of the Neva River.

History. The yard was established in 1856 as a major ship construction facility to build merchant ships. The government soon directed that naval ships be built at the yard, and in 1864 it launched two monitors designed by Johann (John) Ericksson, and in 1892 it launched the famed armored cruiser RIURIK. The yard also built the first Russian submarines and later produced early steel battleships.

Known as the Baltic Shipyard and Engineering Works before the Revolution, after 1918 the yard was renamed Ordzhonikidze for an early Russian communist; subsequently it was changed to the Baltic shipyard.

During the 1930s the yard was extensively modernized and began the construction of cruisers, destroyers, and several classes of submarines. On the eve of World War II the yard began building SOVIETSKIY SOYUZ-class battleships. Shipbuilding stopped during the siege of Leningrad, and the yard was severely damaged.

After the war the Baltic yard built six of the SVERDLOV-class cruisers and began series production of the Whiskey-class submarine. The first Whiskeys built at the yard were completed in 1955 but only 14 of these submarines were built before the yard shifted primarily to building merchant and special-purpose ships.

A variety of ships have been built at the Baltic yard during the past two and a half decades—tankers, refrigerated cargo ships, dry-bulk cargo ships, icebreakers, and trawlers. The yard has also built the large space event support ships KOSMONAUT YURIY GAGARIN and KOSMONAUT VLADIMIR KOMAROV.

Although the Baltic yard is one of four major "first generation" yards in the Soviet Union, it has demonstrated how it can adapt the older facilities to modern techniques. For example, sectional construction techniques were used in building the SOFIA-class tankers (61,000 tons deadweight), with the result that time on the building ways was reduced from six months to three and a half months for the first ship built by the new method.

The yard began constructing nuclear surface ships in the late 1960s. The icebreaker ARKTIKA was launched in 1972 and her sister ships SIBIR' in 1976 and ROSSIYA in 1985. Even more impressive, in 1973 the yard laid the keel for the nuclear-propelled KIROV, the largest surface combatant built by any navy since World War II. Most recently, a large, nuclear-propelled missile range instrumentation ship is being constructed at the yard. Thus, the Baltic became the sixth Soviet yard with a nuclear construction capability.

Baltiya/Klaipeda

Merchant ships are produced at this yard, which is also a former German shipyard, known as the Lindenau yard prior to Soviet takeover of the Memel area at the end of World War II. Baltiya reached major shipyard status in the 1950s and since about 1960 has built only merchant ships. Recent production has included fish-factory ships, trawlers, and floating dry docks.

The yard is located at Klaipeda in Lithuania and was previously known as Memel. It is north of Kaliningrad on the Baltic coast.

Three additional yards at Klaipeda are involved mainly in repairs of merchant and fishing ships as well as small naval units.

Izhora

The Izhora shipyard is located at Kolpino, southeast of Leningrad, where the Izhora River enters the Neva. The yard constructs principally minesweepers and hydrofoil craft, including the T-43, T-58, Natya, and Yurka classes.

The yard was previously named Ust Izhora (mouth of Izhora) and is also called Smeoneva (Middle Neva).

Recently the yard has become a producer of fiberglass-reinforced plastic craft, among them the minesweepers and hunters of the Zhenya and Yevgeniya classes. It also builds the Matka-class hydrofoil missile craft.

Kaliningrad (Shipyard No. 820)

The Yantar/Kaliningrad yard builds surface warships and amphibious ships. It is the former German Schichau shipyard.

The yard is located at Kaliningrad, formerly the East Prussian city of Königsberg. Located near the large Soviet fleet base at Baltiysk (formerly Pillau), the yard comprises almost 200 acres.

History. This yard became a major German shipbuilding facility in the 1880s constructing torpedo boats. After World War II the Soviets rebuilt the yard to produce small commercial and naval ships, among them frigates of the Kola, Riga, and Petya classes.

In the 1960s the Kaliningrad yard began producing the larger Krivak-class frigates and the Alligator-class landing ships. The complexity of the Krivak represents a considerable increase in the yard's capabilities. Subsequently, the yard has produced the UDALOY-class missile destroyers, at 8,200 tons the largest naval ships yet built at Kaliningrad except for the two IVAN ROGOV-class amphibious ships.

Further, the yard modernizes escort ships and performs overhaul and maintenance work for the Baltic Fleet. There has been only limited commercial construction at Kaliningrad since 1960 (e.g., ferries were built there in the 1970s).

Kronshtadt

The naval shipyard on Kronshtadt Island, off Leningrad, is a principal repair base for the Baltic Fleet. Historically this large facility has provided support for warships; no new construction is believed to have occurred in the twentieth century. Kronshtadt has some of the largest dry docks in the Soviet Union.

Petrovskiy (Shipyard No. 5)

This Leningrad yard constructs small combatants. It is located on Petrovskiy Island, in the Small Neva, north of Vasilevsky Island. The Petrovskiy yard became a major shipbuilding facility in the 1930s.

Various mine, patrol, torpedo, and missile boats have been built at Petrovskiy, including large numbers of the Osa missile boats. The largest ships built to date at the yard are Nanuchka and Tarantul classes of missile corvettes.

Sudomekh (Shipyard No. 196)

The Sudomekh yard is a specialized submarine construction facility in Leningrad. It has built several advanced submarines as well as research and experimental undersea craft.

The yard is located in downtown Leningrad, between the Neva and Moika rivers. It is adjacent to the Admiralty yard, and the yards have been administratively joined to form the Leningrad Admiralty Association.

History. The yard became a major shipbuilding facility in the 1930s, at which time it built submarines of the Shch and M or *Malyutka* ("baby") classes. The yard was damaged extensively during the war, but was rapidly rebuilt in the late 1940s for submarine construction. Submarines of the Shch and M-V classes were completed through 1952.

After the war, equipment removed from German submarine construction yards was installed in Sudomekh, and advanced submarine designs and propulsion systems were developed. Long-range Zulu-class diesel submarines were launched at Sudomekh from 1952 on, and smaller Quebec-class submarines, developed for closed-cycle propulsion, were launched from 1954, with the yard building all 30 of the Quebec class.

From the late 1950s Sudomekh produced the long-range Foxtrot class, successor to the Zulu. Foxtrots were built at a steady rate of five or six units per year during the 1960s, with construction for foreign transfer continuing into the early 1980s. (The yard built all 62 Foxtrots for Soviet service plus 17 units built specifically for foreign transfer.)

Sudomekh completed the first Alfa-class SSN in 1967, marking the debut of a submarine significantly faster and deeper diving than any

previous or contemporary combat submarine. After lengthy trials and extensive modification, the Alfa entered limited series production at the Sudomekh and Severodvinsk yards. With the Alfa program, Sudomekh became the fifth Soviet shipyard to construct nuclear-propelled submarines.

The Sudomekh yard also built the research-experimental submarines Uniform, X-ray, and Lima, the first two being nuclear propelled.

Thus, beginning with at least the Quebec class, and continuing with the Alfa and some of the subsequent one-of-a-kind craft, Sudomekh has undertaken the development of submarines with advanced propulsion plants. When this edition went to press, the Kilo advanced diesel submarine was reported under construction at what had been the Sudomekh facilities. Obviously, these facilities also provide support to SSN construction at the adjacent building halls of the now-merged Admiralty yard.

Vyborg

Vyborg is located in former Finnish territory, 75 miles (120 km) northwest of Leningrad, its Finnish name being Viipuri.[13] Vyborg became a major shipyard in the 1960s and almost exclusively constructs dry cargo ships, including large container carriers plus offshore oil rigs and rig support ships.

Zhdanov (Shipyard No. 190)

The large Zhdanov shipyard in Leningrad constructs both commercial and naval ships, the latter being missile cruisers and destroyers. From about 1855 it was known as the Putilov Marine Engine Works and subsequently as the Northern Shipyard. It was later named for A.A. Zhdanov, a major political figure of the later Stalin period and Politburo representative for naval matters.

The yard is located in the commercial port area, in the southern environs of Leningrad. The yard covers more than 200 acres.

History. The Putilov yard built destroyers and had laid down light cruisers prior to the Revolution. The yard again began building naval ships in 1936; ships up to destroyer size were laid down prior to World War II. Extensively damaged during the war, the yard was rehabilitated and became a leading Soviet producer of surface warships in the late 1940s. Initially destroyers were built at Zhdanov (SKORYY, Tallinn, Kotlin, Krupnyy, Kanin, Kashin classes) and then the missile cruisers of the Kynda and Kresta I/II classes. The yard also built six of the Krivak I-class frigates.

The yard is currently constructing missile destroyers of the SOVREMENNYY and UDALOY classes as well as a variety of merchant ships, with about one-third of the yard currently allocated to commercial work.

---

[13] Russian troops of Peter the Great captured Vyborg in June 1710, and it remained under Russian control until 1918, when Finland gained independence from Russia. The city and port were ceded to the Soviet Union in 1940 after the Winter War between Finland and the Soviet Union, but were occupied by Finnish and German forces from August 1941 to June 1944, when they were returned to Soviet control.

The latter includes the construction of roll-on/roll-off, dry cargo, and passenger ships. The yard has both open and covered building facilities.

The largest shipbuilding and repair yard of the River Fleet Ministry is located at Petrokrepost, on the southern shore of Lake Ladoga. This was a shipyard in the time of Peter I, and the adjacent canal contained huge berthing docks where sailing ships could be laid up during the winter months.

Smaller but significant Baltic-area yards include the Kanonerskiy and Petrozavod yards in Leningrad, and ship repair yards in Liepaja, Riga, and Tallinn.

BLACK SEA SHIPYARDS

Black Sea (Shipyard No. 444)

Often referred to as the Nikolayev south yard, this is the largest shipyard on the Black Sea. Aviation ships are constructed at the yard as well as commercial ships and naval auxiliaries. The yard built the two Moskva-class helicopter ships, the four VSTOL carriers of the Kiev class, and in December of 1985 launched the first of at least two nuclear-propelled aircraft carriers; with an estimated displacement of up to 75,000 tons, these last will be the largest warships built in the country.

The yard is located south of the city of Nikolayev, at the mouth of the Southern Bug River. The yard covers almost 500 acres.

History. The yard was established in 1897 as a Belgian-owned enterprise, the Nikolayev Shipbuilding, Mechanical, and Iron Works. It began buildling naval ships in 1901, constructing surface ships up to battleship size (including the Potemkin) as well as submarines.

After the Revolution the yard was renamed for André Marti (Marti south). In the 1930s construction of surface warships and submarines was reinitiated. Destroyer construction was followed by the keel-laying in 1940 of a battleship of the Sovietskiy Soyuz class. Reportedly, the water depth at the yard was limited, and after launching the battleship was to have been towed to Sevastopol' for completion. (Work on the ship stopped in October 1940.) Prewar submarines built at the yard were of the S and M classes.

As German troops approached Nikolayev in 1941, several unfinished cruiser and destroyer hulls were towed from the Marti and 61 Kommuna yards and were towed to Black Sea ports farther east, but only one destroyer, launched in 1940, at the 61 Kommuna yard, was finished at Batum before the end of the war. The yard was occupied by German troops in August 1941 and was not recaptured by Russians until March 1944. Extensive damage was inflicted on both Nikolayev yards by fight-

Northern Black Sea area

ing and German demolitions. The Marti (south) yard was rebuilt and was able to undertake the construction of surface ships and submarines in a relatively short period of time. Several small M-V-type submarines were launched from 1947 to 1950, with the yard starting to launch Whiskey-class submarines beginning in 1951. Submarine construction continued only to the late 1950s, with an estimated 65 Whiskeys being built at the yard.

More impressive were the yard's surface warship programs. The keel for the first STALINGRAD-class battle cruiser was laid down on the rejuvenated battleship ways at Nikolayev south in 1949. Work proceeded rapidly, and the ship is said to have been about 60 percent complete and ready for launching in early 1953 when Stalin died. All work on the project ceased, and the hull was later launched and probably expended in weapon tests. (The second ship was to have been built on the ways vacated by the first hull.)

The yard also built three SVERDLOV-class light cruisers before the mid-1950s cutback in naval construction. The yard then concentrated on merchant construction for the remainder of the decade.

Since the early 1960s the Black Sea shipyard has undertaken the construction of aviation ships for the Soviet Navy—the MOSKVA, KIEV, and new nuclear designs. Naval auxiliaries are also constructed at the yard as well as commercial ships, primarily dry cargo ships, fish-factory ships, and large trawlers.

The yard has two shipbuilding areas, one for naval projects, with end-launch building ways and building docks, and one for commercial projects with a horizontal, dock-launching facility. The aircraft carriers are constructed in a building dock, the largest in the Soviet Union.

Kherson

The yard at Kherson builds merchant ships exclusively, mostly dry cargo ships, tankers, and floating dry docks (steel and concrete), some specifically for foreign transfer. The most impressive to date are the Arctic barge carriers of the ALEKSEY KOSYGIN class, with the lead ship delivered in 1983. These are 40,900-deadweight-ton ships (see chapter 31).

The Kherson yard is located at the mouth of the Dnepr River. It achieved the status of a major shipyard in the 1950s.

61 Kommuna (Shipyard No. 445)

This yard produces surface combatants—SLAVA-class cruisers for the Soviet Navy and Kashin-class destroyers for the Indian Navy. The yard is located at Nikolayev, at the mouth of the Southern Bug River.

History. The 61 Kommuna or northern Nikolayev yard was begun as an admiralty shipyard in 1789 and could be ranked as a major shipyard from about 1800. After more than a century of operation, the yard was closed down in 1910 but reopened the following year as a commercial venture, the Russian Shipbuilding Corporation (Russud).

The yard built warships up to battleship size during the tsarist era. After the Revolution it became the Marti north yard and then the 61 Kommuna yard. During the 1930s, the yard built CHAPAYEV-class light

cruisers, destroyers, and submarines of the Shch class. The second battle cruiser of the KRONSHTADT class was laid down at the 61 Kommuna yard in 1938–1939. The unfinished hull was captured by the Germans in August 1941, having been partially wrecked by Russian demolition. (The ship was never finished, but cut up for scrap after the war.) The yard was heavily damaged during the war.

After being rehabilitated, the yard produced destroyers of the SKORYY, Kotlin, Kanin, and Kashin classes, and then the seven all-gas-turbine cruisers of the Kara class. The single, large replenishment ship BEREZINA was also built at the yard. Nikolayev north has also led in the modernization of the Kashin and Kildin destroyer classes.

Current programs at the 61 Kommuna/Nikolayev north yard are the modified Kashin-class destroyers being built for the Indian Navy and SLAVA-class cruisers.

The yard is one of the few shipyards in the Soviet Union that has only inclined, end-launch building ways and no covered construction halls. It occupies almost 200 acres.

Okean/Oktyabr'skoye

This yard constructs dry cargo and refrigerated cargo ships. It became a major shipbuilding center in the 1950s and has specialized in the construction of large merchant ships and trawlers, including the oil/ore carriers of the BORIS BUTOMA class (130,000 deadweight tons).

The Okean shipyard is in Oktyabr'skoye, near Nikolayev, the third major ship construction yard in the area.

Ordzhonikidze/Sevastopol'

The Ordzhonikidze naval yard is the main repair base of the Black Sea Fleet and additionally builds commercial ships and large floating cranes.

The yard is part of the Sevastopol' port–naval base complex on the bay of that name. It is one of the oldest Russian naval facilities on the Black Sea.

Zaliv/B. Ye. Butoma (Shipyard No. 532)

This yard constructs warships up to frigate size and large commercial ships, including the Soviet merchant fleet's supertankers.

The yard is located at Kerch', on the Crimean Peninsula near the entrance to the Sea of Azov. The yard occupies some 150 acres of land. It was named in 1981 for B. Ye. Butoma, longtime head of the ship production industry.

History. The yard became a major shipbuilding facility in the 1930s. In the postwar period the yard built small combatants as well as merchant ships. There was a major expansion of facilities beginning in the mid-1960s, at which time construction of frigates of the Krivak class was begun. Previously Poti-class corvettes were the largest combat ships built at Kerch'. The merchant ships built at the yard range up to the KRYM-class supertankers, the largest such ships built in the Soviet Union. All eight ships of the class of 150,500 deadweight tons were built here.

The yard is now constructing the SEVMORPUT' class of nuclear-propelled barge carriers for Arctic service. Thus, the yard has become the Soviet Union's seventh nuclear-capable shipyard.

It is also the only one of three Krivak building yards that is still producing these ships, in the Krivak III version for the KGB Maritime Border Troops.

Other construction yards in the Black Sea area are: Feodosiya, on the Black Sea coast of the Crimea, which builds small combatants; Poti, on the east coast of the Black Sea, which builds passenger hydrofoils; and the small commercial ship construction yards at Zhdanov and Rostov on the Sea of Azov.

There are large ship repair facilities at Il'ichevsk, near Odessa, which is the main repair base for Black Sea merchant ships and also builds small commercial ships. Near Sevastopol' is a large repair yard for fishing craft and at Novorossiysk there is a large repair yard that specializes in tankers.

Smaller repair yards are located at Batumi, Kerch', Odessa, Sevastopol', and Tuapse.

PACIFIC SHIPYARDS

Khabarovsk

This yard, at the junction of the Amur and Ussuri rivers in the Far East, produces small combatants, merchant and research ships. Khabarovsk is some 435 mi (695 km) south of the mouth of the Amur River where it enters the Tatar Strait.

The yard became a major shipbuilding facility in the 1950s. It produces patrol craft, small combatants, and minesweepers. Some commercial ships are also built at the yard, including scientific research vessels.

Also on the Amur River is a yard at Blagoveschensk.

Komsomol'sk (Shipyard No. 199)

The Komsomol'sk Shipyard—also known as Leninskaya Komsomola—is a major submarine construction facility where some merchant work is being undertaken. In the 1980s the yard builds the Kilo-class diesel submarines and the Akula-class SSN.

The Maritime shipyard at Nakhodka in the Far East uses automated, horizontal ship-moving systems for the construction and repair of large trawlers. These efficient, horizontal, and modular construction methods are used at most Soviet shipyards, although building docks and inclined ways are still in use at some locations. (Sovfoto)

The Komsomol'sk yard is about 280 mi (450 km) south of the mouth of the Amur River. The depth of water prevents the yard from completing larger ships and submarines, which must be fitted out at a coastal shipyard after being launched at Komsomol'sk.

History. The Komsomol'sk yard was constructed in 1932–1937 to provide a major shipyard for the planned expansion of the Pacific Fleet. During World War II the yard built two heavy cruisers of the older KIROV class (completed 1946–1947) as well as destroyers and submarines (Shch class). Smaller surface combatants and naval auxiliaries as well as some merchant ships were also built at the yard.

In the postwar period the yard has been primarily engaged in submarine construction, although small combatants, up to Petya-class frigates, as well as merchant ships and icebreakers, have been built. During the 1950s the yard constructed Whiskey-class diesel attack submarines (11 units) and Golf-class diesel ballistic missile craft (7 units).

Komsomol'sk became the second yard in the Soviet Union to construct nuclear-propelled submarines. The first of five Echo I-class SSGNs was launched in 1960, followed by 11 of the larger Echo II SSGNs. (The yard subsequently converted the Echo I submarines to an SSN configuration.) It has since built submarines of the Yankee and Delta I classes, sharing these SSBN projects with Severodvinsk. Later SSBN designs have apparently been too large to build at Komsomol'sk.

The yard has continued to develop advanced diesel-electric submarines. In the 1960s Komsomol'sk built four Bravo-class target and training submarines (SST), followed by the two India-class salvage and rescue craft (AGSS), and the Kilo attack submarine (SS). The lead Akula-class SSN, completed in 1985, was the first nuclear attack submarine to be built at Komsomol'sk.

Vladivostok

Vladivostok, the principal Soviet maritime center in the Far East, is located in Peter the Great Bay on the Sea of Japan. The Dal'zavod shipyard constructs merchant and fishing ships, but maintains and overhauls naval units as well. The latter include the KIROV-class nuclear cruiser and KIEV-class VSTOL carriers operating in the Pacific Fleet. A Japanese-built floating dry dock rated at some 80,000-tons lift capacity is at Vladivostok to service these large warships.

During the 1930s this yard constructed destroyers and submarines (L, Shch, and S classes).

There are several yards in the city and vicinity. Among these is the large yard at nearby Slavyanka Bay built in the 1970s as a repair facility for merchant ships, which now employs more than 2,000 workmen. At nearby Nakhodka there are two yards.

There are several other shipyards in the Far East: On remote and isolated Kamchatka Peninsula are large ship and submarine repair yards at Petropavlovsk—the Frenza ship repair yard and the V.I. Lenin yard. Other yards are located at Kholmsk on Sakhalin Island, Sovietskaya Gavan', and Nikolayevsk.

INLAND SHIPYARDS

Krasnoye Sormovo (Shipyard No. 112)

Located at the large industrial city of Gor'kiy, this is one of five Soviet shipyards currently capable of building submarines. In addition, river and inland craft are constructed, including hydrofoils and air-cushion vehicles.

Gor'kiy is located some 200 miles (320 km) east of Moscow on the Volga River at its confluence with the Oka River. Submarines constructed here generally transit down the Volga River to the Black Sea, most for subsequent assignment to other fleet areas.

History. Krasnoye Sormovo is credited with being the oldest significant shipbuilding location in the country.[14] The first "modern" shipbuilding effort there was the Nizhegorodskaya Machine Plant, which started producing river boats and barges in 1849. The facility became one of the major shipyards of the Soviet Union in the early 1940s. At that time the yard built M-class submarines that were fabricated in sections and then taken by barge to various coastal yards for assembly. The larger S-class submarines were also built at Gor'kiy.

After World War II Krasnoye Sormovo became the principal yard for Whiskey submarines. The yard completed 116 units from 1950 to 1957, with 40 submarines completed in the peak year of 1955. The yard then built the Romeo-class attack submarines and the 16 Juliett-class guided missile submarines.

Krasnoye Sormovo was the fourth Soviet shipyard to build nuclear submarines, launching the first Charlie SSGN in 1967. While continuing Charlie I/II construction, in the 1970s the yard initiated the Tango-class diesel attack submarine, successor to the Foxtrot class as a long-range diesel attack submarine. The single advanced Papa SSGN was built at Gor'kiy. The yard is currently building the advanced Kilo-class diesel submarine and the Sierra-class SSNs. Large numbers of commercial inland and river craft are also built at Gor'kiy.

There are three other, smaller yards at Gor'kiy.

Leninskaya Kuznya

The Leninskaya Kuznya yard at Kiev builds large numbers of seagoing trawlers and small naval units. The yard is noted for its highly developed machinery production facilities and fabricates ship components for other shipyards, especially those at Nikolayev and Kherson. The facility is sometimes referred to as the Dnepr yard.

This inland yard is some 500 miles (800 km) up the Dnepr River from the Black Sea.

Zelenodol'sk (Shipyard No. 340)

This yard produces mainly small combatants, trawlers, and hydrofoils. Among its naval products were the Kronshtadt, S.O.-1, Poti, and Grisha

---

[14] Prior to 1932 Gor'kiy was known as Nizhny Novgorod, which was founded in the early thirteenth century and became a major trading center.

classes. In the mid-1970s construction began on the Koni-class frigates, the largest naval units to be built at the yard.

Zelendol'sk is located near Kazan', some 200 mi (320 km) east of Gor'ky, on the Vetluga River. The shipyard was established in 1945–1946.

There are numerous smaller inland yards on the many lakes and rivers of the Soviet Union. These include: the Gorokhovets yard on the Klyazma River near Gor'kiy; the Kama yard at Perm' on the Kama River; three yards at Krasnoyarsk on the Yenisey River; the Limenda and Velikiy Ustuyg yards on the Northern Dvina River; the Moryakovskiy building yard at Tomsk, on the Tom River near its junction with the Ob' River; the Novosibirsk yard on the Ob' River; the Oka yard at Navashino on the Oka River; the Omsk construction and repair yard on the Irtysk River; the newly expanded Osetrovo yard on the Lena River; the Tyumen' yard on the Tobol River, which builds large floating power stations; the Vympel Shipbuilding Association at Andropov (formerly Rybinsk) on the man-made Lake Rybinsk some 300 miles (480 km) north of Moscow; the Volgagrad yard on the Volga River; and the Yaroslavl' yard, about 150 miles (240 km) northeast of Moscow.

On the Caspian Sea the Astrakhan Shipbuilding Association, at the mouth of the Volga River, builds tankers for the Caspian Sea trade as well as passenger ships and offshore oil drilling rigs. There are a total of four yards at Astrakhan and three at Baku.

TABLE 30-1. SUBMARINE CONSTRUCTION YARDS, 1945–1985

Type	Class	First Completed	Severodvinsk	Black Sea† (Nikolayev)	Komsomol'sk	Krasnoye Sormovo (Gor'kiy)	Baltic† (Leningrad)	Admiralty (Leningrad)	Sudomekh* (Leningrad)
SS	Shch	1933			●				●
SSC	Malyutka V	1935		●					●
SS	S	1936				●			
SS	Whiskey	1949		●	●	●	●		
SS	Zulu	1952	●						●
SSC	Quebec	1954							●
SS	Romeo	1957				●			
SS	Foxtrot	1957							●
SSG	Golf	1958	●		●				
SSN	November	1958	●						
SSBN	Hotel	1959	●						
SSGN	Echo I	1960			●				
SSGN	Juliett	1961				●			
SSGN	Echo II	1962	●		●				
SST	Bravo	1967			●				
SSGN	Charlie	1967				●			
SSBN	Yankee	1967	●		●				
SSN	Victor	1968			●			●	
SSN	Alfa	1969	●						●
SSGN	Papa	1970				●			
SS	Tango	1972				●			
SSBN	Delta	1973	●		●				
AGSS	Lima	1978							●
AGSS	India	1979			●				
SSGN	Oscar	1981	●						
SS	Kilo	1982			●	●			●
AGSSN	Uniform	1983							●
SSBN	Typhoon	1983	●						
AGSSN	X-Ray	1984							●
SSN	Sierra	1984				●		●	
SSN	Akula	1985			●				
SSN	Mike	1985	●						

*Since 1972 merged with the Admiralty Shipyard as the Leningrad Admiralty Association.
†No longer constructs submarines.

31
Merchant Marine

The Soviet merchant fleet is increasingly seen on the high seas and in far-flung ports. Here the largest Soviet cruise liner, the MAKSIM GOR'KIY, shares the harbor of Bridgetown in Barbados with the U.S. strategic-missile submarine VON STEUBEN (SSBN 632). The Soviet ship was built in West Germany, and when her operation as the liner HAMBURG was unsuccessful, the 600-passenger ship was purchased by the Soviet Union. (U.S. Navy, Carlos C. Campbell)

Merchant fleets are invaluable to a nation's naval activities in wartime, as evidenced most recently in the British campaign in the Falklands in 1982.[1] Merchant fleets can also provide direct support to naval forces in peacetime—beyond their more obvious role of supporting a nation's political and economic goals. It thus becomes significant to any discussion of the Soviet Navy that the Soviet Union has one of the world's largest, most modern, and most flexible merchant fleets. According to a senior U.S. maritime analyst:

> Soviet shipping is a major force in international maritime affairs. It is the product of a strong national policy dedicated to serving the Soviet Union's military, political, and economic interests. Some may question—with validity—the order of precedence between military and economic interests, considering the merchant navy's contribution of an estimated $2 billion in annual gross earnings to the Soviet Union's need for hard currencies. Nonetheless, the military aspects of the Soviet merchant and fishing fleets are of major strategic importance to the Soviet Navy.[2]

The 1980s have been a period of international merchant fleet decline, with very few new ships being added to Western merchant fleets. The Soviet Union, however, continues to modernize its merchant fleet at a significant rate. Today the Soviet Union has the world's second largest merchant fleet when ranked by number of ships (over 1,000 gross tons) and the seventh largest when measured in terms of carrying capacity, as noted in table 31-1.[3] Recent additions to the Soviet merchant fleet include roll-on/roll-off (RO/RO) vehicle cargo ships, which are of particular value in military operations. The Soviet Union currently operates over 70 of these ships, more than any other nation, and additional ships are on order. Coupled with the Soviet Navy's amphibious ships, these RO/RO ships and certain other cargo units provide a theoretical lift capacity for the entire Soviet Naval Infantry as well as several divisions of the Ground Forces. (The Soviets have exercised merchant ships in this role.)

Current Soviet merchant ship procurement programs also include significant numbers of container and general (break-bulk) cargo ships, large Ore/Bulk/Oil (OBO) ships, tankers, and barge carriers. The last include a series of nuclear-propelled ships for Arctic use (see below).

History. After World War II the Soviet Union had little interest in a buildup of the merchant fleet, in part because of the priorities for rebuilding naval forces and the limited foreign trade. Further, a number of American-supplied merchant ships of recent construction were still held under the Soviet flag.

The Khrushchev period brought a major expansion of the merchant fleet, initially to support overseas clients and then to help trade with other Third World nations. Khrushchev's interest in developing a strong Soviet merchant fleet was further reinforced by the Cuban missile crisis, which demonstrated the need for shipping to support long-range military operations. The ranking of the Soviet fleet rose from twenty-sixth place in the late 1950s to twelfth place in 1962, and to seventh place in 1964 (although since then it has periodically slipped to eighth place as there have been spurts in U.S. merchant fleet development). In the 1970s there was another phase of Soviet fleet expansion as merchant ships became a major earner of "hard" Western currencies.

Regular Soviet cargo service to the United States began in late 1970 after an absence of almost two decades. Soviet passenger ships began calling at New York and other U.S. cities in June of 1973, initiating a service that would extend briefly to the Caribbean cruise route before ending a few years later. Soviet merchant ships called increasingly at almost 60 U.S. ports, reaching a peak of some 1,700 port arrivals per year. (Some of these were multiple U.S. port calls, as this figure includes the same ship calling at different ports.) Soviet merchant service to U.S. ports was halted abruptly in 1979 when U.S. longshoremen protested the Soviet invasion of Afghanistan.

These economic-political goals of the merchant fleet were candidly linked by V. Kudryavtsev, a political observer for the Soviet newspaper *Izvestiya*, who wrote on 15 February 1972 that: "The Soviet Union does not conceal the fact that economic relations with the developing countries are an integral part of the struggle between two world systems, socialism and capitalism. These relations undermine the imperialist powers of economic and trade ties with the developing countries and force the capitalist states to make concessions."

The primary economic emphasis of the Soviet merchant fleet—beyond carrying cargo between Soviet ports—appears to be on earning "hard" Western currencies. Because Soviet ships are largely built in Soviet and Eastern Bloc shipyards with "soft" rubles—which have no exchange value outside of the country—and their operating costs and crews are paid for in rubles, the Western currency earned by the merchant fleet is a profit for the government. (Crew costs are estimated at less than 15 percent of the total cost of Soviet merchant fleet operations, much lower than comparable Western fleets.)

Today this merchant fleet carries cargo and passengers on more than 70 international trade routes, calling at ports in some 140 countries throughout the world. Soviet merchant ships compete effectively with Western shipping on virtually every major trade route throughout the world except those that call at U.S. Ports. The Soviets practice rate cutting to ensure a share of those markets in which they have an interest. For example, when the Soviet Baltic Shipping Company began container service in 1974 to New York, Baltimore, and Philadelphia, the line announced that the service would be 10 percent below regular rates to ensure a certain amount of cargo would be carried. More recently, the Far East Shipping Company has been playing havoc in the Japan-Australia-Hong Kong cross trade by quoting rates as much as 40 percent below those of the Far East Australia Conference. After extensive pro-

---

[1] During the Falklands war the British employed 45 merchant-type Ships Taken Up From Trade (STUFT) as aircraft transports and replenishment, hospital, cargo, and troop ships; five fishing trawlers were also taken on for use as minesweepers but were not used in that role.

[2] Irwin M. Heine, "The Soviet Merchant Navy—A Two-Pronged Force," *Naval Institute Proceedings* (December 1984), p. 142. Mr. Heine was Chief Economist and Statistician of the U.S. Maritime Administration from 1953 to 1965, after which he was Chief for International Maritime Affairs until his retirement in 1970.

[3] The standard measures for merchant ships are gross tonnage or Gross Registered Tons (GRT), the internal cubic capacity of the ship expressed in tons with 100 cubic feet to the ton, and Deadweight Tons (DWT), the carrying capacity of a ship measured in long tons (2,240 pounds). Table 31-1 provides comparative data from a Soviet source.

tests from members of the conference, the Soviet shippers agreed to charge no more than 10 percent below the conference rates.

Soviet shippers—with the world's largest fleet of passenger ships—have greatly encroached on cruise ship operations as well. When the British withdrew the passenger ships QUEEN ELIZABETH 2 and CANBERRA from the cruise trades in 1982 to carry troops to the Falklands, the Soviets seized the opportunity to increase their share of the British market from 10 percent in 1980 to more than 40 percent when this volume went to press. Criticizing the inroads made by Soviet ships in the British cruise-ship market, officials of British shipping lines estimated in late 1984 that they had lost £11.7 million during the two years since the Falklands conflict.

TABLE 31-1. WORLD MERCHANT FLEET RANKING, January 1986*
(Tonnage in thousands)

Number of Ships		Deadweight Tonnage		Gross Tonnage	
Panama	3,620	Liberia	119,080	Liberia	62,126
Soviet Union	2,514	Panama	69,710	Panama	42,101
Liberia	1,852	Japan	60,287	Japan	37,366
Greece	1,835	Greece	57,130	Greece	32,092
Japan	1,604	Soviet Union	24,858	Soviet Union	18,717
China	1,052	United States	21,196‡	United States	13,490§
Cyprus	716	Norway	21,116	Great Britain	12,744
Italy	569	Great Britain	20,256	China	10,278
Great Britain	541	China	15,624	Cyprus	8,900
West Germany	528	Cyprus	15,322	Italy	7,855
(United States	737†)				

* Source: U.S. Maritime Administration listing for ships of 1,000 gross tons and larger.
†The privately owned U.S. merchant fleet had 477 merchant ships (with the international ranking of 14th) and the U.S. government owned an additional 260 ships, with most of the latter laid up in reserve.
‡The 260 government-owned ships totaled an additional 3,143,000 DWT.
§The 260 government-owned ships totaled an additional 2,543,900 gross tons.

TABLE 31-2. SOVIET MERCHANT FLEET, January 1985*
(Tonnage in thousands)

Ship Type	Number	Deadweight Tonnage
Passenger	50	71,087
Passenger and Cargo	152	117,171
Dry Cargo Ships	1,015	9,255,782
Combination Cargo Ships	11	1,194,432
Timber Carriers	368	2,016,989
Container Ships	52	496,204
Rolkers	57	516,126
Tankers	292	6,206,928
Gas Carriers	11	201,519
Chemical Carriers	3	9,960
Special-Purpose Ships	55	134,739
Technical Ships	203	152,326
Totals	2,269†	20,373,263

* Source: Morskoy Flot (Soviet Fleet) (no. 6, 1985.) Ships assigned to the fishing fleet are not included; see table 32-1.
†Does not include 289 tugs, 37 icebreakers, and almost 200 other merchant marine auxiliary ships.

Soviet merchant ships have also supported Soviet military goals. This became evident to the West in the early 1960s, when Soviet and Eastern Bloc merchant ships carried a variety of arms, including long-range missiles and strike aircraft to Cuba. Subsequently, during most of the Vietnam War an average of more than one Soviet ship per day entered North Vietnamese ports carrying equipment, food, building materials, and other supplies from the Soviet Union. (Most of the weapons and munitions from the Soviet Union apparently were transferred by rail through China, possibly because of the fear that the United States would blockade Vietnamese ports.)

Ships of the Soviet merchant marine have carried weapons and other supplies in support of Soviet political-economic-military goals to Third World nations throughout the world. In particular, the large amount of Soviet military assistance to the Middle East is carried largely in Soviet ships.

Finally, the merchant fleet continues to provide direct support to Soviet naval forces. They carry fuel, food, and munitions to ships at sea, and tankers regularly refuel warships on the high seas. Obviously, the merchant ships can also collect intelligence against targets of opportunity, an activity simplified by the fact that captains of most if not all large merchant ships are naval reserve officers. In wartime the merchant fleet would be pressed into service on a full-time basis, as required, for amphibious and logistic duties. In addition to the above-mentioned RO/RO ships, the many break-bulk cargo ships, and the large, barge-carrying ships are particularly well suited for supporting long-range military operations.

A final military-related aspect of Soviet merchant shipping is that several ships have been observed with such military features as CBR "washdown" systems to help clean off the effects of chemical, biological, and radiological (nuclear) weapons, and reinforced deck positions where weapons could apparently be mounted.

ORGANIZATION AND MANPOWER

The Soviet merchant fleet activities are directed by the Ministry of Merchant Marine, which is headed by a civilian minister. Within the ministry there are regional organizations to administer each ocean area, with headquarters at Murmansk, Leningrad, Odessa, and Vladivostok. In Moscow and at each regional headquarters, there is a computing center by which administrators can keep track of all shipping and help plan schedules, port calls, overhauls, and future operations.

Merchant ship operations on the intra-Soviet and international routes are under the jursidiction of 16 shipping lines. Those that have operated most of the ships that called at U.S. ports in the 1970s have been the Baltic Shipping Company of Leningrad and the Far East Shipping Company (FESCO) of Vladivostok.[4]

The Ministry of Merchant Marine also operates ports, research institutes, ship repair yards, and schools. The ship repair yards provide

4 The other shipping companies are: Azov, Black Sea, Caspian, Danube, Estonian, Georgian, Kamchatka, Latvian, Lithuanian, Murmansk, Northern, Novorossiysk, Primorsk, and Sakhalin.

maintenance and overhaul capabilities, while most new construction of the larger units is done at the building yards of the Ministry of Ship Production (see chapter 30). There are an estimated 20 merchant marine and fisheries colleges in the Soviet Union. The merchant schools train ships' officers and crewmen as well as certain specialists to operate shore equipment. Among the more noted merchant marine schools is the Admiral Makarov Higher Marine Engineering School in Leningrad and Odessa Higher Marine Engineering School, which educates merchant marine engineers. Several training ships are operated by these schools (see chapter 24). In addition to training hundreds of Soviet students each year, their cadets include young men from more than 30 East European and Third World nations.

MERCHANT SHIPS

Soviet merchant ships are smaller than the average ships operated by the major maritime powers. This is due in part to the many relatively small Soviet ports and the fact that a large percentage of the Soviet merchant fleet is assigned to intra-country routes. Also, these smaller ships are more suitable for serving on routes to Third World nations, which have few ports that can accommodate the larger merchant ships built in the West and which have insufficient trade to make it "profitable" for Western shipping lines.

In an effort to reduce maintenance requirements, the Soviet merchant fleet has developed an extensive system of preplanned and preventive

The KATUN is the lead ship of a series of seagoing fire-fighting and offshore supply tugs in use by the Soviet merchant fleet and by the Navy. In naval service they are designated PZHS (see page 323).

maintenance. Also, to reduce the expense of overseas repairs for merchant ships in foreign ports, under certain conditions repair teams are sent to sea to perform maintenance, or specialists are assigned to a crew to service new or difficult machinery.

New ships also have reduced manning requirements. More than 400 of the newer merchant ships operated by the Soviet Union have fully automated propulsion plants. And living conditions have been greatly improved; crew members in the newer ships have individual cabins, and some larger ships have gyms and swimming pools for the crew.

The Soviet merchant fleet has been expanding at an annual rate of about 100,000 DWT during the past few years. This number must be considered in the context of the Soviets retiring large numbers of older ships. Still, the size of the fleet has resulted in a significant increase in ship age. By 1985 the average Soviet dry cargo ship was 14.2 years old and the average tanker 14.7 years, an almost doubling of fleet age over a 15-year period.

A reported 250 merchant ships were acquired in the last five-year plan (1981–1985); about the same number is expected to be procured in the current five-year plan. Thus, in a period of worldwide merchant fleet decline, that of the Soviet Union continues to increase in size and capability. The construction of new ships for the merchant fleet (1) provides more lift capability, (2) reduces the higher costs of maintaining the fleet, and (3) helps to justify the modernization of shipyards. A related factor is that new construction can be more carefully measured than repairs, lessening the opportunity for graft and corruption.

About one-half of the current Soviet merchant fleet has been built in the Soviet Union and almost one-half is from Eastern Europe—primarily from East German, Finnish, and Polish shipyards (see chapter 33). The latter ships are purchased with rubles or obtained through various trade and aid agreements. A few merchant ships have been purchased from the Western nations, including Austria, Britain, France, Italy, and Norway. The Soviets appear to buy ships from the West primarily to obtain advanced designs and technologies.

It is beyond the scope of this volume to address specific characteristics of Soviet merchant ships.[5] The remainder of this chapter discusses some of the more significant categories and types of ships in the Soviet merchant fleet.

SEABEE/LASH Ships. These are merchant ships that carry large, fully loaded barges or lighters that can be floated or lifted on and off the ship. This scheme speeds up loading and unloading, and allows cargo to be handled at ports where piers or wharves are unavailable. The two principal barge-carrying designs are known as LASH (Lighter Aboard Ship) and SEABEE (Sea Barge); the former use cranes to lift barges to the cargo decks and the latter employ elevators.

During the 1970s the Soviets purchased plans from a U.S. firm for the SEABEE design and contracted with the Finnish shipyard Valmet

[5] Detailed characteristics of Soviet merchant ships are given in Ambrose Greenway, *Soviet Merchant Ships* (Emsworth, Hampshire: Kenneth Mason, 1985). This volume, in loose-leaf format, is periodically updated.

The STAKHANOVETS YERMOLENKO, seen here departing Antwerp for Cuba with heavy cargo, is one of two large barge carriers built in the 1970s to a U.S. SEABEE design. The two large travelling cranes are stowed immediately abaft the bridge. (L. & L. Van Ginderen)

Another specialized merchant design is the OBO (Ore-Bulk-Oil) ship, with the 101,877-DWT MARSHAL ROKOSSOVSKIY seen here at Antwerp. This ship and others of the MARSHAL BUDYONNYY class were built in Poland; the slightly larger BORIS BUTOMA class was built by the Okean Shipyard in Nikolayev. (L. & L. Van Ginderen collection)

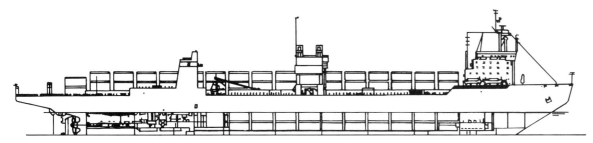

Sketch of the nuclear-propelled SEVMORPUT'

to construct two 37,830-DWT ships, larger than any barge carriers that had been built until that time. These ships, the JULIUS FUCIK (delivered in 1978) and TIBOR SZAMUELI (1979), are 876 ft (267 m), can each carry 26 barges of 1,300 tons. They can offload up to 25,000 tons of cargo in 13 hours without the need of piers.

Obviously pleased with these ships, the Soviets have followed them up with a smaller class of "feeder" barge carriers of the BORIS POLEVOY class, also built by Valmet, and a pair of large ships built at the Kherson shipyard on the Black Sea. The latter ships, the ALEKSEY KOSYGIN class, were designed specifically for Arctic operation and at 40,881 deadweight tons carry 82 barges or 1,480 standard freight containers, or various combinations of both. In 1985 the KOSYGIN was operating between Vladivostok and the mouth of the Yenisey River. (A later ship of this class has been named INDIRA GANDHI, to honor the slain Indian leader.)

More impressive—although smaller—are at least two nuclear-propelled barge carriers being built at Kerch'. These ships, also intended for Arctic operation, are 31,900 tons deadweight and will carry 73 barges of 500 tons or 1,300 freight containers. A single nuclear reactor driving both high- and low-pressure turbines will provide essentially unlimited endurance at 20 knots. The lead ship is named SEVMORPUT'.

The nuclear barge carriers will be the world's first operational nuclear-propelled merchant ships, following one-of-a-kind demonstration ships built by the United States and West Germany.[6] The nuclear barge ships will significantly enhance cargo movement along the Arctic coast of the Soviet Union, where port facilities are limited and the river mouths are shallow. Further, supported by nuclear icebreakers, these ships will greatly extend the shipping season in the Arctic region toward the Soviet long-term goal of year-around shipping between the Arctic and Far East.

General Cargo Ships. A major portion of the merchant fleet consists of general or break-bulk cargo ships. These ships are particularly suited for carrying military cargoes, and their generally small size permits them to call on relatively minor ports. During the past decade the Soviet Union has been the world's largest constructor of general cargo ships and should continue to build this type of ship, albeit at a slower rate, as a greater variety of merchant ship types are procured.

The current design under construction in the Soviet Union is the GEROI PANFILOVTSY-class of 13,500 DWT, being built at Kherson. These ships can carry 320 standard containers in holds plus 68 on deck, or palletized loads or bulk grain.

Container Ships. The Soviet merchant fleet has a large number of container and partial container ships, and combination container-RO/RO ships (see below). The largest all-container ships are the German-built modified MERCUR type, delivered from 1975 onward. The version now being built at Varnemünde in East Germany consists of 17,720-DWT ships that are 571 ft (174 m) long. They can carry 536 containers in holds plus 405 on deck. Eighteen have been delivered, and additional ships are on the building ways.

Roll-On/Roll-Off Ships. The Soviets have more than 70 RO/RO ships in commercial service and more are being built. Again, these ships are particularly valuable for military operations. While they require piers to unload their vehicles, their rapid unloading capability and large vehicle capacity are invaluable in military logistics.

While most Soviet RO/ROs have a speed of 16–17 knots, the eight SKULPTOR KONENKOV-class ships (completed 1975–1982) are capable of 20.5 knots and the three KAPITAN SMIRNOV-class ships (1979–1980) are 25-knot, gas-turbine-propelled ships. The latter, at 20,175 DWT, can lift a significant number of vehicles or 1,246 containers. Additional RO/RO ships are being built for the Soviet merchant marine in East German, Finnish, Polish, and Russian (Zhdanov) shipyards, attesting to the importance of these ships to Soviet planners.

Ore-Bulk-Oil Ships. The OBO ships transport large quantities of liquid fuel, grain, or ore. The first Soviet ship of this type, the MARSHAL BUDENNYY, was completed in 1975 at Gdynia, Poland. At 101,877 deadweight tons, the BUDENNYY is 804 ft (245.9 m) long and has nine large

[6] The U.S. SAVANNAH was completed in 1962 and conducted a number of foreign port visits under President Eisenhower's Atoms for Peace Program. Because of labor problems the ship was economically infeasible and was laid up in 1970. The West German nuclear merchant ship OTTO HAHN, completed in 1968, was also unsuccessful. The Japanese built a nuclear research ship, the MUTSU, completed in 1974, but for mainly political reasons she never became operational.

Large numbers of RO/RO (Roll-On/Roll-Off) ships serve in the Soviet merchant fleet, providing a significant military sealift potential. The East German-built KOSTROMA of 18,020 DWT can carry 529 containers or 232 automobiles or various cargo combinations. (L. & L. Van Ginderen collection)

The MGA is typical of the large number of general cargo ships in Soviet service, this ship being one of the numerous 4,300-DWT KOVEL class built in East Germany from 1958 to 1962. Several are modified to training, research, and naval cargo and missile transport ships. (L. & L. Van Ginderen)

The KAVKAZ, one of the KRYM-class supertankers of 150,500 DWT in heavy seas. The Soviets were late to construct this type of ship, only seven being built by the Kerch' shipyard. (L. & L. Van Ginderen collection)

At over 21,000 DWT, the KOMSOMOLSK is among the largest Soviet container ships, capable of carrying 1,346 standard units. A stern door and folding ramp are provided for vehicles, attesting to the flexibility of the Soviet merchant fleet. (L. & L. Van Ginderen)

cargo holds. A total of 11 ships have been built in Poland and at the Okean yard in Nikolayev for the Soviet merchant fleet.

Reports persist that the Soviets have also purchased up to 14 smaller bulk carriers in secret negotiations with Western brokers. These are secondhand Western ships that have been laid up for lack of cargoes and are available at very low prices.

Tankers. The Soviet merchant fleet operates approximately 400 oil tankers, of which about 100 are subordinated to the Ministry of Fishing to support worldwide fishing activities. These are additionally a number of special-cargo tankers, especially liquified gas and ammonia gas carriers.

The Soviet Union lagged behind the Western maritime nations in the construction of supertankers (i.e., over 100,000 DWT). Belatedly, the Soviets built one series of supertankers, the KRYM class of 150,500 DWT, with seven ships being completed at Kerch' between 1975 and 1980. The ships are highly automated and can pump out a full cargo of 150,000 tons of oil in ten hours.

While the KRYM class was being built, the merchant-ship design bureau in Leningrad began plans for a tanker 1,135 ft (346 m) long with a capacity of some 300,000 to 370,000 tons. These larger ships were never built, however, because the world oil situation of the late 1970s reduced the need for them, and, in any case, there is little domestic use for these large tankers because of the limited size of Soviet ports.

The most recent large tankers acquired for the Soviet merchant fleet are the POBYEDA class, completed from 1981. These 67,980-DWT ships are being built at Kerch'. The majority of the Soviet merchant tankers are smaller than the average in major Western merchant fleets, making them useful for naval and Third World operations in addition to being

The 55,729-DWT LENSOVET is a specialized tanker for Liquid Petroleum Gas (LPG) or ammonia frozen to −480°C. Eleven LPG tankers are currently in Soviet merchant service. The LENSOVET and her sister ship MOSSOVET were built in Venice. (L. & L. Van Ginderen)

The ODESSA, with 590 passenger berths, is another foreign-built ship—by Vickers in England for a Danish firm—but instead she entered service under Soviet colors in 1975. Diesel-propelled, she can steam at 19 knots, and along with other passenger ships provides a significant potential for military troop lift. (International Cruise Center)

more suitable for Soviet ports. Now being built at the Rauma yard in Finland are the VENTSPILS-class ships, which are only 6,297 DWT and 371 ft (113 m) long and are designed for Arctic operations (labeled the *Arktika* type by the Soviets). (Also, the large OBO ships can transport petroleum.)

Specialized Cargo Ships. There are a number of specialized cargo ships in Soviet service, among them heavy-lift ships that have important military support capabilities. The three heavy-lift ships of the STAKHAN-OVETS KOTOV class, completed in 1978–1979, at 5,717 DWT, can carry heavy, outsize loads, and have two 350-ton-capacity gantry cranes.

Another specialized cargo ship that should be of special interest to the Soviet Navy is the oil-drilling rig transport ship under construction at the Wärtsilä yard in Finland. This ship, ordered in 1985, can lift oil rigs and other floating equipment weighing up to 20,000 tons. The ship herself is 34,000 DWT with an overall length of 567½ ft (173 m) and has a broad beam, 131¼ ft (40 m), to provide stability. With a service speed of 14 knots, the ship will carry floating equipment that cannot be easily towed. To load cargo, the ship ballasts down and the rig or other equipment is floated on; the ship's ballast tanks are then emptied by compressed air. (The U.S. government has chartered ships of this type to carry military equipment.)

Passenger Ships. The Soviet Union has one of the world's largest fleet of passenger ships and currently operates about 50. The passenger ships sail on scheduled routes and in cruise service.

Soviet cruise ships tout modern, Western-style accommodations, with bountiful tables and personalized service. These ships earn hard currencies for the Soviet economy while at the same time "showing the flag." (International Cruise Center)

Western passengers relax on board the cruise ship ODESSA. She and other cruise ships operate on worldwide routes as the Soviet merchant fleet bids for all types of commercial service. (International Cruise Center)

A third navigator of the Soviet merchant fleet instructs cadets in the use of a sextant on the Vladivostok-based training ship PROFESSOR YUSHCHENKO. (Sovfoto, Yu. Muravin)

The largest of the Soviet passenger ships is the MAKSIM GOR'KIY, built in West Germany in 1968. The ship was operated by a German shipping line until 1974 when, found unprofitable to operate, was purchased by the Soviet Union. The ship carries more than 600 passengers. Slightly smaller but with a larger passenger capacity are the British-built FEDOR SHALYAPIN (800 passengers) and LEONID SOBINOV (930), both of which served 11 years under the British Red Ensign before being purchased by the Soviet Union in 1973. The four East German-built IVAN FRANKO-class ships, completed 1964–1972, can carry 700–750 passengers.

Five smaller, 2,149-DWT combination RO/RO-passenger ships of the BYELORUSSIYA class are having part of their car deck space converted to additional cabins. This will increase the number of berths from 500 to 650. When employed as day ferries, these ships can accommodate another 500 passengers.

The passenger ships also earn hard currencies for the Soviet Union, help to "capture" trade routes, provide an opportunity for political influence, and offer the potential for moving large numbers of troops by sea.

It should be noted that 1986 was a disastrous year for Soviet passenger ships. The MIKHAIL LERMONTOV of the IVAN FRANKO-class sank on 16 February after striking a rock off New Zealand. Reportedly, only one person was lost in this sinking.

But on 31 August the venerable passenger liner ADMIRAL NAKHIMOV collided with a Soviet freighter in the Black Sea, 45 minutes after sailing from the port of Novorossiysk. Both ships appear to have had radar and visual contact with the other before the cargo ship sliced into the liner. The ADMIRAL NAKHIMOV quickly sank with the loss of 398 passengers and crew (of 1,234 on board). Following the disaster, a Soviet merchant marine official declared, "The ships are not at fault. . . . The people are at fault."

(The ADMIRAL NAKHIMOV was the oldest ship of the Soviet passenger fleet, having been built in Germany in 1925 as the BERLIN. She was sunk in 1945, being salvaged and rebuilt after the war. In Soviet service she was rated at 8,946 deadweight tons with 870 passenger berths.)

Gas-Oil Industry Ships. A relatively new category of "merchant" ships are those developed specifically to support the offshore gas-oil industry. These ships include offshore drilling ships, exploration ships (see chapter 24), and offshore supply and personnel ships that carry men and material to the offshore drilling and pumping facilities.

The Rauma-Repola yard in Finland has recently delivered three large, 7,425-DWT, 490-ft (149-m) drilling ships of the VALENTIN SHASHIN type. Operated by the Ministry of Gas Industry, they are fitted with a dynamic positioning system of bow and stern thrusters so that they can hold precise positions while their drilling rig penetrates the ocean floor.

Training Ships. Several training ships support the merchant marine and fisheries training activities, the best-known being sail-training ships KRUZENSHTERN, SEDOV, and TOVARISHCH (see chapter 24). All German-built, they are the largest sailing vessels in the world, displacing more than 3,000 tons and carrying up to 200 cadets on their far-ranging cruises.

Icebreakers. The Soviet merchant marine operates a large number of icebreakers, including the nuclear-propelled LENIN and ARKTIKA-class ships. These ships are vital for keeping the Arctic sea routes open for commercial as well as military sea traffic as almost 80 percent of the Soviet coastal shipping occurs between Soviet ports in the Arctic and the Far East. Icebreakers are also required for some Baltic and Pacific ports in winter. (Icebreakers are also operated by the Navy, KGB Maritime Border Guards, and Ministry of River Fleet.)

Additional, shallow-water icebreakers with nuclear propulsion are under construction in Finland, which has constructed most of the icebreakers procured by the Soviet Union in the past few years. (The reactor plants for these ships will be installed at the Baltic shipyard in Leningrad.)

32
Fishing Fleet

The 3,541-DWT SPRUT is one of the largest stern-trawler/factory ships in Soviet service. Built in Poland, the five SPRUT-class ships were completed in 1978–1980. They are 365 feet (117.5 m) in length, with diesel engines that provide a maximum speed of 16 knots, and are capable of sustained, long-range operations.

The Soviet Union operates the world's largest fishing fleet with more than 3,500 oceangoing fishing and support vessels. This fleet's annual catch is about 10 million tons, placing the Soviet Union second only to Japan in the size of the annual "catch" of marine life.

The fishing fleet also contributes to Soviet political-military capabilities. In the past, fishing craft performed intelligence collection, and still have at least an overt role in this regard. Also, the support ships of the fishing fleet have in the past provided support to submarines, and still do on an emergency basis. The fishing fleet includes a large number of research ships, training ships, tankers, and refrigerated fish carriers that could be pressed into naval service in wartime, all controlled through an extensive and centralized communications system. Finally, the fishing fleet's construction and repair yards contribute significantly to the viability and flexibility of the Soviet shipbuilding industry.

The Soviet Union exploits fishing grounds throughout the world's oceans with large flotillas of ships. Flotillas of up to 100 and 200 trawlers are not unusual, and on occasion even larger formations have been observed. Some of the larger trawlers can handle up to 50 tons of fish per day and are equipped to filet, salt, and can or freeze the catch on board. Smaller trawlers transfer their catch directly to factory or "mother" ships that process and can or freeze the fish. In many cases, while the trawlers and mother ships remain in the operating area, refrigerated fish carriers take off the catch and carry it to markets in the Soviet Union or other nations. Fishing flotillas in remote areas are often supported by specialized repair ships, tugs, tankers, and fresh-water carriers, in addition to some 260 refrigerated fish carriers.

Most of the fish caught by these vessels—over 90 percent—is for human consumption, being eaten by Soviets or given or sold to other nations. It is estimated that seafood comprises 20 percent of Soviet protein consumption. The part of the catch not used as food is usually processed into fish meal or fertilizer. Fish oil is also produced. However, poor management, storage, and transportation facilities result in the loss of a significant fraction of the catch in the Arctic area.

Soviet fishing operations off U.S. territory have created confrontations between the United States and the Soviet Union. The establishment of a 200-mile economic zone around the United States in 1977 was, in part, an effort to restrict Soviet fishing activities, and the U.S. Coast Guard has occasionally arrested masters of Soviet fishing vessels for violating this zone. The Soviet fishing industry is being faced with protective policies in many areas of the world, thus restricting their fishing and forcing them to exploit new and more remote areas.

At the same time, the Soviet Union is providing technical assistance to the fishing industries of Third World countries. This not only makes for improved relations with those countries, but also allows the Soviets to share area catches and profits, and to export their fishing equipment, including fishing vessels. Among the countries that have received Soviet assistance in this area have been Cuba, Egypt, Ghana, Guinea, India, Indonesia, Senegal, Sri Lanka, Sudan, Tanzania, Vietnam, and South Yemen. The fishing support facility that the Soviets built near Havana, Cuba, encompasses 33 acres and includes repair shops, a floating dry dock, floating and gantry cranes, and other support equipment.

The Soviets, for both domestic and foreign economic reasons, need to increase their catch. With continued advances in technology and the modernization of its fishing fleet, the Soviet Union should in time become the leading harvester of the world's marine life.

ORGANIZATION AND PERSONNEL

As with other Soviet maritime fleets, the fishing industry is highly centralized, with a Ministry of Fish Production directing overall operations and fleet development. The ministry has a central computerized center in Moscow that keeps track of the fleet's worldwide activities.

Under the ministry are specialized port facilities, ship repair yards, processing plants, the fishing fleet itself, fisheries research ships (and previously submarines!), and the various support ships. Personnel to man these ships are trained at several schools and on board special ships, and as in the merchant fleet, many ship captains and masters are naval reserve officers.

Obviously, the fishing fleet—like the merchant fleet—can also provide intelligence to support naval operations. In the past, the tankers supporting the fishing fleet, which is diesel-propelled, also provided fuel to diesel-electric submarines in remote areas.

TRAWLERS AND SUPPORT SHIPS

As with merchant and research-scientific ships, many Soviet fishing vessels are built abroad, mostly in Eastern Europe. During the 1960s a number of trawler-factory ships were built for the Soviet fleet in Danish, Dutch, French, and Japanese yards (and in the 1950s several were built in West Germany). In the 1980s the principal builders of Soviet trawlers are the Black Sea and Okean shipyards (Nikolayev), Baltic shipyard (Klaipeda), Mathias Thesen and Volkswerft in East Germany, and Gdansk in Poland. In 1983, the last year for which full data is available, the Soviet yards produced ten oceangoing trawlers, and the East European yards built another 31 ships as part of a fleet modernization program.

Trawlers. Soviet trawlers come in a variety of sizes and configurations. In numbers of ships, the largest classes of Soviet-built trawlers are the more than 225 ships of the MAYAKOVSKIY type (1,248–1,519 DWT) and the 150 ships of the KRONSHTADT class (1,182 DWT); these are stern-trawler/factory ships. Additional ships of these classes have been completed or converted to fisheries research ships, while several have been transferred to other nations.

Two other large, and hence widely seen, classes are the ATLANTIC and "Super" ATLANTIC designs built in East German yards. There are more than 300 of these ships, whose deadweight tonnage varies from 1,116 for the earlier ships to 2,068 for the later ships. Twenty additional ships of this design are employed for fisheries research and 12 more are fisheries training ships. More than 30 "Super" ATLANTIC factory trawlers are to be delivered by East Germany by 1990.

The largest Soviet ships in the trawler category are three French-built ships of the NATALIA KOVHOVA class, delivered in 1965; these are 419-foot (127.5-m), 4,709-DWT ships that can both harvest and process fish.

The "Super" ATLANTICS apparently are still in production for the Soviet fishing fleet in East German yards as are the stern-trawler/seine factory

The Soviet fishing fleet has an extensive infrastructure to support long-range operations. Factory or "mother" ships process, can, and pack fish—in this instance off the Virginia coast. This is a West German-built RYBATSKAYA SLAVA-class ship; these are 11,086 DWT and 549 feet (167.3 m) long, with eight ships built in the 1960s.

The 2,060-DWT LIMB is one of the East German-built Super ATLANTIC trawler/factory ships. The more than 300 ships of this type are seen continuously on the world's fishing grounds; in some instances relief crews are flown out to overseas ports to increase trawler time on station. (L. & L. Van Ginderen)

The IVAN BORZOV is one of the Polish-built, RODINA-class tuna seiners. These ships are 279 feet (85.1 m) in length, with a helicopter deck fitted over the forward hold area. Ten of these unusual ships were placed in service with the Soviet fishing fleet between 1979 and 1981.

In addition to ocean and scientific research ships, the Soviet Union operates a large fleet of fisheries research ships. The RIFT is a modified stern-haul trawler of the Al'pinist class, one of five completed in 1982-1983 for fisheries and geophysical research work. Here the RIFT has an ARGUS submersible on board. (U.S. Navy)

The EKVATOR is another MAYAKOVSKIY-class conversion; she is considered only a "partial" conversion to a research configuration. Both the EKVATOR and ODISSEY are based in the Soviet Far East. (U.S. Navy)

ships of the ORLYONOK class of 653–669 DWT. Soviet shipyards are building the GORIZONT class of 3,145 DWT (Okean); the PULKOVSKIY MERIDIAN class of 1,815–2,043 DWT (Black Sea); and the BARENSTYEVO MORE class of 556–611 DWT (Klaipeda). All of these are stern-trawler/factory ships.

Factory Ships. The Soviet Union's largest fish factory ship is the VOSTOK, built at Leningrad's Admiralty yard and completed in 1971. The 22,110-DWT ship (43,000 tons displacement) suffered several problems and delays in building and fitting out. She was intended to carry 14 fishing craft of 60 tons each plus helicopters and was designed to process more than 300 tons of fish daily. Even after completion the VOSTOK has not been fully successful, and instead of operating as a small-craft carrier and factory, she has been employed only in the latter role. No additional ships of the class have been built.

Approximately 115 smaller factory ships are in service (in addition to the trawler-factory vessels). These factory ships also provide logistic support, maintenance, and medical services to the trawlers in their working areas.

Support Ships. The Soviet fishing fleet operates a large number of refrigerated cargo ships, fuel tankers, water carriers, repair ships, and

The ODISSEY is one of 15 MAYAKOVSKIY-class trawlers converted to various fisheries research configurations. The ODISSEY and her sister ship IKHTIANDR are fitted to carry research submersibles in their large, amidships hangars.

oceangoing tugs in support of the trawler fleet. There are some 100 tankers and over 500 refrigerated fish carriers (cargo ships) that support the fishing fleet. The two fish carrier classes now being built for the Soviet Union are the 50 LET SSR class, 11,420-DWT ships being constructed at the 61 Kommuna shipyard (Nikolayev), and the ALMAZNYY BEREG, 9,606-DWT ships being produced at the Mathias Thesen yard (Wismar, East Germany). There are about 20 of the former and more than 40 of the latter ships currently in service.

Training Ships. There are several fisheries training ships in service, mostly trawlers modified for student accommodations and classrooms.

Research Ships and Submarines. The fishing industry has several trawlers modified to conduct research into fish hunting and catching techniques. There are some 65 fisheries research trawlers in service, with at least two, the 1,070-DWT IKHTIANDR and ODISSEY, modified to carry research submersibles.

In the 1960s two diesel-electric submarines of the Whiskey class were converted to oceanographic-fisheries research submarines. Renamed SEVERYANKA and SLAVYANKA, their forward torpedo rooms were converted into laboratories, observation stations were installed to permit scientists to see underwater, exterior lights were fitted, and provisions were made to recover sea-floor samples. About six to eight scientists were assigned for these missions. The two undersea craft operated in the research role for several years before being discarded.

Several small submersibles are operated in support of fisheries activities.

TABLE 32-1. SOVIET FISHING FLEET, January 1985*

Ship Type	Number	Deadweight Tonnage
Passenger and Cargo	9	5,383
Dry Cargo	528	1,556,171
Tankers	100	292,566
Gas Carriers	1	270
Fishing Ships	2,646	1,944,736
Special-Purpose Ships	207	1,190,937
Technical Ships	29	8,778
Totals†	3,520	4,998,841

* Source: *Morskoy Flot* (Soviet Fleet) (no. 6, 1985.)
†Does not include some 200 tugs and 150 other auxiliaries assigned to the fishing fleet.

Aircraft. Aircraft are employed periodically to support the fishing industry. Helicopters have been based on the larger ships to help track down schools of fish. In addition, land-based aircraft have been used, especially Il-14 Crate twin-engine aircraft and Il-18D Coot four-engine aircraft. The decision to use the longer-range Coot was made, in part, because of the farther-ranging fishing areas brought about by the 200-mile economic zones. The initial Coot flights in 1980–1981 were sponsored by the Polar Institute of Marine Fishing and Oceanography and the State Scientific Research Institute of Civil Aviation.

33
Warsaw Pact Navies

The Warsaw Pact nations provide the Soviet Navy with (1) a defensive buffer zone, (2) naval and air forces to help control the Baltic and Black seas, (3) amphibious forces to assist in coastal assaults and possible seizure of the Danish straits, and (4) a major shipbuilding capability.[1] Two of the Warsaw Pact navies, East Germany and Poland, have significant capabilities for combat in the Baltic. In the mid-1980s, these two navies began long-awaited modernization programs.

Bulgaria and Romania have smaller naval forces in the Black Sea. While they have only marginal capabilities, the lack of an effective NATO threat in those waters makes this a moot point. The Romanian fleet is undergoing major expansion but, according to one Western analyst, ". . . the expansion of the Romanian Navy, impressive as it is, appears primarily intended to satisfy the country's leadership and national prestige, and not to enable the navy to carry out its wartime tasks."[2]

History. The Soviet Union and seven "satellite" nations in Eastern Europe signed the Treaty of Friendship and Mutual Assistance in Warsaw on 14 May 1955. The treaty was in part a response to the establishment of the North Atlantic Treaty Organization (NATO) in 1949. The Warsaw Pact signatories were Albania, Bulgaria, Czechoslovakia, East Germany, Hungary, Poland, and Romania, in addition to the Soviet

[1] This chapter is based in part on the extensive research of Dr. Milan Vego, a former Yugoslav naval officer. From 1981 he has written an essay on East European navies for the annual (March) issue of the Naval Institute *Proceedings* that addresses international navies; also see Dr. Vego's paper, "The Non-Soviet Warsaw Pact Navies" given at the Sea Power Forum Conference, Center for Naval Analyses, Washington, D.C., 14 November 1985.

[2] Milan Vego, "East European Navies," Naval Institute *Proceedings* (March 1986), p. 49.

The Warsaw Pact navies are undergoing an extensive modernization program. The Koni-class ASW frigates—the East German ROSTOK seen here—have also been transferred to Algeria, Cuba, and Yugoslavia, with construction of the class continuing at the Zelenodolsk shipyard. (West German Navy)

Union. East Germany was only a "political" member of the Warsaw Pact until the existence of its armed forces was officially acknowledged in January 1956.

The Albanian government broke off relations with the Soviet leadership for ideological reasons in 1961 and thus effectively withdrew from the Warsaw Pact. This withdrawal was made official in 1968. Albania's loss to the Soviet Union was significant from a naval perspective because the small country, with a coastline on the Adriatic Sea, had provided the Soviets with Mediterranean bases. In 1960 a Soviet submarine tender and eight submarines had been sent to the Albanian island of Saseno (Sazan) in the Gulf of Valona. This base was abandoned by the Soviets in 1961, with Albania seizing two of the Whiskey-class submarines which it refused permission to leave at the time of the Soviet withdrawal. (Two other Whiskey submarines had been transferred to Albania in 1960.)

The East German and Polish navies are intended primarily for operations in the Baltic, and cannot realistically be considered effective opponents for NATO forces beyond those important, albeit restricted, waters. Beginning in 1957 the Soviet, East German, and Polish navies have conducted joint exercises in the Baltic on a regular basis. A joint command of these three Warsaw Pact navies in the Baltic was apparently established in May 1962, obviously under Soviet direction. Since 1980 they have conducted exercises beyond the Danish straits, in the North Sea. However, these operations appear to be primarily political and not military. At times these exercises have been under the tactical control of non-Soviet admirals.

In wartime the East German and Polish navies would join with Soviet naval forces to (1) provide support for Soviet ground operations along the southern Baltic coast, (2) deny use of the Baltic to NATO naval forces, and (3) seize control of the Danish straits. Amphibious landings would probably be carried out in support of these activities, including the capture of the Danish island of Bornholm, which lies north of Poland, and probably some of the Danish coastline along the straits. (Soviet troops had occupied Bornholm from 1945 to 1947.)

In the Black Sea the Bulgarian and Romanian navies have primarily coastal defense missions against Turkish naval forces that might seek to attack Warsaw Pact territory. Bulgaria, however, because of its proximity to the Turkish straits, may have strategic importance to Soviet military operations. The southern border of Bulgaria is about 50 miles (80 km) from Constantinople, and a Soviet attack on Turkey, presumably to seize the straits, would come through Bulgaria and by sea. The Bulgarian roads and bases could be most important to a thrust against Turkey or, less likely, against Greece or Yugoslavia. Bulgaria—which shares a border with NATO Turkey—has a large number of torpedo and patrol boats, plus two Romeo-class submarines. The Romanian Navy is undergoing a major buildup, but the naval capabilities of both Bulgaria and Romania are limited.

The Warsaw Pact's military activities are totally directed by the Soviet Union, with a Soviet marshal in the post of commander in chief of the Pact military forces. Numerous other Soviet officers—some naval— are assigned to key staff positions, with Admiral N.I. Khovrin currently serving as the deputy CinC for naval forces. It is not clear if Khovrin would be the operational commander of the East German and Polish naval forces in wartime, or whether those forces would be placed under command of the CinC of the Soviet Baltic Fleet.

In peacetime the Warsaw Pact high command directs the Groups of Soviet Forces in Czechoslovakia, East Germany, Hungary, and Poland, certain Soviet forces in the three western military districts of the Soviet Union, and all East German military forces. The military forces of the five smaller Warsaw Pact nations are subordinate to the Pact high command only during periods of external threat. (Efforts by the Soviet Union to establish standing Warsaw Pact armies were attempted in 1956–1957 and again in 1967–1968, but were rejected by the member nations.)

The air, ground, and naval forces of the non-Soviet nations use mainly Soviet equipment, training doctrine, and communications procedures, etc. There have been significant developments in equipment by East Germany and Poland, especially in the naval areas, but these are intended to fit into the Soviet "style" of warfare and often use Soviet components. (This rigidity within the Warsaw Pact is in strong contrast to the NATO nations, who for economic reasons only tend to use significant amounts of some American equipment, but have their own tactical doctrine as well as mostly their own equipment.)

Another major factor for the Soviet Navy is the shipbuilding capability of the Warsaw Pact nations. East Germany, Poland, and to a lesser extent, Bulgaria and Romania, are major suppliers of ships to the Soviet Union. Most of this East European shipbuilding effort for the Soviets consists of research, merchant, and fishing ships; however, the East German and Polish yards also provide the Soviet Navy with amphibious ships, intelligence collection ships, and research ships.

Table 33-1 provides a summary of the major units of the four non-Soviet Warsaw Pact navies.

TABLE 33-1. WARSAW PACT NAVIES

| Ship Type | Baltic Sea | | Black Sea | | Total |
	East Germany	Poland	Bulgaria	Romania	
Submarines	—	3	2	—	5
Destroyers	—	1	—	1	2
Frigates	2	—	2	3	7
Corvettes	18	2	3	3	26
Missile Craft	14	15	5	5	39
Torpedo Boats	48	7	6	30	91
Submarine chasers	—	—	6	—	6
Patrol Boats	16*	54*	5	22	97
Landing Ships	12	23	—	—	35
Land Craft	—	18	19	—	37
Minelayers	2	—	—	—	2
Minesweepers/Minehunters	27	23	6	9	65
Coastal/Inshore Minesweepers	21	24	4	—	49

*Some or all operated by maritime border guards.

BULGARIA

Bulgaria borders on the Black Sea, between Romania to the north and the European portion of Turkey to the south. Bulgaria has a small, outdated navy, consisting primarily of coastal forces, plus river craft that serve on the Danube River.

The transfer of more modern Soviet ships can be expected in the near future.

Bulgaria and Poland are the only Warsaw Pact nations with submarines; Bulgaria has two Romeo-class submarines that were transferred from the Soviet Union in 1971–1972 (replacing two older Whiskey submarines). The submarines can provide limited ASW training as well as serve in the coastal defense role.

The Navy's large surface units are two Riga-class frigates, acquired in 1957–1958 and extensively modernized in 1980–1981. There are also six Osa I/II missile craft and six Shershen torpedo boats. In addition to the Rigas, there is a limited ASW capability in three relatively modern Poti-class corvettes (and a very modern helicopter force).

There is also a minesweeping force.

The Bulgarian Navy has a significant short-range amphibious lift capability consisting of about 20 Vydra-class utility landing craft and a few locally built tank-landing craft.

Significantly, the Bulgarian Navy is upgrading its replenishment force with the 3,500-ton ANLENE, built in Bulgaria in 1980, the first of several expected support ships. There are also three coastal tankers in naval service.

The Danube River Flotilla has about a dozen small patrol craft.

Naval aviation. The naval air arm has recently acquired 12 Haze-A helicopters from the Soviet Union. There are also eight Hoplite and Hound helicopters employed in search and rescue.

Special forces. No naval or ground troops specifically trained for amphibious landings have been identified.

There is a coastal defense force with a battalion of SSC-2b Samlet missiles plus several gun batteries.

Command and personnel. Vice Admiral V.G. Yanakiev is CinC of the Navy. The Bulgarian Navy has some 8,500 uniformed personnel, of whom 1,800 are assigned to ships and craft, some 2,200 to coastal defenses, 1,800 to training activities, and 2,500 to shore support. There are about 5,000–6,000 conscripts in the Navy on three years' obligated service.

Bases and ports. The principal bases and ports on the Black Sea are Sozopol; Varna at the mouth of the Provadiya River with commercial and naval facilities; and Burgas, the nation's most important harbor and center of its fishing industry. The Danube Flotilla has bases at Atiya, Balchik, and Vidin.

Shipyards. The major Bulgarian shipbuilding facilities are the George Dimitrov shipyard at Varna and yards at Burgas and Ruse (on the Danube, near the Romanian border). The principal customer of these yards has been the Soviet Union; the most significant recent deliveries have been from the Dimitrov yard—another group of 24,354-DWT bulk

TABLE 33-2. BULGARIAN NAVY

Number	Type	Class	Builder
2	submarines	Romeo	USSR
2	frigates	Riga	USSR
3	corvettes	Poti	USSR
2	missile craft	Osa I	USSR
3	missile craft	Osa II	USSR
6	torpedo boats	Shershen	USSR
6	submarine chasers	S.O.-1*	USSR
5	patrol boats	Zhuk	USSR
4	minesweepers	Vanya	USSR
2	minesweepers	T-43	USSR
4	inshore minesweepers	Yevgenya	USSR
19	landing craft	Vydra	USSR
1	replenishment ship	Mesar (ANLENE)	Bulgaria
1	survey ship/tender	Moma	Poland
1	salvage tug	Type 700	East Germany

*None is reported serviceable.

carriers of the SOVIETSKIY KHUDOZHNIK class and smaller, 9,370-DWT container ships.

Merchant marine.[3] One hundred and seventeen ships of 1,877,700 DWT are reported in the Bulgarian merchant fleet, consisting of 37 general cargo ships, 12 container and partial container ships, 2 Roll-On/Roll-Off (RO/RO) ships, 4 passenger ships, 17 tankers, and 45 bulk carriers and coal ships. These ships are operated by the Bulgarian Maritime Shipping line.

CZECHOSLOVAKIA

Czechoslovakia has no coastline, but army personnel operate several armed motor launches on the Danube River. The government owns a large number of river craft.

Shipyards. There is a major shipyard—the Gabor Steiner yard—for building and maintaining river craft in Komarno, as well as lesser facilities along the Danube. The Komarno yard has built more than 250 river and coastal ships for the Soviet Union since the late 1940s.

Merchant marine. The Czechoslovak International Maritime Company operates 19 ships totaling 274,500 DWT. These are 13 general cargo ships, 1 partial container ship, and 5 bulk/ore carriers.

EAST GERMANY

East Germany—the German Democratic Republic—is of considerable naval significance to the Soviet Union because of its proximity to Denmark and the Danish straits. The East German National Peoples Navy (*Nationale Volksmarine*) ranks after the Polish Navy in size and is characterized by a large number of small combatants with considerable

---

[3] Merchant fleet data from U.S. Maritime Administration, as of January 1986.

The East German and Polish navies have large numbers of small combatants to help the Baltic Fleet obtain control of the Baltic in wartime. Here the East German Shershen-class torpedo boat JOSEPH ROEMER (852) closes on the Osa I-class missile boat EGELHOFWE (752). (West German Navy)

missile (SS-N-2 Styx and SS-N-9), minesweeper, and amphibious capabilities. The missions of this force are apparently to help to control the western Baltic, and to conduct amphibious operations against the West German and Danish coasts.

During the past few years the East German Navy has been undergoing an extensive modernization program. Among the more recent acquisitions are two new, Soviet-built frigates of the Koni class, transferred in 1978–1979, to replace two ineffective ships of the Riga class, and the first of a series of Soviet Tarantul I guided missile corvettes delivered in late 1984. The latter, carrying the SS-N-9 missile with a range of some 60 n.miles (110 km), have improved seakeeping and attack capabilities over the older Osa missile craft operated by the *Volksmarine*.

Also joining the East German Navy since 1980 have been the PAR-CHIM-class 1,100-ton anti-submarine corvettes. An estimated 18 ships of this class will be operational when production ends in 1986–1987. These are German-built ships that are fitted with Soviet weapons and electronics.

But the most potent *Volksmarine* combat capability is found in the fast attack craft—14 Osa I-class missile boats, each with four SS-N-2 Styx missiles, and 18 Shershen-class torpedo boats, all built in the Soviet Union.There are also 30 smaller Libelle-class "light" torpedo boats that were built in Germany. The larger (540-ton), more heavily armed Tarantuls are to replace the Osas and probably Shershens, but at a less than one-for-one rate because of the newer ship's size and complexity.

The East German mine countermeasure force is composed of 28 Kondor II sweeper/hunters. Two of these currently serve as training ships for petty officers.

The Navy has a significant amphibious lift in 12 Frosch-class medium landing ships (LSM) of 1,950-tons displacement. These are similar to the Soviet Ropucha class, but smaller and more heavily armed.

Another area of naval modernization has been the acquisition of two support ships of the Frosch II class (which can also be employed as minelayers) and seven of the 1,200-ton DARSS class. These ships can support smaller units operating in the western Baltic or beyond the Danish straits. The Navy also has five support tankers and five harbor tankers plus two repair ships, several survey and salvage ships, icebreakers, and three intelligence collection ships (AGI). The AGIs consist of one Okean and two Kondor I types configured for the ELINT role.

Naval aviation. The *Volksmarine* flies only helicopters, with the current strength estimated at about nine of the Haze-A type configured for ASW, 15 Hip type flown in the transport role, and three older Hip type employed for search and rescue.

Special forces. A limited amphibious assault force is provided by the Army's 29th motorized rifle regiment ("Ernst Moritz-Arndt"), which is especially trained in amphibious operations. The regiment, numbering some 2,000 men, is based at Prora (Rügen Island).

There is a Coastal Border Brigade that provides patrols and defenses along the Baltic coast. The brigade has some 4,100 men; it operates 20 Kondor I minsweepers plus about 50 patrol craft. For coastal defense there are at least two missile battalions and five coastal gun batteries, the former having been rearmed about 1984–1985 with the SSC-3 anti-ship missile.

Command and personnel. The Navy commander is Vice Admiral Willi Ehm. (Dr. Ehm was appointed CinC of naval forces with the rank of rear admiral in August 1959.) The East German Navy has an estimated 15,500 personnel (not including the 29th rifle regiment). Of these, an estimated 4,700 are assigned afloat, 4,100 to coastal defense, 2,000 to training activities, 4,200 to shore support, and about 500 to naval aviation. Some 8,000 of the men are conscripts with 18 months of required service in the Navy and the remainder officers (1,800) and long-term enlisted men.

Bases and ports. Rostock is the largest and most important port in East Germany, being located on the Warnow River near where it enters the Baltic Sea. Among the commercial and naval activities at Rostock are the Navy's headquarters (Rostock-Gehsdorf), a major oil terminal, and a large fishing center. The port has recently undergone a major expansion.

Warnemünde, the outer port of Rostock, is a seaside resort with naval and commercial facilities. Wismar, on the gulf of that name, is mainly a commercial port; Stralsund, on the Strela Sund, is a naval base and commercial port, as is Sassnitz on the opposite side of Rügen Island; Wolgast, near the mouth of the Peene River, appears also to be a naval and commercial port; and nearby Peenemünde, former center for German wartime missile development, is a major naval facility.

The Navy's helicopters are based at Parow (near Stralsund) and Peenemünde.

Shipyards. There are several shipyards in East Germany, most being employed to construct and repair fishing, coastal, and river craft. There are five major shipyards: The Warnow yard at Warnemünde; the Matthias Thesen yard at Wismar; the Neptun yard at Rostock; the Volks yard at Stralsund; and the Peenewerft yard at Wolgast. All five yards build commercial ships, while Peenewerft also builds small combatants and the Frosch-class landing ships for the East German Navy, while Wolgast is constructing the PARCHIM-class corvettes.

Most of the merchant ships built in East German yards are for the Soviet Union. Since 1946 the Soviet Union has received over 1,300 of the merchant and fishing ships built in East Germany. This represents over 60 percent of the ships built in the country.

Recent commercial shipbuilding programs for the Soviet Union include some 25 refrigerated fish carriers of the ALMAZNYY BERG class built by the Matthias Thesen yard; a class of 19,240-DWT dry-bulk carriers of the modified DMITRIY DONSKOY class for Arctic service, 18,020-DWT RO/RO ships of the ASTRAKHAN class, and an additional 17,720-DWT container ships of the MERCUR II series—the largest in the Soviet fleet—at the Warno yard; and several classes of stern trawler/factory ships at the Volks yard. The Volks yard is currently under contract for more than 30 trawler/factory ships of the Super ATLANTIC type, to be delivered to the Soviet fishing fleet by 1990.

Merchant marine. The East German merchant fleet has 161 ships of 1,715,100 DWT. These consist of 87 general cargo ships, 41 container ships, 8 RO/RO ships, 3 tankers, 17 bulk/ore ships, and 3 passenger ships. The firm of VEB Deutfracht/Seereederei operates East Germany's merchant ships.

HUNGARY

Hungary, like Czechoslovakia, has no coastline, but operates river patrol craft under army command on the Danube River. The army also has a few small landing craft. The smaller of these craft have been built at the minor shipyards along the Danube. Some of these yards have built large numbers of river tugs and other small craft for the Soviet Union. In particular, the Ganz shipyard and crane factory has delivered more than 1,200 small craft and about 2,000 gantry cranes to the Soviet Union since 1945.

Merchant marine. Twenty-one ships totaling 111,000 DWT are registered to Hungary, 15 general-cargo ships and 6 partial container ships operated by the Mabart line.

POLAND

The Polish Navy is the largest of the non-Soviet Warsaw Pact forces in terms of ship size, ship tonnage, and naval personnel. The Navy (*Ludowa Marynarka Woyenna*) is reported to be the best trained and best maintained of the four satellite navies, based on a serious naval tradition.[4]

Like those of East Germany and Romania, the Polish fleet is currently being modernized with significant ship transfers from the Soviet Union

TABLE 33-3. EAST GERMAN NAVY

Number	Type	Class	Builder
2	frigates	Koni	USSR
18	corvettes	PARCHIM	East Germany
2	missile craft	Tarantul I	USSR
14	missile craft	Osa I	USSR
18	torpedo boats	Shershen	USSR
30	light torpedo boats	Libelle	East Germany
16*	patrol boats	(various)	East Germany
27	minesweeper/hunters	Kondor II	East Germany
21*	inshore minesweepers	Kondor I	East Germany
12	landing ships	Frosch	East Germany
2	support ships/minelayers	Frosch II	East Germany
6	support ships	Darss	East Germany
2	repair ships	VOGTLAND	East Germany
2	intelligence ships	mod. Kondor I	East Germany
1	intelligence ship	Okean	East Germany
6	survey ships	(various)	Poland, East Germany
8	buoy tenders	(various)	East Germany
5	tankers	(various)	USSR-East Germany
1	training ship	WODNIK	Poland
1	salvage ship	Piast	Poland
6	experimental-research ships	(various)	East Germany

*Operated by the maritime border guards.

[4] A Polish Navy was established between the World Wars. After the fall of Poland in 1939, a Polish-Navy-in-exile was organized with headquarters in England. At war's end the Polish Navy had in service one light cruiser, six destroyers, six submarines, and several smaller craft. Another cruiser, four destroyers, and two submarines were lost during the war. In the postwar period the Polish Navy was the first of the satellite navies to receive submarines, M-class boats in 1956, and the first to receive destroyers (SKORYY class) in 1957.

anticipated. Poland and Bulgaria are the only fleets with submarines. Three of four ex-Soviet submarines of the Whiskey class, transferred to Poland in 1962–1965, remain in service. While kept in excellent condition, they are overage and of limited capability. In June of 1985 the CinC of the Polish Navy stated that in the near future Poland would commission a modern submarine as well as new escort ships and minesweepers. The first of probably several Kilo-class submarines was transferred to Poland in 1986.

Poland was long the only non-Soviet Warsaw Pact fleet with a destroyer, the WARSZAWA, a SAM Kotlin transferred to Poland in 1970. This ship is also outdated and will probably be discarded in the next few years. (Romania has recently acquired destroyers.)

The Soviet replacement of the submarines and destroyer was probably delayed because of the political unrest in Poland during the early 1980s. The small combatant force is being modernized, with the first Tarantul I-class missile corvette being acquired from the Soviet Union in December 1984. These ships, however, have the SS-N-2c Styx missile, and not the longer-range SS-N-9 found in East German and Soviet ships of this class. These will replace 13 former Soviet Osa I-class missile boats and the few surviving, Polish-built Wisla torpedo boats.

The absence of Koni or other modern anti-submarine ships now limits the ASW capabilities of the fleet. However, a class of 1,000-ton frigates has been started, the first major surface combatants to be built in Poland since before World War II. A large number of patrol craft as well as several minesweepers are also in service. The Polish-built Notec class, 160-ton ships with glass-reinforced plastic hulls, are now entering service.

The Polish Navy has a significant amphibious lift capability in 23 Polnocny-class medium landing ships plus several smaller landing craft.

There are several auxiliary ships (see table 33-4) in naval service, including a large sail training ship. One other noteworthy ship of recent construction is the sail-driven oceanographic research ship OCEANIA, operated by the Polish Academy of Sciences. Completed in early 1986,

this 550-ton ship has a hydraulic-operated sail system that can be operated by one man. (An auxiliary, 3,200-horsepower diesel is also fitted.) The ship's total crew is 15 plus 12 scientists.

Naval aviation. Poland has a large although outdated naval air arm, the only one among the Warsaw Pact navies with fixed-wing aircraft. There are 10 Il-28 Beagle light bombers and about that number of MiG-17 Fresco fighters flown in the reconnaissance role. Another 30 MiG-17s and MiG-19 Farmer aircraft fly in the fighter-attack role. (The MiGs are Polish-built aircraft.) The Navy has about 25 helicopters—Hoplite, Hound, and Hip types employed for various duties.

A few training planes are also available. Again, all of the aircraft are overage and in need of replacement.

Special forces. The Polish Army's 7th Sea Landing Division regularly exercises with the Navy's amphibious ships. The division—with some 12,000 men—is based in the Gdansk area.

There is a large coastal defense force with several battalions armed with the SSC-2b Samlet missile and a small number of gun batteries.

Command and personnel. Admiral Ludwik Janczyszyn commands the Polish Navy. There are a reported 19,100 men in this Navy, with 5,200 afloat, 2,300 with the naval air arm, 4,100 assigned to coastal defense, 2,500 involved in training activities, and 5,000 in shore support assignments. Of this force, about 6,000 are conscripts, drafted for 18 months.

Bases and ports. Most Polish ports and naval bases are in territory that was German through World War II. All were heavily damaged during the war and then stripped by the Soviets of their useful machinery and other material.[5]

The principal Polish commercial port and naval base are in Gdynia,

[5] The Polish state that existed between the two world wars had Danzig (now Gdansk) as the country's only port. It was connected to the rest of Poland by a narrow corridor separating East Prussia from the rest of Germany.

The Polish Navy training ship WODNIK is one of two similar craft developed from the MOMA-class hull. She appears to be employed mainly for navigation and gunnery training; note the twin 30-mm gun mounts forward and aft and paired 25-mm mounts aft of the twin funnels.

known as Gotenhafen from 1939 to 1945. It was a small fishing village until the mid-1920s when there was a period of rapid growth and development, making it a major port. It is now the main base of the Polish Navy, a large commercial port (especially for the shipment of coal from Upper Silesia), and a major shipbuilding center.

Just south of Gdynia, also on the Gulf of Danzig, is the city of Gdansk, which is also a major commercial port and naval base, with a large shipyard.

There are smaller naval bases at Hel (formerly Hela) on the Polwysepottel Peninsula, and at Świnoujście (Swinemünde) on the Polish–East German border. Nearby Szczecin (Stettin), on the Oder River, is a commercial port. The naval aircraft and helicopters fly from fields at Elblag (formerly Elbing), Gdansk, Koszalin, Sliepsk, and Szczecin.

Shipyards. Poland has one of the world's most advanced shipbuilding industries, with ship construction having long been the nation's largest "export" industry after coal. The Polish and former German shipyards, which were devasted in World War II, were totally rebuilt from the late 1940s onward with heavy Soviet assistance.

Since the first oceangoing ship was laid down in 1948, the Polish yards have produced more than 800 commercial ships for some two dozen nations. Most ships have gone to the Soviet Union, but other recent export customers have included Bulgaria, Czechoslovakia, France, West Germany, India, Mexico, the Netherlands, and Sweden.

Polish shipyards have also produced some 60 landing ships of the Polnocny series and 11 of the Ropucha class as well as large numbers of intelligence-collection ships, survey ships, and other naval units for the Soviet Union, with landing ships also being built for the Polish and several Third World navies. While large naval ships are not built in Poland, the shipyards have built supertankers and large bulk carriers as well as relatively complex merchant ships.

There are five major shipyards and several smaller building and repair facilities. The principal shipbuilding facilities are the V.I. Lenin (ex-Schichau) and Stocznia Polnocny (ex-Danziger) in Gdansk;[6] the Paris Commune in Gdynia; and the Adolf Warski (ex-Vulcan) yard in Szczecin. Most recently a major yard was built at Ustka (formerly Stolpmunde). All five yards build commercial ships and some naval auxiliaries. The Polnocny yard produces amphibious ships, while the Paris Commune yard concentrates on large merchant ships, including tankers to carry petroleum and liquified gas.

Also, on 6 March 1982, the Lenin yard launched the hull of the large sail-training ship ISKRA for use by the Polish Navy. Another sail-training ship, the DAR MLODZIEZY, has been built at that yard for the Polish merchant marine academy (replacing the DAR POMORZA, which was retired after 70 years of service), with additional ships of this type being built for the Soviet Union. Recent construction programs for the Soviet Union, Poland's largest foreign customer, have included the RO/RO ships, fish factory/mother ships, refrigerated fish carriers, and the VITYAZ-class research ships at the Szczecinska yard; the impressive, 18,462-DWT SKULPTOR KONENKOV RO/RO ships, refrigerated cargo ships (reef-

ers), stern trawler/factory ships, Arctic timber carriers, and Shel'f-series geological research ships at the Gdansk yard; and both of those yards plus the Gdynia yard produce the NEFTEGAZ-class offshore supply ships.

The Soviet five-year merchant-fishing plan for 1986–1990 provides for Polish yards to construct some 300 fishing, merchant, and technical ships for the Soviet Union. The value of these contracts—more than three billion rubles—represents an increase of 300 percent over the previous five-year construction program for the Soviet merchant and fishing fleets.

(While Poland exports large numbers of ships, in 1985–1986 the Polish merchant marine took delivery of eight grain carriers of 27,000 DWT and two bulk carriers of 61,000 DWT built in Argentina.)

Polish shipyard workers have generally been among the leaders of political unrest in postwar Poland. The political crises of the early 1980s began in August 1980 when 17,000 workers at the Lenin shipyard went on strike. The workers sought major labor and union reforms. But one of their key demands was for construction of a monument to shipyard workers killed by police in the 1970 riots that toppled the government of Wladyslaw Gomulka and brought to office the government in power when the 1980 unrest began.

Merchant marine. The Polish merchant marine has a reported 285

TABLE 33-4. POLISH NAVY

Number	Type	Class	Builder
1	submarine	Kilo	USSR
3	submarines	Whiskey	USSR
1	missile destroyer	SAM Kotlin	USSR
2‡	missile corvettes		Poland
2	missile craft	Tarantul I	USSR
13	missile craft	Osa I	USSR
7	torpedo boats	Wisla	Poland
5*	patrol craft	Obluze	Poland
9*	patrol craft	Gdansk	Poland
40*	coastal patrol craft	(various)	Poland
12	minesweepers	KROGULEC	Poland
11	minesweepers	T-43	Poland
2	coastal minesweepers	Notec (GOPLO)	Poland
24†	inshore minesweepers	K-8	Poland
23	landing ships	Polnocny	Poland
3	landing craft	Marabut	Poland
15	landing craft	Eichstaden	Poland
2	intelligence ships	Moma	Poland
1	intelligence ship	B-10 (trawler)	Poland
6	tankers	(various)	Poland
2	survey ships	Fenik	Poland
1	survey ship	Moma	Poland
2	salvage ships	Piast	Poland
2	training ships	WODNIK	Poland
4	training ships	BRYZA	Poland
1	sail training ship	ISKARA II	Poland

*Operated by maritime border guards.
†Most are laid up in reserve.
‡NATO designation Balcom-6.

[6] This yard is also known as the Heroes of Westerplatte North Shipyard.

ships of 4,385,300 DWT. These consist of 154 general-cargo ships, 24 container ships, 6 RO/RO ships, 90 bulk/ore ships, 9 tankers, and 2 passenger ships. Poland is building a major fleet of RO/RO cargo ships and has also purchased ships from France and Spain.

Because of the political unrest in the country, the three shipping lines—the Polish Steamship Company, Polish Baltic Ship Company, and Polish Ocean Lines—have suffered a large number of crew desertions during the early 1980s, as has the large Polish fishing fleet.

There is also a joint shipping venture between China and Poland, *Chinsko-Polskie Towarzystwo* SA, which operated 28 ships on liner services between the two nations in 1986. This liner fleet is equally divided between the two flags, with most ships having been acquired secondhand from other countries.

ROMANIA

Romania lies on the western coast of the Black Sea, between Bulgaria and the Soviet Union. The newly built 40-mile (64-km) canal between Cernavoda and the new port of Constanta-South connects the Danube River and the Black Sea, shortening the shipping route by some 300 miles (480 km). The canal gives the Romanians full control over all shipping entering and leaving the Danube River.

Although Romania has the smallest of the four significant non-Soviet Warsaw Pact navies, it is currently undergoing a major modernization and expansion. The Navy (*Marina Militara Romana*) had consisted mainly of coastal torpedo and patrol boats until the commissioning in August 1985 of the 4,500-ton, guided missile destroyer MANTENIA. A second ship of this class is under construction. These ships, with surface-to-air missile launchers fore and aft, a helicopter hangar and landing deck, and pyramid mast structures, bear a resemblance to the Soviet Kresta I-class cruisers.

The Navy also took delivery in 1983–1985 of three 1,800-ton Tetal-class light frigates. And, rumors persist that the Romanians are seeking submarines.[7]

There are almost 70 combat craft in Romanian service, most outdated or of limited combat capability. These include six Osa I type, 22 Huchuan hydrofoils, and 14 Epitrop-class units. The Soviet-built Osas are outdated; the Huchuan-type torpedo boats were built in Romania between 1973 and 1983 to a Chinese design; and the 200-ton Epitrop-class torpedo craft were built in Romania from 1980 onward. More of the last are being built.

The remaining small combatants are Shanghai II gunboats and obsolete P-4 torpedo boats.

There are also a few landing craft and minesweepers in service.

In addition to the larger combat units, the Romanian naval modernization includes the recent construction of two 3,500-ton CROITOR-class support ships, which supplement three older coastal tankers.

For operations on the Danube River, there is a flotilla of modern Brutar-class monitors plus some 40 patrol craft.

Naval aviation. Romania was the latest of the Warsaw Pact nations to establish a naval air arm. Formed in 1983, the squadron has six Haze-A ASW helicopters.

Special forces. There is a coastal defense force that is believed to have an SSC-2 missile battalion plus several gun batteries.

There is no trained amphibious assault force.

Command and personnel. Rear Admiral Ioan Musat is commander of the Romanian Navy. The Navy has an estimated 7,700 personnel—up about 1,000 men in the past three years. Of these, some 3,600 are assigned to ships and craft, 600 to coastal defense, 900 to training activities, and 2,600 to shore support. Conscripts are required to serve for two years on active duty.

[7] Early in World War II the Romanian Navy had two domestically built submarines and one Italian-built submarine.

The Romanian MANTENIA shown fitting out in 1985 at the Mangalia Shipyard No. 2. Note the SS-N-22-type anti-ship missile tubes, paired on each side of the superstructure, forward and aft, for a total of eight missiles. Also visible are the pyramid towers and twin 30-mm gun mounts amidships and at the after end of the superstructure; there is a twin 76.2-mm gun mount forward. (Agerpress)

Bases and ports. Romania, with the shortest coastline of those Warsaw Pact nations that border on seas, has two major seaports. Constanta handles most of the country's overseas trade, is the terminal point for the Ploesti oil pipeline, and is the country's major naval base. Constanta's port facilities are being expanded beyond the current capacity of handling 60 million tons of cargo per year. The expansion is to the south, toward Agigea, with a capacity goal of 250 million tons of cargo per year by 2000.

The port at Vilovo at the mouth of the Danube—called Ust'-Dunaysk—was opened in 1980 to handle bulk cargoes. Mangalia to the south has recently been enlarged to handle ships of up to 55,000 DWT.

Sulina at the central mouth of the Danube, and Tulcea and Braila on the Danube have limited port facilities. A new port has been built during the past decade at Calarasi, an industrial center. It is connected with the Danube through a 3-mile (5-km) canal.

Shipyards. The country has four shipyards that build mostly coastal and small seagoing ships, as well as several minor facilities. The significant yards are at Braila, Constanta, Galati, Mangalia, and Sulina.

The Mangalia yard is building the new destroyers and light frigates as well as smaller naval craft. Constanta builds large bulk ore carriers. The Galati yard, located on the Danube, constructed two submarines at the beginning of World War II, but subsequent naval construction has been limited to smaller units.

The Soviet Union is a major customer for these yards while several merchant ships have also been built for Cuba during the past few years. Current programs for the Soviets include a class of 7,410-DWT shallow-draft tankers of the SERGEY KIROV class.

Merchant marine. Romania has a reported 268 merchant ships in service of 4,605,900 DWT. There are reported to be 142 general-cargo ships, 46 partial container ships, 6 RO/RO ships, 64 bulk/ore carriers, 1 passenger ship, and 9 tankers flying the Romanian flag for the Navrom line.

TABLE 33-5. ROMANIAN NAVY

Number	Type	Class	Builder
1	guided missile destroyer	MANTUNIA	Romania
3	frigates	Tetal	Romania
3	corvettes	Poti	USSR
5	missile craft	Osa I	USSR
10	torpedo boats	Epitrop	Romania
20*	torpedo boats	Huchuan	Romania
19	patrol boats	Shanghai II	China-Romania†
3	patrol boats	Kronshtadt	USSR
5	minesweepers	T-301	USSR
4	minesweepers	DEMOCRATIA	Romania
2	mine support ships	Cosar	Romania
1	ocean research ship	mod. Cosar	Romania
2	support ships	Croitor	Romania
3	coastal tankers	(various)	Romania
2	ocean tugs	Roslavl	USSR
1	headquarters ship	FRIPONNE	France (1916)
1	survey ship	FRIPONNE	France (1916)
1	sail training ship	MIRCEA	Germany (1938)

*Three units were built in China and the remainder in Romania.
†Some operated by maritime border guards.

An East German Frosch-class medium landing ship at high speed in the Baltic. These German-built ships are generally similar to the Polish-built Ropucha class, but smaller and more heavily armed. They demonstrate the national-design ships operated by Eastern Bloc navies as well as by Soviet-type naval units.

A
Senior Naval Officers, 1986

MINISTRY OF DEFENSE[1]

Position	Rank	Name	Year
Deputy Minister of Defense	Adm. Fleet	V. N. Chernavin	1985
General Staff of the Armed Forces			
Deputy Chief	Adm.	N. N. Amel'ko	1978
Main Political Directorate of the Army and Navy			
1st Deputy Chief	Adm.	A. I. Sorokin	1981
Main Directorate of Navigation and Oceanography			
Chief	Adm.	A. I. Rassokho	1963
External Relations Directorate			
Deputy Chief	Rear. Adm.	V. Z. Khuzhokov	1978

JOINT ARMED FORCES OF THE WARSAW PACT

Position	Rank	Name	Year
Deputy CinC for Naval Forces	Adm.	N. I. Khorvin	1983

NAVY

Position	Rank	Name	Year
Commander in Chief	Adm. Fleet	V. N. Chernavin	1985
1st Deputy Commander in Chief	Adm. Fleet	N. I. Smirnov	1974
Representative of the Central Apparatus	Rear Adm.	L. M. Zhiltsov	1983
Deputy CinC for Combat Training	Adm.	G. A. Bondarenko	1973
Deputy	Rear Adm.	I. F. Uskov	1978
Deputy CinC for Naval Educational Institutions	Vice Adm.	A. M. Kosov	1978
Deputy	Engr. Rear. Adm.	V. S. Yefremov	1981
Deputy CinC for Rear Services	Adm.	L. V. Mizin	1974
Deputy and Chief of Staff	Maj. Gen. Quartermaster	N. I. Kobelev	1977
Chief Navy Finance Service	Maj. Gen. Quartermaster	V. Belov	1977
Chief Navy Fuel Service	Engr. Col.	Ye. Stankevich	1981
Chief Navy Medical Service	Maj. Gen. Medical Serv.	N. Potemkin	1981
Deputy CinC for Shipbuilding and Armaments	Engr. Adm.	P. G. Kotov	1966
Deputy	Engr. Vice Adm.	I. I. Tynyankin	1980
Chief Main Directorate of Ship Repair Plants	Engr. Rear Adm.	A. M. Gevorkov	1975
Deputy CinC	Engr. Adm.	V. G. Novikov	1970

Main Naval Staff

Position	Rank	Name	Year
Chief	. . . . . .	. . . . . .	
1st Deputy Chief	Adm.	P. N. Navoyster	1976
Deputy Chief	Vice Adm.	Y. P. Kovel'	1968

Position	Rank	Name	Year
Deputy Chief	Vice Adm.	I. A. Sornev	1973
Deputy Chief	Rear. Adm.	O. M. Kalinin	1981
Chief Observation Directorate	Rear. Adm.	M. M. Krylov	1977

Political Directorate

Position	Rank	Name	Year
Chief	Adm.	P. N. Medvedev	1981
1st Deputy Chief	Rear Adm.	S. P. Vargin	1981
Deputy Chief	Rear Adm.	Ya. Grechko	1978
Deputy Chief for Agitation and Propaganda	Rear Adm.	E. Yu. Zimin	1980
Chief Organizational Party Work Department	Rear Adm.	S. M. Yefimov	1979
Party Commission Secretary	Rear. Adm.	A. Kolchin	1982

Auxiliary Fleet and Salvage-Sea Rescue Service

Position	Rank	Name	Year
Chief	Rear. Adm.	P. M. Yarovoy	1981

Inventions Bureau

Position	Rank	Name	Year
Chief	Engr. Rear. Adm.	N. Popov	1980

Naval Air Defense

Position	Rank	Name	Year
Chief	Rear. Adm.	S. P. Teglev	1982

Naval Aviation

Position	Rank	Name	Year
Commander	Col. Gen. Aviation	G. A. Kuznetsov	1982
Deputy Commander	Col. Gen. Aviation	V. I. Voronov	1985
Deputy Commander for Political Affairs	Maj. Gen. Aviation	I. M. Tropynin	1978
Chief of Staff	Lt. Gen. Aviation	V. Budeyev	1985

NORTHERN FLEET

Position	Rank	Name	Year
Commander in Chief	Adm.	I. M. Kapitanets	1985
1st Deputy	Vice Adm.	V. S. Kruglyakov	1976
Deputy for Combat Training	Rear Adm.	V. Ryabov	1981
Deputy for Rear Services	Vice Adm.	V. M. Petrov	1978
Chief of Staff	Rear Adm.	V. Denisov	1981
Chief Finance Department	Maj. Gen. Quartermaster	I. Burnayev	1978
Deputy Commander	Rear Adm.	A. V. Akatov	1980
Chief of Staff	Vice Adm.	V. K. Korobov	1981
1st Deputy	Rear Adm.	M. D. Iskanderov	1979
Chief Political Directorate	Vice Adm.	N. V. Usenko	1980
1st Deputy	Rear Adm.	V. T. Polivanov	1976
Deputy Chief	Rear Adm.	V. Losikov	1978

[1] Abbreviations for ranks are listed at the end of this appendix; dates are for appointment to position. Admiral Chernavin succeeded Admiral of the Fleet of the Soviet Union S. G. Gorshkov as Deputy Minister of Defense and Commander in Chief of the Soviet Navy in early December 1985.

Commander Naval Aviation	Maj. Gen. Aviation	V. P. Potapov	1981
Chief Political Department	Maj. Gen. Aviation	M. S. Mamay	1969
Chief Military Procuracy	Maj. Gen. Justice	M. Guzeyev	1981
Chief Military Tribunal	Maj. Gen. Justice	V. Bobkov	1981
Chief Personnel Department	Rear Adm.	V. Ya. Zuyev	1977

BALTIC FLEET

Commander in Chief	Adm.	K. Makarov	1985
1st Deputy	Vice Adm.	Ye. Semyonkev	1985
Deputy for Rear Services	Vice Adm.	P. P. Belous	1976
Chief Political Department	Rear Adm.	V. Kabanov	
Deputy for Construction	Maj. Gen. Engr.	O. Anikanov	1979
Chief of Staff	Rear Adm.	V. Kolmagorov	1985
Chief Political Directorate	Vice Adm.	I. F. Alikov	1980
1st Deputy	Rear Adm.	A. Korniyenko	1976
Commander Naval Aviation	Col. Gen. Aviation	A. I. Pavlovskiy	1977
Chief Political Department	Maj. Gen.	B. I. Grekov	1976
Chief Military Tribunal	Maj. Gen. Justice	D. Zhdanov	1982
Commander Leningrad Naval Base	Adm.	V. A. Samoylov	1982
1st Deputy	Rear Adm.	Ye. V. Butuzov	1978
Deputy	Rear Adm.	I. M. Kolchin	1974
Deputy for Rear Services	Rear Adm.	V. N. Bashkin	1982
Chief Political Department	Vice Adm.	A. A. Plekhanov	1971
Deputy Chief	Rear Adm.	A. P. Prosvernitsyn	1978

BLACK SEA FLEET

Commander in Chief	Rear Adm.	M. N. Khronopulo	1985
1st Deputy	. . . . . .		
Deputy	Rear Adm.	P. T. Zenchenko	1978
Deputy for Rear Services	Rear Adm.	N. A. Yermakov	1979
Chief of Staff	Rear Adm.	L. Y. Dvidenko	1981
Chief Political Department	Rear Adm.	A. Morozov	
Deputy for Combat Training	Rear Adm.	F. T. Starozhilov	1982
Chief of Staff	Vice Adm.	N. G. Klitnyy	1981
Chief Political Directorate	Rear Adm.	R. N. Likhvonin	1981
1st Deputy	Rear Adm.	V. I. Popov	1980
Deputy	Rear Adm.	S. Rybak	1981
Commander Naval Aviation	. . . . . .		
Chief of Staff	Lt. Gen. Aviation	F. G. Nefedov	1973
Chief Political Department	Maj. Gen. Aviation	Yu. Sinyakov	1975
Chief Hydrographic Directorate	Rear Adm.	L. I. Mitin	1979

CASPIAN FLOTILLA

Commander	Rear Adm.	V. V. Tolkachev	1984
1st Deputy	. . . . . .		
Deputy	Capt. 1st Rank	V. M. Zhuchkov	1976
Deputy for Rear Services	Capt. 1st Rank	B. R. Knyazchyan	1979
Chief of Staff	. . . . . .		
Chief Political Directorate	Capt. 1st Rank	V. Kalinin	1983

PACIFIC FLEET

Commander in Chief	Adm. Flt.	V. V. Sidorov	1981
1st Deputy	Vice Adm.	N. Ya. Yasakov	1979
Deputy	Engr. Vice Adm.	V. Novikov	1983
Deputy for Rear Services	Rear Adm.	I. Makhonin	1984
Chief Finance Service	Maj. Gen. Quartermaster	V. Novikov	1976
Deputy for Construction	Maj. Gen. Engr.	V. Skuratov	1980
Chief of Staff	Vice Adm.	G. A. Khvatov	1985
Deputy Chief	Rear Adm.	V. N. Perelygin	1978
Chief Observation & Communications Directorate	Rear Adm.	A. Morev	1981
Chief Political Directorate	Rear Adm.	A. M. Slavskiy	1984
1st Deputy	. . . . . .		
Deputy Chief	Rear Adm.	V. V. Abramov	1976
Deputy Chief	Rear Adm.	V. G. Semiletenko	1978
Chief Personnel Department	Rear Adm.	A. Shebanin	1977
Commander Naval Aviation	Lt. Gen. Aviation	Yu. S. Gudkov	1980
Deputy Commander	Maj. Gen. Aviation	P. Ryzhkov	1979
Chief Auxiliary Fleet	Rear Adm.	A. E. Yakimchik	1981

NAVAL EDUCATIONAL INSTITUTIONS

Leningrad Naval Academy	Vice Adm.	V. N. Ponikarovskiy	1981
Dzerzhinsky HNS (Engineering)	Vice Adm.	N. K. Yegorov	1975
Frunze HNS	Rear Adm.	N. K. Fedorov	1980
Kaliningrad HNS	Vice Adm.	V. S. Pilipenko	1970
Kiev HNS (Political)	Vice Adm.	N. S. Kaplunov	1980
Kirov Caspian HNS	Vice Adm.	V. A. Arkhipov	1976
Chairman, Sports Committee	Rear Adm.	V. Kandalintsev	
Lenin HNS (Engineering)	Engr. Vice Adm.	B. A. Lapshin	1975
Leninsky Komsomol HNS (Submarine Warfare)	Vice Adm.	G. L. Nevolin	1974
Makarov Pacific HNS	Rear Adm.	I. Karmadonov	1982
Nakhimov Black Sea HNS	. . . . . .		
Popov HNS (Radio-Electronics)	Vice Adm.	A. A. Rulyuk	1975
Sevastopol' HNS (Engineering)	Engr. Vice Adm.	A. A. Sarkisov	1972

MISCELLANEOUS ASSIGNMENTS

Editor, *Morskoy Sbornik*	Rear Adm.	A. Pushkin	
Military Attaché, Havana, Cuba	Rear Adm.	G. A. Mikhalov	1981
Naval Attaché, Washington, D.C.	Rear Adm.	I. P. Sakul'kin	1984

Abbreviations:
Adm. Fleet = Admiral of the Fleet
Adm. = Admiral
Vice Adm. = Vice Admiral
Rear Adm. = Rear Admiral
Lt. Gen. = General Lieutenant
Maj. Gen. = General Major
Capt. = Captain
Engr. = Engineer

B
Commanders in Chief of the Soviet Navy

Admiral of the Fleet of the Soviet Union Sergei Georgiyevich Gorshkov, twice Hero of the Soviet Union, served as commander in chief of the Soviet Navy from January 1956 until December 1985. He was succeeded by Admiral of the Fleet Vladimir Nikolayevich Chernavin, Hero of the Soviet Union, the change of command occurring on 6 December 1985, almost simultaneous with the launching of the first Soviet nuclear-propelled aircraft carrier and the keel laying of a second ship.[1]

The Soviet decision to construct large aircraft carriers could be viewed as the crowning achievement of Admiral Gorshkov's tenure of 29 years, 11 months, and 2 days as CinC of the Navy. During that period the Soviet Navy changed from essentially a coastal defense force to an oceangoing, multi-function fleet.

Admiral Gorshkov, born in 1910, had served in surface ships prior to World War II. Shortly after Germany invaded the Soviet Union in July 1941, he was promoted to flag rank and was given command of a cruiser division in the Black Sea. He was among the youngest of the Soviet flag officers, a situation caused by the massive purges of military and naval officers by Stalin during the late 1930s.

The rapid advance of German forces across the Ukraine led to the increasing importance of the Sea of Azov, and Gorshkov was assigned to command the flotilla of small craft on that inland sea. When the coastlines fell into German hands, the flotilla was abolished and in November 1942 he was assigned as naval deputy for the 47th Army, fighting in the Novorossiysk area. During this period he served under Generals R.Ya. Malinovskiy and A.A. Grechko, both later ministers of defense; he met Nikita Khrushchev, at that time a political officer in the area, and possibly encountered Leonid Brezhnev, also a political officer who saw combat in one of the amphibious landings in the area.

Subsequently, when the Azov Flotilla was reestablished in 1943, Gorshkov again took command, then commanded the Danube Flotilla during the Soviet campaign to recapture the Balkans. After the war he commanded units in the Black Sea and from August 1951 was commander in chief of the Black Sea Fleet. He held that position in the summer of 1955, when he was selected to come to Moscow as the 1st deputy CinC of the Navy and as the probable successor to Admiral N.G. Kuznetsov as CinC.

Admiral Gorshkov was advanced to his Navy's highest position because of his accomplishments and contacts: His contacts were men with whom he had worked or who knew of his reputation. According to Khrushchev's purported memoirs, "The question arose of whom we should appoint to replace Kuznetsov as commander in chief of the navy. We asked Malinovsky [a Khrushchev confidant and at the time CinC of Soviet Forces in the Far East], and he recommended Gorshkov. I knew Gorshkov only slightly; I'd met him at the end of the war when he was in charge of our river defenses. Malinovsky's recommendation was good enough for me."[2] The men who knew Gorshkov included Khrushchev's protégé Leonid Brezhnev, who had served briefly as head of the Political Administration of the Navy during 1953.

Gorshkov had a reputation for innovation; he was a tested combat leader, who had been in action with large ships as well as small craft; he had commanded troops ashore; and had experience in staff work. Khrushchev, in his memoirs at least, erred in his description of Gorshkov's background, writing: ". . . we counted it very much in his favor that he was a former submarine captain. He appreciated the role which German submarines had played in World War II by sinking so much English and American shipping, and he also appreciated the role which submarines could play for us in the event that we might have to go to war against Britain and the United States."[3]

(At the time of his appointment as CinC, Gorshkov was 46 years old. Of his six U.S. contemporaries who served as Chief of Naval Operations, Admiral E.R. Zumwalt had become CNO at age 49, Admiral James L. Holloway at age 52, Admirals Arleigh Burke and Thomas Hayward at age 54, Admirals George Anderson and James Watkins at age 55, and Admirals Leslie Macdonald and Thomas Moorer at age 57.)

In addition to being CinC of the Navy, Gorshkov was a 1st deputy minister of defense (the position later changed to simply deputy minister), the equivalent of the U.S. political-administrative position of Secretary of the Navy.

Gorshkov apparently was directed by Khrushchev to preside over the dismantling of the battleships and cruisers of the Stalin era, and to provide a cheaper, more technologically advanced fleet based on sub-

---

[1] The carrier was launched on 5 December 1985.

[2] Nikita Khrushchev, *Khrushchev Remembers, The Last Testament* (Boston: Little, Brown & Company, 1974), p. 28.
[3] Khrushchev, p. 31.

marines and missiles. The admiral succeeded in doing this and, in time, also building and deploying large warships. The KIEV-class VSTOL carriers are the largest warships yet completed in the Soviet Union; the KIROV-class battle cruisers are the largest surface warships other than aircraft carriers built by any nation since World War II. The now-building, full-deck carriers represent a still greater commitment of industrial facilities, raw materials, people, and other resources than any ships in history except for U.S. supercarriers.

Of equal significance, the Soviet large-ship programs have been undertaken with essentially no reduction in the important submarine, land-based aviation, and small combat programs. At the same time, three other cruiser-destroyer programs are under way, and the largest warships yet built for the KGB Maritime Border Troops are being constructed (Krivak III class).

The precise reasons why Admiral Gorshkov stepped down are not publicly known. Certainly the series of changes in national-political leadership in the Soviet Union following the death of Brezhnev in November 1982 and the subsequent changes in the commanders of three of the four other military services, coupled with Gorshkov's age (75) and reports of medical problems, lead to an opinion that no "dissatisfaction" or "political revolt" occurred. (Of Brezhnev's three successors, Yuri Andropov honored Gorshkov on 28 December 1982, presenting him with a second award of Hero of the Soviet Union, and on 26 February 1985, Konstantin Chernenko awarded Gorshkov his sixth Lenin Medal.)

Some observers, however, have seen the events as an indication of the Soviet leadership's displeasure with Gorshkov and his having been "relieved" because of his strong stand for an "independent" role for the Soviet Navy. This analysis sees Chernavin as more of a "team player."[4]

Admiral Gorshkov's replacement, Admiral Chernavin, sailed with a Soviet naval squadron for Tunisia four days after assuming his new post. Chernavin, age 57 at the time of his appointment, brings to the position extensive fleet and staff experience.

Chernavin served in submarines as a young officer, rising to command a nuclear-propelled unit and subsequently to command all submarines in the Northern Fleet. From 1972 to 1975 he reportedly was a deputy CinC of the Navy, although his specific responsibilities are unknown. He then returned to the important Northern Fleet as chief of staff and, from 1977 to 1981, as commander in chief.

In December 1981 he was given the most important staff positions in the Soviet Navy: that of chief of the Main Naval Staff, and at the same time, a 1st deputy CinC of the Navy. Heretofore there had been only one 1st deputy; from that point there were two—the other being Admiral of the Fleet N. I. Smirnov. But Smirnov was obviously no longer a contender for the position of CinC. (Admiral Smirnov, who has been 1st deputy CinC since 1974, was age 68 at the time of Chernavin's appointment.)

Accordingly, in December 1985 the watch was changed.

Admiral Gorshkov's tenure was remarkable for its accomplishments as well as for its longevity. Several efforts have been made to compare Admiral Gorshkov with "revolutionaries" in the West, in particular Admiral Sir John Fisher (British First Sea Lord from 1904–1910 and 1914–1915) and Admiral H. G. Rickover (head of the U.S. Navy's nuclear-propulsion program from the late 1940s to 1982). Obviously, Gorshkov had far more influence on the Soviet Navy than Fisher had on the Royal Navy, while Rickover's authority was limited to the development of nuclear-propelled ships and their crews, and his efforts to influence other aspects of the Navy were largely failures, Admiral Gorshkov held full responsibility for the development and operations of the total Soviet fleet.

According to one Western observer, "Gorshkov achieved his greatest success in connection with his . . . demand—that the Soviet Naval Fleet be used as a political tool of the state. Without actually deploying his divisions, the Soviet Union can today demonstrate its power throughout the world by means of its naval fleet. The presence of the Soviet Navy has limited the West's naval operational options. In addition, the Soviet Union is influencing the countries of the Third World, and its influence in this area is increasing.

"The build-up of the Soviet Naval Forces is not yet complete. There will be no dramatic changes in numbers, but the improvement of the deployment capabilities of the fleet will continue. The climax of the Soviet naval armament program is the construction of the aircraft carriers."[5]

Also significant, Admiral Gorshkov has provided his own service and the West with considerable detail on his views of the development and needs of naval power. His writings are unprecedented for a serving naval commander in chief; his book *The Sea Power of the State*, based on his earlier magazine series "Navies in War and in Peace," must be considered an invaluable text in this area, albeit from the Soviet perspective. (See appendix E.) These and other Gorshkov writings have been given various interpretations by Western analysts; they have been called the visible manifestations of major debates within the Soviet defense establishment as well as simple expositions of his views. Most likely, Gorshkov's writings were his means of informing the Soviet Navy (and to some extent the defense establishment) what was already decided in closed councils, and providing the rationale for such decisions. (In contrast to the prolific efforts of Gorshkov, there have been only a few substantive articles by U.S. secretaries of the Navy and chiefs of naval operations published during the same three decades.)

The following are the principal dates in the careers of Admirals Gorshkov and Chernavin:

Admiral S. G. Gorshkov   (born 26 February 1910)

1927–1931	attended Frunze Higher Naval School
1931–1932	navigator in destroyer FRUNZE (Black Sea Fleet)
1932–1936	flag navigator of minesweeping and harbor defense brigade (Pacific Fleet); commanding officer of guard ship BURUN (Pacific Fleet)

---

[4] Two recent commentaries on this subject are Dr. Robert C. Suggs, "Silently, In Darkness and Fog," U.S. Naval Institute *Proceedings* (June 1986), pp. 40–48, and Captain William H.J. Manthorpe, Jr., USN (Ret), "The Soviet View," U.S. Naval Institute *Proceedings* (June 1986), pp. 138–139.

[5] Ulrich-Joachim Schulz-Torge, "Sergei G. Gorshkov—the end of an era!" *Military Technology* (1/86, 1986), p. 139.

	1937	attended course for destroyer commanding officers (Pacific Fleet)
	1938	commanding officer of destroyer
	1939	chief of staff destroyer brigade (Pacific Fleet)
	1939	commander of destroyer brigade (Black Sea Fleet)
	1941	attended command course at Voroshilov Naval Academy
Sep	1941	promoted to rear admiral
Oct	1941–Nov 1942	commander Azov Flotilla
	1942	admitted to Communist Party
Nov	1942–1943	deputy commander of Novorossiysk area and acting commander of 47th Army
	1943–1944	commander Azov Flotilla
Apr	1944–Dec 1944	commander Danube Flotilla
Sep	1944	promoted to vice admiral
	1945–1948	commander of squadron (eskadra) in Black Sea
	1948–1951	chief of staff Black Sea Fleet
Aug	1951–June 1955	commander in chief Black Sea Fleet
	1954	promoted to admiral
July	1955–Jan 1956	1st deputy commander in chief of Soviet Navy
Jan	1956	appointed commander in chief of Soviet Navy and 1st deputy minister of defense*
	1956	elected candidate member of Central Committee
	1961	elected full member of Central Committee
	1962	promoted to admiral of the fleet
Oct	1967	promoted to admiral of the fleet of the Soviet Union
Dec	1985	retired

Admiral V. N. Chernavin (Born 22 April 1928)

	1947–1950	attended Frunze Higher Naval School
	1951–1958	navigation division in submarine (Baltic Fleet); deputy commanding officer of submarine (Northern Fleet)
	1959	commanding officer of nuclear-propelled submarine (Northern Fleet)
	1964–1965	attended Grechko Naval Academy
	1968–1969	attended Voroshilov General Staff Academy
	1970	commanding officer of nuclear-propelled submarine (Northern Fleet)
Sep	1970	deputy commander for combat training of submarine unit (Northern Fleet)
	1970	promoted to rear admiral
	1970–1972	chief of staff, submarine force; commander, submarine force (Northern Fleet)
	1972–1975	deputy commander in chief Soviet Navy [one of several]
Apr	1975	promoted to vice admiral
	1975–July 1977	chief of staff Northern Fleet
July	1977–Nov 1981	commander in chief Northern Fleet
Feb	1978	promoted to admiral
Dec	1981–Dec 1985	chief of the main naval staff and 1st deputy commander in chief of the Soviet Navy
Nov	1983	promoted to admiral of the fleet
Dec	1985	promoted to commander in chief of the Soviet Navy

* Subsequently changed to deputy minister of defense.

The Soviet Navy's leadership has continually stressed submarine development; the new Commander in Chief of the Soviet Navy, Admiral Chernavin, a nuclear submarine veteran, can be expected to continue—and possibly accelerate—the rate of submarine development. In particular, large-scale production of new SSNs, like this Akula, may be forthcoming.

C
Soviet Naval Order of Battle, 1945–1985

This appendix lists the major ships of the Soviet Navy in active service at five-year intervals since the end of World War II. Sources vary as to the numbers because of differing methodologies of keeping track of Soviet warships, different dates for data in the various categories, and other counting problems.

	1945	1950	1955	1960	1965	1970	1975	1980	1985
Submarines—Nuclear									
SSBN	—	—	—	1	9	31	60	70	63
SSGN	—	—	—	—	20	36	40	45	50
SSN	—	—	—	3	15	23	40	55	86
SSQN	—	—	—	—	—	—	—	—	1
AGSSN	—	—	—	—	—	—	—	1	3
Submarines—Diesel									
SSB	—	—	—	13	29	25	23	17	15
SSG	—	—	—	1	25	33	25	25	16
SS/SSQ/SSR	—	—	117	285	259	208	143	155	143
SST/AGSS	—	—	—	—	—	4	4	few	15–20
Pre-1950 Designs	241	286	249	131	—	—	—	—	—
(Total Submarines)	(241)	(286)	(366)	(434)	(357)	(360)	(335)	(372)	(395)
Aircraft Carriers	—	—	—	—	—	—	1	2	3
Helicopter Carriers	—	—	—	—	—	2	2	2	2
Battleships	3	2	2	—	—	—	—	—	—
Heavy Cruisers (180 mm guns)	7	7	7	5	2	2	—	—	—
Light Cruisers (150–152 mm guns)	2	6	21	20	12	9	11	11	11
Guided Missile Cruisers	—	—	—	—	6	10	19	24	29
Destroyers	41	52	115	120	81	44	36	30	48
Guided Missile Destroyers	—	—	—	—	6	26	35	36	34
Guided Missile Destroyers (SSM only)	—	—	—	6	12	10	1	1	1
Guided Missile Frigates (Krivak class)	—	—	—	—	—	1	10	27	32
Frigates/Ocean Escorts	19	29	67	88	56	45	} 106	} 135	} 160
Light Frigates	—	—	—	—	34	64			

D
Soviet Ship Transfers

The Soviet Union is the principal supplier of arms to the Third World, including surface ships and submarines.[1] The current Soviet ship transfer policy has none of the constraints seen in Western arms policies. The Soviets provide weapons to nations that are allies, neutrals, or even historically aligned with the West; they will provide new as well as used weapons; the recipient countries may or may not be capable of operating the weapons; and the terms of payment are highly flexible.

From the Soviet viewpoint, arms transfers have up to five purposes: they can (1) earn hard foreign currency for ships that are built in Soviet or Eastern European shipyards for "soft" rubles; (2) provide the means for establishing a training-support infrastructure in the host country; (3) increase the receiving country's dependency upon the Soviet Union for spare parts and other logistics support; (4) provide a potential weapons reserve in the region for Soviet forces; and (5) cause problems for the West.

In many respects the last is the most significant, as evidenced by the cost to the United States of Soviet weapons supplied to North Vietnam during the 1962–1972 conflict, and the more recent arms transfers to such countries as Cuba, Grenada, and Nicaragua.

These arms transfers have not, however, been without problems for the Soviet Union. In some cases recipients have not been able to pay as promised or pay in hard currencies, causing a financial loss to the Soviets. By Western standards, the training and support personnel assigned to Third World countries have been of poor quality, while spare parts have been in short supply. The results has been dissatisfied customers, and in some instances has strained relations between the Soviets and their clients.

But at the same time, by establishing major support and even production facilities overseas, as in India (for ships and aircraft) and Peru (for aircraft), the Soviets have made important political-military inroads in those countries. Also, such facilities and spare parts stores could be used under certain conditions by Soviet forces operating in the region.

The current Soviet arms transfer policy had its beginnings shortly after the death of Josef Stalin in 1953. Under the Stalin regime Moscow viewed the world as bi-polar: a nation was either in the Soviet camp or was against it. Only China, North Korea, and allied Eastern European nations received ships as part of Soviet military assistance in the first decade after World War II.

Stalin's successors, led by Nikita Khrushchev, saw political and economic advantages in recognizing the "third" world of so-called non-aligned nations. The first major Soviet arms transfer was announced in 1955, with the arms going to Egypt with Czechoslovakia as the intermediary. Previously the Egyptians had been dependent upon Britain for arms. This Soviet arms agreement—valued as high as $200 million by some sources—was thus significant for breaking a Western monopoly as well as for its size. The agreement was in essence a barter deal with the Egyptian government to pay for the arms with cotton and rice over a 12-year period. Thus, for more than a decade, a good percentage of the major Egyptian crops was pledged for arms that were, in the view of some authorities, of poor quality. Moreover, most of the arms that were transferred in the first year were lost in the October 1956 conflict between Egypt and Israel and the ensuing Anglo-French invasion of Suez. After the 1956 war the Egyptians continued to rely on the Soviets for weapons.

There were naval arms involved in the initial Egyptian deals. Over the next 15 years, a large fleet was provided to Egypt: several submarines of the Whiskey and Romeo classes, Skoryy-class destroyers, Komar and then Osa missile boats, torpedo boats, patrol craft, and landing craft. The Komars, each armed with two SS-N-2 Styx anti-ship missiles, made history on 21 October 1967, when, from the safety of Alexandria harbor, a pair of the boats launched missiles that sank the Israeli destroyer ELATH. That was the first sinking of a ship by guided missiles fired from another ship.[2]

By the early 1970s the Egyptian Navy had 12 submarines plus the destroyers (albeit outdated) and missile and torpedo boats, providing a considerable naval capability—at least on paper. In addition, the Soviets transferred Tu-16 Badger strike aircraft armed with AS-1 Kennel missiles, Be-12 Mail and Il-38 May patrol/anti-submarine aircraft, and An-12 Cub electronic reconnaissance aircraft. The patrol and electronic aircraft flew with Soviet crews.

[1] In overall military arms transfers for 1984—the last year for which comprehensive data are available—the Soviet Union exported a total of $9.4 billion in arms to other nations, of which $8.6 billion went to the so-called developing or Third World nations. In comparison, U.S. arms transfers in 1984 totalled $7.7 billion, of which $4.8 billion went to developing countries. During the last five years the Soviets have averaged more than $11 billion per year in arms transfers.

[2] The first sinking of a warship by guided missiles occurred in September 1943 when German aircraft launched guided bombs to sink the Italian battleship ROMA.

The HAMEENMAA is the largest warship in the Finnish Navy. The former Soviet Riga-class frigate has been provided a twin 30-mm gun mount on her bow; a sister ship has been stricken. A variety of such old as well as new Soviet ships are operated by non-Warsaw pact navies. (L. & L. Van Ginderen)

A Cuban Turya-class hydrofoil torpedo craft. The Soviets have provided Cuba with air and naval forces suitable for interdicting U.S. merchant shipping in the Caribbean in time of war.

The Indian Foxtrot-class submarine KARANJ. When this edition went to press, India was receiving its first Soviet-built submarines of the more-advanced Kilo class. (Giorgio Arra)

The Arab nations have been major recipients of Soviet arms, with a major buildup of the Syrian Navy now under way. This Syrian Petya II was photographed off the Dardanelles; she and a sister ship have been followed by Romeo-class submarines plus a Natya-class corvette and missile boats. (L. & L. Van Ginderen)

Soviet military assistance to Egypt ended in 1972, when Soviet advisors and air-defense units were ordered out of the country. (The aircraft flown by Soviet crews returned to the Soviet Union at that time.) Although the Egyptians subsequently turned to the West as well as to China for arms, the Soviets continue to make most of their arms sales to the Middle East. By dollar volume more than one-third of the Soviet arms sales during 1979–1983 went to Middle East nations—estimated at $20 billion by the U.S. government. The primary Soviet customers in the Middle East are Iraq, Libya, and Syria. (U.S. transfers to the Middle East in that five-year period were $14 billion, while those of other NATO nations totaled $18 billion.) The other major areas receiving Soviet arms are Africa (almost $14 billion in 1979–1983), Eastern Europe ($6.8 billion), East Asia ($6.5 billion), Southeast Asia ($5.3 billion), and Latin America ($3.6 billion).

The only other nation to receive as large a Soviet fleet as the Egyptians was Indonesia. During the Sukarno regime, from the late 1950s ship transfers to Indonesia included a SVERDLOV-class cruiser, at 17,200-tons the largest warship ever transferred by the Soviet Navy, a dozen Whiskey-class submarines, several destroyers, and lesser craft. Again,

the terms of the deal were simple, with long repayment periods. Yet the capability of the receiving navy to operate the equipment was highly questionable; reportedly, some of the ships never left port under the Indonesian flag.

Some of the Soviet arms agreements had significant naval implications even if only minor naval craft were involved. For example, in the 1968–1976 period the Soviets provided Somalia with several torpedo boats and a Polnocny landing ship. In return, the airfield at Berbera was enlarged to handle strike aircraft, and a Soviet missile assembly facility was built. Because of Somalia's location at the southern entrance to the Red Sea and the Suez Canal, this Soviet presence had major strategic implications for the West. (Somalia's going to war against Ethiopian-backed rebels in 1977 caused embarrassment to the Soviets because of Ethiopia's Marxist government; Soviet aid to Somalia ended and the estimated 1,500 Soviet and Cuban advisors were expelled.)

Since the mid-1950s 33 nations have received Soviet naval ships and submarines. Some, like Somalia, no longer have diplomatic relations with the Soviet Union. The ships transferred during those 30 years are shown in table D-1. All of the landing ships transferred by the Soviet

Union—one Ropucha LST and 31 Polnocny LSMs—were built in Poland.

Foreign-built ships of these types are among the several that the Soviets have available for transfer. The others are new construction specifically for foreign navies, new construction of the types of ships in production for the Soviet Navy, and units that have seen service under the Soviet naval ensign.

The most impressive of new-construction ships being built for transfer are the 4,950-ton modified Kashin-class destroyers that are going to India. The 61 Kommuna shipyard at Nikolayev on the Black Sea had by 1986 delivered four Kashins to the Indian Navy and at least two more are being built. Another batch of at least three larger ships—probably a variation of the Kresta II cruiser class—is on order from the Soviet Union as are Kilo-class submarines.

Also being built for foreign transfer is the 1,900-ton, Koni-class frigate or patrol ship. This ship, oriented toward anti-submarine warfare, may have initially been intended for Soviet service. Only the lead ship, however, was retained by the Soviet Navy, apparently for training foreign crews. The ten additional units built to date have been transferred to Algeria, Cuba, East Germany, Libya, and Yugoslavia. The Yugoslav ships have additionally been fitted with four Styx anti-ship missiles.

Another new warship that has become a major foreign sale item is the Kilo-class submarine. This diesel-electric craft, with a submerged displacement of 3,000 tons, was introduced into the Soviet Navy in 1982. Production is under way at three shipyards in the Soviet Union and at least nine units are in Soviet service. The first foreign transfers, in 1986, were to Poland and India. No other diesel submarines are being built in the Soviet Union, and while older units are available for transfer, from 1967 to 1983 the Foxtrot production line was kept open to build 17 units for Cuba, India, and Libya. All of these nations are candidates for additional diesel submarines, as are Syria, which received two Romeo-class submarines late in 1985, and Vietnam.

A number of other ship classes that are being built for the Soviet Navy are also being transferred. In some instances there are significant modifications for foreign use. For example, Nanuchka-class missile corvettes being sold have the Styx missile in place of the more-capable SS-N-9 of Soviet units, and the Square Tie targeting radar instead of the Band Stand (although the lesser radar is housed in the same dome).

In the 1980s very few older, used ships are being transferred by the Soviets. Rather, the Soviet government is committed to providing relatively modern and capable ships to its allies and to non-aligned nations. This policy will continue to cause problems for the West while garnering several benefits for the Soviet Union and the Soviet Navy.

TABLE D-1. SOVIET SHIP TRANSFERS

SUBMARINES

Golf		1 assembled in China with Soviet components (1964)
Malyta V	China	4 (1954–55)
	Poland	6 (1956–57)
S-class	China	2 (1955)
Whiskey	Albania	4 (1960–61)
	Bulgaria	2 (1958)
	China	5 (1956–57) + units built in China
	Cuba	1 (1979)*
	Egypt	6 (1957–62 + 2 replacements in 1972)
	Indonesia	12 (1959–62)
	North Korea	4 (1960s)
	Poland	4 (1962–65)
Romeo†	Algeria	2 (1982–83)
	Bulgaria	2 (1971–72)
	Egypt	6 (1966–69)
	Syria	2 (1985)
Foxtrot	Cuba	3 (1979, 1980, 1984)
	India	8 (1968–74)
	Libya	6 (1976–83)
Kilo	India	1 (1986) more on order
	Poland	1 (1986) more on order

CRUISERS

Sverdlov	Indonesia	1 (1962 ex-Soviet Orzhonikidze)
Mod. Kresta II	India	(3 reported on order)

GUIDED MISSILE DESTROYERS

SAM Kotlin	Poland	1 (1970)
Mod. Kashin	India	3 (1980–83 + 3 on order)

DESTROYERS

Skoryy	Egypt	6 (2, 1956; 2, 1962; 2, 1967)
	Poland	2 (1957, 1958)
	Indonesia	7 (1959–64)
Gordy	China	4 (1954–55)

FRIGATES

Riga	Bulgaria	2 (1957–58)
	East Germany	5 (1957–58)
	Finland	2 (1964)
	China	4 (1954–57) + 4 units built in China
	Ethiopia	2 (1964 ??)
	Indonesia	6 (1962–64)
Petya II	Ethiopia	2 (1983–84)
	India	10 (1969–75)
	Syria	2 (1975)
	Vietnam	5 (2, 1978; 2, 1981)

CORVETTES

Koni	Algeria	3 (1980–84)
	Cuba	2 (1981, 1984)
	East Germany	2 (1978, 1979)
	Libya	2 (1985)
	Yugoslavia	2 (1980, 1983)

* Transferred for use as battery-charging barge; not operational.
† Romeo-class submarines also built in China and North Korea.

CORVETTES (continued)

Poti	Bulgaria	3 (1975)
	Poland	3 (1970)
	Romania	3 (1970)
Nanuchka II	Algeria	4 (1980–83)
	India	3 (1976–78 + 3 on order)
	Libya	4 (1981–85)
Tarantul I	East Germany	2+ (1984–)
	Poland	2+ (1984–)

MISSILE BOATS

Komar	Algeria	6 (1967)
	China	7–8 (1960–61) + units built in China
	Cuba	18 (1962–66)
	Egypt	7 (1962–67) + units built in Egypt
	Indonesia	12 (1961–65)
	Iraq	3 (1972)
	North Korea	10
	Syria	9 (1963–66)
	North Vietnam	4 (1972)
Osa I	Algeria	3 (1967)
	Benin	2 (1979)
	Bulgaria	3 (1970–71)
	China	4 (1960s) + units built in China
	Cuba	6 (1972–74)
	Egypt	10 (1966)
	East Germany	15 (1966)
	India	8 (1971)
	Iraq	6 (1971–74)
	North Korea	12 (1968–73) + units built in North Korea
	Poland	13 (1960s)
	Romania	6 (1964)
	Syria	8 (1966)
	Yugoslavia	10 (1965–69)
Osa II	Algeria	9 (1976–80)
	Angola	6 (1982–83)
	Bulgaria	2 (1978, 1982)
	Cuba	13 (1977–82)
	Ethiopia	4 (1978–82)
	Finland	4 (1975)
	India	8 (1976)
	Iraq	8 (1974–77)
	Libya	12 (1976–80)
	Somalia	2 (1975)
	Syria	12 (1978–85)
	Vietnam	8 (1979–81)
	South Yemen	8 (1979–83)
	North Yemen	2 (1982)

TORPEDO BOATS

(Some units delivered without torpedo tubes for use as patrol boats.)

P-4	Albania	6 (1956) + 6 from China (1965)
	Benin	2 (1979)
	Bulgaria	8 (1956)
	China	few (1950s + units built in China
	Cuba	12 (1962–64)
	Cyprus	6 (1964–65)
	Egypt	4 from Syria (1970)
	East Germany	27 (1957–58)
	North Korea	12 (1952–53)
	Romania	12
	Somalia	4 (1972)

	Syria	17 (1958–60)
	Tanzania	4 (1972–73)
	North Yemen	4 (1, 1960; 3, 1970–71)
	South Yemen	4
	North Vietnam	14 (1961–64)
P-6	Algeria	10 (1963–68)
	China	few + units built in China
	Cuba	12 (1962)
	Egypt	20 (1956–68)
	East Germany	27 (1957–60)
	Guinea	4 (1965–67)
	Guinea-Bissau	4 (1975–76)
	Indonesia	14 (1961–62)
	Iraq	10 (1960–62)
	North Korea	few + several from China + units built in North Korea
	Poland	20 (1957–58)
	Somalia	4 (1968)
	Tanzania	3 from East Germany (1974–75)
	North Vietnam	3 (1967)
	South Yemen	2 (1973)
Shershen	Angola	5 (1977–83)
	Bulgaria	6 (1970–71)
	Cape Verde Islands	2 (1979)
	Congo	1 (1979)
	Egypt	6 (1967–68)
	East Germany	18 (1968–76)
	Guinea	3 (1978–79)
	Guinea-Bissau	1 (1978)
	North Korea	4 (1973–74)
	Vietnam	14 (1979–83)
	Yugoslavia	4 (1965) + 10 units built in Yugoslavia
MOL	Ethiopia	2 (1978)
	Somalia	4 (1976)
	South Yemen	2 (1978)
	Sri Lanka	1 (1975)
Turya	Cuba	8 (1979–83)
	Kampuchia	1 (1984)
	Vietnam	14 (1979–83)

PATROL CRAFT

Artillerist	North Korea	1–2 (1950)
M.O. IV	North Korea	20 (1957–60)
	Bulgaria	10
	Nigeria	3 (1967)
	Guinea	4 (?) (1972–75)
S.O.-1	Algeria	6 (1965–67)
	Bulgaria	6 (1963–64)
	China	2 (1960)
	Cuba	12 (1964–67)
	East Germany	16 (1960–61)
	Egypt	12 (1962–67)
	Iraq	3 (1962)
	North Korea	6 (1957–61) + 9 units built in North Korea
	Mozambique	2
	North Vietnam	8+ (1980–83)
	South Yemen	2 (1972)
Kronshtadt	Albania	4 (1961)
	Bulgaria	2 (1957)
	China	6 (1955)
	Cuba	6 (1962)
	Indonesia	14 (1958)

PATROL CRAFT (continued)

	Poland	6 (3, 1950; 3, 1956)
	Romania	3 (1950)
Stenka	Cuba	4 (1985)
Zhuk	Algeria	1 (1981)
	Angola	2 (1977)
	Benin	5 (1979–80)
	Bulgaria	5 (1980–81)
	Cape Verde Islands	1 (1980)
	Congo	3 (1982)
	Cuba	27 (1972–84)
	Ethiopia	2 (1982)
	Iraq	5 (1975)
	Mauritius	2 (1980s)
	Mozambique	6 (1979–81)
	Nicaragua	2 from Algeria (1982–83)
	Seychelles	2 (1981–82)
	Syria	12 (1981–85)
	Vietnam	6 (1978–79)
	North Yemen	4 (1978–80)
	South Yemen	2 (1975)

AMPHIBIOUS SHIPS

Ropucha	South Yemen	1 (1980) built in Poland
*Polnocny-C	India	4 (1975–76) + 6 on order
	Iraq	4 (1977–79)
	Libya	3 (1977–79)
	Syria	1 (1984)
*Polnocny-B	Angola	3 (1977–79)
	Cuba	2 (1982)
	Ethiopia	2 (1981, 1983)
	Vietnam	3 (1979–80)
	South Yemen	4 (1973–79)
*Polnocny-A	Algeria	1 (1976)
	Egypt	3 (1974)
	India	2 (1966)
	Somalia	1 (1976)
	Vietnam	1 (1979)
	South Yemen	1 (1979)
T-4	Angola	5 (1976)
	Cuba	6 (1967–74)
	Ethiopia	4 (1977–78)
	Guinea	4 (1974)
	Guinea-Bissau	4 (1975–78)
	Kampuchia	2 (1985)
	Somalia	4 (2, 1968; 2, 1979)
	North Vietnam	15 (1967–69)
	North Yemen	2 (1970)
	South Yemen	5 (3, 1970; 2, 1982)
MP-4	Egypt	1 (1970?)
MP-6	Indonesia	1 (about 1962)
Vydra	Bulgaria	24 (2, 1956; 10, 1970; 12, 1977–79)
	Egypt	10 (1967–69)
SMB-I	Egypt	4 (1965)

MINESWEEPERS

T-43	Albania	2 (1960s)
	Algeria	2 (1968)

	Bulgaria	2 (1953)
	China	4 (1954 55) + about 20 units built in China
	Egypt	3 (1956–59 + 3 1970s)
	Indonesia	12 (1962–64)
	Iraq	2 (1969)
	Poland	4 + 12 units built in Poland 1955–60
	Syria	2 (1962?)
T-58	Guinea	1 (1979)
	South Yemen	1 (1978)
T-301	Albania	6 (1957–60)
	Bulgaria	4 (1955)
	Egypt	2 (1962, 1963)
	Indonesia	1 (about 1962)
	Poland	8 (1957)
	Romania	14 (1956–59)
Natya	India	6 (1978–80)
	Libya	7 (1981–85)
Yurka	Egypt	4 (1970–71)
	Vietnam	1 (1979)
Vanya	Bulgaria	4 (1970–71)
	Syria	2 (1972)
Sonya	Bulgaria	1 (1983)
	Cuba	2 (1980, 1985)
Yevgenya	Bulgaria	4+ (1977–)
	Cuba	11 (1978–84)
	India	6 (1983–1984)
	Iraq	3 (1975)
	Syria	1 (1978)
	North Yemen	2 (1982)
K-8	Cuba	1 (1978) built in Poland
	Poland	22 (some possibly built in Poland)
	Vietnam	5 (1980) built in Poland

TORPEDO RECOVERY CRAFT/PATROL CRAFT

Poluchat I*	Albania	1 (1958)
	Algeria	1 (1979)
	Angola	2 (1979)
	Bangladesh	1 (1973)
	Congo	2 (1978–79)
	Egypt	2
	Ethiopia	1 (1982)
	Ghana	4 (1967)
	Guinea	2 (1972, 1973)
	Guinea-Bissau	2 (1978)
	India	5 (1967–69)
	Iraq	2 (1966)
	Mozambique	1 (1977)
	Somalia	6 (5, 1966–67; 1, 1977)
	Tanzania	1 (1970s)
	Vietnam	2 (1963)
	North Yemen	4 (1970)
	South Yemen	1 (1970s)

AUXILIARY SHIPS

A large number of auxiliary ships built in the Soviet Union and Poland have been transferred to other Warsaw Pact as well as Third World nations.

---

* 23 additional Polnocny-class used by Polish Navy; all ships of this class built in Poland.

*Virtually all of these craft are employed in the role of patrol craft.

E
Reading List

This appendix describes writings about the Soviet Navy and Soviet sea power since World War II that are available in English.

At the end of World War II—almost four decades ago—Soviet dictator Josef Stalin initiated a massive naval buildup. The West knew little of the details of this buildup, and there was a dearth of English-language writings on the Soviet Navy. Little of what was happening behind the "iron curtain" was known in the West, and in the opinion of many of the contemporary observers, little that was happening was worthy of note. That judgment was based more on the indications of the quality of Stalin's fleet-building program and not the quantity, which was, in some respects, remarkable for any country in peacetime.

For the first two decades after the war, only three significant works appeared. Marin Mitchell's *The Maritime History of Russia 848–1948* (London: Sidgwick and Jackson Limited, 1949) had little coverage of the Soviet period. However, there were discussions of naval and ship-building matters, and of the personalities that affected postwar developments.

More useful was M.G. Saunder's *The Soviet Navy* (New York: Praeger Publishers, 1958), which comprised a set of essays by Western naval officers, analysts, and journalists. Saunders, a commander in the Royal Navy, provided a most valuable overview in his introduction to the book.

The first significant American effort in this field was Robert Waring Herrick's *Soviet Naval Strategy* (Annapolis, Md.: U.S. Naval Institute, 1968). With the subtitle "Fifty Years of Theory and Practice," Herrick's heavily annotated work suggested that the Soviet Navy was defensively oriented. The book encountered significant opposition within the U.S. Navy, which was attempting to rationalize new ships and aircraft on the basis of the emerging Soviet threat, especially the new missile-armed ships and nuclear submarines being produced under the direction of Admiral S.G. Gorshkov, who had become commander in chief of the Navy and a deputy minister of defense in January 1956. Herrick, a retired U.S. naval intelligence officer had, like Saunders, served in Moscow as an assistant attaché. A lengthy version of Herrick's thesis was also published in the U.S. Naval Institute's annual *Naval Review 1967*.

Similar to the book situation, there were few articles on the Soviet Navy appearing in Western publications into the early 1960s, and those were mostly superficial or historical, and in some instances, both.

This situation began to change radically in the 1960s as the Soviet Navy significantly increased at-sea (out-of-area) operations, making their ships and aircraft more visible to Western observers. Also, enhanced Western intelligence-collection activities by these observers provided Western navies with much more information about the Soviet fleet. A steady flow of books and articles on Soviet naval and maritime subjects began in the 1960s, and the flow continues unabated. In addition to the specific books listed below, the so-called "Dalhousie papers" are recommended reading. These are published collections of papers presented at a series of conferences on the Soviet Navy chaired by Michael MccGwire, a formal Royal Navy intelligence officer, at Dalhousie University, Halifax. (MccGwire also served as an assistant naval attaché in Moscow.) The papers, by many of the leading Western analysts of Soviet naval developments, have been published as *Soviet Naval Developments: Capability and Context* (1973), *Soviet Naval Policy: Objectives and Constraints* (1975), and *Soviet Naval Influence: Domestic and Foreign Dimensions* (1977), all by Praeger Publishers, New York. Together, these volumes cover most aspects of the Soviet Navy, most of them in a scholarly manner.

(Several years later MccGwire summarized his views in the May 1980/Naval Review issue of the Naval Institute *Proceedings* under the title "The Rationale for the Development of Soviet Seapower." A complementary, albeit different, view is provided in a comprehensive article by Dr. Norman Friedman, "The Soviet Fleet in Transition" in the May 1983/Naval Review issue.)

More recent assessments of the "Future of the Soviet Navy" from a 1984 conference, sponsored in part by the U.S. Defense Intelligence College, have been published under that title (Boulder, Colo.: Westview Press, 1986). The essays are by Messrs. John Jordan (submarines), Friedman (carriers), Norman Polmar (surface ships), A.D. Baker III (small combatants), Frank Uhlig, Jr. (amphibious), Jan S. Breemer (mine warfare), and Commander Bruce W. Watson, USN (evolution of strategy).

One other set of conference papers, while now somewhat dated, made a significant contribution to the understanding of Soviet naval issues. Published as the *The Soviet Union in Europe and the Near East: Her Capabilities and Intentions* (London: Royal United Service Institution), this was the result of a seminar sponsored by Southampton University and the RUSI at Milford-on-Sea in March 1970.

WESTERN BOOKS

Among the books that appear to have significance in this field are: Captain Robert B. Bathurst, USN (Ret.), *Understanding the Soviet Navy: A Handbook* (Newport, R.I.: Naval War College Press, 1979), an effort to put the modern Soviet Navy into perspective as a navy and an institution; this soft-cover book is by a retired U.S. Navy captain and intelligence specialist.

Alexander Boyd, *The Soviet Air Force Since 1918* (London: Macdonald and Jane's, 1977). This is probably the best of several books on the Soviet air force; the subject is significant because of the position of Soviet naval aviation within the overall scheme of Soviet "air power."

James Cable, *Gunboat Diplomacy* (New York: Praeger Publishers, 1971). This is an excellent analysis of this subject with appropriate coverage of Soviet efforts; a revised edition appeared in 1981 (New York: St. Martin's Press).

John Erickson, *The Soviet High Command 1918–1941* (London: Macmillan, 1962). Professor Erickson, the dean of analysts of the Soviet defense establishment, covers the development of that establishment and the Soviet military philosophy behind it that continues to prevail today. Although Erickson's research and coverage of the Soviet Navy is limited, he has written a useful—but now quite dated—essay "The Soviet Naval High Command" for the *Naval Review 1973*. Erickson's *Soviet Military Power* (Washington, D.C.: United States Strategic Institute, 1973) is a soft-cover volume with a valuable overview of the Soviet armed forces. It is an updated version of the author's *Soviet Military Power* published by the RUSI in 1971.

David Fairhall, *Russian Sea Power* (Boston: Gambit, 1971). Fairhall, an English journalist, provides a highly readable account stressing Soviet commercial activities at sea. (The English edition's title, *Russia Looks to the Sea,* was closer to the mark; the American cover shows a Soviet submarine missile streaking skyward—an example of a misreading of the coverage of the book by the publisher.)

Robin Higham and Jacob W. Kipp, eds. *Soviet Aviation and Air Power* (Boulder, Colo.: Westview Press, 1977). This is a collection of essays on Soviet aviation, albeit mostly historical, with adequate mention of the naval air arm.

David R. Jones, ed, *The Military-Naval Encyclopedia of Russia and the Soviet Union* (Gulf Breeze, Fla.: Academic International Press). This ambitious project, relying extensively on Russian-language sources, is historically oriented, but does cover the post–World War II period. Four volumes (through *Adzhariia*) have been published, with the articles mostly by members of the academic community, relying extensively on Russian sources. Of particular value in these early volumes are the discussions of Soviet shipyards (mostly under "Admiralty" listings).

John Jordan, *Soviet Surface Fleet* (London: Arms and Armour press, 1983). The author provides detailed and particularly well-illustrated discussions of the features of modern Soviet aircraft carriers, cruisers, and destroyers.

Captain John Moore, RN (Ret.), *The Soviet Navy Today* (London: Macdonald and Jane's, 1975) sought to provide a single-volume overview of the Soviet Navy with basic data listings on Soviet ships and aircraft.

Norman Polmar, *Soviet Naval Power—Challenge for the 1970s* (New York: Crane, Russak & Company, 1972). This second edition of a college text, by the author of this volume, describes Soviet naval developments since World War II in a simplified style.

Harriet Fast Scott and William Scott, *The Armed Forces of the USSR* (Boulder, Colo.: Westview Press, 1979). While not specifically emphasizing the Soviet Navy (and there are some errors in the naval section), this is a detailed and highly annotated description of the structure of the Soviet military establishment. Both authors served in the U.S. embassy in Moscow, he for two tours as U.S. Air Force attaché. (The Scotts have also produced several excellent articles on Soviet command and organization for *Air Force* magazine.)

James D. Theberge, *Soviet Seapower in the Caribbean: Political and Strategic Implications* (New York: Praeger Publishers, 1972). This volume is limited in scope and to some extent overtaken by events, but it does explain Soviet naval efforts in this area and their significance.

Edward L. Warner III, *The Military in Contemporary Soviet Politics* (New York: Praeger Publishers, 1977). This "institutional analysis" is more philosophical than the Scotts' work, and covers more of the institutional factors. However, it is useful and heavily annotated.

U.S. Department of Defense, *Soviet Military Power* (Washington, D.C.: Government Printing Office, 1986). This is the fifth edition (first published in September 1981) of a heavily illustrated, impressive exposition by the Secretary of Defense on the Soviet "threat." Produced to help support the administration's defense programs, these "slick," soft-cover volumes provide significant data on Soviet naval issues while they are "hard line" in the message.

U.S. Navy, *Understanding Soviet Navy Developments* (Washington, D.C.: Government Printing Office, April 1985). This is the fifth edition of a basic reference book on the Soviet Navy, first published in 1974. Prepared by the Director of U.S. Naval Intelligence and Chief of Information, this soft-cover book is a valuable introduction to the subject, although lacking specifics. The book is also published in a hard-cover, updated edition by the Nautical & Aviation Publishing Co. (Baltimore, Md.).

Bruce Watson's *Red Navy at Sea* (Boulder, Colo.: Westview Press, 1982), subtitled "Soviet Naval Operations on the High Seas, 1956–1980," is an excellent description and assessment of Soviet fleet operations, with emphasis on port visits and their political-military significance. Watson is a commander in the U.S. Navy.

Commander Bruce W. Watson, USN, and Sue Watson, ed., *The Soviet Navy: Strengths and Liabilities* (Boulder, Colo.: Westview Press, 1986). This is a collection of essays that vary greatly in quality and provide little new material.

Two other books are often cited in bibliographies of Soviet naval matters: Rear Admiral Ernest M. Eller, USN (Ret.), *The Soviet Sea Challenge* (Chicago: Crowles Book Co., 1972) and Donald W. Mitchell's *A History of Russian and Soviet Sea Power* (New York: Macmillan, 1974). Eller, a distinguished former director of U.S. Naval History, tells little about the Soviets and much about the U.S. Navy—past and present. The Mitchell book, a tome of more than 600 pages, has little to recommend it; errors of fact and understanding abound in that work.

SOVIET WRITINGS

A number of books written in the Soviet Union addressing naval matters are readily available in English. Most important are the writings of Admiral Gorshkov, who has directed the development of the Red fleet for almost three decades. While he has been a prolific writer in Soviet journals, particular significance was attached to his 11 articles on "Navies in War and in Peace," originally published in *Morskoy Sbornik* [Naval Digest] in 1972–1973. Gorshkov explained the development of modern navies, rationalizing the need for the Soviet Union to have a large, far-ranging fleet. These articles were, in turn, reprinted in the Naval Institute *Proceedings* in 1974, each article being accompanied by a commentary by a U.S. naval officer. Subsequently, the Naval Institute published the articles and commentaries as the soft-cover book *Red Star Rising* (Annapolis, Md.: Naval Institute Press, 1974).

Gorshkov's "second" book, *The Sea Power of the State* (Annapolis, Md.: Naval Institute Press, 1979), expanded his views on the importance of sea power to a nation, arguing that the Soviet Navy should have a dominant role in all areas of the world except Europe.

(A useful effort at placing Gorshkov and his views in perspective is German historian-author Dr. Jürgen Rohwer's "Admiral Gorshkov and the Influence of History Upon Sea Power" in the May 1981/Naval Review issue of the *Proceedings*.)

Nikita Khrushchev, *Khrushchev Remembers, The Last Testament* (Boston: Little, Brown & Company, 1974). Khrushchev, who had appointed Gorshkov to head the Navy, is reputed to have written two volumes of memoirs. This second volume provides major coverage of military developments during his tenure as First Secretary of the Communist Party (1953–1964), especially the chapter "The Navy," which gives his perspective on "The Fall of Admiral Kuznetsov" and "The Rise of Admiral Gorshkov."

Marshal of the Soviet Union V.D. Sokolovskiy, *Soviet Military Strategy* (Stanford, Calif: Stanford Research Institute, 1975). This is the third edition of Sokolovskiy's classic work, which provides a defense-level look at naval missions and requirements. This volume is edited by Harriet Fast Scott and includes her commentary and analysis of differences in the three editions.

Although not dealing specifically with Soviet naval subjects, the reader should be aware of the "Soviet Military Thought" series, translated and published under the auspices of the U.S. Air Force. These books are written largely by Soviet officers on a variety of national security and military subjects, among them military psychology and pedagogy, operational art and tactics, and the relationship between the Soviet state and the military. While heavily laden with political verbiage that makes them slow reading, these publications do convey the basis of Soviet military thinking. The translations are available in paperback from the Government Printing Office.

The Soviets publish the monthly journal *Soviet Military Review* in several languages, including English. Although intended for foreign readers, it contains numerous articles on naval subjects that also appear in internal Soviet publications.

REFERENCE WORKS

During the past few years *Combat Fleets of the World* (Annapolis, Md.: Naval Institute Press) has emerged as probably the best "annual" reference addressing the world's navies, especially the Soviet and Warsaw Pact fleets. This volume is adapted from the French *Flottes de Combat* edited by Jean Labayle-Couhat and is published every second year in a revised, English-language edition edited by A.D. Baker III.

Weyer's Warships of the World is similarly published in English in alternate years (Baltimore, Md.: Nautical & Aviation Publishing Co.), being originally produced in German. While this is a highly "abbreviated" pocket-size book, it is a handy and relatively affordable volume, although its publication has been erratic.

Jane's Fighting Ships, published annually, continues as the largest and most expensive naval reference work (London: Jane's Publishing Co.). Unfortunately, of late *Janes* appears to be declining in quality while increasing in price.

Valuable for its descriptions of contemporary Soviet aircraft is *Jane's All the World's Aircraft* (London: Jane's Publishing Co.), edited by J.W.R. Taylor. And while not an annual, another valuable reference on this subject is Bill Sweetman's *Soviet Military Aircraft* (Novato, Calif.: Presidio Press, 1981). The best historical work on Soviet military aircraft is by Bill Gunston, *Aircraft of the Soviet Union* (London: Osprey, 1983).

The Soviet merchant fleet is best covered in Ambrose Greenway's *Soviet Merchant Ships* (Emsworth, Hampshire: Kenneth Mason, 1985). This very useful, loose-leaf book is updated every few years. It provides characteristics and photographs of Soviet merchant, fishing, and research ships as well as icebreakers.

Also noteworthy is David R. Jones, ed, *Soviet Annual Review* (Gulf Breeze, Fla.: International Press). When this edition went to press, the last available book was volume 8 (1985). There are essays on naval subjects; again, the quality varies, but the significant information of the past year is provided.

Soviet weapons, with an emphasis on electronic systems, are described annually in *The International Countermeasures Handbook* (Palo Alto, Calif: EW Communications, Inc.).

CONGRESSIONAL DOCUMENTS

The U.S. Congress annually publishes copies of the hearings held by the various committees that consider defense programs. These hearings include periodic briefings from the Director of Naval Intelligence on Soviet naval matters as well as limited discussions by other senior naval officials. Of particular interest during the 1960s and 1970s were the statements of Admiral H.G. Rickover, at the time head of the U.S. Navy's nuclear-propulsion program, before various committees of the House and Senate and, especially, the Joint Committee on Atomic Energy.

Also during the 1970s, the Congressional Research Service (CRS) prepared a series of compendiums entitled *Soviet Oceans Development* that were published by the Senate Committee on Commerce. These included essays on a variety of Soviet naval and maritime subjects.

John M. Collins and Patrick M. Cronin of the Library of Congress, at the request of several members of congress, have prepared a comprehensive comparison of the *U.S.-Soviet Military Balance 1980–1985,* that reviews progress made by both nations in this period in improving their military capabilities. This is an excellent, broad-coverage volume (available commercially through Pergamon-Brassey's International Defense Publishers, McLean, Va.).

GOVERNMENT REPORTS

Beyond the *Soviet Military Power* and *Understanding Soviet Naval Developments* cited above, less elaborate unclassified reports on various aspects of Soviet naval activity are published on occasion by the Central Intelligence Agency, Defense Intelligence Agency, and the Navy-supported Center for Naval Analyses (CNA). The usefulness of these documents varies. Each agency has lists of its publications available.

Messrs. Bradford Dismukes, Robert Weinland, and James McConnell, senior CNA analysts, have produced several significant reports over the past few years as well as articles in various defense journals.

JOURNALS AND MAGAZINES

Since the early 1960s there have been a vast number of articles in the professional and public press on Soviet naval and maritime matters. The principal English-language journals addressing the subject are the Naval Institute *Proceedings* and *Naval War College Review* in the United States, and *Navy International, International Defense Review,* and *Military Technology* in Europe. Articles of particular merit in the last include those by Ulrich-Joachim Schulz-Torge.

The enlarged May/Naval Review issue of the *Proceedings* and its predecessor, the separately published *Naval Review,* have had special features on Soviet naval developments. These articles are most useful, especially ones by the late Naval Academy Professor Robert Daly; Captain William Manthorpe, USN (Ret.); Captain James Kehoe, USN (Ret.); Kenneth Brower; Dr. Norman Friedman; and Dr. Robert Suggs. The *Proceedings* has also presented an excellent series of articles based on the comparative analysis of U.S. and Soviet warship design by Captain Kehoe and Mr. Brower, while John Jordan has prepared more popular articles of this type for the British magazines *Navy International* and *Defence.*

The May/Naval Review issue of the *Proceedings* generally has a review of the past year's Soviet naval activities. The current authors of this feature are Donald C. Daniel and Gael D. Tarleton.

The October 1982 issue of the *Proceedings* was devoted entirely to the Soviet Navy. The articles in that issue were written by Messrs. Polmar and Friedman (missions and tactics); Commander Dean Sedgwick, USN (command and control); Lieutenant Kevin Lynch, USN (command and control); Andrew Hull (surface forces); Dr. Milan Vego (attack submarines); Lieutenant Commander Gerry Thomas, USN (Pacific Fleet); Dr. Suggs (training); Captain Roger Barnett, USN, and Dr. Edward Lacey (*Morskoy Sbornik*); Brigadier General E.F. Black, USA (Ret.) (national leadership); Lieutenant Commander Ted Wile, USN (mine warfare); Lieutenant Colonel Dominik Nargele, USMC (naval infantry); Captain Robert Wyman, USN (Baltic Fleet); Captain Robert McKeown, USN (merchant fleet); and A.D. Baker III (ship types). Extensive updates of that special issue have been published in January 1984 and December 1985. Beginning in 1986 a regular column on the Soviet Navy and one on the Soviet viewpoint, by Messrs. Polmar and Manthorpe, respectively, are being published in the *Proceedings.*

Several perceptive articles on Soviet military manpower—with significant implications for the Soviet Navy—have been authored by Dr. Ellen Jones of the Defense Intelligence Agency. Among them are "Soviet Military Manpower: Prospects in the 1980s" in *Strategic Review* (Fall 1981) and "Minorities in the Soviet Armed Forces" in *Comparative Strategy* (vol. III no. 4, 1982). Dr. Jones has expanded her views on Soviet military manpower issues in her book *Red Army and Society* (Boston: Allen & Unwin, 1985).

Subjects on which relatively little has been written are the use of tactical nuclear weapons and electronic warfare at sea. Two excellent works are by Captain Linton F. Brooks, USN, "Tactical Nuclear Weapons: The Forgotten Facet of Naval Weapons" in the January 1980 *Proceedings,* and Lieutenant Commander Guy Thomas, USN, "Soviet Radio Electronic Combat and the U.S. Navy," in the *Naval War College Review,* July-August 1982. Dr. Friedman has also touched on the related command-and-control issues in "C³ War at Sea," *Proceedings,* May 1977, as has Polmar in "Soviet C³," *Air Force Magazine,* June 1980, while the December 1984 and December 1985 issues of *Signal* magazine were devoted to Soviet C³ issues. All have significance for dealing with the Soviets at sea. Commander Floyd Kennedy, Jr., USNR, has written a useful article on EW in "The Evolution of Soviet Thought on Warfare in the Fourth Dimension" in the *Naval War College Review* (March-April 1984).

Beyond articles on Soviet naval and maritime subjects that appear regularly in the journals listed above, relevant articles in the periodicals *Problems of Communism* (published by the U.S. Information Agency), *Strategic Review* (U.S. Strategic Institute), and the commercial publications *International Defense Review, Armada,* and *Naval Forces.* The annual March issue of *Air Force Magazine* is a Soviet Aerospace Almanac that contains a wide range of articles, some of which relate to naval activities.

Finally, the British magazines *Air International* and *Flight International* are recommended for details of Soviet naval aircraft.

Soviet Maritime Flags

National Flag

Naval Ensign

Fleet Commander

DEP. Min. DEF

Nav. Aux

Squad Commander

Red Banner

Salv & Rescue

Form CDR

Guards

Hydro. Serv.

Form CDR

Div. CDR

Senior CDR

KGB

Jack

Combat

Commissioning Pennant
of an Auxiliary

Combat Efficiency Awards

The Soviets conduct regular operational readiness inspections of their ships and those rated as outstanding are allowed to display the appropriate emblem.

Below are depicted the various awards–there will usually be painted on the bridge, except the individual gun or combat action stations award which is printed on the winning station.

| Outstanding Ship of the Soviet Navy | Outstanding Ship of a Fleet | Outstanding Ship | Stern Emblem (Larger Ships) |

| Individual Guns or Combat Stations | Artillery | Minelaying | Rockets (AAW) and Radar |

| Torpedoes | Rockets (SSM) | Propulsion | Minesweeping |

| Air Defense/AAW | Rocket and Radar Technology
(Gold border indicates three or more awards) | ASW
(circles indicate awarded by Fleet Commander) | Artillery
(Gold circle indicates awarded by CINC of the Soviet Navy) |

Naval Rank Insignia

(Service Uniforms and Dress Overcoats Have Black Shoulderboards Vice Gold)

Higher Officers

  *

Admiral of the Fleet of the Soviet Union (Admiral Flota Sovetskogo Soyuza)	Admiral (Admiral)	Vice Admiral (Vitse-Admiral)	Rear Admiral (Kontr-Admiral)

Senior Officers

'Scrambled Eggs' and
Gold Chin Strap on Dress Service
Caps of Officers
and Service Caps
of Senior Officers

Captain, 1st Rank (Kapitan Pervogo Ranga)	Captain, 2nd Rank (Kapitan Vtorogo Ranga)	Captain, 3rd Rank (Kapitan Tretyego Ranga)

Junior Officers

Captain-Lieutenant (Kapitan-Leytenant)	Senior Lieutenant (Starshiy-Leytenant)	Lieutenant (Lelytenant)	Junior Lieutenant (Miadshiy-Leytenant)

Ornamentation on Collars of the
Full Dress and Dress Coats

Fleet Admiral	Admirals and Generals	Other Officers

Line Engineering Officer Wear The Same Insignia but with the Silver Engineering Device Mounted on Shoulderboards.

*Fleet Admiral (Not Shown) Insignia 15 similar to FASU except Shoulderboard has only the large star and sleeve has 3½ bars above broad stripe.

Enlisted Shoulderboards
Afloat

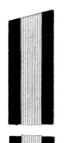     

Senior Chief Petty Officer	Chief Petty Officer	Petty Officer 1st Class	Petty Officer 2d Class	Senior Seaman	Seaman

Shore-Based Units and Naval Aviation

Master Sergeants	Senior Sergeants	Sergeants	Junior Sergeants	Senior Seaman	Seaman

Naval Infantry

Master Sergeant	Senior Sergeant	Sergeant	Junior Sergeant	Corporal	Private

Cap Devices

Hat Ribbon (With Name of Fleet)	On Winter Cap	On Service Cap	On Service Cap of Naval Infantry	Unit Citation Hat Ribbon Worn by Enlisted Personnel Serving In Units or Vessels Honored by "Guards" Designation

General Index*

Ship Name and Ship Class Index*

*Tables are not indexed. (Ger. = German, Pol. = Polish, U.S. = United States)

Norman Polmar is an internationally known naval analyst and author. He has directed analytical and historical studies for the U.S. Navy, various agencies of the Department of Defense, the Army, the Maritime Administration, the National Oceanographic and Atmospheric Admin- istration, and American and foreign shipbuilding and aerospace firms. From 1982 to 1986 he was a member of the Secretary of the Navy's Research Advisory Committee, and served on the steering group for the Secretary's analysis of the lessons of the Anglo-Argentine war in the Falklands.

Mr. Polmar is the author of fifteen books on naval and aviation sub- jects, including the reference work *The Ships and Aircraft of the U.S. Fleet*, published at three-year intervals by the Naval Institute Press, and coauthor of the biography *Rickover: Controversy and Genius*. He is now developing a reference book on the Soviet armed forces.

His articles appear frequently in U.S. and foreign military journals, and he writes a regular column on the U.S. and Soviet navies in the Naval Institute *Proceedings*. These and other literary efforts have won him the Navy League's Alfred Thayer Mahan award and the Naval Institute's award of merit as distinguished author.

Mr. Polmar has visited the Soviet Union as a guest of the Soviet Navy and the Institute of U.S. Studies, and China as a guest of the Chinese Navy and the Beijing Institute of Strategic and International Studies.

Addenda

The ill-fated Yankee with severe hull damage visible abaft the sail, showing where the hatch for the third missile on the port side was blown off; wisps of smoke are evident. In this view the submarine is underway on her own power, her sail planes are in the vertical position (probably due to a hydraulic or electric failure), and a launch from an accompanying ship is off the starboard bow. (U.S. Navy)

SUBMARINES

One of the approximately 20 Yankee-class SSBNs remaining in service was lost at sea in the Atlantic on the morning of 6 October 1986. The submarine had surfaced three days earlier after apparently suffering an explosion and fire involving one of the craft's 16 SS-N-6 ballistic missiles.

The explosion wrenched the hatch from the third missile tube on the port side and holed the side of the submarine below the waterline. After surfacing, the submarine was briefly underway on her own power but was then taken in tow by a Soviet merchant ship, with about one-half the submarine's crew of some 120 being taken off. There was difficulty with the tow, and the submarine was observed settling in the water. About 3:30 A.M. lifeboats and rafts were observed, and the remaining crewmen abandoned ship just before the submarine sank at 4 A.M. (EDST). The Soviet government stated that three crewmen were killed in the explosion but that all survivors (some apparently injured) were safely taken off before the submarine sank.

The submarine sank in 18,000 feet of water some 600 miles east of Bermuda and 1,200 miles east of Cape Hatteras, North Carolina.

Stern view of the damaged Yankee, showing damage to upper hull; the hull was also holed below the waterline. (U.S. Navy)

COLLECTION SHIPS

...GI class went to sea in 1986, being given the NATO ...ed Vishnya. The hull bears some resemblance to that of the ...ge Bal'zam-class AGI (5,000 tons full load, 348⅙ feet overall); however, the mast and funnel features as well as deck arrangement differ considerably. The first unit, designated SSV-520, sailed on trials in the Baltic in July 1986.

The Vishnya has the heaviest gun armament of any AGI yet seen, with two 30-mm multi-barrel (Gatling) guns fitted forward and another pair aft.

The lead ship of the Vishnya AGI class observed during the NATO exercise NATO Northern Wedding in 1986. Additional electronic antennas are expected to be installed. (Royal Netherlands Navy)

Stern view of the missile range instrumentation ship MARSHAL NEDELIN, the largest scientific ship operated by the Soviet Navy. Additional and larger ships of this type are under construction. (Royal Netherlands Navy)